THE PEOPLE'S JOURNAL

Pickens, South Carolina
1894–1903

*Historical and
Genealogical Abstracts*

Compiled by
Peggy Burton Rich and
Marion Ard Whitehurst

Heritage Books
2025

HERITAGE BOOKS
AN IMPRINT OF HERITAGE BOOKS, INC.

Books, CDs, and more—Worldwide

For our listing of thousands of titles see our website
at
www.HeritageBooks.com

Published 2025 by
HERITAGE BOOKS, INC.
Publishing Division
5810 Ruatan Street
Berwyn Heights, MD 20740

Copyright © 1991 Peggy Burton Rich and Marion Ard Whitehurst

Heritage Books by the authors:

The Pickens Sentinel: *Favorite Newspaper of Pickens County: Volumes 1 and 2*
Peggy Burton Rich

Alexander Families of Upper South Carolina: Volumes 1–3
Marion A. Whitehurst, Peggy B. Rich, Jerry L. Alexander

All rights reserved. No part of this book may be reproduced or transmitted in any form or by any means, electronic or mechanical, including photocopying, recording or by any information storage and retrieval system without written permission from the author, except for the inclusion of brief quotations in a review.

International Standard Book Number
Paperbound: 978-1-55613-428-9

CONTENTS

Introduction	v
Key	vii
Pickens County, South Carolina School Districts	viii
The People's Journal 1894	1
The People's Journal 1895	41
The People's Journal 1896	79
The People's Journal 1897	124
The People's Journal 1899	172
The People's Journal 1900	202
The People's Journal 1901	227
The People's Journal 1902	266
The People's Journal 1903	298
Bibliography	314
Index	315

INTRODUCTION

The material presented in this compilation was gleaned from original issues of *The People's Journal* published in Pickens, South Carolina from 1891 to 1903 under the editorship of T. C. Robinson and T. J. Mauldin. Extant issues of the paper cover, with the exception of some few missing issues, the years 1894 to 1897 and 1899 to March, 1903, and fully represent those issues of the paper available. Microfilm is currently available at The Caroliniana Library (Columbia, S. C.), the Greenville County Library (Greenville, S. C.), the Pickens County Library (Easley, S. C.), and perhaps other institutions. Hopefully a wider distribution and scholarly use of this newspaper will result from the publication of this work.

Presented in this volume in abstract form are births, deaths, marriages, Sheriff's Sales, Clerk of Court Sales, Mortgagee's Sales, Final Estate Settlements, Notices to Creditors and Debtors, and a variety of other county records. Information is provided on stores, as they appear in numerous ads, churches, area schools, teachers and honor students. Although the newspaper principally covered events and happenings within Pickens, Oconee and Anderson counties, many items of interest are to be found relating to the counties of Greenville and Spartanburg. *The People's Journal* was an extremely "chatty" newspaper rich in happenings, events and personalities of north western South Carolina. The picturesque area lifestyle is often vividly portrayed.

Many buildings, churches and homes in the Pickens area are mentioned, and in some instances the date of construction is provided as is the name of the contractor. During the late 1890's, fire was a persistent problem in Pickens and the listing of the date of these fires and the buildings destroyed is particularly valuable. In addition, the structure(s) erected to replace the destroyed properties are normally listed.

Obituaries provide extremely valuable information on older members of the community, many having been born in the early 1800's. Sadly, tombstones were not always placed on graves as a result of the economic depression of the 1890's, and these persons are not identified in the various cemetery surveys published on Pickens and Oconee counties. Except for a few statistical figures maintained for a short period during the late antebellum years, South Carolina did not require registration of births, deaths and marriages until about 1915. As a result, newspapers often provide the only source of this valuable information on births, deaths and marriages.

Reference is also made within the body of this work to major newspaper entries at the national, state and local level, with issue dates provided and abstracts presented for many of the articles. These articles show the lifestyle and views of Americans in the late 1800's and early 1900's.

This compilation, perhaps the first attempt to abstract and reference major events from a South Carolina newspaper, was facilitated by the relatively short run of this publication and the cooperation of Dr. Allen Stokes of the Caroliniana Library. We also wish to express our appreciation to Frederick C. Holder, historian and map collector, and Jane B. Morris, author of the in press book, *Pickens, The Town and The First Baptist Church*, for their help and support of this project.

Peggy Burton Rich and Marion Ard Whitehurst

KEY

T.J. - Trial Justice
N.P. - Notary Public
Hon. - Honorable
Mag. - Magistrate
UDC - United Daughters of the Confederacy

PICKENS COUNTY, SOUTH CAROLINA
SCHOOL DISTRICTS 1895 - 1905

G - grade school   H - high school   W - white   C - colored
District, School and Type

#1 Lathem
    Lathem Academy
    Crosswell G (W)
    Crosswell G (C)
    Turner's Hill

#2 Dayton G (W)
    Dayton G (C)

#3 Zion G (W)
    Rocky Knob

#4 Flat Rock G (W)

#5 Ruhamah G (W)

#6 Symmes G (W)
    White Oak G (C)

#7 Tabor
    Mt. Tabor G (W)
    Able G (C)

#8 Calhoun-Clemson G H (W)
    Calhoun G (C)

#9 Central G (W)
    Central G (C)

#10 Johnston
    Johnston's Chapel
    Johnsonia Female
    Norris G (W)
    Norris G (C)

#11 Liberty G & H (W)
    Liberty G (C)

#12 Reunion G (W)
    Easley G (C)

#13 Easley
    West End G (W)
    Central H (W)
    Glenn Wood G (W)
    North Side G (W)
    Arial G (W)
    Bright's Station G (C)
    Alice G (W)
    Pickensville
    Lendhardt ?

#14 Cateechee G (W)
    Mauldin

#16 Farr's
    Vineland Academy
    Vineland G (W)
    Vineland G (C)
    Lendhardt ?

#17 Dacusville G & H (W)
    Dacusville G (C)

#18 Maynard G (W)
    Cross Plains G (C)

#19 Cedar Rock G (W)
    Piney Grove G (C)
    Holly Bush
    Tabor

#20 Bethlehem G (W)
    St. Stephens

#21 Roanoke G (W)
    Holly Springs G (C)

#22 Gates G (W)

#23 Long Branch G (W)
    Poplar Springs (C)

#24 Garvin
    Pleasant Hill G (W)

#25 King's G (W)

#26 Palestine G (W)
    Crow Creek

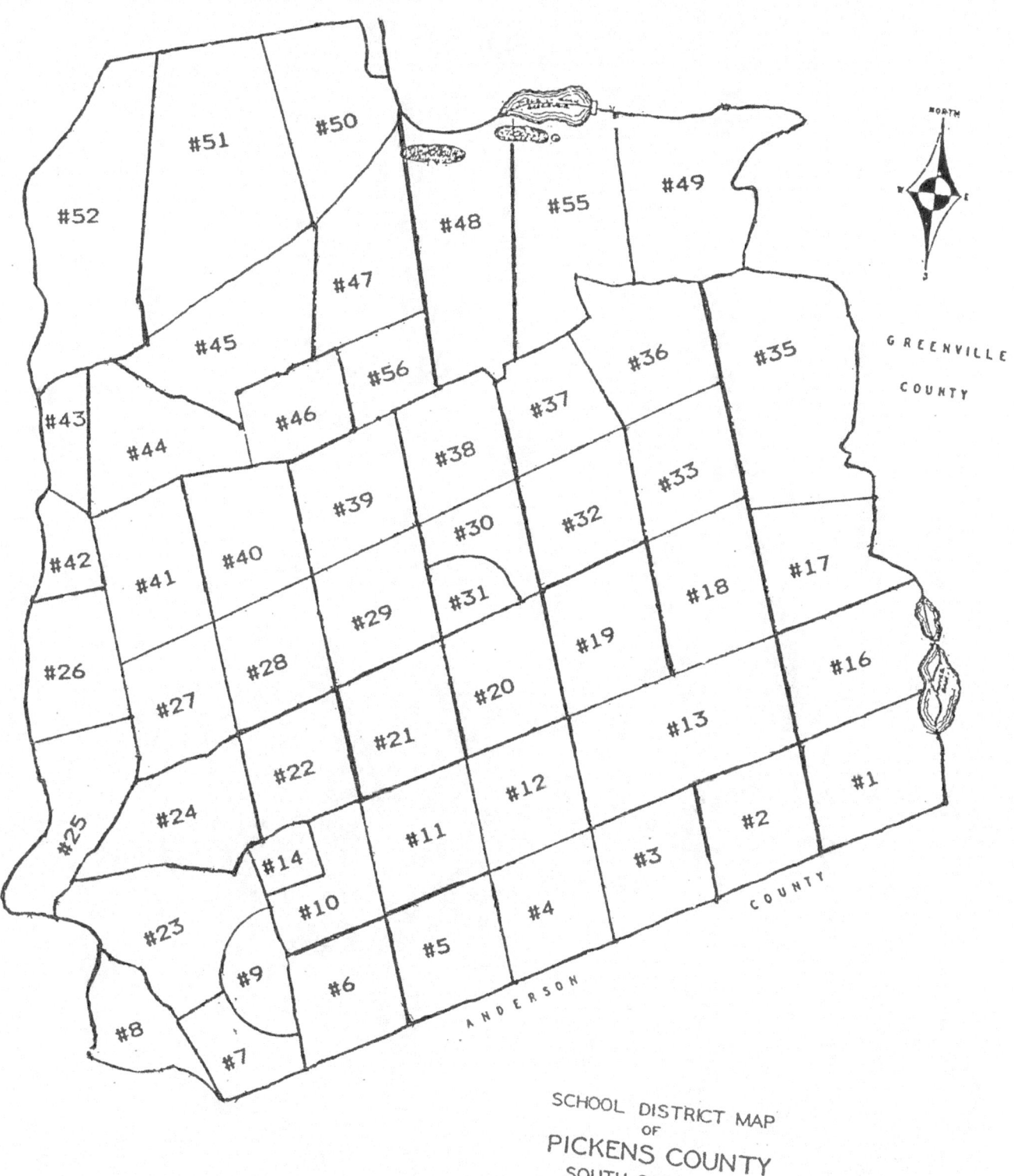

SCHOOL DISTRICT MAP
OF
PICKENS COUNTY
SOUTH CAROLINA

#27 Six Mile G (W)
   Camp Creek G (W)
   Mountain View G (C)

#28 Praters G (W)

#29 Wolf Creek G (W)
   Wolf Creek G (C)
   Concord G (W)
   Cross Roads G (C)

#30 Town Creek G (W)
   Field

#31 Pickens G & H (W)
   Pickens Mill G (W)
   Pickens G (C)
   Pickens H (C)
   Academy Hall
   Aiken Hotel
   Piedmont Academy
   Griffin Ebenezer G (C)

#32 Glassy Mountain G (W)

#33 Mica G (W)

#35 Olga
   Peter's Creek G (W)
   Carpenter's Creek
   Shoal Creek G (C)

#36 Oolenoy G (W)
   Oolenoy Academy

#37 Ambler G (W)

#38 Hagood G (W)
   Midway G (W)
   Cold Springs G (C

#39 Twelve Mile G (W)
   Twelve Mile G (C)
   Mountain Grove

#40 Martin G (W)

#41 Mile Creek G (W)

#42 Keowee G (W)
   Gap Hill

#43 Bethel

#44 Shady Grove

#45 Antioch G (W)
   Hazel

#46 Hampton G (W)
   Pinder

#47 Holly Springs G (W)

#48 Rock G (W)

#49 Pleasant Grove G (W)
   Soapstone G (C)
   Saluda Hill

#50 Rocky Bottom G (W)

#51 Eastatoe G (W)

#52 Cane Creek G (W)
   Horse Pasture G (W)

#55 Newton (New Town) G (W)
   Table Rock

#56 Montvale G (W)

Given above are approximate locations of schools in Pickens County, South Carolina. There may be errors due to combining of districts, addition of districts and other districts being dissolved. The assistance of Mrs. Julia Woodson, Earl Freeman and Fred Holder is greatly appreciated.

THE PEOPLE'S JOURNAL - 1894

Pickens Court House, South Carolina

Issue of: Thursday 4 January 1894:

Married the 24 December 1893 at Mount Tabor Church, MR. MATT (?ROPER - torn) to MISS LEIAR SIMMONS all of Dacusville, S.C., by Rev. J.E. Foster (details).

C.E. ROBINSON soon to rebuild his office in the burnt district.

MISS ALMA KAY to teach school near Six Mile, S.C.

REV. E.M. McKISSICK and family left for their new home in Orangeburg, S.C.

W.B. MOORE formerly of Anderson Co., S.C. has moved to his farm in Central Township.

Married the 31 December (1893) FOREST ARTHUR and MARY McKINNEY, both colored, by M.F. Hester, N.P.

Married the 27 (Dec. 1893) at the residence of the bride's mother, by Rev. W.B. Singleton, MISS E.R.B. MILLER to MR. B.H. WHITMIRE.

Married the 21 December (1893) at MR. BUD BROWN'S by Rev. B. Holder, MR. GEORGE LANDERS to MISS LUCY ANDERSON.

Married the 31 (Dec. 1893) by Trial Justice B.D. Garvin at his residence, ANDREW ANDERSON and TEXIE CONNOR, both colored.

SAMUEL EARLE of Georgia is visiting DR. W.T. FIELD. Mr. Earle is extensively engaged in mining.

Married the 24 (Dec. 1893) at the residence of the bride's father MR. J.I. HOLLIDAY by Trial Justice W.K. Merck, MISS LILLIE E. HOLLIDAY to MR. J.H. DRIVER of Oconee Co., S.C.

JEFFERSON FERGUSON, colored, died at his home in town the 1 (Jan. 1894) at the age of about 70 years (minor details).

NOAH R. HENDRICKS of Texas is visiting his parents MR. and MRS. JAMES F. HENDRICKS near Liberty, S.C. His son MASTER JAMES HENDRICKS accompanied him.

HENRY D. HENDRICKS, son of JAMES F. HENDRICKS, who has been in Texas several months returned to his home in Pickens County.

EARLE HANNA, son of OLIVER HANNA, died at the residence of his father about 4 miles from town on the 27 (Dec. 1893) from congestion of the brain.

Pickens Co., S.C. Salesday:
Property of GEORGE HENDRICKS. Tract #1 - 140 acres for $365. Tract #2 - 122 acres for $800 sold to J.M. STEWART. Tract #3 - 136 acres for $1,000 sold to E.L. WILLIAMS.

From Liberty
HENRY HENDRIX, MRS. JOHN HENDRIX and MRS. MINNIE BRUCE all of Texas and G.L. BOGGS of Arkansas are visiting relatives here.
B.F. PARSON moved out of town. J.W. DAWSON and McJAMESON moved in town from the Slabtown Section of Anderson Co., S.C.

If you have occasion to visit Fort Hill, S.C. see W.H. HESTER at HOTEL DE CLEMSON.

AD - T.C. ROBINSON is selling a tract of land in Pickens County on the head waters of Gregory's Creek of Twelve Mile River, 4 miles from Pickens.

Pickens Co., S.C. Tax Assessment Notice.

AD - HAGOOD, BRUCE & CO., Selling General Merchandise, Pickens, S.C.

AD - JOHN T. LEWIS & SON, Selling Groceries and General Merchandise, Pickens, S.C.

AD - A.G. WYATT, Selling General Merchandise, Easley, S.C.

AD - W.C. BRAMBLETT, Selling General Merchandise, Pickens, S.C.

AD - W.T. McFALL, Selling Tools, Baskets, Seed, Shoes, Harnesses, Leather Goods, etc., Pickens, S.C.

AD - JOHN T. BOGGS, Selling Jewelry and Watches, Liberty, S.C.

AD - T.D. HARRIS, Selling Groceries and General Merchandise, Pickens, S.C.

AD - JAMES E. BROWN, Selling Groceries and General Merchandise, Central, S.C.

AD - C.N. WYATT, at QUILLIANS Old Stand, Easley, S.C. - Selling Drugs, Garden Seed, Paint, Oil, etc.

AD - J.H. BROWN, Selling General Merchandise, Liberty, S.C. Clerks: MR. C.H. PARKINS and MR. RICHARD T. HALLUM.

Issue of: Thursday 11 January 1894:

Pickens Co., S.C. Clerk's Sale - CHARLES T. HUTCHINGS, et al. vs J.B. CLYDE, et al. 55 acres on Rice's Creek to be sold.

DR. J.D. CURETON has moved to his new residence on Jail Street.

MISS MATTIE KAY is teaching in Anderson Co., S.C.

J.W. SUTHERLAND of Knob, S.C. will move into the MILES house on Main Street.

MELVIN M. HOLDER left for Davis Military School at Winston, North Carolina.

J.L.O. THOMPSON formerly of *The Westminster Banner* will soon move into his new residence on Pendleton Street.

"SIS" AMBLER, colored, daughter of WILLIS AMBLER who lives one mile north of town died Monday.

Married the 4 (Jan.) at the residence of Rev. B.F. Murphree, ELIJAH WINCHESTER to MISS FLORENCE WINCHESTER all of Pickens County.

W.R. MAJOR'S residence burned the night of the 3 (Jan.). The building belonged to J.C. WILSON who now lives in Pelzer, S.C. (details).

REV. R.A. CHILDS is to marry the 12 (Jan.) MISS MAGGIE ROPER. The Rev. John Owens will perform the ceremony. Rev. Childs is the pastor at Clio, Chester Station, S.C.
Marlboro Democrat

MISS NANNIE HARKNESS is teaching at Vinland (Vineland).

From Liberty
Married, MR. BOWDEN to MISS MARY BOGGS, last Thursday at the residence of the bride's mother near Slabtown, S.C. They boarded the train for California where they will make their home. Mr. Bowden is in the fruit business.

AD - A.M. MORRIS, Selling Groceries, Pickens, S.C.

AD - Patrick Military Institute, Anderson, S.C.

AD - H.O. BOWEN & L.E. CHILDRESS, Lawyers in Pickens, S.C.

AD - B.A. MORGAN, Lawyer in Greenville and Pickens, S.C.

AD - DR. J.F. WILLIAMS' office is at his residence at the GRIFFIN house in Pickens, S.C.

AD - F.B. MORGAN, Selling General Merchandise, Central, S.C.

AD - J.E. HAGOOD & J.L. THORNLEY, Selling General Merchandise, Easley, S.C. Also, Livery Stable, Feed, etc., Easley and Pickens, opposite the Hotel.

AD - B.P. GRIFFIN, Veterinary Surgeon, Pickens, S.C.

Issue of: Thursday 18 January 1894:

From Liberty
MESDAMES WINNIE BRUCE and JOHN M. HENDRICKS have returned to Sherman, Texas after visiting in this area.
MRS. W.L. BOGGS opened a Public School here last week.
J.A. BOGGS died the 10 (Jan.) at the age of 69 years. He leaves a host of friends.

Central
The firm of D. FRICKS is dissolved by mutual consent.
DAVID FRICKS is now clerking for MORGAN BROS.
T.L. WATKINS has moved to his new residence in the fork of the Pendleton and Fort Hill Roads.
MR. and MRS. LON DAVIS have made Central, S.C. their new home.
CAPTAIN JAMES H. ROWLAND is the popular RAILROAD HOTEL man of Central, S.C. *Keowee Courier*

SAMUEL JAMESON, colored, was shot the 13 Jan. by WILLIAM FERGUSON, colored, at the residence of PINK BLASSINGAME in Easley Township. Jameson is not expected to live.

T. ADDISON BOGGS of Liberty, S.C. died at his home the 10 (Jan.). He was a member of the Presbyterian Church. Mr. Boggs leaves a large family.

Issue of: Thursday 25 January 1894:

JOHN MEARS will probably locate near Asheville, North Carolina.

MRS. LETTIE NEWTON wife of REV. J.C.C. NEWTON, missionary in Japan, is visiting relatives and friends near town.

Married the 18 (Jan.) at the office of Rev. G.R. Shaffer, MISS DAMIE MAULDIN of Pickens Co. to MR. LEWIS GOSLIN of Greenville Co., S.C.

Two children of MR. and MRS. A.B. LEWIS of Eastatoe Township died last week. One was 3 years old and the other 3 months old.

MRS. MOSER, wife of G.W. MOSER of "Old Pickens", Oconee Co., S.C., died at her home the 16 (Jan.). She was about 50 years old and a member of the Methodist Church. Mrs. Moser leaves a husband and four children. (MRS. E.J. MOSER, born 1836, died 15 Jan. 1894, buried Old Pickens Presbyterian Church Cemetery - Oconee County, S.C. Cemetery Survey, Vol. 2, p. 258).

MRS. NAOMI MAULDIN widow of the late BENJAMIN MAULDIN died the 16 (Jan.) at the home of her son ALLEN MAULDIN of Dacusville Township. She was about 77 years old and was a member of the Methodist Church. Mrs. Mauldin leaves 3 sons and 2 daughters. (MRS. NAOMI MAULDIN, nee CAMPBELL, died 15 Jan. 1894, buried Tabor Methodist Church Cemetery - Pickens County S.C. Cemetery Survey, Vol., 1 p., 158).

MISS JOSIE ROBINSON of Pickens Co. is teaching school at St. Paul.

Issue of: Thursday 1 February 1894:

HOWARD JENKINS son of W.L. JENKINS has gone to work at the PELZER COTTON MILLS.

B.A. BOWEN has been appointed Postmaster of Pickens.

ROBERT DAVIS of Dacusville, S.C. died the 27 (Jan). He was about 70 years old. Mr. Davis leaves a wife and several children.

TONEY FERGUSON, colored, who has been living on JOHN FERGUSON'S farm near town, died in Greenville, S.C. on Monday (details).

S.T. PRYOR of Dacusville Township has been appointed Trial Justice.

JAMES J. GARVIN died at his home at Central Township the 24 (Jan.). He was about 70 years old and was the District Surveyor. Mr. Garvin served in the late war. He leaves a large family. (Buried, Mt. Zion Cemetery - Pickens Co., S.C. Cemetery Survey, Vol. 2, p. 31).

MR. MARK PRINCE died at the home of his son E.J. PRINCE the 24 (Jan.). He was 82 years old and was buried from the Presbyterian Church. Mr. Prince leaves many relatives and friends. He was a Mason.

DR. JAMES H. HARRISON died the 25 January at Micanopy,

Florida. He was 44 years old and leaves a wife and 4 children. Dr. Harrison was the third son of the late DR. JAMES HARRISON of Greenville, S.C. and brother of MRS. SAMUEL MAULDIN of Greenville and MRS. J.J. WIDEMAN of Bradley, North Carolina.

FRANK HUNT of Transylvania Co., North Carolina was killed by a falling limb on the 27 (Jan.) 1894. He was almost 60 years old and a member of the Methodist Church. Mr. Hunt was a brother of T.J. and M.H. HUNT of Dacusville, S.C.

Married the 24 (Jan.) at the residence of A.H. CURETON on Pendleton Street (place not given), LIZZIE M. CURETON of the city to GEORGE E. LATIMER of Chester, S.C., by the pastor of the St. Paul's Methodist Church. *Greenville News* - 25 Jan.

Liberty News
MISS FLORENCE MOORE is teaching at Hickory Flat.

The condition of the Crosswell #1 School was found to be good.

Roll of Honor for Pupils of the Liberty School

TUNIS PARSONS	ANNIE GANT
FLORA BOGGS	SUSIE WHITLOCK
FRANK BOGGS	MAY DAWSON
ARTHUR BOGGS	BETTIE DAWSON
HATTIE BOGGS	AMANDA DAWSON
ARTHUR W. BOGGS	HARRY PRESLEY
ELLA BOGGS	ADDIE YOUNG
PARKER BROWN	CONNIE STEWART
JESSE FORD	AGNES WILLARD
VERA FORD	WILLIE PARSONS
ALIENE GREEN	NETTIE PARSONS
IDA GANT	KATE SMITH
JONNIE GANT	ANNIE SMITH
ESSIE GANT	PEARL ROBINSON
CLIFFORD GANT	JOHNNIE ROBINSON
OSCAR BOGGS	MADALENE MOORE
OFFREY LOOPER	DORCAS MOORE

Greenville Tragedy - ED DAVIS, well known Negro, killed his wife and then himself (details).

Issue of: Thursday 8 February 1894:

Married the 31 Jan. (1894) at the residence of the bride's parents, by Rev. Robert Springfield, MRS. SARAH ALLISON to MR. JOHN SUTHERLAND all of Dacusville, S.C.

MISS CORA BOWEN returned home after taking special courses at Williamston Female College in reference to teaching.

Ambler School District building is near completion.

W.A. PALMER is pushing to completion the new store house of LEWIS & SONS.

Married the 4 Feb. 1894 at the residence of the bride's father J.M. PORTER, ESQ. by Rev. J.M. Stewart, MR. HARRISON HUNTER to MISS LIZZIE PORTER all of Pickens.

Married the 4 Feb. 1894 at the residence of the bride's parents, by Rev. J.M. Stewart, MR. NORMAN ALEXANDER to MISS ANNA PORTER, eldest daughter of E.R. and LUCINDA PORTER.

Pickens Co., S.C. Final Settlement - Estate of MASON BURDINE, deceased by JAMES M. BURDINE, Executor.

Issue of: Thursday 15 February 1894:

Spartanburg - Disaster at SPARTAN COTTON MILLS (details).

Calhoun
The school under J.E. LIBBY will run 10 months.
MR. T.P. CAMPBELL one of the oldest citizens died the 11 (Feb.) leaving a widow and one daughter. (THOMAS P. CAMPBELL buried Mt. Tabor Baptist Church - Pickens Co., S.C. Cemetery Survey, Vol. 1, p. 203).
MR. D.B. SLOAN and family of Greenville, S.C. will move to town soon.

From Golden Creek
RICHARD HALLUM is teaching at Shoal Creek.

Dots from Central
J.E. BROWN is building a 20 foot addition to his store.
C.S. STEPHENS is building a new store.
L. ROSS EATON is building a nice cottage to rent on the street that leads to Madden's Bridge.
JIM ROWLAND has built a livery stable.

Union, S.C. - HON. JOHN R. JEFFERIES of Union Co., S.C. died the 10 Feb. from blood poison at Jonesville, S.C. (details).

GUY MAULDIN is attending Clemson College.

MRS. JENNINGS, the mother of the JENNINGS ORPHANAGE, died Thursday afternoon.

The Six Mile Church burned the 6 Feb. 1894.

LEWIS & SONS have moved their stock and goods into their new store on Main Street.

MAJOR W.A.C. DOGGETT was crushed to death between the bumpers of two railroad cars at Gaffney, S.C. on Thursday. He had charge of the guano business at CARROLL & CARPENTER. Major Doggett leaves a wife and 4 grown sons.

Raleigh, North Carolina - 10 Feb.
HENRY MILLER died here today of consumption at the age of 35 years. He had been the business manager for the *News and Observer* for 10 years. Mr. Miller was the son of SARGENT THOMAS A. MILLER of the Confederate Army.

GENERAL LUCIEN B. NORTHROP of the Confederate Army died Friday at the CONFEDERATE SOLDIER'S HOME, Pikesville, Maryland. He was a native of that state.

A.K. PARK bought the interest of A.J. JONES in the business of PARK & JONES of Greenville, S.C.

DANIEL BALDWIN died at his home in Eastatoe Township the 7 (Feb.) at the age of about 75 years. He was a member of the Baptist Church and leaves relatives and friends.

MRS. M.L. HUNT died Sunday at her residence at George's Creek. She was buried from Antioch Methodist Church of which she was a member. Mrs. Hunt leaves a daughter, the wife of REP. C.H. CARPENTER.

Maynard
The new schoolhouse site is near MR. B.A. GREEN'S store. The building will be 40 X 24 and 12 feet high (details).

Issue of: Thursday 22 Feb. 1894:

From Liberty
MRS. W.L. BOGGS is to teach a subscription school.
Married at the residence of W.H. CHAPMAN by Rev. J.T. McBride, MR. J.R. CHAPMAN to MISS JULIA CALAHAN.
The colored Baptists and Methodists are both putting up good new church buildings.

COLLECTOR TOWNES has appointed R.G. GAINES of Central, S.C. storekeeper and gauger.

Married at the residence of MR. T.L. ROBINSON by Rev. W.C. Seaborn, MR. S.W. O'DELL and MISS FRANKIE ROBINSON. She is the only daughter of MR. and MRS. ROBINSON. The groom is the oldest son of SENATOR O'DELL. He graduated from Furman last June (details).

From Liberty - 19 Feb. 1894
J.C. O'DELL telegraph operator of Griffin, Georgia is

visiting his father A. O'DELL.

JAY BOGGS, who is in service with the SEABOARD AIR LINE RAILROAD, is visiting his old home for reason of the serious illness of his brother ROSS BOGGS.

Calhoun
MRS. SARAH CHAPMAN and daughter MRS. J.T. FORD moved to Calhoun, S.C. where they will keep a boarding house.

Resolutions of Respect for J.A. BOGGS (details).

Pickens Co., S.C. Court Jury List and Report.

JAMES A. WHITNER and HOMER A. RICHEY are to be admitted to Clemson College.

JAMES JAMESON died at his residence near Maynard, S.C. the 19 (Feb.). He leaves two children, J.B. JAMESON and MRS. A.E. DAVIS.

Married the 11 (Feb.) at the residence of the bride's parent REV. L.T. LEWIS by J.M. Stewart, L.E. CHILDRESS to MISS KATE LEWIS all of Pickens.

Married Wednesday the 14 Feb. at the residence of the bride's father MR. W.L. ROBERTSON by Rev. W.D. Seaborn, MR. WYATT O'DELL to MISS FRANKIE ROBERTSON all of Pickens County.

Died last Saturday at Briggs Post Office, S.C., MRS. E. LYDIE ANN WILSON wife of SAMUEL WILSON. She was 71 years old and died of old age. Mrs. Wilson was buried from Antioch Methodist Church of which she was a member. She leaves 5 children.

Pickens Co., S.C. Township Boards of Assessors to meet.

Notice - ESSIE HENDRICKS, colored, my wife has left my bed and board. Signed, DAVE HENDRICKS - 8 Feb. 1894.

B.P. GRIFFIN, Veterinary Surgeon, Pickens Co., S.C.

Issue of: Thursday 1 March 1894:

MAJOR WHITNER SYMMES must serve 3 years for the murder of WILLIAM GARY (details).

MISS NANNIE KIRKSEY is teaching in Easley Township.

MISS LENA BOWEN was teaching in the Six Mile School.

ZADE COX will have a position in the GOVERNMENT PRINTING OFFICE, Washington, D.C.

J.H. RABORN was accidently killed the 24 Feb. near Greenwood, S.C. He was a conductor on the COLUMBIA AND GREENVILLE RAILROAD.

Married at the Presbyterian Church (Pickens) the 21 Feb. by Dr. Rile and Dr. Curry of Gainesville, Florida., MISS OLA HOLLINGSWORTH to DR. ROBERT LANCASTER of Gainesville, Florida. MR. JOSEPH and MISS SALLY NORTON attended the wedding (minor details).

Issue of: Thursday 8 March 1894:

From Nimmons - 3 Feb. 1894
MRS. WINEFRED WINCHESTER died at the home of J.M. WINCHESTER of heart failure. She was 87 years old and a member of the Baptist Church.

From Liberty
MRS. MAMIE BOLT died the 6 (March). She was the daughter of MRS. B.F. MORGAN of Dacusville, S.C. and sister of MRS. R.A. BOWEN and MRS. FLORENCE GRIFFIN. Mrs. Bolt leaves two children, a boy and a girl.

FRANK H. WORD of New York is registered at the HESTER HOUSE.

MR. W. PRICE and MR. McDADE of Asheville, North Carolina are registered at the THORNLEY HOUSE. Also, JUDGE I.D. WITHERSPOON, of York, S.C., M.G. ANSEL of Greenville, S.C. and D. WYATT AIKEN of Cokesbury, S.C.

PROF. O'HANLON is a local schoolmaster.

DR. ROBERT KIRKSEY is at his office at his new residence on Main Street.

WILLIE STANSELL died the 1 (March) at his home at Oolenoy, S.C. He was about 80 years old and leaves a wife and 7 children.

Pickens County, S.C. Court Session Report - Criminal cases (details).

Married the 4 (March) at the residence of the bride's parents by Rev. B.F. Murphree, MR. B.S. CHILDRESS to MISS MATILDA SANDERS of Oconee Co., S.C.

Issue of: Thursday 15 March 1894:

MISS ROSA LEWIS is teaching school in Oconee Co., S.C.

LEE P. ORR has moved into the house recently occupied by REV. E.M. McKISSICK on Cedar Rock Street.

Married the 11 (March) at the residence of the bride's father THOMAS HESTER by James E. Boroughs, N.P., MISS JANE HESTER to RILEY BEARDEN.

DR. W.F. AUSTIN will be in Pickens soon. He has graduated from the School of Dentistry, Atlanta, Georgia.

B.T. McDANIEL, son of J.H.G. McDANIEL, has been appointed storekeeper and gauger of E.F. ELLISON'S DISTILLERY near Easley, S.C.

WILLIAM ANTHONY son of J.T. ANTHONY, has entered Clemson College. Clemson College has 560 students and several new buildings have been erected.

Issue of: Thursday 22 March 1894:

Married the 14 (March), MR. JOS. L. LOOPER of Maynard S.C. to MISS LILY BAILEY of Georgia.

Died last Thursday THOMAS CANNON, colored, at the age of 87 years. He was buried from Bethlehem Church.

WALTER O. HESTER is working at DARBY JOB OFFICE in Washington, D.C.

Married the 1 (March) at the residence of the bride's father MR. B.S. LYNCH by Rev. James T. Burdine, MR. JOSEPH M. CHASTAIN to MISS LILLY L. LYNCH all of Pickens County.

H.O. BOWEN will leave here to practice law in Sherman, Texas.

Issue of: Thursday 29 March 1894:

WILLIE GAINES died the 1 (March) in Central America.

MR. CAUBLE and family will move back to Central, S.C.

MISS ALMA KAY is teaching school at Mile Creek, S.C.

MISS GERTRUDE HAGOOD is attending Converse College, Spartanburg, S.C.

Married the 18 (March) at the residence of the bride's father MR. SHARP CHAPMAN, MR. GEORGE W. POWELL to MISS VISA A. CHAPMAN. James T. Burdine officiated.

WILLIAM BLAIR, colored farmer, of near Central, S.C. was

accidentally shot and killed by EUGENE WRIGHT white, age 14 years (appears to have been a hunting accident).

PROF. O'HANLON has been called to the bedside of his dying wife in Rome, Georgia.

Died the 25 (March) at her home near Cross Roads Church, MRS. MARY LARK wife of L.A. LARK. She was buried at Cross Roads Church of which she was a member.

The Trustees of Mica School District #33 have their school house nearly ready.

The Trustees of Glassy Mountain School #32 have completed their schoolhouse. Size 24 X 36.

Roanoke School District #21 is being completed. Size 20 X 30, with a good fire place and chimney that does not smoke and some blackboards (see for details).

MR. H.W. STEELE of Gap Hill District will graduate from North Georgia Agricultural College in June.

AD - J.E. ROBINSON, Selling General Merchandise, Easley, S.C.

Issue of: Thursday 5 April 1984:

MISS LAURA ELLIS of Lebanon, Ohio is visiting with her parents.

The state convicts, who have been at Clemson College for the past year, were carried back to Rock Hill, S.C. last Friday in the charge of CAPTAIN PERRY.

W.C. BRAMBLETT moved his stock of goods into the storeroom on the corner of Main and Jail Street. The building was recently occupied by LEWIS & SONS.

Married Sunday the 1 April 1894 at the residence of the bride's parents, by Rev. J.M. Stewart, MR. EDWARD HUNTER to MISS MARTHA PARRETT all of Pickens County.

Married Sunday last at the Nine Forks Church, by Rev. D.C. Freeman, MR. P. MARTIN to MISS EMMA OWENS all of Dacusville, S.C.

Married Sunday the 25 March by Rev. I. Holder:
WILLIAM SULLIVAN to MANDY PRICE.
JAMES PRICE to HESTER WARD.
DANIEL ALEXANDER to STELLA BOWEN.
MARION HALL to ANNIE PACE.

Issue of: 12 April 1894:

MR. JOHN GRADY son of MR. HENRY W. GRADY will be a conductor on a cable car in Washington, D.C. *Easley Democrat* - 6 April

MR. WILLIAM W. PHILLIPS, better known as" WIG" PHILLIPS, died the 28 March of cancer at his residence four miles below Easley, S.C.

From Liberty

C.H. PARKINS left for Texas where he plans to join the rest of his family near Sherman.

J.L.O. THOMPSON moved into his new house on Garvin Street, Pickens, S.C.

MAJOR J.J. LEWIS has been appointed United States Raiding Deputy Marshall.

Married the 11 March at the residence of the bride's father MR. JOSEPH PACE by Rev. B. Holder, MARION HALL to MISS ANNIE PACE.

Pickens County Commissioners will receive bids for the old court house.

Pickens Co., S.C. Sheriff's Sale - Land of JEREMIAH POWELL which he bought from W.R. PRICE to be sold.

Pickens Co., S.C. Final Settlement - Estate of DAVID G. HUMBERT, deceased, J.M. STEWART, C.C.P., Administrator.

Pickens Co., S.C. Final Settlement - Estate of MRS. CANTRELL, deceased, J.M. STEWART, C.C.P., Administrator.

Issue of: Thursday 19 April 1894:

Pinder has built a new school.

Plans to Improve the Town of Pickens, S.C. (details).

MRS. JOSEPH LOOPER of the Cross Road Section died the 11 April. She was over 86 years old and leaves a husband and children. She raised 16 children. MR. JOSEPH LOOPER, JR. had an accident while returning home with a coffin for his mother (details). *Easley Democrat* - 13 April

GENERAL J.B. KERSHAW died Thursday night at his home in Camden, S.C.

ETTA GARRETT the 2 year old daughter of MR. and MRS. JAMES

GARRETT died last Monday. She was buried from Prater's Church.

W.L. JENKINS left for Rock Hill, S.C. where he will work on the Woman's Industrial School.

Carpenter Creek Schoolhouse in Dacusville, S.C. has been finished by THOMAS H. WILLIAMS and W.H. JONES.

SENATOR ZEBULON B. VANCE of Asheville, North Carolina died the 18 April.

Two new post offices have been established in the Brushy Creek Township. One called WHITE'S, postmaster JAMES W. WHITE. The other called BURDINE'S, postmaster J. THEODORE SMITH.

MRS. DAVIS of Williamston, S.C. died the 17 (April) leaving 6 orphan children. Her husband has deserted her (details). *Anderson Advocate*

From Liberty
FRANK GLENN and WARREN BOGGS are living in Slabtown, Anderson Co., S.C.

Issue of: Thursday 26 April 1894:

JUNIUS BOGGS of Liberty, S.C. and PROF. RICHARD HALLUMS were in town the 14th. These boys shine in their new uniforms.

MRS. W.L. BOGGS closed her school last week.

REV. R.W. SEYMOUR died at his home in Walhalla, Oconee Co., S.C. last Friday of heart failure. He was pastor of the Baptist Church. Rev. Seymour was born in Charleston, S.C. and was the son of ROBERT WILLIAM SEYMOUR.

LEE P. ORR will open a photograph gallery here.

The young men of Pickens have organized a militia company of 60 men.

Married last Saturday by Trial Justice J.J. Lewis, AMOS SUTHERLAND and MISS NETTIE CHASTAIN.

Married last Sunday by Rev. J.M. Stewart, MR. SAMUEL EDENS and MISS MAMIE LIGON.

Married at the residence of HARRISON HUNTER on Sunday the 22 April 1894, by Trial Justice Jesse J. Lewis, MR. JOHN HUNTER and MISS MARY HUNTER.

Married the 17 (April) by Rev. B.T.(sic) Murphree, MR. R.K. LEWIS to MISS M.E. LEWIS daughter of H.J. LEWIS.

Married Sunday the 22 April 1894 at the residence of the bride's grandmother, the widow of J.C.C. PARSON by Rev. W.C. Seaborn, MR. JOSEPH HOLCOMB to MISS LENER COX both of Pickens.

From Hughes
MISS ALICE TOMPKINS is postmistress.

Pickens Co., S.C. Final Settlement - MRS. MARY ANN CANTRELL, deceased by J.W. SUTHERLAND, Administrator.

Issue of: Thursday 3 May 1894:

MISS MATTIE KAY is teaching at Double Springs School, Anderson Co., S.C.

Military Company organized at Pickens, S.C. (details).

MRS. SUSA HILL widow of the late LOUIS HILL died the 30 (April) at her home near Dacusville, S.C. She was 70 years old and leaves 6 children. (SUSAN HILL, buried Hill Family Cemetery - Pickens Co., S.C. Cemetery Survey, Vol. 1, p. 10).

SAM J. ASHMORE left Pickens for Rutherford, North Carolina to work as Publisher on the *Rutherford Herald*.

Issue of: Thursday 10 May 1894:

MR. JOHN GEDDES died at his home on Main St. Sunday. He was a native of Scotland. He first settled in Charleston, S.C. but during the war moved to Cherokee Ford near Gaffney, S.C., after the war he came here. He was engaged in the marble business. *Spartanburg Herald* - 1 May

The seventeen year locust are swarming in on the Keowee River.

Died last Sunday, the infant son of MR. and MRS. STANSELL of Pumpkintown, S.C.

W.F. METTS has been appointed postmaster in Greenville, S.C.

The old court house (Pickens, S.C.) was sold to C.L. HOLLINGSWORTH for $310 last Monday.

LEE P. ORR has opened a dry goods and notions store at W.C. BRAMBLETT'S old stand.

Fire destroyed the dwelling of E.S. GRIFFIN. Neighbors and friends helped build him a neat and commodious cottage where the former dwelling stood (details).

MRS. MARTHA CLAYTON wife of F.V. CLAYTON died at her home near Central, S.C. the 5 (May). She was buried from Sharon Church of which she was a member. Mrs. Clayton leaves a husband and 3 children.

There will be a program for the laying of the corner stone for the Winthrop Normal and Industrial College at Rock Hill, S.C.

Pickens Co., S.C. Citation Notice - Estate of B.S. PORTER, deceased. J.M. STEWART applied for Letters of Administration.

Pickens Co., S.C. Citation Notice - Estate of WILEY MOSELEY, deceased. RICHARD BROOKINS applied for Letters of Administration.

Issue of: Thursday 17 May 1894:

Liberty - 13 May 1894
Married the 5 (May), MR. JAMES SMITH and MISS JANE SMITH all of Pickens.
W.A. STEWART is the depot agent at Green's Station.

The post office has moved to the MASONIC HALL until a new office is finished.

M.F. HESTER has purchased from J.B. CLYDE his late residence in Pickens which is now occupied by H.B. HENDRICKS.

MRS. NANNIE SMITH wife of W.A. SMITH died the 14 (May) at her residence in Pelzer, S.C. She was buried at the family cemetery in Central Township. Mrs. Smith leaves a husband and several children.

MRS. MARTHA WILLIAMS wife of HENRY WILLIAMS died the 14 May of dropsy. She was a member of the Peter's Creek Baptist Church. Mrs. Williams was 48 years old and leaves a husband and 1 child.

Issue of: Thursday 24 May 1894:

The Main Building at Clemson College burned Tuesday morning (see issue of the 31 May 1894 - details).

Liberty
MRS. R.M. WORTS (WERTZ) died last Tuesday in Greenville, S.C. She was buried from the Presbyterian Church and

interred in the Liberty Burying Ground. Mrs. Wertz leaves a husband and 2 children. (ADA B. WERTZ, died the 15 May 1894 - Pickens Co., S.C. Cemetery Survey, Vol. 2, p. 212).

MRS. LEE P. ORR has opened a millinery store in the FREEMAN BUILDING.

DR. EARLE is constructing a very neat building for the post office on his lot on Main Street.

Died Friday, the infant daughter of JOHN BRAZEALE of Dacusville, S.C. Burial at Cross Roads Church.

T.A. WALKER & BROS. will open a business at the same old stand.

Special train rates to the unveiling of the Confederate Soldier's and Sailor's Monument in Richmond, Virginia on the 30 May.

A Reporter of the Journal visited several places of business in Greenville, S.C. and reports on trade there (details).

AD - New Store opposite the court house (FREEMAN BUILDING), Selling Dry Goods and Notions, LEE P. ORR, Agent.

AD - NEW YORK RACKET STORE, General Merchandise, J.M. RAMPEY, Easley, S.C.

AD - JOHN T. LEWIS & SON, Selling Shirts and Pants.

Issue of: Thursday 31 May 1894:

Article - "The Indian Empire". Correspondent - Boston Herald

The Main Building at Clemson College burned Tuesday the 22 May (see issue of the 24 May 1894 - details).

There is a new post office at THOMAS' STORE near Dacusville, S.C.

Married Sunday the 13 May, the second daughter of JAMES C. WILSON by Rev. D. Weston Hiott, MR. M.B. DAVENPORT of Pelzer, S.C. to MAGGIE WILSON of Williamston, S.C.

LEE P. ORR has finished his building where he will have a photograph gallery.

Married at the residence of the bride's father, by Rev. J.E. Foster, MR. B.T. McDANIEL to MISS ROSA LEWIS.

DAVE ARIAL is engineer, conductor, baggage master, flag man and express agent on the Pickens and Easley road during CAPTAIN HESTER'S absence.

Married at the residence of the bride's aunt MRS. JANE WYATT on the 20 May by Rev. J.E. Foster, MR. W.F. CRENSHAW of Oconee Co. S.C. to MISS ESSA KILBY of Anderson Co., S.C.

W.T. ROWLAND is editor of the *Central Tyro*.

Married the 3 May at Hellanis Crossing by Rev. J.E. Foster, MR. BEN E. BURNS of Marietta, S.C. to MISS S.F. POWEL (sic) of near Hellanis Crossing, Greenville Co., S.C.

MRS. ABECROMBIE wife of JOHN ABECROMBIE died near Twelve Mile Camp Ground on Tuesday last. She was about 48 years old.

The report of W.H. SUMMEY'S death in the issue of the 17 May 1894 is incorrect. He is still living. Signed, W.H. SUMMEY.

GERTRUDE PRITCHARD, little daughter of MR. and MRS. W.L. PRITCHARD, died the 20 (May) in Anderson Co., S.C. from cholera infantum (sic). She was buried from Prospect Church.

Card of Thanks, to neighbors and friends at the time of JAMES HENRY FORTNER'S death. He was the son of MR. HENRY FORTNER. Family of James Henry Fortner.

AD - DR. ROBERT KIRKSEY, Physician and Surgeon, has his office at his residence on Main Street.

Pickens Co., S.C. Court of Common Pleas - JOHN T. ANTHONY, Administrator of the Estate of HENRY J. ANTHONY, et al. vs SAMUEL BLASSINGAME, et al. Summons for Relief.

NO PAPER FOUND FOR THURSDAY 7 JUNE 1894:

Issue of: Thursday 14 June 1894:

Married the 10 (June) at the residence of Rev. J.M. Stewart, MR. DAVIS BROWN to MISS MARY HESTER.

MRS. AVERY and son ALBERT of Atlanta, Georgia are stopping at the MOUNTAIN VIEW HOTEL, Easley, S.C.

PROF. O'HANLON'S wife died at her home in Rome, Georgia the 5 June.

M.D. KEITH died the 11 (June) at his home in Pumpkintown Township. He was 76 years old. Mr. Keith leaves 2 sisters. (MARCUS D. KEITH, born the 19 Sept. 1817, died the 11 June 1894, buried Oolenoy Cemetery - Pickens Co., S.C. Cemetery Survey, Vol. 1, p. 247 - see issue of the 21 June 1895).

LOUI HAGOOD, the 1 year old son of MR. and MRS. W.M. HAGOOD, died Sunday and was buried at the family burying ground 5 miles north of Pickens. (Died the 10 June 1894, buried Hagood Cemetery - Pickens Co., S.C. Cemetery Survey, Vol. 1, p. 183).

Clemson College to Organize a Fire Department.

Pickens Co., S.C. Court of Common Pleas - Estate of ROBERT E.T. HOLCOMBE, deceased. RICHARD LENHARDT vs MARTHA ELVIRA HOLCOMBE, et al. Summons for Relief.

Issue of: Thursday 21 June 1894:

From Table Mountain
MARCUS KEITH, SR. died the 11 (June) of Bright's disease of the kidneys. He was buried at Oolenoy (see issue of the 14 June 1894).

D.F. SUTHERLAND & BROS. store and stock were burned the 14 (June) in Pumpkintown, S.C.

ELIJAH FOSTER is the father of a son born the 8 (June).

M.M. HOLDER is attending the Military School at Winston, North Carolina.

MISS MINNIE KIRKSEY graduated with distinction last week from Winthrop Training School in Columbia, S.C.

LEO HARTWELL ORR infant of MR. and MRS. L.P. ORR died the 13 (May) at the home in Pickens.

AD - Winthrop State Normal School, Columbia, S.C.

From Pinder
Corner stone laying for the Hampton School on the 6 (June).

Issue of: Thursday 28 June 1894:

Pickens Co., S.C. Treasurer's Annual Report (details).

DR. C.E. FLEMING of Spartanburg, S.C. died of heart disease (details).

PROF. LANG CLAYTON is teaching at Townville, S.C.

ANTHONY STEWART died at his residence in Oconee Co., S.C. the 5 (June). He was a resident of Pickens Co. until 1890. Mr. Stewart leaves a brother.

NELLIE WILLIAMS, the 2 year old daughter of MR. and MRS. B.H. WILLIAMS, died the 24 (June) at the home of her parents at Cedar Rock, S.C. She was buried at the family cemetery.

MRS. JAMES THOMPSON would like to have a few boarders.

Those wishing to spend the summer in Pickens will find comfortable quarters at reasonable rates at MRS. JAMES RAINES.

Investigation into the Cross Roads Church Matters (continued).

Issue of: 5 July 1894:

GEORGE W. SINGLETON'S birthday is the 15 June.

Pickens Co., S.C. Treasurer's Report (continued).

Pickens Co., S.C. Petit Jury List.

W.T. BRYANT lost his house to fire last Saturday night.

J.M. WARD is living on JOHN FERGUSON'S place.

DR. AND MRS. LANCASTER of Gainesville, Florida. are visiting Mrs. Lancaster's parents MR. and MRS. C.L. HOLLINGSWORTH.

HARLSTON PILGRIM died Sunday night at the age of 50 years. He was buried from Prater's Church.

COL. W.C. PICKENS of Anderson Co., S.C. married MRS. LOUIS PHILLIPS. This is the third marriage for each. *Keowee Courier*

LEVINA MILLER of Seneca, S.C., died the 18 (June) at the age of 70 years. She was a member of the Methodist Church. Mrs. Miller leaves 8 children and a host of grandchildren.

Dacusville
Letter from TYLER HILL of Texas (details of life in Texas).

Fairview Methodist Episcopal Church will apply for a charter to incorporate - 28 June 1894 Pickens, S.C.

Issue of: Thursday 12 July 1894:

From Liberty
J.S. O'DELL'S house burned the 5 (July).

MAJOR E.B. MURRY of Anderson, S.C. drowned the 7 July (details).

Pickens Co., S.C. Court Of General Sessions Report - Criminal cases (details).

BENJAMIN F. MARTIN has a position in Washington, D.C. with the DEPARTMENT OF INTERIOR.

MR. F.C. PARSON is building a good substantial schoolhouse, free of charge, for the New District cut off from Mile Creek District near J.N. MURPHREE'S.

MISS MARY ALLGOOD is to teach in Bethlehem School District.

JUDGE DAVID JOHNSON of Spartanburg, S.C. died Saturday night.

Issue of: 19 July 1894:

From Six Mile
REV. SAMUEL CHAPMAN died the 13 (July) at the age of 81 years. He leaves a wife and several children.

Democratic Primary Election Managers Named (details).

REUBEN FOLGER has been attending the Business College in Lexington, Kentucky.

CAPTAIN IVY M. MAULDIN of Clemson College has been visiting his parents MR. and MRS. JOAB MAULDIN.

MR. E.M. KENNEMORE has a new 7 room house in Liberty Township. The house was built by BABB BROS.

PROF. JOHN O. DAVIS taught at the new Dacusville School.

GOVERNOR B.R. TILLMAN offers a reward for information on the person who burned the barn of JOHN FERGUSON.

INTERNAL REVENUE SERVICE seized property in Pickens Co., S.C. (details).

Issue of: Thursday 26 July 1894:

Letter to the Editor from R.R. SINGLETON of Mallard, Montague Co., Texas (details).

Pickens Co., S.C. Court Proceedings - Minor criminal cases (details).

MISS BERRY daughter of L.M. BERRY to receive a Winthrop Scholarship.

The infant of DR. and MRS. J.J. MORGAN of Dacusville, S.C. died the 20 (July). Burial was from the Methodist Church.

The infant of MR. and MRS. MERRITT LOOPER died the 20 (July) and was buried from Nine Forks Church.

Died the 18 (July), a little son of MR. and MRS. L.D. STEPHENS of Redmond, S.C.

The Trustees of Pickens Court House School have elected PROF. MARSHALL STRIBLING to teach.

NO PAPER FOUND FOR THURSDAY 2 AUGUST 1894.

Issue of: Thursday 9 August 1894:

Report of the County Democratic Convention (details).

Work has commenced on a Public Well for Pickens, S.C.

JOE E. KINCH is working on the *Sentinel*.

CHARLEY ROBINSON will soon finish his building on Main Street and will have it ready for occupancy.

A.C. TILDEN left here for Greenville, S.C. where he will take a position on the *Baptist Courier*.

DR. J.C.C. NEWTON, missionary from Japan, is preaching at the Methodist Church.

J.W. SIMPSON is teaching at Turner's Hill School.

Zion School is being taught by J.A. McWHORTER.

Pickensville School is being taught by MISS LULA GLAZENER in a tenant house on AUDITOR BRYANT'S place.

Liberty Colored School is being taught by REV. G.W. SHACKLEFORD in a new log building 16 X 20. The school is not yet in good condition.

Liberty White School is being taught by R.E. BOGGS.

Issue of: Thursday 16 August 1894:

The Candidates in Anderson Co., S.C. - Campaign Meeting (details).

ROE KEITH, colored, is the mail carrier in the Pickens area (details). *Greenville News* - 8 Aug.

Liberty - 13 Aug. 1894
Liberty, S.C has a brass band.

JAMES N. RICHEY died near Hamilton, Anderson Co., S.C. He had been married about 4 times. By the first wife he had one child, MR. WARREN RICHEY. By the second wife he has 4 living children and 3 dead: H.A. RICHEY, Ex-Sheriff of Pickens Co., W.O. RICHEY living a few miles from Easley, S.C., JOHN T. RICHEY of Fair Play, Oconee Co., S.C. and only surviving daughter MRS. TEMPLETON WYATT of Anderson Co., S.C. His last wife a MISS TOMPKINS survives him. Mr. Richey was buried from Fairview Church (details). *Easley Democrat*

Tribute of Respect - RUSSELL DUKE who recently passed away. He was one of the largest contributors of the rebuilding of the Tabor Methodist Church (details).

JOHN SMITH is building a new dwelling on his farm near town. BABB BROS. have the contract.

Died, the 5 day old infant of M.F. HESTER on Monday.

Married the 8 (Aug.) at the residence of MRS. THOMAS STEWART by Rev. B.F. Murphree, MR. C.N. FOSTER to MISS M.A. TAYLOR.

The BABB BROS. are to build a large and commodious dwelling house for GEORGE KENNEMORE on his farm between Liberty and Easley, S.C.

MISS HASSIE LESLEY daughter of MR. and MRS. W.A. LESLEY died at the home of her parents near Easley, S.C. the 10 (Aug.).

Bridge to be let on Wolf Creek - road leading from Pickens to Easley, S.C. (details).

MRS. LILY RIVES is teaching at Ruhamah School, assisted by MR. RIVES. The new school is not yet complete.

Tabor School #7 is being taught by MISS LIZZIE MAULDIN.

MISS HESTER is teaching at the Long Branch School.

J.W. WILLIAMS is teaching at Johnston's School.

MARY KIRKSEY is teaching at Lenhardt School in a tenant house of B.D. LENHARDT.

JAMES RICHARDSON is teaching at Bright's Station School in a tenant house on R.R. HILL'S land.

AD - Pickens High School, M.S. STRIBLING, Principal.

AD - Furman University, Greenville, S.C.

AD - *People's Journal*, Job Press and Type by JAMES RAINES, Job Printer.

AD - PROF. J.M. LOOPER will teach classes in Music.

Issue of: Thursday 23 August 1894:

J.F. WELLS is completing the law office of C.E. ROBINSON on Main Street.

The School House in town is being repaired and remodeled.

C. ARTHUR RAINES and family of Richmond, Virginia are visiting his father JAMES RAINES. Mr. Raines holds a position in the freight department SOUTHERN RAILWAY COMPANY.

List of guests at the AMBLER HOUSE: MR. and MRS. A.H. PETSCHE, MISS ALICE MOROSO, MISS BETTIE MOROSO, MRS. T.R. JORDAN, MISS M. JORDAN, MISS GERTRUDE BURGESS, MR. BURCHMEYER, MISS LAURIE M. BORNEST, MISS MARIE H. MICHEL all of Charleston, S.C. and MISS MAY McPHAIL of Greenville, S.C.

REV. HARTWELL R. MOSELEY of the Baptist Church is in jail in Mexico due to tracts circulated among the Mexicans. He is a missionary (details).

St. Stephens in School District #20 is being taught by L.A. JENKINS.

Mauldin School #14 is being taught by W.J. BOGGS.

Colored School #12 in the Easley, S.C. area is being taught at MR. CHAPMAN'S tenant house for want of a house. The teacher is J.N. MILLER of Oconee Co., S.C. (details).

The Trustees could not agree in Cedar Rock, S.C. - They will have 2 schools, Holly Bush to be taught by MISS HATTIE WYATT and Tabor to be taught by MISS MARY BOWEN.

Issue of: Thursday 30 August 1894:

Pickens Co., S.C. Campaign Closes - Candidates for County Offices to be Voted on (details).

MRS. REBECCA CURTIS wife of SILAS CURTIS died at her home on Crow Creek the 23 (Aug.). She was buried from the Six Mile Church. Mrs. Curtis leaves a husband and several children.

WILLIAM MAULDIN of Hurricane Township has been visiting his brother AMERICUS MAULDIN at Waco, Georgia.

Pickens Co., S.C. Election Returns (details).

REV. HARTWELL R. MOSELY was released from the Mexican jail.
Greenville Mountaineer

The Trustees of Bethlehem School have moved their house to the center, a little off Main Street in a shady grove. MISS MARY HAGOOD is the teacher (minor details).

Mica School is being taught by MISS LOU M. PHILPOT. The building is 20 X 36 and not yet finished.

Roanoke School #21 is being taught by S.W. O'DELL.

Carpenter's Creek School #34 is being taught by MISS JOSIE ROBINSON (details).

MRS. A.J. BUTLER is teaching at Olga, S.C. (details).

Issue of: Thursday 6 September 1894:

Election News - Anderson Primary and Oconee Primary (details).

MAJOR SANDERS GLOVER, a clerk in the UNITED STATES DISTRICT ATTORNEY'S OFFICE, spent 2 days with his old army friends last week.

FANNIE HARRIS infant daughter of MR. and MRS. ROBERT L. HARRIS died the 26 (Aug.) at the home of her parents near Rice, S.C. and was buried from Enon Church.

MRS. ALICE BOGGS wife of MR. HAMILTON BOGGS, JR. died the 31 (Aug.) at the home of her husband in Slabtown, Anderson Co., S.C. She was 25 years old. *Anderson Advocate*

Pickens Co., S.C. Petit Jury List.

Soapstone School in District #49 is being taught by JOHN A. BAKER. The schoolhouse is 16 X 26 (details).

Grove School in District #49 is taught by MISS NETTIE SOUTHERLAND. The schoolhouse is 18 X 26 (details).

Oolenoy School is taught by MR. W.F. HENDRICKS. The building is rather small (details).

School #48 is being taught by E.C. EDENS. The building is 20 X 30 (minor details).

From Dacusville
Letter to the Editor, 28 Aug. 1894, about his trip to Texas, from J.E. HILL (details).

Pickens Co., S.C. Notice to Creditors and Debtors - Estate of MARQUIS D. KEITH by J.D.M. KEITH, Executor.

Pickens Co., S.C. Notice to Debtors and Creditors - Estate of B.S. PORTER, deceased by J.M. STEWART, Administrator.

Pickens Co., S.C. Final Settlement - W.T. FIELD, Guardian of GEORGE H. HENDRICKS.

For Sale - Thorough-bred Poland China and White Chester pigs. Call on MRS. J.B. WATKINS or W.A. ARNOLD at Central, S.C. or R.J. WATKINS at Stewart, S.C.

Issue of: Thursday 13 Sept. 1894:

S.C. State Democratic Committee Report on Democratic Convention (details).

From Liberty
B.F. PARSONS is clerking for J.D. SMITH.
R.C. ROBINSON is clerking for HUNTER & BOGGS.

Pickens Co., S.C. Election Returns (details).

List of guest at the AMBLER HOUSE:
MRS. J.F. DARAGAN and daughter Miss MAGGIE of Charleston, S.C.

Married Sunday the 2 September 1894 by O.S. Stewart, N.P., MR. C. EARLE NEWTON to MISS ROSA GARRETT.

The 7 month old child of MR. and MRS. W.P. STEWART died the 30 August 1894 and was buried at Keowee Burying Ground.

LEE HUNT and family are living on JAMES PEEKS' farm near Central, S.C.

Married Thursday the 6 September 1894 at the residence of the bride's father MR. JOHN ROPER by Rev. W.C. Seaborn, MR. FRANK SMITH to MISS ESSIE ROPER all of Pickens County.

HEYMAN HUNT the 5 year old son of T.J. HUNT died the 3 (Sept.) at the home of his father at Dacusville, S.C. He was buried at Dacusville, S.C.

WADE HEATON, white, was stabbed to death, at Salem, Oconee Co., S.C., by a Negro on Sunday.

WILLIAM U. HUNT died Monday at his home in Easley Township. He was buried at the Martin Hunt Family Cemetery. Mr. Hunt was about 64 years old and leaves 5 sons and 4 daughters.

MRS. AMANDA E. BAKER wife of WILLIE P. BAKER died the 5 September 1894. She was buried at Mountain Grove Baptist Church Cemetery. Mrs. Baker leaves a husband and 5 children. She was 41 years old and a member of the Baptist church.

Pickens Co., S.C. Petit Jury List.

Pickens Co., S.C. Sheriff's Sale - A.R. HARRIS, Administrator and Plaintiff vs JOHN CRAIG. 250 acres of land on the Keowee River to be sold.

W.C. BRAMBLETT - Sale before moving to the new store room recently erected by C.E. ROBINSON opposite the *Journal* office.

Pickens Co., S.C. Final Settlement - Estate of GEORGE H. HENDRICKS, deceased.

Pickens Co., S.C. Final Settlement - Estate of W.S. CLAYTON, deceased.

Wolf Creek School is taught by B.A. ALLGOOD in a tenant house on Mr. GER LOOPER'S land.

Gates School #22 is taught by MISS DAISY BUROUGHS and Shoal Creek School is taught by MRS. DARTHULA WILLIAMS.

Garvin School is taught by MISS GEORGIA BOGGS.

King's School is taught by MISS SALLIE MULLIKIN.

Six Mile School is taught by MRS. FLORENCE BOWEN. This is a new school with an enrollment of about 60.

Prater's School #28 is taught by MISS MYRTIE BOUROUGHS in a new school not yet complete.

Issue of: Thursday 20 September 1894:

Two deaths near Clemson - Clemson College, S.C. *Daily News* - 11 Sept.
MR. BEATTIE an old gentleman who lives in the vicinity died yesterday (10 Sept.) from a fall. He was on the scaffolding of a 2 story building.
CAPTAIN PERRY, lately in charge of the convict guard, died last night (10 Sept.) of typhoid fever. He leaves a young wife.

Blood Shed, Oconee Co., S.C.
BILL WHITE, colored, was thought to be shot by ANDY LESTER and BILL ROACH, 2 Negroes, on Saturday night near Westminster, S.C. Bill White may die (details).
FRANK THREFT cut JOHN and IRA QUARLES on Sunday morning on Whetstone Creek. JOHN QUARLES may die (details).

J.H. BROWN is preparing to build a new store in Liberty, S.C. L. REID SMITH will be the clerk and W. LEE SAMMONS will serve customers in the cotton business.

J. SMITH'S baby died (no other details).

From Looper's
MR. N.H. JONES is building a dwelling, barn, stable, etc. on land he recently purchased from MR. S.F. ROBINSON.
MR. TRAINUM has his store house at Nine Fork Church about ready for goods.
MESSRS. HUGHES are to build a new store house, then we will have an ALLIANCE STORE here.

MRS. SARAH M. MANLY widow of the late REV. DR. BASIL MANLY died at the home of her son REV. DR. CHARLES MANLY in Greenville, S.C. Wednesday night. She was 88 years of age.

MISS LETTIE GRICE is to teach at Zion School in District #8.

C.T. MILLER, colored, has opened a flourishing school on the mountain near Bald Knob, S.C.

J.W. SUTHERLAND of Oolenoy, S.C. will move his family to town in a few days. He will occupy the new house recently erected by B.D. STEWART. Mr. Sutherland comes to educate his children.

MR. J.E. KINCH'S family arrived in Pickens from Mississippi last week. They will occupy the MAJOR house owned by REV. J.M. STEWART.

MISS ESSIE EARLE will attend the Presbyterian Female College, Greenville, S.C.

MISS EUGENIA CURTIS daughter of SILAS CURTIS of Hurricane Township died the 15 (Sept.) of typhoid fever and was buried at Six Mile Church Cemetery.

Death at Briggs
BENTAN S. FREEMAN, JR. age 15 died. He was the son of BENTAN FREEMAN who lives near Briggs, S.C.

NORMA WILSON daughter of MR. and MRS. J.C. WILSON formerly of Pickens Co., died the 7 (Sept.) at the home of her parents in Pelzer, S.C.

Twelve Mile Cross Roads School, colored, is being taught by A.G. BOWEN.

Concord School #29 is being taught by J.G. SEABORN.

Mile Creek School is being taught by MISS ALMA KAY in a tenant house on MR. DAVIS MORGAN'S place.

Parson's Grove School is being taught by MISS NANNIE KIRKSEY in a new school house not yet complete. We understand it belongs to the district.

Gap Hill District #42 is being taught by J.S. HIMES (sic) of Newberry, S.C. He is a Chafflin man (details).

Keowee School is being taught by W.E. BARTON. The house used is the Keowee Church.

Issue of: Thursday 27 September 1894:

Democratic State Convention, Columbia, S.C.

Married the 2 September 1894 in the city of Asheville, North Carolina, ALONZO PACE to MISS ALICE KUYKENDALL. They are visiting in Pickens.

Pickens Co., S.C. Court Records - Criminal cases. (details).

MISS LIZZIE ESTHER LOOPER daughter of MR. and MRS. E.F. LOOPER died at her parent's home the 22 (Sept.). She was 14 years old and was buried in the family cemetery. Another daughter Viola is critically ill. (LIZZIE LOOPER, buried Baker Family Cemetery - Pickens Co., S.C. Cemetery Survey, Vol. 1, p. 11).

Martin School District is being taught by MISS FANNIE DALTON in a new schoolhouse.

The school at Twelve Mile is being taught by MISS VIRGINIA LIGON. The new 20 X 40 house is not yet complete.

District #32 School is being taught by ANDREW BRAMBLETT in a new school (details).

Anthony's Fork School is being taught by JAMES RICHARDSON. The school is small but a good log house.

Ambler School is being taught by W.E. HENDRICKS. The new school is to be completed by Christmas with little aid from school funds.

Pickens Co., S.C. Grand Jury - Report on conditions of buildings, bridges, etc. in the county.

Issue of: Thursday 4 October 1894:

Tragedy at Pickens
WILL LATHEM was shot and killed by L.E. CHILDRESS the 26 (Sept.) (details).

Pickens Co., S.C. Salesday:
R.L. McCRACKIN vs W.A. BARR. 51 acres sold to R.L. McCRACKIN for $100.
JOSEPH HARDIN vs JAMEE F. CAULEY, et al. 350 acres sold to R.E. BROWN for $311.

B.D. STEWART is a salesman in WALKER'S CASH STORE in Greenville, S.C.

MISS ELLA MEARS of Pickens is attending school in Leesville.

W.A. PALMER and family have moved to Pelzer, S.C.

Married the 23 (Sept.) by T.J. Cureton at his residence, MISS MARTHA CAPPS of Anderson Co., S.C. to MR. WILLIAM GRIFFIN of Pickens County.

McALISTER & BEATTIE of Greenville, S.C. have moved into a new store.

HUNTER & BOGGS CO. of Liberty, S.C. have been granted a charter to do general merchandise business. Members: WILLIAM HUNTER, SR., T.N. HUNTER, C.E. HAMILTON, M.A. BOGGS, B.D. BOGGS, B.D. MAULDIN and JOHN HUNTER. *Columbia Register*

A huge dam is being built by the PELZER COMPANY two and a half miles from Pelzer, S.C. (details). *Greenville News*

Married Tuesday the 2 (Oct.) at the residence of J.B. NEWBERRY, ESQ. of Easley, S.C., by Rev. G.R. Shaffer, MR. A.R.N. FOLGER to MISS CHARLOTTE MURFF of Pickens.

Pickens Co., S.C. Tax Notice.

Hampton School is being taught by JOHN D. EDENS. The building is 20 X 32 with no heat.

Cold Spring School, colored, is being taught by T.M. ELROD. The building is 18 X 20.

Issue of: Thursday 11 October 1894:

The hotel at Clemson is about completed (details).

From Liberty
MISS LIZZIE BOGGS is in the millinery business in Pelzer, S.C.
LEE SAMSON has located here to buy cotton and cotton seed.

MR. F.C. PARSONS has added a cane mill to his machinery and is now making molasses.

The funeral service for MR. B.S. PORTER will be preached on the 2nd Sunday in October by Rev. G.R. Shaffer.

Married the 2 (Oct.) at the residence of the bride's father MR. MARION ELLISON, MR. J.D. MORGAN of Pickens to MISS NETTIE ELLISON of Anderson, S.C.

MISS EMMA CHAPMAN daughter of HARLESTON CHAPMAN formerly of this county died at the home of her father in Pelzer, S.C. the 3 (Oct.). She was 16 years old.

MRS. ELIZABETH CHANDLER died the 6 (Oct.) at the home of her son J.J. CHANDLER near town. She was 88 years old and a member of the Baptist Church. Burial from Secona.

MAY VAUGHN the 3 year old daughter of MR. and MRS. JOHN VAUGHN died the 6 (Oct.) at her home 3 miles south of town. She was buried from Enon Church.

AD - LEE P. ORR, Photographer, FREEMAN BUILDING, Pickens, S.C.

AD - L.S. WILLIAMS will be located at Newry, the new mill town on Little River, Oconee Co., S.C.

AD - DR. W.F. AUSTIN, Dentist, will be in Central, S.C. and Pickens certain days (details).

Pickens Co., S.C. Citation Notice - Estate of SUSAN E. LATHEM, deceased. E.B. LATHEM applied for Letters of Administration.

Pickens Co., S.C. Citation Notice - Estate of A.M. NEAL, deceased. J.M. STEWART applied for Letters of Administration.

Pickens Co., S.C. Clerk's Sale:
Furman University vs W.P. TATE and M.P. HALL. 160 acres and 40 acres on the Saluda River to be sold.
RICHARD LENDHARDT vs MARTHA ELVIRA HOLCOMBE, et al. 100 acres and 120 acres on Bushy Creek to be sold.

Pickens Co., S.C. Sheriff's Sale - Estate of R.A. STEWART, deceased. J.M. STEWART, Administrator vs SARAH A. STEWART, et al. 31 acres on Crow Creek to be sold.

MRS. SUSAN E. LATHEM wife of ENOCH B. LATHEM died the 4 (Oct.) at her home near Easley, S.C. She was the daughter of JOHN S. CLEMENTS of New Prospect, Spartanburg Co., S.C. and a member of Mount Carmel Baptist Church. Mrs. Lathem leaves a husband and several children. (ELLEN S. LATHEM, born 5 Oct. 1867, died 4 Oct. 1894, buried Lathem Family Cemetery - Pickens Co., S.C., Cemetery Survey, Vol. 1, p. 42).

The infant of MR. and MRS. JOHN CHILD died the 6 (Oct.) at their home near town. Burial from Griffin Church.

Pickens Co., S.C. - List of County Commissioners (details).

MRS. BETSY CASSON died near Flat Rock Church the 4 (Oct.) at the age of 76 years, 3 months and 4 days. She was buried at Old Liberty Burying Ground. Mrs. Casson was a member of the Six Mile Baptist Church.

Issue of: Thursday 18 October 1894:

Letter to the Editor, from R.R. SINGLETON, Mallard, Texas (details).

MRS. ELLA ROBINSON wife of T.C. ROBINSON died last Monday of consumption at the age of 39 years. She was buried at the family burying ground Liberty, S.C. Mrs. Robinson leaves a husband and 6 children.

Cadets attending Clemson College from Pickens County, S.C.
J.T. BOWEN	I.M. MAULDIN
W.L. CLYDE	B.F. ROBERTSON
R.F. HALLUM	E.L. HAMILTON
E.E. LEWIS	F.A. LEWIS

Contractors are ready to rebuild the building that was burned at Clemson College.

From Table Rock
Messrs. HOLBERT LYNCH, ALONZO EDENS and SIDNEY EDENS formed a company for mercantile business to be located about 1 mile above Pumpkintown, S.C. The firm is named EDENS BROS. & LYNCH.
D.F. SUTHERLAND & BROS. of Pumpkintown, S.C. are filling up rapidly since their burn out.

J.W. SUTHERLAND and family and SILAS HINKLE and family have moved to town to school their children.

Pickens Co., S.C. Commissioners of Election Meeting (details).

JAMES RAINES has moved from the BABB house to the FOLGER house. H.B. HENDRICKS has moved from the CLYDE house to the BABB house and M.F. HESTER has moved from the DURANT house to the CLYDE house.

AD - Good building lot for sale on Garvin St., Pickens, S.C., by JAMES RAINES.

Pickens Co., S.C. Notice to Creditors and Debtors - Estate of JACOB M. KING by MARGARET C. KING and J. MONROE KING, Administrators.

Issue of: Thursday 25 October 1894:

Election Managers named for Pickens Co., S.C. for State and Federal Elections (details).

H.B. HENDRICKS is making improvements on the BABB place.

PROF. S.W. O'DELL has a neat and commodious new dwelling house on his farm near Roanoke Schoolhouse. It was built by J.F. WELLS.

JIM ALEXANDER, colored, was killed by CHARLES SPENCER, white, at B.J. WILLIAMS' gin the 20 (Oct.) (details).

MRS. ELIZABETH FINLEY died the 10 Oct. 1894 at the residence of her husband MR. CHARLES B. FINLEY near Gap Hill, Pickens Co. She was the daughter of MR. ELISHA ALEXANDER of Pickens Co. and was 55 years old. Mrs. Finley married first MR. JOHN KNOX and he died during the Civil War, they had 2 sons, ROBERT E. KNOX of Pickens and JAMES E. KNOX of Oconee Co., S.C. After the war she married Mr. Finley, by this marriage she leaves 2 daughters, 4 sons and 2 step-sons. Early in life she joined the Baptist Church but at her second marriage joined the Methodist Episcopal Church. *Oconee News*

MRS. AMANDA BOYD wife of MAJOR WAREN BOYD died at her home near Pickens Court House the 18 October 1894 at the age of 66 years. Services were held at Secona Baptist Church.

MR. NIX MEDLIN who lived about 5 miles north of town died the 23 (Oct.) at the age of 96 years.

Pickens Co., S.C. Clerk's Sale - Court of Common Pleas - J.D. SMITH vs JACKSON CANNON. 161 acres known as the BELL SHOAL place to be sold.

Issue of: Thursday 1 November 1894:

Pickens Co, S.C. State Elections (details).

DR. W.A. COX died the 11 (Oct.) at his home in Hart Co., Georgia. He was the son of MR. S.M. COX of Pickens County. Dr. Cox was buried from George's Creek Church. He leaves a wife and 2 children.

W.O. SINGLETON of Dacusville, S.C. will move to Oconee Co., S.C.

MR. BLANTON is running the KEOWEE HOTEL in Seneca, S.C.

AD - Selling General Merchandise, SHEPPARD & ELLISON, Easley, S.C.

Issue of: Thursday 8 November 1894:

Facts about the THORNWELL ORPHANAGE (details).

W.H. THOMAS of Six Mile, S.C. has moved to Georgia.

THOMAS MADDEN was killed by THOMAS ALEXANDER at Salem, Oconee Co., S.C. the 1 (Nov.).

JESSE SIMMONS who lives about 8 miles east of Pickens died the 2 (Nov.). He was about 84 years old.

M.F. HESTER is repairing his house on the east side of Main St. which he recently purchased of J.B. CLYDE.

Married the 4 (Nov.) at the Methodist Parsonage by G.R. Shaffer, MISS JANIE McWHORTER to MR. CHARLES N. DURHAM.

Married the 4 (Nov.) by J.A. Robinson, N.P., MR. BENJAMIN BOYDE to MISS MARY SKELTON all of Dacusville, Pickens County.

Married the 4 Nov. at the residence of the bride, by J.A. Robinson, N.P., MISS SALLY OWENS to MR. ABRAHAM BANKS.

Married the 4 (Nov.) at the residence of MRS. ELIZABETH HOLDER by I.H. Philpot, N.P., MISS VALLENIE HOLDER to MR. FORD McCULLUM.

MR. JAMES RAINES employed by the *Journal* office for the last four years will leave for Richmond, Virginia where he will make his future home.

MR. JOHN G. CAPERS of Columbia, S.C. son of BISHOP CAPERS, has been appointed to a position in the Attorney General's Office (details).

EARLE HUNT oldest son of MR. and MRS. JAS. T. HUNT of Pendleton, S.C. died at his father's home of peritonitis. He was 18 years old.

The small child of MR. and MRS. ROBERT HUGHES who live on JAMES HENDRICK'S farm, Liberty Township died the 3 (Nov.). She fell into the fire.

MRS. JOHN F. ARNOLD died in Greenville, S.C. last Sabbath. She is buried at a cemetery here (place not given). *Central Tyro*

THOMAS JENKINS and JOSEPH MAULDIN will resume work in the factory at Pelzer, S.C.

MRS. HINTON mother of SAMUEL HINTON died at her residence in Dacusville Township the 4 (Nov.) at the age of about 80 years. She was buried from Griffin Church.

Pickens Co., S.C. Salesday:
C.H. JUDSON vs W.P. FATE. 160 acres bought by C.H. JUDSON for $300.
J.D. SMITH vs JACKSON CANNON. 160 acres bought by J.D. SMITH for $150.
RICHARD LENHARDT vs MARTHA E. HOLCOMBE, et al. 113 acres bought by M.E. HOLCOMBE for $1,245.
J.M. STEWART, Administrator vs SARAH A. STEWART. 31 acres bought by C.E. ROBINSON for $25.
NORA E. ALEXANDER, et al. vs R.W. HOLCOMBE, Administrator. Tract #1 - 70 acres bought by J.B. ROBINSON for $660.
Tract #2 - 2 lots in Easley, S.C. bought by J.E. BOGGS for $295. Tract #3 - 100 acres bought by J.E. BOGGS for $825.
JACOB ALEXANDER, et al. vs GEORGE K. HENDRICKS, et al. 500 acres sold to EPHRIAM GILSTRAP for $350.
MARY P. GARRICK (sic) vs S.D. COOPER, et al. 144 acres sold to J.P. CAREY for $800.
ROBERT G. HUNT, et al. vs J.P. CAREY, et al. 90 acres sold to M.V. HUNT for $410.
EASLEY BANK CO. vs W.J. CRENSHAW. 52 acres sold to T.H. STEWART for $52.
EASLEY BANK CO. vs W.W. CHILDRESS. 6 acres bought by J.E. BOGGS for $300.
NANNIE ROBINSON vs JOSEPH BOATWRIGHT. 7 acres sold to C.E. ROBINSON for $300.
D. McD. KENNEDY vs N.A. CHRISTOPHER, et al. 86 acres bought by J.E. BOGGS for $500.

Pickens Co., S.C. Executor's Sale - Estate of JOHN B. CLARDY, deceased by JOHN L. CLARDY and W.R. KENNEMUR, Executors. 160 acres on the Keowee River to be sold.

AD - LEE P. ORR leaving Pickens, S.C.

Issue of: Thursday 15 November 1894:

Married the 11 (Nov.) by Rev. L. Jones, MISS LIZZIE PORTER to MR. D. LEWIS.

Married at the residence of the Rev. W.C. Seaborn, MR. JOHN ABERCROMBIE to MISS ANNIE DAY all of Pickens County.

Married Sunday the 4 (Nov.) at the residence of the bride's father, by Rev. L.T. Weldon, MR. PEARCY ROBINSON to MISS SALLIE NELSON.

Married Sunday the 7 (Nov.) at the residence of the bride's father, by Rev. L.T. Weldon, MR. WILL YOUNG of Anderson Co., S.C. to MISS ELIZA McWHORTER of Pickens County.

MR. FLOWERS originally from Mecklenburg Co., North Carolina, who was born in 1806 is living on CAPTAIN F.L. GARVIN'S place 4 miles north of town. He has been married 4 times and has raised 35 children (details).

Pickens Co., S.C. Sheriff's Sales:
JAMES P. JONES vs E. FOSTER KEITH. 119 acres in Pumpkintown Township to be sold.

Pickens Co., S.C. Clerk's Sale:
VESTA ELIZABETH KING, et al. vs MARGARET C. KING, et al. 64 acres near the town of Easley, S.C. to be sold
P.A. PORTER, et al. vs DAVID PORTER, et al. Tracts of land at Hagood's Mill Creek, waters of the Twelve Mile River to be sold as the estate of B.S. PORTER, deceased. Tract #1 - 12 acres; Tract #2 - 68 acres; Tract #3 - 32 acres and Tract #4 - 47 acres.
JESSE CRENSHAW vs J.W. BRADLEY. 182 acres to be sold.
JOHN T. ANTHONY, Administrator, et al. vs SAMUEL BLASSINGAME, et al. Tract #1 - 146 acres on Town Creek; Tract #2 - 270 acres. The two tracts to be sold are the home place of H.H. ANTHONY, deceased.
SAMUEL EDENS vs JAMES P. JONES. 92 3/4 acres on Oolenoy Creek to be sold.

Issue of: Thursday 22 November 1894:

MRS. ELLEN CLEMENTS LATHEM wife of MR. E.B. LATHEM died at her home near the town of Easley, S.C. the 4 Oct. Two little boys died ahead of her. She leaves a husband and two little girls (lengthy details).

Dacusville
Married at the home of the bride's mother MRS. M.M. MORGAN of Dacusville, S.C. yesterday, by Rev. John O. Wilson, MR. JEPTHA NORTON MORGAN and MISS MINNIE EVA MORGAN daughter of the late B.F. MORGAN and sister of MESSRS. J.H., M.A. and B.A. MORGAN of this city. Mr. Morgan is a junior member of the mercantile business in Central, S.C. *Greenville News* - 15 Nov.

N.J. WILLIAMS of Table Rock, S.C. is building a dwelling on his farm and will move in soon.

F.G. HILL of Dacusville Township is about to complete an elegant and commodious residence on his farm.

Married the 18 (Nov.) at the residence of Rev. J.M. Stewart, THOMAS KIRKSEY to MISS LILLIE HENDRICKS, both colored.

Married the 15 Nov. 1894 at the residence of the bride's parents, by Rev. J.M. Stewart, MR. FOREST MURPHREE to MISS ELLEN LOOPER.

Married in Central Township Sunday the 11 (Nov.) at the residence of the bride's father J.H. CLAYTON by Rev. G.R. Shaffer, MR. WILLIAM PARROTT to MISS IOLA CLAYTON.

Married the 11 (Nov.) at the residence of the bride's father MR. WILLIAM BAKER by Rev. M.L. Jones, MR. M.A. LEWIS to MISS LIZZIE BAKER.

Married Sunday the 18 November 1894 at the residence of the bride's father MR. B.M. BOLDING by Rev. W.C. Seaborn, MR. DANIEL ABBECRUMBIE (sic) to MISS EMMA BOLDING both of Pickens County.

MRS. SINGLETON wife of DAN SINGLETON died the 16 (Nov.) at her residence about four mile south east of town and was buried from Enon Church where she had been a member. She leaves a husband and 2 children.

Issue of: Thursday 29 November 1894:

The Work at Clemson College - Enlarging, etc. (details).

Westminster, S.C. - 24 (Nov.)
W.H. SHELDON'S house was struck by lighting and burned.

Correspondent Spartanburg, S.C. - 24 Nov. (1894) *The Daily News*
Lynching at Landrum, S.C. Thursday night DICK WOFFORD of Polk Co., North Carolina was lynched (details).

Pickens Co., S.C. Tax Assessment Notice.

Married the 25 (Nov.) by Rev. T.F. Nelson at Nine Forks Baptist Church, MR. WILLIAM PERRY to MRS. M.C. TRAINER.

Married the 25 (Nov.) at the residence of Rev. Thomas Looper, MR. BREAZEALE to MISS FANNIE TURNER.

JAMES PEEK'S residence near Central, S.C. burned the 24 (Nov.).

MRS. HANNAH COOPER who lived 6 miles north of town died the 26 (Nov.) at the age of 76 years. She was buried from Porter's Chapel.

Married Wednesday the 21 (Nov.) at the residence of the bride's father MR. DAVID C. TOMPKINS by Rev. W.C. Seaborn, MR. ELFRED M. BOLDING to MISS ALICE TOMPKINS all of Pickens County.

WILLIE PAYNE, age 2 years, died the 16 (Nov.) at the home of his parents MR. and MRS. J.H. PAYNE of Calhoun, S.C. He was an only child.

ELIJAH EDENS died the 26 (Nov.) at the age of 22 years at the residence of his father SAMUEL EDENS in Pumpkintown Township. Mr. Edens was buried from Oolenoy.

Married the 13 (Nov.) at the office of Trial Justice A.L. Edens, MR. JOHN GALLOWAY to MISS CORRIE ROBINSON.

EMMA BRUCE relict of the late S.P. BRUCE, ESQ. of Elberton, Georgia died at her residence in town the 23 (Nov.) and was buried from the Presbyterian Church. She was 64 years old. Mrs. Bruce was a native of Pickens Co. but since her marriage resided in Georgia until 1878 when she returned to this county. She leaves four children: MRS. MINNIE BOGGS wife of HON. J.E. BOGGS, MR. J.McD. BRUCE, MISS CORRIE BRUCE and MR. JULIAN BRUCE of Anderson Co., S.C.

The Work at Clemson College Continues (details).

Issue of: Thursday 6 December 1894:

Organization of the South Carolina General Assembly (details).

GOVERNOR TILLMAN'S Message (details).

REV. G.R. SHAFFER and family will leave for their new home in Princeton, Laurens Co., S.C.

W.A. MILLER has moved his family to Sherman, Texas.

MR. BILL MOORE of Pendleton, S.C. died the 4 November 1894 at the age of 70 years. He was a brother of J.A. MOORE of Prater's Creek.

Married Sunday the 25 (Nov.) at the residence of MR. LARON GARRETT by O.S. Stewart, N.P., MR. G.H. NEWTON to MISS EMMA KELLEY all of Pickens.

Married the 25 (Nov.) at the residence of the bride's father MR. DAVID PARROTT in Oconee Co., S.C., by O.S. Stewart, N.P., MR. SAMUEL KELLY to MISS MAMIE PARROTT.

SENATOR JOSEPH EMERSON BROWN of Georgia died in Atlanta the 30 (Nov.) at the age of 72 years. He was born in Pickens District the 15 April 1821 and married in 1847 MISS ELIZABETH GRESHAM. Senator Brown was a member of the Baptist Church. He leaves a wife, 4 sons and 2 daughters.

DR. J.B. CARPENTER of Marietta, S.C. died the 25 (Nov.) in Columbia, S.C. at the age of 42 years. He was buried from Ebenezer Church.

BARNETT BOWEN, the 3 year old son of MR. and MRS. MARTIN H. BOWEN who live about 4 miles east of town, burned to death last Friday (details).

REV. C.C. BROWN is publishing a map of all the baptist churches in the state, their distance from the court house and directions from same and date of their constitution and oldest churches in the county. B. HOLDER of Pickens request clerks to send information on their churches.

Pickens Co., S.C. Salesday:
O.H.P. FANT vs REBECCA G. CRAWFORD. 228 acres sold to O.H.P. FANT for $1,900.
RANSOM DUKE, et al. vs RHODA MAULDIN. Tract #1 - 36 1/2 acres sold to A.M. MAULDIN for $171; Tract #2 - 39 acres sold to RANSOM DUKE for $196; Tract #3 - 50 acres sold to J.I. WILLIAMS for $400; Tract #4 - sold to RANSOM DUKE for $400; Tract #5 - 184 acres sold to RANSOM DUKE $1,000; Tract #6 - 192 acres sold to A.M. MAULDIN for $350; Tract #7 - 1/2 interest in 28 acres sold, gin, etc. sold to J.S. LATHEM $200; Tract #8 - 1/2 interest in 20 acres to RANSOM DUKE $5; Tract #9 - 1/2 interest in 404 acres to RANSOM DUKE for $605.
ELIZABETH KING, et al. vs MARGARET C. KING, et al. 64 acres sold to MARGARET KING for $495.
P.A. PORTER, et al. vs DAVID PORTER, et al. Tract #1 - 68 acres sold to C.E. ROBINSON for $392; Tract #2 - 32 acres sold to AUTHER (sic) PORTER for $270; Tract #3 - 41 acres sold to D.A. COOPER for $200.
JESSE CRENSHAW vs J.W. BRADLEY. 182 acres sold to JESSE CRENSHAW for $270.
SAMUEL S. EDENS vs J.P. JONES. 93 3/4 acres sold to J.P. JONES for $1,901.
The executors of the estate of J.B. CLARDY, deceased sold 160 acres to J.E. BOGGS for $346.

Issue of: Thursday 13 December 1894:

GOVERNOR TILLMAN'S Message (continued).

From Pinder
Three new stores are underway: SHIRLEY & PERKINS STORE is receiving finishing touches.

From Liberty
MR. B.F. PARSONS has moved into MRS. J.A. SMITH'S house.
REV. W.F. WORKMAN of Clarendon Co., S.C. moved into the CHAPMAN house.

Married Sunday the 9 (Dec.) at the residence of Trial Justice B.D. Garvin, MR. JOSEPH GAINES to MISS LILLIE RAMPEY.

Married the 6 (Dec.) at the residence of the bride's father MR. JERE PRINCE by Rev. W.C. Seaborn, MR. M.B. GARRETT to MISS LILA PRINCE.

Married the 9 (Dec.) at the residence of W.C. SCOTTY of Anderson Co., S.C., by Rev. W.C. Seaborn, MR. JOHN P. BRYANT of Anderson Co., S.C. to MISS ETTIE CLARDY of Pickens.

Married Thursday the 6 (Dec.) at the residence of the bride's father MR. W.R. GARRETT by Rev. W.C. Seaborn, MR. C.R. ABERCROMBIE to MISS DORA M. GARRETT all of Pickens County.

Married the 9 (Nov.) at the residence of the bride's father -- W. BARKLEY, MR. W.H.---- of Madison Co., Georgia. to ---- (unable to read this record).

NO OTHER ISSUES FOUND FOR DECEMBER 1894.

THE PEOPLE'S JOURNAL 1895

Issue of: Thursday 3 January 1895:

"Looking Backward - The Year 1894 in Review" - (the entire United States, major fires, crimes, industrial, educational, etc.).

DR. ROBERT KIRKSEY is a physician and surgeon located on Main Street.

Married the 22 Dec. (1894) at the home of the bride's father MR. JAMES BYARS by Rev. B. Holder, MISS BYARS to MR. RILEY DODGENS.

Married the 26 Dec. (1894) at the residence of MRS. HARRIET BOWIE by Trial Justice Lewis, MR. A.A. ALEXANDER to MISS L.A. NIMMONS.

Married the 24 Dec. (1894) at the residence of the bride's parents MR. and MRS. J.A. CRAIG by Rev. J.R. Riley, D.D., MISS SARAH CRAIG to MR. ROSS HENDERSON of Anderson Co., S.C.

Married the 24 Dec. (1894) at the bride's residence in Walhalla, S.C., MISS EUGENIA MOSS to DR. JOEL BOWEN of Mt. Pleasant, S.C. After visiting the HON. W.T. BOWEN father of the groom the couple went to Mt. Pleasant (details).

CHARLES W. GARRISON of Easley Township died the 21 (Dec. 1894) at the age of 38 years. He leaves a wife and 4 children. Buried (unable to read). (CHARLES W. GARRISON, born 31 Oct. 1854, died 21 Dec. 1894, buried Antioch United Methodist Church Cemetery - Pickens Co., S.C. Cemetery Survey, Vol. 1, p. 4b).

J.B. BOWEN son of THOMAS H. and MANCY E. BOWEN died. Mr. and Mrs. Bowen lived in Pickens until they went to Texas in 1853.

MRS. M.F. ANSEL wife of SOLICITOR ANSEL died at her home in Greenville, S.C. the 25 (Dec. 1894).

J.E. CRAIG of Waxahachie, Texas is visiting his parents.

MR. JAMES F. LAY of Alexander, S.C. has moved to Heardmont, Georgia and is engaged in business with COL. MATTOX of that place.

Married the 25 (Dec. 1894) at Antioch Church by Rev. J.F. Anderson, HENRY E. BATSON of Greenville, S.C. to SALLIE T. GOSSETT daughter of Mr. PINK GOSSETT.

Married the 26 Dec. 1894 at the residence of the bride's parents, by Rev. J.M. Stewart, MR. WILLIE LAURENCE of Central, S.C. to MISS HESTER LEWIS of Anderson Mills, S.C.

For Rent - Two good horse farms, need tenants, by C.L. HOLLINGSWORTH.

Pickens Co., S.C. Clerk's Sale:
Estate of H.J. ANTHONY, deceased. JOHN T. ANTHONY, Administrator, et al. vs SAMUEL BLASSINGAME. Tract #1 - 146 acres on Town Creek and Tract #2 - 270 acres, the homeplace of H.J. ANTHONY.
Estate of JOHN P. PORTER, deceased. P.A. PORTER, et al. vs DAVID PORTER, et al. Tract #2 - 68 acres at Hagood Mill Creek and Tract #3 - 32 acres, part of the homeplace of B.S. PORTER.

Pickens Co., S.C. Citation Notice - Estate of C.W. GARRISON. VARINA GARRISON and JAMES N. GARRISON apply for Letters of Administration.

Pickens Co., S.C. Mortgagee's Sale - JOSEPH BOATWRIGHT vs J.H. NEWTON, Mortgagee. 2 acres of land with 2 good springs adjoining the town of Pickens, S.C. to be sold.

Pickens Co., S.C. Court of Common Pleas - Summons for Relief - F.M. MORRIS & CO. vs J. FRANK WELLS.

Greenville Co., S.C. Master's Sale - G.W. TAYLOR vs P.B. WASTON, et al. 450 acres of land in Central, S.C.

AD - DR. W.F. AUSTIN, dentist of Seneca, S.C. will be in Central, S.C. and in Pickens part of each month.

AD - SHEPPARD & ELLISON, General Merchandise Store, Easley, S.C.

Issue of: Thursday 10 January 1895:

"Looking Backward - The Year 1894" (continued - details).

Pickens Co., S.C. County Board of Trustees (names of members).

Pickens Co., S.C. Land Sales and County Court Records:
J.A. STEWART vs S.S. STEWART. 300 acres sold to N.M. MADDEN for $300.
JOHN T. ANTHONY vs SAMUEL BLASSINGAME. Tract #1 - 146 acres sold to E.O. ANTHONY for $500; Tract #2 - 270 acres sold to S.P. FREEMAN for $800.
P.A. PORTER, et al. vs DAVID PORTER, et al. Tract #2 - 68 acres sold to M.F. HESTER for $163; Tract #3 - 52 acres sold to W.R. PRICE (amount not given).

Executor's Sale of lots of W. ALLEN, deceased. Three acres in the town of Easley, S.C. were sold to W.M. HAGOOD for $350.

Executor's Sale of lots, in the town of Liberty, S.C., as the property of J.A. BOGGS, deceased. Lot #1 sold to WALTER BOGGS for $40.50; Lot #2 sold to T.N. HUNTER for $50; Lot #3 and lot #4 sold to WALTER BOGGS for $45 each; Lot #5 sold to J.D. SMITH for $6; Lot #6 sold to WALTER BOGGS for $23.

G.S.W. TAYLOR vs P.B. WATSON. 450 acres sold to P.B. WATSON for $1,200.

Fires at Seneca

The home of MRS. LIVINGSTON was burned but some of the furniture was saved. MRS. JOHN C. CARY daughter of Mrs. Livingston had a narrow escape with her daughter and nurse.

From Liberty

New inhabitants in Liberty, S.C.: REV. W.H. WORKMAN and family of Clarendon Co., S.C.
DR. J.F. WILLIAMS of Pickens.
W.S. PARSONS has taken charge of the Hotel.
PROF. McCRARY of Laurens Co., S.C.
B.F. PAPRSON.

NENA SPENCER is postmaster at Farris, S.C.

B.A. ALLGOOD has returned to school in Dahlonega, Georgia after visiting during the holidays.

MRS. PERMELIA COLYER, formerly MISS BARTON, sister of HARLSTON BARTON of Easley, S.C., will preach at McKinney's Chapel on the 2nd Sunday in January.

Married the 30 December 1894 in Piedmont, S.C. by W.W. Wright, N.P., MR. JOHN O. MAULDIN of Pickens Co. to MISS MARGARET M. COWARD of Piedmont.

ROSWELL GAILLARD EATON died the 17 December 1894 of typhoid fever. He was born the 24 October 1852 Anderson Co., S.C. and moved to Central, S.C. the 1 December 1881. Mr. Eaton married the 5 February 1890 MISS LOU E. WALTHALL. He removed to Chuta, Virginia the 25 Nov. 1890 where he died. *Central Tyro*

W.H. SUMMEY was postmaster at Goodwin, S.C. (details).

Pickens Co., S.C. Tax Assessment Notice.

Issue of: Thursday 17 January 1895:

LINCOLN GRANT, colored, sentenced to be hanged today (date not given) Berkley Co., S.C. for the killing of his colored companion, had his life saved the 11 (Jan.) by GOV. EVANS who commuted his sentence to life imprisonment.

ROBERT MOORE, a revenue officer and ROBERT T. THRIFT, a moonshiner, shot and killed each other about 15 miles from Walhalla, S.C.

MISS KITTY KIRKSEY to teach school at Holly Springs.

MRS. R.C. WATTS wife of JUDGE WATTS died the 14 (Jan.) at Cash's Depot.

J.E. KINCH has moved into the ASHMORE house recently vacated by DR. J.F. WILLIAMS.

ALFRED J. MOSELEY died last night at the residence of his father-in-law LEWIS GREEN in Greer's, this county. He was a native of Abbeville Co., S.C. and was about 40 years old. Mr. Moseley was a nephew of MAJOR BENJAMIN McDANIEL. *Greenville News*

MISS LIZZIE GRANT of Oconee Co., S.C. died last night at a Columbia Hospital. She was a student in the Winthrop Training School. Her remains will be taken to Walhalla, S.C. *Columbia Register* - 13 January

Pickens Co., S.C. Final Settlement - Guardianship of MAUD and MARY E. BARTON by MELVILLE BARTON, Guardian.

Issue of: Thursday 24 January 1895:

CHICAUMAUGA - Continuing story Chapter I.

JAMES SMITH is now running the HOLLINGSWORTH LIVERY STABLE at Liberty, S.C.

J.H. BROWN of Liberty, S.C. will soon have his new store completed.

Married the 16 (Jan.) at the residence of the bride's father A.E. KELLY in this county, by Rev. John Attaway, MR. M.C. GRAVELEY to MISS MAGGIE KELLY.

Married the 13 January 1895 at the residence of the bride's father MR. JOSEPH CHAPMAN by Rev. M.L. Jones, MR. BRIGHT GILSTRAP to MISS MARY CHAPMAN all of this county.

PROF. W.H. STEELE will teach a six months school in the Gap Hill District at Keowee Church. Prof. Steele graduated last year at North Georgia Agricultural College, Dahlonega, Georgia.

MISS ALICE FARR daughter of MRS. FRANCIS FARR of this county died last Tuesday at the home of her aunt MRS. MOORE in Greenville, S.C. She was buried in Berea, S.C.

WILLIAM H. PILGRIM of Prater, S.C. accidently shot himself the 19 (Jan.). He was 19 years old.

Pickens Co., S.C. Board of Commissioner's Meeting (details).

Issue of: Thursday 31 January 1895:

Married the 16 (Jan.) by Rev. J.E. Foster at his residence, MR. BEN FINDLEY to MISS MARY SIMMONS all of this county.

Married the 23 January by J.A. Robinson, MR. JOHN WIMPHEY to MISS MILLIE HENDRICKS all of Dacusville, S.C.

Married the 13 (Jan.) at the residence of Rev. J.E. Foster, MR. JERRY BATSON to MISS DORA STROUD both of Greenville, S.C.

Married Sunday the 27 (Jan.) by John O. Davis, Esq., MR. W. ELBERT HINTON to MISS MATTIE R. RIDDLE eldest daughter of MR. M.V. RIDDLE all of Dacusville, S.C.

Married the 30 (Jan.) at Griffin Ebenezer Colored Baptist Church in the town of Pickens, by Rev. A.L. Jones of Piedmont, S.C., MR. RICHARD A. GOLDMAN to MISS ADDIE ROSEMOND.

Married Wednesday the 23 January 1895 at the residence of P.A. PORTER, ESQ. uncle of the bride and by consent of all parties, by Rev. J.M. Stewart, MR. WARREN BOYD to MISS MARTHA ADCOX.

MRS. WILLIAM J. PONDER died at Dacusville Township on the 23 (Jan.). She was about 50 years old and was a member of Mt. Caramel Church. Mrs. Ponder leaves a husband and 6 children.

JAMES WATKINS has bought the PICKLE LIVERY STABLE.

AD - J. McD. BRUCE, is the successor to HAGOOD, BRUCE & CO.

Issue of: Thursday 7 February 1895:

MISS TERZA HUGHES will teach at Hagood Schoolhouse.

Married at the residence of bride's father MR. J.L. LAFOY by J.E. Boroughs, N.P., MISS AVERILLA LAFOY of Greenville Co., S.C. to MR. THOMAS TURNER of Pickens County.

MISS STELLA NEWBERRY has transcribed the Index Book in the Pickens Co., S.C. Probate Office in a neat and legible hand.

COTHRAN ANSEL youngest son of SOLICITOR ANSEL died of measles (no date). *Greenville News*

Pickens Co., S.C. Salesday:
J.L. CLARDY and WILLIAM KENNEMORE, Executors of JOHN B. CLARDY, made their final return and were discharged.
W.E. HOLCOMBE made a return in the estate of R.E. HOLCOMBE, deceased, and settlement was continued. Notes were sold.
E.S. BATES, notes of the estate were sold.
H.G. ANTHONY, notes of the estate were sold.
The BOATWRIGHT lot containing 2 acres was bought by J.H. NEWTON for $37.

Issue of: Thursday 14 February 1895:

C.T. MILLER is teaching in town and has 44 students.

MISS ELIZA McCASLAN will teach in the city schools of Columbia, S.C.

The mercantile business of MR. J.D. MORGAN at Six Mile, S.C. will move to Central, S.C.

JAMES M. BURDINE of this county died the 31 (Jan.) at his home near Easley, S.C. He was about 55 years old and leaves a wife and several children.

GOODLOE DAVIS, colored, and wife POLLY of near Pendleton, S.C. appear to have poisoned JASPER ARTHUR. The cause seems to be the lack of a divorce law in the state (details).

Married the 7 (Feb.) at the residence of SQUIRE PRICE by John T. Lewis, THOMAS HAGOOD to MISS LUCY CLAYTON both colored. All of the town of Pickens.

MRS. GRESHAM nee MISS SEP SLOAN and her son drowned at Fish Dam, Union Co., S.C. when the ferryboat overturned. She was the sister of R.E. SLOAN of Pendleton, S.C. and MAJOR BEN SLOAN of S.C. College.

Issue of: Thursday 21 February 1895:

A schoolhouse is to be built at Town Creek by B.L. HOLDER.

R.T. HALLUM and B.F. ROBERTSON have been teaching at the Gates District School but are now pursuing their studies at Clemson.

PROF. W.A. DOGNALL of Easley, S.C. has the largest school in the county.

Married the 14 (Feb.) at the residence of the bride's father, by J.M. Stewart, MR. ALLEN DURHAM to MISS ELLEN DUNCAN all of Pickens County.

Married at the residence of the bride's father, by J.M. Stewart, MR. ANDREW P. PERRIT to MISS NANNIE STEPHENS all of Pickens County.

MISS MARY ALLGOOD is teaching in the Bethlehem School District.

W.F. BEATTY of Clinton, S.C. died last Sunday in Easley, S.C. at the home of his brother-in-law G.C. HOLLMAN at the age of 22 years. He was buried at the Methodist Church Cemetery (location not given).

MRS. MARY E. DILWORTH, wife of B.F. DILWORTH formerly of this county, died at her home near Westminster, Oconee Co., S.C. of pneumonia. She was 62 years old. Mrs. Dilworth was buried at Coneross Baptist Church Cemetery. She was a member of Mt. Carmel Baptist Church. Surviving are a husband, 1 son and 2 daughters.

Pickens Co., S.C. Jury and Petit Jury Lists.

JOSEPH LAWRENCE MANSELL has left the house of his father without his consent or knowledge. Signed, J.C. and JANE MANSELL, 13 Feb. 1895.

Issue of: Thursday 28 February 1895:

Letter from ROBERT R. SINGLETON formerly of South Carolina now of Mallard, Montague Co., Texas (lengthy).

Married at Pelzer, S.C. the 18 (Feb.), MR. WILLIAM OSBY to MISS VAN DAILY.

J.E. BOGGS and T.J. MAULDIN have formed a law partnership.

Married the 24 (Feb.) at the residence of L.O. LATHEM by Rev. W.S. Singleton, MR. SILAS CURTIS to MISS LOU AARIAL (sic) of Pickens County.

Pickens Co., S.C. Court Proceedings - Criminal cases (details).

Married Tuesday the 26 (Feb.) at the residence of the bride's father JAMES R. HARRIS by Rev. J.M. Stewart, MISS SALLIE HARRIS to MR. JAMES HENDRICKS son of COUNTY SUPERVISOR HENDRICKS.

Pickens Rifles has been reorganized. Gives names of officers and non-commissioned officers.

Pickens Co., S.C. Final Settlement - Estate of BAILEY B. MOSELEY, deceased by J.M. STEWART, Administrator.

Issue of: Thursday 7 March 1895:

CORA BOWEN is teaching at Dacusville, S.C.

W.H. FINDLEY son of J.B. FINDLEY who has been on an extended prospecting tour in Texas and California returned home the 4 (March).

MR. FORSYTHE son of ATTORNEY J. ADGER FORSYTHE of Brevard, North Carolina will attend Clemson College.

Married the 28 February at the residence of the bride's father J.B. JETT, 78 Jones Avenue, Atlanta, Georgia, J.D. YOUNG and BELL JETT. The couple left for the groom's home in Birmingham, Alabama. Mr. Young is a native of Pickens County.

Pickens Co., S.C. Court Proceedings - Criminal cases (lengthy details).

Pickens Co., S.C. Grand Jury Report - County affairs, condition of jail, poor house, court house, etc.

MR. W. HENRY WILLIAMS attended this session of North Greenville Baptist High School.

Liberty
New storehouse of the CORPORATE COMPANY is about complete.

Card of Thanks, for kindness shown during the illness and death of my wife NANCY HIOTT. Signed, DEAL HIOTT and Family.

NORRIS COTTON MILLS of Central, S.C. apply for a charter.

Issue of: Thursday 14 March 1895:

HOMER A. RICHEY matriculated at Clemson College Monday.

W.N. HUGHES and G.M. LYNCH were appointed Township Commissioners the 11 March by GOVERNOR EVANS.

MISS LILLIE BOWIE of Eastatoe, S.C. enrolled Monday as a pupil in PROF. STRIBLING'S school. She is boarding at MRS. J.K. KIRKSEY'S.

Pickens Co., S.C. Court Proceedings - Minor criminal cases, foreclosures, etc. (details).

Dots from Kings
M.D. FARMER will soon have his mills running on Six Mile Creek at PHILLIPS' old mill.

Anderson, S.C. - 8 March.
GENERAL LEWIS M. AYER died today at the age of 74 years. Mentions daughter MRS. VANDIVER (details).

Pickens Co., S.C. Citation Notice - Estate of HENRY HADDEN, deceased. J.M. STEWART applied for Letters of Administration.

Issue of: Thursday 21 March 1895:

FRIENDLY CISSON died the 17 (March) at the POOR HOUSE at the age of 93 years. He was buried at Concord Baptist Church (see correction 28 March 1895 - FRIENDLY CHASTAIN died).

Married the 7 March 1895 in Dacusville, S.C., by John O. Davis, Esq., MR. JAMES W. CLEMENTS to MISS CORDELIA WILLIAMS all of this place (appears Dacusville).

W.B. ALLGOOD received a valuable present last week from his sister MRS. ADALINE KEITH of Cherokee Co., Georgia. Gold rimmed spectacles of the finest pebble.

Closing exercises were held at the colored school taught by C.T. MILLER on the 8 (March).

MRS. ADALINE ALEXANDER died the 18 (March) at her home on Crow Creek and was buried in the family cemetery. She was about 64 years old. Mrs. Alexander leaves 2 sons, G.W. and E.M. ALEXANDER.

JEFF GREEN son of PHILIP GREEN of Central, S.C. was killed by an explosion the 13 (March) (details).

Pickens Co., S.C. Jury List.

WARREN SPEARMAN died the 8 (March) near Pelzer, S.C. at the age of about 60 years. He was buried at Old Liberty Cemetery. Mr. Spearman leaves a wife and several children. He was a citizen of Pickens County for many years but moved to the factory last fall.

MISS LOU PHILPOT is teaching at Mica School District.

MR. DANIEL BOYD and MISS ELIZA BLAKELY were married by J.A. Robinson. They walked through the mud to get married (details).

G.B. LOOPER moved his family to Pelzer, S.C. a few days ago.

Married at the residence of J.L. GARY on Main St. opposite the coach factory yesterday (date not given), by Rev. J.R. Riley, D.D. of Easley, S.C., THOMAS W. BRADLEY of Pickens County, conductor of E.T.V. & G. RAILROAD CO. and MISS ETTA GARY, daughter of MR. and MRS. J.L. GARY formerly of Fort

Hill, S.C. They will live in Atlanta, Georgia.
Greenville News - 15 March

RACHEL MOODY formerly of Pickens died the 10 March in Pelzer, S.C. of pneumonia. She was born in 1816. Mrs. Moody leaves 3 sons and 2 daughters.

Louisville, Ky. - 16 March
DR. JOHN A. BROADUS died the 16 March. He was one of the best Greek scholars of the world and one of the most noted divines.

Issue of: Thursday 28 March 1895:

Stabbing Affray at Pickens
On Sunday at the colored church near Thomasville, Pickens Co. JEFF WALKER stabbed a man named BLAKE. He is not expected to live.

SNIDER PRICE son of W.R. PRICE of Eastatoe Township is very ill.

Married at the residence of RILEY SUTHERLAND in town, by Rev. I.B. Jones, JAMES GRIFFIN to LILA ALEXANDER both colored.

CORRECTION:
It was FRIENDLY CHASTAIN not FRIENDLY CISSON who died last week.

DR. SAMUEL J. HESTER formerly of this county died at his home at Becca, Spartanburg Co., S.C. on the 24 (March) at the age of about 40 years. He was a member of the Baptist Church. Dr. Hester leaves a wife and 1 child.

LAWRENCE SHIELDS of Carthage, North Carolina a salesman for ALEXANDER BROS. & CO. of Greenville, S.C. died last Sunday in that city. His remains were sent home for interment.

Notice - MORGAN and ROBINSON have formed a law partnership.

W.A. STEWART son of SQUIRE STEWART was robbed and had his throat cut at Blacksburg, S.C. He is the night telegraph operator for SOUTHERN RAILROAD CO. Several Negroes have been arrested on suspicion (Stewart is still living).

Pickens Co., S.C. Board of Tax Assessors named.

Issue of: Thursday 4 April 1895:

LEWIS JEWEL died at the residence of his son THOMAS JEWEL near here the 22 (March) at the age of 83 years. He was buried from the Marietta Church., Greenville Co., S.C. Mr. Jewel was a member of the Baptist Church.

Twelve Mile has a new schoolhouse. MR. GRAVELY did the wood work and CHARLES CHILDRESS the brick and rock work.

Married the 24 March at the residence of JAMES HOLDER by A.L. Edens, MR. JOHN HOLDER to MISS MINNIE HUGHES all of Pickens.

Pickens Co., S.C. County Commissioner's Meeting (details).

Liberty
J.H. BROWN is moving into his new store.

Table Rock
The colored people are very interested in securing registration certificates. We did not know we had so many colored Democrats.

Issue of: Thursday 11 April 1895:

DR. R. KIRKSEY is prospecting in Florida.

A.R.N. FOLGER of Easley, S.C. is now in Greenville, S.C. with MESSRS. JAMES M. and E.B. DICKSON.

DR. H.E. RUSSELL of Easley, S.C. graduated with first honors from Atlanta Medical College.

Married Sunday the 7 April 1895 at the residence of the bride's parents, by J.M. Stewart, MR. BLUFORD SMITH to MISS BETTIE CLEMENTS all of Pickens County.

BETSY RACKLEY is expected to die. At her bedside are all of her children, among them MRS. J.S. BARKER of Calhoun, S.C. MRS. ELIZABETH RACKLEY died at her home near Nine Forks Church (Dacusville Township) on last Saturday the 6 (April) at the age of 78 years. The funeral was held from the Nine Forks Church. She was buried beside her husband at the family burying ground. Mrs. Rackley was a sister of JOSEPH LOOPER, REV. THOMAS LOOPER and JERRE LOOPER who reside 2 miles west of Pickens (the two articles above were in the same issue).

MISS JOSIE ROBINSON is teaching at Centerville, S.C. on the subscription plan.

MISS NETTIE ROBINSON is teaching a public school in Liberty Township.

B.D. STEWART and J.C. PRICE left last week for Montgomery, Alabama to engage in fire insurance business.

Pickens Co., S.C. Sheriff's Sale:
AMERICAN BANK vs JAMES ROSAMOND, et al. 1/2 acre in the town of Easley, S.C., known as Lot #33 to be sold.

F.M. MORRIS & CO. vs J. FRANK WELLS. Several pieces of land to be sold.

Pickens Co., S.C. Clerk's Sale:
C.L. HOLLINGSWORTH vs A.R. HUNT. Two parcels of land sold.
C.L. HOLLINGSWORTH vs PETER C. MARCHBANKS. Several parcels of land sold (details).

Pickens Co., S.C. Final Settlement - Estate of JACOB M. KING, deceased by MARGARET C. KING and J. MONROE KING.

Issue of: Thursday 18 April 1895:

Oconee News - Westminster's New Enterprise
E.G. SPALDING has just arrived with his wife from Lachute, Canada and has located in Westminster, S.C. to start a shuttle factory. The shuttles are to be made of dogwood and persimmon wood and will be sold to woolen and cotton manufacturers.

CANNING FACTORY to opened in Westminster, S.C.

Married at the residence of PINKNEY DUNCANS the 31 (March) by Johnson Sheriff, MISS MARY NORRIS to JOHN STEGALL.

Married at the residence of BLUFORD SMITH the 11 (April) by Rev. John T. Lewis, MRS. MARY WRIGHT to DANIEL WINCHESTER.

Married the 10 (March) at the residence of MR. P. WHITTEN by B.D. Garvin, MR. JNO. CHAPMAN to MRS. JUDA NICE all of Pickens.

Married at the residence of the bride's father JOSHUA BURGESS the 7 (March), by Rev. H.M. Fortner, MISS ELZARIE BURGESS to JAMES SIMMONS.

MICHAEL SMITH KENNEMORE known as "Uncle Mike" died at his home in this place from paralysis. He was born in this county on Golden Creek near the old Battalion Muster Ground. Mr. Kennemore moved to Pickens Court House in 1869 and was a drayman. He was buried at Secona Church.

A child was born on the 4 April to JESSE CRENSHAW of Mica, S.C. He is now 70 years old and has three families to prattle on his knee.

Issue of: Thursday 25 April 1895:

South Carolina Voter Registration Laws (details).

S.A.S. PORTER is building a neat and substantial cottage on his lot recently purchased from F.M. MORRIS. He expects to occupy it soon as a residence.

A survey is being made of Twelve Mile River by NORRIS COTTON MILLS. They may build a cotton mill there.

CRAYTON PRICE returned home Monday. He has been working insurance in Alabama.

F.M. MORRIS will locate at Central, S.C. after a tour of Alabama and Florida (details).

MISS AIRY WHITMIRE of East Fork, North Carolina is visiting her grandmother MRS. T.R. PRICE. She spent a week with her uncle W.R. PRICE of Sunny Dale, S.C.

Some more of the Pickens "colony" in Alabama are expected to arrive in a few days.

Liberty
Married at the residence of the bride's uncle W.H. SANDERS two miles west of town, by Rev. L.T. Weldon, MR. G.W. ROBINSON and MISS MELINDA SANDERS daughter of J.E. SANDERS.

NO ISSUE FOUND FOR THURSDAY 2 MAY 1895

Issue of: Thursday 9 May 1895:

Pickens Rifles will soon get guns and uniforms.

MRS. NALLEY wife of W.T. NALLEY died at her home in Pickensville, S.C. Sunday the 5 (May) of consumption. She leaves a husband and 2 children.

Wolf Creek Camp is being used by the Confederate Soldiers (veterans).

ISAAC COX of Washington, D.C. is visiting his parents in town.

JOSEPH DODGINS died at the home of B.W. TRAMMEL near town on Saturday the 4 (April) at the age of 75 years. He served in the Mexican War and drew a pension. Mr. Dodgins was buried from Secona Church. He has no immediate relatives in the county except for a niece MRS. B.W. TRAMMEL.

Issue of: Thursday 16 May 1895:

South Carolina Voter Registration Decision (details - two articles).

MR. J.McD. BRUCE joined the order of wheelmen. He purchased a wheel last week.

MR. BEN M. McDANIEL who has been storekeeper at PONDER'S DISTILLERY has moved to town and occupies the PALMER house.

LEO MAXEY who lives at COL. HOLLINGSWORTH'S "MAJOR" place met with an accident (details).

LAWRENCE STEWART, son of CARTER STEWART of this county, died at his home in Pelzer, S.C. last Sunday the 12 (May) of consumption at the age of 24 years. He was buried at the Old Stewart Burying Ground in this county. Mr. Stewart leaves a wife.

Married at the residence of MR. JESSE JULIAN of this place, by Rev. T.J. Rooke, MISS STELLA CLARK to MR. PERRY McKEE all of Oconee Co., S.C.

WILLIAM SMITH the brick mason of Easley, S.C. is putting brick pillars under the Presbyterian Church and doing other fixing up.

The guns have arrived for the Pickens Rifles.

JUDGE GOFF Essays - "Constitutionality of South Carolina Voter Laws" (details).

Issue of: Thursday 23 May 1895:

GOVERNOR EVANS' Address on Voter Registration (details).

Democratic Executive Committee Meeting (details).

Dacusville, S.C. - 18 May 1895 - Shooting Affray at Thomasville
ISAAC BENTLY shot and killed WILLIAM AUSTIN the only son of CHARLEY AUSTIN of Pickens. The shooting took place near JOHN W. THOMAS' store. The cause was whiskey and pistols (details).

There was a "White Frost" on the morning of the 18 May 1895.

FRANK MILES, colored, was arrested for setting fire to SUTHERLAND BROS. store house about 18 months ago.

MISS OLIVE KENNEMORE daughter of E.E. KENNEMORE of Easley Township is visiting. She is attending the graded school in Greenville, S.C.

Pickens Co., S.C. Guardianship Notice - L.P. ELLISON, Guardian of M.O. ELLISON.

AD - MORGAN & ROBINSON LAW FIRM. B.A. MORGAN is in Greenville, S.C and T.C. ROBINSON is in Pickens.

Issue of: Thursday 30 May 1895:

Pickens Co., S.C. Voter Registration to go on.

MISS ELLA MEARS is visiting here, she attends school in North Carolina.

Married the 26 May at the residence of B.D. Garvin, MR. CLAYTON DOBSON to MISS SALLIE ROPER all of Pickens.

HENRY A. DURANT who has been living in the lower part of the state at Cartersville, S.C. is visiting. He is the son of O.L. DURANT of Pickens.

S.D. GLENN of Tumbling Shoals, Laurens Co., S.C. has had one of his store buildings moved, remodeled and painted which adds much to the appearance.

The cotton has died out badly.

MRS. LIZZIE HYDE of Missouri is visiting her aged mother MRS. H. RICHARDSON at her old home.

W.A. STEWART has recovered from having his throat cut by robbers. He is a railroad agent.

Issue of: Thursday 6 June 1895:

"Memorial Day Tribute to the Confederate Soldiers" - Talk at Greenville, S.C. by COL. B.W. BALL of Laurens, S.C.

Tribute to MAJOR ERNEST A. GARLINGTON of South Carolina. He was born in 1853, Newberry County, South Carolina (details).

Tribute to GENERAL WALTER QUENTIN GRESHAM of Harrison County, Indiana. He was born the 17 March 1832 (details).

Clinton, S.C. - 1 June
EX-CONSTABLE J.B. WORKMAN was killed by E.M. DUNCAN (details).

Married the 26 (May) at the residence of J.A. McWhorter, N.P., MR. HIMER WATKINS and MISS ----- MASSEY.

DR. G.W. EARLE, assisted by DR. J.R. GILLAND (GILLILAND), cut out a tumor of 4 years standing of the body of THOMAS DUKE'S wife, colored.

Married the 2 (June) at the residence of the bride's father on Little Eastatoe, by Rev. B.F. Murphree, MR. CLAYTON MARTIN and MISS IDA WINCHESTER all of Pickens.

MOSES CREW, colored Methodist Minister, died at his home on Pea Ridge last Sunday at the age of 73 years. He was well liked by white and black.

An attempt is being made to raise a band fund for the Pickens Rifles.

WARREN EDENS son of SAMUEL EDENS died of erysipelas. He was about 25 years old.

Cotton stills looks sorry.

MR. O.P. FIELD and daughter JANIE are visiting MR. J. BENNETT HILL of Oconee Co., S.C. (near Old Pickens). They are also to visit Mr. Field's brother EX-JUDGE W.G. FIELD of Elberton, Georgia.

South Carolina New Militia - by regiments, etc. (lengthy details).

Pickens Co., S.C. Court of Common Pleas - Summons for Relief - PLANTER'S BANK, Plaintiff vs W.H. SUMMEY, Defendant.

AD - Coming Friday the 31 May TEET'S BROTHERS MAMMOTH SHOW. They will also be at KING'S Old Stand, Pickens County on the 1 June (see issue of the 13 June 1895).

Issue of: Thursday 13 June 1895:

South Carolina Voter Registration Case before the Circuit Court of Appeals (details).

Confederate Veterans Meet in Chicago - Making plans for a monument to the Confederate dead (details).

Article - "Fall of the Alamo".

J.M. STEWART is Clerk of Court Pickens Co., S.C.

MAJOR WHITNER SYMMES was pardoned on the 7 (June) by the Governor's act. The action is commended by many.

Married Sunday the 9 (June) at the residence of the bride's parents at Central, S.C., by Rev. J.M. Stewart, MR. J.S.H. PRICE to MISS JULIA E. WILSON all of Pickens County.

South Carolina Voter Registration Matters (details).

DANIEL GASTON, colored, died Sunday at his home near town of consumption. He left a wife and a number of children.

Hazel Nuts Cracked
Married today at the residence of the bride's father J.M. WINCHESTER by Rev. B.F. Murphree, MR. CLAYTON MARTIN to MISS IDA WINCHESTER (see issue of 6 June 1895)..

AD - Railroad wreck stock, 10 car loads, being sold by J.M. and E.B. DICKSON of Greenville, S.C.

TEET'S BROS. SHOW did not come to KING'S Old Stand at W.W. AIKEN'S store.

Issue of: Thursday 20 June 1895:

South Carolina Voter Registration Law Stands (details).

Annual Report of J.T. YOUNGBLOOD, Treasurer of Pickens Co., S.C. (lengthy details).

S.D. GLENN is having his home in Liberty, S.C. overhauled and repainted.

D.W. HOPKINS the shoemaker has moved back to his old quarters in the HOLLINGSWORTH BUILDING.

MISS ESSIE EARLE is attending Chicora College, Greenville, S.C. She took part in the commencement exercise with a piano solo.

MRS. ELIZA GRIFFIN died the 12 (June) of heart disease at the residence of her nephew ALLEN DURHAM near town. She was a member of the Baptist Church and was of an advanced age.

B.A. ALLGOOD is attending North Georgia Agricultural College, Dahlonega, Ga.

PROF. ---- LESENE of Kingtree, S.C. a graduate of Wofford College and now teaching in Marlboro Co., S.C. is visiting in Pickens County.

MISS ELIZABETH GAILLARD died the 23 (May) at the home of her son B.H. GAILLARD 2 miles north of Easley, S.C. She was buried at Sandy Springs, S.C. Mrs. Gaillard leaves 9 children, 7 sons and 2 daughters (details).

HENRY BIRD who shot J.E. BROWN merchant of Central, S.C. at a campmeeting of the colored people two years ago was arrested in Greenville, S.C. Results not known by the *Journal*.

Invitations are out for the wedding of MISS AVA STODES OMBERG daughter of SUE GREGORY OMBERG of Rome, Georgia and niece of MRS. W.C. CLEVELAND of this city, to MAJOR JAMES M. FERGUSON of Greenville, S.C. The wedding will take place the 19 June at the Methodist Church in Rome, Georgia.

Born a girl on last Friday to MR. and MRS. J.E. KINCH.

Issue of: Thursday 27 June 1895:

Article - "HORACE GREELEY".

Annual Report T.J. YOUNGBLOOD, Treasurer Pickens Co., S.C. (continued).

Crow Creek Dots
M.C. WINCHESTER has returned to his old home.

C.D. CURETON is a dentist in Pickens, S.C.

MRS. MAUR died at her home about 2 miles north of Central, S.C. on the 24 (June). She was about 90 years old and was buried at Mt. Zion Cemetery. Mrs. Maur leaves several children.

MRS. SARAH A. CLYDE wife of W.A. CLYDE died at her home in Easley, S.C. the 24 June. She leaves a husband and 5 children.

REV. JAMES T. BURDINE'S house at Bald Knob, S.C. on the Oolenoy River was entered and robbed. His wife was able to escape (details).

Pickens Co., S.C. Citation Notice - Estate of JAMES GANTT, deceased. FRANCES SIMPSON applies for Letters of Administration.

Pickens Co., S.C. Citation Notice - Estate of WARREN EDENS. J.M. STEWART, applies for Letters of Administration.

Issue of: Thursday 4 July 1895:

Spartanburg, S.C. - 28 June 1895
JACK FISHER and BILL DURHAM were killed near the Pisgah Church. This was a "Dispensary Battle" (details).

Details of the Civil War Battle at Staunton River Bridge the 25 June 1864.

Will of MRS. ELIZA GRIFFIN entered probate the 26 (June). Her property will go to ALLEN DURHAM.

Married the 23 (June) by A.L. Edens, MR. HAMPTON BURGESS to MISS MATTIE TROTTER all of Pickens County.

Liberty Dots
R.E. BOGGS of Liberty, S.C. graduated with distinction from the Citadel Academy in Charleston, S.C. and will engage in teaching. He is some what fatigued by camp life at Camden, S.C.

ROBERT GLENN is living on the NELSON farm of C.L. HOLLINGSWORTH in Liberty Township (details).

Married the 23 June at the residence of the bride's mother MRS. W.N. SMITH by O.S. Stewart, N.P., MR. SLOAN H. COLLINS to MISS RETTER SMITH all of Oconee Co., S.C.

The colored Methodist Episcopal Church has been repurchased and ELDER G.A. BROWN preached last Friday night.

The prospect that Liberty, S.C. may have an oil mill is no longer in doubt.

Pickens Co., S.C. Board of Commissioner's Meeting (details).

From Farr's - 17 June 1895
The wife of MR. JOHN EDWARDS died the 14 (June). She leaves several children to grapple in the world of sin (details).

GEORGE HAWTHORNE, colored, who lives on the J.T. GASSAWAY farm in Central Township was bitten on the head by a water moccasin Saturday. He is very sick but his condition is better and not dangerous.

Notice - Several bids for bridges to be let in Pickens Co., S.C.

Pickens Co., S.C. Jury List.

Issue of: Thursday 11 July 1895:

Meeting of the Pickens Co. Democratic Executive Committee at Pickens Court House. Appointments were made (details).

JOHN T. BOGGS has school books for sale.

L.T. WINPY (WIMPEY) & CO. of Maynard, S.C. have started them a jug factory (appears to be pottery).

Cotton has been damaged by lice.

R.K. LEWIS who cultivates a part of the farm of H.L. LEWIS has good cotton blooms.

G.W. BOWEN of Pickens Rifles is now a full fledged major (details).

Married the 7 (July) at the residence of Trial Justice B.D. Garvin, MISS COLUMIE SMITH to MR. JOHN MATTOX all of Central Township.

Interesting Court Scene Pickens Court House - Court room almost vacant due to a large storm (details).

Pickens Co., S.C. Court Records - Minor criminal cases (lengthy details).

Pickens Co., S.C. Court of Common Pleas - Summons for Relief - Estate of J.G. FERGUSON, deceased. JOHN FERGUSON, Executor vs SARAH McFALL, ANNA DEAN, JAS. M. FERGUSON, et al.

Pickens Co., S.C. Citation Notice - J.M. STEWART, C.C.P. applied for Letters of Administration for the estate of WARREN D. EDENS, deceased.

Sunny Dale Dots
PRICE & DURANT have alligators on exhibition.

Issue of: Thursday 18 July 1895:

Article - "Facts of ANDREW JACKSON'S Duel".

"An Appeal to UNCLE SAM by the Negroes of South Carolina" - They want help from the army in defense of their rights.

Lynching of IRA JOHNSON, colored, Columbia, S.C. for the accused murder of FRANK LANGFORD of Piedmont, S.C. (details - see issue of the 25 July 1895). *Greenville News*

CONSTABLE PETTIGREW who was shot in the battle with moonshiners in Spartanburg, S.C. died the 18 (July).

Married the 14 (July) at the residence of Mr. ALONZO FORTNER by Trial Justice A.L. Edens, MR. VARDERY RIGDON to MISS MALISSA FORTNER.

Pickens Co., S.C. Court (continues) - Minor crimes, etc. (lengthy details).

Issue of: Thursday 25 July 1895:

Lynching of IRA JOHNSON in Columbia, S.C. Johnson shot FRANK LANGSTON at Piedmont, S.C. (lengthy details - see issue of the 18 July 1895).

"Mystery of AARON BURR'S Daughter's Death" (details).

MISS IDA ROSAMOND of Mexico, Missouri has been appointed by GOVERNOR STONE of Missouri one of the commissioners of that state at the Atlanta Exposition. She is the granddaughter of the late JAS. ROSAMOND and a relative of MR. JNO. W. ROSAMOND of Brushy Creek, Anderson Co., S.C.

MRS. SARAH C. BURGESS wife of J.D. BURGESS died at her home near Pumpkintown, S.C. on the 16 (July) at the age of 45 years. She was buried from the Saluda Hill Baptist Church of which she was a member. Mrs. Burgess leaves a husband and 8 children.

Guests at the AMBLER HOUSE:
MR. A.G. WHITNEY, wife and 2 children from Palatka, Florida.
MRS. S. WEINBERG and 2 children from Charleston, S.C.
MRS. W.E. DICKSON and 1 child from Ocala, Florida.
REV. J.R. RILEY, MISS LIDA RILEY, FANNIE RILEY, A.B. RILEY and REV. A.B. FOWLER, Easley, S.C.

MRS. C.P. BARRETT and 2 children, Spartanburg, S.C.

Girls State College, Winthrop Normal and Industrial College, will open to the women of the state on the 3 October.

"The Catawba Indians" - Article.

JAMES D. LEWIS is on trial for the murder of HENRY RUTLEDGE. *Greenville News* - 21 July

H.C. SHIRLEY, G.W. DORR and J.N. MURPHY were named Pickens Co., S.C. Commissioners of Elections.

REV. M.L. JONES has the job of making shelves in the vaults in the office of the Pickens Co., S.C. County Clerk and Auditor - he is doing the work in good style.

FRANK M. GLENN of Anderson Co., S.C. died Thursday the 18 (July) at the residence of his son J.M. GLENN of Equality, S.C.

WILLIE WORKMAN died at Liberty, S.C. the 23 (July). He was the son of REV. and MRS. W.H. WORKMAN. Burial was at Liberty Cemetery.

Issue of: Thursday 1 August 1895:

Notice of upcoming election in Pickens Co., S.C., names of managers, etc.

Born a boy and a girl the 23 (July) to MR. and MRS. A.R.N. FOLGER of Greenville, S.C.

COL. W.E. NIMMONS died at his home at Eastatoe, S.C. last Saturday. He was 89 years old and was buried in the family burying ground.

The editor of the *Journal* learned of the death of his only brother JOE M. ROBINSON by drowning. He was 35 years old and unmarried (details unclear).

Married the 24 (July) at the residence of Squire B.D. Garvin, JAY GILSTRAP son of MR. JOHN GILSTRAP and MISS HESTER HUGHES daughter of MR. T.A. HUGHES (details).

Pickens Co., S.C. Commissioner's Meeting.

Liberty Dots
BOWEN & WYATT are to make bricks for the oil mill.

Pickens Co., S.C. Election Notice (details).

A Tornado hit Liberty, S.C. last Monday (details of damage).

MR. NEIL STRIBLING has the contract to make the bricks for the NORRIS COTTON MILL.

The Pickens Co., S.C. Election Primary.

MRS. T.F. NELSON nee MRS. McDUFFIE RAMPEY nee MISS FANNIE PERRY gave birth to triplets last Thursday, one boy and 2 girls. The combined weight was 20 pounds, the boy's weight was 7 pounds. Mrs. Nelson is the daughter of W.H. PERRY and a sister of MRS. J.T. YOUNGBLOOD. Rev. Nelson lives near Townville, S.C.

HON. JOHN G. PRESSLEY died. He was born in May 1833, Williamston, S.C. and entered the Citadel in 1848, graduating with honors in 1851 (details). *News and Courier*

J.M. ROBINSON died the 22 July (details).

Pickens Co., S.C. Citation Notice - MRS. S.G. OATS and WILLIAM R. OATS apply for Letters of Administration for the estate of THOMAS WATSON, deceased.

Pickens Co., S.C. Commissioners of Elections (list).

Pickens Co., S.C. Primary Election Results.

Pickens Co., S.C. Homestead Exemption Notice - BANISTER S. LYNCH as guardian of the children of JOHN F. STEWART, deceased, applies for Homestead Exemption.

Issue of: Thursday 8 August 1895:

Article - "Battle of Horseshoe at Spottsylvania Co., Virginia the 12 May 1864" (details). *Greenville News* - 10 Dec. 1894

Notice of Election - Three delegates to represent Pickens Co., S.C. at the South Carolina Constitutional Convention.

Born a 14 pound son last Saturday the 3 August to MR. and MRS. J.C. JENNINGS. This is the sixth boy at this house.

JOHN ELFORD HILL is visiting in Dacusville, S.C. and is enroute to "Old Pickens", Oconee Co., S.C. to visit relatives and friends. He is accompanied by his three children.

CADETS H.A. RICHEY and IVY M. MAULDIN returned to Clemson College last Monday.

Married at the residence of the bride's father T.W. STEWART the 1 (Aug.), MISS JULIA STEWART to CHARLES KELLEY.

MISS LAURA BOWEN is teaching in the Wolf Creek School District #30 near town.

Married the 3 (Aug.) at Pleasant Hill Church by Trial Justice Merck, MISS MARY REAVES to JAMES YATES.

Married the 28 July at the residence of Trial Justice Merck, MISS JULIA MERCK and WILLIAM KELLEY.

T.K. HUDGENS has resurrected the *Easley Messenger* and with CAPTAIN A.W. HUDGENS as Editor-in-chief, is publishing the paper (details).

Dacusville News
A child belonging to a colored woman living on MRS. ELIZA ANN LATHAM'S place burned to death Friday evening. Particulars not known.

DR. R.A. ROSS has purchased a small lot of land from MR. JOSEPH LOOPER and is preparing to erect a dwelling and office on the same.

From Liberty
S.D. STEWART and wife attended the old soldier's reunion below Williamston, S.C. last week.

Information on the South Carolina Constitution (details).

Issue of: Thursday 15 August 1895:

Article - "The Charms of Caesar's Head".

Rev. J.M. Stewart is to preach the funeral service of MRS. SUSAN E. SANDERS at the Griffin Church the 4th Sunday in September.

Pickens County has another Military Company, one is being organized at Pumpkintown, S.C. A.R. HUNT was elected captain with 55 men.

MR. S.B. NEWTON is teaching at Newton District.

Election will be next week. Registration certificates are needed.

MRS. DURHAM wife of CARTER DURHAM died at her home near Redmond, S.C. the 8 (Aug.) with burial at Secona Church of which she was a member. She was about 75 year old and leaves a husband and several children.

Table Mountain News
The infant of MR. WILLIAM MASTERS died the 1 (Aug.) of cholera infantum and was interred from Saluda Hill Church.

The infant of MR. and MRS. NILES GRAVELY died the 8 (Aug.) near Ambler and was buried at Oolenoy Cemetery.

ALICE GLENN, colored, wife of WILLIS GLENN of Rock, S.C. died the 7 (Aug.) of cancer of the breast. She was buried at Soapstone Church.

Article - "Greenville Legends - Paris Mountain", by PROF. F. MUENCH, Ph.D.

Issue of: Thursday 22 August 1895:

"The Dispensary and Prohibition" (details).

Winthrop Normal College (details).

W.R. and MRS. S.G. OATS have qualified as administrators of the estate of THOMAS WATSON, deceased.

MR. W.W. MARTIN of Mile Creek moved to his property in the southern portion of town last Tuesday.

Married the 13 (Aug.) at the residence of the bride, by Rev. J.T. Anderson, MR. JOHN M. BARR to MISS MARY JOHNSON.

The infant, about 6 months old, of MR. and MRS. STEPHEN GALLOWAY, died at the residence the 17 (Aug.) and was buried from Holly Spring Baptist Church.

PROF. M.S. STRIBLING will open school the 2 September.

Married the 18 (Aug.) at the residence of Trial Justice B.D. Garvin, MR. LEE SAMMONS to MISS FLORENCE MOORE daughter of MR. and MRS. T.H. MOORE of Liberty, S.C.

Born the 17 (Aug.) a daughter to MR. and MRS. BEN M. McDANIEL.

R.E. LATHEM is erecting a commodious dwelling on his farm below Easley, S.C.

MISS ELLA MEARES is teaching in the lower part of the state.

Election to be held for Cotton Weighers.

Issue of: Thursday 29 August 1895:

Clemson Trouble - Dissention among the faculty (details).

Article - "ABRAHAM LINCOLN as a Native of North Carolina - Another Version". *Carolina Spartan*

Letter to the Editor - Battle of Manassas (lengthy sketch).

Cards are out announcing the approaching marriage the 4 (Aug.) at the Presbyterian Church in Easley, S.C., of J.E. HAGOOD, JR. and MISS DORA A. FOLGER.

THORNLEY BROTHERS have sold their interest in the livery business in Easley, S.C. to their partner J.E. HAGOOD. They will continue in the business at this place.

Married the 18 August 1895 in Dacusville, S.C., by John O. Davis, Esq., MR. F.M. HINTON of Dacusville, Pickens Co. to MISS EULA LANCE of Greenville Co., S.C.

The dwelling of GEORGE KENNEMORE who lives about 2 miles west of Easley, S.C. along the SOUTHERN RAILROAD was destroyed by fire. Most of the furniture was saved. The smoke house also burned (details).

B.H. WILLIAMS is building an elegant and commodious residence on his farm at Cedar Rock, S.C. MR. SLOAN of Easley, S.C. is the contractor.

The Pickens Rifles got their uniforms last week.

STEPHEN SIMMONS died the 24 (Aug.) at his residence in Piedmont, S.C. of cholera morbus at the age of 45 years. He was originally from Liberty, Pickens Co., S.C. *Greenville News* - 25 Aug.

Dacusville
MISS NETTIE ROBINSON left Easley, S.C. the 23 (Aug.) for Greenville, Tennessee where she will attend Greenville and Tusculum College.

Pickens Co., S.C. Supervisor's Cabinet (details).

"Greenville Legends - KATE DILLARD'S Ride", by PROF, F. MUENCH Ph.D, (an episode of the Revolutionary War written in poetry style).

Article - "A Visit to the Cherokees", by PROF. J.A. GAMEWELL.

No Trouble at Clemson - Harmony between President, Faculty and Trustees. The college is accomplishing its mission (details).

Issue of: Thursday 5 September 1895:

"Confederate Gold" (details).

Arrivals at the HEADRICK HOUSE this week:
MRS. M.S. SEABROOK of Charleston, S.C.
MISS H.R. BLACK of Charleston, S.C.

MRS. J. SWINSTON WHALEY and three children of Edisto Island, S.C.

ROBERT STEWART of Six Mile, S.C. sold his plantation Tuesday to W.E. PINSON of Dacusville, S.C., 58 acres for $450.

There was a railroad accident in Central, S.C. last Friday. A man named MOORE from Asheville, North Carolina died (details).

Pickens Co., S.C. Jury List.

Pickens Co., S.C. Homestead Exemption - Estate of SAMUEL M. EDENS, deceased. MRS. MARY L. EDENS, Administrator applied for Homestead Exemption.

Pickens Co., S.C. Sheriff's Sale - At the residence of J.L. OWINGS, Dacusville, S.C. Property of A.R. HUNT. Bale of cotton, seed cotton and cotton seed to be sold.

Issue of: Thursday 12 September 1895:

Pickens Co., S.C. Supervisor's Report by MATTHEW HENDRICKS.

LIBERTY OIL MILL pushing to completion.

Born a son the 5 (Sept.) to MR. and MRS. M.F. HESTER.

MISS LOLA HOLDER is teaching at Rehoboth in Greenville Co., S.C.

MRS. D.W. McDONALD died Thursday the 5 (Sept.) and was buried at Bethlehem Cemetery the next day.

MRS. BETSY ROPER mother of SPENCER ROPER died at her home near Cedar Rock, S.C. last Monday at the age of about 70 years. She was buried at Tabor Cemetery.

Married Sunday the 8 (Sept.) by Rev. J.E. Foster, MISS MATTIE MOSELY to MR. AARON BISHOP both parties of the Looper Section of this county.

MR. P. EUGENE ALEXANDER left the *Sentinel* to go to Atlanta, Georgia.

A bridge is to be built over Twelve Mile Creek near the NORRIS COTTON MILLS (details).

Married Sunday the 1 September at the parsonage of Rev. J.F. Anderson, WILLIAM A. CANTRELL and MISS FANNIE C. SMITH. *Easley Messenger*

MRS. MARGARET UNETTY McDONALD nee MORRIS died the 5 September 1895, at 46 year of age. She was the daughter of JESSE MORRIS of Anderson Co., S.C. Mrs. McDonald married D.W. McDONALD the 25 February 1875. She was a member of the Methodist Episcopal Church and was buried at Bethlehem Church Cemetery leaving a husband and 6 children.

Married the 4 (Sept.) by pastor Dr. Riley at the Presbyterian Church, Easley, S.C., MISS DORA FOLGER and MR. J.E. HAGOOD (details).

Issue of: Thursday 19 Sept. 1895:

S.C. State Convention - 10 Sept. - Framing the South Carolina Constitution (details).

A picnic was given by the patrons of MISS GRICE's school at Zion. Picture were taken by MR. LON YOUNG of those attending.

Married Sunday the 15 September at the residence of the bride, by Rev. Benjamin P. Moore, MR. ANDREW RACKLEY to MRS. ELIZABETH VICKERY.

MRS. FRANCES BARRETT died at her home in Dacusville Township the 13 (Sept.) at the age of 95 years. She was a member of the Methodist Church of Dacusville, S.C. Mrs. Barrett leaves 4 children.

Married at the residence of Trial Justice Garvin, MR. WILLIAM CONNOR, colored, to MISS MARTHA BAKER, colored.

MR. G. SINCLAIR WHITMIRE died at his home near Peter's Creek the 11 (Sept.) at the age of 78 years. He was a member of Nine Forks Church from which he was buried. Mr. Whitmire leaves a wife and 2 children.

Pickens Co., S.C. Report of the General Sessions Court. Comments on conditions at the court house and jail (lengthy details).

"Greenville Legends - The Legend of White Horse Road" by PROF. F. MUENCH, Ph.D. (poetry style). *Greenville Mountaineer*

Card of Thanks, to neighbors and friends for kindness during illness and death of wife. D.W. McDONALD and Family.

Issue of: Thursday 26 September 1895:

South Carolina Constitutional Convention, Columbia, S.C. - 5th day (details).

JAMES G. SEABORN, who is teaching a large school at Concord near Seneca, S.C. is home for vacation.

Pickens Co., S.C. Court Cases and Convictions (details).

Report of an attempt by citizens to hang a prisoner (details).

In Memory of M.S. KENNEMORE - died the 16 April 1895 at his home in Pickens, S.C., written by his niece EVA D. JAMES of Cateechee, S.C.

ANDREW BRAMBLETT of Pickens has been awarded a scholarship to the Citadel Academy.

Special rates to students wishing to enter the Easley Graded School at the EASLEY HOTEL. S.N. WYATT, Proprietor.

Issue of: Thursday 3 October 1895:

South Carolina Constitutional Convention (details).

U.S. District Judge, GEORGE D. BRYAN died the 28 (Sept.) at Flat Rock, S.C.

Married the 1 September 1895 at the residence of the bride's father J.D. HOLDEN by Rev. J.L. Mullinix, NARNADA PARROTT to MISS HATTIE HOLDEN all of Pickens.

MR. S. DREIFUS of DREIFUS & CO., Greenville, S.C. will make that city his permanent home, having rented the elegant residence of J. WALTER GRAY on Coffee Street.

Shooting in Pickens - Friday
DR. ROBERT KIRKSEY and DEPUTY MARSHALL FRANK COX. Cox was injured (details).

JULIAN W. BRUCE died at the home of his sister MRS. J.E. BOGGS on the 30 (Sept.). He came from his home in Anderson, S.C. to Pickens this summer. Mr. Bruce was 27 years old and a member of the Presbyterian Church. He leaves 1 brother MR. J.McD. BRUCE and 2 sisters MRS. J.E. BOGGS and MISS CORRIE BRUCE (see issue of the 10 Oct. 1895).

Married the 20 (Sept.) at the residence of Rev. J.M. Stewart, MISS DORA MASSINGALE to MR. JAS. SMITH all of Pickens.

Married the 26 (Sept.) at the residence of W.T. BRYANT by W.H. Bryant, MR. BOSS SPENCER of Anderson Co., S.C. to MISS JANIE SMITH of Pickens County.

Pickens Co., S.C. Final Settlement - Estate of G.W. LATHEM, deceased by NANCY L. LATHEM and J.K. LATHEM, Executors.

Pickens Co., S.C. Final Settlement - Estate of E.H. BATES, deceased by B.A. GREEN and W.W.F. BRIGHT, Executors.

Issue of: Thursday 10 October 1895:

South Carolina Constitution Convention (details).

The Divorce Question in South Carolina (details).

Factory Towns - Compulsory Incorporation or not? Voted against Compulsory Incorporation (details).

Pickens Co., S.C. Commissioner's Meeting (details).

Central Notes
MR. JAMES F. LAY was shot and killed by GEORGE E. HINSON near the factory. He was buried at Shanon.
We now have the largest school in the county, 110 students.
Mrs. ROE has moved back here from Pelzer, S.C.

REV. LEWIS, colored, of Easley, S.C. will preach at the colored Methodist Episcopal Church on the 11 (Oct.).

Married the 1 (Oct.) at the residence of MANSEL GLASPIE (sic) by Rev. J.T. Dobson, MISS IDA ROGERS to MR. H.N. MANLEY all of Pickens.

MISS JESSIE BERRY who has a scholarship at Furman University, has matriculated in the Greenville Female College.

Married the 3 (Oct.) at the residence of MR. S. MEDLIN the bride's father near Prather, S.C., by Rev. W.C. Seaborn, MISS MAMIE MEDLIN to MR. JOHN DUNCAN of Greenville, S.C.

JOHN PERRITT died at his home 4 miles from town on the 6 (Oct.) at the age of 65 years. He was buried from the Concord Baptist Church of which he was a member. Mr. Perritt leaves a wife and 4 children.

W.O. WILLARD of Liberty, S.C. has leased the ARMSTRONG HOTEL in Rome, Georgia.

MR. JULIAN W. BRUCE died at the residence of his brother-in-law J.E. BOGGS, ESQ. at Pickens Court House of consumption. He was the youngest son of the late SIDNEY BRUCE of Elberton, Georgia. Mr. Bruce was born 28 years ago. He was buried at the Presbyterian Church of which he was a member. (details - see issue of the 3 Oct. 1895). *Anderson Intelligencier*

AD - COURTNAY MANUFACTURING CO., NEWRY MILL on Little River, Oconee Co., S.C.

Pickens Co., S.C. Tax Notice.

Issue of: Thursday 17 October 1895:

GENERAL WILLIAM MAHONE of Virginia died the 8 (Oct.) in Washington, D.C. He was born in Southhampton Co., Virginia in 1826 (lengthy details).

Twelve Mile Baptist Association Report (details).

EDDIE DURRANT has returned home after working insurance in Alabama.

B.T. McDANIEL has been transferred to York Co., S.C. where he will continue to serve the U.S. Government as store keeper and gauger.

The child of MR. and MRS. J.B.R. FREEMAN died Saturday of diphtheria and was buried from Griffin Church.

EARLE N. KENNEMORE, who enlisted in the regular army about 4 years ago in Battery A, 4th Artillery, has been discharged. *Easley Messenger*

EFFIE and ADDIE EVATT daughters of W.H. EVATT, formerly of this county, died the 6 (Oct.). His wife died 3 months ago. Mr. Evatt is living at Fowler Station, Woodlawn near Birmingham, Alabama.

Voter Registration Case (details).

Issue of: Thursday 24 October 1895:

South Carolina Constitutional Convention (details).

The South Carolina Homestead Exemption (details).

Exposition Dots (Atlanta, Georgia - details).

J.P LEWIS' house burned last week.

HENRY GRACE MASTERS, age 7 years, son of J.C. MASTERS died. He was buried from Saluda Hill Church, Greenville Co., S.C.

FRANCIS M. ELLENBURG of Crow Creek died at his farm from a relapse of measles the 20 (Oct.) at the age of 64 years. He was buried from Shady Grove Church.

"BUN" BRANCH, colored, who lives at the railroad crossing on the road to Easley, S.C. died last Monday.

WILLIAM BOWEN, colored, died at his home beyond Secona Church last Saturday. He was buried from Tabor Church.

Brushy Creek Correspondent - *Anderson People's Advocate*
MR. HAMPTON CELY'S residence burned.

MRS. M.L. JONES wife of REV. M.L. JONES died at the age of 46 years. She was buried from Griffin Baptist Church on the 19 October 1895.

Issue of: Thursday 31 October 1895:

South Carolina Constitutional Convention (details).

Township Plan of New England suggested for use in South Carolina (details).

ED ARAIL, colored, age about 13 years died the 23 (Oct.) and was buried near Enon.

The infant of MR. and MRS. SRLAS (sic) HINKLE died the 23 October of measles at his home on Cane Creek.

Last will and testament of JOHN P. PERRITT was admitted to probate on the 22 (Oct.) and ANDREW L. PERRITT obtained Letter Testamentary. The property goes to his son ANDREW L. PERRITT and he is charged with the support of his mother.

JOHN A. MOROSO of the *News and Courier* died. *Greenville News*

JOHN J. CANTRELL will soon become a citizen of Pickens County having purchased the farm of TILLMAN G. FENNEL on Three and Twenty Creek.

Married the 20 (Oct.) at the residence of ROBERT DAVIS in Central, S.C., by Rev. J.J. Beck, MISS LAURA HUGHES to MR. SAMUEL NEAL.

Married the 27 (Oct.) at the Methodist Church in Central, S.C., by Rev. S.H. Zimmerman, MISS NELLIE RAMSUER to MR. C.G. ROWLAND.

Married the 27 (Oct.) in Pelzer, S.C. at the residence of the bride's father DR. GEORGE ROBINSON by Rev. Mr. Graveley, MR. J.D. GRANDY to MISS BETTIE ROBINSON.

LIZZIE SARGENT, age 10 years old, daughter of MR. and MRS. J.B. SARGENT died the 27 (Oct.) at the home in Hurricane Township. She was buried from Prater's Creek Church.
MARCUS SARGENT another victim of fever from that family died at the age of 21 years. He was buried from Prater's Creek Church.

TOM BOLDING son of B.M. BOLDING died from an accident that occurred last Thursday. He was buried from Prater's Creek Church (details).

Central, S.C. - 26 Oct.
MRS. B.A. HENRY wife of D.R. HENRY of Fort Hill, Georgia (sic) died yesterday (25 Oct.) and was buried at the Old Stone Church Cemetery. She was the daughter of OVERTON LEWIS and sister of DR. THOMAS L. LEWIS. *Greenville News* - 27 Oct.

MARGIE BOATWRIGHT, the 3 year old, daughter of MR. and MRS. J. BOATWRIGHT died the 25 October 1895 at Pelzer, S.C.

Issue of: Thursday 7 November 1895:

South Carolina Constitutional Convention (details).

Qualification for Voters (details).

J.T. LANGSTON is improving his premises and is erecting an elegant cottage residence on his farm near town.

MRS. CORDELIA CLEMENTS wife of JAMES CLEMENTS died the 30 (Oct.) and was buried from Tabor Church. She was the daughter of the late JOSEPH WILLIAMS.

F.P. McALISTER of Anderson Co., S.C. has purchased the J.L. COX farm 2 miles north of town and will make it his future home from the first of December.

Married the 31 (Oct.) at the residence of the bride's father MR. IRVIN ALEXANDER by Rev. W.C. Seaborn, MR. T.O. ALLGOOD to MISS IDA ALEXANDER.

The 7 year old daughter of MR. and MRS. JAMES SIMMONS was badly burned at her home near Table Rock. She was burned on Wednesday and died on Thursday.

CHOICE WILLARD of Hot Springs, Arkansas is visiting his aged father F.E. WILLARD.

The oil mill is to start this week.

From Liberty
DR. ROBINSON has moved back to his old home in town. He likes Liberty, S.C. better than Pelzer, S.C.
REV. W.H. WORKMAN moved to Easley, S.C. last week.

Married the 30 (Oct.) at the residence of the bride's father MR. S.M. COX, MR. HERBERT THOMPSON of Seneca, S.C. to MISS JULIA COX (lengthy details).

MILTON W. LAND of Atlanta, Georgia has made a request for a divorce from CORDELIA ANN LAND formerly of South Carolina (details). *Atlanta Journal*

JUSTICE CURETON'S Court - Minor criminal cases (details of decisions). *Easley Messenger*

Pickens Co., S.C. Clerk's Sale:
SALLIE ALEXANDER, et al. vs W.E. ALEXANDER. 110 acres of land to be sold.
RICHARD LENHARDT vs GEORGE E. MOON. 135 acres of land to be sold.

Pickens Co., S.C. Salesday - Court of Common Pleas:
TEMPY C. STEWART, et al. vs CORRIE J. BLAYLOCK, et al. 11.5 acres of land in the town of Easley, S.C. sold to J.P. CAREY for $495.
J.P. CAREY, Attorney vs F.M. MORRIS, et al. Lot in the town of Pickens on Main and Ann Streets, 26 feet X 80 feet sold to B.M. GRIFFIN for $265. One acre lot on the road to Secona Church sold to H.B. HENDRICKS for $68.
COOPER vs COOPER. 126 acres sold to MRS. ELIZABETH COOPER for $320.
R.A. HESTER vs ELIZABETH BARKER. 173 acres sold to J.E. BOGGS for $100.

Issue of: Thursday 14 November 1895:

South Carolina Constitutional Convention (details).

Progress in Pickens Co., S.C. (details).

The PICKENS RAILROAD (details).

MR. B.T. McDANIEL has been transferred from York Co., S.C. to Edgefield Co., S.C.

MR. W.D. CHAPMAN formerly section master of the SOUTHERN RAILROAD in Easley, S.C. has a good job in Chicamauga, Georgia and has removed there with his family.

V.E. HUDGENS who has been the night operator in the telegraph office in Salisbury, North Carolina has been promoted and given the position of day operator in Greenville, S.C.

DR. W.J. BRAMBLETT and family will move to Charleston, S.C. *Keowee Courier*

LARKIN HENDRICKS son of DAVID HENDRICKS of this county died at his home in Asheville, North Carolina the 5 (Nov.) at the age of 35 years. He was buried from Tabor Church. Mr. Hendricks married a daughter of THOMAS J. CHILDS who lives near town. He leaves a wife and 1 child.

Married the 6 (Nov.) at the residence of G.K. MAXWELL in Walhalla, S.C., by Rev. G.G. Mayes, MISS SUE MAXWELL to MR. CHARLES M. NIELD. They will live at NIELD'S HOTEL. *Keowee*

Courier (Both buried Walhalla Westview Cemetery - <u>Oconee Co., S.C. Cemetery Survey</u>, Vol. 2, pp. 118-119).

MRS. SUSAN HENDRICKS wife of B.L. HENDRICKS died at her home about 6 miles north east of Pickens on the 6 (Nov.). She leaves a husband and several children. (??SUSANAH HENDRICKS, born 6 June 1852, died 28 Nov. 1894, buried Oolenoy Baptist Church Cemetery - <u>Pickens Co., S.C. Cemetery Survey</u>, Vol. 1, p. 243).

FRANK E. McKENZIE who lived near Piedmont, S.C. died yesterday (5 Nov.) at his residence. *Greenville News* - 6 November

JOHN O. DAVIS, ESQ. died at his home near Thomasville, S.C. the 6 (Nov.) of pneumonia. He leaves a wife and several children (details).

MR. E.F. WALDROP of Greenwood, S.C., wife and four children have rented the farm of MRS. ELIZA AIKEN.

CONSTANT HUGHES died at his home in Austin Township near Bethel Church at the age of 102 years. His birthday was in June. He was buried from Bethel Church of which he was a member. Mr. Hughes had a number of children, one daughter survives. *Greenville News*

Married the 30 (Oct.) at the residence of MR. H.C. HUNT near Calhoun, S.C., by Rev. Mr. Porcher, MISS MAUD LEE HUNT and MR. WILLIAM A. GRESHAM (details).

MRS. SUSAN EDENS wife of the late SAMUEL EDENS died at the residence of her father J.T. LIGON the 8 (Nov.) at the age of 24 years. She was buried from Mountain Grove Baptist Church. Mrs. Edens leaves an infant child.

ABRAHAM STEWART died at his residence on the Eastatoe the 8 (Nov.) at the age of 88 years. He was a member of the Antioch Baptist Church. Mr. Stewart was buried in the family cemetery on the banks of the Eastatoe. He leaves several children.

<u>From Liberty</u>
Married the 6 (Nov.) at the residence of the bride's father, MISS IDA TEMPTON (TEMPLETON) of Powers, Laurens Co., S.C. to DR. W.A. SHELDON. The groom's parents are from Westminster, S.C. (see below).

<u>Powers, S.C.</u> - IDA TEMPLETON married DR. WILLIE SHELDON of Liberty, S.C. Miss Templeton is the eldest daughter of DAVID TEMPLETON (lengthy details - see above).

Married a few nights ago MR. SMITH about 48 years old to MISS ANNIE CULBERSON age 15 years. Her family lives a few miles from town. *Greenville News*

Issue of: Thursday 21 November 1895:

South Carolina Constitutional Convention (details).

DR. FIELDS of Pickens gave a speech at the Constitutional Convention.

MISS ESSIE EARLE is attending Chicora College at Greenville, S.C.

Married the 13 (Nov.) by J.A. McWhorter, N.P., MR. GEORGE COTHRAN to MISS ELLA GILLISPIE both of Anderson Co., S.C.

Married the 10 (Nov.) by J.A. McWhorter, N.P., MR. W.O. TROTTER of Anderson Co., S.C. to MISS LILLIE BRYANT of Pickens County.

PROF. JOHN O. DAVIS died the 4 (Nov.). He was an area teacher.

Looper's
MRS. CARRIE HUNT wife of W.E. HUNT and daughter of REV. M.L. JONES died the 14 (Nov.) of typhus fever. She was buried from Nine Forks Baptist Church of which she was a member. Married Sunday the 17 (Nov.) at Peter's Creek Church by W.N. Hughes, N.P., MR. PINKNEY REID of Greenville Co., S.C. to MISS TALITHA HENDRICKS of Looper, S.C. (details).

Issue of: Thursday 28 November 1895:

South Carolina Colored State College (details).

The Confederate Veteran (details).

Schools of the State of South Carolina (details).

COL. E.M. SEABORN died at the home of his daughter MRS. JAMES S. HAMILTON of Atlanta, Georgia. He was Clerk of the U.S. District Court. *Greenville News* - 26 November

PROF. S.W. O'DELL has opened his school in the Roanoke District.

F.N. MOODY who is living near town will move to Whites in Anderson Co., S.C.

Married the 17 (Nov.) at the residence of Rev. Thomas Looper, MR. DEAL HIOTT to MISS JENNIE DUNCAN daughter of W.A. DUNCAN.

PHILIP HUNTER, colored, died at his home in town at the age of about 75 years (details).

MRS. LIZZIE WINONA FOLGER wife of W.A. FOLGER died at her residence in Washington, D.C. Tuesday the 17 (Nov.). She was married during the Christmas holidays last year. Mrs. Folger leaves an infant baby 12 days old, a husband and an aged father.

Easley Messenger - Buildings and Residences Burned.
A one story frame house of MARIA GRIFFIN, colored.
W.M. HAGOOD & CO.'S two story frame furniture and coffin store and a brick store.
HOWARD'S STORE was saved but the EASLEY BANK was damaged.
T.K. HUDGENS building and printing office were damaged.

DR. W.A. SHELDON has moved to his place west of DR. W.R. HOLLINGSWORTH'S house.

Issue of: Thursday 5 December 1895:

GENERAL THOMAS JORDAN died the 27 (Nov.) at his home in New York. He was born in Luray, Page Co., Virginia in 1819 (details).

ALICE LESLEY, colored, wife of DENNIS LESLEY died at her home near town on the 28 (Nov.) at the age of 36 years.

Married the 17 (Nov.) at Tigerville, Greenville Co., S.C. JAMES M. HAYNES of Pickens to MISS MARY E. PEARSON of Tigerville, S.C.

W.R. ROSEMAN, colored, is living on JOHN LATHEM'S place.

MR. THOMAS CHRISTOPHER, grandfather of the Auditor, died at his home near Reidville, Spartanburg Co., S.C. the 28 Nov. at the age of 94 years. He was buried from Abner's Creek Methodist Church of which he was a member.

Pickens Co., S.C. Salesday:
L.M. RIGDON vs LEWIS TERRELL. 125 acres sold to J.E. BOGGS.
P.E. ALEXANDER vs REBECCA J. HENDRICKS, et al. 12 acres sold to A.T. WYATT for $235.
LOUISA RHODES, et al. vs EPHRIAM GILSTRAP, et al. 1/3 interest in 500 acres bought by EPHRIAM GILSTRAP for $13.
RICHARD LENHARDT vs GEORGE E. MOORE. 135 acres sold to J.P. CAREY for $1,316.
SALLIE ALEXANDER, et al. vs W.E. ALEXANDER. 110 acres sold to W.E. Alexander for $585.

Issue of: Thursday 12 December 1895:

The President's Message (details).

CHARLES B. ROUSE wants to establish a CONFEDERATE MUSEUM.

B.H. WILLIAMS of Cedar Rock, S.C. has completed his new residence.

WILLIAM WILKINS died the 5 (Dec.) at his residence in the suburbs of West Greenville, S.C.

PLEASANT M. STEWART died at his home in Tucumseh, Oklahoma Territory in November. He was formerly of this county. Mr. Stewart leaves a wife and one child.

TOM PETERSON was hanged at Abbeville, S.C. (details).

WILLIS AMBLER, colored, is living on J.W. EARLE'S farm.

MRS. ALEXANDER wife of A.A. ALEXANDER died at her home on the Eastatoe the 8 (Dec.) and was buried at the family cemetery on that beautiful stream. She leaves a husband and many relatives. Mrs. Alexander was the daughter of COL. WILLIAM NIMMONS and was 41 years old.

JOHN W. FINLEY age 35 and daughter about 8 years old died at their home in Hurricane Township. They were buried from Six Mile Church. He leaves a wife and several children. Mr. Finley moved here several years ago from Oconee Co., S.C.

D.B. JONES died at his home the 6 (Dec.) and was buried from the Baptist Church at "Old Pickens", Oconee Co., S.C. of which he was a member. Mr. Jones married the youngest daughter of REV. D.H. KENNEMORE. He leaves a wife and 7 children.

Issue of: Thursday 19 December 1895:

South Carolina New State Constitution (details).

B. MOONEY, colored, is living in Liberty Township.

J.H. KENNEMORE, Superintendent of Registration, has removed to town and is occupying one of W.C. BRAMBLETT'S houses.

Married the 1 (Dec.) in Central, S.C. at the residence of W.H. Moore, N.P., MR. JAS. SUMMY to MISS MAGGIE EVATT.

Married the 12 (Dec.) at the residence of Rev. B. Holder, JOHN TROTTER and MISS SALUDA LESLEY.

Married the 15 (Dec.) near Table Mountain, S.C. at the residence of the bride's mother MRS. WRIGHT, MISS CARRIE WRIGHT to JAMES FRIDDLE, JR.

AUDITOR CHRISTOPHER has changed his domicile to the WILLIAM FERGUSON farm 2 miles from town.

Married the 8 (Dec.) at the residence of Trial Justice B.D. Garvin, THOMAS RAMPEY to MISS JANIE DARK all of Pickens County.

R.C. YOUNG and family of Fairfield Co., S.C. are visiting DR. J.D. CURETON, father of Mrs. Young.

REV. OLIN L. DURANT and family left for their new home on the Greenville Circuit at Ready River.

MISS LULA GLAZENER is teaching in the Zion District in a new schoolhouse.

The Easley, S.C. bridge fell the 10 (Dec.) (details).

Issue of: Thursday 26 December 1895:

B.F. MARTIN of Central, S.C. is teaching at Ridge Springs, Saluda Co., S.C.

C.B. MARTIN is teaching in Greenville, S.C.

Born the 7 (Dec.) a daughter to MR. and MRS. O.D. McCRAVEY.

Married at the residence of the bride's father (?JASPER) NIX by B.D. Garvin, SAMUEL GRAY to MISS --- NIX all of Pickens.

ROBERT W. STEWART, formerly of Six Mile, S.C., is living on the HAGOOD place about 5 miles from Pickens.

Married at the Baptist Church in Easley, S.C. the 22 (Dec.), by Rev. Weldon, MISS EMMA GRIFFIN daughter of E.-- GRIFFIN to STOKELY FARR.

JAMES A. BROWN who has been living near Field, S.C. has moved to near Pelzer, Greenville Co., S.C.

Johnston Chapel
R.F. TERRELL of Red Hill, Georgia is teaching at this place.
MISS DARTHULA WILLIAMS is teaching at this place.

Married the 18 (Dec.) at the residence of the bride's father CAPT. J.H. BOWEN by Rev. Mr. Williams of Honea Path, S.C. MISS ELLA BOWEN to MR. LUTHER HUNT both of Pickens County. (details). *Greenville News* - 20 December

Married the 21 (Dec.) at the Methodist Parsonage by Rev. W.J. Elkins, DR. W.F. AUSTIN to MISS ETTA LOWREY both of Seneca, S.C.

An iron bridge is to be built across the Saluda River at Easley, S.C.

Article -" The Death of GEORGE WASHINGTON" (details).

THE PEOPLE'S JOURNAL 1896

Issue of: Thursday 2 January 1896:

The BILTMORE HOUSE was open for Christmas (for the Vanderbilt family).

Married the 26 (Dec. 1895) at the residence of T.J. HERD by Hon. C.H. Carpenter, JOHN HERD and FLORENCE ANDERSON both colored.

LEWIS F. ROBINSON will attend college at Greenville and Tusculum in Tennessee.

P. EUGENE ALEXANDER formerly of Pickens is in the brokerage business in Atlanta, Georgia.

Married the 27 (Dec. 1895) at the residence of the bride's father, MR. J.A. CISSON by M.F. Hester, N.P., MRS. ALICE TROTTER and MR. THOMAS SUDDETH of near Greer's Station, S.C.

MR. J.F. LATHEM of the Cross Plains Section died the 25 (Dec. 1895) at the age of 66 years. He was buried Lathem Burying Ground.

Married on Wednesday the 25 December 1895 at the residence of the bride's father CAPT. R.S. LEWIS by Rev. J.M. Stewart, MR. ROBERT LYNCH to MISS MAGGIE LEWIS.

MISS MAMIE CHILD died the 25 (Dec. 1895) at the home of her father MR. R.R. CHILD at the age of 22 years. She was a member of the Baptist Church and was buried from Camp Creek Church.

MISS MARY BOWEN is teaching school at Hagood's District #38.

Married the 26 (Dec.) at the home of the bride's father ARKELUIS (sic) YATES by Jas. E. Bouroughs, N.P., MR. WILLIE MEDLIN to MISS ADDIE YATES all of Pickens County.

M.S. STRIBLING, Superintendent of Pickens High School has MRS. J.D. CURETON as his assistant.

Married the 25 December 1895 at the residence of the bride's parents MR. and MRS. W.B. ALLGOOD by Rev. J.M. Stewart, WALTER J. BOGGS to MISS MARY ALLGOOD (details).

From Central
MARIAH GAINES, the 10 year old daughter of R.G. GAINES, died and was buried the 27 December (1895) at the Methodist Church.

From Liberty
BILL LEMONS, a Negro, died just below here the other day (details).

Article - "The Last Christmas Dinner in the Union Army".

Pickens Co., S.C. Commutation Tax - For Road Repair.

AD - For Sale, a car load of rust proof red oats grown by NOAH HENDRICKS of Texas. Apply to JAMES F. HENDRICKS of Liberty, S.C.

T.C. ROBINSON selling 300 acres of land on Gregory's Creek, 3 miles from Pickens.

Pickens Co., S.C. Probate Sale:
Estate of JOHN F. STEWART, deceased. GIDEON M. LYNCH, Administrator vs OSCAR STEWART, EMMA STEWART, et al. Two parcels of land, 1,000 acres. Also, part of a parcel of land known as the WILLIS place to be sold.

Pickens Co., S.C. Clerk's Sale:
J.B. NEWBERRY, Judge of Probate vs MARY T. HESTER, et al. 700 acres of land known as the ABRAHAM STEWART home place to be sold.
800 acres of land conveyed to J.F. STEWART by HARRIET BOWIE.

Issue of: Thursday 9 January 1896:

ROBERT E. KNOX of the Stewart Section has moved to Piedmont, S.C.

MISS MARGARET WELBORN will teach at Hagood School District #38.

MR. J.D. SMITH an old citizen died the 1 (Jan.).

An infant of GEORGE B. LOOPER died Saturday the 4 (Jan.). This is three deaths in his family within 3 months.

Married the 5 (Jan.) at the residence of MRS. MARTHA MORGAN the bride's mother by Major Merck, MRS. E.M. McNAMIRE to C. PELFRY.

Married the 5 Jan. at the residence of MRS. J.J. ROBINS by M.F. Hester, N.P., MR. JOE FINDLEY to MISS ROSEY ROBINS.

Married the 1 Jan. 1896 at the residence of the bride's mother, by J.M. Stewart, MR. DAVID A. HERD to MISS ALICE ROBINS all of Pickens County.

Married the 24 Dec. 1895 at the residence of Trial Justice W.K. Merck, MR. J.L. DURHAM to MISS GEORGIA MARCHBANKS all of Pickens County.

MR. JAMES EVANS of the Liberty Section died the 1 January.

Married the 5 January 1896 at the home of the bride's mother MRS. CAROLINE FREEMAN by Rev. J.E. Foster, MR. ALLGOOD MOON to MISS MATTIE FREEMAN all of Pickens County.

Married the 17 December 1895 at the residence of the bride's father D.H. ELLIS by Trial Justice W.K. Merck, MR. J.H. GUNNELLS of Honea Path, S.C. to MISS E.T. ELLIS of Pickens.

A.R. HUNT, age 24, died of pneumonia at Simpsonville, S.C. He was the son of J. HUNT. Funeral services were held at Dacusville, S.C. where he was a member of the Methodist Church. Mr. Hunt leaves a widow and 1 child.

MISS LOLA HOLDER is teaching school in Greenville Co., S.C.

W.W. ORR of Texas is visiting in this county.

M.D. BOWEN of Hill Co., Texas is visiting in the area.

MR. FLAVOR HAYNES died the 4 (Jan.) at his home near Mount Caramel. He leaves a wife and relatives.

DR. ENSOR, Ex-Raiding Deputy Marshall, has gone into the drug business in Columbia, S.C. having purchased DR. HEINITSH'S stock.

Married Wednesday the 25 (Dec. 1895) at the residence of the bride's father T. WYATT, MISS MATTIE WYATT of Anderson Co., S.C. and J.R. FOSTER of Olga, S.C. (details). *Observer*

From Liberty
W.A. GRIFFIN will clerk in Rome, Georgia.
The LIBERTY HOTEL is closed to the public, W.H. PARSON having moved to MRS. J.A. SMITH'S place.
B.F. PARSONS moved to J.P. SMITH'S place east of town.
Married the 12 Dec. (1895) at the residence of Magistrate S.D. Stewart, W.O. ROPER of Rice's, S.C. and MISS D.D. SMITH of Easley, S.C. Married by the same, LEVI SPEARMAN and MISS ELIZABETH RACKLEY all of Pickens.
Liberty has four private boarding houses.

Pickens Co., S.C. Commissioner's Meeting and Report (details).

Issue of: Thursday 16 January 1896:

Article - "MR. DAVIS as the Confederate President".

Article - "MRS. CATHERINE LADD an Outstanding South Carolina Teacher and Poet". She was born in October 1809 in Virginia by the name of CATHERINE STRATTON. She was married at the age of 18 to MR. LADD, portrait and miniature painter.

Dots from Olga
GUY PHILLIPS the infant son of W.P. PHILLIPS died the 10 Jan. at his home near Olga, S.C.

MRS. PERMELIA HUNT wife of MR. JAMES HUNT died the 6 Jan. at her home in Cross Plains, S.C. and near Mount Carmel Church of which she was a member. She leaves a husband and 2 daughters. Mrs. Hunt was buried from Mount Carmel Church (details - 2 articles in the same issue).

MAGISTRATE W.C. BRAMBLETT sold his farm adjoining the town to M.F. HESTER.

MISS LULA GURLEY of Texas is visiting her aunt MRS. J.L. THORNLEY of this place.

CAPTAIN JAMES A. GRIFFIN of this town moved back to his old home place (place not given).

Married in Easley, S.C. at the residence of Dr. J.R. Riley, MR. G.L. McWHORTER TO MISS ROSA LEE YOUNG.

UNCLE BILLY MARTIN who moved from his farm sometime ago to his property in town has moved back to his farm for reasons of health.

COL. JOEL WELBORN died at his residence in Shubuta, Mississippi the 28 November 1895. He moved from Anderson, S.C., his native county and state to Mississippi in 1835. Col. Welborn was Mayor of Shubuta for 8 years. He was 84 years old and leaves a brother and 2 sisters in Anderson County.

Died the 8 January 1896 at Edgefield, S.C., NORA McDANIEL age four months 20 days, infant daughter of MR. and MRS. B.T. McDANIEL. The remains were brought to Pickens for burial. The funeral was at the residence of the child's grandparents MR. and MRS. J.H.G. McDANIEL on the 10 (Jan.) and burial was at Secona Cemetery.

Born the 12 Jan. a girl to MR. and MRS. JAMES CANTRELL near Glassy Mountain, S.C.

Married last Sunday at the residence of D.W. Garrison, N.P., MR. E.B. LATHEM to MISS CLEO McMAHAN.

BALUS ARTER, colored, an old and respected man who was living on HAGOOD'S place just east of town but recently living in Greenville, S.C., died in that city Sunday at the age of about 60 years. His body was brought back to this place and buried at Bethlehem.

W.M. HAGOOD & CO. of Easley, S.C. are preparing to rebuild on the burnt out site. The new building will be brick. The EASLEY BANK also will erect a brick building.

Pickens Co., S.C. Board of County Commissioner's Meeting (details).

From Mica
MISS REBECCA HUNT opened her school the 6 (Jan.) at Mica, S.C.

G.B. LOOPER of Pelzer, S.C. buried an infant child at Cross Roads Church on the 4 (Jan.). This is the fifth child that has been brought from Pelzer, S.C. in the last 4 months and 3 have been in Mr. Looper's family.

From Briggs
W.J.F. HAYNES died the 4 (Jan.) of cancer of the mouth at about 60 years of age. He was an old veteran.
MR. MORAN of Mississippi is visiting the family of J.T. KAY.

From Liberty
PROF. R.E. BOGGS is in charge of the public schools at Liberty, S.C.

Bids for the rock pillars for the bridge over Twelve Mile Creek at NORRIS COTTON MILLS to be let.

Pickens Co., S.C. Executor's Sale:
Estate of JAMES F. LATHEM, deceased by J.S. LATHEM and J.K. LATHEM, Executors (details).

Issue of: Thursday 23 January 1896:

The South Carolina Governor's Message (details).

MISS CORA BOWEN is teaching at Dacusville, S.C.

B.A. ALLGOOD is teaching a large school at Wolf Creek District just west of Secona.

MR. J.F. JAMES returned by train to Texas the 12 January. He had been visiting his uncle TREASURER J.T. YOUNGBLOOD (details).

Pickens Co., S.C. Salesday - No information found.

CLARK MILLER, colored, a son of C.T. MILLER died at his residence near town Friday night at the age of about 9 years.

Married the 14 (Jan.) at the residence of Magistrate B.D. Garvin, MR. THOMAS C. JOHNSON to MISS MARY BALLENTINE.

Married the 30 December 1895 at the residence of SAMUEL CHAPMAN by B.D. Garvin, JAMES YOUNG to HESTER COLLINS both colored.

Letter discussing the organized Militia in Pickens Co., S.C. (details).

Issue of: Thursday 30 January 1896:

Article - "Confederate Records" - Interesting report by historians.

Article - "The Monroe Doctrine".

South Carolina Legislature Report.

PROF. J.M. LOOPER moved into his new house last Monday in the Mica neighborhood.

MR. W.L. JENKINS of this place has been invited to the wedding of his son HOWARD JENKINS.

Born a daughter to MR. and MRS. JOHN W. LOOPER of near Table Rock, S.C. the 23 (Jan.).

MRS. E.S. GRIFFIN'S new, neat and commodious dwelling is nearing completion between here and Easley, S.C.

MISS MINNIE KIRKSEY is teaching at the Three and Twenty School. *Anderson Advocate*

MRS. BETTIE GAINES wife of the late WILLIAM GAINES died at Central, S.C. the 24 (Jan.). She leaves 2 sons ages 10 and 12 years old.

PAUL FOLGER infant son of MR. and MRS. A.R.N. FOLGER died at Gaffney, S.C. the 23 (Jan.). His remains were brought to Easley, S.C. for burial which took place the 25 (Jan.)

JOHN T. LANGSTON moved into his new house last week.

MESSRS. WALKER & OWENS have a genuine bargain store, 117 Main St., Greenville, S.C. (details).

REV. GEORGE W. SINGLETON died at the residence of his nephew MR. SILAS F. ROBINSON in the eastern section of this county, last Thursday of dropsy of the heart. He was a member of the Baptist Church and was buried from Peter's Creek Church. Rev. Singleton lost a leg in the war for his country (2 notices in the same issue).

Married at the home of W.E. GALLOWAY in the Jeptha Section on Wednesday this week by Rev. E. Allison, PROF. J.L.

MURPHREE to MISS KANNIE GALLOWAY of Pickens, S.C. Prof. Murphree is a teacher of music in Pickens. *Brevard News*

Dacusville Dots
WARRIE RUSSELL JONES son of N.H. JONES died the 21 Jan. at the age of 19 years of pneumonia and was buried from Nine Forks Church.

MISS CORA BOWEN commenced teaching public school at Lathem School District. Many students are absent due to measles.

From Mica
MISS REBECCA HUNT'S school (at Mica, S.C.) is not as large as last week due to measles.

MISS SUSAN ABERCROMBIE died at the home of her nephew ARWELL ABERCROMBIE last Thursday at the age of 95 years. She was a member of the Methodist Church and was buried at Cross Roads Church on Sunday.

REV. T.J. BOOK to leave for Florence Co., S.C. (details).

V.E. HUDGENS day operator for the SOUTHERN RAILROAD DEPOT of this city has transferred to the "rock pit" near Easley, S.C. at the 530 mile post where a telegraph office will be established. MR. C.W. BOSTICK former night operator will take over his duties.

Article - "ATTICUS G. HAYGOOD, Methodist Bishop of Georgia".

Issue of: Thursday 6 February 1896:

Information from the South Carolina School Commissioners (details).

The LIBERTY BELL went through Easley, S.C. on the AIR LINE last Thursday enroute to its resting place in Philadelphia, Pennsylvania.

J.E. HAGOOD'S MILL DAM at the PORTER MILL place is no more, it succumbed to torrents of rain last Sunday.

SQUIRE HALLUMS, colored, was knocked on the head by JOHN TEASLEY, colored. Teasley was arrested at Liberty, S.C. (details).

MRS. M.M. MORGAN relict of the late B.F. MORGAN of Dacusville, S.C. died the 28 (Jan.) at her home. Her birthday was on the 30 (Jan.) and she would have been 71 years old. Mrs. Morgan was buried from the Dacusville Methodist Church of which she was a member. She was a sister of the late COL. H.P. HAMMETT and mother of JAMES H., M.A. and B.A. MORGAN of Greenville, S.C. and DR. J.J. MORGAN of Dacusville, MRS. FLORENCE GRIFFIN of Pickens, MRS. R.A.

BOWEN of Pickens and MRS. J.N. MORGAN of Central, S.C. MRS. MAMIE BOLT of Laurens, S.C. another daughter died 2 years ago.

Married the 26 (Jan.) at Pleasant Grove Church by Magistrate A.L. Edens, MR. PHILLIP RIGDON to MISS NANNIE EVANS.

Married the 30 Jan. 1896 in Spartanburg Co., S.C. by Rev. C.L. Craig, MR. JESSE ROSS of Pickens Co. to MISS DORA VAUGHN of Spartanburg County.

Married the 23 (Jan.) at the residence of the bride, by Rev. Thomas Looper, MR. JOHN H. BOWEN of Pickens County to MRS. EMMA HUNT of Greenville Co., S.C.

REV. THOMAS LOOPER of Farr's, S.C. now 80 years old, has married 480 white couples and 150 black couples.

Married Sunday the 2 Feb. 1896 at the residence of the bride's father MR. LAFAYETTE PACE by M.F. Hester, MR. D.D.B. JONES of Greenville Co., S.C. to MISS DARCUS PACE of Pickens County (details).

MRS. ELIZABETH HESTER nee WHITMIRE, widow of the late CARR HESTER, died at her residence in this county Sunday the 26 (Jan.) at an advanced age. She was born the 21 March 1798 and was almost 98 years old. Mrs. Hester was a member of the Methodist Church and was buried in the family burying ground at Jocassee, S.C. *Keowee Courier*

Pickens Co., S.C. Sheriff's Sale:
J.M. STEWART, Administrator vs THOMAS CANNON et al. Tract #1 - 140 acres sold to J.E. BOGGS for $300. Tract #2 - 23 1/2 acres bid in by C.L. HOLLINGSWORTH for $23. Tract #3 - 100 3/4 acres sold to J.E. BOGGS for $449.50. Tract #4 - 78 acres sold to J.E. BOGGS for $75.

Reporter from the *People's Journal* visits Easley, S.C.
MESSRS. W.M. HAGOOD & CO. and EASLEY BANKING CO. are constructing new buildings.
J.H. "JAKE' MARTIN has a large stock of goods on the corner.
ANDY WYATT is selling a line of merchandise.
W.H. PICKENS' place is selling stoves, tin ware, etc. and has every facility for repairing.
W.C. SMITH is a cashier at the EASLEY BANK.
The MOUNTAIN VIEW HOTEL still occupies a prominent place in Easley, S.C. not only in site but in patronage. MRS. CORRIE M. BLAYLOCK, the proprietor is one of the best hostesses that exist in South Carolina.
MAGISTRATE CURETON is still dispensing justice.
MAJOR D.F. BRADLEY has a magnificent residence just on the edge of town.

A.W. FOLGER is still looking after the beam at the cotton warehouse. "Gus" is a mover and has handled lots of cotton this season.

A.S. AIKEN is still pegging shoes and mending harness. Mr. Aiken is a #1 shoemaker and is always busy.

MR. J.M. RAMPEY is at the same old place dealing out general stock to a good trade.

From Easley
Married the 2 Feb. at the residence of the bride's father by Rev. J.R. Riley, MISS LIZZIE KELLY to MR. FITZHUGH BRADLEY.

The closing exercises of Soapstone School, colored, taught by C.T. MILLER were held the 31 Jan. (details).

W.C. BRAMBLETT is selling his property, houses, lots, etc. in Pickens and closing - his store is going out of business.

Story - "ANDREW JACKSON - Hero of New Orleans".

Issue of: Thursday 13 February 1896:

The General Assembly - What is Going on in Columbia, S.C. (details).

The infant child of DR. J.J. MORGAN died the 3 (Feb.).

Born a boy and a girl last Friday to MR. and MRS. FRANK R. McCLANAHAM.

Married Sunday the 9 Feb. 1896 at the residence of THOMAS R. PRICE in Pickens, by Rev. J.M. Stewart, B.F. PARSONS to MISS CRECY ROGERS daughter of MR. FRANCIS ROGERS.

MR. R.A. BOWEN will have been postmaster for 2 years on the 17 (Feb.). He has only lost 2 days from his duties, one day at the burial of his mother-in-law the late MRS. M.M. MORGAN and the other to attend the funeral of his sister-in-law the late MRS. MAMIE BOLT who died some 20 months ago.

ISAAC McDANIEL, age about 19, son of HARRY McDANIEL died the 5 (Feb.) of typhoid fever and measles. He was buried from the Dacusville Methodist Church.

List of new boarders who have had their names entered on the register of HOTEL De McDANIEL (jail) since the sitting of the U.S. Court at Greenville, S.C.

Married the 2 (Feb.) at the residence of Magistrate W.F. Hendricks, MISS LUCY WHITMIRE of Table Mountain, S.C. to MR. T. WHITE of Pelzer, S.C.

MR. S. CHERRY McWHORTER celebrated his 76 birthday the 2 (Feb.). He is a member of Carmel Presbyterian Church. He has a son B.W. McWHORTER (details).

From Maynard
MESSRS. WIMPER (WIMPEY) & ROPER, the pottery firm, have dissolved partnership and each has his own factory.

Awful Tragedy at Blacksburg, S.C.
Murder - CHARLES WILLIAMS of Tunnel Hill, Georgia (sic) was shot and killed by MARION R. REESE and DAN LUCKIE was an accessory (details).

South Carolina Legislative Notes (details).

MR. GEORGE ROBINSON is now clerking for MR. J.E. ROBINSON at Easley, S.C.

MR. JOHN CRAIG has opened a general stock of merchandise in the J.N. HOWARD stand at Easley, S.C.

Issue of: Thursday 20 February 1896:

Married Friday the 14 February in Easley, S.C. by Rev. J.F. Anderson, MR. BUD NALLEY to MISS LETTIE MOORE.

Married the 11 February at the residence of Rev. W.J. Sheriff, MR. B.F. HOLCOMBE to MISS VESTA KING both of Pickens County.

HOMER A. RICHEY has been appointed to a position in the railway mail service. He will report for duty in Charlotte, North Carolina the latter part of the month.

Married the 12 (Feb.) at the residence of the bride's father MR. SILAS HINKLE on Cane Creek, by Rev. B.F. Murphree, MISS LEONIA HINKLE and C. EUGENE THOMAS (details).

A child of MR. R.M. HENDRICKS of the Mica Section died the 17 (Feb.) from measles and was buried at Cross Roads Church.

MR. W.F. SNIPES recently of Anderson, S.C. has moved to the Meet Section and has become one of our county's citizens.

Pickens Co., S.C. Jury List.

From Liberty
T.H. MOORE has started a dwelling and J.H. BROWN is enlarging his house with a view of taking in boarders.

Pickens Co., S.C. Final Settlement - Estate of W.A. PERRY, deceased by J.T. DARWIN, Administrator.

Article - "WESTFIELD & HELLAM'S FURNITURE BUSINESS, Greenville, S.C."

Issue of: Thursday 27 February 1896:

South Carolina General Assembly - Election Bill (details).

Affairs at Clemson College - Clemson College Trustees and the Clemson Committee (details).

GEORGE ROOKE and THOMAS JENKINS left Friday for Pacolet, S.C. where they will take positions in one of the cotton mills there.

JOHN W. BROCK is a merchant at Central, S.C.

Died Sunday the 23 (Feb.) the infant of MR. and MRS. OLIVER HANNAH.

W.M. LOGAN is a conductor on the SOUTHERN RAILROAD.

Married the 12 (Feb.) at the residence of MR. A.A. CASTLE by Magistrate Edens, MR. MALONE to MISS REBECCA CLARK both of Greenville, S.C.

Married Sunday the 23 February 1896 at the residence of the bride's mother MRS. ROBINS by W.C. Seaborn, MR. JOHN P. ALEXANDER to MISS GUSSIE C. ROBINS both of Pickens County.

MR. BAYLUS STEPHENS, father of BUD and J.L. STEPHENS, is in much better health.

Easley
Married last Sabbath at the Baptist Church by Rev. Weldon, MR. T.R. HENDRIX to MISS EMMA HOLDER.

Married the 18 (Feb.) at the residence of Dr. Riley, MR. JOHN BERKLEY to MISS BESSIE ELLENBURG.

South Carolina House Discusses Clemson College (details).

AD - W.C. BRAMBLETT selling 2 dwellings and 2 3/4 acres of land in Pickens, S.C.

Issue of: Thursday 5 March 1896:

South Carolina General Assembly - The College and the Citadel (details).

BILL NYE noted humorist died the 22 February.

STATE CONSTABLES JENKINS and REDMOND were shot and wounded at Walhalla, S.C. near the Court House (details).
Greenville News

Pickens Co., S.C. Court Records - Criminal cases (details).

DR. FLETCHER S. PORTER of Westminster, S.C. has moved to Pickens for the practice of his profession. He occupies the D.B. STEWART house on Pendleton Street.

MRS. CLARA MAULDIN wife of MR. JOSEPH MAULDIN living in the north west portion of this county died the 29 (Feb.) at the age of 40 years. She was a member of the Methodist Church.

EDDIE BRYSON, age 2 months and 24 days, son of MR. and MRS. JOHN A. BRYSON died Saturday night last. Buried Pickens Cemetery.

Married Wednesday the 26 February 1896 at the home of the bride's mother MRS. M.J. HARRIS, MR. ROBERT HUGHES to MISS ESSIE HARRIS both of Greenville, S.C. The bride is the sister of MR. T.D. HARRIS our townsman.

Easley
Little BLANCHE ANTHONY daughter of MR. and MRS. W.B. ANTHONY died at the home of her parents on Main Street.
S.N. WYATT is host of the EASLEY HOTEL.

Dacusville Dot
Married Sunday the 2 March by Rev. Thomas Looper, MR. THOMAS LOOPER to MISS ANNA CHILDRESS all of Pickens County.

Clemson
Clemson College Faculty has been Reorganized (details).
The New Presbyterian Church on College Ave. is Nearing Completion.

STATE CONSTABLES W.R. CROWFORD (sic), Chief, A.T. DAVIS, J.A. MAYS, T.B. PETTIGREW and T.E. REMBERT are in Pickens this week.

Liberty
MR. VIC HUDGENS of Easley, S.C. moved into J.S. O'DELL'S house last week. He is the railroad agent at the UNION ROCK QUARRY.

Married the 26 (Feb.) at McKinney's Chapel by Rev. Inabonett of the North Pickens Circuit, MISS H.E. McKINNEY to MR. W.A. GRAVELEY, son of L.B. GRAVELEY (details).

Issue of: Thursday 12 March 1896:

South Carolina General Assembly on the Metropolitan Police Law (details).

Article - "The Birth Place of ANDREW JACKSON".

Spartanburg, S.C. - 5 March
U.S. STATE DEPUTY MARSHALL JOHN KIRBY was shot and killed at Holly Springs, S.C. (details).
H.B. HENDRICKS is remodeling the old MORRIS COTTON GIN HOUSE and will make a dwelling house out of it for RICHARD ROSEMOND.

B.M. WHITMIRE of Oconee Co., S.C. will make his home with his brother B.H. WHITMIRE near Cedar Rock, Pickens County.

Married the 23 (Feb.) near Camp Creek by Rev. S.G. Sloan, MR. J.L. PRESSLEY to MISS MINDIE EADS (sic) all of Pickens County.

Married the 5 March 1896 at the residence of the bride's mother, by Rev. D. Tally, MR. FRANK PACE of Pickens Co. to MISS CARRIE JONES of Greenville Co., S.C.

Maynard
MISS MINNIE WILLIAMS and MISS ESSIE COX are teaching in the Maynard School.
Married the 8 (March) at the residence of R.P. Freeman, N.P., MR. W.R. LARK to MISS MARY WIMPY of Maynard, S.C.

From Field
D.E. HENDRICK'S has a flour mill.

J.B.R. FREEMAN expects to build a new cottage.

B.F. ROBERTSON and wife, living just over the line in Oconee Co., S.C., died within 48 hours of each other.
MRS. ROBERTSON died on Saturday night last and MR. ROBERTSON followed her on Monday. They were buried Tuesday. Several years ago they lived just west of town on Twelve Mile Creek (two above articles in same issue).

Sale of the CALHOUN ESTATE - JOHN EDWARD CALHOUN. *Abbeville Press and Banner*

Pickens Co., S.C. Mortgagee's Sale - T.W. FOLGER vs H.N. MORGAN, Mortgagee. Land in the town of Central, S.C. to be sold.

Pickens Co., S.C. Court of Common Pleas - CHARLES R. BATES, et al. vs G.E. HAMMOND. 742 acres of land (details).

Issue of: Thursday 19 March 1896:

Married the 19 (Feb.?) at the residence of MR. GEORGE K. HENDRICKS some 5 miles north of Pickens, by M.F. Hester, N.P., MR. B.L. HENDRICKS to MISS MARTHA JANE PORTER.

LAURENCE BOWEN of Grayson Co., Texas is visiting his brothers POSTMASTER R.A. BOWEN, HON. T.W. BOWEN and G.W. BOWEN. He went to Texas about 20 years ago. Mr. Bowen will remain in the area to regain his health.

Liberty - A Tour of Businesses in Liberty, S.C. by the *People's Journal*.
The LIBERTY OIL MILL & MANUFACTURING CO. and HUNTER & BOGGS CO. have been the stimulus of a great deal of Liberty's growth.
LIBERTY OIL CO. is located a short distance to the east of the railroad depot and is officered by: WILLIAM HUNTER, President, T.N. HUNTER, Secretary and Treasurer, H.B. HUNTER, Business Manager. The building was completed last year and commenced operating the beginning of cotton season 1895-96. They also sell hulls and meal.
HUNTER & BOGGS CO. is part of the parcel of the OIL MILL CO. It is officered by WILLIAM HUNTER, President, T.N. HUNTER, Secretary, Treasurer and Business Manager. The store is located on the corner just as you go into town from Pickens on Main Street. They have a new business house about 40 X 80 (nice details). Clerks are BOB ROBINSON and Mr. Hunter's cousin WASH HUNTER.
MESSRS. SHIRLEY & PARKINS are located in a new building diagonally from HUNTER & BOGGS CO. They commenced business in the summer of 1894. MR. H.C. SHIRLEY is the senior member of the firm and has been in business 21 years. MR. C.H. PARKINS is the other partner (details).
CHAPMAN & CALLAHAM carry a good stock of goods.
J.D. SMITH on the corner of Front and Main Streets has been in business for many years. They are in the general merchandise business.
MR. W.S. PARSONS, our coroner, has purchased the livery stable on Front Street. He has ordered some new vehicles and will shortly purchase several head of horses.
MR. J.H. BROWN is located on Front Street just west of J.D. SMITH'S. He has new and commodious quarters. Mr. Brown was previously located in a building of moderate proportions on the west side of Main Street. Mr. Brown is now erecting a new and commodious building on the lot adjoining his store house for hotel purposes.
DR. J.F. WILLIAMS is fast gaining a good practice. He has cute twin girls (details).
MR. RUFUS M. WERTZ, the marble man, is now engaged in building the new hotel for MR. JOE BROWN.
MR. T.H. MOORE is building a nice dwelling house just in the rear of his blacksmith shop. He expects to build a new shop soon. Mr. Moore is also the cotton weigher for Liberty, S.C. (details).

Cross Plains
There will be a new post office at the store of FREEMAN & WILLIAMS to be known as Clement, S.C.

MR. JOE HENDRICKS son of SUPERINTENDANT MATTHEW HENDRICKS disappeared the 8 (March). He is a student at Clemson College (details).

From Field
R. HARRIS and J.M. HAYES have improved their places.
W.F. HAYES has built a new dwelling.

Dots from Olga
Married Sunday the 8 (March) at the residence of the bride's parent PICKENS HARRIS by Rev. J.E. Foster, MISS SUNIE HARRIS to LUM BAYNE.

BASWELL RAINES of near Dacusville, S.C. died Thursday the 5 (March) and was buried from Peter's Creek Church.

Board of Registration - Appointments made by GOVERNOR EVANS for the state (details).

New Pension Laws (details).

New South Carolina Dispensary Law (details).

Pickens Co., S.C. Mortgagee's Sale:
J.H. PAYNE, Assignee of W.H. TUCKER, by authority given to him by CLARISSA SMITH. 1 acre of land to be sold.

AD - F.S. PORTER, Physician and Surgeon, Pickens, S.C.

Issue of: Thursday 26 March 1896:

New Registration Law for South Carolina (details).

J.G. SEABORN is a traveling agent with NORTHWESTERN YEAST COMPANY.

WALHALLA COTTON MILLS have opened. *Keowee Courier* - 19 March

MR. BAYLUS STEPHENS died last Friday at the residence of his son L.D. STEPHENS about 3 miles from town and was buried in the family cemetery. He was 81 years old and leaves 7 children.

MRS. CLINELIA HAMILTON widow of the late LEMUEL HAMILTON died at the residence of her son W.A. HAMILTON the 18 (March) and was buried from Carmel Church. She was 82 years old and leaves 5 children.

Maynard
B.A. GREEN is building the Maynard Schoolhouse.
G.H. HENDRICKS will soon build an elegant storehouse near his mill and gin about a mile from Cedar Rock, S.C.

From Liberty
D.H. TEMPLETON and daughter LAURA are visiting his son-in-law DR. SHELDON.
PERCY ROBINSON and CHARLEY HUTCHINS have recently become citizens of Easley, S.C.

Crosswell
MR. T.C. SPENCER is selling guano.

Requirements for Confederate Pensions (details).

GEORGE VANDERBILT'S Estate (details).

Article - "LAMAR FONTAINE, The Scout".

Issue of: Thursday April 2 1896:

Table Mountain
The wife of JAMES SIMMONS, of near Mica, S.C., died Sunday the 22 (March) of peritonitis and was buried at Oolenoy Cemetery. She leaves an infant son.
AMANDA GILLESPIE the 11 year old daughter of MR. JOSEPH A. GILLESPIE of East Fork, North Carolina died of pneumonia following measles. Mr. Gillespie also reports the death of BENJAMIN AIKEN of near Brevard, North Carolina.

A.J. JONES is doing business at 205 Main St., Greenville, S.C.

MISS MARY KIRKSEY is teaching at the Hampton Schoolhouse.

Voter Registration books are to be open 6 weeks.

MR. FRANK LOOPER has a new son born the 21 (March).

W.C. BRAMBLETT closed his store yesterday and with his family moved to the country in the Mica, S.C. area. He had lived in Pickens for 6 years.

MR. L. (LARRY) C. THRONLEY purchased the stock of merchandise of J.T. LEWIS & SON and moved it to the HOLLINGSWORTH BUILDING on the corner just opposite.

B. LEWIS is traveling for a Baltimore hardware house.

JOHN T. LEWIS moved back to his farm at Anderson Mill, S.C.

MISS JANE STEELE died at the home of her sister MRS. HARPER in the Six Mile Section on the 30 (March) at the age of about 50 years. She was buried at Old Pickens, Oconee Co., S.C.

Clemson College - List of Cadet Commissioned Officers.

Issue of: Thursday 9 April 1896:

G.W. BELL a mechanic for the NORRIS FACTORY has moved to town.

D.R. PLUMMER, car inspector, and family are boarding with J.M. SMITH.

CHARLIE HUTCHINS opened a stock of goods in W.R. HOLLINGSWORTH'S old drug store.

Married the 5 (April) at the residence of MR. J.E. OWENS by B.D. Garvin, MR. LEE PRESLEY to MISS ESTELLE THOMAS.

MR. BEN McDANIEL who has been in Lexington Co., S.C. for some time returned home.

WILLIE McCOMBS age about 19, son of MR. and MRS. JOHN A. McCOMBS of the Cedar Rock, S.C. neighborhood, died the 1 (March). He was buried at the JOHN I. WILLIAMS Burying Ground. (2 notices in the issue of the 9 April 1896 - with no other details).

The contract has been let for the Easley, S.C. covered wooden bridge (details).

Born a girl the 28 March to MR. CONNIE GRAVELY.

JOHN WYATT formerly of Pickens County is running the GREENVILLE HOTEL in the west end of town.

RUBIE ROBINSON daughter of MR. and MRS. A.P. ROBINSON of near Easley, S.C. died the 29 (March) at the age of 3 years. She was buried from Enon Baptist Church.

Married Sunday the 5 April 1896 near Easley, S.C. at the residence of the bride's parents, by A.W. Folger, J.P. "PAUL" BLASSINGAME to MISS MARY BRANCH who is living on JUDGE M. WELBORN'S place just north of Pickens, both colored.

150 CSA VETERANS met at the Court House to hold an election for the members of the Examining Board for Pensions (details).

From Maynard
MAT JULIAN has gone to Izard County, Arkansas to visit his brother and may locate there.

MISS BETTIE BOWEN is teaching at Maynard, S.C.

A child of MR. A.P. ROBINSON died and was buried last Monday.

Married the 5 April at the home of the bride's parents MR. and MRS. V.A. FERGUSON, MR. W.T. FREEMAN to MISS TUCKY FERGUSON (lengthy details).

Issue of: Thursday 16 April 1896:

A letter from THOMAS C. LYNCH, Middleton, Canyon Co., Idaho, written the 1 March 1896 to his brother (name not given - details).

Married the 12 April at the residence of the bride's father MR. J. MATT RAMPEY by B.D. Garvin, MR. ROBERT CANTRELL to MISS JANNAH RAMPEY.

REV. T.J. ROOKE and family have moved to Florence Co., S.C.

MRS. MALINDA STEWART wife of REV. J.M. STEWART died Tuesday morning at the age of 54 years. She was a member of the Baptist Church and was buried at Secona. Mrs. Stewart leaves a husband and 4 grown children. (MELINDA STEWART, born 14 June 1843, died 14 April 1896, buried Secona Baptist Church Cemetery - Pickens Co., S.C. Cemetery Survey, Vol. 1, p. 206).

MR. W.F. BLASSINGAME, lawyer of Anderson Co., S.C. can be found at the HOLLINGSWORTH BUILDING adjoining L.C. THORNLEY'S STORE.

EX-MAYOR W.W. GILREATH of Greenville, S.C. shot and killed himself (details).

Hazel Nuts Cracked
MR. E.F. DePRIEST is teaching school in this section.
MISS MARY KIRKSEY is teaching a large subscription school at Hampton, S.C.
MR. W.W. AIKEN has the largest store at Hazel, S.C. It is known as KING'S OLD STAND. His other store is at Central, S.C. with MR. E.M. CORN as clerk.

Pickens Co., S.C. Clerk's Sale:
PLANTER'S BANK OF GREENVILLE, S.C. vs W.H. SUMMEY. 75 acres of land to be sold.

Issue of: Thursday 23 April 1896:

South Carolina State Convention (details).

The South Carolina Exhibit at Chicago, Illinois (details).

Confederate Pension Instructions (details).

Dispatch - MRS. SARAH SMITH wife of REV. Z.H. SMITH committed suicide at her home 3 miles from here - Bourbon, Missouri, Monday morning the 7 April. Rev. Smith is a brother of FOSTER and WILLIAM SMITH and his wife is a sister to MR. N.M. MADDEN of this county. Rev. Smith and family moved to Missouri in 1870. Mrs. Smith's daughter MRS. McGREGOR died a few months ago. She leaves a husband, 2 sons, REV. T.M. SMITH and ELIJAH SMITH and a daughter MRS. WILLIAM DIXON.

Letter concerning the building of the Easley Bridge from MATTHEW HENDRICKS. The Easley Bridge fell about the 28 Dec. 1895. The Keowee Bridge at "Old Pickens", Oconee Co., S.C. fell in April 1890 and was rebuilt and ready by the 11 June 1891 (details).

Letter to the Editor from H.M. LOOPER, Bowie, Texas. Mr. Looper moved there about 2 years ago (details).

MRS. THOMAS BOGGS of Birmingham, Alabama is visiting relatives in Pickens County.

Married the 19 April 1896 at the residence of the bride's mother by J.J. Herd, N.P., MISS SARAH ANGELINE BURGESS to MR. J.H. HUDSON all of Pickens County.

MRS. D.P. ORDWAY of Camden, Maine is at the residence of DR. F.S. PORTER. She brought her little daughter here to be treated for spinal curvature.

MESDAMES DR. WILLIAMS and J.S. O'DELL of Liberty, S.C. were in Pickens Wednesday of last week. They come to attend to the obsequies of the late MRS. J.M. STEWART which occurred yesterday.

From Liberty
MRS. LIZZIE HYDE of Indiana is visiting her brother E.B. RICHARDSON.
S.D. GLENN died at his old home in Laurens Co., S.C. He has been living here and keeping a furniture store for the last few years. Quite feeble (details).

From Maynard
The 3 month old infant of MR. ARTHUR ROBINSON died from whooping cough the 12 April 1896.

From Mica
ESSIE the infant daughter of MR. and MRS. H.A. ROBINSON died the 12 (April) and was buried from George's Creek Church.

Pickens Co., S.C. Voter Registration Notice (details).

GENERAL JOHN D. KENNEDY is dead (details).

Notice - Do not hire MARIAH BLAKE or her son ED BLAKE or JOHN TEESE as they are under contract to JOHN W. THOMAS.

Issue of: Thursday 30 April 1896:

Married the 19 April at the residence of MR. MILTON NALLEY by Rev. W.J. Sheriff, MR. J.L. NALLEY and MISS LIDA CARTER all of Pickens.

ORA LEE BOWEN infant daughter of MR. and MRS. MARTIN BOWEN died Friday and was buried at the family cemetery at Cedar Rock, S.C.

Article - "Pendleton District 90 Years Ago" (lengthy details).

From Crosswell
ELIAS HUNT, colored, lost his house to fire Friday night, also corn, bacon and flour.

From Liberty
There was a fire at HUNTER & BOGGS CO. It was close to being serious (details).
JIM BROWN, colored, lost his arm in a railroad accident (details).

Article - "Slaves and Slavery - Facts and Figures from the History of the Traffic".

Peabody Scholarship to be awarded. Gives names of those of South Carolina now holding scholarships.

Issue of: Thursday 7 May 1896:

Article - "Last Cabinet Officer of the Confederacy - Scraps of Unwritten History".

Pickens Co, S.C. Convention (details).

From Mica
Married Thursday the 23 (April) at the residence of MRS. SUCKIE TROTTER by Rev. A.S. Whitmire, MR. DAVID HENDRICKS, JR. to MISS MARY JANE TROTTER all of Pickens County.

MR. BEN McDANIEL and family have moved into the ASHMORE house opposite the Methodist Church.

MRS. JOSEPH GILSTRAP died Friday the 1 May and was buried at New Friendship Methodist Church.

Married the 26 April 1896 at the residence of the bride's brother GEORGE HOLCOMBE by J.A. Mullinax, N.P., MR. JOHN D. GILLARD to MISS KATE HOLCOMBE all of Anderson Co., S.C.

Married the 3 May 1896 at the residence of Rev. M.L. Jones, THOMAS TURNER to MISS AXIE GRAVELEY.

An infant of MR. and MRS. THEODORE LEWIS died last Thursday and was buried at Mountain Grove Church Cemetery.

V.S. MEDLIN is living on JERRE LOOPER'S place.

MISS TIRZAH HUGHES of Pickens has been visiting her sister MRS. J.A. DAVIS in Kershaw, S.C. Miss Hughes left for Baltimore, Maryland where she goes to learn the millinery business. *Kershaw New Era*

From Field
MR. SAM BROWN celebrated his 79 birthday the 25 (April). MR. and MRS. BROWN have been married 53 years (details). Married the 28 April at the residence of the bride's father ANDERSON EVATT by Rev. M.L. Jones, WILLIAM BYARS to MISS ELVINA EVATT.

Pickens Co., S.C. Commissioner's Meeting (details).

Married the 28 April 1896 at Prater's Creek Baptist Church, MR. JAMES G. SEABORN to MISS MYRTIE BOUROUGHS. The bride's father is MR. J.E. BOUROUGHS and the groom's father is REV. W.C. SEABORN (details).

MR. DANIEL MILLS died the 5 May 1896 at the age of 73 in the Six Mile Section. He was buried at the Six Mile Church Cemetery and leaves a wife and numerous relatives.

Issue of: 14 May 1896:

South Carolina Exhibit at Chicago, Illinois (details).

Clemson
An infant of PROF. and MRS. S. THOMPKINS died last week and was buried at the Pendleton Presbyterian Church Cemetery.

Letter to the Editor from ROBERT R. SINGLETON, Montague, Texas (details).

Married Wednesday evening the 6 Mary by Rev. Dr. Baldwin, ISAIAH COX formerly of Pickens to MAUDE MEACHAM 3rd daughter of CAPTAIN and MRS. JOHN F. MEACHAM at their residence, 810 5th St. N.E., Washington, D.C.

JOSEPH HUNT, colored, was killed on the BRUNSON farm 3 miles from Easley, S.C. SAMUEL RIPLEY has been arrested.

MR. J.E. PARSON teacher at the Keowee School in Pickens Co. held a closing ceremony. A dinner was served at OLD FORT GEORGE SPRING which is said to have been walled up by Indians.

NERO HALLUMS, prosperous and highly respected colored citizen of Central Township killed RICHARD ANTHONY, also colored. Anthony died Sunday (details).

From Clement
Married the 3 May by Robert P. Freeman, MR. LEIGH OWENS to MISS FANNIE TATE all of Pickens County.

Issue of: Thursday 21 May 1896:

Article - "Notable Women of the Civil War Conflict" - The sister of JOHN MORGAN and wife of GENERAL A.P. HILL.

SOUTH CAROLINA STATE MUSEUM to Collect CSA Relics (details).

Article - "Pendleton District, South Carolina 90 Years Ago" (continued).

Married the 10 May 1896 at Hickory Flat, S.C. by J.A. Mullinax, N.P., MR. W.A. GILLESPIE to MISS OLA MULLINAX all of Anderson County, S.C.

Converts at the Griffin Ebenezer Colored Church, C.T. MILLER and wife.

NERO HALLUMS is out on bail.

MRS. HUGH ELLISON died Friday the 15 May in Anderson Co., S.C. She was buried at George's Creek Church. Mrs. Ellison leaves a husband and 4 children.

MR. W.D. JAMES, foreman of the CLEMSON FARM, was shot Tuesday the 12 (May) by MR. PETER LINDSAY. Mr. James died the 13 May (details).

MAJOR JOHN J. LEWIS, daughter JENNIE and son JESSIE are visiting his brother-in-law MR. HUNTER in Seneca, S.C.

DOR CLAYTON, colored, took a snooze on the sidewalk near the front of W.H. ASHMORE'S Blacksmith Shop (details).

Account of Memorial Day at Pendleton, S.C. (details).

Looper
MR. G.T. HENDRICKS has put up a big store on Malyer Street near the corner of Tamy.

Issue of: Thursday 28 May 1896:

South Carolina State Convention.

Article - "Pendleton District 90 Years Ago".

An infant of WILLIAM RACKLEY died Friday the 21 May of whooping cough.

HENRY MILLER living in Sherman, Texas, son of IRVIN MILLER, was badly injured in a disastrous storm. A brother and sister of his wife were killed (information from a letter with no indication of writer).

JOHN I. WILLIAMS died the 21 (May) at his residence near Cedar Rock, S.C. He was buried with MASONIC HONORS at the family cemetery near his home. Burial was from the Cross Roads Baptist Church of which he was a member. He was 72 years old and leaves a wife and several children.

MRS. ELLEN BROCK, relict of CAPTAIN ANDREW BROCK, died the 14 (May) at the residence of her daughter MRS. ANDREW PARSONS 4 miles from Easley, S.C. She was 103 years old and was buried from Mt. Zion Church. Mrs. Brock leaves 4 children, 2 sons and 2 daughters.

Article - "Exploits of Patriots in the Piedmont Region".

AD - A.J. BOGGS, Selling Goods, Calhoun, S.C.

Pickens Co., S.C. Citation Notice - Estate of RICHMOND ANTHONY, deceased. OLA ANTHONY applied for Letters of Administration.

Issue of: Thursday 4 June 1896:

Article - "ABRAHAM LINCOLN as a Grocery Clerk".

Letter to the Editor from R.R. SINGLETON, Montague, Texas (details).

New School Law - Trustee's Notice (details).

PROF. W.H. STEELE is teaching at Elgin, Georgia.

MRS. DURHAM wife of MR. BUCK DURHAM died the 29 (May) in the Mile Creek Section at the age of 83 years. She was buried the next day in the family burying ground.

MRS. R.A. LANCASTER nee OLA HOLLINGSWORTH and little daughter of Gainesville, Florida are visiting her parents MR. and MRS. C.L. HOLLINGSWORTH. They will remain for the summer.

MRS. MARY NORRIS died the 27 May 1896 near Needmore, S.C. at the age of 77 years. She was buried the following day at the Lathem Grave Yard. Mrs. Norris leaves three sons and 1 daughter.

The 10 month 6 day old daughter of MR. and MRS. A.N. FOLGER died Friday the 29 May 1896 at Gaffney, S.C. Her remains were brought to Easley, S.C. and interred.

MRS. HESTER RICHARDSON an aged widow died at the residence of her son-in-law J.F. HENDRICKS in Liberty Township last week. She was buried at Carmel. Mrs. Richardson leaves several children.

MR. T.D. HARRIS has moved into the LEWIS BUILDING temporarily. He will erect a new and commodious building on the site where his old one now stands. The building will be 24 X 70 (details).

Hughes
There was a killing near Mayfield, S.C. on the Greenville side. BUD ROBINSON stabbed and killed WILLIAM LANCE (no other details).
A baby of MR. and MRS. A.H. DULIN died last night (24 May) and was buried from Peter's Creek Church.

A child of ANNIE CUNNINGHAM, colored, living on JOAB MAULDIN'S place near town burned to death Tuesday afternoon.

Democratic Convention - New Party Constitution (details).

Article - "GOVERNOR CLAUDE MATTHEWS - A Brief Sketch of Indiana's Favorite Son".

Issue of: Thursday 11 June 1896:

South Carolina State Campaign (details).

Mica
WASHINGTON JULIAN died the 3 June at his home and was buried from Peter's Creek Baptist Church. He leaves a wife and 6 children.

MR. JAS. P. LEWIS will fill the position of foreman at the CLEMSON FARM due to the death of MR. W.D. JAMES.

MRS. E.A. GARLINGTON of Washington D.C. is visiting the family of CAPTAIN E.B. FULLER of Clemson College, S.C. and COL. R.W. SIMPSON of Pendleton, S.C.

Homicide: JOSIAH CHAPMAN, JR. died on the Keowee River. He was shot by deputies and died at his home (details).

Card of Thanks, to both white and black during the trying times of our crippled baby. Signed, C.T. and ANNA E. MILLER

Pickens Co., S.C. Sheriff's Sale:
WILLIAM THOMPSON - 100 acres in Pumpkintown Township to be sold (tax execution).

Land conveyed to W.E. PATTERSON by ROBERT L. GILSTRAP - 144 3/4 acres in Eastatoe Township to be sold (tax execution).
L.O. HENDERSON - 1/4 acre lot in Liberty, S.C. to be sold. (tax execution).
Unknown land - 400 acres in Central Township to be sold.
S.W. MAJOR - 7 1/2 acres in Pickens Court House Township to be sold.

Issue of: Thursday 18 June 1896:

Spartanburg and Commencement - Wofford and Converse.

SOUTHERN RAILROAD is issuing a book on Summer Homes and Resorts.

B.A. HAGOOD and bride arrived in Pickens Saturday evening.

J.E. HAGOOD has taken charge of the CAESAR'S HEAD HOTEL.

LT. FRANK G. MAULDIN of the U.S. Army is visiting his parents MR. and MRS. J.A. MAULDIN.

MISS ESSIE EARLE is attending Converse College.

A boy named FRANK GRIFFIN was murdered and his body found in the Saluda River with gunshot wounds. OSCAR SIMMONS has been arrested and is in the Greenville, S.C. jail (details).

Confederate Reunion is being held in Richmond, Virginia. (details).

Article - "North Carolina Veterans". *Brevard News*

Article - "History of Gold Pieces".

The State Executive Committee arranges dates for the Campaign and Primary (details).

Pickens Co., S.C. Citation Notice - H.J. MARTIN applies for Letters of Administration for the estate of CARRY DOBBINS, deceased.

Pickens Co., S.C. Citation Notice - W.W. ORR applies for Letters of Administration for the estate of MRS. S.A.R. ORR, deceased.

Pickens Co., S.C. Sheriff's Sale - Numerous tracts of land being sold to satisfy tax execution (details).

Issue of: Thursday 25 June 1896:

National Republican Convention (details).

MR. WILLIAM PICKLE an old citizen died at the COUNTY POOR HOUSE near Pickens on Tuesday the 23 June at the age of 62 years.

COL. J.J. NORTON died at his residence in Walhalla, S.C. the 20 (June) at the age of 61 years.

An infant of MR. J.F. WELCH of Clement, S.C. died the 14 June 1896 and was buried by Rev. T. Looper.

Married Sunday the 21 June at the residence of Rev. B. Holder, MR. JAMES CHAPMAN of Mica, S.C. to MISS NANCY GILLILAND all of Pickens County.

Married Sunday the 31 (May) at the residence of MR. M. BARTON by C.H. Carpenter, N.P., MR. WALES CARUTH of Campobella, S.C. to MISS MATTIE ALTOM (sic) of Pickens County.

From Mica
An infant child of MR. and MRS. EDDIE HENDRICKS of Olga, S.C. died and was buried at Peter's Creek Church.

Table Mountain
The infant son of JAMES SIMMONS of near Mica, S.C. died the 15 (June). The child survived its mother who died back in the winter.
An infant of SAMPSON BURGESS of near Table Rock, S.C. died the 16 June due to dysentery and whooping cough.
A 3 year old child of JAMES JONES of near Rock, S.C. died the 17 June of intercolitis and dentition. All 3 of the above named children were interred at Oolenoy (details).

Article "THE STAR SPANGLED BANNER - Effort to Build Monument to the Author - The Origin of the Poem" (details).

The Six Mile Baptist Church applies for a charter of incorporation.

Issue of: Thursday 2 July 1896:

Cross Plains
MR. W.M. PODER is teaching at Roseland Academy.
MR. OSCAR CHILDRESS son of MR. and MRS. W.P. CHILDRESS died the 20 (June) at his home in Newry, S.C. of an accidental gun shot wound. He was 18 years old (details).
The grandson of W.L. SMITH of this place was buried at Mt. Carmel.

Roundabout
MR. JESSE WARD is the manager of the FERGUSON farm.
MR. PET ELLENBURG bought the BOATRIGHT place from W.T. McFALL.

The infant son of ARTHUR PORTER died last week.

MR. J.E. STANSELL died Tuesday afternoon at his home on the Big Eastatoe at the age of 26 years. He was buried Wednesday at Nimmons, S.C.

Liberty
The passenger depot at Liberty, S.C. will be a handsome affair when completed.
HUNTER & BOGGS, General Merchandise Store at Liberty, S.C. has dissolved. MR. WASH HUNTER will continue business at the present stand. T.N. HUNTER and C.E. HAMILTON have formed a partnership and will continue business in a vacant store room on the same street above their present place of business. BOB ROBINSON will be with HUNTER and HAMILTON.
J.H. BROWN had fine touches put on his new hotel (Liberty, S.C.) by MR. MARSHALL late from Vanderbilt Palace, North Carolina where he has been working.
A baby of LEE SAMMON'S died last Friday near Marietta, S.C. and was buried by his mother's side at Ruhamah Church. The baby survived but a short time.

R.M. WERTZ is engaged in building a mill near Marietta, S.C. on the Greenville, S.C. side.

Pickens Co., S.C. Jury List.

New Mail Routes in Pickens Co., S.C. (details).

Pickens Co., S.C. Voter Registration Notice (details).

Issue of: Thursday 9 July 1896:

Mail carrier J.W. ADCOX has moved in to the old LESLIE house now owned by W.T. MEARS.

CAPTAIN R.E. STEELE owns among one of the finest farms on the Keowee River on which the historical FORT GEORGE (Field, S.C.) lies just below Birche's (Burch's) Ford, which all lovers of fish generally visit during the summer months.

Married Sunday the 7 June 1896 at the residence of the bride's father MR. WILLIAM SINGLETON by Mr. Elias Raines, N.P., MR. W.E. PACE of Pickens Co. and MISS FANNIE SINGLETON of Greenville Co., S.C.

The Carolinian is a new paper published at Seneca, S.C. by MESSES. CAPERS and McWHORTER.

Married the 5 July 1896 by Rev. W.B. Singleton, MR. W.D. DUNCAN to MISS L.A. DUNCAN (sic) all of Pickens County.

MISS MARGARET WELBORN will have charge of the Hagood District School.

MISS WILLIAMS daughter of B.H. WILLIAMS will teach at King's Schoolhouse.

Issue of: Thursday 16 July 1896:

National Democratic Convention (details).

MRS. ARIAL wife of MR. ALBERT ARIAL died the 12 July 1896 and was buried at Ruhamah.

MR. C.A. DURHAM and daughter MAY DURHAM of Limestone County, Texas are on a visit with his brother L.R. DURHAM of this county.

MRS. REBECCA DURHAM died the 14 (July) at 1:00 A.M. at the age of 84 years. She was buried at Bethlehem the 14 (July) (sic) at 4:00 pm. Mrs. Durham was a member of the Methodist Church (REBECCA DURHAM, born 12 Sept. 1812, wife of CHARLES DURHAM - Pickens Co., S.C. Cemetery Survey, Vol. 1, p. 18).

MR. M.L. SHIPMAN, Editor of the *Brevard Hustler* and MISS LULA OSBORNE daughter of W.K. OSBORNE of Brevard, North Carolina were married last Saturday (minor details).

Born Saturday last EARLE BRYAN GILSTRAP son of MR. ELISHA GILSTRAP.

Pickens Co., S.C. Court of General Sessions - Minor criminal cases (details).

Tribute of Respect
Died the 21 May JOHN I. WILLIAMS of the Cedar Creek area at the age of 72 years (details).

Table Mountain
MR. DANIEL LOOPER of near Looper, S.C. died Monday the 29 June and was buried at Nine Forks Cemetery.
MR. AMOS C. SUTHERLAND is building a large and commodious storehouse in the forks of the Pumpkintown and Caesar's Head Road at Rock Post Office, S.C. He will, in the near future, erect a fine dwelling near his storehouse. His brother D.F. SUTHERLAND will move in September to Pickens and will sell goods at that place.

Article - "A Soldier's Memory - Confederate Account".

Issue of: Thursday 23 July 1896:

Article - "The Oldest Confederate Commissioner".

CADET OSSIE MAULDIN of Clemson is at home on a visit.

MR. ANDREW BRAMBLETT is on vacation from the Citadel and is visiting with his parents MR. and MRS. W.C. BRAMBLETT.

Liberty - 13 June
Liberty has a new passenger depot (details).
MRS. A.H. ARIAL died yesterday (12 May).

Old Soldier's Picnic (details).

Pickens Co., S.C. Court Actions - Criminal cases (details).

Briggs
MRS. NANCY BRIGGS wife of W.D. BRIGGS died the 14 June and was buried at George's Creek Church of which she was a member. She leaves a husband and 5 children.

Issue of: Thursday 30 July 1896:

The work on the bridge at DODD'S place on the Keowee River to be let.

MR. N.A. COTHRAN of Seguin, Texas is visiting his cousin D.F.S. PORTER.

MR. ANDERSON TURNER is a pensioner (details).

MR. A.C. DURHAM of Armour, Texas has been visiting his brother L.R. DURHAM of this county.

FOREST BRYAN JACKSON son of J.R. JACKSON was born 2 weeks ago.

JAMES CAMPBELL is living on the E.F. LOOPER place.

W.F. BLASSINGAME is in the law business in the firm of MORGAN and BLASSINGAME.

J.H. ABERCROMBIE, SR. will be 75 on the 31 August.

Issue of: Thursday 6 August 1896:

South Carolina State Campaign Schedule (details).

MR. SILAS M. DAVIS' house burned and an infant died the 30 July (details).

Pickens Co., S.C. Executive Committee Report (details).

Dacusville
WILL WHITMIRE son of ANDY WHITMIRE died Friday the 31 (July) and was buried at Oolenoy. JAMES CLEMENT and BERRY MEDLIN are mentioned as being present at the time Whitmire was killed (details).

T.D. HARRIS broke dirt for his storehouse on Main Street.

MRS. J.L. MURPHREE is teaching the Field Schoolhouse.

A.M. MORRIS is having bricks made on Town Creek to build a 2 story storehouse at his present site.

PROF. J.L. MURPHREE who was teaching at Mountain Grove will begin a school at Pleasant Hill the 10 August.

REV. J.K. MENDENHALL prominent Baptist Minister of Greenville, S.C. died at his home Thursday.

Liberty
The GIN and MILLING CO. is changing their building, moving and enlarging and are preparing to put in new modern machinery.
HUNTER & HAMILTON is the new firm being part of the old firm HUNTER & BOGGS.

Pickens Co., S.C. Executor's Sale - MARION B. LEACH vs B.J. WILLIAMS, E.M. HUNT and W.J. PONDER. Steam engine, saw mill and cotton gin to be sold.

Pickens Co., S.C. Citation Notice - Estate of LICENEY A. ALEXANDER, deceased. J.M. STEWART applied for Letters of Administration.

Issue of: Thursday 13 August 1896:

Pickens Co., S.C. Executive Committee Appoints Managers for Election (details).

PROF. M.F. STRIBLING has been appointed principal of the Westminster High School, Oconee Co., S.C.

WILLIAM FEATHERSTONE is living on the R.A. BOWEN place.

MRS. HENRIETTA BRAMBLETT wife of W.B. BRAMBLETT died the 7 (Aug.) near Cedar Rock, S.C. at the age of 60 years. She was buried the next day (place not given).

Married Wednesday the 5 (Aug.) at the residence of MAJOR D.F. BRADLEY at Easley, S.C., by Rev. J.F. Anderson, MISS MARY W. CLYDE to MR. H.H. MARTIN of Easley.

MRS. ELLA SINGLETON nee MISS ELLA E. JONES daughter of MR. and MRS. W.D. JONES of Pickens County died the 5 August 1896. She was born the 18 October 1869 and married the 5 August 1888 MR. T.P. SINGLETON. Mrs. Singleton leaves 2 children a son 4 years old and a daughter six months old.

MISS WYATT of Easley, S.C. is teaching school at Long Branch.

Calhoun
MR. A.J. BOGGS and MR. S.O. SKELTON entered into co-partnership. They have an immense stock of goods of great variety.

A girl was born to agent MR. L.W. CRISP last Thursday.

Pickens Co., S.C. Notice to Creditors - Estate of JAMES F. LAY, deceased. MARY LAY, et al. vs SAVILLA LAY, et al.

Issue of: Thursday 20 August 1896:

Campaign Meeting at Greenville, S.C. (details).

THORNWELL ORPHANAGE Needs Assistance (details).

Pickens Co., S.C. Executive Committee Report.

T.B. HAYES is living on DR. FIELD'S place.

MRS. MATILDA MILLS, relict of the late DANIEL MILLS, died the 17 Aug. at Six Mile, S.C. and was buried at the Six Mile Church. She was 70 years old. Mrs. Mills leaves no children but leaves a brother MR. S.B. MANN and an aunt MRS. J.T. YOUNGBLOOD.

Liberty
The depot has been rolled back from the railroad track to make room for another side track. The furniture has been fitted up in the new passenger waiting room.

J.M. LOOPER is growing cotton on W.N. HUGHES plantation.

Issue of: Thursday 27 August 1896:

Brief Sketch of South Carolina's Next Lt. Governor, M.B. McSWEENEY (details).

MR. PERRY F. THORNLEY arrived in Pickens from Fort Worth, Texas.

LULA GLAZENER is teaching at Zion School District.

MRS. LOUIS GILSTRAP died Saturday and was buried from Mountain Grove Church. She was 35 years old.

MRS. HENRY MILLER came from Texas and said she and her husband expect to make Pickens County their home.

D.F. HENDRICKS son of D.E. HENDRICKS will attend Tusculum College, Nashville, Tennessee.

Married Tuesday the 18 August 1896 at the residence of Rev. J.F. Anderson, MR. W.H. FARR to MISS LILLIE BYARS. Rev. J.F. Anderson and Rev. W.B. Singleton officiated (details).

I.N. EARLE is living in the Bald Mountain Section.

W.S. DURHAM the shoemaker has his shop at the SMITH GRIFFIN MILL.

MISS CARRIE O. SAMS of Gaffney, S.C. will open school in the Pickens High School Building.

Pickens Co., S.C. Board of Supervisor's Meeting and Report.

Born a baby boy to J.D. GRANBY.

Flat Rock Church to apply for a charter (details).

Issue of: Thursday 3 September 1896:

The Election in the State (details).

MR. WALTER GRIFFIN is a clerk for MR. J. McD. BRUCE.

MR. AARON MORRIS moved his stock of goods to the FREEMAN BUILDING pending the erection of a new brick storehouse.

WILLIAM W. MARTIN died Friday the 28 (Aug.) at the age of 70 years. He requested that he be buried at Secona Cemetery by the old soldiers (WILLIAM W. MARTIN - born 12 Aug. 1829, died 29 Aug. 1896 - Pickens Co., S.C. Cemetery Survey, Vol. 1, p. 206).

Liberty
CHAMBERLIN & BOGGS CO. started the new gin mill.
The OIL MILL CO. will start soon.

Hazel Nuts Cracked
MR. E.J. PRINCE sold his farm 2 miles south of Pickens and rented the farm of DANIEL WINCHESTER.

Pickens Co., S.C. Court of Common Pleas - MALINDA HOPKINS, ELIZA HOLLIDAY, ELIZA YOUNGBLOOD, et al. vs ELIZA PILGRIM, WILLIAM MANN and the heirs at law of MILSTEAD MANN, deceased.

Issue of: Thursday 10 September 1896:

Sketch of South Carolina's New Governor, WILLIAM HASELDEN ELLERBE (details).

MRS. JAMES G. SEABORN daughter of MR. JAMES E. BURROUGHS died the 6 September of consumption. She married the 28 April 1896. Mrs. Seaborn was buried from Prater's Creek

Baptist Church of which she was a member and is buried in the family burying ground. (MARY MYRTIE BOROUGHS, wife of JAMES G. SEABORN, born 10 Aug. 1868, died 10 Sept. 1898 (sic), buried Boroughs, Gillespie Cemetery - <u>Pickens Co., S.C. Cemetery Survey</u>, Vol. 1, p. 17).

The 12 or 14 year old son of MR. JAMES E. BURROUGHS died the 8 (Sept.) (EARNEST J. BOROUGHS, born 5 Dec. 1881, died 8 Sept. 1896, buried Boroughs, Gillespie Cemetery - see documentation above).

<u>Dots from Alexander</u>
MR. JULIUS E. PARSON who is teaching at Keowee will place a stock of nice goods in the store of F.C. PARSON'S MILL.
MISS OLA STEELE, Dear Lodge, Montana is visiting her aunt and uncle MR. and MRS. W.E. ALEXANDER of Mile Creek, S.C.

MISS LIDIE PORTER is teaching at Table Rock, S.C.

Married Sunday the 30 August at the residence of the bride, by T.N. Hunter, MR. A.T. STEPHENS to MISS DAISY CRUMPTON.

MINNIE SNIPES died Wednesday morning at the home of her father in the Six Mile Section. She was 9 years old.

MRS. ADALINE GALLOWAY late of Piedmont, S.C. died at BERRY STEPHENS' residence last Tuesday. She was about 50 years old (details).

MISS TIRZAH HUGHES of Pickens has accepted a position as head milliner at the house of JAS. O. BRAGG at Winnsboro, S.C.

JOHN B. SEXTON originally from North Carolina but now living near Liberty, S.C. fell about 8 feet from a tree and broke his neck. Mr. Sexton was the son-in-law of L.A. BROWN. He was between 35 and 40 years old and leaves a wife and several small children (two notices in the same issue).

PROF. W.W. FISHER is teaching the colored school.

<u>Liberty</u>
J.S. O'DELL and family have moved to Georgia and C.N. ENGLISH of North Carolina now has charge of the depot agency here.
B.H. CALHOUN will build a dwelling.
WILLIAM TAYLOR and JAMES MILLER were injured by a blast at BEVERLEY QUARRY three miles above Liberty, S.C. William Taylor died the 6 Sept.

T.H. MOORE has moved in to his new house south of the depot.

Pickens Co., S.C. Citation Notice - J.T. YOUNGBLOOD applies for Letters of Administration for the estate of DANIEL MILLS, deceased.

Issue of: Thursday 17 September 1896:

JOSEPH E. EARLE of Greenville, S.C. was nominated by the Democratic Party for the U.S. Senate.

Bowie, (Texas) Cross Timbers
MISS JEANETTE DAY the 15 year old daughter of MR. M.V. DAY committed suicide. She was buried from the Methodist Church (details).

MR. LAWRENCE BOWEN returned to his home in Texas after visiting relatives for 4 months in Pickens.

O'DELL HENDRICKS, 2 year old son of MR. and MRS. W.F. HENDRICKS, died Sunday and was buried at Oolenoy Church.

MESSRS. SUTHERLAND & GRIFFIN will open a stock of general merchandise in the MASONIC TEMPLE BUILDING. They will move to their new store on the corner when it is completed.

Fires Set in the Table Rock Neighborhood: MR. FRANK FERGUSON'S dog was shot and his out house filled with fodder burned. MR. J.L. TROTTER was shot and house burned (details).

Dots from Alexander
MISS ANNIE NIMMONS is teaching school on the Eastatoe.
MR. F.C. PARSON'S cane mill is in operation.

Calhoun
MESSRS. BALLINGER and GILLERSON'S cotton gin is operating. The telephone line from Clemson College to Calhoun was completed by the 14 Sept. 1896.

Pickens Co., S.C. Citation Notice - SARAH E. MARTIN and J.T. YOUNGBLOOD apply for Letters of Administration for the estate of W.W. MARTIN, deceased.

Issue of: Thursday 24 September 1896:

MRS. T.J. HUNT died at her home in Dacusville, S.C. Sunday morning at the age of about 36 years.

MISS ARTIE LEWIS of Anderson, S.C. entered Pickens High School.

BENNETT PERRY, the 18 year old son of S.M. and S.J. PERRY of the Keowee side, died Saturday the 19 (Sept.) of typhoid. He was buried at Six Mile Church.

MISS LILLIE WILLIAMS daughter of MR. and MRS. B.H. WILLIAMS of Cedar Rock, S.C. died last Tuesday morning and was buried in the family burying ground.

MRS. LOUISA HESTER mother of M.W. HESTER of Dacusville, S.C. died the 19 (Sept.) at the age of 66 years. She was a member of the Dacusville Methodist Church where she was interred. Mrs. Hester was left a widow when she was quite young with 5 children, 3 sons and 2 daughters. One daughter married MR. RIDDLE and the other MR. ALVA GRIFFIN.

Married Tuesday the 15 (Sept.) near Pickens at the residence of MR. A.E. KELLEY, MISS M. CARRIE KELLEY to REV. L.L. INABINETT (details).

Calhoun
MISS ELLA HENRY of Middleton, Georgia is visiting.
Born a son the 14 (Sept.) to MR. W.P. SLOAN.
The Episcopal Church of Pendleton, S.C. has purchased the residence of J.H. MOUNCE (sic) to be used as a parsonage.
Married the 20 September by Rev. Mr. Watson at the residence of the bride's father, MR. T.M. DODD of Calhoun, S.C. and the widow MRS. RICE of Anderson Co., S.C. This is the third wife for Mr. Dodd and the third husband for Mrs. Rice (details).

Pickens Co., S.C. Citation Notice - J.M. STEWART applied for Letters of Administration on the estate of W.R. BOWEN, deceased.

Issue of: Thursday 1 October 1896:

BEN B. GRIFFIN, colored, is a professional stockman (details).

Pickens Co., S.C. Tax Notice.

The will of STEPHEN BURDINE was admitted to Probate on the 28 (Sept.). JOSEPH NALLEY obtained Letter Testamentary.

MISS MARY BOWEN the daughter of W.T. BOWEN, MISS MAY ROBINSON daughter of C.T. ROBINSON, MISS NETTIE BOEN (sic) of Easley, S.C. and MISS MARTIN daughter of C.T. MARTIN also of Easley, left for Rock Hill, S.C. to attend Winthrop.

Liberty
WILL GANTT and FRANK CRANE bought W.A. PARSON'S LIVERY STABLE.
REDMOND HENDERSON of the Brushy Creek Section is clerking for J.H. BROWN.

Calhoun - 28 Sept. 1896
MRS. S.E. LEWIS and MISS LASIENE LEWIS are teaching dancing.

Resolutions of Respect - DANIEL GRICE died in May 1896 at the age of about 70 years. He was born in Georgia and married MISS BOGGS (details).

Article - "Piedmont's Early Days - GENERAL ROBERT MAXWELL, Revolutionary War Hero". His tombstone says, "In Memory of ROBERT MAXWELL, died in 1797, he was a Whig, a Soldier and a Christian" (details). *Piedmont Sun*

AD - R.S. HILL, Merchant at South Main St., Anderson, S.C.

AD - Land for Sale - Old HAMILTON homestead 4 miles south of Easley Station on the waters of Twenty-Three Mile Creek, 94 acres, by W.A. and A.R. HAMILTON.

Issue of: Thursday 8 October 1896:

Pickens Co., S.C. Annual Supervisor's Report.

Married in Central, S.C. at the residence of Magistrate B.D. Garvin, MR. DAVID DORSEY to MISS EFFIE EVANS all of this county.

MR. CHARLIE BOWEN son of POSTMASTER MR. R.A. BOWEN will attend Furman University.

MR. CALVIN BAGWELL is living on THOMAS GRIFFIN'S place.

Married the 4 (Oct.) near Liberty, S.C. by T.J. Boggs, N.P., ELISHA SANDERS to MARY ANN STEPHENS.

WALTER HUGHES was killed near Easley, S.C. last Thursday by JOHN HARPER (details).

Married THE 27 September 1896 at the residence of the bride's father AARON GARRETT in the Six Mile Section by Squire W.K. Merck, MR. JACOB MERCK to MISS EMMA GARRETT.

A new baptismal pool has been erected at Secona just below the church.

Calhoun
MR. W.H. HESTER and family are moving to Westminster, S.C. to take charge of the WESTMINSTER HOTEL. Mr. and Mrs. Hester are competent hotel managers. MISS MYRA LAY of Charlotte, North Carolina will take charge of HOTEL De CLEMSON at Calhoun, S.C.
The Old Stone Church has been destroyed by fire three times. MR. and MRS. C. RANDALL of Pendleton, S.C. have sold their old house and are moving away. They have lived there 40 years.

Issue of: Thursday 15 October 1896:

Married the 11 (Oct.), at the residence of Magistrate W.F. Hendricks of Pumpkintown, S.C., WILLIAM OWENS to MISS ALICE GLENN both colored.

MR. T.H. BOGGS and wife of Birmingham, Alabama are here to attend the funeral of his brother REV. W.K. BOGGS who died in Liberty, S.C. Sunday.

List of letters remaining in the Pickens Post Office.
W.R. ROBERTS
R.R. REACH
MISS P.E. WILSON
MISS EVA WRIGHT
V. GREER CLEMENT
HARRY LINEBURG
P.F.M. FURR (2)
A.W. LAWMAN

DR. W.T. FISHER of Gatesville, Texas is visiting relatives in Pickens Co. He was born and raised in S.C.

Pickens Co., S.C. Jury List.

Thomasville
MR. MILTON PONDER will attend 2 courses of lectures at the Medical College of Charleston, S.C. Dr. Ponder had charge of Lathem Academy all summer.

PROF. BEN F. FREEMAN will teach at Bethlehem Schoolhouse.

Waxhaw, North Carolina - 10 October
W.K. BOGGS died at his home the 9 October at the age of 46 years. The funeral will be at Liberty, S.C. He leaves a widow and 7 children. Special - *News and Courier*

MR. W.K. BOGGS was the brother of JULIUS E. BOGGS (see above).

Pickens Co., S.C. Clerk's Sale:
Land of the estate of JAMES F. LAY, deceased. MARY LAY, et al. vs SAVILLA LAY, et al. Tract #1 - 220 acres to be sold.
Tract #2 - 200 acres in Central Township to be sold.
Tract #3 - 74 acres to be sold.
Tract #4 - 45 3/4 acres to be sold.
Tract #5 - 242 acres in Central Township to be sold.
Tract #6 - 111 9/10 acres in Central Township to be sold.
Tract #7 - 69 8/10 acres to be sold.
Tract #8 - 7 1/2 acres on Twelve Mile River to be sold.
Tract #9 - 27 3/4 acres on Twelve Mile River to be sold.

Issue of: Thursday 22 October 1896:

Pickens Co., S.C. Appointments of Election Managers (details).

W.S. DURHAM will open a shoe shop at D.W. HOPKINS old stand.

Married Wednesday the 14 October 1896 at the residence of the bride's parents by Rev. J.M. Stewart, MR. GEORGE W. KEITH to MISS JULIA NIX all of Pickens County.

CLINT BURRLES died from gun shot wounds. He was shot by ERNEST WASHINGTON at the edge of Easley, S.C. Both colored.

COL. LEMUEL THOMAS died at his home in Oconee Co., S.C. the 17 October 1896 at the age of 82 years. He was the father of JOHN W. and JOSEPH L. THOMAS of this county. Col. Thomas was Sheriff of Old Pickens Co., S.C. (now Oconee Co., S.C.).

HONEST PONDER died at his home in Dacusville, S.C. the 18 (Oct.) at the age of about 20 years. He was the third son of W.J. PONDER. His mother died about 2 years ago. Mr. Ponder was a member of the Baptist Church. He leaves a father, brothers and sisters.

AD - J.T. CLYDE, New Store Selling General Merchandise, Easley, S.C.

Issue of: Thursday 29 October 1896:

South Carolina State Fair (details).

MISS LAURA ELLIS died in Gainesville, Georgia of malaria fever. The funeral was held from Bethlehem Church. Miss Ellis' remains were accompanied by her brother JOHN L. ELLIS (details). *Pickens Sentinel*

MRS. C.B. DAVIS of Newberry, S.C. died the 17 (Oct.) and was buried at Rosemont Cemetery. She was a sister of MR. R.M. WERTZ of Liberty, S.C.

FOSTER ARTER son of BAYLUS ARTER is living on FOREST ALLGOODS' place.

Married Sunday the 25 October at Antioch by Rev. J.F. Anderson, MISS KATIE KAY daughter of J. THOMAS KAY and MR. CHARLES A. DAVIS (details).

Liberty
W.H. SANDERS died at Pelzer, S.C. the 9 October 1896 of fever. He was buried at Old Liberty Burying Ground. Mr. Sanders moved to Pelzer last winter. He leaves a wife.

Sale of land of the estate of J.F. LATHEM known as the McADAMS' place, 175 acres, by J.K. and J.S. LATHEM.

Pickens Co., S.C. Court Cases - Minor criminal cases (details).

Issue of: Thursday 5 November 1896:

Pickens Co., S.C. Criminal Court Records - Minor criminal cases - continued (details).

Born a boy Wednesday the 4 November 1896 to MR. and MRS. WILL PITTS.

MR. ZADE COX and wife of Washington, D.C. are visiting Mr. Cox's parents MR. and MRS. J.E. COX of this place.

Married Tuesday the 3 November 1896 at the residence of Rev. J.M. Stewart, MR. G.A. KELLEY to MISS V.G. ABERCROMBIE all of Pickens County.

Married Wednesday the 28 October at the residence of the bride's father MR. REX DALTON by Rev. W.B. Singleton, MR. JOHN TOMPKINS to MISS TAMA DALTON.

Married Sunday the 25 October 1896 at the Pelzer Methodist Church by Rev. A.B. Earle, MR. J.A. LEONARD of Lexington, North Carolina to MISS EDITH BOATWRIGHT formerly of Pickens Co. now of Pelzer, S.C. She is the eldest daughter of MR. and MRS. J. BOATWRIGHT.

Pickens Co., S.C. Real Estate Sales Report:
MARY LAY, et al. vs SAVILLA LAY, et al. 200 acres sold to J.E. BOGGS for $1,051. 200 acres, the home place, sold to F.V. CLAYTON for $511. Tract #5, 242 acres sold to ELISHA KELLEY for $836. Tract #6, 111 acres sold to T.C. ROBINSON for $250. 7 1/2 acres sold to J.F. WILLIAMS for $13. 27 acres sold to WARREN MARTIN for $41.
HARRIET BOWIE, et al. vs HESTER LYNCH, et al. 65 acres sold to DOC ALEXANDER for $502. --- ELLENBURG bought 210 acres for $1,237. 279 acres were sold to --- for $85.
JOHN WATSON, et al. vs SALLIE G. OATS. 250 acres were bought by some of the heirs at law for $900.

Table Mountain
B.L. HENDRICKS of near Field, S.C. is putting up a GOVERNMENT DISTILLERY.

Field
J.F. ANTHONY will improve his mill call a "dirt mill".
SQUIRE BRAMBLETT of Pickens Court House is moving to J.B.R. FREEMAN'S place.

Pickens Co., S.C. Citation Notice - Estate of LAURA ELLIS, deceased. GIDEON ELLIS applies for Letters of Administration.

Pickens Co., S.C. Citation Notice - Estate of W.H. SANDERS, deceased. J.M. STEWART applies for Letters of Administration.

Issue of: Thursday 12 November 1896:

Electoral Vote for McKINLEY and BRYAN Given by States (details).

Card of Thanks, to friends and neighbors at the death of MATTIE FREEMAN the 3 November, daughter of T.M. and M.E. FREEMAN.

Pickens Co., S.C. Clerk's Sales - Court of Common Pleas: MARTHA A. BOWEN, et al. vs D.F. BRADLEY, et al.
Tract #1 - 68 1/2 acres of land in Easley Township to be sold.
Tract #2 - 4 1/4 acres of land to be sold.
Tract #3 - 3/4 acre to be sold.
J.H. MORGAN, et al. vs J.J. MORGAN, et al. 227 acres of land being the home plantation of REV. B.F. MORGAN to be sold.

Pickens Co., S.C. Sheriff's Sale - CITY NATIONAL BANK OF GREENVILLE, S.C. vs S.C. DICKSON, et al. 142 1/2 acres of land in Dacusville to be sold.

MISS MARGARET WELBORN is teaching at Hagood School.

BOYCE EUGENE FARR son of MR. and MRS. S.E. FARR died the 25 October 1896 at Avondale, Alabama at the age of 1 month.

MISS FLORENCE BOWEN has been appointed assistant teacher at Bishop's Branch School, Anderson Co., S.C. MISS OLIVIA NEWTON is the principal.

Married the 8 November 1896 at the residence of J.A. NORRIS by W.J. Sheriff, MR. WILL NORRIS to MISS SUSIE NEELSON both of Pickens County.

Married the 5 November 1896 at the residence of the bride's father MR. THOMAS HAINES by Jas. E. Borough, N.P., MR. WILLIAM TURNER of Pickens to MISS NETTIE HAINES of Oconee Co., S.C.

MISS CORA BOWEN is teaching at Johnston's Chapel.

BARRY WHITNER, colored, who lived on ROBERT STEWART'S plantation on Crow Creek died Friday the 6 November of typhoid. He leaves a wife and 6 children.

Union Meeting to be held at "Old Pickens", Oconee Co., S.C.

Married Thursday the 5 (Nov.) by Rev. J.E. Foster, MISS OMECCA LEWIS daughter of ROBERT LEWIS of Anderson Mills, S.C. to MR. THOMAS KELLEY son of A.E. KELLEY.

Dacusville
LOOPER BROTHERS have moved into their new and commodious storehouse at LOOPER'S GIN.

Issue of: Thursday 19 November 1896:

Sketch - "McKINLEY and HOBART, President and Vice-President of the United States".

Married the 15 (Nov.) at the Central Baptist Church by Rev. L.T. Weldon, MISS CORA MARTIN to MR. DAVID FRICKS.

MISS NANCY GUNTER of Pickens County, age 106, cut and made a skirt without the help of eye glasses.

Married Wednesday the 11 November 1896 at the residence of the bride's father MR. C.A. HOLCOMBE by Rev. W.C. Seaborn, MR. WALTER DAVIS to MISS SUE LEE HOLCOMBE all of Pickens County.

MRS. HANNAH CANTRELL died at the home of her brother MR. W.T. AIKEN, Sunday the 15 November 1896 at the age of about 45 years. She was buried at her home on the Toxaway in North Carolina.

J.W. CAPPS, shoemaker, has opened a shop in the D.W. HOPKINS old stand.

Married the 17 November at the home of the bride's parents MR. and MRS. R.K. HILL by Rev. J.F. Anderson, MISS MARGARET HILL to MR. HENRY W. NIX.

The BEVERLY GRANITE CO. has stopped working.

FARMER'S PUBLISHING CO. of Pickens to hold a Stockholder's meeting. W.W.F. BRIGHT, Secretary and Treasurer.

Pickens Co., S.C. Tax Notice.

Issue of: Thursday 26 November 1896:

Pickens Co., S.C. Clerk's Sale:
Land to be sold Salesday in December.
MARTHA A. BOWEN, et al. vs D.F. BRADLEY, et al.
Tract #1 - 69 1/2 acres in Easley Township.
Tract #2 - 4 1/4 acres.
Tract #3 - 3/4 acre.
J.H. MORGAN, et al. vs J.J. MORGAN, et al.
Home plantation of B.F. MORGAN, deceased. 200 acres in Dacusville Township.

Pickens Co., S.C. Sheriff's Sale:
CITY NATIONAL BANK OF GREENVILLE, S.C. vs S.C. DICKSON, et al. 142 1/4 acres Dacusville, S.C.

J.B.R. FREEMAN has moved to town and is at home in the BRAMBLETT house which he traded for.

The brick work has been completed on the A.M. MORRIS new storehouse.

Married Sunday the 15 November 1896 at the residence of the bride's father MR. THOMAS GARRETT by Rev. W.C. Seaborn, MR. JOHN B. SARGENT to MISS NANCY ANN GARRETT all of Pickens County.

Married the 19 (Nov.) at the residence of the bride's father ISAAC EPPS in Greenville Co., S.C., by Rev. J.E. Foster, MR. RUFUS N. HENDRICKS of Pickens County to MISS FANNIE EPPS.

Married the 22 November at Monticello, Fairfield Co., S.C., MISS ANNIE CURETON daughter of DR. and MRS. J.D. CURETON of Pickens to MR. JAMES WILKES of Beuna Vista, Fairfield County, S.C.

JAMES ERNEST STEWART died the 12 November 1896 at the age of 1 year and 11 months. He was the son of MR. and MRS. D.T. STEWART.

MR. D.R. SUTHERLAND of the firm SUTHERLAND & GRIFFIN has rented the property recently vacated by PROF. M.S. STRIBLING and will move there.

Sale of the estate of NAOMIE L. CLAYTON is expected in January.

Ad - WILLIAM A. MAULDIN & CO. are selling a car load of mules.

SOUTHERLAND & GRIFFIN are in their new store located on the corner.

Issue of: Thursday 3 December 1896:

Married the 30 November at the home of the bride's father T.O. JAMESON by Rev. W.B. Singleton, MISS NORA JAMESON to MASON B.T. BURDINE.

Married at the residence of the bride's brother ANDREW ARNOLD in Anderson Co., S.C. by Rev. S.H. Zimmerman, MR. J.W. McDONALD of Pickens County to MISS EMMA ARNOLD.

Liberty
DR. J.F. WILLIAMS bought a beautiful lot and will build a dwelling.

Calhoun

Calhoun has a shingle mill.

MR. HAMILTON CRAIG is up from Keowee and is boarding with MRS. W.N. PAYNE and studying telegraphy under MR. L.W. CRISP.

Pickens Co., S.C. Final Settlement - Estates of S.M. and MARY L. EDENS, deceased by T.J. LIGON, Administrator.

Pickens Co., S.C. Guardianship Papers - N.T. MARTIN applies for guardianship papers for MATTIE, LETTIE and JESSE DOBBINS, minors.

Oolenoy River Colored Church Report (details).

Pickens Co., S.C. Tax Assessment Notice.

Issue of: Thursday 10 December 1896:

Information for Pensioners (details).

BROTHER SAMUEL T. CLYDE eldest son of REV. THOMAS J. CLYDE, Presiding Elder of Greenville District died at Easley, S.C., Wednesday night the 25 November at the age of 28 years. He was buried from the Methodist Church. Brother Clyde, wife and baby moved to Easley the 3 September (details).

Born the 14 November, twin boys to MR. and MRS. THOMAS WELBORN.

Married the 7 (Dec.) at the residence of Magistrate B.D. Garvin, MISS ADDIE ROPER daughter of MARION ROPER to MR. DUROD OWENS.

MR. B.T. McDANIEL who is employed as storekeeper and gauger for the GOVERNMENT DISTILLERY has been transferred from Rigdon, S.C. to Abbeville, S.C.

CAPTAIN J.J. HERD served in the Confederate Army.

T.D. HARRIS has moved into a new store. He has leased the LEWIS BUILDING to sell furniture and stoves.

ELIZABETH PRICE widow of HARDIN PRICE died at the home of her grandson McD. MURPHREE the 1 (Dec.) at the age of 96 years. She was a member of the Keowee Baptist Church for more than 50 years. Mrs. Price was buried at Keowee Baptist Church Cemetery.

Born Monday a boy named BEN to MR. BEN McDANIEL - a Christmas present?.

Married at the home of MR. and MRS. W.T. SPENCER (better known as MAJOR JACK BANNISTER) of Farrs, S.C., their baby girl MAUDIE SPENCER to MR. N. DANA TAYLOR of Dixon, Pennsylvania, by Rev. Thomas Looper (details).

Issue of: Thursday 17 December 1896:

The President's Message (details).

Pickens Co., S.C. Executor's Sale:
Estate of MRS. NAOMI L. CLAYTON, deceased by J.M. STEWART, Executor.

Bring the children to HARRIS' for SANTA CLAUSE.

Married the 10 December at the residence of the bride's father A.W. KAY by Rev. M.L. Jones, MISS VESTA KAY to MR. KING MASSENGALE.

CHARLES S. ROBINSON died at his home at Twelve Mile last Monday at the age of about 56 years. He leaves a widow and a brother DR. G.E. ROBINSON of Liberty, S.C. Mr. Robinson served in the Confederate Army, 1st S.C. Sharpshooters, later Quartermaster, 2nd Rifles, Orr's Regiment. He was buried at the family burying ground.

Pickens Co., S.C. Final Settlement - L.G. HAMILTON, deceased by W.A. and A.R. HAMILTON, Executors.

Pickens Co., S.C. Executor's Sale:
To be sold Salesday in January 1897.
Estate of MRS. NAOMI L. CLAYTON, by J.M. STEWART, Executor.
Tract #1 - 58 acres and dwelling, the homestead.
Tract #2 - 97 acres.
Tract #3 - 84 acres on both sides of Golden Creek.
Tract #4 - 125 acres.
Tract #5 - 80 acres on the east side of Twelve Mile River.
Tract #6 - 70 acres on the south side of Gassaway Bridge.
Tract #7 - 100 acres on the west side of Gassaway Bridge.
Tract #8 - 140 acres on the west side of Gassaway Bridge.
Tract #9 - 130 acres bounded on the west by Twelve Mile
          River (details).

Pickens Co., S.C. Probate Sale:
J.M. STEWART, Administrator of the estate of W.H. SANDERS, deceased vs NANCY E. SANDERS, et al.
Tract #1 - 50 acres to be sold.
Tract #2 - 15 acres to be sold.
Tract #3 - 35 acres on Golden Creek to be sold (details).

Issue of: Thursday 24 December 1896:

J.H. ABERCROMBIE, JR. of the Hughes Section has moved to the R.A. BOWEN plantation.

Liberty (continued):

MR. IRVIN MILLER has moved to the PAYNE place close to Glassy Mountain, S.C.

Married the 15 (Dec.) at the residence of the bride's father by Magistrate Edens, MISS MARGARET MILES to LAKE GOWEN son of R.P. GOWENS (sic).

MRS. WILLIAM ALEXANDER died the 17 December 1896 at the age of 56 years. She was buried at Shady Grove where she had been a member for 30 years.

Cards are out announcing the marriage on Thursday the 24 instant, at the residence of the bride's father HON. W.T. BOWEN, MISS BETTIE BOWEN to MR. WADE O'DELL son of STATE SENATOR O'DELL.

MRS. PARMELIA GALLION died the 19 (Dec.) at her home on the HAGOOD place 5 miles north of Pickens at the age of about 40 years. She was buried at the Mosley Family Burying Ground.

MRS. GAZELIA DURHAM died Saturday at her residence near Pickens at the age of about 67 years. She was buried at Secona Church of which she was a member. Mrs. Durham was the mother of ALLEN DURHAM.

Article - "Anderson Co., S.C ".

NO ISSUE FOUND FOR 31 DECEMBER 1896.

THE PEOPLE'S JOURNAL 1897

Issue of: Thursday 7 January 1897:

Dots from Coon Creek
A.A. FIELD has erected a new dwelling.

Married the 3 (Jan.) at the residence of the bride's mother, by Rev. W.G. Mauldin, MISS N.J. LANGLEY to MR. W.J. RAMPEY.

MISS CARRIE O. SAMS is teaching school at Gaffney, S.C.

Married the 24 Dec. 1896 at the residence of the bride's father, by Magistrate S.D. Stewart, MR. HAMPTON ROPER to MISS BELLE CHANDLER.

MAJOR STEWART purchased the J.K. KIRKSEY lot on Main Street.

Married the 3 January at the residence of the bride's father MR. HOPE GALLOWAY by M.F. Hester, N.P., MR. LOUIS GILSTRAP to MISS CANNIE GALLOWAY.

MR. HENDERSON the photographer will be working for a short time in Pickens.

HARBIN BROWN son of W. SILAS BROWN formerly of Pickens now of Gordon Co., Georgia died a few days ago after having a fall from a mule in December (1896).

SAMUEL A. BARR died at his residence in Easley Township the 28 (Dec. 1896). He left 1 child. Mr. Barr's wife died about 3 years ago.

Married Wednesday the 30 (Dec. 1896) at the residence of the bride's parents, by Rev. R.J. Williams, MR. FRANK E. COX to MISS LENA STEWART daughter of MAGISTRATE J.M. STEWART.

W.O. WILLARD and T.H. MOORE of Liberty, S.C. have a store under the name of WILLARD & MOORE and are now dealing in wagons, carriages, buggies, etc.

Married the 23 December (1896) at the home of the bride's father MR. JOAB MAULDIN by Rev. J.R. Riley, MR. LAFAYETTE LESESNE of Kingstree, S.C. to MISS HORTENSE MAULDIN of Pickens. They will live at Kingstree.

MR. S. CLEMENT died at the home of his sister MRS. M.F. WILLIAMS last Sunday at the age of about 45 years. He was well known as the newspaper correspondent using the name "Lost Boy".

Married yesterday at the residence of MRS. BRIGGS of Easley, S.C., by Dr. J.R. Riley, E.P. GAINES of Honea Path, S.C. to

MISS JANE WYATT of Easley. *Greenville News* - 29 December (1896)

Married the 24 December (1896) by Rev. J.E. Foster, W.C. O'DELL to MISS BETTIE BOWEN, 2nd daughter of HON. W.T. BOWEN.

Liberty
REV. W.H. BOWEN'S new dwelling is nearly complete.
MR. B.H. CALLAHAN will commence his dwelling soon.

MISS LILA BOGGS is attending school in Greenville, S.C.

MASTER CONNIE STEWART has been attending school in Spartanburg, S.C.

From Field
MISS UNITY RIGDON is teaching in the Ambler School District.
D.E. HENDRICKS has employed MELVILLE BARTON as a miller.
ED HENDRICKS lost a house by fire.

The *People's Journal* enters the sixth year of operation.

Issue of: Thursday 14 January 1897:

T.D. HARRIS is at his new store at his old stand in Pickens.

PROF. I.M. MAULDIN has taken charge of the Liberty School.

MR. MARCUS DUCKWORTH has moved into the DURANT house.

An infant of MR. and MRS. W.F. BARRON died the 9 (Jan.) and was buried at Secona Church.

MRS. MURPHY who lives on MAJOR AMBLER'S farm had her dwelling burned on Saturday.

MR. J.C. "SWEET" ALEXANDER of Alexander, S.C., a salesman for T.D. HARRIS, has moved into the MRS. JAMES house on Liberty Street.

The house of WILL ARIAL of the Oolenoy Section burned last Sunday.

MR. T.A. WALKER is with EBAUGH & JORDAN on the corner of Main and Coffee Streets in Greenville, S.C.

AD BLASSINGAME and ROBERT BLASSINGAME sons of D.W. BLASSINGAME of Grayson Co., Texas were struck by lightning. Ad was seriously injured and Robert was killed.

MRS. CORRIE FULLER died at her home near Briggs, S.C., the 5 (Jan.) at the age of 33 years. She leaves a husband DANIEL FULLER and 2 children. Mrs. Fuller was a member of the

George's Creek Baptist Church. She was buried at Antioch Church Cemetery.

MRS. MARTHA MULLINAX died the 6 (Jan.) at her home in Dacusville, S.C. at the age of 30 years. She was buried from Griffin Baptist Church of which she was a member. Mrs. Mullinax leaves a husband and 3 children.

Married the 7 (Jan.) by Rev. J.E. Foster, MISS NORA WATSON of Dacusville, S.C. to MR. THOMAS WEST of Spartanburg, S.C. They will live in Spartanburg. Nora Watson is the daughter of MR. L.W. WATSON (details).

Calhoun
The Calhoun Christmas tree (details).
A ball was given (during the holidays).
Married Thursday the 7 (Jan.) by Rev. W.H. Workman, MR. S.O. SKELTON of Calhoun, S.C. to MISS EMMA SMITH of Liberty, S.C. She is the daughter of MR. JOB SMITH.
CARTER MERCHANDISE CO. has a nice stock of goods in the DOYLE BUILDING at Calhoun, S.C. MR. FRANK CARTER is in charge.

MISS JONES age about 17 and almost grown and ELBERT JONES, children of REV. M.L. JONES burned to death Wednesday. Rev. Jones' wife died a year ago. He has 4 other children (details).

Pickens Co., S.C. Final Settlement - Estate of WILLIAM and HESTER NIMMONS, deceased by W.E. NIMMONS, Administrator.

Pickens Co., S.C. Citation Notice - Estate of SALATHIEL CLEMENT, deceased. M.F. WILLIAMS applies for Letters of Administration.

Pickens Co., S.C. Tax Assessment Notice.

AD - NEW YORK RACKET STORE, Easley, S.C. CLYDE & NALLEY, Proprietors.

Pickens Co., S.C. Mortgagee's Sale - Property of ELIZABETH SMITH. 22 acres where THOMAS SMITH now lives to be sold.

Issue of: Thursday 21 January 1897:

The Governor's Message (details).

MR. W.T. ALEXANDER son of MR. and MRS. J.B. ALEXANDER died the 11 January 1897 at the age of 23 of typhoid and bilious fever. He leaves a father, mother, four brothers and four sisters. Mr. Alexander was a member of the Little River Baptist Church. He was buried at the family burying ground.

MR. J.H. BROWN has an elegant hotel in Liberty, S.C.

DR. KIRKSEY has moved from town to the Twelve Mile plantation of his father.

Married at the residence of the officiating officer W.N. Hughes, MR. JESSE WADE to MISS LUDA FOREST both of Mayfield, Greenville Co., S.C.

MR. SMITH of Westminster, S.C. will open a watch repair shop in the front part of the LEWIS stand. He will move into one of MR. J.B.R. FREEMAN'S houses.

Married the 15 (Jan.) at the residence of the groom's father MR. J.M. DUCKWORTH by Frank E. Cox, N.P., MR. J.M. DUCKWORTH to MISS MARY MURPHREE.

JAMES K. KIRKSEY and family removed from town to his old home on Twelve Mile River.

Married the 14 (Jan.) at the residence of the bride in Greenville, S.C., by Rev. Dr. McConnell, MR. R.L. AMBLER to MRS. LILY GOODWIN.

MARTHA SIZEMORE, colored, wife of WILLIAM SIZEMORE died at their residence near town the 14 (Jan.) at the age of 67 years. She was buried from Cold Springs Church of which she was a member.

WALTER MULLINAX son of J.E. MULLINAX died at his home in Easley Township at the age of 16 years. He was buried from Zion Methodist Church of which he was a member.

Information on the fire at REV. M.L. JONES' house.

From Mala
MR. IREY SMITH has moved to the area.

From Liberty
MR. C.E. HAMILTON and family have moved to this place.
MR. BARNES the well known blacksmith and wood workman has moved to Liberty, S.C. and will open a shop.
MR. WOOD from near Mauldin, Greenville Co., S.C. has rented from MR. J.P. SMITH.

From Mica
MR. BUTLER of Greenville, S.C. is teaching the Mica School.

From Maynard
REV. W.C. SEABORN of Cross Roads Church is leaving and REV. W.L. ANDERSON of Greenville Co., S.C. will fill the vacancy. There is a new post office at S.H. BROWN'S known as PEARL, S.C. MRS. NANCY C. BROWN is the postmaster.

Married Tuesday at the residence of the bride's father, by Rev. W.A. Rogers, MISS VIRGINIA HUNT daughter of CAPTAIN

W.P. HUNT to J.A. OWINGS of Owings Station, S.C. They will live in Laurens, S.C. *Greenville News*

BOGGS & SKELTON, Selling General Merchandise, Fort Hill, S.C.

Issue Of: Thursday 28 January 1897:

MR. A.M. MORRIS moved into a new store last week.

MR. J.B.R. FREEMAN and MR. JOHN HENDRICKS will open a general merchandise store in the FREEMAN BUILDING.

Born the 25 (Jan.) a son and a daughter to MR. and MRS. JORDAN BREAZEALE.

Married at the residence of Rev. Johnson Sheriff, MR. W.B. BRAMBLETT to MISS REBECCA STEPHENS all of Pickens County (no date given).

C.T. MILLER, colored, is teaching the colored school at Easley, S.C..

Married the 20 January 1897 near Townville, S.C. at the residence of the bride's parents MR. and MRS. C.D. GILES by Rev. W.B. Singleton, MR. GEORGE E. SINGLETON to MISS LEILA GILES all of Oconee Co., S.C.

From Clement
Married the 17 January at the residence of the officiating officer, T. Looper, MR. THOMAS NORRIS son of WILLIAM NORRIS to MISS ANNIE FENDLEY only daughter of J.P. FENDLEY (details).

From Liberty
MRS. CAROLINE BROCK widow of GEORGE BROCK of Central, S.C. died the 21 January at the residence of her son-in-law H.C. SHIRLEY at the age of 76 years of paralysis.
SARAH E. ROWLAND wife of W.T. ROWLAND died at Piedmont, S.C. on the 19 January at the age of about 35 years. She leaves a husband and 3 children.

MR. BELL will build a new schoolhouse.

B.H. CALLAHAN commenced his new dwelling house.

Article - "The Town of Gaffney, S.C."

Inaugural Address - GOVERNOR WILLIAM H. ELLERBE.

Issue of: Thursday 4 February 1897:

South Carolina General Assembly (details).

Article - "The New Judge" - JUDGE J.C. KLUGH age 39 was born in Abbeville Co., S.C. (lengthy sketch).

ANDERSON BABB has completed a neat and substantial cottage for B.B. GILSTRAP.

W.A. GRESHAM and BEN CRAWFORD are attending Clemson College.

Cards are out announcing the marriage of MR. J.F. BANISTER of Cateechee, S.C. to MISS LENA BOWEN of Pickens on the 10th (appears Jan.).

Married the 18 January at the residence of the bride's mother, by Rev. W.B. Singleton, MR. WILLIAM J. PONDER to MRS. FRANCIS HUNT.

MRS. TOLLISON wife of THOMAS TOLLISON died at her home in Dacusville Township at the age of about 60 years. She was buried from Oolenoy Baptist Church of which she was a member.

REDDEN CRANE was found dead at RACKLEY MILL at Dacusville, S.C. He was very old and leaves a wife.

MRS. LAURA BAKER relict of the late LEMUEL BAKER died at the residence of her son B.C. BAKER the 30 (Jan.) at the age of about 60 years. She was a member of the Methodist Church. Mrs. Baker was buried in the family cemetery. She leaves a son B.C. BAKER and 2 daughters MRS. E.F. LOOPER and MRS. J.W. EARLE. (LAURA BAKER, born 30 Aug. 1834, died 31 Jan. 1897, wife of L.M. BAKER, buried Baker Family Cemetery - Pickens Co., S.C. Cemetery Survey, Vol. 1, p. 12 - see issue of the 25 Feb. 1897).

From Easley
JUDGE LATHEM is doing a rousing business in furniture and undertaking goods.

MRS. CLYDE has sold, so it is said, her stock of goods to A.G. WYATT.

Married yesterday at the residence of WILLIAM GOLDSMITH, SR., 2 miles from the city, by Dr. C.S. Gardner, MISS MAY GOLDSMITH of Greenville, S.C. to J. MILTON KING (details). *Greenville News* - 28 January

Issue of: Thursday 11 February 1897:

REV. M.L. JONES is erecting a neat and substantial cottage for ED HENDRICKS near Field, S.C.

SHERIFF McDANIEL will have a substantial fence put around the jail.

MR. PETE FERGUSON and wife of Texas are visiting his brother MR. V.A. FERGUSON who lives 5 miles south of town.

MR. AMBROSE E. GRIFFIN of Ohatchie, Alabama is visiting his father CAPTAIN JAS. A. GRIFFIN who lives 5 miles north of Pickens.

JEREMIAH TRAINUM died the 7 (Feb.) at the age of 83 years of natural causes. He was a member of the Methodist Church. Mr. Trainum leaves a wife and friends.

Oconee News - Officers for Oconee Co., S.C. Appointed (details).

EUGENE GARY DRAKE son of MR. and MRS. JOHN J. DRAKE died the 28 (Jan.) at the age of 9 years and was buried at Tabor Church.

From Mica
JAMES RICHARDSON, colored, is teaching school at Shoal Creek.

Pickens Co., S.C. Special Meeting of the Board of Commissioners (details).

From Calhoun
Born a daughter to DR. and MRS. E.A. HINES the 3 (Feb.).
MR. RAMSEY DOYLE and family have moved back to their Keowee farm after 2 years absence.
BOGGS & SKELTON are selling fancy groceries and dry goods.

Liberty Items
DR. W.A. SHELDON bought part of a lot belonging to DR. W.R. HOLLINGSWORTH.

Issue of: 18 February 1897:

South Carolina General Assembly (details).

MR. W.W. BALL of the *Charleston Sun* will be the Editor of the *Greenville News*.

Barnwell, S.C. - 12 February
EX-JUDGE A.P. ALDRICH died at his home this afternoon at the age of 83 years. He was born in Charleston, S.C. and married MISS MARTHA AYERS. They have six children: MRS. HAL RICHARDSON of Columbia, S.C., MRS. MILLEDGE BONHAM of Anderson, S.C., MRS. WILLIAM DUNCAN of Barnwell, S.C., MRS. (sic) ROSE ALDRICH of Barnwell, COL. ROBERT ALDRICH of Barnwell and ALFRED ALDRICH of Barnwell (details). *The State*

EMALINE JAMISON, colored, died last Sunday the 14 (Feb.) at the age of about 65 years.

Married at the residence of Rev. J.T. Looper, MR. FRANK LARK to MISS LIDA WILLIAMS all of Pickens County.

MRS. MARGARET KAY widow of the late DORAN KAY died at the home of her brother (name not given) on the 15 (Feb.) at the age of about 50 years. She was buried at the family cemetery on the Keowee River. Mrs. Kay leaves 3 brothers.

Married at the residence of Rev. Thomas Looper, MR. JAMES EUBANKS of Union Co., S.C. to MISS LAURA DARNOLD of Pickens County.

MAY ALICE STEWART daughter of JOHN and SARAH STEWART and granddaughter of BANNISTER LYNCH died of congestion at the home of DR. and MRS. M.M. KING on Saturday the 6 (Feb.). She was born the 10 December 1882 Pickens Co., S.C. being 14 years 1 month and 27 days old. She was buried from the Methodist Episcopal Church. *The Sylvan Valley News*

SUSAN TROTTER of Pumpkintown Township died the 27 (Jan.) at the home of her son-in-law REV. A.S. WHITMIRE at the age of about 80 years. She was buried from the Oolenoy Baptist Church of which she was a member. Mrs. Trotter leaves many children and grandchildren.

Married the 14 (Feb.) at the residence of Rev. J.M. Stewart, MR. THOMAS McKINNEY to MISS NETTIE ARTER.

W.H. WILLIAMS & CO. are doing general merchandise business in Olga, S.C.

GEORGE WASHINGTON FARR died at his home near Farr's Post Office, S.C. at the age of 86 years. He leaves a son and 2 daughters: J.P. FARR, DELILIA and FRANCES FARR. Mr. Farr was buried from the Berea Baptist Church of which he was a member. *Greenville News*

Married the 10 February in Pickens by Rev. W.M. Harden, MISS LENA LUCILLE BOWEN 2nd daughter of MR. ROBERT A. BOWEN to MR. J.F. BANISTER of Cateechee, S.C. The groom is a merchant at Norris, S.C. (details).

Olga News
STEPHENS R. RAINES died the 5 February and was buried at Peter's Creek Cemetery.

Pickens Co., S.C. Grand Jury and Petit Jury Lists.

Issue of: Thursday 25 February 1897:

South Carolina General Assembly (details).

J.A. WOOD is opening a barber shop in part of the FREEMAN BUILDING.

THOMAS WILLIAMS of Thomasville, S.C. is now 77 years old.

Married Sunday the 21 (Feb.), by Rev. J.M. Stewart, MR. TOM McKINNEY and MISS IDA ARTHUR both colored.

Married the 18 (Feb.), MISS EVA HUNT daughter of MR. and MRS. M. HUNT of Dacusville, S.C. to MR. MULL of North Carolina.

Married the 11 (Feb.) at the residence of the bride's parents, by Rev. B. Holder, MR. RICHARD HAYES to MISS QUEEN MASSINGALE.

---- WHITESIDES who was shot last week by EUGENE MILLS, colored, on CAPTAIN J.R. SUTHERLAND'S farm in Dacusville, S.C. died the 20 (Feb.).

Clemson College has an enrollment of 250.

Died MRS. LAURA BAKER (see issue of the 4 Feb. 1897).

MRS. MARGARET KAY (sister of Mrs. Laura Baker above) widow of DORAN KAY, who died several years ago, of Westminster, S.C. died the 14 (Feb.) at the home of her brother MR. JOHN CRAIG at Newry, S.C. at the age of 59 years. She was a member of the Baptist Church. Mrs. Kay leaves no children. She was buried at the Craig Family Cemetery.

From Clement
WALTER COX who has been residing in Georgia for the past year returned to his native home and is erecting a new dwelling and store house near Cox's Bridge. He thinks there is no place like Briggs, S.C.
MR. WILLIE HAMILTON son of WARREN HAMILTON married Sunday the 14 (Feb.) MISS GUSSIE DAY.

Pickens Co., S.C. Citation Notice - Letters of Administration applied for by ROBERT STEWART for the estate of JOHN STEWART, deceased.

Issue of: Thursday 4 March 1897:

South Carolina General Assembly (details).

MISS ADA GOUDELOCK entered the Liberty High School. She is boarding at the BROWN house.

ARTHUR CHRISTOPHER has entered the Vinland School in Farr's School District. MISS LIDIE BOWEN is teaching there.

Married the 28 (Feb.) by Rev. J.M. Stewart, MR. ROBERT DOWNS to MISS SALLIE ARTHUR both colored.

DeFOREST MILLER of Indiana is visiting. He left Pickens Co. many years ago.

Appointments of Magistrates in several Pickens Townships (details).

REUBEN ARNOLD died at his home in Central, S.C., the 25 (Feb.) at the age of 33 years. He was buried at Mt. Zion Methodist Church of which he was a member. Mr. Arnold leaves a wife and 3 children.

MRS. CYNTHIA MARTIN relict of the late EDMUND MARTIN died at her residence near Central, S.C. at the age of 83 years. She was buried from Mt. Zion Methodist Church of which she was a member. Mrs. Martin leaves 2 sons and 3 daughters.

GEORGE BLAKE will soon complete a handsome villa on the windy point of "Possum Ridge".

Article - "A Visit to Brevard, North Carolina", by the *People's Journal*.

Pickens Co., S.C. Court of General Sessions Report - Minor criminal cases (details).

Clement
Vineland Academy will soon have a bell.

From Liberty
REV. W.H. WORKMAN and family moved to their new residence. J.D. SMITH one of oldest merchants sold out his town property to PARSONS BROS. and T.N. HUNTER bought his residence. Mr. Smith contemplates moving to Georgia.

Issue of: Thursday 11 March 1897:

South Carolina General Assembly (details).

Inauguration of PRESIDENT McKINLEY.

Pickens Co., S.C. Special Meeting of the Board of Commissioners (details).

Married the 7 (March) at the residence of MR. FOSTER MASTERS by Magistrate Alonzo Edens, MR. WILL McJUNKIN of Pickens Co. to MISS MATTIE PHILLIPS of Piedmont, S.C.

Born a son and a daughter to MR. and MRS. HUGH REVIS on the 2 (March).

Married Tuesday the 3 (March) at the residence of the bride's parents MR. and MRS. BARNES by Rev. L.T. Weldon, MISS ADA BARNES to MR. JOE LINK of Anderson Co., S.C.

MRS. JAMISON wife of JOHN JAMISON who lives near Liberty, S.C. died the 4 March at the age of about 58 years. She was a member of the Methodist Church and was buried from Ruhamah. Mrs. Jamison leaves a husband, 4 sisters and 3 brothers.

The *Pickens Sentinel* is under new proprietorship. It has been purchased by MESSRS. HOMER A. RICHEY and J.L.O THOMPSON. MR. CHARLES E. ROBINSON, Editor will be in charge (details).

The 16 month old infant of MR. and MRS. RICH ROSEMOND died the 5 (March), colored.

REV. THOMAS JOHNSON of this county died the 3 (March) of pneumonia at the age of about 64 years. He was a member of the Methodist Church and was buried from Mt. Bethel Methodist Church. Rev. Johnson leaves a wife and 7 children.

Greenville News - 2 March
MRS. JANE E. CAUBLE died in Baltimore, Maryland at the age of 66 years. She was the mother of J.O. CAUBLE, MRS. MATTIE GILREATH and MRS. W.C. GIBSON and the sister of MRS. R.E. BOWEN of Pickens, MRS. JOHN W. ROSAMOND of Brush Creek and MISS LOU OLIVER of Pickens. Mrs. Cauble was the widow of the late H.A. CAUBLE one of the oldest citizens of Greenville, S.C. and the daughter of DR. OLIVER of Anderson Co., S.C.

Pickens Co., S.C. Court Cases - Minor criminal cases (details).

AD - HUTCHINS & MORRIS of Hughes, S.C. want to rent, hire or buy a 10, 12 or 15 horse engine.

Issue of: Thursday 18 March 1897:

Account of the VANDERBILT PALACE at Biltmore, North Carolina.

CHARLES L. CURETON has been appointed State Constable.

REV. J.T. LEWIS sold his property south of town to "BEE" LEWIS on Monday.

Born a son to MR. and MRS. FRED WILLIAMS of near Easley, S.C. on the 12 (March).

C.E. ROBINSON has torn away his dwelling house, preparatory to building a new one.

The estate of J.F. LATHEM, deceased, was wound up Thursday the 11 (March) by the executors J.S. and J.K. LATHEM.

New bridge across Coon Creek between Liberty and Easley, S.C. (details).

Re-enlistment of Pickens Rifles the 13 March (details).

J.M. HALL carries the U.S. Mail between here and Easley, S.C.

MRS. TABITHA LOGGINS, who lived at Briggs, S.C., died the 13 (March). She was buried from the Antioch Church of which she was a member. Mrs. Loggins leaves 3 sons.

Pickens Co., S.C. Citation Notice - E.T. CRAIG applies for Letters of Administration for the estates of MARGARET M. KAY and JOSEPHINE CRAIG, deceased.

Issue of: Thursday 25 March 1897:

Pickens Co., S.C. Township Commissioners (details).

Clemson College now has 330 students.

Married the 12 (March) by M.F. Hester, N.P., MR. THOMAS CANNON to MISS ELOWEE BOWEN both colored.

MRS. C.C. CUMMINGS and family have returned to Anderson, S.C. to live. They are now occupying a neat cottage on East Avenue on the height near the laundry. *Anderson Journal*

REV. A.J.S. THOMAS, Editor of the *Baptist Courier*, has been called to the pastorate of the Pickens Baptist Church.

ROBERT WILLIS TODD living just in the corporate limits of Anderson, S.C. died last Sunday at the age of 77 years. *Anderson Journal*

MR. JOHN A. LOGAN died the 13 March 1897 at his home near Tunnel Hill, S.C. at the age of 92 years. He was born at George's Creek, Pickens Co. but moved to this county many years ago. Mr. Logan was a member of the Baptist Church. He was buried from the Neville Schoolhouse near Walhalla, S.C. *Oconee News*

Married the 23 (March) at the residence of the bride's father MR. E.S. GRIFFIN by Rev. J.M. Stewart, MR. GEORGE H. HENDRICKS to MISS LAKE GRIFFIN (details).

Pickens Co., S.C. Court of Common Pleas - Estate of JOHN STEWART, deceased by GIDEON M. LYNCH, Administrator.

Issue of: Thursday 1 April 1897:

Pickens Co., S.C. Sheriff's Sales - Court of Common Pleas: JOHN M. GLENN, Administrator of the Estate of W.D. GLENN, deceased vs JOHN J. JAMISON, et al (details).

A.B. RILEY has been elected principal of Central High School.

Married the 21 (March) at the residence of the bride's parent HON. FRED GARVIN at Central, S.C., MR. WILLIAM WERNER to MISS GEORGIA GARVIN.

MISS ANNIE CLAYTON daughter of the late DR. S.W. CLAYTON who lived near Central, S.C. died the 23 (March) of consumption at the age of about 20 years.

MISSES DUCKWORTH and WYATT have opened a full line of millinery in Easley, S.C.

W.R. PRICE has a store near Sunny Dale, S.C.

Calhoun News
MR. L.W. CRISP, depot agent, is now with with CLIFTON MILLS. W.D. GRIFFIN of Norcross, Georgia fills his place.

Oolenoy School is under the management of MISS JANIE GILLESPIE of East Fork, North Carolina.

Issue of: Thursday 8 April 1897:

Notice to Confederate Veterans of Meeting to elect Township Pension Board.

Citizens of Pickens are making ready to welcome the railroad when it is completed.

Married the 5 (April) at the Methodist Parsonage by Rev. W.M. Harden, MR. W.H. MAULDIN to MISS MARY JANE CLEMENT.

MR. JOHN FREEMAN who lives near Maynard, S.C. and JACK BYRD, Negro, who lives with him, accidently drowned while crossing the river. Freeman leaves a wife and relatives (JOHN M. FREEMAN, born 2 April 1866, died 5 April 1897, buried Cross Roads Baptist Church Cemetery - Pickens Co., S.C. Cemetery Survey, Vol. 1, p. 116 - see issue of the 15 the April 1897).

Liberty News - 3 April 1897
J.H. BROWN and PARSONS & BROS. put street lamps in front of their shops.

Pickens Co., S.C. Board of Commissioner's Meeting and Report (details).

Pickens Co., S.C. Citation Notice - C.L. GASSAWAY applies for Letters of Administration for the estate of JOSEPH S. GASSAWAY, deceased.

Issue of: Thursday 15 April 1897:

J.W. CAPPS has moved his shoe shop into part of the old FREEMAN BUILDING.

DANIEL WOLSEY VORHEES, U.S. Senator from Indiana, died at his home in Washington, D.C. the 10 (April).

Cards are out announcing the approaching marriage of MISS MAMIE FOLGER of Easley, S.C. to MR. MILTON CLAPP of Central, S.C. The wedding will occur the 27 April. (see issue of the 6 May 1897).

Married Sunday the 4 (April) at the home of the bride's father MR. WILLIAM ARNOLD near Central, S.C., by Rev. W.C. Seaborn, MR. W. PRESTON CAMEL of Anderson Co., S.C. and MISS HOPE ARNOLD of Pickens County.

From Maynard
MR. JOHN M. FREEMAN drowned in Cox Creek and was buried from Cross Creek Church (see issue of the 8 April 1897).

MRS. MANDANAH WILLIAMS wife of BENAJAH WILLIAMS died at her residence in Easley, S.C. the 30 (March). She was the daughter of the late GENERAL FREDERICK GARVIN and was a member of the Baptist Church. Burial was at Mullinix Cemetery by Dr. J.R. RILEY. Mrs. Williams leaves a husband and 5 children.

CHARLEY GLASBY, colored, drowned the 5 April.

Article - "Reminiscence of Confederate Times".

Pickens Co., S.C. Notice to Debtors and Creditors - Estate of JEREMIAH TRAINUM by W.U. ROPER and N.H. JONES, Executors.

Pickens Co., S.C. Executor's Sale - 250 acres of land known as the estate of McDUFFIE HAMILTON, deceased to be sold.

AD - DR. L.G. CLAYTON, Central, S.C. has a Morgan Stallion.

Issue of: Thursday 22 April 1897:

From Clemson College
The Seneca River busted (sic) the dyke on the 14 (April) and damaged farms with much loss.
The uniforms have arrived for Rats.

Maynard Items
Twenty Confederate Veterans met at Looper, S.C. the 17 (April) and organized (details).

D.C. FREEMAN died and was buried at Cross Roads Church. He entered the Confederate Army the 19 January 1862 and was wounded the 29 November 1863 (details). He died of heart failure on the 11 (April) at Montgomery Co., Alabama where he had recently entered the drug business.

Married the 15 (April) by Rev. J.M. Stewart at the Colored Baptist Church, MISS TEXIE MILLER to MR. WILLIAM ANDERSON both colored (details).

J.McD. BRUCE is furnishing dynamite as a means of getting a well - at last water came (details).

Liberty
A company of Gypsies struck this town and spent 2 nights.

Pickens Co., S.C. Citation Notice - H.B. HENDRICKS applied for Letters of Administration for the estate of C.W. CUMMINGS, deceased.

Issue of: Thursday 29 April 1897:

Vineland School is being taught by MISS LIDA BOWEN.

MISS MARGARET WELBORN will teach the summer term at the Union School.

ROBERT WERNER son of MR. and MRS. JOSEPH WERNER died at the home of his parents the 23 (April) at the age of about 19 years. He was a member of the Mt. Zion Church.

Wednesday last MR. JAMES CRAIG who lives on the Easley Road took an overdose of morphine and passed away at the age of 63 years. He was a member of the Baptist Church. Mr. Craig was buried at the Craig Family Burying Ground. He leaves a wife and 2 children.

Calhoun Items
A nice sidewalk is being built between Calhoun and Clemson College. We hope soon spring water will be furnished.
DR. E.A. HINES and family have moved to Seneca, S.C.

Praise to MISS LOLA HOLDER teacher at Town Creek School.

Issue of: Thursday 6 May 1897:

Article on Liberty High School (lengthy details).

Pickens Co., S.C. Commissioner's Meeting (details).

Daily Record is a new newspaper being published at Columbia, S.C.

Lightning struck the telephone wire at MR. BRUCE'S store.

MR. J.M. HAll is the mail carrier from here to Easley, S.C.

MR. E.F. KENNEMUR is a photographer in Pickens County.

Married the 27 (April) at the Presbyterian Church at Easley, S.C., by Rev. D.J.R. Riley and REV. DR. CLAPP of Newton, North Carolina the father of the groom, MISS MAMIE FOLGER to MR. MILTON CLAPP of Central, S.C. Miss Folger is the daughter of MRS. LOU and the late ORLANDO C. FOLGER.

Married the 27 (April) at the residence of the bride's parents in Easley, S.C., by Rev. L.T. Weldon, MR. THOMAS K. HUDGENS son of CAPTAIN A.W. HUDGENS to MISS LILLIE KING daughter of MR. J. MONROE KING (in this issue twice).

BUTLER BOWEN, colored, died at his home in Toccoa, Georgia the 26 (April). He was employed by the SOUTHERN RAILROAD and was buried at that place.

Article - "The History of Postage Stamps - 60 Years".

Issue of: Thursday 13 May 1897:

Information on the Corporate Limits Law.

BARNUM and BAILEY CIRCUS is to be in Greenville, S.C.

Married the 2 (May) by Rev. W.M. Harden at the Methodist Parsonage, MR. IRA FEW to MISS LILY McCOLLUMS all of Pickens County.

MR. T.E. CLYDE is opening a stock of general merchandise in the old BRAMBLETT stand opposite the *Journal* office.

MRS. JONES wife of CAPTAIN MANNING JONES died at her home near Looper on the 8 (May), age of about 70 years. She was a member of the Baptist Church and was buried in the Jones' Family Burying Ground. Mrs. Jones leaves a husband and relatives. (TELITHA G. JONES, born 11 Aug. 1819, died 8 May 1897, buried Captain Jones' Cemetery - Pickens Co., S.C. Cemetery Survey, Vol. 1, p. 68 - see issue of the 20 May 1897).

MRS. J.M. GLENN wife of HON. JOHN M. GLENN a representative from Anderson Co., S.C. died at her residence at Equality, Anderson Co., S.C. on Sunday the 9 (May). She was the daughter of the late MAJOR THOMAS H. McCANN. Mrs. Glenn was buried at the Slabtown Presbyterian Church of which she was a member. She leaves a husband and 7 children.

ROBERT P. FREEMAN resident of Clement Post Office, Pickens Co. died at his home the 10 (May) at the age of about 30 years. He was manager of WILLIAM & FREEMAN at Clement, S.C. Mr. Freeman was buried at Mt. Carmel Cemetery. He leaves a widow and 4 young children (see issue of the 20 May 1897).

Account - Memorial Day, Anderson, South Carolina.

Pickens Co., S.C. Executor's Sale - Property of A.R. FOWLER, deceased by WILLIAM THOMPSON and MRS. LOU MOORE. Tract #1 - 178 acres in Hurricane Township, Tract #2 - 100 acres in Pumpkintown Township and Tract #3 - 50 acres in Eastatoe Township to be sold.

Issue of: Thursday 20 May 1897:

OSSIE MADDEN a cadet at Clemson College is visiting his parents.

Pelzer Herald is a new paper published at Pelzer, S.C. by MR. P.B. LANGSTON.

Married the 16 (May) on Town Creek Bridge, by the Rev. J.M. Stewart, MR. GEORGE McD. COOPER to MISS EMMA PORTER all of Pickens County.

Married the 13 (May) in Eastatoe Township at the residence of the bride's parents, by Rev. Cling Boren, MRS. ELIZABETH PATTERSON to MR. CONNIE BOREN all of Pickens County.

MESSRS. SOUTHERLAND & GRIFFIN have purchased the soda fountain and fixtures from L.C. THORNLEY.

Married the 8 (May) at the residence of W.K. Merck, N.P., MISS MAGGIE E. SMITH daughter of MRS. O.G. SMITH to MR. F.C. STEWART.

WARD HENDRICKS, colored, was hit in the head with a weight by DAVE HENDRICKS, colored, Wednesday 12 (May). Ward Hendricks is not expected to live. The quarrel took place at G.H. HENDRICKS' store.

Report on the Graded School at Easley, S.C. (details).

Central News
The residence of J.R. McNEELY one mile north of Central, S.C. was destroyed by fire Sunday the 2 (May).

From Clement
MR. ROBERT P. FREEMAN postmaster at Clement, S.C. died the 10 (May) of catarrh fever and typhoid fever at the age of about 28 (sic) years. He was buried at Mt. Carmel. Mr. Freeman leaves a wife, 4 children, an aged father, 4 brothers and 2 sisters (see issue of the 13 May 1897).

Married the 9 (May) at the residence of Rev. Thomas Looper, MR. LAWRENCE GRANGER of Greenville Co., S.C. to MISS JANIE MOODY of Anderson Co., S.C. Also on the same day at the residence of the bride's father MR. SAMUEL PITMAN, MISS ARCIS PITMAN to MR. BENJAMIN CENTER all of Greenville Co.

Olga Dots
Rev. J.E. Foster conducted funeral services for MRS. MANNING JONES the day following her death at the family burying ground (see issue of the 13 May 1897).

Mt. Carmel Baptist Church has applied for a charter - 20 May 1897.

Pickens Co., S.C. Tax Execution Sales:
To be sold Salesday in June.
A.R. FOWLER - 178 acres in Hurricane Township.
WILLIAM TOMPSON - 100 acres in Pumpkintown Township.
MRS. LOU MOORE - 50 acres in Eastatoe Township.

Issue of: Thursday 27 May 1897:

Article - "Sketch of GENERAL THOMAS PINKNEY'S HOME".

GENERAL ANDREW PICKENS' monument at the Old Stone Church was mutilated and is now in Greenville, S.C. for repairs. Clemson students were arrested, etc. (details).

Greenville Mountaineer - 22 May 1897
SENATOR JOSEPH H. EARLE died. He was a native of Greenville Co., S.C. having been born the 30 April 1847. Sketch of his life and a picture (lengthy details).

Trustees of Zion School District known as Rocky Knob in Easley Township apply for a charter and incorporation of said schoolhouse and grounds.

Born a girl Tuesday at the home of MAJOR WARREN BOYD.

W.T. McFALL is making some improvements on his store. He will also put goods in the old *Sentinel* office.

T.D. HARRIS is enlarging his store. He is having a furniture store erected in the rear of the main store.

An 11 month infant of MR. and MRS. JOHN CHILDS died the 19 (May) at the home of Mrs. Child's father J. MATTIE STEWART. The infant was buried at Griffin Baptist Church.

MR. T.W. TOWNES who lives near Porter Post Office, S.C. lost his house to fire the 19 (May). It was a new house and he had just moved in.

MRS. HARRIET NIX died at her home in Oconee Co., S.C. Thursday the 20 (May). She was buried at the Keowee Burying Ground. Mrs. Nix leaves relatives and friends.

Married Sunday the 16 May at Pisgah Church, Equality, S.C., by Rev. G.B. Moore, MISS EMMA ALLGOOD and REV. JESSE VERMILLION from the Slabtown Section. Rev. Vermillion is to assume the Presidency of an institution of learning in Rush, Texas. *Anderson People's Advocate*

Issue of: Thursday 3 June 1897:

Anderson Mill News
MR. WADE TOWNES whose house was destroyed by fire is now building a new one.

From Liberty
C.T. HUTCHINS occupies the GLENN Store and DR. W.A. SHELDON has moved his Drug Store to the stand MR. HUTCHINS vacated. Dr. Sheldon now owns that property.

HOMER A. RICHEY is a constable under MAGISTRATE JENKINS.

CADET BERTRAN THORNLEY of Clemson College is visiting his parents.

Married Sunday the 23 (May) at the residence of Rev. Thomas Looper, MR. CALVIN LOGGINS to MISS OLA HUGHEY all of Pickens County.

FRED P. DAY who has a position with SOUTHERN AGRICULTURAL WORKS of Atlanta, Georgia is visiting his mother in Easley, S.C.

A child of MR. and MRS. FRANK SMITH died the 25 (May) and was buried at the Williams Grave Yard. Mr. Smith lives on the JOHN ROPER place near Maynard, S.C.

Issue of: Thursday 10 June 1897:

Pickens Co., S.C. Commissioner's Meeting (details).

MR. A.M. FOLGER was sworn in as postmaster of Easley, S.C.

CHARLES BOWEN is taking a course at Furman University.

JOHN TROTTER, who lived on J.T. ANTHONY'S farm near Griffin Church, died the 1 June at the age of about 55 years. He was buried from the Oolenoy Baptist Church.

Married the 9 June at the residence of MR. J.D. MOORE by J.E. Boroughs, N.P., MR. E.D. BRADLEY of Polk Co., North Carolina to MISS BECKAY REEVES of this county.

Pickens Co., S.C. Salesday:
Two tracts of land. 178 acres in Hurricane Township sold to W.A. HUDSON for $12. 50 acres in Eastatoe Township sold for $9.26.

SOUTHERLAND & GRIFFIN are to erect a shelter in front of their store.

JUDGE J.H. NEWTON who is in the insurance business in Alabama is visiting family here.

CAPTAIN T.J. MAULDIN, lawyer, is moving to Anderson, S.C.

Married the 2 June 1897 by Rev. J.M. Stewart, MISS CORNELIA LEWIS daughter of MRS. (sic) H.J. and N.J. LEWIS to MR. WADE TOWNES (details).

Issue of: Thursday 17 June 1897:

Easley

CLYDE & NALLEY and J.T. LATHEM have exchanged stores.

J.O. BROCK the jeweler, has moved from the FREEMAN & HENDRICKS STORE to the magnificent brick store of MR. A.M. MORRIS.

E.B. CRAIGHEAD has resigned as President of Clemson College to accept the presidency of a college in Missouri.

OLIVER M. HANNAH, who lived on J.E. PARSON'S Twelve Mile River farm, died the 14 of (June) of pneumonia at the age of about 48 years. He was buried at Secona Cemetery. Mr. Hannah leaves a wife and 6 children.

Married the 13 (June) at the residence of Rev. W.M. Harden, MR. DAVID E. PORTER of Piedmont, S.C. formerly of this county to MISS LOLA HOLDER daughter of REV. B. HOLDER.

CAPTAIN H.C. GRADY who lives about 3 miles east of Pickens will move nearer town by the first of November. He has purchased MR. H.A. RICHEY'S Bermuda farm just north west of Pickens.

Methodists, Baptists and Mormons are using the Holly Bush Schoolhouse for services.

Issue of: Thursday 24 June 1897:

MRS. ANNIE KEELER is New Jersey's second woman lawyer.

B.D. STEWART will go into business in Greenville, S.C.

W.T. McFALL is having improvements made on his dwelling on Factory Street.

An eleven pound boy was born the 20 (June) to MR. and MRS. J.H. MARTIN.

MRS. FLORA LATHEM is teaching at Fairview, Anderson Co.

MISSES OLGA and SADIE RICHEY have been attending school in Anderson, S.C.

SHERIFF McDANIEL had the jail covered last week.

A daughter of ZEDAR LAWRENCE, colored, died Tuesday at the age of 15 years and was buried at Cold Springs Church.

DR. JOSHUA F. ENSOR has been appointed postmaster at Columbia, S.C.

Married the 15 (June) at Fairview Schoolhouse near Sheriff, Anderson Co., S.C., by Rev. George Nalley, MISS NORA RICHEY daughter of EX-SHERIFF H.A. RICHEY of Pickens to MR. B.A. LABOON of Anderson, S.C.

MRS. HARRIET KEITH relict of the late CORNELIUS KEITH died at her home near Table Rock, S.C. on the 22 (June) at the age of 72 years. She was buried from Oolenoy Church of which she was a member. Mrs. Keith leaves 8 children.

Six Mile
Born a boy the 17 (May) to MR. and MRS. JAKE MERCK.

Born a son to MR. and MRS. J.B.R. FREEMAN the 27 (May).

Notice - Do not hire ELA YOUNG, colored, as he is under contract to me. W.L. JENKINS.

Issue of: Thursday 1 July 1897:

A. BABB is building a fine 2 story, 10 room house for MRS. NAOMI MOSELEY of near Sunny Dale, S.C.

LT. FRANK MAULDIN who is stationed at West Point Military Academy is visiting his parents here.

An infant son of MR. and MRS. FRANK FERGUSON of Table Mountain died the 24 (June) and was buried at Oolenoy Cemetery.

FELIX STEPHENS, colored, who lives on MR. FOREST ALLGOOD'S farm died the 23 (June) and was buried at Secona Church.

R.M. WERTZ was elected Superintendent of the LIBERTY OIL MILL and J.H. BROWN was elected Secretary and Treasurer.

CAPTAIN T.J. MAULDIN resigned as Captain of the Pickens Rifles.

MR. JOHN BRINSDON died at his home near Charleston, S.C. on the 25 (June) at the age of 53 years. He was buried in Pendleton, S.C. Mr. Brinsdon leaves a wife and 2 children. He was an uncle of MRS. J.J. LEWIS of this place.

JOHN TURNER of near Rock Post Office, S.C. died the 9 (June) of fever at the age of about 40 years and was buried at Oolenoy. He leaves a wife and several children.

BEN MASTERS of near Rock Post Office, S.C. died the 24 (June) at the age of 60 years. He was buried from the Saluda Hill Baptist Church of which he was a member. Mr. Masters leaves a wife and several children.

CLIFTON EARLE, son of MR. and MRS. J.W. EARLE who live near Pickens, died the 23 (June) of pneumonia at the age of about 8 years. He was buried at the Baker Family Burying Ground.

MRS. EFFIE MORHORN, wife of MR. SAM MORHORN of Auburn, Georgia, died the 24 (June) at the age of 17 years. She was buried from the Baptist Church of which she was a member. Mrs. Morhorn was the daughter of W.S. DURHAM of near this place.

CHARLIE LOOPER son of MR. and MRS. J.B. LOOPER of near Mica, S.C. died Friday the 25 (June) at the age of 6 years and 3 months. He was buried at Cross Roads Church.

MISS DORA JONES daughter of MR. THOMAS JONES of Table Mountain, S.C. died the 26 (June) at the age of 18 years. She was buried at Oolenoy Church of which she was a member.

MRS. ALEXANDER wife of MR. JAKE ALEXANDER of Reedy Cove, S.C. died the 23 (June) at the age of 70 years. She was buried from Holly Springs Church of which she was a member. Mrs. Alexander leaves a husband and several children. (MARY E. "POLLY" (HOLDER) ALEXANDER - <u>Alexander Families of Upper South Carolina</u>, p. 391).

Pickens Co., S.C. Petit Jury List.

<u>From Easley</u>
MR. T.B. HIGGINS has a position with the SEABOARD AIR LINE RAILROAD at Lawrenceville, Georgia and is moving his family there.

Article - "United Confederate Veteran's Convention in Nashville, Tennessee".

For Sale - One Scofield power cotton press, by JAS. A. WHITEN, Central, S.C.

Pickens Co., S.C. Final Settlement - Estate of RACHEL CHAPMAN, deceased by J. HARVEY CHAPMAN.

Issue of: Thursday 8 July 1897:

Article - "Celebrated TURNER BYNAM Duel".

Article - "Surviving Confederate Generals and their Places of Residency" (lengthy details).

Born a girl to MR. and MRS. W.B. LOOPER of Mica, S.C. last week.

ANDREW BRAMBLETT is attending the Citadel Academy.

Born a boy to the V.S. MEDLINS who live near town on the 22 (June).

J.C. JENNINGS has purchased the soda fountain of B.M. GRIFFIN and can now be found in the LEWIS old stand.

MAJOR STEWART has his new house on Main Street complete. It was built by MR. W.A. PALMER and MR. F.E. COX.

Letter from BAILY A. LANGSTON of Eureka Springs, Arkansas, a brother of MR. J.T. LANGSTON. Baily A. Langston has six children.

Pickens Co., S.C. Commissioner's Meeting and Report (details).

AD - G.W. EARLE, Selling Drugs of all Kind, Pickens S.C.

AD - New Store, F.H. CARTER, General Merchandise, DOYLE BUILDING, Calhoun, S.C.

Pickens Co., S.C. Jury List.

THE ISSUE OF: THURSDAY 15 JULY 1897 IS MISSING.

Issue of: Thursday 22 July 1897:

South Carolina State Board of Health - Report on fever at Clemson College (details).

Story - "STONEWALL JACKSON at Fredericksburg".

Pickens Co., S.C. Citation Notice - Estate of MARY A. OATS, deceased. N. OATS applied for Letters of Administration.

Pickens Co., S.C. Citation Notice - Estate of J.G. FREEMAN, deceased. W.B. FREEMAN applied for Letters of Administration.

Pickens Co., S.C. Citation Notice - Estate of R.P. FREEMAN, deceased. W.B. FREEMAN applied for Letters of Administration.

Notice - Do not hire ELLA McGRAW, colored, as she is under contract to me. SCIPIO McELWANE.

LEO GILLESPIE is teaching at the Wolf Creek School.

Born a daughter to MR. and MRS. THOMAS KELLEY of near Pickens the 17 (July).

PROF. W.J. BOGGS is teaching the Shady Grove School.

MRS. JULIA WOOD of Elmont, Texas was badly hurt by a cow. She is well known in this county.

MISS JANIE GILLESPIE of East Fork, North Carolina is teaching in the Oolenoy School District #36.

Married the 10 (July) on a mountain near Caesar's Head by, Rev. Joe McJunkin, GEORGE KIRKLAND, colored, to MISS ELLA KIRKLAND, colored.

Married Sunday the 18 July at the residence of Rev. J.T. Dobson near Central, S.C., MR. BENNIE ROPER to MISS MINNIE HOW (sic) all of Pickens County.

List of Guest at the AMBLER HOUSE: MRS. G.D. OSWALD and family of James Island, S.C., MRS. WILLIAM C. DAVIS of Charleston, S.C., MRS. R.L.R. BENTZ and children of Greenville, S.C.
MISS DORA LA ROCHE of Greenville, S.C.
MRS. A.M. BECKUTE of Greenville, S.C.

MRS. JULIA KELLY of the Six Mile Section died Thursday the 15 July and was buried from the Keowee Church by Rev. W.C. Seaborn.

The little son of MR. and MRS. AMOS SUTHERLAND of Rock, S.C. died the 20 (July) of typhoid fever and was buried at Oolenoy Church.

REV. W.C. SEABORN'S son JAMES SEABORN is seriously ill with typhoid at Williamsport, Pennsylvania (see issue of the 29 July 1897).

Born a daughter to MR. and MRS. J.A. ROBINSON the 13 July.

MR. J.G. FREEMAN a citizen of the Cross Plains Section died the 17 (July) at the age of 67 years and was buried from Cross Roads Church. He leaves 7 children.

Easley Dashes
MISS MARY MARTIN is teaching at Dayton.
MR. RAGSDALE is the manager of COL. W.A. NEAL'S, Pickensville, S.C. farm.

MR. MARION DAY has purchased the CALHOUN GRIFFIN CORN MILL and will move it here to be run by steam at his plaining mill plant.
MISS BLANCHE HUDGENS is teaching at Holly Bush.
The DRUCKENMILLER family entertained at the Academy Hall.

From Liberty
W.A. STEWART a telegraph operator at Charlotte, North Carolina is visiting his father MAGISTRATE STEWART.
W.O. WILLARD has moved into his hotel. CONTRACTOR BELL has moved into the house vacated by W.O. Willard.
PROF. R.E. BOGGS is teaching the Walker and McElmoyle School.
CONTRACTOR BELL has finished the new school and has commenced to work on C.T. HUTCHIN'S dwelling house.

Olga
WILLIE BURNS died the 11 (July) at the home of his father near Marietta, S.C. He was buried from Ebenezer Church.
JESSE MILLER, colored, who lived on the J.S. WILLIAMS' farm died at her residence the 9 (July) and was buried from Shoal Creek Church.
WILLIAMS & BARKER are doing business at the FOSTER old stand.

Issue of: Thursday 29 July 1897:

Article - "Dead Town in Oconee County, S.C. - Tunnel Hill", by W.A. DICKSON.

Dacusville
PROF. W.W.F. BRIGHT is teaching at Maynard, S.C. and LEWIS F. ROBINSON is assisting.
PROF. S.A. HUNT is teaching the Lathem School and MISS NETTIE ROBINSON is assisting.
MR. JAMES K. LATHEM is to build a new brick house (using 1,000 bricks) near Mt. Carmel Church.
W.P. HOGSED father of our neighbor FRANK W. HOGSED died a few days ago and was buried at Dacusville, S.C. He was a native of North Carolina and served in the Confederate Army.
JOHN BIRD, colored, stole a 15 year old daughter of A.N. BOGGS, colored. Reports say this is his 4th woman (details).

Born a son to MR. and MRS. JEFF HOLDER on the 24 (July).

Pickens High School to be taught by PROF. DARGAN.

W.A. CHRISTOPHER is teaching the Town Creek School.

An infant of MR. and MRS. R.L. HARRIS of near Pickens died the 24 (July) and was buried at Enon Baptist Church.

The 4 year old daughter of MR. DEAN SINGLETON who lives near town died the 24 (July) and was buried at Enon Cemetery.

NANCY BOWEN, colored, was jailed for infancide.

J.A. WOOD opened a barber shop in the rear end of the old LEWIS stand.

MR. BERRY CHILDRESS who lived near town died the 24 (July) at the age of 76 years. He was a member of the Baptist Church and was buried at Secona Cemetery. Mr. Childress leaves 5 sons and 4 daughters (see issue of 5 Aug. 1897).

MRS. A.E. BRAWNER died at the home of her daughter MRS. T.J. ROOKE of Bostick, Florence Co., S.C. on the 13 (July) at the age of about 70 years. She was a member of the Baptist Church. Mrs. Brawner was buried at that place (where she died). She leaves 2 daughters.

FREEMAN LYNCH died from a gun shot wound at his residence 10 miles north of Pickens Sunday at the age of 34 years. He was buried at Mountain Grove Church with MASONIC HONORS. Mr. Lynch leaves a wife and 4 children.

JAMES G. SEABORN died the 21 (July) at Williamsport, Pennsylvania of typhoid fever at the age of 28 years. He was the son of REV. W.C. SEABORN. Mr. Seaborn was buried at the Boroughs Family Cemetery where his wife is buried. She died 8 years ago. A brother JOSEPH SEABORN went to Pennsylvania to care for him but his death occurred prior to his arrival (see issue of the 22 July 1897 - details).

DR. W.L. RYDER was lynched six miles from Waverly Hall, Georgia at the "WILLIS PLACE" on Monday night (details).

Pickens Co., S.C. Citation Notice - Estate of NANCY L. LATHEM, deceased. J.K. LATHEM applied for Letters of Administration.

AD - A.W. HUDGENS & SON, Selling Fire Insurance.

Issue of: Thursday 5 August 1897:

Campaign in Pickens Co., S.C. for U.S. Senate Seat (details).

Pickens Co., S.C. Commissioner's Meeting and Report (details).

MISS KATE MAYFIELD is teaching the Rock School.

REV. W.C. VENELL, wife and daughter of Lincoln, Alabama are visiting relatives and friends in this area.

Married the 1 (Aug.) at the residence of MR. JEFF MOON of near town, by Rev. J.E. Foster, MR. JAMES UNDERWOOD to MISS DORA GROGAN.

W.W. HAMMOND will soon have the Gap Hill Church near Stewart Post Office, S.C. completed.

MR. CHILDRESS died of paralysis not typhoid (see issue of the 29 July 1897).

PROF. MOORE of Georgia has been elected Principal of Central High School.

Merchants at Table Mountain, S.C., A.C. SUTHERLAND, EDENS BROS., KEITH and HENDRICKS, LYNCH and EDENS and JEFF GALLOWAY are all within 1 mile of each other.

MR. R.M. WERTZ made marble tombstones for MR. B.C. BAKER'S father and mother.

REV. ELIJAH ROPER of Dawson, Georgia is visiting relatives in the Table Mountain and Knob Section. He has not been here in 13 years.

JAMES JONES, JR., son of JAMES JONES, died the 31 (July) at his home near Table Mountain, S.C. of typhoid at the age of almost 25 years. He was buried at Oolenoy Baptist Church. Mr. Jones leaves a wife and 1 child.

Pickens - W.A. PALMER and J.M. DUCKWORTH have purchased the BYARS lot near the livery stables and will soon erect a building for a machine shop, the front for a buggy establishment and the rear for a blacksmith shop.

MRS. JAMES ALEXANDER died the 27 (July) at her home in Piedmont, S.C. at the age of 40 years. She was the daughter of MR. CARTER DURHAM of near town. Mrs. Alexander was a member of the Baptist Church and was buried from the Concord Church. She leaves a husband and 7 children.

Pickens Co., S.C. Citation Notice - Estate of W.B. CHILDRESS, deceased. CHARLES and J.T. CHILDRESS apply for Letters of Administration.

Issue of: Thursday 12 August 1897:

Campaign Meeting at Anderson, S.C. - Senatorial Candidate.

From Liberty
FRANK CRANE sold his livery business to GANTT BROS.

Born a son to MR. and MRS. WILLIAM LAWRENCE of Anderson Mills, S.C. the 6 (Aug.).

PROF. E.F. DuPRIEST of Galloway, North Carolina is teaching at Horse Pasture.

MISS FANNIE MOORE is teaching at Ruhamah.

MAJOR J.M. STEWART moved into his new dwelling on Main Street.

MR. McCARLY of Seneca, S.C. died the 8 (Aug.) and was buried from the Methodist Church of which he was a member. He leaves a wife and several children. (W.C. McCARLY, born 23 Aug. 1850, died 8 Aug. 1897, buried Seneca Mountain View - Oconee Co., S.C. Cemetery Survey, Vol. 1, p. 186).

JUDGE SAMUEL McGOWAN died at his residence in Abbeville, S.C. the 9 (Aug.) at the age of 79 years. He leaves 3 children: MRS. W.C. BENNETT, W.G. McGOWEN, and MISS LUCIA McGOWEN.

MRS. R.R. CHILD died the 3 (Aug.) at her home near Cateechee, S.C. at the age of about 40 years. She was a member of the Baptist Church and was buried from Camp Creek Church. Mrs. Child leaves a husband and 5 children. (IDA T. CHILD, born 16 Nov. 1857, died 3 Aug. 1897 - Pickens Co., S.C. Cemetery Survey, Vol. 1, p. 186).

A dwelling belonging to MR. W.H. HESTER in Central, S.C. burned Tuesday. The house was unoccupied.

FRANK HOLCOMB who lives with his son BERRY HOLCOMB three miles east of Easley, S.C. will have a reunion of his 16 children, 10 sons and 6 daughters are living. He has been married 3 times. His last wife who is living, was the widow of the late JOHN GOSSETT of near Easley. Mr. Holcomb will be 80 years old the 30 April next. *Anderson Intelligencer*

MISS NORA HENDRICKS died the 5 August at the home of her uncle MR. BENNETT HILL of Old Pickens, Oconee Co., S.C. of brain fever. She was the eldest daughter of MR. and MRS. D.E. HENDRICKS. Miss Hendricks was buried from Griffin Church of which she was a member.

Issue of: Thursday 19 August 1897:

Pickens Co., S.C. Executive Committee Report (details).

Married Saturday the 15 August at the residence of J.M. HALLUMS by R.T. Hallum, N.P., MR. PRESLEY to MISS NORRA BOLEN.

Married the 10 (Aug.) at the residence of Rev. J.T. Lewis, MR. OSCAR COTHRAN late of Texas but now of Oconee Co., S.C. to MISS JANIE FIELD daughter of MR. and MRS. O.P. FIELD of Pindor, S.C.

J.E. BOGGS and T.K. HUDGENS have re-organized the PICKENS LAND AGENCY with offices at Pickens and Easley, S.C.

Oconee News - WILLIAM GOSS committed suicide at Old Pickens, Oconee Co., S.C. He is thought to be from Madison Co., Georgia. A woman with him claims to be his wife (details).

MR. J.W. PACE held a reunion. He was 50 years old the 10 August 1897 (details).

Easley
MR. W.H. PICKENS is making a 35 foot addition to his storehouse.
WYLIE ELLISON purchased the interest of J.A. SHEPPARD of the firm of SHEPPARD & ELLISON. It will now be known as ELLISON BROS. MR. SHEPPARD will open a grocery store in the west end of Greenville, S.C.
MISS EMILY JOHNSON is teaching at Carson, Anderson Co., S.C.
ELMER FOLGER will work in Gaffney, S.C. on the SOUTHERN RAILROAD.

Pickens Co., S.C. Court of Common Pleas - Summons for Relief - Estate of RUFUS OATS, deceased. NEWTON OATS, FRANCIS A. SHECK et al. vs S. C. ROPER, et al.

Issue of: Thursday 26 August 1897:

J.O. BROCK has moved into the AMBLER HOUSE on Main Street.

The convicts have been moved from George's Creek to Hunt's Bridge.

List of Guests at the AMBLER HOUSE:
MR. CHARLES F. HARD, MRS. ELLA W. HARD, MISS ELLA S. HARD, MISS CLARA T. HARD and MISS ELIZABETH W. HARD of Greenville, S.C. MISS HARRIET J. HARD of Williamston, S.C.
MISS MARGARET H. SMITH and MR. JOSIAH E. SMITH of Charleston, S.C.
MISS MARY E. HARD of Bessemer, Alabama

MRS. MAMIE WARD wife of J.M. WARD died the 17 (Aug.) 2 miles east of Pickens at the age of about 24 years. She was a member of the Baptist Church and was buried from Laurel Creek Church Cemetery, Greenville Co., S.C. Mrs. Ward is survived by her husband.

MR. JAY HUNT a citizen of Dacusville, S.C. died the 20 (Aug.) at his home of dropsy at the age of 60 years. He was buried at the Methodist Church Cemetery at that place. Mr. Hunt leaves several children.

Liberty
W.H. CHAPMAN has commenced a commodious residence.

Married last Sunday by J.M. Stewart, MR. W.M. MURPHREE to MISS OCTAVE NEELY at the home of the bride's parents.

Born a son to JOHN LOOPER 16 Aug. 1897 - which makes 16.

Article - "Recollection of GENERAL R.E. LEE".

Issue of: Thursday 2 September 1897:

Confederate Veteran's Reunion at Greenville, S.C. (details).

Old Soldiers' Picnic at LOOPER'S SHOP last Saturday (details).

HENRY LANGSTON and wife have moved from Mauldin's Mill, S.C. to one of J.B.R. FREEMAN'S houses in town.

MR. W.S. KIRKSEY is building a mine on the Easley road south of Pickens. He has employed the services of a mineralogist and indications are there is gold there.

Liberty
T.E. WILLARD a well known citizen died Monday at the age of 80 years. He was originally from Union Co., S.C. but has been here over 40 years. Mr. Willard was buried at Ruhamah Cemetery. He leaves a large family.

MR. JOSIAH TROTTER is living on Hill Street.

MR. ASHMORE HINTON rented a house on "HUDSON HILL" to move here to educate his children.

Pickens Co., S.C. Court of Common Pleas - Summons for Relief - LIDA OWINGS, RAYMOND O. HUNT by T.F. HUNT, Guardian vs AMANDA HUNT, JESSE HUNT, et al.

Pickens Co., S.C. Notice to Debtors and Creditors - Estate of G.W. FARR, deceased by J.P. FARR, Administrator.

Issue of: Thursday 9 September 1897:

Sketch - "Old St. Philip's Church, Charleston, S.C.".

Pickens Co., S.C. Commissioner's Report (details).

PROF. MILES ALLGOOD closed his school at Bethel District #43 (for the session).

EX-SHERIFF H.A. RICHEY bought the stock of SUTHERLAND & GRIFFIN.

S.P. FREEMAN started the STANDARD FURNITURE FACTORY last week.

Pickens Rifle Company to have new guns.

ROBERT FOSTER who was buried near Olga, S.C., was re-buried (sic) the 26 (Aug.) at Peter's Creek Cemetery. He has been dead 40 years. A great part of his coffin was sound (Note: stone found at Peter's Creek Cemetery).

MRS. PERMELIA McDANIEL, wife of JAMES M. McDANIEL, deceased, died at her home in Greenville Co., S.C. the 23 (Aug.). She was a member of the Baptist Church. Mrs. McDaniel was buried at the family cemetery.

The cotton gin at White Post Office, S.C. called CELY & CO. burned the 2 (Sept.).

Students from a distance who are attending the Graded School at Easley. MISS SALLIE LOU STARKE and MISS REBECCA SWELLING of Elbert Co., Georgia (details).

MR. J.T. SINGLETON moved to Oconee Co., S.C. from Pickens Co. in the fall of 1891 and settled on the old THODE place on Cane Creek 2 miles above Walhalla, S.C. (details).
Oconee News

Liberty
The RAILROAD COMPANY is having the old depot recovered and repaired.

Pickens Co., S.C. Final Settlement - Estate of A.T. CLAYTON by MRS. T.C. CLAYTON and W.T. O'DELL.

Issue of: Thursday 16 September 1897:

RUFUS ASHMORE is a clerk for J. McD. BRUCE.

D.F. SUTHERLAND moved back to his home on the Oolenoy last week.

FRANK E. COX and wife moved into the house recently vacated by MAGISTRATE STEWART.

Born a daughter the 19 (Aug.) to MR. and MRS. FRANK PORTER of near town.

PROF. ANDREW P. MONTAGUE of Columbia University, Washington, D.C. has been elected President of Furman University, Greenville, S.C.

The Academy here is improved with an enrollment of 50 students.

LAWRENCE LOOPER of Huntington, Arkansas is in Pickens County visiting relatives. He is the son of the late ANDERSON LOOPER and JERRIMIAH (sic) LOOPER is his grandfather.

Married the 7 (Sept.) in Atlanta, Georgia GENERAL JAMES LONGSTREET and MISS ELLA DORTCH. Mrs. (sic) Dortch is 26 years old and an assistant librarian at the State of Georgia. General Longstreet is in his 77 year (see issue of the 23 Sept. 1897).

Sketch - "Furman's New President".

AD - A. ELLISON BROS., Selling General Merchandise, Easley, S.C.

AD - J.A. SHEPPARD, Selling General Merchandise, Easley.

Pickens Co., S.C. Clerk's Sale:
Land to be sold Salesday in October.
R.G. GAINES vs W.H. HESTER. 3 lots in Central, S.C., 1/4 acre each, known on the plat of the town as Lot #1, #2 and #3.
D.F. BEASLEY vs GAINES SMITH. 55 acres on Twenty-Three Mile Creek.

Pickens Co., S.C. Final Settlement - Estate of MARY NORRIS, deceased by W.T. NORRIS, Executor.

Pickens Co., S.C. Final Settlement - Estate of STEPHEN BURDINE, deceased by JOSEPH NALLEY, Executor.

Issue of: Thursday 23 September 1897:

Maynard Dots
REV. W.L. ANDERSON is leaving Cross Roads Church to go west. REV. T.C. HOLSCLAW of North Carolina to supply the church next year.

Born a girl to MR. and MRS. J.L.O. THOMPSON on the 18 (Sept.)

J.C. JENNINGS and family have moved into the BRADLEY house on Main Street.

REESE BOWEN who lives east of Pickens erected himself a commodious dwelling.

HENRY S. HARTZOG of Barnwell Co., S.C. was elected President of Clemson College last Thursday.

Married the 19 (Sept.) at the residence of Magistrate Garvin of Central, S.C., SYDNEY COLLINS to JULIA McCANN both colored.

BEE LEWIS and family will shortly occupy the house recently vacated by J.C. JENNINGS.

MISS TIZAH HUGHES of Roanoke, S.C. is now employed with the firm of NESBITT, TROWBRIDGE & CO. of Piedmont, S.C. as head trimmer of the millinery department.

ALBERT AIKEN, son of TOMPS AIKEN of near Sunny Dale, S.C., died the 7 (Sept.) at the home of his brother (name not given) near Galloway, North Carolina. Age about 18 years.

MRS. JAMES RAINES wife of JAMES RAINES died the 10 (Sept.) at her home in Gaffney, S.C. with fever. Mr. Raines worked at the *Journal* office.

The 11 month old child of MR. and MRS. JAS. BAKER of Central, S.C. died last week (accident - see for details).

Liberty
The firm of HUNTER & HAMILTON has dissolved co-partnership. HAMILTON is selling his interest to HUNTER.
Married the 20 September 1897 by John T. Boggs, N.P., J.H. MOORE to MISS S.J. SPEARMAN all of Pickens County.

The infant child of THOMAS BRADLEY of Atlanta, Georgia died last week and was buried at Ruhamah Cemetery.

J. MEDE SMITH a citizen of this county died the 7 (Sept.) at Columbia, S.C. at the age of about 90 years. He was buried at Zion Burying Ground. Mr. Smith leaves a large family.

Article - "Clemson College's New President".

AD - J.H. MORGAN & BROS., 211 North Main St., Greenville, S.C., Selling General Merchandise.

Pickens Co., S.C. Clerk's Sale:
Firm of GAINES, LEWIS & CO., Central, S.C., notes, accounts, mortgages and assets to be sold.

Pickens Co., S.C. Final Settlement - Estate of W.W. MARTIN by SARAH E. MARTIN and J.T. YOUNGBLOOD, Administrators.

Issue of: Thursday 30 September 1897:

Article - "A Confederate Story, Abbeville, South Carolina" - Letter 21 September 1897, telling the story of JOHN GABRIEL CHRISTOPHER KRUSE, born the 25 August 1821 in Germany and lived in Walhalla, S.C. until 1861 (details).

Olga
MISS MINNIE FOSTER is postmaster at Olga, S.C.
Married the 19 (Sept.) by Rev. F.H. Schuler, MR. BUD COLEMAN to MISS JENNIE KEITH of Traveler's Rest, S.C.

Church House Dedicated - Baptist Church known as Corinth #1 at Anderson County, S.C. (details).

A Negro woman was admitted to the bar in Tennessee.

COL. JAMES A. HOYT of Greenville, S.C. to publish and edit the *Cotton Plant* for next year.

JOHN E. STEELE son of CAPTAIN R.E. STEELE studies at Easley Graded School.

RUFUS J. WATKINS and W.K. MERCK are erecting a store building at Six Mile, S.C. for general merchandise.

Married the 26 (Sept.) at the residence of MR. JOHN D. BURGESS of Greenville Co., S.C. by Rev. J.T. Burdine, MR. J.R. JONES to MISS L.A. KEITH all of Pickens County.

R.G. GAINES and GASSOWAY BROS. has secured the services of O.S. STEWART of Alexander, S.C. They are dealers in stock, cotton buyers, etc.

Hazel Nuts
DAVID WINCHESTER has his grist mill completed now.

Liberty
C.C. STEEL of Trinity, North Carolina is clerking for J.H. BROWN.

Pickens Co., S.C. Notice to Debtors and Creditors - Estate of MRS. E.M. KAY and\or JOSEPHINE CRAIG, deceased by T.E. CRAIG, Administrator.

Pickens Co., S.C. Clerk's Sale:
Foreclosures.
R.E. GAINES vs W.H. HESTER. 3 lots of 1/4 acre each in Central, S.C. Known as Lots #1, #2 and #3 on the town plat made by J.J. GARVIN to be sold.
D.F. BRADLEY vs GAINES SMITH - Foreclosure - 55 acres on Twenty-Three Mile Creek to be sold.

A New Feature for Clemson College. Plan to make a Textile Department in the Farmer's College (details).

Issue of: Thursday 7 October 1897:

Married the 3 (Sept.) at the residence of J.D. MOORE by J.E. Boroughs, N.P. MISS JOSIE REAVES to JACOB BEARDIN.

Born a baby girl to MAGISTRATE JENKINS (2 articles).

Liberty
MRS. L.R. SMITH and family have moved to Dacusville S.C. where MR. SMITH is selling goods.

REV. R.J. WILLIAMS was elected to replace R.L. WELDON as pastor of the Baptist Church here (Liberty, S.C.).

Issue of: Thursday 14 October 1897:

Seneca, South Carolina - 6 October
DR. O.M. DOYLE died and was buried at the Old Stone Church. He was born in Oconee Co. S.C. 66 years ago. Dr. Doyle served in the Confederate Army. He leaves 4 children: MRS. & Dr. C.C. JONES of Greenville, S.C., O.R. DOYLE of Calhoun, S.C., DR. W.R. DOYLE of Seneca, S.C. and DR. E.C. DOYLE of Laurens, S.C. Special - *Greenville Daily News*

CALVIN LAND of Greenville, S.C. has moved to near town.

MR. CLAYTON NEWTON has erected a neat and substantial dwelling - "wedding bells"?

MRS. J.T. HINTON died the 6 October at her home 4 miles from Easley, S.C. (N. ELIZABETH FENNELL, wife of J.T. HINTON, born 21 Jan. 1835, died 6 Oct. 1897, buried Carmel Presbyterian Church - Pickens Co., S.C. Cemetery Survey, Vol. 2, p. 169).

Married the 6 October at the residence of Rev. J.T. Dobson of Central, S.C, MR. HOKE SMITH to MISS TALLEY PATRICK both of Pelzer, S.C.

EX-GOVERNOR JOHN GARY EVANS and MISS EMILY PLUME of Connecticut will be married the 14 December next (see issue of the 23 Dec. 1897). *Hampton Guardian*

LOUIS BURGESS son of WILLIAM BURGESS who lives in the Dacusville Section died the 8 (Oct.) at the age of 13 years. He was buried at Mt. Carmel Church.

Married Thursday the 7 (Oct.) at the residence of the bride's parents, by Rev. J.R. Riley, MR. J.E.M. STEELE to MISS JOSIE ALEXANDER all of Alexander, S.C.

J.B. STEWART erected a neat and commodious dwelling at Liberty Township.

Married Sunday the 10 (Oct.) at the residence of the bride's parents, by Rev. J.M. Stewart, MR. JOSEPH SEABORN to MISS IDA GILLESPIE.

LOUIS W. CAREY died Sunday at his home in Seneca, S.C. He leaves a wife and 2 children. J.P. CAREY is a brother.

PROF. C.T. MILLER will teach in the Griffin Ebenezer School.

A.T. WINCHESTER of Eastatoe, S.C. will accept a position with W.W. AIKEN in Greenville, S.C.

MR. JOSEPH C. DODGENS says he has a rich gold and silver mine on his land on the head waters of Cane Creek in Pickens Co., 7 miles from Toxaway, North Carolina. His Post Office is Hazel, S.C. *Keowee Courier*

Locals from Easley
MR. JOHN B. ROBINSON purchased the beautiful home of MR. W.J. ROARKE last Saturday on the east side of Main Street and will move there soon.
MR. W.H. HAMILTON has purchased MISS TEXIE BOWEN'S house and moved here to get the advantage of our excellent schools.
MR. CLINGMAN HARRIS formerly of this county but more recently foreman in *The Spartanburg Herald* office will move here this week (details).
J.H. MARTIN has again opened a store on Sardine Avenue. He recently moved his family to a house on Spring Street vacated some time since by MRS. WILLIAMS.
MISSES DUCKWORTH and WYATT have opened their millinery establishment.

Married Wednesday at the Easley Presbyterian Church by Rev. J.R. Riley, MR. JOHN B. ROBINSON of Easley, S.C. and MISS ESTELLE BOGGS eldest daughter of the late REV. W.K. BOGGS. The bride was given in marriage by her uncle HON. J.E. BOGGS. MRS. E.C. ROBINSON is the mother of the groom (details).

Clemson College will have an exhibit at the State Fair.

Pickens Co., S.C. Petit Jury List.

Pickens Co., S.C. Sheriff's Sale - R.F. WYAT (sic) vs JOHN G. WYATT, et al. Steam engine, cotton gin, etc. to be sold.

AD - B.M. GRIFFIN, Livery Stable and General Store, at LEWIS' old stand.

Issue of: Thursday 21 October 1897:

Columbia State - 14 October
Death of EX-SENATOR THOMAS J. ROBERTSON, Columbia, S.C. He died yesterday (details).

PERRY F. THORNLEY left Pickens last week for Atlanta, Georgia where he will engage in business.

Born a son the 12 (Oct.) to MR. and MRS. ELBERT CHRISTOPHER.

WILL LOOPER a student in a school in Saluda, North Carolina is visiting his mother MRS. MATILDA LOOPER of Mica, S.C.

R.L.R. BENTZ has added a shoe department to his dry goods business.

A.E. GRIFFIN has rented the LEWIS WAREHOUSE fronting on Anne Street and will run a first class beef market.

Cross Plains News
JOHN O. SHECK is erecting a commodious residence on the Greenville and Pumpkintown Road for J.K. LATHEM.

Liberty
DES W. HOPKINS has opened a shoe shop here.
L.R. SMITH and family have moved to Donaldsville, South Carolina not Dacusville, South Carolina.

Pickens Co., S.C. Jury List.

AD - DUCKWORTH & PALMER, Proprietors, Factory Making Wagons and Buggies. Located in new quarters near the livery stable.

Issue of: Thursday 28 October 1897:

Sketch -"GENERAL HAMPTON P. BEE". He was born the 22 July 1822 in S.C. and died the 3 Oct. 1897 at his home in San Antonio, Texas. General Bee served in the Confederate Army. *San Antonio Daily Express*

Six Mile
Born a boy to MR. and MRS. JOHN SARGENT (no date given).
MERCK & WATSON'S store is complete and will open soon.
MR. NASH died the 19 October of cholera-morbus at the home of his brother-in-law MR. DAVID RIGGINS. He was buried at Six Mile Burying Ground. Mr. Nash leaves a widow.

Born a son the 21 (Oct.) to REV. and MRS. L.L. INABINETT.

Rock steps have been put in from McFALL'S STORE to RICHEY'S STORE.

MR. CLING HARRIS of Spartanburg, S.C. will move to Pickens and engage in Life Insurance Business.

Married the 17 October 1897 at the residence of Rev. J.H. Stone, MR. JOHN F. HUNT of Pickens Co. to MISS ORAH STRIBLING of Oconee Co., S.C.

Married the 20 (Oct.) at the residence of the bride's parents MR. and MRS. SHERIFF BROWN of Pearl, S.C., by Rev. Charles L. Craig., MR. W.E. HENDRICKS to MISS LIDA BROWN.

REV. M.L. JONES and MR. JOHN W. WILLIAMS have completed the dwelling of Mr. Williams of Dacusville, S.C.

Married Sunday the 24 (Oct.) at the residence of Rev. M.L. Jones at that old home near Field, S.C., MR. SAMUEL COX only son of MR. GEORGE COX of Dacusville Township and MISS LOU HENDRICKS second daughter of MR. D.E. HENDRICKS of Field.

Married last night at the residence of the bride's father CAPTAIN W.P. HUNT by Rev. W.J. Langston, C.A. POWER and MISS MAUDE HUNT. They will live in Owens, South Carolina. *Greenville News* - 21 Oct.

Pickens Co., S.C. Court Sessions Report - Criminal cases (details).

GEORGE M. PULLMAN the famous PALACE CAR MANUFACTURER died the 19 (Oct.) in Chicago, Illinois at the age of 66 years.

AD - J.H. MORGAN & BROS., Greenville, S.C. CHARLES M. BOWEN of Pickens Court House is a clerk.

AD - A.M. MORRIS, Selling General Merchandise. Located in a new brick store, Pickens, S.C.

Issue of: Thursday 4 November 1897:

Article - "History of STANDARD OIL".

A.D. GAILLARD who was born near Pendleton, S.C. died. He served in the Confederate Army (details). *Greenville Mountaineer*

Olga News
G.C. FOSTER has moved into his new house near his mother. B.A. FOSTER and family moved to his home near Looper, S.C. last week.

Married the 14 (Oct.), MRS. MAGGIE PICKENS of Anderson, S.C. and J. MONROE SMITH of Eastman, Georgia.

MRS. AIKEN has moved to her farm near Maynard, S.C. from Cedar Rock, S.C.

A.C. HARRIS and family of Spartanburg, S.C. have moved into the house of DR. G.W. EARLE on Main Street.

Married at the residence of J.B. Jameson, N.P., WILL NESBITT to KANIE BARTON both colored.

HARLIN SIMMONS who lives near Ambler Post Office, S.C. had his house burned last week.

Pickens Co., S.C. Salesday:
J.J. SITTON, Cashier vs R.L. GILLESPIE. 256 acres on waters of Little Eastatoe sold to J.E. BOGGS for $250.
W.M. PRINCE, et al. vs JAMES SPEARMAN. 55 acres on waters of Crow Creek sold to J.P. CAREY for $35.

J.M. BARR, Administrator vs SAMUEL BARR, et al. 50 acres sold to J.P. CAREY for $710.
R.F. WYATT vs JOHN G. WYATT, et al. Steam engine, cotton gin, feeder and condenser, one press, one saw mill and fixtures sold to J.E. BOGGS for $30.

REV. JAMES T. BURDINE and MRS. BURDINE died Thursday the 28 October near Sunny Dale, S.C. both of about the age of 52 years. He shot her then himself. He was a Baptist preacher. They were buried from Holly Springs Church of which they were members. Rev. and Mrs. Burdine leave 1 child ROBERT BURDINE (details).

Liberty
JOHN HUTCHINS blacksmith at BEVERLEY GRANITE WORKS received a telegram last Sunday telling of the death of his father-in-law (name not given) in Jefferson Co., Georgia.
MRS. HARVE SMITH died last Wednesday at the age of about 35 years and was buried at Ruhamah Cemetery. She leaves a husband, several children and several brothers.

Pickens Co., S.C. Sheriff's Sale:
S.A. GOSNELL vs MARY A. SMITH. 10 to 15 acres on the west side of Pumpkintown Road to be sold.
C.L. HOLLINGSWORTH vs AMANDA HUNT, et al. 59 acres to be sold.

Pickens Co., S.C. Notice to Debtors and Creditors - Estate of JOHN STEWART, deceased - SUSAN STEWART vs ROBERT STEWART, et al.

Issue of: Thursday 11 November 1897:

The Confederate Rolls - Companies that are needed to complete the Roster of Soldiers from the State of South Carolina (details).

New Regime at Clemson College (details).

Pickens Co., S.C. Clerk's Sale - Court of Common Pleas:
Land to be sold Salesday in December.
NEWTON OATS, et al. vs RUFUS C. ROPER, et al.
Lot #1 - 29 3/10 acres, Lot #2 - 23 acres, Lot #3 - 30 1/2 acres, Lot #4 - 26 1/8 acres, Lot #5 - 31 1/5 acres, Lot #6 - 2 1/2 acres, Lot #7 - 15 7/10 acres, Lot #8 - 46 3/4 acres, Lot #9 - 24 2/3 acres, Lot #10 - 34 1/2 acres and Lot #11 - 28 2/5 acres.
Estate of JAMES F. FREEMAN. EMPS FREEMAN, et al. vs W.B. FREEMAN, et al.
Tract #1 - 37 1/2 or 31 1/2 acres, Tract #2 - 30 acres, Tract #3 - 36 1/2 acres, Tract #4 - 44 acres, Tract #5 - 41 1/2 acres , Tract #6 49 1/2 acres, Tract #7 31 acres and Tract #8 - 33 1/4 acres.
SUSAN STEWART vs ROBERT STEWART, et al.

60 acres on Mile Creek waters to be sold.
JAMES B. JONES, et al. vs M.L. JONES, et al.
216 acres in Dacusville Township to be sold.

Pickens Co., S.C. Final Settlement - Estate of MRS. S.A.R. ORR, deceased by W.W. ORR, Administrator.

Rock steps to be put in from the POST OFFICE to the COURT HOUSE.

Photographs of Pickens Rifles are now ready.

Married the 3 (Nov.) by Rev. J.T. Clyde. MR. W.A. CLYDE of Easley, S.C. to MISS MAJOR of Greenwood, S.C.

Married the 31 October 1897, MR. ADOLPHUS BAGWELL to MISS EMMA PACE by Magistrate Jones all of Pickens.

W.R. MAJOR and family who live near town are moving to Piedmont, S.C.

The infant daughter of MR. and MRS. A.C. SUTHERLAND died the 4 (Nov.) and was buried at Holly Springs Church.

PRIESTLY MAXWELL living near Easley Bridge died Thursday the 4 (Nov.) of paralysis at the age of 62 years. Mr. Maxwell is survived by 4 sisters. He was buried at Pendleton, S.C. the old home of Mr. Maxwell.

Pickens Co., S.C. Commissioner's Meeting and Report. A four room cottage to be built for the sheriff at the jail.

Liberty
MR. ARCH SMITH who lost his wife last week has a daughter very sick.

Pickens Co., S.C. Clerk's Sale - Estate of RUFUS and MARY OATS. NEWTON OATS vs RUFUS C. (or S.C.) ROPER, et al. Eleven Tracts of land to be sold.

Pickens Co., S.C. Citation Notice - J.R. BURDINE applied for Letters of Administration for the estate of J.T. BURDINE, deceased.

Issue of: Thursday 18 November 1897:

Pickens Co., S.C. Clerk's Sales - Property of JAMES G. FREEMAN, deceased by W.B. FREEMAN, Administrator (details).

Pickens Co., S.C. Citation Notice - HENRY BRIGGS applied for Letters of Administration of the estate of PRIESTLY E. MAXWELL, deceased.

MRS. MARY LOOPER of Mica, S.C. moved into her new house recently.

Born a son to MR. and MRS. HENRY LANGSTON the 11 (Nov.).

MISS FLORENCE BOWEN is teaching at Cateechee, S.C.

FRANK E. COX is now storekeeper and gauger for MR. MARK HUNT who is running a GOVERNMENT DISTILLERY.

Married the 14 (Nov.) at the residence of Rev. M.L. Jones, MR. JOHN EVATT to MISS CANNA BYARS all of Pickens County.

W.W. CLAYTON of Rice, S.C. died the 14 (Nov.) of dropsy at the age of 65 years and was buried at the family burying ground. He leaves 1 daughter.

Born a son to MR. and MRS. WILLIAM NALLEY near town.

MR. J.M. WILLIAMS of Cedar Rock, S.C. has a new home.

GEORGE T. JOHNSON son of the late REV. THOMAS JOHNSON of Crow Creek, S.C. died the 13 (Nov.) at his home in Pelzer, S.C. He was a member of the Methodist Church and was buried from Mt. Bethel Methodist Church.

List of people having pensions in the Clerk of Court's Office, Pickens Co., S.C.:

Pensioners   (List as given)

Males	Females
W.J. KING	RACHAEL HENDRICKS
J.F. SMITH	MARY J. KING
W.D. DAVIS	MRS. ELLIOTT WILLIAMS
I.L. SMITH	ELIZABETH HOLDER
LEWIS HARRISON	JOANNA ELLENBURG
EZEKIAL HUNT	ABLE SANDERS
C.T. HOLCOMBE	KEZIAH DUNWOODY
JOSEPH DAVIS	N.E. BALLENTINE
	MICHAIL ROGERS

Married yesterday at the home of the bride's father W.P. HUNT by Rev. William A. Rogers pastor of Buncombe St. Methodist Church, Greenville, S.C., T.C. ROBINSON of Pickens and MISS CORRIE HUNT of this city. *Greenville News* - 11 November.

ARCH SMITH married the WIDOW TRAMMELL last Sunday, the Rev. W.H. Workman officiating.

The year old daughter of ARCH SMITH died last week and was buried at Ruhamah Burying Ground.

Issue of: Thursday 25 November 1897:

DR. THOMAS LAWTON LEWIS died at his home in Greenville, S.C. on Monday of peritonitis.

Married the 11 (Nov.) at the residence of the mother of the bride MRS. LUCY FOLGER of Easley, S.C., by Rev. J.R. Riley, MISS ESTELLE FOLGER to MR. WILLIAM STEWART telegraph operator of the SOUTHERN RAILROAD.

W.H.H. CHILDRESS died the 19 (Nov.) at the age of 44 years and was buried at Cross Roads Baptist Church of which he was a member. He leaves a wife.

Pickens Co., S.C. Tax Assessment Notice.

Pickens Co., S.C. Notice to Debtors and Creditors - Estate of MRS. L.A. ALEXANDER, deceased by J.M. STEWART, Administrator.

Issue of: Thursday 2 December 1897:

Easley
MR. EDWARD NALLEY is building a 4 room cottage on Hudson Street.
A. JAMISON sold his farm on the Greenville Road to a MR. McCOY of Greenville, S.C. He has rented and moved in the TROTTER house.
F.M. COUCH "the butcher" will move in the TALLEY house in the eastern part of town.

WILL BARR has completed a new dwelling near CEMP JOHNSON'S and it will be rented.

Easley
MISS EMILY JOHNSON is teaching at Roberts, Anderson Co., S.C.
JOHN WYATT father of MAYOR WYATT will soon occupy the dwelling recently vacated by W.A. HAMILTON.
DR. and MRS. E.F. WYATT of Lavonia, Georgia are visiting his parents. Ed (Dr. Wyatt) married a MISS COX of Athens, Georgia.
REV. W.T. WELDON has accepted at call to the Baptist Church.
MR. S. HOMER GOSSETT has a position with SOUTHERN RAILROAD in Buford, Georgia. He has been promoted to the dispatcher's office in Atlanta, Georgia. Mr. Gossett is visiting his parents here.
CAPTAIN A.W. HODGENS who is working for LEA BROS. & CO. of Philadelphia, Pennsylvania is visiting family.
The PICKENS LAND CO. sold the JONES place near the Baptist Church to MRS. J.L. ROARK. She will move there as soon and T.K. HUGENS can move out.

Born an heiress the 27 (Nov.) to MR. and MRS. R.A. HESTER.

Married Sunday the 28 November by M.F. Hester, N.P., THOMAS DUKE to EMALINE McKINZIE both colored.

MR. CAMERON and family of Fairfield Co., S.C. have moved into the house of W.T. MEARS and will make Pickens their home.

MR. R.E. YOUNGE and family of Fairfield Co., S.C. moved to town.

Married the 18 November at the residence of the bride's parents, by Rev. B. Holder, MR. ROBERT RIGDON to MISS L.D. PORTER.

Died EX-SHERIFF JOAB MAULDIN (see issue of the 9 December 1897 for details).

H.G. ANDERSON, colored, killed BUTLER ANDERSON, colored (details).

DOC CASSELL, son of BEN CASSELL, died at Table Rock, S.C. Saturday from a hunting accident. He was 20 years old.

G.H. HENDRICKS is now living near Easley, S.C.

MR. A.C. HARRIS has moved into the house of DR. G.W. EARLE on the corner of Main and Factory Streets.

Married the 28 (Nov.) at the residence of the bride's parents MR. and MRS. S.R. DAY by Rev. J.M. Stewart, MR. GEORGE GRIFFIN to MISS ZARA DAY.

CAPTAIN H.C. GRADY and family who live near town will soon leave for Washington, D.C. where they will make their home.

Married the 30 (Nov.) at the residence of the bride's parents, by Rev. J.M. Stewart, MR. M.M. HOLDER to MISS MARY MAULDIN daughter of MR. and MRS. A.M. MAULDIN of Easley, S.C.

MISS JANIE STEWART, daughter of the late THOMAS STEWART, died at the home at Nine Times Post Office, S.C. the 25 (Nov.) and was buried from Shady Grove Baptist Church of which she was a member.

Married in Anderson, S.C. at the home of the bride's mother, by Rev. W.R. Richardson, MISS CANZADA FISHER to MR. D.B. FINNEY of Pickens.

Easley
Some stores were closed part of Thanksgiving Day.
MISS MARIE RICHARDSON who is attending college in Greenville, S.C. is visiting her father E.B. RICHARDSON.

MRS. LIZZIE HYDE of Cincinnati, Ohio is visiting her brother E.B. RICHARDSON.

Married near Dacusville, S.C. at the home of the bride's mother MRS. ELIZA AIKEN, her second daughter MISS MATTIE WILLIAMS to MR. W.M. HENRY of Brevard, North Carolina, by Rev. T.C. Holsclaw (details).

Liberty, S.C. Land Sales - Estate of THOMAS E. WILLARD, deceased by W.O. WILLARD and T.G. BOGGS, Executors.

Pickens Co., S.C. Tax Assessment Notice.

Issue of: Thursday 9 December 1897:

J.W. ADCOX has charge of the mail route between here and Easley, S.C.

J.T. ANTHONY is running a beef market in the rear of B.M. GRIFFIN'S STORE.

DANIEL WINCHESTER of Hazel, S.C. has purchased a nice farm from JAS. NIMMONS on the Eastatoe.

EX-JUDGE COTHRAN died in New York, Sunday. His remains were sent to Abbeville, S.C. for burial.

Married the 6 (Dec.) by Rev. W.B. Singleton, EARL HENDRICKS to MISS LULA WALDROP, both colored.

The general merchandise goods of O.P. BRIGHT will be sold at Public Auction.

S.P. BURBAGE died the 4 (Dec.) at his home in Greenville, S.C. at the age of about 62 years. He was a merchant in that place.

Married the 1 (Dec.) at the residence of the bride's grandmother MRS. JOHN I. WILLIAMS by Rev. W.C. Seaborn, MISS REBECCA SMITH to MR. CHARLES R. FERGUSON.

Married the 1 (Dec.) at the residence of the bride's parents in Denver, S.C., by Rev. Mike McGee, DR. R. BOLT DAY to MISS KATE ESKEW. Dr. Day is the son of ELIAS DAY who lives in Easley, S.C. Dr. Day has been in Denver for awhile practicing medicine.

J.J. LEWIS' plantation near town burned last Thursday.

Pickens Co., S.C. Salesday:
OATS vs ROPER. 29 3/10 acres sold to A.G. WYATT for $1,270; 23 acres sold to JASPER OATS for $500; 30 1/2 acres to JASPER OATS for $415; 36 1/2 acres sold to J.E. OATS for $600; 24 1/2 acres sold to A.G. WYATT for $780; 15 7/10

acres sold to FRANCES A. SHECK for $610; 46 3/4 acres sold to JASPER OATS for $1,000; 24 2/3 acres sold to JASPER OATS for $375; 28 2/5 acres sold to W.R. OATS for $850; 1 1/2 acres, the family grave yard, sold to JASPER OATS for $5.00.
SUSAN STEWART vs ROBERT STEWART. 60 acres sold to ROBERT STEWART for $430.
ROBERT TROTTER vs THOMAS TROTTER. 127 acres sold to I.A. WHITMIRE for $530; 102 1/2 acres sold to I.A. WHITMIRE for $75; 97 1/2 acres sold to J.E. HAGOOD for $75.
LIDA OWNES vs AMANDA HUNT. 41 1/2 acres to be continued.
HOLLINGSWORTH vs AMANDA HUNT. 59 acres sold to J.J. MORGAN for $870.
S.A. GOSNELL vs MARY A. SMITH. 10 to 15 acres sold to C.H. HOLLINGSWORTH FOR $81.
W.A. McDANIEL vs REDEN RACKLEY. 176 acres sold to C.M. HART for $35.
W.A. RICHARDSON vs E.M. ALEXANDER. 50 acres sold to R.M. RICHARDSON for $51.
HAGOOD, BRUCE & CO. vs ELIZABETH STANSELL. 150 acres sold to J.McD. BRUCE for $52.
J.J. SITTON, Cashier vs R.M. STEWART. 273 acres sold to J.E. BOGGS for $106.

JOAB MAULDIN died the 30 November 1897 at his residence 2 miles south of Pickens at the age of 58 years. He was buried at the Pickens Cemetery with MASONIC HONORS. Mr. Mauldin leaves a widow and 9 children (see issue of the 2 Dec. 1897).

Liberty
J.J. WAKELIN has moved to his new residence.

C.E. HAMILTON will move back to his farm near Majors' Post Office, S.C.

JAY BOGGS died last Thursday and was buried at Ruhamah Cemetery. (JAY L. BOGGS, born 12 June 1862, died 2 Dec. 1897 - Pickens Co., S.C. Cemetery Survey, Vol. 1, p. 177).

Issue of: Thursday 16 December 1897:

Story - "An Echo at Antietam".

Article - "Tribute to ROBERT E. LEE".

Mica
JAMES RICHARDSON has erected a nice little cottage.

Pickens Co., S.C. Citation Notice - Estate of MRS. BETTIE BOYD RAINES, deceased. JAMES RAINES applied for Letters of Administration.

Pickens Co., S.C. Citation Notice - I.M. MAULDIN applied for Letters of Administration of the estate of JOAB MAULDIN.

MRS. McKINLEY, mother of PRESIDENT McKINLEY, died the 12 (Dec.) at her home in Canton, Ohio.

J.M. PHILLIPS of Central, S.C. bought the stock of O.P. BRIGHT.

The six year old son of MR. and MRS. GUS DURHAM of Nine Times, S.C. died the 7 (Dec.) and was buried at Secona Cemetery.

MRS. SALLIE LESLEY wife of W. ANDERSON LESLEY died Monday at her home 2 miles south of Easley, S.C. at the age of 83 years. She leaves a husband and several children. (SALLIE LESLEY, born 18 Feb. 1816, died 13 Dec. 1897, buried Zion Methodist Church Cemetery - Pickens Co., S.C. Cemetery Survey, Vol. 3, p. 71).

MRS. ZEILA ROBERTSON TALLEY of Oconee Co., S.C. died the 9 (Dec.) at her home at the age of 45 years. She was a member of the Baptist Church and was buried in the family burying ground. Mrs. Talley leaves 5 children.

Liberty
The infant son of F.M. MORRIS died the 8 (Dec.) and was buried at Roberts Church, Anderson Co., S.C.

Easley
MISS LIZZIE MAULDIN has purchased the millinery business of MISSES DUCKWORTH and WYATT.

PRESIDENT McKINLEY'S Message (details).

Issue of: Thursday 23 December 1897:

The SOUTHERN RAILROAD train will come to Pickens in January (details). *News and Courier*, Charleston, S.C.

LOUIS WERNICKE died at his home in Pickensville, S.C. last week at the age of about 65 years. He was buried in Easley, S.C. (LOUIS WERNICKE, born 3 Dec. 1821, died 15 Dec. 1897, buried Easley City Cemetery - Pickens Co., S.C. Cemetery Survey, Vol. 3, p. 51).

Married Tuesday the 7 (Dec.) by W.C. Seaborn at his residence, MR. ALEXANDER SMITH to MISS ANNA BANKS both of Pickens County.

EX-GOVERNOR EVANS married the 15 (Dec.) MISS EMILY PLUME of Waterbury, Connecticut (see issue of the 14 Oct. 1897).

Married Wednesday the 15 (Dec.) at the residence of the bride's father MR. SAMUEL NEAL near Central, S.C., by Rev. W.C. Seaborn, MISS FLORENCE NEAL to MR. JOHN TEAT of Franklin Co., Georgia.

Liberty - 20 December 1897

F.M. MORRIS will move to his old home near Roberts, Anderson Co., S.C. He has bought part of the place.

MR. THOMAS RANKIN and ROARK of Slabtown, S.C. bought a lot in town and plan to build a dwelling.

T.C. ROBINSON has a 1/2 acre lot on Garvin St. for sale.

Married Thursday the 15 (Dec.) at the residence of the bride's mother in Greenville Co., S.C., by Rev. J.W. Shell, MISS HATTIE HARRIS daughter of MRS. M.J. HARRIS to MR. J.T. HARRIS of Glassy Knob, North Carolina. Miss Harris is a sister of T.D. HARRIS merchant here.

Methodist Conference Appointments (details).

Born the 20 (Dec.) an heir to MR. and MRS. GEORGE BREAZELE of near town.

Issue of: Thursday 30 December 1897:

Liberty

V.E. HUDGENS, F.M. MORRIS and MRS. ROE have moved out of town. JOHN HUTCHENS, DES HOPKINS and --- BARNES have moved in town.

MRS. EMILY HUNTER widow of the late N. HUNTER died Sunday with apoplexy. Services were held at the Presbyterian Church with burial at the family burying ground 2 miles below town. Mrs. Hunter leaves 2 children.

Married last week at the residence of the bride's parents near Mica, S.C., by Rev. Thomas Looper, MR. GRADY JONES to MISS MAGGIE KAY.

Married at Olga, S.C. the 23 (Dec.) at the residence of Rev. J.E. Seaborn, MR. JAMES MEDLIN to MISS NANCY FORTNER.

Married the 23 (Dec.) at the residence of the bride's parents MR. and MRS. JOSEPH PACE by Rev. J.M. Stewart, MR. J.M. WARD to MISS SUNIE PACE.

Married the 23 (Dec.) at the residence of the bride's parents, by Rev. W.L. Richards, MR. O.B. MARTIN of Greenville, S.C. to MISS DORA COOK.

Married the 22 (Dec.) at the residence of the bride's parents MR. and MRS. JNO. L. GRAVELEY of Sunny Dale, S.C., by Rev. J.M. Stewart, MR. WILLIAM STEWART to MISS DALLA (sic) GRAVELEY.

Married Sunday the 26 (Dec.) at the residence of the bride's father MR. B.L. HENDRICKS of Field, S.C., by M.F. Hester, N.P., MR. JAMES COOPER to MISS LIDA HENDRICKS.

Married Sunday the 26 (Dec.) at the residence of the groom's parents, by F.E. Cox, N.P., MR. LEMUEL DUCKWORTH to MISS MYRA MURPHREE.

Married the 23 (Dec.) at the residence of Rev. J.R. Riley, MR. ELMER FOLGER of Easley, S.C. to MISS LENA HIGGINS daughter of MR. and MRS. J.A. HIGGINS.

MRS. SANDERS wife of JACK SANDERS died Tuesday the 21 (Dec.) at her home in Greenville, S.C. at the age of about 40 years. She was a member of the Baptist Church and was buried from the Flat Rock Baptist Church. Mrs. Sanders leaves a husband and 5 children.

Pickens Co., S.C. Salesday:
The following tracts of land to be sold in January.
LIDA OWENS, et al. vs AMANDA HUNT, et al. Tract #1 - 41 1/2 acres; Tract #2 - 62 acres in Dacusville, S.C.
W.A. McDANIEL, C.C.G. vs REDEN RACKLEY. 21 acres of land, being part of the DEAN tract.

REV. W.M. HARDEN and family left last week for Lexington, S.C. which is his new field of ministry.

Married Thursday at Ruhamah School by Rev. J.R. Riley, MISS FANNIE MOORE to MR. W.A. BURDETT of Piedmont, S.C. They will live in Piedmont, S.C. (details).

For Sale - 1 house and a 5 acre lot. The house has 5 rooms and 3 fireplaces and is located on the corner of Main and Liberty Streets, by J.H. AMBLER, Ambler, South Carolina.

NO ISSUES AVAILABLE FOR 1898

THE PEOPLE'S JOURNAL 1899

Issue of: Thursday 5 January 1899:
(The first two issues of 1899 give the year as 1898)

CADET LEO GILLESPIE is visiting his parents.

CADET ROSS O'DELL is visiting relatives and friends.

DR. W.F. AUSTIN will be in Pickens the 10th, 11th and 12th of January.

PROF. B.F. ROBERTSON and CADET SAM ROBERTSON spent the holidays with their parents.

Married the 28 Dec.(1898), MR. LUTHER BURNS to MISS DORA HANES. Magistrate A.A. Jones officiated.

Married the 21 Dec. (1898) at the residence of Rev. Seabrook Atkinson, MR. B.D. DUNCAN and MISS ELLENOE EVANS.

SGT. JAMES T. JONES of Battery C, 7th Ill. Light Artillery has been visiting his father, W.D. JONES of Briggs, S.C. He left the 20 Dec. 1898 for Puerto Rico.

Married Sunday the 25 Dec. 1898 at the residence of the bride's father WARREN TURNER by G.A. Ellis, MR. JOHN NIX to MISS AMANDA TURNER.

Married at MR. BENNETT SATTERFIELD'S the 25 Dec. 1898 by Rev. W.G. Mauldin, MR. LAWRENCE MERCK and MISS LIZZIE SATTERFIELD. Also married at the same time were JOHN PERRY and MISS MAGGIE ROSS.

Married at the residence of the bride's parents MR. and MRS. RICHARD HILL in Easley, S.C. the 21 Dec. 1898, by Rev. J.R. Riley, MR. JOHN L. THORNLEY, JR. to MISS BIDDIE HILL. A reception was given by THOMAS HILL, brother of the bride at Welford (details).

Married Wednesday the 21 Dec. 1898 by Rev. J.M. Stewart at the residence of the bride's parents, JOB L. PARSONS to MISS NANNIE MURPHREE (details).

MRS. AMANDA KNIGHT nee ROBINSON died the 22 Dec. 1898. She was the wife of W.W. KNIGHT. Mrs. Knight was of Scotch-Irish extraction and has been a member of Carmel Church for 67 years. She was buried at Carmel (details). *People's Advocate*

Pickens Co., S.C. Notice to Creditors and Debtors - Estate of CASLEY W. CUMMINGS, deceased by J.M. STEWART, Administrator.

Pickens Co., S.C. Notice to Creditors and Debtors - Estate of W.B. SINGLETON, deceased by H.D. SINGLETON, Executor.

Issue of: Thursday 12 January 1899:

REV. JOHN B. ADGER, D.D. died the 3 Jan. at Pendleton, S.C. at the age of 88 years. He was born the 2 Dec. 1810 and married MISS ELIZABETH K. SHREWSBURG. Rev. Adger was a member of the old Adger family of Charleston, S.C. (see issue of the 19 Jan. 1899).

T.J. MAULDIN came to Pickens on Thursday to attend the funeral of his uncle COL. C.L. HOLLINGSWORTH.

Married at the residence of Rev. J.W. Sheriff, MISS ARTIE ROBINSON and MR. JULIUS SMITH both of this county (date not given).

Married the 24 Dec. 1898, Dacusville, S.C. at the home of the bride, MISS HETTIE ROBINSON to SAMUEL MAULDIN of Anderson County, S.C.

A large barn of JOHN FERGUSON fronting the residence of J.M. WARD burned last Friday morning.

DR. J.L. BOLT offers his services to the people of Pickens. He can be found at HENDRICKS' BOARDING HOUSE.

COL. COLUMBUS L. HOLLINGSWORTH died Friday evening last about 12 P.M. He was a lawyer from Pickens. Service and burial were at the Presbyterian Church by Dr. J.R. Riley.

Pickens Co., S.C. Sheriff's Sale - W.O. STEWART, et al. vs P.E. ALEXANDER. 1,000 acres on the branches of Big Eastatoe Creek to be sold.

Issue of: Thursday 19 January 1899:

B.E. GRANDY moved into his new residence on Factory Street.

DR. J.R. RILEY moved into a residence recently vacated by MRS. J.C. JENNINGS.

WESTER KAY, formerly of this county, now of Greenville, S.C. died at his home the 14 Jan. of pneumonia. He left a wife and 1 or 2 children.

HENRY COUCH died at his residence, 3 miles south of Easley, S.C., the 9 Jan. at the age of 58 years. He was a member of the Methodist Church and leaves 7 sisters.

Two Negro Regiments, encamped at Macon, Georgia are to be mustered out because of their general incapacity for military duty and because of the continual rioting and murderous conduct of a number of their members.

REV. JOHN B. ADGER, D.D., died Tuesday night the 3 Jan. at his residence in Pendleton, S.C at the age of 87 years (see issue of the 12 Jan. 1899).

JAMES B. WILLIAMS, the murderer of CHARLES P. POTTS, who was sentenced to be hung the 27 Jan., died in his cell in the Greenville, S.C. jail last Friday the 14 Jan. of dropsy. He was a native of this county and a son of MR. GUS WILLIAMS.

Whitewright, Texas
Married 25 Dec. 1898 at the residence of the bride's father MR. JAMES HENDRICKS, MR. JOHN DONAGHEY of this city and MISS EMMA HENDRICKS of Liberty, Pickens Co., S.C. John Donaghey is our popular south side grocer.

Issue of: Thursday 26 January 1899:

The new school building has been completed and is now occupied by Pickens High School.

J.K. LATHEM was in town last Friday and made the Final Settlement of the estate of MRS. NANNIE L. LATHEM.

HARDY GILSTRAP, a Pickens County boy of the 2nd S.C. Regt., having received an honorable discharge, returned home Saturday to live the quiet and peaceful life of a civilian.

Stockholder's meeting of NORRIS COTTON MILLS CO. will be held 28 Feb. 1899. D.K. NORRIS, President and Treasurer.

Looper's Notes
Married the 15 Jan. at the residence of the groom, by W.N. Hughes, MR. JOHN T. COOK of Dacusville, S.C. to MISS MAZILDA (sic) HOLDER of North Carolina.
Married at the residence of the bride's father MR. JASPER JONES by W.N. Hughes, MR. HENRY WADE to MISS MALINDA JONES, both of Greenville Co., S.C.

JOSEPH H. MURPHREE native of this county but later of Piedmont, S.C. died at his home last Friday the 20 Jan. at the age of 60 years of pneumonia. He was a manufacturer of wool in Pickens County.

Issue of: Thursday 2 February 1899:

Article - "Account of the Civil War".

Pickens Co., S.C. Public Schools (details).

Married at Mt. Bethel Methodist Episcopal Church on Sunday the 29 Jan. 1899, by John T. Lewis, MR. JENKINS A. HUDSON to

MISS LARTIE (LOTTIE) SPEARMAN, eldest daughter of MR. and MRS. W.D. SPEARMAN.

Married at the residence of J.M. Hallums, MR. WILLIAM GREEN and MISS JULIA JAMES daughter of JOHN JAMES of Cateechee, S.C. R.T. Hallums officiated.

MRS. J.N. McELRATH of Easley, S.C died the 28 Jan. 1899 of pneumonia at the age of 73 years. She leaves a husband and one son.

Article - "Where Our Pioneers and Heroes Sleep". Information on the Old Stone Church. DR. THOMAS REESE, D.D. a native of Pennsylvania died 1796 at the age of 54 years. He is buried at the Old Stone Church. The Old Stone Church Cemetery Commission desires to build a fence. Send contributions to REV. B.P. REID, Pendleton, S.C. *Anderson Advocate*

J.M. NASH of Atlanta, Georgia, railroad conductor, married MISS ZEUELLA McCORKLE daughter of J.M. McCORKLE, proprietor of the CENTRAL HOTEL, the 25 Jan at 8:00 P.M. by Rev. B.P. Reed of Pendleton, S.C. (details).

Article - "The Use of Monkeys as Cotton Pickers".

Pickens Co., S.C. Citation Notice - J.J. CHASTAIN applied for Letters of Administration for the estate of J.R. BURDINE, deceased.

Pickens Co., S.C. Administrator's Sale - To be sold the 23 Feb. 1899 the property of C.L. HOLLINGSWORTH, deceased. Horses, mules, cattle, etc. by MRS. M.A. HOLLINGSWORTH and R.G. SMITH, Administrators.

Issue of: Thursday 9 February 1899:

ISAAC BENTLEY convicted of murder in this county was pardoned last Wednesday by GOV. ELLERBE. He reached his home in Pelzer, S.C. the next day and died of consumption on Saturday morning. Bentley leaves a wife and little girl (details).

THOMAS A. McMAHAN who lives near Easley, S.C. died at his home Wednesday the 1 Feb. 1899 at age 48 years of Bright's disease. He leaves a wife and five children. The service was conducted by Rev. Dr. Riley. (T.A. McMAHAN, born 22 May 1850, died 1 Feb. 1899, buried McMahan Family Cemetery - Pickens Co., S.C. Cemetery Survey, Vol. 1, p. 156).

Married at the residence of the bride's parents CAPTAIN and MRS. J.L. THORNLEY the 1 Feb. 1899, MISS OLIVIA THORNLEY and R.E. OLIVER of Langley, S.C. (details).

Central Dots
R.G. GAINS has another son.
MRS. THOMAS JOHNSON died the 31 Jan. 1899 and was buried at Mt. Zion Church. The funeral was conducted by Rev. H.M. Allen. She leaves a husband and several children.
MISS NANNIE BLACKERBY died at her home the 1 Feb. 1899 and was buried at Mt. Zion by Rev. C.C. Fricks. She leaves a brother and 2 sisters.

The Confederate Flag is said to have originated with MRS. CATHERINE LADD. She is still living at the age of 91 years.

New Store - MAHON & ARNOLD located at 213 North Main Street in Pickens, S.C. (details).

MRS. E. LADD died Monday the 30 Jan. 1899 at her home in Blairs, S. C. with burial at Solan Church. She was the mother of MRS. J.D. CURETON.

Issue of: Thursday 16 February 1899:

A daughter was born to MR. and MRS. J.M. STEWART the 11 February.

EARLE and RETT MAULDIN came home from Texas where they have been for only a short time.

MR. CLAYTON NEWTON married MISS ELLA MILLER, at the residence of the bride's father MR. IRVIN MILLER on Wednesday the 8 (Feb. 1899), by Rev. J.S. Porter.

B.J. WILLIAMS died at his residence near Cedar Rock, S.C. last Monday. He was about 75 years old and was a member of the Baptist Church. Mr. Williams leaves a wife and several children. (BENJAMIN JOSIAH WILLIAMS, born 3 Aug. 1822, died 13 Feb. 1899, buried Cross Roads Baptist Church Cemetery - Pickens County, S.C. Cemetery Survey, Vol. 1, p. 118).

DOCK BRECKINRIDGE, a young colored man, employed by SUPERVISOR LOOPER died Sunday night (froze to death - details).

Married last Tuesday evening at the residence of the bride's father JUDGE I.H. PHILPOT, THOMAS V. HELLAMS and MISS MINNIE VIRGINIA PHILPOT (details).

Pickens Co., S.C. Court of Common Pleas - T.B. BOGGS, Executor of the Estate of E.E. WILLARD, deceased vs MARY F. WILLARD, W.O. WILLARD, et al. Summons for Relief.

Issue of: Thursday 23 February 1899:

MISS MINNIE KIRKSEY closed a flourishing school in Wolf Creek School District last Friday.

CADET L.O. MAULDIN has been elected President of the Calhoun Literary Society.

Married the 22 Jan. at the residence of Mr. J.I. MADDOX, MR. THOMAS D. SMITH of Pickens Co. and MISS BESSIE WHITMIRE of Anderson Co., S.C. B.D. Garvin, Magistrate officiated.

HON. W.B. WIDEMAN of "Hit the Grit" fame will give his latest lecture entitled "Fools in the Court House at Pickens, S.C." on Thursday the 23rd at 8:00 P.M. General admission 25 cents, children 15 cents.

MR. AARON BOGGS who lives near Clemson College, S.C. has been in Atlanta, Georgia for several weeks under the treatment of DR. A.W. CALHOUN. Mr. Boggs had almost lost his sight but now thinks that Dr. Calhoun will fully restore it. *Oconee News*

Died Thursday the 16 Feb. 1899, MRS. CARRIE MARTIN wife of WARREN C. MARTIN. She was 26 years of age and leaves a husband and 2 children. Burial was at Prater's Creek Church Cemetery. Rev. W.C. Seaborn paster of Prater's Creek Church, where she was a member, conducted the service.

JAMES O. MOORE of Pendleton Township died on the streets of Anderson, S.C. He was about 60 years of age and leaves a wife and 6 children (details).

CAPTAIN JOHN McFALL of this city died last night at the home of his daughter, MRS. H.L. ODIORNE (sic), 116 Highland Ave. He was born at High Shoals, Anderson Co., S.C. and was 72 years and 12 days old. His wife was the former MISS SULLIVAN. Captain McFall was a Confederate Veteran. Surviving are three daughters, MRS. ORDIORNE (sic), MRS. W.M. SHANNON of this city and MRS. DR. HARRIS of Anderson, S.C. and two sons, A.C. McFALL of Bennettsville, S.C. and J.S. McFALL of Chattanooga, Tennessee. *Greenville News*

Card of Thanks, for kindness shown during the sickness and death of our little son HORACE, by MRS. D.H. DAVIS (details).

Issue of: Thursday 2 March 1899:

Married the 23 Feb. 1899 at the residence of the bride's father MR. J.W. EARLE, MR. AUGUSTUS G. WOOD of Union, S.C. and MISS NINA EARLE of Pickens. Rev. J.S. Porter officiated.

JAMES ROSS son of J.R. ROSS has returned home after an absence of 6 years. He spent most of the time in Oklahoma. He was in Pickens on Monday.

MR. J.H. JONES of near Field Post Office, S.C. had a 10 pound baby girl born the 22 Feb. 1899.

MISS DAISY JENKINS daughter of T.N. JENKINS died Monday at her home town, she was buried at Porter's Chapel by the side of her mother who died about 3 months ago. She was 16 years old and a member of the Methodist Church. The funeral was conducted by J.A. Porter and Rev. Mr. Burgess.

Married the 22 Feb. 1899 at the home of the bride by Rev. J.G. Schaid (sic), GEORGE J. HUNTER and MISS JULIA ANNA BRANDT daughter of MR. and MRS. L. and H. BRANDT (details). *Oconee News*

THOMAS LYNCH son of MR. GIDEON LYNCH of Sunny Dale, S.C. is in from an 11 year sojourn in Idaho. He will leave in 2 weeks for his home in the west (details - appears approaching marriage).

WILLIE AMBLER and WILLIAM GILREATH are putting up a snug little store near MAJOR AMBLER'S for the purpose of a merchandise business.

Issue of: Thursday 9 March 1899:

Pickens County, S.C. Court Cases - Criminal Cases (details).

MRS. ELIAS DAY wife of CAPT. ELIAS DAY died on Wednesday evening. She was a member of the Baptist Church and leaves a husband and 7 children (nearly all of whom are grown). She was 50 years of age and was a sister of SHERIFF BOLT of Anderson, S.C. Burial was in the family cemetery with the service being conducted by Rev. J.E. Rushton.

Married Wednesday at high noon at the home of the bride's father REV. D.W. HIOTT of Townville, S.C., MISS MYRTLE HIOTT to JOHN TERRELL of Lockhart, S.C. They came immediately to the home of the groom's father M.A. TERRELL (details).

Married the 22 Feb. at the residence of N.S. Reese, N.P., MR. W.W. BRISSEY to MISS JULIA ASTISON (sic) all of Pickens County.

Married the 22 Feb. at the residence of JULIUS MILLIKIN by N.S. Reese, N.P., MR. JOHN ROYLSTON and MISS MOLLIE BRACHER all of Pickens County.

Married at Tigerville, Greenville, Co., S.C. the 2 March 1899 at the residence of the bride's father JAMES HAYES, MISS LILA HAYES and MR. W.E. HENDRICKS by Rev. J.E. Foster.

WYATT AIKEN, after serving his country in the late war, has returned to his post as stenographer of the 8th Circuit.

ROBERT TROTTER died at his home near Dacusville, S.C. at the age of 84 years. Cause of death was dropsy. His wife and one son survive.

Article - "Ex-Slave Pension Scheme for the Negroes of Greenville, S.C." *Greenville News*

Issue of: Thursday 16 March 1899:

Article - "Pickens, S.C. County Government Laws" (details).

Married at the residence of Rev. B. Holder the 12 March, MR. I.R. MAULDIN and MISS DAISY DILLARD all of Pickens.

Married Sunday the 12 March at the residence of Rev. B. Holder, MR. JOSEPH MASSENGALE to MISS SIMMONS all of Pickens Co., S.C.

MRS. WILLIAM MILLINAX died at her home Friday the 10 March. Burial was Sunday at Bethlehem Church by B.B. Grandy.

Married the 12 March at the residence of Rev. B. Holder, MR. WHIT McDANIEL of Greenville Co., S.C. and MISS EFFIE FERGUSON of Pickens, S.C. Both colored.

WILLIAM MAYFIELD died at the age of 82 years at his home at Mayfield Post Office, S.C. on Sunday morning. He was the father of Ex-Superintendent of Education, W.D. MAYFIELD and State Senator, S.G. MAYFIELD of Barnwell, S.C. Mr. Mayfield was a native of Tennessee but had lived in Greenville County, S.C. since the Civil War. The widow is the sister of CAPTAIN A. BLYTHE of this city. MRS. BURGE and MRS. MARTIN of Indian Territory, GEORGE R. MAYFIELD and MISS KATE MAYFIELD are the other children. *Greenville News*

Liberty Letter
P.H. BYARS died the 1 March at his home near Gaffney, Cherokee Co., S.C. He was the only brother of REV. D.D. BYARS of this county.

Local TELEPHONE SYSTEM BUILDING is the latest construction.

Letter concerning the growth of Gaffney, S.C. (details).

Pickens Co., S.C. Clerk's Sale - Court of Common Pleas: J.H. SIMMONS vs A.M. SIMMONS. 144 3/4 acres of land on the waters of Oolenoy River to be sold.

Pickens Co., S.C. Notice to Creditors and Debtors - Estate of HENRY S. COUCH, deceased by J.D. SMITH, Executor.

Issue of: Thursday 23 March 1899:

Article - "Battle of Cowpens".

Taking of the Census (details).

The Penitentiary Board came from Columbia, S.C. to look over the convict farms. They spent the night with MR. A.T. NEWELL in Hopewell, S.C. and visited WATSON, HAMMOND, ALLEN and FOWLER STOCKADES (details).

Best cigars can be bought from G.W. EARLE.

CADET ROSS O'DELL of Clemson College was visiting at home last Sunday.

MISS DAISY BOROUGHS closed a flourishing school in Glassy Mountain School District.

HOME TELEPHONE CO. has a central office in town (Pickens).

WILL ANDERSON is painting the front of the new brick drug store owned by DR. EARLE.

Married the 16 March at the residence of the bride's parents, MISS EVSIE (hard to read) NEIGHBORS to DAVIE HOLDER all of Mica, S.C. Rev. J.E. Foster officiated.

W.C. WYATT of Mica, S.C. lost a barn by fire.

Cateechee
MRS. ELIZABETH CHILD widow of JAMES W. CHILD died the 11 March at the residence of her son MR. R.R. CHILD. She was 87 years old and was left a widow 42 years ago. Mrs. Child leaves 3 children: REV. R.A. CHILD of Greenwood, S.C. MRS. DR. ROBINSON of Liberty, S.C. and R.R. CHILD, ESQ. of Cateechee, S.C. She was a member of the Methodist Episcopal Church and was buried at Camp Creek Church by Rev. Mr. Attaway.

Card of Thanks, to neighbors and friends at the time of E.E. HENDRICKS' death, from MRS. E.H. HENDRICKS.

Issue of: Thursday 30 March 1899:

Tribute to COL. C.H. HOLLINGSWORTH (lengthy details).

The 2nd S.C. Regiment has arrived in Savannah, Georgia where it will be mustered out soon.

Married at the residence of the bride's father at Liberty, S.C., MISS WILLIE PARSONS youngest daughter of W.S. PARSONS and MR. ROBERT C. ROBINSON all of Liberty, S.C. Rev. W.H. Workman officiated.

REV. ROBERT MASON of Pickens died at his home in the city of Greenville, S.C. last Wednesday at the age of 74 years.

Burial was at "Old Pickens Chapel" Burying Ground, Oconee Co., S.C.

MR. W.T. MEARES recently moved from Pickens Co. and bought the old PERRITT farm on Cane Creek of the Seneca River.

Issue of: Thursday 6 April 1899:

CADET OSSIE MAULDIN of Clemson College was at home last week.

MRS. ELIZABETH H. HOLLOWAY died the 24 Feb.(1899) at the home of her granddaughter in Easley, S.C. (see issue of the 13 April 1899).

MARCUS STEPHENS died at his home near Six Mile, S.C. the 31 March at the age 35 years and was buried at Six Mile Church. The funeral was conducted by Rev. T. Osborne.

COL. JAMES W. NORRIS of Anderson, S.C. died the 24 March at the age of 83 years. The cause of death was a rupture of a blood vessel in his head. At one time he was a citizen of Pickens District.

J.H. GILSTRAP received a loss due to a fire.

J. ALONZO BROWN is teaching a subscription school at Camp Creek Church.

The 10 year old daughter of MR. and MRS. A.B. RIGGINS died and was buried at Six Mile Cemetery.

Pickens Co., S.C. Final Settlement - Estate of MARY JANE CHAPMAN, deceased by SARAH M. KING, Administratrix.

Issue of: Thursday 13 April 1899:

Married the 9 April, MISS JANIE GILLIARD to MR. JOE SHERIFF both colored. M.F. Hester, N.P. officiated.

MRS. ELIZABETH HOLLOWAY of near Humphries died at the home of her granddaughter near Easley, S.C. the 24 Feb. 1899. She was born the 26 Aug. 1826 and first married MR. GARRIEN GREEN. In 1843 she married MR. O.A. HOLLOWAY, who survives and several children (see issue of the 6 April 1899).

DR. T.G. UNDERWOOD died the 27 Nov. 1898. He was born the 21 Oct. 1826, in Elbert Co., Georgia but moved to Habersham Co. (now White Co., Ga.) while still an infant. Dr. Underwood was in the medical profession and was a minister. The funeral services were at Carnesville Baptist Church and were with MASONIC RITUALS (lengthy article).
Easley Correspondent to *Daily News* - 10 April

WARREN KING son of J.B. KING of this town died at the age of 38 years and was buried beside his mother. He left a father, sister and brother. Services were at the Methodist Church.

Pickens Co., S.C. Sheriff's Sale:
ANNIE W. EARLE vs W.H. COX. 117 acres on Crow Creek.

Issue of: Thursday 20 April 1899:

Married Sunday the 16 April, MR. WILLIAM LITTLEJOHN and MRS. HANNAH MORGAN both colored.

Free Delivery of Mail, RFD, etc. Abbeville, S.C. and surrounding area (details).

Issue of: Thursday 27 April 1899:

JOHN MEARS and bride of Pacolet, S.C. passed through town last week.

MRS. ANNIE HEMPHILL NEUFFER daughter of R.R. HEMPHILL, Editor of *The Abbeville Medium* died at her father's home in Abbeville, S.C. the 23 April.

Married the 16 April at Central Baptist Church, MR. L.D. SPAN of Sumter, S.C. and MISS MATTIE JOHNSON the adopted daughter of HON. B.J. JOHNSON.

Died last Monday ROWLAND CHASTAIN. He was shot by MARTIN WELBORNE (details).

Married Tuesday the 18 April by Rev. C.L. Craig, MR. A. CALLOWAY STONE to MRS. MOSS. The groom is 70 and the bride is 65 years old. This is the third marriage for each.

A list of Pickens County boys who enlisted in the 2nd S.C.V.I. who were mustered out of service the 19 April:
CAPTAIN M. MAULDIN
SARGEANT G.R. HENDRICKS
QUARTER MASTER SARGEANT J.C. JENNINGS
MUSICIAN W.O. HESTER
CORPORAL G.B. SMALLEY and CORPORAL W.W.H FIELD
PRIVATES: JAMES W. HESTER, ROBERT ANTHONY, WYLIE MILLER, AMOS DODGENS, MED F. DAY, JACOB A. PICKEL and CLAUDE R. ELLISON.
They all enjoyed their stay in the army especially in Cuba.

Married the 12 April, MR. BEN BOWLIN and MISS LILA DALTON by Rev. J.E. Foster (details).

Clemson College Trustees to Meet (details).

Pickens Co., S.C. Final Settlement - Estate of P.E. MAXWELL, deceased by HENRY BRIGGS, Administrator.

Issue of: Thursday 4 May 1899:

An infant son of MR. and MRS. W.H. PERRY of Dacusville, S.C. died the 29 April and was buried the 30 April at Nine Forks Church.

Married last Sunday at the residence of the bride's father, MISS MATTIE BOLDING to MR. McDUFFIE MAULDIN both of Cateechee, S.C.

MRS. W.A. GRESHAM (nee) MISS MATTIE HESTER of Atlanta, Georgia, who has been visiting her parents MR. and MRS. M.F. HESTER, was called home due to the illness of her husband.

MR. J.P. CARY of Pickens is in Seneca, S.C. making arrangements to have the KEOWEE HOTEL remodeled. *Oconee News*

Married at the residence of the bride's parents MR. and MRS. E.F. LOOPER on Saturday the 30 April, MISS VIOLA LOOPER and MR. R.L. HENDERSON of Saluda Co., S.C.

Married at the residence of the bride's parents on Wednesday the 26 April 1899, by J.M. Stewart, MR. ABRAHAM T. WINCHESTER and MISS FLORA THOMAS (details).

HENRY McCORD of Atlanta, Georgia died at the residence of his brother-in-law J.H. BROWN, Friday night (May 5) at about 22 years of age. He left a father, mother, 1 brother and 2 sisters. Burial was at Enon Burying Ground.

State Summer Schools for Graded School Teachers and others.

Issue of: Thursday 11 May 1899:

Married near Sassafras Gap last week, MISS CAMIE CHAPMAN of Upper East Fork and JOHN CONLEY of Pickens, S.C. by Rev. W.A. Gigney.

MISS MARY STEWART, age 23, died Monday at the home of her parents MR. and MRS. THOMAS STEWART of Easley Township. Burial was at Antioch Methodist Church.

Issue of: Thursday 18 May 1899:

I.P. ALEXANDER'S house burned the 8 May.

Married at the home of the bride's parents in Brevard, North Carolina the 14 May, MISS IDA SHIPMAN to ROBERT L. BRYANT. Rev. I T. Newton officiated.

Obituary in verse (very wordy, etc.)
Dedicated to the memory of JAMES GAINES SEABORN and his beloved wife MYRTIE by his loving and affectionate mother, MRS. M.E. SEABORN.

Issue of: Thursday 25 May 1899:

J.B. MERRILL, a first class shoe maker of Walhalla, S.C. has moved his shoe shop to the FREEMAN BUILDING of this place.

MRS. J.G. HUGHES died at her home hear Looper, S.C. the 18 May. She leaves a husband and 6 children. Burial was at Peter's Creek Church.

G.T. McGREGOR, STROTHER FORD, C.B. DOUGLAS, JR. and N.D. WALKER, Cadets at Clemson worshiped at Six Mile, S.C..

Pickens Co., S.C. Notice to Creditors and Debtors - Estate of HENRY C. MILLER by CARRIE M. SIMONS, RESSIE E. MILLER HOOK and W.W. SIMONS, Executors.

JOHN GEORGE and MISS ALICE ALEXANDER were married the 14 May at the residence of Mr. W.L. VICKERS by Rev. Mauldin.

Issue of: Thursday 1 June 1899:

The HAGOOD Reunion was held at" Old Pickens", Oconee Co., S.C. last Friday.

Married, MR. D. COUCH and MISS MAMIE OWENS of Pickens Co. at the residence of THOMAS OWENS last week, Rev J.T. Dobson officiated.

CHARLES H. TOLBERT first class shoe maker has moved his shop to the back of the barber shop.

MR. MOSES GILLESPIE of Central, S.C. died of dropsy the 25 April. He leaves a wife and 7 children. Mr. Gillespie was a member of the Methodist Episcopal Church and a Confederate Veteran.

JOHN WESLEY COCHRAN of Calhoun, S.C. died of typhoid fever. He leaves a wife and 8 children. His wife was a daughter of AARON BOGGS. Mr. Cochran was 45 years of age and a member of the Wesleyan Methodist church. Burial was at Old Stone Church Cemetery.

B.R. TOLBERT is a professional barber.

Pickens Co., S.C. Homestead Exemption - MARY ALICE COCHRAN, Administrator of the estate of JOHN W. COCHRAN, deceased applies for Homestead Exemption.

Issue of: Thursday 8 June 1899:

Article - "Battle of Cowpens".

GOV. W.H. ELLERBE died the 2 June. Burial was at Ellerbe - Godbold Cemetery near Sellers, S.C. (details).

Born a son the 11 May to MR. and MRS. H.W. FARR.

Married Saturday last by Rev. C.T. Miller, JIM ELLISON to MAGGIE RICHARDSON all persons colored.

MILTON ARNOLD is a clothes cleaner and dyer.

An infant son of MR. and MRS. J.W. SNELLINGS died Monday the 5 June. Burial was at Secona Church.

Married at the residence of Mr. DEAL HIOTT the 4 June, MISS MINNIE GILLILAND to MR. WILLIAM DARNELL. H. Hendricks, N.P. officiated.

COL. W.A. NEAL bought H.A. RICHEY'S immense brick yard on Town Creek.

JANE PRICE, colored, died at her home on MR. JOHN FERGUSON'S farm last Monday the 5 June. Burial was at Cold Springs Church.

The funeral service of ELDER JESSE SIMMONS and wife MATILDA SIMMONS will be held at Oolenoy Baptist Church on the 3rd Sunday in June by Rev. J.M. Stewart and Rev. M.L. Jones.

CAPTAIN I.M. MARTIN, Lawyer, has an office over DR. EARLE'S DRUG STORE.

MISS HATTIE FERGUSON of Pickens and HARRY VALENTINE of Trenton, N.J. were married Wednesday the 31 May at the home of the bride's father MR. JOHN FERGUSON. Mr. Valentine was a lieutenant in the army in the late war. The couple will live in New Jersey.

Issue of: Thursday 15 June 1899:

Article - "A Monument to the Dead at Winchester, Virginia".

Article - "The Confederate Seal".

Death of ROSA BONHEUR, noted animal painter. She was born in France in 1821 (details).

Pickens Co., S.C. Sheriff's Sale:
Land to be sold next Salesday.
HENRY M. FINDLEY. Tract of land in Eastatoe Township.

T. JACKSON MORTON. 100 acres in Eastatoe Township.
MARY M. SMITH. 50 acres in Eastatoe Township.
HATTIE MARTIN. Lot in Central, S.C.
STOVALL SMITH. 2 acres in Central Township (details).

Married the 11 June at the home of the bride's parents, by Mr. L.L. Smith of Clement, S.C., MR. JAMES L. THOMPSON of Newry, S.C. and MISS ORA L. CHILDRESS.

Pension Roll 1899, Pickens County, S.C.:

Class B $17.60

JACOB KENNEMORE	J.J. JAMERSON
W.J. KING	T.J. LIGON
F. BAGWELL	S.R. DAY
E.B. STEPHENS	W.B. GAINES
SAMMIT NEAL	PETER SUMMEY
J.T. O'BRYANT	JAMES HOPKINS
S.M. PERRY	M.L. SMITH
W.G. SMITH	I.H. PHILPOT
	F.M. CASSELL

Class C. $13.20

RICHARD ANDERSON	JEFFERSON ARNOLD
J.H. ABERCROMBIE	ORWELL ABERCROMBIE
ALBERT BABB	WARREN BOYD
A.J. BRADLEY	W.J.M. BURTON
J.M. BOWLIN	M.A. BARRE
MARTIN C. BRAMBLETT	JOHN F. CONNELLY
W.A. COLLINS	THOMAS CHILD
R.C. CRAWFORD	I.D. COLEMAN
J.H. CHILDRESS	FRANK P. CRANE
ANDERSON CHAPPELL	HENSON CHAPMAN
S.B. CARSON	WILLIAM CAMPBELL
W.H. CAMPBELL	J.T. CANTRELL
W.M. DICHERT	JAMES R. DICKERSON
W.S. DAVIS	J.H. DAVIS
LEWIS H. DALTON	J.H. ELLIS
A.T. EPPS	J.B. ERVIN
A.F. EPPS	J.M. INTREKIN
M.L. ELLENBURG	J.N. EARLE
L.G. FENNELL	J.W. FRIDDLE
MOSES GILLESPIE	W.R. GILSTRAP
HENRY GRIFFIN	DAVID GILSTRAP
J.A. GILSTRAP	S.J. GASSOWAY
JAMES HAMMOND	M.B. GRANGER
O.W. HALLOWAY	G.R. HENDRICKS
JAMES A. HUGHEY	C.T. HOLBOMBE
T.H. HAMLEY	E.C. HITT
JOHN HAWKINS	S.W. HOWARD
J.W. HOPKINS	THOMAS HESTER
B.F. HOLDEN	JOBERRY HESTER
WILLIAM HAWKINS	J.H. HUNT
E.C. HAYWARD	TYRA HOLDER
MARTIN HOLDER	J.W. HUNTER

DANIEL HENDRICKS	EMEZIAH HUNT
HARRISON JONES	C.L. JOHNSON
A.W. KAY	W.S. KIRKSEY
CLARINDA LASH	JOHN LESLEY
G.W. LESLEY	F.A. LEWIS
ISAAC LANGSTON	F.M. MOODY
GEORGE McADAMS	WILLIAM McGAHA
D.T. MAHAFFY	D.C. MERIDITH
S.P. MAW	ANSIL McGILL
JOHN McSWEAR'GTON	S.B. McJUNKIN
HARRISON MAULEY	ALEXANDER MAULDIN
WILLIAM NIX	JOSEPH NALLEY
T.F. NELSON	G.W. OWENS
B.M. PRESLEY	W.H. PERRY
R.W. PHILLIPS	JOSEPH REEVES
JORDAN RICE	J.H. RAINES
R.E. RAINES	G.W. ROPER
MICHAEL ROGERS	P.P. SHERIFF
WILEY SMITH	RUBEN SMITH
MOSES SMITH	A.C. STEPHENS
ELISHA SKELTON	W.K. STEWART
W.M. STANSELL	J. FOSTER SMITH
W.S. SMITH	LEWIS SIMMONS
JOHN N. SMITH	J.D. STEPHEN
STEPHEN SMITH	J.S. SANDERS
A.A. SWANGNAM	JOHN T. TURNER
S.T. TUMBLIN	G.W. THOMAS
JAMES TROTTER	K.H. VAUGHT
JOHN R. WHITE	JAMES WALDROP
J.T. WATSON	G.W. WILLIAMS
	N.H. WELBORN

JULIUS PARSONS, Surveyor, Pickens Co., S.C.

OLD SOUTH CAROLINA was the first railroad built in the United States.

Pickens Co., S.C. Notice to Debtors and Creditors - Estate of B.F. McKENZIE by W.C. McKENZIE.

Issue of: Thursday 22 June 1899:

MRS. BENNETT HILL of Old Pickens, Oconee Co., S.C. is very sick.

Born a son to MR. and MRS. JORDAN BRAZEAL the 15 June.

Married Sunday the 18 June by Rev. W.C. Seaborn, MR. JOHN MEDLIN and MISS ALLIE REEVES.

DR. J.L. BOLT is having a telephone put in.

W.J. OLIVER and CO. built the PICKENS RAILROAD.

Died the 15 June, SARAH C. MILLER widow of the late TILLMON MILLER. She leaves many children and grandchildren. Burial was at George's Creek Church. Mrs. Miller was 80 years old.

Born a boy to MR. and MRS. MARCUS O. LOOPER of near Pickens the 20 June.

DR. LITTLEJOHN of Gaffney, S.C. is attending MISS STELLA NEWBERRY.

DR. J.W. NORWOOD of Greenville, S.C. died last Thursday.

GEN. JOHN B. GORDON'S home "THE SOUTHERLAND" burned. It was located at Kirkwood, near Atlanta, Georgia.

Pickens Co., S.C. Citation Notice - FRANCIS RICHARDSON applied for Letters of Administration for the estate of GEORGE RICHARDSON, deceased.

Issue of: Thursday 29 June 1899:

Table Mountain Dots
ELBERT ROPER, son of IRA THOMAS ROPER, deceased, died the 22 June near TABLE ROCK HOTEL. He leaves a mother, brother and 2 sisters. Burial was at Oolenoy Church.

DR. BOLT'S new drug store is to be completed by the 15 August.

Died an infant of MR. and MRS. JOHN D. HARRIS of Lenderman, Greenville Co., S.C. the 22 June.

Born the 23 June a son to MR. and MRS. BART NEELY.

MR. HOMUTH, known in Pickens as the "Texas Dutchman", is a buggy and sign painter.

Issue of: Thursday 6 July 1899:

J. McD. BRUCE is to move into his new dwelling next week.

Pickens Co., S.C. Petit Jury List.

J.P. O'DELL repairs gins.

WILL ARIAL is home from Birmingham, Alabama where he has been working in the railroad shops.

MRS. ADDIE CURTIS and little daughter of New Orleans, Louisiana are on a visit to her brother MR. B.E. GRANDY of Pickens.

Pickens Co., S.C. Salesday - 100 acres of land sold for $11.50 (no additional information).

Issue of: Thursday 13 July 1899:

EX-GOVERNOR JOHN P. RICHARDSON was buried at Camden, S.C. the 7 July.

An infant child of MR. and MRS. JAMES COOPER died the 6 July. Burial was at Oolenoy Church.

DR. J.W. EARLE died at the home of his son J.W. EARLE, JR. the 5 July at the age of 87 years. He was buried from Carmel Presbyterian Church. Surviving children: MRS. ALICE BRUCE of Easley, S.C., MRS. E.B. O'NEAL of Texas, DR. G.W. EARLE and J.W. EARLE of this place.

Issue of: Thursday 20 July 1899:

Pickens Co., S.C. General Court Session - Criminal Cases (details).

Born the 13 July, a boy to MR. and MRS. C.E. ROBINSON.

J.T. ANTHONY is constructing a new building on Ann Street.

Born the 13 July, a boy to MR. and MRS. S.W. O'DELL.

Born a girl to MR. and MRS. J.D. HOLDER the 17 July.

Married Sunday the 16 July by G.W. Ellis, N.P., ANDERSON HUNTER to LIZZIE ALEXANDER, both parties colored.

MRS. THOMAS PARKINS who moved with her husband and children to Texas several years ago, died the 7 July at 48 years of age. She leaves a husband and several children. She was a sister of MRS. JOAB MAULDIN and COL. HOLLINGSWORTH.

Married the 16 July at the home of the bride's parents MR. and MRS. SAMUEL ROBINSON of Blaine, MISS BETTIE ROBINSON to MR. GEORGE HONEY of Kansas. John D. Sitton, N.P. officiated. The bride's mother is a sister of J.R. HARRIS who lives near Pickens.

MRS. J.P. YOUNG died at her home near Cateechee, S.C. the 15 July at 35 years of age. She leaves a husband and 2 children. Burial was at Six Mile Cemetery.

J.S. HENDRICKS of Cross Roads died the 17 July at about 50 years of age. He leaves a wife and 7 children. Burial was at Tabor Church Cemetery.

Issue of: Thursday 27 July 1899:

COL. ROBERT G. INGERSOLL died the 21 July at Dobbs Ferry, New York.

NORA HENDRICKS is teaching at Oolenoy Schoolhouse.

PROF. FRANK HENDRICKS is teaching at Town Creek.

Married the 23 July at the home of the bride's parents on Crow Creek, MISS ANNETTA WINCHESTER to MR. J. FRANK GARY. Rev. B. F. Murphree officiated.

PROF. R.E. MILLER is teaching in the Garvin District.

MRS. MATHEW EDENS of Pelzer, S.C. formerly of this county, died of typhoid the 23 July at the home of her parents MR. and MRS. BAKER LYNCH of Knob, S.C. She was 38 years of age and leaves a husband and several children. Burial was at Oolenoy. Mrs. Edens was a member of the Baptist Church.

DR. FRANK FERGUSON son of JOHN FERGUSON of Greenville, S.C. returned from Texas to Greenville. He will be with DR. W.M. NORWOOD in dentistry.

Issue of: Thursday 3 August 1899:

Crosswell School will be taught by MR. BOYCE MILLER and MR. HENRY GARRISON. They have 85 students.

J. SALTER HENDRICKS died the 17 July. He was born in Pickens Co. in 1854 and leaves a wife and 9 children.

The wife of WILL FEATHERSTONE, colored, died the 29 July.

Born a girl to MR. and MRS. MACK DURHAM the 30 July.

Bricks were being laid Tuesday on the ANTHONY BUILDING. WILLIAM SMITH of Easley, S.C. is the contractor.

PROF. A.B. RILEY is the principal of Laurens High School.

Born a baby boy to J.L.O. THOMPSON the 26 July.

CRAIG BROTHERS will open a store with general merchandise in the store room of the MASONIC LODGE in September.

Maynard School Building will have a new addition.

Died an infant of MR. and MRS. C.L. CRAIG of Seneca, S.C. the 25 July. Burial was at Griffin Church.

J.R. WILLIAMS a good carpenter, worked on the drug store and the home of J. McD. BRUCE.

A son was born to MR. and MRS. W.R. LYNCH of Sunny Dale, S.C. last month.

Born a boy to REV. J.A. BOND of Six Mile, S.C. the 30 July.

PROF. ARTHUR CHRISTOPHER is teaching at Bethlehem. There are 75 students.

PINCKNEY GOSSETT who resides near Easley Bridge Road, Greenville Co., S.C. died Sunday at 79 years of age. His wife died a few years ago. Burial was at Antioch Church. He leaves a large family. (W.P. GOSSETT, born 12 April 1821, died 30 July 1899 - Pickens County, S.C. Cemetery Survey, Vol.1, p. 4b).

MRS. BRYANT wife of TALBERT BRYANT who lives near Easley, S.C. died the 30 July at the home of her son in North Carolina at 57 years of age. Burial was at Mt. Pisgah Baptist Church Cemetery. She leaves a husband and several children.

W.K. MERCK of Pelzer, S.C., formerly of this county, died the 26 July of typhoid. He was about 50 years of age and leaves a wife and several children. Burial was at Six Mile Cemetery.

Issue of: Thursday 10 August 1899:

Article - "The Civil War".

An infant of MR. and MRS. W.L. GILLESPIE died the 3 August. Burial was at Camp Creek.

MISS CORA BOWEN is teaching at Olga, S.C. She has 60 students.

PROF. J.B. DANIELS is principal of Pickens High School.

Married at the residence of Rev. W.H. Workman of Liberty, S.C. the 20 July, MR. J.P. HYDE to MISS SALLIE CRAIG. They are both from Cateechee, S.C.

MISS AMANDA NIX died at the home of her parents MR. and MRS. W.D. NIX of Eastatoe, S.C. the 30 July. Burial was at the family burying ground. She was a member of the Baptist Church.

R.P. SNODDY of near Crosswell, S.C. died the 27 July. Burial was at George's Creek. Mr. Snoddy was a Confederate Veteran and leaves a wife and 6 children, 2 boys and 4 girls.

BANISTER LYNCH, age about 65, died at his home near Sunny Dale, S.C. the 6 Aug. leaving a wife and 2 children. He was a member of Holly Springs Baptist Church. Burial was at the family burying ground.

CALVIN LYNCH, who moved to Parker Co., Texas in 1852, is visiting his brothers BANISTER and GIDEON LYNCH who live at the old homestead near Table Rock, S.C. Their father was NATHANIEL LYNCH.

ANDY SMILER, colored, who lives in Laurens, S.C. died by drowning in Pickens County. He was 27 years of age.

Issue of: Thursday 17 August 1899:

A girl was born the 13 Aug. to MR. and MRS. MARCUS PRINCE.

O.P. FIELDS has a new house at Pinder, S.C.

RILEY RAINES died the 13 Aug. of typhoid at 18 years of age. He was a member of Secona Baptist Church.

The brick building of J.T. ANTHONY on Ann Street is nearly completed.

MINNIE CLARDY, age 13, daughter of JOHN W. CLARDY died after being accidently shot by her 18 year old brother JAMES CLARDY. Burial was at Secona Baptist Church.

JOHN RICHEY died Tuesday of last week after being shot by WILLIAM K. POWERS.

Origin of "Dixie" (details).

Pickens Co., S.C. Final Settlement - Estate of J.F. BRUCE, deceased by MRS. A.M. BRUCE and H. EARLE RUSSELL, Administrators.

Pickens Co., S.C. Tax Execution Sales:
Land to be sold.
W. AUSTIN HUDSON. 41 acres in Hurricane Township.
MILTON T. HUDSON. 41 acres in Hurricane Township.
Estate of DR. J.T. ANDERSON, deceased. 35 acres in Dacusville Township.
WILLIAM THOMSON. 100 acres in Pumpkintown Township.
MRS. MARY J. CHAPMAN. 1 lot in Central, S.C.
Estate of MRS. NAOMI HOLDEN. 160 acres in Eastatoe Township.

Issue of: Thursday 24 August 1899:

Married WILL ROSEMOND, colored, Sunday the 20 Aug. to MISS NORSISSIE SIZEMORE, colored, by Alonzo M. Folger, N.P. of Easley, S.C.

MR. and MRS. W.T. DAY of Maynard, S.C. celebrated 10 years of marriage the 15 August.

PROF. WYER of Virginia is to be principal of the school, PROF. DANIEL being unable to accept.

Married the 16 August at King's Mountain, North Carolina, HOWARD JENKINS to MISS HUBBARD.

MRS. LEVISA HINTON wife of S.P. HINTON of Sampson Mill and a native of Pickens Co. died. She leaves a husband and 9 children. Burial was at Griffin Baptist Church Cemetery.

HAMPTON CRAIG is teaching at the Keowee School.

Issue of: Thursday 7 September 1899:

An infant of MR. ED WILSON died on Friday and was buried at Mt. Zion.

MRS. DR. LONG is teaching at Cateechee, S.C.

MISS NORA HOLDER closed a school at Martin Schoolhouse. They had 60 students.

Married Sunday the 3 Sept. at the residence of MRS. GEORGE RIDDLE of Dacusville, S.C., MR. W.E. HUNT of this county to MISS ELLA GLAZENER of Brevard, North Carolina. Rev. B.E. Grandy officiated.

SAMUEL BROWN, who lived near Field Post Office, S.C., died Monday at 82 years of age. He leaves a wife and 7 children and was a member of the Methodist Church. Burial was in the family cemetery. (SAMUEL BROWN, born 25 April 1817, died 4 Sept. 1899, buried Brown Family Cemetery - Pickens County, S.C. Cemetery Survey, Vol. 1, p. 17).

MISS CORA BOWEN is teaching at Olga, S.C.

A new church is being built at Friendship, S.C. The old one burned more than a year ago.

REV. J.E. FOSTER is building a new home on his farm near Peter's Creek.

An infant of MR. PICKENS HARRIS of Pelham, S.C. died and was buried at Peter's Creek last second Sabbath.

Pickens Co., S.C. Notice to Debtors and Creditors - Estate of B.S. LYNCH by MRS. ELIZABETH LYNCH, Administrator.

Sale of personal property of W. PINKNEY GOSSETT at the old homeplace, six miles from Easley, S.C., to be held the 13 September, by T.F. GOSSETT, Administrator (details).

Issue of: Thursday 14 September 1899:

DR. WILLIAM MOFFETT GRIER died at his home in Due West, S.C. He was President of Erskine College and was born the 11 Feb.

1843 in York County, South Carolina. Dr. Grier was a Confederate Veteran.

Married Wednesday the 6 Sept. at the residence of Rev. F. R. McClanahan of Liberty Township, MR. W.C. HARPER of this county and MRS. S.E. GALLOWAY of North Carolina.

MRS. MEADY HOLDER wife of TYLER HOLDER died the 31 August. Burial was at Oolenoy.

Born a son to MR. and MRS. BARNETT PORTER the 7 August.

WILLIAM BENTON FREEMAN, the little son of MR. and MRS. W.B. FREEMAN of Greenville, S.C., died the 13 Sept. of pneumonia. He was buried in Greenville.

MRS. MISSOURI EDENS wife of the late CATO EDENS died at her home at Knob, S.C. the 9 Aug. at the age of 37 years. She leaves several children. Burial was at Oolenoy Baptist Church Cemetery.

Card of Thanks, to neighbors and friends for sympathy shown at the death of our father SAMUEL BROWN. Signed, MRS. SALLIE CHAPMAN, JOHN BROWN, R.B. BROWN, S.H. BROWN and J.A. BROWN.

Issue of: Thursday 21 September 1899:

JULIA VESTA MAULDIN eldest daughter of PERRY J. and KATE MAULDIN who live near Dalton, S.C. died at the age of 22 years. Burial was at Gap Hill Methodist Church.

A Memorial Service will be conducted for SAMUEL BROWN at the Old Home Place the third Sunday in October.

Five Indians stationed on Crow Creek near JORDAN RICE'S place are making some nice baskets out of cane. They arrived here a few days ago.

MRS. MARY O'DELL wife of CALVIN O'DELL died the 10 Sept. at her home near Easley, S.C. at about 60 years of age. She leaves a husband and several children. She was a member of the Methodist Church. Burial was in the family cemetery (see issue of the 28 Sept. 1899).

MRS. LOOPER wife of WILLIAM LOOPER of Mica, S.C. died the 15 Sept. at about 25 years of age. Burial was at Nine Forks Baptist Church Cemetery. She leaves a husband and several children.

CORNELIUS VANDERBILT died in New York the 12 Sept. of paralysis at 56 years of age. He was head of the world's richest family.

Pickens Co., S.C. Citation Notice - JOSEPH T. MURPHREE, deceased. J.M. STEWART, C.C.P. applies for Letters of Administration.

Pickens Co., S.C. Notice to Debtors and Creditors - Estate of SAMUEL BROWN, deceased by LUCIAN HENDRICKS, Executor.

Issue of: Thursday 28 September 1899:

A son was born the 23 Sept. to MR. and MRS. JOHN HAYNES of Liberty Township.

JOHN A. HENDRICKS is erecting a large and commodious home at his farm at Table Rock, S.C.

J.O. BROCK does watch repairs.

A new hotel for Easley, S.C. with 40 rooms. It will be located where HAGOOD's LIVERY now stands.

A daughter was born to MR. and MRS. A.R. FOLGER of Gaffney, S.C.

Married the 18 Sept. at the residence of MR. RIAL BARNETT by Rev. Johnson Sheriff, MISS CURRY to MR. D. BARNETT all of Pickens County.

W.E. CHESWELL of Newry, S.C. is to establish a cotton mill at Westminster, S.C. (details).

MRS. MARY ANN O'DELL relict of the late CALVIN O'DELL and sister of H.B. HENDRICKS died the 19 Sept. at 60 years of age. She was a member of the Methodist Church and was buried at the family burying ground. (MARY A. O'DELL, born 3 May 1832, died 19 Sept, 1899, buried Kennemore, Mauldin, O'Dell Cemetery - Pickens County, S.C. Cemetery Survey, Vol.1, p. 197 - see issue of the 21 Sept. 1899).

Announcing the approaching marriage of MISS MARIE HUFFMAN to DR. JOHN JAMES LINDSAY next Tuesday at the Presbyterian Church in Seneca, S.C. The announcement is made by her aunt and uncle, MR. and MRS. FRANK M. CARY of Seneca, S.C.

Issue of: Thursday 5 October 1899:

A son was born to MR. and MRS. FRANK CRANE of Liberty, S.C. the 29 September.

Married at the home of the bride's parents, MR. ELIJAH BAGWELL to MISS LEOTO CANTRELL by Magistrate A.A. Jones.

Born an heir to MR. and MRS. P.B. LANGSTON of Liberty, S.C. the 27 September.

MRS. D.B. FINNEY has a new store in Pickens at the old drug store of DR. G.W. EARLE. She will have millinery, etc.

MRS. LIZZIE WIGGINGTON of Six Mile, S.C. died the 28 Sept. and was buried at Six Mile Baptist Church Cemetery. She leaves a husband and several children.

HANNAH PARSONS widow of the late BENJAMIN PARSONS, who was killed in the late war, died at the home of J.H. HUDSON of Sunny Dale, S.C. the 1 Oct. at 59 years of age. She had lived here for 7 years. Burial was at Concord Church Cemetery.

Married, MISS HATTIE GRADY daughter of CAPT. H.C. GRADY of Washington, D.C. formerly of Pickens to MR. M.A. HOLSTEIN of Batesburg, S.C. the 29 Sept. They were married in Washington, D.C., by Rev. J.J. Miner.

Bids are being accepted for tenement houses for the EASLEY COTTON MILLS.

Issue of: Thursday 12 October 1899:

D.F. PACE has opened a complete line of merchandise.

Married the 2 Oct. at the residence of R.J. MATTISON, MR. E. SUTHERLAND to MISS EMMA SHIPMAN both of Pickens County. B.W. McWhorter, N.P. officiated.

Pickens Co., S.C. Petit Jury List.

Pickens Co., S.C. Final Settlement - J. MASON HENDRICKS, Guardian of WILLIAM WALKER HENDRICKS, et al., minors.

Issue of: Thursday 19 October 1899:

A son was born the 15 Oct. to MR. and MRS. JAMES COOPER of near Pickens.

A son was born the 14 Oct. to MR. and MRS. ANDREW BLACKSTON of near town.

MRS. FLORA LATHEM has purchased the old BRADLEY house and lot and has moved to town.

MESSRS. HANBY and THOMPSON are to build 50 tenant houses for the EASLEY COTTON MILL.

Married at the home of the bride's parent CAPTAIN W.H. HUNTER the 10 Oct., MR. SHERMAN GILLESPIE of Cateechee, S.C. and MISS MARY HUNTER.

MR. and MRS. S.O. COTHRAN formerly of this county and late of Texas have moved to Pickens and will make it their future home. They occupy one of JUDGE NEWBERRY'S houses.

Married the 12 Oct. at the residence of the bride's father EZEKIEL McALISTER by Magistrate B.D. Garvin. MR. THOMAS G. JOHNSTON to MISS MIRANDA McALISTER all of this county.

Married the 10 Oct., MR. S.O. SKELTON of Liberty, S.C. to MISS LOUIE ROBINSON of Level Land, Abbeville County, S.C. Rev. W.H. Workman officiated.

C.B. HAGOOD entered Clemson College and JOHN W. HALLUMS, South Carolina College.

BATES and FREEMAN purchased the livery stable of B.M. GRIFFIN near ASHMORE'S SHOP.

THURMAN GOUDELOCK son of MR. and MRS. M.N. GOUDELOCK of Prater's Creek died the 4 October. He was born in Pickens Co., S.C. the 7 Aug. 1882. Burial was at Prater's Creek Church Cemetery (two items in same issue).

CALVIN CISSON died at the home of his son CHARLES CISSON near Table Rock, S.C. the 11 Oct. at about 50 years of age. He leaves a wife and 8 children. Burial was at Saluda Hill Baptist Church Cemetery.

Issue of: Thursday 26 October 1899:

MRS. CAROLINE INABINETT wife of REV. L.L. INABINETT died in Townville, S.C. the 19 October. She was born the 15 Sept. 1866 in Pickens Co. to ASHBURY and ANNA KELLY. In Sept. 1896 she married REV. INABINETT. Burial was at Porter's Chapel Cemetery. Surviving are her husband and 2 children.

ANNA MARCELLA INABINETT infant daughter of L.L. and MARY CAROLINE INABINETT was born the 13 Oct. 1899 and died the 22 Oct. 1899. She is buried beside her mother.

Issue of: Thursday 2 November 1899:

Pickens County young men at Clemson College:
J.M. BURGESS	L.O. MAULDIN
W.A. BURGESS	S.M. ROBERTSON
F. CRAWFORD	B.C. ROBERTSON
L.D. GILLESPIE	S.C. STEWART
C.B. HAGOOD	J.C. STRIBLING (post graduate)
D.G. HUMBERT	C.W. MAULDIN

MAJORS: G. SHANKLIN, W.W. KLUGH and S.M. MARTIN
Football Management: MR. J.N. WALKER and PROF. W.M. RIGGS.

MR. GRANDY has a new house on Glassy Mountain Street. It is a neat cottage.

The new house of DR. G.W. EARLE on Factory Street is nearing completion.

MRS. PORTER wife of SMITH PORTER who lives near Pinder Post Office, S.C. died Sunday the 29 Oct. at about 48 years of age. Burial was at Porter's Chapel Cemetery. She leaves a husband and 8 children.

Pickens Co., S.C. Court of General Sessions - Criminal cases (details).

Issue of: Thursday 9 November 1899:

The Confederate Battle of Williamsburg and a tribute to DR. GRIER (details).

Building and equipment of the OLD SOUTH CAROLINA RAILROAD (details).

Estate of J.W. COCHRAN is selling land in Calhoun, S.C. Wife, ROSA COCHRAN. Children: WALTER D., LELAND A., MAMIE, SALLIE BESSIE, THURMAN, and GEORGIA COCHRAN. G.B. COCHRAN and A.J. BOGGS, Administrators.

Town Schools to open the 6 Nov. under FRANK HENDRICKS, Principal.

Married the 1 Nov. at the residence of the bride's parent . A.B. CHASTAIN of Knob, S.C., MR. JAMES LIGON of Pindor, S.C. to MISS MALINDA CHASTAIN. Rev. T.C. Holsclaw officiated.

Married this morning, MR. JAMES MANCHESTER PAGET and MISS MARY ELISE MAULDIN at the home of the bride's parents MR. and MRS. B. FRANK MAULDIN of North Main Street, this city. Rev. O.L. Martin officiated (details). *Anderson Intelligencer* - 1 Nov. 1899

Pickens Co., S.C. Sheriff's Sale:
MARY ALICE COCHRAN, et al. vs G.B. COCHRAN and A.J. BOGGS, Administrators of the estate of J.W. COCHRAN, deceased. 1 acre in the town of Calhoun, S.C. to be sold.
SENECA BANK vs G.B. COCHRAN, et al. 12 acres of land to be sold.

Pickens Co., S.C. Clerk's Sale:
Land to be sold next Salesday.
VAN B. ELLISON vs ELIAS F. ELLISON, et al. 5 acres in Easley Township.
T.H. SMITH, et al. vs A.F. SMITH. Tract #1 in the estate of H.A. SMITH, deceased, 71 1/5 ACRES. Tract #2 - 64 acres and Tract #3 - 63 1\5 acres (details).
RICHARD LENHARDT vs DARCUS P. ROBINSON. 135 acres in Easley Township.

R.F. SMITH vs JAMES AGNEW. 2 lots in the town of Calhoun, S.C. and 89 acres in Central Township.

Issue of: Thursday 16 November 1899:

Central News - 8 Nov. 1899
MRS. GARVIN has moved from near Six Mile, S.C. to our town. She will get the advantage of graded school for her daughter.
MRS. JAMES H. ROWLAND has left her beautiful home to take charge of the Hotel. The railroad authorities may consider themselves fortunate and if we are correctly informed it was a mere accident they succeeded in getting her. MRS. McCORKLE who formerly kept the Hotel has moved to Atlanta, Georgia.

The new HOTEL EASLEY will be completed in a short time.

MRS. FLORA LATHEM is a teacher at Bethlehem School.

E.H. BARTON who lives below Easley, S.C. on the Greenville Road is storekeeper and gauger at HOLCOMBE'S DISTILLERY.

JOHN JOHNSON, colored, and SAMANTHA MANSELL, colored, were married the 5 Nov. by W.N. Hughes, N.P. All of Looper, Pickens County.

Married at the residence of the bride's parents Sunday the 12 Nov. 1899, MR. NELSON GARRETT to MISS MAMIE DILLARD. Rev. J.M. Stewart officiated.

Married the 5 Nov. at the residence of HAYNES JONES of Dacusville, S.C., MR. JOHN HUNT to MISS VICTORIA HILL by Rev. B.E. Grandy.

Married the 14 Nov. at the residence of the bride's parent MR. ELIAS DAY of below Easley, S.C., MR. WALTER WYATT of Greenville, S.C. to MISS MAY DAY of Easley, by Rev. J.E. Roushton.

NATHANIEL J. WILLIAMS died at his home at Table Rock, S.C. the 11 Nov. at 58 years of age. Burial was from Oolenoy Church. He leaves a wife and large family. (NATHANIEL J. WILLIAMS, born 1 May 1843, died 12 Nov. 1899 - Pickens County, S.C. Cemetery Survey, Vol. 1, p. 247).

Issue of: Thursday 30 November 1899:

A teacher is wanted for Hagood School.

B.A. ALLGOOD is principal of Wolf Creek School.

The infant daughter of MR. and MRS. V.S. MEDLIN died from burns and was buried on Friday at Secona.

Issue of: Thursday 7 December 1899:

A daughter was born the 28 Nov. to MR. and MRS. J.W. EARLE.

CADETS CLEON MAULDIN, BAYLUS ROBINSON and CHARLES OWENS of Clemson, S.C. were here last week.

Married the 3 Dec. at the residence of the bride's father N.R. KENNEMORE by Rev. W.C. Seaborn, MR. THOMAS S. RAMSEY to MISS SULA KENNEMORE all of Pickens County.

Requesting sealed bids for a new editor of the *People's Journal*.

Married the 3 Dec. 1899 at the residence of the bride's father MR. JOHN FERGUSON, MR. FRANK ROPER to MISS THURSIE FERGUSON all of Pickens County. Rev. W.C. Seaborn officiated.

Norris Station News
R.T. HALLUMS is principal of the school.

MISS RICHARDSON of Greenville, S.C. is teaching the school at Cateechee, S.C.

Issue of: Thursday 14 December 1899:

Born an heiress the 8 Dec. to MR. and MRS. C.T. HUGHES of near this town.

LUCIUS EARLE is at Baltimore Medical College in Pharmacy.

Married at the residence of the bride's parents MR. and MRS. THOMAS WELBORN last Monday, MISS FLORENCE WELBORN and MR. J.A. PICKLE. Rev. J.M. Stewart officiated.

Born the 9 Dec. a daughter to MR. and MRS. W.M. MURPHREE of near town.

Easley Dots
S.C. STATE BOARD of HEALTH has instructed DR. WYATT and DR. GILLILAND to force compulsory vaccination (small pox).

Born a boy the 17 Dec. to MR. and MRS. R.E. OLIVER.

MISS CORA BOWEN closed school at Peter's Creek on Friday.

Hagood School will open the 1st Monday in Jan. with JOHN D. EDENS, Principal.

Married the 17 Dec. at the residence of MR. SNOW MASTERS by Magistrate A.L. Edens, MR. GEORGE SUTHERLAND to MISS MARTHA CANTRELL all of Pickens County.

LT. THOMAS M. BRUMBY of Georgia, ADMIRAL DEWEY'S flag officer died Sunday at Garfield Hospital, Washington, D.C.

E.C. COOPER died the 12 Dec. at his home near Thomasville, S.C. He was born the 9 July 1845 in Anderson County, S.C. Burial was at Antioch Methodist Church. He leaves 7 children.

Married at the residence of the bride's parents MR. and MRS. T.C. SPENCER of Spencer Post Office, S.C. the 13 Dec., MR. MOSES PINSON of Thicketty, S.C. to MISS FANNIE Z. SPENCER. W.D. Garrison, N.P. officiated. The couple will live in Gaffney, S.C.

WEST HEAD died on Sunday after being shot by JOE KELLEY. They are both white. Inquest Tuesday. *Greenville News*

Card of Thanks, to neighbors and friends for kindness at the death of our son MANLEY CLARK by parents, J.E. and M.E. CLARK.

Article - "Tuskegee Institute".

THE PEOPLE'S JOURNAL 1900

Issue of: Thursday 4 January 1900:

Born a boy to MR. and MRS. JOHN F. HARRIS the 26 (Dec. 1899).

Born a girl to MR. and MRS. GEORGE COOPER, four miles north of town, the 14 (Dec. 1899).

Born a boy to MR. and MRS. JAMES TROTTER, who live near Glassy Mountain, the 16 (Dec. 1899).

Married the 27 (Dec. 1899) at the residence of the bride's mother MRS. MARY MARTIN, MR. REED McCRAREY to MISS LIZZIE MARTIN all of Pickens County.

Married the 24 (Dec. 1899) at the residence of Rev. B.E. Grandy, MR. J.R. KELLEY to MISS HATTIE SMITH all of Pickens County.

Married the 24 (Dec. 1899) at the residence of Rev. J.E. Foster, MR. LEM EPPS of Marietta, S.C. to MISS BETTIE STROUD of Dacusville, S.C.

Married the 24 (Dec. 1899) at the residence of Magistrate B.D. Garvin of Central Township, MR. HENRY ENTREKIN to MISS LUCY GAINES.

Married the 29 (Dec. 1899) by Rev. J.T. Dobson, MR. WILLIAM DORSEY to MISS LIZZIE MAULDIN all of Central Township.

Married the 26 (Dec. 1899) by Magistrate B.D. Garvin, COLUMBUS JAMESON to NINEVAH HALLUMS, both colored.

Married the 24 (Dec. 1899) at the residence of Magistrate B.D. Garvin of Central Township, MR. TRAINUM MAULDIN to MISS MARY DORSEY.

Married the 31 (Dec. 1899), MR. WILEY ROPER of near town, to MISS MINNIE DACUS of Knob, S.C.

Married the 24 (Dec. 1899) at the residence of the bride's father MR. WARREN TURNER by Rev. W.C. Seaborn, MR. BUTLER SCRUGGS to MISS MAGGIE TURNER all of Pickens County.

Married the 24 Dec. 1899 at the home of the bride's mother MRS. NANCY CRUMPTON, by Rev. W.C. Seaborn, MR. SAMUEL A. PERRY to MISS LIDIA M. CRUMPTON all of Pickens County.

Married the 24 Dec. 1899, at the residence of the bride's parents at Cateechee, S.C., MR. J. ALONZO BROWN to MISS _____ JOHNSON by Rev. W.G. Mauldin (this was an error see issue of the 18 Jan. 1900).

Married the 24 (Dec. 1899) at the residence of the bride's father J.C. GARRETT of Prater, S.C., MISS LULA GARRETT to PROF. RICHARD T. HALLUM of Liberty, S.C. by Rev. W.C. Seaborn.

Married the 31 Dec. 1899 at the home of the bride's parents MR. and MRS. H.A. RICHEY, MISS CORA RICHEY and MR. WARREN MARTIN by Rev. M.L. Jones.

Pickens Co., S.C. Final Settlement - Estate of J.G. FREEMAN, deceased by W.B. FREEMAN, Administrator.

Pickens Co., S.C. Citation Notice - L.P. JAMES applied for Letters of Administration for the estate of T.E. JAMES, deceased.

Pickens Co., S.C. Citation Notice - R.J. ROGERS and J.D. ROGERS applied for Letters of Administration for the estate of HENRY ROGERS, deceased.

Issue of: Thursday 11 January 1900:

The work on the tenement houses of the EASLEY COTTON MILL is progressing nicely under the supervision of CONTRACTOR GRANDY of Pickens.

Married the 7 (Jan.) at the residence of Magistrate B.D. Garvin of Central Township, MR. CHARLIE GASSAWAY to MISS MARY MAW.

Married the 31 (Dec. 1899) at the residence of the bride's father EDWARD EARRICK (GARRICK) of Maynard, S.C., MR. JOHN LOOPER to MISS MELLIE GARRICK by Rev. A.J. Manley.

Married the 7 (Jan.) at the residence of Rev. J.M. Stewart, MR. SMITH PORTER to MISS HELLEN JARRETT all of Pickens County.

MRS. DICKSON of Calhoun, this county, died the 1 (Jan.). She was about 50 years old and leaves a husband and many relatives. Mrs. Dickson was buried at the cemetery in Duncan, S.C.

FRANK CAUWELL, colored, died the 22 (Dec. 1899) while working on a well for J. FRANK CRANE.

HENSON CHAPMAN died at his home on the Eastatoe the 7 (Jan.). He was a Confederate Veteran of about 60 years of age. Burial was at McKinney's Chapel.

Married at the home of the bride's parents MR. and MRS. D.B. WERTZ of Silver Street, Newberry, S.C. the 3 (Jan.), MISS LILLIAN WERTZ and MR. S. ARTHUR HUNT of this place by Rev. D.P. Boyde. They will live in Pickens.

REV. A. McSWAIN ATTAWAY living 6 miles west of Pickens died last Thursday. His son died a few days before. Rev. Attaway was a prominent young Methodist Minister who leaves a wife and seven children (lengthy article).

Pickens County, S.C. Citation Notice - J.P. ATTAWAY applied for Letters of Administration for the estate of A. McSWAIN ATTAWAY, deceased.

Pickens Co., S.C. Clerk's Sale - Court of Common Pleas: H.B. HENDRICKS vs EPHRIAM GILSTRAP and J.F. HENDRICKS. Tract #1 - 1/3 interest in 735 acres; Tract #2 - 153 acres more or less. The land is to be sold Salesday in February.

Issue of: Thursday 18 January 1900:

A daughter was born to MR. and MRS. ROSS MOON the 16 (Jan.).

WILLIAM H. BILLINGSLEY formerly of this county, committed suicide by hanging himself during the Christmas Holidays.

Married the 7 (Jan.) at the home of Rev. John T. Lewis, MR. THOMAS EDENS to MISS MARIA ALEXANDER all of this county.

Married the 7 (Jan.) at the residence of NILES GRAVELEY by Magistrate A.L. Edens, MR. TYLER HOLDER to MISS NANCY TURNER all of this county.

JOHN SMITH has bought all the land that P.B. WATSON owned on the east side of Cateechee Road. Mr. Smith has just completed a nice residence on his "home place".

Married the 11 (Jan.) at the residence of S.W. HOWARD by Rev. W.G. Mauldin, MR. JACOB KNIGHT and MISS EULA EADES.

Issue of: Thursday 25 January 1900:

MISS FLORENCE BOWEN is assisting MISS BLANCHE HUDGEN in a very large school at Bishop Branch, Anderson County, S.C.

Twin boys were born to MR. and MRS. J.L. STANSELL near Ambler, S.C. Another pair of cotton choppers.

Issue of: Thursday 1 February 1900:

The Golden Wedding Anniversary of MR. and MRS. AARON BOGGS was celebrated the 17 Jan. 1900. The bride is 69 and the groom is 77 years old.

A flourishing school in Calhoun, S.C. is under the direction of PROF. H.C. McCRACKIN.

DR. W.T. FIELD was in the office the other day and says the

first deed ever recorded in this county was the 28 Oct. 1828.

Married at the residence of MRS. COOPER near Thomasville, S.C. the 23 (Jan.), MR. WILLIAM CORBIN to MISS EMMA SMITH by Rev. A.J. Manly.

MRS. A.C. CARSON of Liberty, S.C. died the 24 (Jan.) at the age of 55 years. She leaves several children.

J. ALONZO BROWN says he is not married, nor don't want to be (see also issue of the 4 Jan. 1900).

Receiving bids on the Maw Bridge near Central, S.C.

From Norris
NEWT COOK our resident contractor and builder has erected a dwelling on Factory Street.
HON. B.J. JOHNSON has erected a nice storehouse on Main Street.
J.C. GARRETT has erected a warehouse on Railroad Street.

Issue of: Thursday 8 February 1900:

MR. HOWARD died at his home near Dacusville, S.C. the 5 (Feb.).

LEUMAS SINGLETON, age 4, died the 27 (Jan.). He was the son of MR. and MRS. JOHN E. SINGLETON and was buried at Peter's Creek Cemetery.

A boy was born to MR. and MRS. THOMAS LYNCH the 6 (Feb.).

Married the 1 Feb. at the residence of Magistrate A.L Edens, MR. ARTHUR ROBINSON to MISS NANCY NEIGHBORS all of Pickens County.

A concert by several of the colored people of town was given at the Court House Monday night. A very large crowd of both white and colored people were present. BEN R. TOLBERT was the manager. Admission fee was a dime.

MRS. LAWRENCE LATHEM (nee ARIAIL) died at her home near Easley, S.C. the 1 (Feb.). She was about 35 years of age and leaves a husband and 3 children. Burial was at Lathem Burying Ground.

JACK JACKSON was killed on the FERGUSON place on Saturday by a falling tree.

TUDE REEVES was killed by JOHN MASSINGALE on Wednesday afternoon. ED WALKER and SILAS HINCKLE were accessories (details).

Pickens Co., S.C. Final Settlement - Estate of MRS. HESTER RICHARDSON, deceased by A.N. RICHARDSON, Executor.

Issue of: Thursday 15 February 1900:

WYATT PRICHARD the infant son of MR. and MRS. W.L. PRICHARD died the 8 (Feb.). He was one month old and was buried at Enon.

DAVID FRANKLIN GAILLARD, the 3 month old, son of MR. and MRS. B.H. GAILLARD died the 2 (Feb.) and was buried at Rock Springs Baptist Church. Rev. W.J. Sheriff conducted the funeral service.

A girl was born to MR. and MRS. W.W. HAMMOND.

The Palestine School at Stewart, S.C. will have MISS JANIE BRIGHT as a teacher.

My wife SADIE WALDROP has left me and I will not be responsible for her debts. SANFORD S. WALDROP.

Pickens Co., S.C. Final Settlement - Estate of G.W. FARR, deceased by J.P. FARR and E.M. HUNT, Administrator.

Pickens Co., S.C. Final Settlement - Estate of J.F. LAY, deceased by SAVILLA LAY and H.J. MARTIN, Administrators.

Pickens Co., S.C. Final Settlement - Estate of CARRY DOBBINS, deceased by H.J. MARTIN, Administrator.

Issue of: Thursday 22 February 1900:

The Times is a new weekly paper published at Westminster, S.C. The first issue made its appearance the 8 (Feb.).

REV. S.P.H. ELWED (ELWELL) died in Columbia, S.C. the 17 (Feb.). He leaves a wife and several children (tribute in issue of the 15 March 1900).

Pickens Co., S.C. Final Settlement - Estate of J.T. BURDINE, deceased by J.J. CHASTAIN, Administrator.

Issue of: Thursday 1 March 1900:

Married MR. WALTER KESTER of Calhoun, S.C. to MISS ELLA MEARES of Seneca, S.C. the 14 (Feb.).

M.F. HESTER is making arrangements to have a new dwelling erected on his lot on East Main Street.

A seven year old daughter of MR. and MRS. JOHN BEARDEN who live near the Campground died the 26 (Feb.) of typhoid fever.

The Progress a new five column, 12 page paper is being published at Union, S.C. MR. D.J. CARTER, Editor and MR. ALLEN NICHOLSON, Publisher.

A son was born to MR. and MRS. RUBEN MAULDIN of Field, S.C. the 22 (Feb.).

REV. R.N. STONE has moved into the new parsonage at Perritt Chapel.

MRS. SARAH MEDLIN wife of S.H. MEDLIN of West Union, Oconee County, S.C. died at her home the 21 (Feb.). She was 56 years old and leaves a husband and 11 children. Burial was at Wolf Stake Baptist Church.

J.R. GOSSETT died at his home in Easley, S.C. the 21 (Feb.). He was 68 years old and a former Confederate Soldier. He leaves a wife and several children. Burial was at the Methodist Church Cemetery. (JOHN R. GOSSETT, born 7 Sept. 1831, died 20 Feb. 1900, Co. E, 2nd S.C. Rifles, CSA, buried Easley City Cemetery - Pickens Co., S.C. Cemetery Survey, Vol. 3, p. 53).

MRS. ELIZABETH CAPEHART died at the home of her daughter, MRS. J.C. JENNINGS the 23 (Feb.). She was 69 years of age. Rev. J.G. Henderson conducted the funeral service. (ELIZABETH A. CAPEHART, born 1832, died 1900, buried Pickens Sunrise Cemetery - Pickens Co., S.C. Cemetery Survey, Vol. 2, p. 139).

JAMES R. HARRIS died the 22 Feb. at 62 years of age. His wife died 16 years ago. He leaves six daughters: MRS. W.T. GRIFFIN, MRS. J.B.R. FREEMAN, MRS. JAMES HENDRICKS, MISSES LILA, RACHAEL and HATTIE HARRIS. Burial was at Griffin Baptist Church.

Pickens Colored High School has C.T. MILLER as principal.

Issue of: Thursday 8 March 1900:

MR. B. LEWIS' house on Factory Street is nearing completion.

ALBERT KAY died at his home in Anderson County, S.C. the 14 (March) at 83 years. He leaves a wife and 8 children. Burial was in Pickens County at Griffin Baptist Church. Rev. M.L. Jones conducted the service.

MRS. DANIEL C. DURHAM of Pickens died the 1 (March). She was 56 years old and leaves a husband and 4 children. Burial was at Secona Baptist Church. (EMMA DURHAM, wife of D.C. DURHAM, born 12 Feb. 1843, died 1 March 1900 - Pickens Co., S.C. Cemetery Survey, Vol. 1, p. 211).

Walhalla is having a Semi-Centennial Celebration.

Issue of: Thursday 15 March 1900:

Married the 5 (March) by T.D. Harris, N.P., JAMES SMITH of Illinois to SARAH POOL of this county.

A twelve year old son of PINK EARLE died Monday.

Married on Monday last in the Clerk's Office by Rev. J.M. Stewart, MR. J.D. SUTHERLAND to MISS A.J. BALDWIN all of this county.

Married the 1 (March) at Glady Fork Church by Rev. A.S. Whitmire, MR. PORTER CLARK of Greenville County, S.C. to MISS LUCY GRAVELEY of Transylvania County, North Carolina.

MRS. BOWEN widow of JOHN BOWEN died at the home of her son COL. R.E. BOWEN below Easley, S.C. the 10 (March). She was 88 years, 3 months and 21 days old and was the first person to join George's Creek Baptist Church when it was established 40 years ago. She leaves 10 children. Burial was at George's Creek Baptist Church. Rev. A.J.S. Thomas and Rev. Aiken conducted the service. (ELVIRA HUNT BOWEN, born 17 Oct. 1811, died 10 March 1900 - Pickens Co., S.C. Cemetery Survey, Vol. 2, p. 183).

Issue of: Thursday 22 March 1900:

POWERS who killed JOHN RICHEY was tried in Walhalla, S.C. last week and found guilty of murder. He was sentenced to life imprisonment.

Married at the residence of Rev. W.C. Seaborn the 18 March, MR. JOHN T. ROBERTS and MISS EMMA MERCK both of Pickens County.

JACK SUTHERLAND died at his home in Pumpkintown, S.C. the 16 (March). He was 79 years old and was a gallant soldier in the Mexican War. He leaves a wife and 3 children. Burial was at Oolenoy Baptist Church.

Pickens Co. Court of General Sessons - Minor Criminal Cases.

NO ISSUE FOUND FOR THURSDAY 29 MARCH 1990

Issue of: Thursday 5 April 1900:

PROF. WALTER J. BOGGS is at the school in Reunion, S.C.

HIRAM SLOAN, colored, died while plowing near Olga, S.C., last week.

Born a boy and a girl to MR. and MRS. JAMES CHILDRESS near town the 3 (April).

Married the 1 (April) at the residence of the bride's parents of Marietta, S.C., MR. SIDNEY BURNS to MISS JENNIE COLEMAN. Rev. J.E. Foster officiated.

Married the 27 (March) at the residence of the bride's parents MR. and MRS. THOMAS STEWART of Maynard, S.C., MR. JULIUS EUGENE SMITH to MISS MAUDE STEWART by Rev. Mr. Wiggins. The couple will live in Spencer, North Carolina.

MRS. T.W. TOWNES, nee MISS LEWIS, died at her home near Porter Post Office, S.C. the 2 (April). She was a daughter of HENRY J. LEWIS of Anderson Mills, S.C. Burial was at Mountain Grove Baptist Church. (CORNELIA J. TOWNES, born 31 Jan. 1870, died 2 April 1900 - Pickens Co., S.C. Cemetery Survey, Vol. 2, p. 79 - see issue of the 12 April 1900).

SOLOMON LOOPER of near Dacusville, S.C. died the 31 (March). He was about 80 years old and leaves a wife and 2 children. Burial was from Nine Forks Baptist Church.

Issue of: Thursday 12 April 1900:

MRS. CORNELIA TOWNES wife of T.W. TOWNES died at the home of her parents MR. and MRS. H.J. LEWIS the 2 (April). She was 29 years old and leaves a husband, mother, father, one brother and two sisters (see issue of the 5 April 1900).

Married the 14 (March) at the residence of MR. MASTER by Rev. John T. Lewis, MR. R.D. SUTHERLAND to MISS LAURA E. CANTRELL all of Pickens County.

An infant son of J.R. MAULDIN who lives near town died Sunday. Burial was at Tabor Church with Rev. R.R. Dagnall conducting the funeral service.

Married the 4 April at the residence of the bride's father MR. J.S. BARKER of Calhoun, S.C., by Magistrate Thomas L. Grant, MR. JOHN HUNT of Pickens Co. to MISS SUDIE BARKER.

Article - "A Story of the Revolution - The Heroic EMILY GEIGER".

Pickens Co. Clerk's Sale:
JOHN C. O'DELL vs A. O'DELL - 110 acres near the town of Liberty, S.C. to be sold.

Issue of: Thursday 19 April 1900:

A girl was born to MR. and MR. W.A. GRESHAM of 29 Johnson Ave., Atlanta, Georgia the 10 (April).

Married the 10 (April) at the residence of the bride's father T.W. COCHRAN of near Pickens, MISS MATTIE COCHRAN to REV. STEWART T. IRVIN of Lincoln, Nebraska. Rev. Daniel

Avery of Tennessee and Rev. R.B. Hayes officiated.

Valuable Land For Sale - The BARRET farm - 250 acres - 1/2 mile north west of Pickens (name of seller not given).

Issue of: Thursday 26 April 1900:

Married the 4 April 1900, MR. D.W. REESE of O'Neal, Greenville County, S.C. and MISS OLA FOSTER second daughter of MR. R.B.A. FOSTER by Rev. Mr. Attaway. *The Observer*

Married last Sunday morning, MR. M.M. KNIGHT to MISS DELLA EADES at MR. J.C. HOWARD'S residence near Cateechee, S.C. Rev. W.G. Mauldin officiated.

MRS. ENTREKIN daughter of MR. and MRS. CHARLES E. WHITE died last Tuesday night. She leaves a husband, her parents and a seven month old child. Mrs. Entrekin is the niece of MRS. E.F. TAYLOR of Pickens County. MR. ENTREKIN is the son of JOHN ENTREKIN. Guntersville, Alabama - *Democrat*

A girl was born to MR. and MRS. ARTHUR MASSINGALE the 23 (April).

A boy was born to MR. and MRS. THOMAS FREEMAN of near town the 22 (April).

Married MR. BAGWELL of Pickens and MISS _____ HOPKINS of Piedmont, S.C on Sunday morning. Rev. J.B. Marsh officiated. *Piedmont Sun-Herald* - 20 April 1900

MISS STELLA HOLCOMBE daughter of the late R.E. HOLCOMBE died at the home of her mother the 17 (April). Burial was at George's Creek Cemetery.

MRS. TILDA GROGAN died at her home the 19 (April). She was 65 years old and leaves 2 daughters. Burial was at Bethlehem Methodist Church.

MRS. J. ADDISON BOGGS died at her home near Liberty, S.C. the 19 (April) and was buried at the cemetery in Liberty. She was 65 years old. Rev. J.R. Riley conducted the service.

MRS. MALINDA BROWN wife of FRANK BROWN died at her home near Travelers Rest, S.C. the 17 (April) at the age of 45 years. Burial was at Mount Carmel, with Rev. T.C. Holsclaw conducting the service. She leaves a husband, four children, a father, three sisters and two brothers. Mrs. Brown was the youngest daughter of WILLIAM L. SMITH of Cross Plains, S.C.

Issue of: Thursday 3 May 1900:

A girl was born to MR. and MRS. C.M. GRAVELEY the 25 (April).

Married the 29 (April) at the residence of Rev. J.M. Stewart, MR. F.B. DILLARD to MISS VINDA (VINDIE) MAULDIN daughter of MR. and MRS. PERRY MAULDIN who live near this place.

G.W. BANKS died at his home near Maynard, S.C. the 23 (April). Burial was at Cross Roads Baptist Church with Rev. Thomas Looper conducting the service. Mr. Banks was about 87 years old and leaves a wife and several children.

G.W. RICHEY a brother of H.A. RICHEY of this place died Monday at his home in Piedmont, S.C. He was about 60 years old and leaves a wife and several children. Burial was at Siloam (sic) Baptist Church.

Married the 25 (April) at the home of the bride, MISS CARRIE WYATT to MR. J. FLETCHER BROOK. Rev. R.R. Dagnall officiated.

Issue of: Thursday 10 May 1900:

Married the 6 (May) at the residence of M.F. Hester, N.P., MR. EARLE STEPHENS to MISS LEILA MAULDIN all of Pickens County.

Married the 6 May at the residence of M.F. Hester, N.P., MR. AMOS DODGENS to MISS MYRTIE PACE all of Pickens County.

MISS LUCINDA JOHNSTON died the 26 (April) at 63 years of age and was buried in the family burying ground. She was a sister of the HON. B.J. JOHNSTON of Central, S.C. (LUCINDA E. JOHNSTON, born 28 Aug. 1836, died 26 April 1900, buried Johnston Family Cemetery - Pickens Co., S.C. Cemetery Survey, Vol. 1, p. 14).

Issue of: Thursday 17 May 1900:

Pickens Co., S.C. Citation Notice - SUSAN WILSON applied for Letters of Administration for the estate of JOHN D. WILSON, deceased.

Married the 18 (May) at the residence of Magistrate B.D. Garvin, MR. FRED GAINES of Norris, S.C. to MISS LIZZIE MAULDIN of Liberty, S.C.

ANDERSON LESLEY died at his home at Old Pickensville, S.C. He was about 80 years old and was buried at Zion Methodist Church. He leaves three sons and one daughter.

Married at the residence of the bride's parents MR. and MRS. A.B. WILLIAMS near Cateechee, S.C. the 10 (May), MISS DORTHULA L. WILLIAMS and MR. TURNER T. ARNOLD. Rev. W.C. Seaborn performed the ceremony.

Issue of: Thursday 24 May 1900:

SERGEANT E.A. PRICE died at Petersburg, Virginia the 30 July 1864. There are two letters written from the line of battle near Cold Harbor, (Va.) concerning this death. One is from J.W.T. to Col. THOMAS and the other from A.J. PENDLY to COL. THOMAS. The second letter is continued in the next issue.

A girl was born to MR. and MRS. JOHN VAUGHN the 21 (May).

A boy was born to MR. and MRS. J.E. KINCH the 19 (May).

CHARLES H. CURTIS died the 19 (May) at his home in Pickens. He was a native of Indiana and had only been in Pickens a short time. His wife is the daughter of REV. B.E. GRANDY. Mr. Curtis was 42 years old and leaves a wife and one child. The funeral was conducted from the Baptist Church by Rev. A.J.S. Thomas.

Pickens Co., S.C. Court of Common Pleas - Summons for Relief - F.V. CLAYTON vs J.H. DEAN, et al. (details).

Issue of: Thursday 31 May 1900:

A son was born to MR. and MRS. W.T. NALLEY the 25 (May).

JERVEY REED, colored, was captured in Anderson County, S.C. He is wanted for murder in Pickens County. Reed is about 19 years of age. *Anderson People's Advocate* - 28 May 1900

Names and ages of people who died at the Poor Farm since 14 Apr. 1900.
NANCY COOPER   age 86
POLLY GROGAN   age 70
MAHALEY ELLENBURG   age 82
FRANK DRYMOND   age 84

Issue of: Thursday 7 June 1900:

Twelfth Confederate Soldier's Reunion is being held in Louisville, Kentucky (details).

A son was born to MR. and MRS. HENRY MAULDIN the 29 (May).

A son was born to MR. and MRS. FIELD ROPER who live south of town the 31 (May).

An infant of MR. and MRS. JOHN WALDROP died and was buried at Secona.

Married at the home of the bride's parents the 23 May, MR. ROBERT H. HOLCOMBE and MISS BELLE Z. MAULDIN by Rev. L.L. Inabinet.

GEORGE JOHNSON a native of this county, who left here many years ago for Texas, was killed by lightning week before last.

WILLIAM CANNON was killed by his brother THOMAS CANNON near Highlands, Oconee Co. (sic).

Married the 3 (June) at the residence of the bride, MRS. ANNA WHAM to MR. DANIEL C. DURHAM. Rev. W.C. Seaborn officiated.

MR. JOSEPH SMITH died at his home near Easley, S.C. the 25 (May). He was born the 18 Dec. 1814 and was a member of Enon Baptist Church. Mr. Smith leaves three sons and 2 daughters.

Issue of: Thursday 14 June 1900:

LINDA STURKEY died at the Poor House the 3 (June). She was 42 years old.

JOHN McTINDALL of Anderson County, S.C. shot and killed his uncle JAMES W. ROPER on Friday night (details).

Married the 10 (June) at the residence of M.F. Hester, N.P., MR. MODE HAYES to MISS LOLA WARD all of Pickens County.

Pickens Co., S.C. Court of Common Pleas - Summons for Relief - WILLIAM S. PARSONS vs JOHN WOOLEY (details).

Issue of: Thursday 21 June 1900:

A son was born to MR. and MRS. J.M. WARD the 17 (June).

Married the 8 (June) by Rev. T.F. Nelson, MR. E. WILSON and MISS NORA LESLEY. The bride is the daughter of PROF. J.F. LESLEY of near Easley, S.C.

Issue of: Thursday 28 June 1900:

A son was born to MR. and MRS. BEN M. GRIFFIN the 20 (June).

The father of TROPE PARTRIDGE died in Floville, Georgia last week.

Contract for bridge to be let to the lowest bidder - Hagood Bridge on the Saluda River.

Issue of: Thursday 5 July 1900:

Article - "BELLE BOYD'S Career - Noted Confederate Spy had a Varied Life".

HAYNES JONES died the 26 June at the age of 54 years. He leaves a wife, 2 daughters and one son. Burial was at Peter's Creek Baptist Church Cemetery. Rev. J.E. Foster conducted the funeral service.

An infant of MR. and MRS. W.C. KEITH of Table Mountain, S.C. died the 25 (June) and was buried at Griffin Cemetery.

JULIUS JOEL PARSONS, age one year and four months, a son of JULIUS E. and LILLIE PARSONS died the 28 June. Burial was at Secona Church with Rev. J.M. Stewart conducting the service assisted by Rev. Z.P. Hamilton and Rev. M.L. Jones (see issue of the 19 July 1900).

A two story, 3 room front, brick building 90 X 90 will be erected on the lot just above this office. The firm's name will be HEATH, BRUCE, MORROW and COMPANY.

Issue of: Thursday 12 July 1900:

A son was born to MR. and MRS. JOHN BLACKSTON the 1 (July).

A son was born to MR. and MRS. ED HENDRICKS of Field, S.C. the 3 (July).

MISS OLIVE NEWTON will teach the Town Creek School.

Married the 8 (July) at the residence of Alonzo M. Folger, N.P. of Easley, S.C., MR. ROSS SMITH to MISS JANIE SATTERFIELD.

Married at Liberty, S.C. the 8 (July), MR. V.S. CARSON to MISS DORA DAVIS the eldest daughter of MR. and MRS. D.H. DAVIS by Rev. L.T. Weldon of Greenville County, S.C.

MRS. G.B. WATSON of Newry, S.C. died the 2 (July). She was the sister of MRS. J.D. HOLDER. Burial was in the Seneca Cemetery.

MRS. P.B. WATSON of Greenville, S.C. died. *Greenville News* - 3 July 1900

MISS CARRIE McFALL daughter of the late ANDREW McFALL died the 4 (July) at her home near High Shoals, S.C. She was 68 years old and had lived all her life in Anderson County, S.C. Funeral service was held at the Presbyterian Church with Rev. J.N.H. Summerall officiating.

REESE BOWEN died the 7 (July) at his home. He was 86 years

old and leaves a wife and 11 children. Burial was at Tabor Methodist Church. The service was conducted by Rev. J.M. Stewart, Rev. B.E. Grandy and Rev. R.R. Dagnall.

Issue of: Thursday 19 July 1900:

The Mile Creek School will have MISS CORA ROBERTSON as a teacher.

H.A. PRICE of Sunny Dale, S.C. will teach at the Garvin School.

A daughter was born the 14 (July) to MR. and MRS. R.L. HENDERSON who live at SUPERVISOR LOOPER'S.

The Wolf Creek School will have MISS BETTIE ALLGOOD as a teacher.

Pickens Graded School will have PROF. W. ERSKINE DENDY of Walhalla, S.C. as principal and MISS JANIE FERGUSON of this place as assistant.

Pickens Co., S.C. Final Settlement - Estate of A.T. CLAYTON, deceased by W.T. O'DELL, Executor.

Pickens Co., S.C. Court of General Session - Criminal cases (details).

Issue of: Thursday 26 July 1900:

Article - "CONGRESSMAN A.C. LATIMER".

AUDITOR HUNT and his wife moved into their new residence last week.

The Keowee School will have R. EARLE MILLER as a teacher.

The new residence of C.L. CURETON on Liberty Street is very near completion.

The work on the PICKENS BENDING FACTORY is progressing nicely and in a short time wagon spokes, realms, etc. will be manufactured.

Issue of: Thursday 2 August 1900:

MISS MARY KIRKSEY will teach at Martin School.

Married the 8 (July) at the residence of John T. Boggs, N.P. of Liberty, S.C., MR. ISAAC KING to MISS ETTA BRITTON all of Pickens County.

RICHARD K. HILL "DICK HILL" of Easley, S.C. died last Saturday at the age of 62 years. He leaves four children:

MR. THOMAS HILL of Welford, S.C., MRS. B.M. HESTER of Brownwood, Texas, MRS. HENRY NIX of Spencer, North Carolina and MRS. JOHN L. THORNLEY, JR. of Pickens. Burial was at the Methodist Church in Easley. (RICHARD K. HILL, born 24 Jan. 1838, died 28 July 1900, Co. F, 1st S.C. Cavalry, CSA, buried Easley City Cemetery - Pickens Co., S.C. Cemetery Survey, Vol 3, p. 31).

Pickens Co., S.C. Citation Notice - Estate of R.K. HILL, deceased. T.M. HILL and A.W. FOLGER apply for Letters of Administration.

Issue of: Thursday 9 August 1900:

ELMER SIMMONS, son of FRANK SIMMONS, died at his home at Pearl, S.C. the 18 (July). He was eight years old and was buried at Griffin Church. Rev. B. Holder conducted the service.

THOMAS A. BOLT of Piedmont, S.C. died Wednesday. He was 36 years of age. Mr. Bolt was a brother of DR. J.L. BOLT and the son of EX-SHERIFF WILLIAM BOLT of Anderson, S.C. He leaves a wife and several children.

MRS. IRVIN ALEXANDER of Stewart, S.C. died Saturday at her home. She leaves a husband and several children. (CAROLINE ELIZABETH ALEXANDER, born 21 Jan. 1854, died 4 Aug. 1900, buried Keowee Baptist Church Cemetery - Pickens Co., S.C. Cemetery Survey, Vol. 1, p. 91).

J. MATTISON WINCHESTER died at his home in Hazel, S.C. last Sunday. He leaves a wife and several children. Burial was at Antioch Baptist Church Cemetery.

A girl was born to MR. and MRS. ADOLPHUS BAGWELL the 27 (July).

Married the 5 (Aug.) by Magistrate Garvin of Central, S.C., ANDREW HAMILTON, colored, to MARY HALLUM, colored.

Issue of: Thursday 16 August 1900:

JOHN THOMPSON LOVETT died the 24 July at Liberty, S.C. His home was in Jefferson County, Florida. He was a cousin of T.N. HUNTER and is survived by his parents. Burial was at the Old Liberty Cemetery. Mr. Lovett was 19 years old.

MRS. PAULINE BOGGS died the 19 April. (E. PAULINE BOGGS, born 21 Dec. 1828, died 19 April 1900, wife of J.A. BOGGS, buried Liberty City Cemetery - Pickens Co., S.C. Cemetery Survey, Vol. 2, p. 211).

Married at Norris, S.C. the 12 (Aug. 1900) by Magistrate

B.D. Garvin, NOAH G. BOWLIN of Chick Springs and MISS MARY GAINES.

Issue of: Thursday 23 August 1900:

A son was born to RICH ROSAMOND, colored, the 20 (Aug.).

A son was born to MR. and MRS. BEN FRANK FREEMAN the 18 (Aug.).

Married the 21 (Aug.) by G.H. Hendricks at his residence, MR. JAMES HEATHERBY and MISS MAMIE RHODES of North Carolina.

Married at Liberty, S.C. the 20 (Aug.) by Magistrate B.D. Garvin, MISS LIDIE MAULDIN daughter of KIRK MAULDIN to MR. M.A. YOUNG.

The colored teachers of this county met on the 18 (Aug.) and organized a teachers institute to meet monthly. C.T. MILLER, President, W.W. COOK, Vice President and A.G. BOWEN, Secretary.

JOE LOLLIS, colored, has opened a first class barber shop in the shop on Main Street formerly occupied by B.R. TOLBERT.

The North Greenville High School situated at Tigerville, S.C. in the northern part of Greenville County is becoming one of the most prominent preparatory schools in the state.

Issue of: Thursday 30 August 1900:

B.E. GRANDY has the contract to build a brick store for J.D. MOORE on the west end.

Married the 23 (Aug.) at the residence of WILLIAM McCOLLUM, MISS ADA LEE McCOLLUM to RUTH (sic) HUDSON. Rev. B.E. Grandy officiated. All of Enon, Pickens County.

Married the 26 (Aug.) at the residence of the bride's father HENRY WRIGHT, MR. EDWARD HAYNES to MISS ADA WRIGHT. R.T. Hallum, N.P. officiated. All of this county.

Married the 26 (Aug.) by Magistrate B.D. Garvin, at his residence, MR. JOHN DILLARD of Calhoun, S.C. and MISS CORNELIA ARNOLD, daughter of ANDREW ARNOLD of near Central, S.C.

Issue of: Thursday 6 September 1900:

A son was born to MR. and MRS. PERRIN PRICE of Pendor, S.C. the 1 (Sept.).

Married on Wednesday before the 3rd Sunday in August by Rev. B.F. Murphree, MISS JANE LYNCH to MR. BEN CANTRELL all of

Pickens County.

Married the 4 (Sept.) at the residence of George H. Hendricks, N.P., MR. HENRY GAILLARD to MISS MARIE HOESH all of Pickens County.

MRS. JENNIE MASSINGALE died at her home at Table Mountain, S.C. last Saturday. She was about 78 years old and leaves four children. Burial was at Oolenoy Baptist Church.

BAZ HALLUM son of ISAAC HALLUM was killed at R.H. BOWEN'S saw mill on Monday by _____ JOHNSON. Both parties colored.

Pickens Co., S.C. Final Settlement - Estate of J.W. COCHRAN, deceased by A.J. BOGGS, Executor.

Pickens Co., S.C. Final Settlement - Estate of H.C. MILLER, deceased by CARRIE M. SIMMONS, RESCIE (sic) C.M. HOOK and W.W. SIMMONS, Executors.

Land for sale at the late residence of M.A. O'DELL on the 15 November:
Tract #1 - 51 41/100 acres with a good dwelling house.
Tract #2 - 43 77/100 acres with a good dwelling house.
Tract #3 - 56 15/100 acres.
The land is being sold by F.V. O'DELL, L.B. O'DELL, J.P. O'DELL, N.L. WILLIAMS and L.K. KELLY.

Issue of: Thursday 13 September 1900:

ARTHUR SEWALL, Democratic Candidate for Vice-President in 1896 died (details).

MRS. MILDRED ANN FANT wife of MR. O.H.P. FANT died in Anderson, S.C. the 6 (Sept.) at the residence of her son MR. J. REESE FANT. She was the daughter of TILLMAN McGEE and was born in Oconee Co., S.C. near Townville the 12 July 1822. Mrs. Fant married the 16 Jan. 1844 and had 11 children, 10 are still living. Burial was at Silver Brook Cemetery, Anderson County, S.C. *Anderson Daily Mail*
Mrs. Fant was the mother of MRS. J.L. THORNLEY of this place (two notices in same issue).

A son was born to MR. AND MRS. WILLIAM BAGWELL of near town the 8 (Sept.).

The Oconee News, published at Seneca, S.C. has suspended publication for awhile.

A son was born to MR. and MR. EARLE GILSTRAP of Cedar Rock, S.C. the 7 (Sept.).

A six month old son of THOMAS STEWART of Crow Creek, died the 3 (Sept.). Burial was at Shady Grove Baptist Church.

Married the 9 (Sept.) at the residence of M.F. Hester, N.P., MR. JOHN STEPHENS to MISS CORA PACE all of Pickens County.

LUCAS LYNCH, 15 month old son of MR. and MRS. ROBERT LYNCH of Sunny Dale, S.C., died the 8 (Sept.). Rev. J.T. Lewis conducted the service at Holly Springs Baptist Church. (R. LUCUS LYNCH, born 14 June 1895, died 8 Sept. 1900 - Pickens Co., S.C. Cemetery Survey, Vol. 2, p. 63).

Married at the residence of the bride's parents the 5 (Sept.), MR. FRANK STEPHENS to MISS ESSIE DURHAM. Rev. J. M. Stewart officiated. All of Pickens County.

MRS. WILLIAM KELLEY died at her home on Crow Creek the 5 (Sept.). She was about 40 years old and leaves a husband and 2 children. Burial was at Shady Grove Baptist Church.

Issue of: Thursday 20 September 1900:

The Vote for South Carolina State Officers (details).

Married at the residence of MR. and MRS. J.B. RIGDON, MISS MANNIE RIGDON to MR. TOM MASSINGALE, by Rev. J.T. Singleton.

Issue of: Thursday 27 September 1900:

Article - "STONEWALL JACKSONS' Surgeon Dies, DR. HUNTER H. McGUIRE".

CAPT. JOHN LEWIS THORNLEY, who was born near Charleston, S.C. died. He was the proprietor of the THORNLEY HOTEL. Burial was at the Presbyterian Church. (JOHN L. THORNLEY, born 30 Sept. 1828, died 19 Sept. 1900 - Pickens Co., S.C. Cemetery Survey, Vol. 2, p. 94 - lengthy details).

Married, MR. WILLIE MAW and MISS MAUD McNEALEY, on Sunday at the home of Magistrate B.D. Garvin.

Central Graded School is under the management of PROF. RUFUS RAY and his assistant MISS EFFIE CARR. Both are from Greenville, S.C.

Issue of: Thursday 4 October 1900:

The BENDING FACTORY at this place commenced work last Monday. R.M. WERTZ, Manager.

The Graded School at this place is under W.E. DENDY, Principal.

Married the 30 Sept. at the residence of M.F. Hester, N.P., MR. BEN PACE to MISS MAMIE HAYES. The parents of the groom are MR. and MRS. JOE PACE.

MRS. POLLIE C. HENDRICKS wife of MR. GEORGE HENDRICKS and daughter of MR. JOHN and CATHERINE NALLEY died at her home the 10 August. Burial was at Fairview Church. She leaves a husband and 4 children (lengthy details).

AD - CRAIG BROS., located in the MASONIC HALL BUILDING, Pickens, S.C., Selling General Merchandise and Groceries.

AD - The "BIG STORE", HEATH, BRUCE & MORROW COMPANY will open the 1 October.

Issue of: Thursday 11 October 1900:

J.P. CAREY, ESQ. moves into his new and elegant law office this week.

MARTHA SMITH wife of JOE SMITH, colored, living on the HOLDER place near town, died Saturday. She was about 20 years old.

Married the 3 Oct. by Rev. Stewart, MR. ARTHUR ALLEN of Williams, S.C. to MISS SALLIE LOOPER daughter of G.B. LOOPER.

MR. RICHARD ELROD of the Bushy Creek Township, Anderson County, S.C. died on Saturday. Mr. Elrod was the brother-in-law of MRS. W.H. ASHMORE of this place.

An 18 month old daughter of JULIUS MAYFIELD died Saturday. She was buried in Anderson County, S.C.

Issue of: Thursday 18 October 1900:

Pickens Co., S.C. Notice of Election Managers (details).

MRS. WILCOX living near Easley, S.C. died last Saturday. She was buried at Antioch Church.

RAY BRADLEY, the little son of THOMAS D. BRADLEY, died at the home of his parents in Atlanta, Georgia last Thursday. Burial was at Ruhamah Church near Liberty, S.C. Mr. Bradley is the son of A.J. BRADLEY of this county.

Pickens Co., S.C. Citation Notice - J.M. STEWART, C.C.P. applied for Letters of Administration for the estate of MRS. N.F. PONDER, deceased.

Issue of: Thursday 25 October 1900:

Pickens Co., S.C. Court of General Sessions - Criminal cases (details).

A son was born to MR. and MRS. JEROME PALMER the 23 October.

A girl was born to MR. and MRS. ARTHUR HUNT on Monday night.

Married, REV. L.L. INABINETT of the S.C. Conference, West Pickens Circuit and MISS IDA KELLEY daughter of MR. A.E. KELLEY at the Methodist Parsonage in Pickens the 23 (Oct.). Rev R.R. Dagnall officiated.

A son was born to MR. and MRS. B.C. BAKER the 18 October.

MRS. S.A. PORTER'S funeral will be preached at Porter's Chapel on the first Sun. by Rev. R.R. Dagnall. (SARAH GRAVELY PORTER, born 1 April 1858, died 11 Oct. 1900 - Pickens Co., S.C. Cemetery Survey, Vol. 2, p. 121).

Married the 14 (Oct.) at the residence of WILLIAM FARMER by B.J. Johnston, N.P., MR. SHADY BALLENGER of Greenville Co., S.C. to MISS CORNELIA FARMER of Norris, S.C.

A girl was born to MR. and MRS. SLOAN MEDLIN the 18 (Oct.). She has five brothers.

Married last Sunday, MR. RILEY MAULDIN and MISS CATHERINE STEPHENS, only daughter of MR. HENRY STEPHENS at the residence of M.F. Hester, N.P.

Pickens Co., S.C. Sheriff's Sale:
To be sold at Salesday in November.
J.L. McCRACKIN - 20 acres in Easley Township (tax execution).
MRS. SARAH J. SMITH - One town lot, Liberty, S.C. (tax execution).
WHITNER SYMMES - 2 lots and 3 buildings in Central, S.C. (tax execution).
M.B. DUNCAN - 100 acres in Pumpkintown Township (tax execution).
MRS. M.J. CHAPMAN'S Estate - One lot in Central, S.C. (tax execution).
GEORGE WHITE'S Estate - 50 acres in Hurricane Township on Keowee River to be sold.

Issue of: Thursday 1 November 1900:

Article - "Confederate Wagon Making Factory at Augusta, Georgia".

Pickens County Court of General Sessions - Criminal cases.

C.L. CURETON moved into his new residence last week.

MRS. HARRIS is erecting a commodious dwelling on her lot near the Court House Square.

Married at the residence of the bride's parents in Pelzer, S.C. the 17 Oct., by Rev. G.W. Russey, MISS ANNIE BOATWRIGHT to MR. C.M. DAWKINS.

Issue of: Thursday 8 November 1900:

Pickens Co., S.C. Court of Common Pleas:
T.C. SPENCER, Administrator of the estate of MARGARET HILL, deceased, Plaintiff, vs IDA SPENCER, G.W. HILL, ALICE HILL, FELIX HILL, JOHNNIE HILL, LEWIS HILL, JENNIE HILL, FRANK HILL, and BELLE HILL, Defendants (details).

A son was born to MR. and MRS. SMITH PORTER the 4 (Nov.).

A girl was born to MR. and MRS. BEN LaBOON the 4 (Nov.).

Married the 4 (Nov.) at the residence of Magistrate B.D. Garvin, MISS PRUDENCE GILLESPIE of Anderson Co., S.C. and MR. WILLIAM DOBSON of Pickens County.

Married the 4 (Nov.) at the residence of Mag. B.D. Garvin, MISS ORA COOK and MR. ROBERT OWENS. All of Pickens County.

Married the 4 Nov. at the residence of Magistrate Thomas L. Grant at Calhoun, S.C., MR. JULIUS ANDERSON to MISS HASSIE BARKER. All of Pickens County.

REV. DR. and MRS. JOHN SIMS WATKINS will hold a wedding reception for their daughter, LAVINE FRANCES WATKINS and MR. RALPH ERWIN BOGGS, the 15 Nov. 1900, Spartanburg, S.C.

Gaffney, S.C. - 2 Nov.
MR. ROBERT E. LEAVELL and MISS KATE FOLGER were married last evening at the home of the bride's parents MR. and MRS. A.R.N. FOLGER on Grenard St. by Rev. W.S.B. Ford and Rev. W.H. Hodges. The groom is lately from Newberry, S.C.

A.S. SALLY, JR. has published a lot of correspondence in the *News and Courier* to show that EMILY GEIGER may have carried some messages between American leaders. Her famous ride of a hundred miles with a message from GEN. GREEN to GEN. SUMTER must have been mostly fiction.

Issue of: Thursday 15 November 1900:

CHARLES CLARDY, the 2 year old son of MR. and MRS. JOHN L. CLARDY, died the 13 November. Burial was at Secona.

MISS ELLA JAMISON daughter of MR. ARCHIBALD JAMISON married MR. JOHN BABB on Thursday. Rev. D.W. Key officiated. *Greenville Mountaineer*

Pickens Co., S.C. Sheriff's Sale:
67 3/4 acres for sale, unknown land.

Pickens Co., S.C. Clerk's Sale - Court of Common Pleas:
CALVIN McDUFFIE SMITH vs WILLIAM HOLDEN, et al. 625 acres in Eastatoe Township to be sold (details).
N.A. HENDRICKS, et al. vs WILLIAM HOLDEN, et al. 100 acres in Eastatoe Township to be sold (details).
CHARLIE HUGHES, et al. vs W.M. GARRETT, et al. Land in Greenville Co., S.C. and 51 acres and 3 acres in Pickens Co., total 54 acres to be sold together and 2 tracts in Easley Township, and 104 1/2 acres to be sold (details).
The BRITISH and AMERICAN MORTGAGE CO. vs MARY M. MURPHREE, et al. 37 18/100 acres, 25 78/100 acres and 48 96/100 acres to be sold.
S.E. HESTER, et al. vs E. OBEDIENCE THORNLEY to be sold:
LOT #1 - A lot of land in the town of Easley, S.C. known as the R.K. HILL home place.
Lot #2 - A lot in the town of Easley.
Lot #3 - A lot in the town of Easley.
Lot #4 - A lot in the town of Easley.
Lot #5 - A lot in the town of Easley.
Lot #6 - A lot in the town of Easley.
Lot #7 - Land in Pickens County.
Tract #8 - Land on George's Creek.
Tract #9 - Land in Dacusville Township.
Tract #10 - Land known as the ROSWELL HILL estate.

Issue of: Thursday 22 November 1900:

Wolf Creek School has J.W. LANGSTON as principal.

A son was born to MR. and MRS. ROBERT KELLEY who live near town the 13 (Nov.).

Married at the home of the bride's father MR. E.O. SINGLETON near Tabor, S.C. the 11 (Nov.), MR. W.P. TEAL of Norris Cotton Mills, S.C. to MISS LILLIE SINGLETON. Rev. P.J. Vermillion officiated. *Keowee Courier*

W.I. GRAVELEY oldest son of MR. and MRS. W.I. GRAVELEY of Hall Post Office, S.C. died on Monday. The burial service was conducted by Rev. I.N. Stone. He was a member of Porter's Chapel Methodist Church.

AD - Seven acres of land for sale within 10 minutes walking distance of the Court House, by FRANK E. COX.

Issue of: Thursday 29 November 1900:

Little WILLIE RICHARDSON, the infant daughter of MR. and MRS. S.L. RICHARDSON, died at their home near Old Pickens, Oconee Co., S.C. the 11 Nov. at the age of one year. Burial was at Seneca Cemetery, conducted by Rev. D.W. Hiott. *Keowee Courier*

THOMAS CONNER, S.H. CHAPMAN, B.J. WASHINGTON and L.H.T.

CONNER, Deacons of a Baptist church at Central, Pickens Co., S.C. have applied for incorporation of the New Olive Grove Baptist Church. Charter will be granted the 26 Dec. 1900. J.M. Stewart, Clerk of the Court.

The telephone line is nearly completed from Easley to Pickens.

Married at Calhoun, S.C. the 18 Nov. by Magistrate Thomas L. Grant, MR. FRANK H. BARKER to MISS MAMIE DILLARD all of Pickens County.

HENRY DAVIS of California is visiting relatives in Oconee Co., S.C. He has been in California for 15 years and is the son of the late SIDNEY DAVIS.

Go to the Court House the 29 Nov. to see the wonderful optograph (sic) moving picture machine - Admission 15 cents.

HENRY BOGGS, 13 year old son of MR. and MRS. R.L. BOGGS, died after being struck by a falling tree the 13 (Nov.). Burial was at New Hope Cemetery with Rev. J.M. Sanders conducting the service. *Keowee Courier*

Issue of: Thursday 6 December 1900:

Dacusville School has MR. W.A. CHRISTOPHER as principal. ARTHUR is a model young man.

MISS MARY BOWEN has a flourishing school at Bethlehem Academy.

Married the 21 Nov. by Rev. R.L. Duffie, MR. JOHN L. SINGLETON and MISS EMMA GOOD at the residence of the bride's parents MR. and MRS. I. GOOD. All of Oconee Co., S.C. *Keowee Courier*

MR. TYLER GILLESPIE died the 23 (Nov. 1900). MRS. GILLESPIE is critically ill. *Keowee Courier*

A son was born to MR. and MRS. W.T. McFALL the 4 (Dec.).

Married the 25 Nov. at the residence of Magistrate B.D. Garvin, WILLIAM HENDRICKS to GRADA ARIAIL.

Married, MR. WILLIAM OWENS and MISS JOSEY GILSTRAY (sic), the 3 Dec. at the residence of Magistrate B.D. Garvin. All of Pickens County.

The infant of MR. and MRS. HAMP BRYANT was buried at Pisgah Cemetery the 26 November. *Anderson Daily Mail*

MR. JERRY WILLIAMS of Kansas died, while visiting his sister, MRS. H.A. RICHEY and other relatives, last Monday.

He was 71 years old and leaves 4 sisters and 2 brothers: MRS. E.J. MAULDIN of Forsythe, Georgia, MRS. M.A. GRANT of Georgia, MR. T.J. WILLIAMS and MRS. FANNIE EVATT of Gainesville, Georgia, MRS. H.A. RICHEY of Pickens and MR. A.S. WILLIAMS of Kansas City, Kansas. He was buried at Pickens Cemetery. (JEREMIAH WILLIAMS, died 3 Dec. 1900, buried Pickens Sunrise Cemetery - Pickens Co., S.C. Cemetery Survey, Vol. 2, p. 132).

Issue of: Thursday 13 December 1900:

MRS. MARY B. PICKRELL died at the home of her daughter MRS. KATE NORRIS at Broyles, S.C. on Friday. She was the widow of the late JONATHAN PICKRELL and a worker in the first cotton mill in S.C. (long article). *Anderson Daily Mail*

Reference to the newspaper, *Piedmont Headlight* (probably in Piedmont, S.C.).

Married the 9 (Dec.) at the residence of Rev. W.J. Sheriff, MR. G.R. GILSTRAP to MISS E.R. THOMAS all of Pickens County.

Married the 9 (Dec.) at the residence of Rev. T.F. Nelson, MR. LUCIUS WILSON to MISS AMY SWANGLING all of Pickens County.

HENRY GANTT, colored, died at the home of his son-in-law LEWIS EARLE on Elford Street this city on Saturday. He was 85 years old. *Greenville News*

Married last Sunday at the home of the bride, MISS EMMA LYNCH and MR. ABNER LOOPER. Rev. J.E. Foster officiated.

School opened at Olga, S.C. with G.R. MAYFIELD as principal.

MR. BENTON ROBINSON and family and MR. BOB JONES and family left last Saturday to try their fortune in the "Lone Star State".

Issue of: Thursday 20 December 1900:

Article - "Great Records of the Past".

MR. TOM JOE MAULDIN will take over as editor of the *People's Journal* the 1 Jan. 1901.

Married the 8 (Dec.) by Rev. J.T. Dolson, MR. JERRY GLENN to MISS LUCY SADLER.

Married at the residence of Rev. J.T Dolson the 6 (Dec.), MR. GEORGE LOCKHART to MISS MATTIE OGLESBY.

Married the 18 Dec. at the home of Rev. J.T. Dolson, MR. F. BAGWELL to MRS. FRANCIS GILLESPIE all of Anderson, S.C.

DAVID DUNCAN, who lives 3 miles south of Pickens, died at his residence on Monday. He was about 60 years old and leaves a wife and several grown children. (DAVID A. DUNCAN, born 28 Aug. 1822, died 18 Dec. 1900, buried Bethlehem Methodist Church Cemetery - Pickens Co., S.C. Cemetery Survey, Vol. 1, p. 19).

MR. JOHN J. KEITH died this Wednesday. He was 54 years old and a son of the late J.M. KEITH and a brother to MRS. NOAH A. BURLEY, MRS. W.W. BURLEY and MRS. J.H. KILE. He leaves one daughter MRS. W.M. FENNELL. His wife predeceased him by a few months. Services were conducted at Richland Presbyterian Church by Rev. R.L. Rogers. *Keowee Courier*

J.B.R. FREEMAN died at his residence the 12 (Dec.). He was about 37 years old and leaves a wife and 5 children. (JAMES B.R. FREEMAN, born 24 March 1863, died 12 Dec. 1900, buried Pickens Sunrise Cemetery - Pickens Co., S.C. Cemetery Survey, Vol. 2, p. 139).

Issue of: Thursday 27 December 1900:

A daughter was born to MR. and MRS. GEORGE GRIFFIN the 17 December.

MR. LEO GILLESPIE who has closed a school in Palestine is now at home.

Married the 25 Dec. at the North Pickens Parsonage, MR. GEORGE B. PORTER to MISS ARDELLA E. STONE the daughter of REV. I.N. STONE.

The mother of MRS. O.F. BACON died in Seneca, S.C. last week. *Oconee News*

PRESIDENT JOHN M. GEER of the EASLEY COTTON MILL went to Belton, S.C. to attend the marriage of his brother PROF. B.E. GEER to MISS RENA RICE. *Greenville News* - Friday

THE PEOPLE'S JOURNAL 1901

NO ISSUE AVAILABLE FOR 3 JANUARY 1901:

Issue of: Thursday 10 January 1901:

Article - "Immigration for 1900".

Married the 6 Jan., MR. CHARLES FOSTER and MISS LILLIE McJUNKIN at Secona Church. Rev. J.E. Foster officiated.

Married by Rev. R.R. Dagnall the 7 Jan. at the residence of I.C. FEW near Twelve Mile Church, MR. JAMES E. STOKES to MISS DAISEY B. McCULLUM all of Pickens County.

Married the 6 (Jan.) at the residence of Rev. W.C. Seaborn, MR. JAMES M. SPEARMAN to MISS MARY A. ATES (sic) all of Pickens County.

Married at the residence of Magistrate B.D. Garvin the 6 (Dec.), MR. JULIUS MAW to MISS CORRIE PERKINS all of Pickens County.

AD - B.E. GRADY, Selling Hardware, the office and warehouse are located near the depot in Pickens, S.C.

Land for Sale - 85 acres located 1 mile north of Central, S.C. being sold by J.R. MADDOX, Central.

Issue of: Thursday 17 January 1901:

The Governor's Message - Review of Conditions in S.C.

MISS MAY ROBINSON has charge of a school at Oolenoy, S.C.

Married the 10 Jan. at the home of the bride, MR. WALTER TURNER to MISS_____ADAMS. M.F. Hester officiated. All of Pickens County.

Married by Rev. J.M. Stewart at the residence of the bride's father the 13 Jan., MISS CORRIE DILLARD to MR. HENRY RIGGINS. They are both of Hurricane Township this county.

The new telephone arrangement connecting Pickens with the outside world is about completed.

MRS. O'BRYAN an aged widow of TIMOTHY O'BRYAN died last Thursday at Hagood Mill. She was buried in the western section of the county.

NORA RAINES, the youngest daughter of W.A. RAINES who lives near Maynard, S.C., died the 8 Jan. at the age of 18 years. Burial was at Cross Roads with Rev. W.C. Seaborn conducting the service (see issue of the 24 Jan. 1901).

ADAM MANSEL, colored, is the boss slaughterer of swine. Last season he killed 69 in the town of Pickens and vicinity.

MR. WILLIS STEVENSON of Abbeville, S.C. died here Monday. His sister is MISS LILA STEVENSON. Mr. Stevenson was about 32 years of age and unmarried. Burial was in Abbeville, S.C.

Married the 16 Dec. 1900, MR. THOMAS PORTER to MISS CORRIE CROW at Porter's Chapel. Rev. I.N. Stone officiated.

MRS. NANCY WOOTEN (nee PRESSLEY) died the 10 (Jan.). She was almost 75 years old and leaves a son and 2 grandchildren. Burial was at New Friendship Cemetery with Rev. John T. Lewis conducting the service.

From Liberty
TOM (BLUE) SMITH has built and moved to town.
S.O. SKELTON has moved to his new residence.
THOMAS HUNTER of Twelve Mile side has built a dwelling on his lot near J.D. SMITH and has moved in.

Pickens Co., S.C. Notice to Debtors and Creditors - Estate of J.R. HARRIS, deceased by W.T. GRIFFIN, Administrator.

Pickens Co., S.C. Homestead Exemption - CATHERINE ROGERS has applied for Homestead Exemption on the property of her husband HENRY ROGERS, deceased.

AD - Lumber for Sale - W.F. HENDRICKS & BROS., Table Mountain, S.C.

Letter to the *Journal* dated the 6 Jan. 1901 from SAM LARK, Valley View, Texas (details).

Issue of: Thursday 24 January 1901:

Inaugural Message - South Carolina Governor and Lt. Governor Inducted into Office (details).

MARY P. GARRICK relict of the late J.C. GARRICK died the 10 (Jan.) and was buried at Antioch Cemetery. She was 81 years old and leaves 4 sons, one daughter, over 30 grandchildren and 6 great grandchildren.

Married, DR. J.M. PONDER of Thomasville, S.C. to MISS KATE MAYFIELD of Mayfield, S.C., over the Christmas Holidays.

Married at Central, S.C. the 15 Jan. by Rev. D.T. Hayes, REV. ANDREW S. DAVIS of Central, S.C. to MRS. ANNA E. (?CATO - paper torn) of Oconee Co., S.C.

Married the 15 Jan. at the residence of the bride's father

by Rev. B.F. Murfree (sic), MISS ELIZABETH CRENSHAW to MR. J.T. BENJAMIN.

Married the 26 Dec. 1900 by Rev. D.T. Hayes at his residence near Fair View Church, MR. DAVE LAROY (sic) to MISS MATTIE BEARDEN all of Oconee Co., S.C.

Married at the residence of the bride's father MR. ELIAS DAY near Easley, S.C., MISS ESTHER DAY to MR. WILLIAM D. SITTON of Bushey Creek, Anderson Co., S.C. by Rev. W.E. Wiggins of Easley, S.C. (date not given).

Married the 17 Jan., MR. WALTER O. HESTER foreman of the *Pickens Sentinel* office to MISS LUCIA PERRY at the Methodist Parsonage in Easley, S.C., by Rev. W.E. Wiggins. The bride is the daughter of MR. ELBERT E. PERRY.

There was a lynching in Barnwell, S.C. of CHARLIE LANG ROBINSON. His mother lives in Denmark, S.C. (details).

Pickens Co., S.C. Auditor's Notice (details).

Issue of: Thursday 31 January 1901:

A family reunion was held the 22 Jan. 1901 to celebrate the birthday of CHARLIE N. DURHAM. His parents MR. and MRS. L.R. DURHAM were present and it was their marriage anniversary. Mrs. Durham's parents MR. and MRS. W.W. McWHORTER were also present and it was Mrs. McWhorter's birthday (details).

Letter from J.S.L. of Valley View, Texas, dated the 26 Jan. 1901 (perhaps SAM LARK).

Pickens Co., S.C. Final Settlement - Estate of JOHN F. STEWART, deceased by GIDEON M. LYNCH.

Pickens Co., S.C. Notice to Debtors and Creditors - Estate of R.A. COCHRAN, deceased by R.B. COCHRAN, Executor, Fort Hill, S.C.

Married at the residence of MACK CANTRELL of this county the 27 (Jan.), MISS LIZZIE CANTRELL to MR. J.E. DURHAM by Rev. B.E. Grandy.

MRS. MILLIE LADD who lived with NANCY GRAVELEY died the 24 (Jan.). Burial was on the Little Eastatoe.

Persons indebted to the estate of J.B.R. FREEMAN must settle with AMANDA E. FREEMAN, Administrator.

The SOUTHERN RAILROAD placed on its line a new fast train last Sunday known as the "Atlanta and New York Express".

Married the 23 (Jan.) at the residence of BAYLUS GOWENS, ZIM MILES to HATTIE GOWENS, all colored. A.L. Edens, Magistrate officiated.

MRS. JENNIE CRANE died in the Little Eastatoe Section the 24 (Jan.) at nearly 104 years of age (see issue of the 7 Feb. 1901).

Eulogy - "ROBERT E. LEE" (details).

A letter to the *Journal* from BEN HILL DAY of Decatur, Texas (details).

Issue of: Thursday 7 February 1901:

South Carolina General Assembly (details).

HON. GEORGE D. TILLMAN died at his home near Clark's Hill the 2 Feb. (1901) and was buried at Clark's Hill Cemetery. He was born the 21 Aug. 1826 at Curryton, Edgefield Dist., S.C. Mr. Tillman was a son of BENJAMIN RYAN and SOPHIA HANCOCK TILLMAN.

MR. MILES MOSS died at his home near Salem, S.C. the 25 (Jan.) and was buried at Ross Burying Ground. He was about 70 years old and had raised 6 children of his own and 10 adopted children. (MILES MOSS, died 25 Jan. 1900, 66 years old, buried Ross-Wilson Cemetery - <u>Oconee Co., S.C. Cemetery Survey</u>, Vol. 2, p. 16).

DR. BOLT now occupies his new residence near the depot.

Married at the residence of Rev. P.E. Grandy on the 3 (Feb.), MR. W.B. MANN to MISS JENNIE YOUNGBLOOD.

MR. and MRS. J.M. STEWART visited her parents MR. and MRS. W.R. HAMILTON near Easley, S.C. last Sunday.

Died the 13 Jan. (?)1900 (sic) MRS. MARTHA JOHNSON, wife of J.W. JOHNSON aged about 35 years. Burial was at Bethel Cemetery. She leaves a husband and 6 children.

MRS. JENNIE CRANE died the 24 Jan. at the home of her son FRANK CRANE who lives on Little Eastatoe. She was born in Pickens Co. the 11 June 1797. Burial was at New Hope Methodist Cemetery. Mrs. Crane leaves 3 sons, one in Alabama and 2 in this county (see issue of the 31 Jan. 1901).

From Hazel
MR. W.W. AIKEN has purchased from MR. J.S. PARROTT a tract of land including his storehouse to erect a commodious dwelling.

The congenial hotel keeper feeds the new train. The people look brighter and seem to feel better after 20 minutes in MRS. ROWLAND'S dining hall.

From Seneca
MRS. SUSANNAH BEARDEN died the 24 Dec. at the home of her son MR. JOHN BEARDEN near Fair View Church. She was 84 years old. Burial was at New Hope Church with the service being conducted by Rev. D.T. Hayes. Mrs. Bearden leaves children, grandchildren and great grandchildren.

A daughter was born to MR. and MRS. J.W. SHERIFF the 22 (Feb.).

MISS ALLIE EICHELBURGER of Laurens, S.C. has charge of the Reunion School.

WILLIAM T. KING died at the home of his son-in-law, W.R. DAVIS near Welcome Church on Friday. He was in his 87th year. Mr. King was a native of Anderson Co., S.C. but lived most of his life in Pickens County. Burial was at George's Creek Baptist Church Cemetery. His children are: JOHN T. KING of Oconee Co., S.C., MRS. E.E. DAVIS of Pickens, MRS. MARY ELLIS of Atlanta, Georgia and MRS. VERRELL of Alabama.

MISS MAY ROBINSON has had charge of the Grove Schoolhouse.

ADDIE MAY WELBORN, infant daughter of MR. and MRS. JUDGE M. WELBORN who was born the 10 Nov. 1899, died the 7 (Feb.) at their home 3 miles north of Pickens Court House. She was buried at Secona Church (see issue of the 14 March 1901).

Issue of: Thursday 14 February 1901:

South Carolina General Assembly (details).

Married the 10 (Feb.) at the residence of Rev. J.M. Stewart, MR. T. JEFF McDONALD of Pickens and MISS EVA E. NALLEY, daughter of MR. W.W.T. NALLEY of Easley, S.C.

Married the 10 (Feb.) at the residence of MR. FRANK SIMMONS the bride's father, MR. JOHN HOOD to MISS TEXIE SIMMONS both of Pickens County. Mr. M.F. Hester performed the ceremony.

MR. HENRY ROBINSON died last Sunday. He was buried at Enon Burying Ground.

Married the 10 (Feb.) at the residence of Rev. J.M. Stewart, MR. FEASTER CAMERON to MISS MAGGIE WATSON.

Six Mile, S.C.
B.D. MAULDIN has erected a blacksmith shop and WILL STEWART has a store and a very good corn mill.

Issue of: Thursday 21 February 1901:

Memorial to CAPT. JOHN L. THORNLEY who died the 19 Sept. 1900 at Pickens. He married first MISS McFALL and second MISS EVA FANT, the eldest daughter of O.H.P. FANT of Anderson, S.C. (details).

LESLEY MATTHENEY has returned to Pickens from Candler, North Carolina and has accepted a position with the *Sentinel*.

MRS. HARDY GILSTRAP, who lives at the home of MRS. PATTERSON near Seneca, S.C., died the 10 (Feb.) and was buried at Bethlehem (in this issue twice - see next page).

PROF. RUFUS RAY has resigned as teacher in Central, S.C. and is now in Greenville, S.C.

JAMES B. HOLCOMB is in his new quarters and is doing all kinds of blacksmithing.

Married, MISS CORRIE BRUCE to MR. LARRY C. THORNLEY, at the Presbyterian Church today (see issue of the 28 Feb. 1901).

MRS. ELIZA ZINK died at her home near Oconee Station, S.C. the 6 Feb. at the age 81 years. The service was conducted by Rev. D.T. Hayes at Pleasant Ridge Baptist Church.

Populations of Incorporated Towns in Pickens County, S.C.

	1890	1900
Easley	421	903
Calhoun		209
Central	396	349
Liberty	368	216
Pickens	283	449

MRS. MARY ANN SMITH daughter of the late WILLIAM GILSTRAP and widow of ANDREW SMITH died the 14 (Feb.). She was 73 years old and leaves 3 sons and 2 daughters. Burial was at Tabor Cemetery.

Married the 27 Jan. 1901 at 11:25 A.M. at the residence of the bride's mother MRS. MARY ANN GILSTRAP, MR. LEE REEVES to MISS JOSIE GILSTRAP. Magistrate Philip Chapman officiated. Parties all of Pickens County (in this issue twice). *Keowee Courier*

From Hazel
MR. LEE W. WREAVES (sic) and MISS JOSIE GILSTRAP were married Sunday, Feb. 4 at the residence of the bride's mother (in this issue twice - details).

MRS. LAVINA GILSTRAP aged 74, relict of the late HARDY GILSTRAP, died at her home in Easley, S.C. on Tuesday. Burial was at Bethlehem. Her first husband was the late

JASYER (JASPER) N. HAWTHORNE by whom she leaves one son, J. LUD (LUDLOW) HAWTHORNE of Lavonia, Georgia. By her second marriage to HARDY GILSTRAP she leaves one son HARDY GILSTRAP of near Seneca, S.C. (in this issue twice).

Married the 31 Jan. 1901, S.S. EDENS of Anderson, S.C. at the home of Mr. PRINCE near Abbeville, S.C., by Rev. T.C. Holtsclaw (name of bride not given).

MRS. DEANNIE FERGUSON SHUEY, daughter of W.M. and C.A. FERGUSON formerly of Pickens Co. died at her home near Bunker Hill, Russell Co., Kansas the 30 July 1901 (sic). She leaves a husband ALEXANDER SHUEY, 4 children (one a few hours old), her parents, and one sister, MRS. EFFIE LEWIS. She married the 14 July 1893.

Pickens Co., S.C. Court of Common Pleas - Summons - 21 Feb. 1901 - PEOPLE'S BANK of GREENVILLE, S.C. vs B.T. JOHNSON and J.M. HUTCHINS.

Issue of: Thursday 28 February 1901:

Married the 17 (Feb.) at the residence of Rev. P.S. Butler, MR. RUFUS MAHAFFY to MISS MAGGIE McCALL all of Brandon Mills, Greenville Co., S.C. Mr. Mahaffy is a former Pickens County boy.

MRS. ELIZA HELLAMS died on Tuesday at her home in Gray Court, Laurens Co., S.C. She is the mother of MRS. R.R. DAGNALL of Pickens.

MRS. MATILDA BOSWELL of Easley, S.C. died at the home of her daughter MRS. MAG SMITH the 20 (Feb.) at the age of 86 years. She was the grandmother of EX-AUDITOR N.A. CHRISTOPHER. She leaves six children: MR. SIMEON BOSWELL and MRS. J.H. BARNETT of Alabama, MRS. J.A. PICKENS and MRS. B.A. PELUM of S.C. and MRS. C. VAUGHN of Greenville, S.C. Burial was at George's Creek Church.

Issue of: Thursday 7 March 1901:

Information on the Anderson Co., S.C. Stockades (two articles in this issue).

A son was born to MR. and MRS. FRANK GRAY the 26 (Feb.).

Twin daughters were born to MR. and MRS. W.J. BOWEN of Mount Pleasant, this county, the 26 (Feb.).

A son was born to MR. and MRS. TYLER HOLDER of Rock, S.C. the 1 (Feb.).

MISS LEONA HENDRICKS daughter of EX-COMMISSIONER HENDRICKS held closing exercises at Oolenoy School of which she is principal.

Pickens Co., S.C. Jury List.

Issue of: Thursday 14 March 1901:

Anderson Co., S.C. Labor Contracts (details).

On the 2 Feb. MR. S.C. McWHORTER of the Carmel neighborhood celebrated his 80th birthday. His wife is about 72 years old.

MR. A.B. WILLIAMS who lives near Cateechee, S.C. died.

MRS. NANCY ACKER died at her home in Easley, S.C. the 7 March and was buried from St. Paul's Church in Brushy Creek Township, Anderson County, S.C. (NANCY ACKER, born 10 Aug. 1835, buried Williamston Memorial - Smith's Book of the Dead, Anderson Co., S.C., p. 3).

ADDIE MAE WELBORN born the 10 Nov. 1899, died Thursday the 7 Feb. 1901. She was a daughter of MR. and MRS. J.M. WELBORN. (see issue of the 7 Feb. 1901).

MRS. ELIZA A. BOGGS relict of the late A. MATTHEW BOGGS died the 7 (Mar.) at her home near Liberty, S.C. at about 65 years of age. She was buried at Ruhamah and leaves 5 children.

MRS. JULIA A. BOGGS relict of M.R. BOGGS died the 10 (Mar.) at her home near Calhoun, S.C. in her 70th year. Burial was at Mt. Zion Cemetery in Central, S.C. She leaves several children.

RANSOM DUKE died at his home about 3 miles east of Pickens the 7 (Mar.). The service was conducted by Rev. R.R. Dagnall at Tabor Church.

MISS ADELINE NEIGHBORS died at her home near Liberty, S.C. the 28 Feb. at the age of 66 years. Burial was at Ruhamah Church.

PROF. JAMES MOSS has a school in Walhalla, Oconee Co., S.C. and MISS HELEN MOSS a school on the Factory Hill.

PROF. JOHN O. HICKS is teaching in a school near the town of Walhalla, S.C.

A son was born to MR. and MRS. ROBERT LYNCH the 25 February.

A son was born to MR. and MRS. FRANK GRAY the 26 February.

Married on Wednesday afternoon at Equality, S.C., MISS BESSIE MARIE GLENN of Greenville, S.C. and DR. WALTER MONROE

SMITH by Rev. J.C. Shive. MISS JESSIE GLENN is a sister of the bride. The groom is the brother of DR. R.F. SMITH of Easley, S.C. and J.P. SMITH, President of LIBERTY COTTON MILL. They will live in Liberty, S.C. *Greenville News*

Pickens Co., S.C. Citation Notice - A.M. MAULDIN applied for Letters of Administration for the estate of RANSOM DUKE, deceased.

AD - Going Out of Business, T.D. HARRIS.

AD - WHITE & CO., WALTER W. WHITE and WILL E. WHITE, Marble, Granite and Iron Fencing, Anderson, S.C.

Issue of: Thursday 21 March 1901:

Sketch - "GENERAL BENJAMIN HARRIS".

Negro Burned at the Stake in Corsicana, Texas the 13 March (details).

Anderson, S.C. Matters - Additional Information on the Stockades.

Pickens Co., S.C. Court Proceedings - Criminal cases (details).

ETHEL AMBER HUNT died the 5 March at the home of her uncle W.J. PONDER. Rev. T.C. Holtzclaw conducted the service. Burial was at Hunt Burying Ground. She was 17 years old.

Died last Friday, an infant son of WYLIE ROPER. Burial was at Bethlehem.

Married the 14 March 1901 at the residence of Rev. D.T. Hayes, Fairview Church, Oconee Co. S.C., MR. J.R. BELL of Oconee County to MISS EVA WATSON of Ocala, Florida.

Married at Central, S.C. the 6 March 1901 at the residence of Dr. L.G. Clayton, REV. JAMES H. LAWRENCE of Calhoun, S.C. and MISS LAURA GOOD of Walhalla, S.C. The bride is the daughter of MR. and MRS. I. GOOD. *Keowee Courier*

Eastatoe Church Organized (details).

MR. JAVANN (sic) FOSTER died the 14 (March) at his home. Burial was at Shady Grove. He leaves a wife and 2 children.

W.W. GOODMAN died the 2 March at the age of 79 years. He was born the 19 May 1822 in Hadley, Massachusetts. Burial was at Old Stone Church. He leaves a wife and several children. *Keowee Courier*

Pickens Co., S.C. Citation Notice - T.T. ARNOLD and SUSAN E.

WILLIAMS apply for Letters of Administration for the estate of A.B. WILLIAMS, deceased.

Issue of: Thursday 28 March 1901:

Sketch - "JUDGE WILLIAM H. WALLACE".

South Carolina State News and Notes (details).

MR. HENRY DAY, son of the late BASS DAY and about 30 years of age, died the 19 (Mar.) at the house of Mrs. CLARINDA SMITH near Fair View Church of small pox.

A bank is being organized in Liberty, S.C.

MRS. BAKER (sic) relict of W.H. BAKER (sic) of near Wattacoo, in this county, died the 20 (Mar.). Burial was at Peter's Creek. She was in her 82nd year and leaves 6 sons and one daughter. Rev. J.E. Foster conducted the service. (A.P. BARKER, wife of W.H. BARKER, born 9 Sept. 1820, died 19 March 1901 - Pickens Co., S.C. Cemetery Survey, Vol. 2, p. 91).

The seven month old son of MR. and MRS. R.P. PRINCE, who died recently, was named OSSIE WALTON PRINCE. Burial was at Mountain Grove Church with Rev. J.T. Lewis conducting the service. (OSSIE WALTON PRINCE, son of R.P. and N.J. PRINCE, born 31 Aug. 1900, died 20 March 1901 - Pickens Co., S.C. Cemetery Survey, Vol. 2, p. 81).

Issue of: Thursday 4 April 1901:

The *Easley News* appeared in its initial issue last Friday. Edited and published by J.E. KINCH from his office in Pickens. It will be "helplike" for Easley, S.C. and the county.

Married the 24 March 1901, MR. W.F. TOMPKINS to MISS JOICIE J. MOORE at the residence of the bride's father. Rev. W.C. Seaborn officiated.

JAMES WALKER was shot and killed at Central, S.C. last Sunday night by DAN SMITH, both colored (details).

Two weddings among the negroes last week. CATER SIMS and LULA WRIGHT and BILL FOSTER and HATTIE BROWN.

JOHN TYLER YOUNGBLOOD died at his home near the western part of town last Tuesday, leaving a widow and seven children. He was elected Treasurer of Pickens Co., S.C. in 1890 and served until the term just ended. Burial was at Secona. (JOHN T. YOUNGBLOOD, born 23 Dec. 1850, died 2 April 1901 - Pickens Co., S.C. Cemetery Survey, Vol. 1, p. 207 - see issue of the 11 April 1901).

DANIEL ROGERS died in Louisiana at the age of 70 years. He leaves a wife, one son and 5 daughters in Louisiana and 3 brothers and one sister in S.C. His mother was the late MRS. CASSANDRA ROGERS (details).

Married the 13 (April) at the residence of R.A. Graveley, N.P., MR. THOMAS POWELL of Rocky Bottom, S.C. to MISS MARY DRYMAN.

Easley News suspends publication.

JAMES NEWBERRY KEITH infant son of MR. and MRS. E. FOSTER KEITH, died at their home in Pickens the 4 (April), at the age of 4 months. Burial was at Oolenoy Cemetery.

MRS. SALLIE CHAPMAN died at her home in Liberty, S.C. the 7 (April) in her 74th year. Burial was at Ruhamah. She leaves several children.

Issue of: Thursday 11 April 1902:

Additional Information on the Death of JOHN TYLER YOUNGBLOOD. Also, Resolutions of Respect (see issue of the 4 April 1901).

Pickens Co., S.C. Final Settlement - Estate of B.F. McKENZIE, deceased by W.C. McKENZIE, Administrator.

Issue of: Thursday 18 April 1901:

Pickens County, S.C. Church Directory (details).

A daughter was born to MR. and MRS. J.E. PARSONS at Pickens the 14 (April).

W.A. GILREATH is erecting a substantial residence on Main Street opposite the AMBLER HOUSE.

MRS. EMMA COUCH wife of MR. OSCAR COUCH died at her home near Walhalla, S.C. the 3 (April) at the age of 41 years, leaving a husband and 3 children. Burial was at Rocky Springs near Easley, S.C., with Rev. Johnson Sheriff conducting the service. She was the daughter of the late SPENCER STEGALL.

Married last evening, MR. GEORGE HILL and MISS KATE BOHART in Chickasha, Indian Territory by Rev. L.B. Grogan. The bride is the daughter of MR. and MRS. J.C. BOHART. Chickasha, Indian Territory - *Evening Telegraph*, 21 March 1901
Mr. Hill is the son of J. TYLER HILL, formerly of this county (two notices in this issue).

Pickens Co., S.C. Citation Notice - ELIZA J. YOUNGBLOOD and W.W. YOUNGBLOOD apply for Letters of Administration for the estate of J.T. YOUNGBLOOD, deceased.

Issue of: Thursday 25 April 1901:

Article - "Easley, S.C.".

Married in Pickens the 22 (April) by M.F. Hester, N.P., JAKE GRAY to ALICE CONNER, both colored.

MISS FLOY FOLGER of Central, S.C. until recently a teacher at Chicora College, Greenville, S.C. is visiting Pickens.

A memorial service will be held at the Old Stone Church the 4 May 1901.

MRS. ELIZABETH SMITH widow of TURNER SMITH died at her home in Central, S.C. the 13 (April). Burial was at Mount Zion Church Cemetery with the service being conducted by Rev. T. C. Potter.

The graves of the Confederate Soldiers at the Old Stone Church were decorated the 16 April (details - gives names of the ladies decorating graves).

Issue of: Thursday 2 May 1901:

Article - "JOHN C. CALHOUN'S Old Home". A Northern Correspondent describes the FORT HILL MANSION at Clemson, S.C. (details).

WILLIAM HAGOOD, colored, known as "Uncle Buck", died at his home in the west end of Pickens the 26 April at the age of about 80 years. Burial was at Cold Springs Cemetery.

A son was born to MR. and MRS. CLAYTON MARTIN on the 30 (April).

A model mill building was completed in Liberty, S.C. and the machinery will soon be in place.

A daughter was born to MR. and MRS. J. CONNEY GRAVELEY the 12 April.

From Beverly - 21 April 1901
A daughter was born to MR. and MRS. W.J. BOGGS on the 14 (April).
A daughter was born to MR. and MRS. T.N. SMITH the 13 (April).

Proclamation by the Governor of South Carolina, M.B. McSWEENEY, offers a reward for DAN SMITH said to have murdered JAMES S. WALKER on the 31 March.

Issue of: Thursday 9 May 1901:

Article - "Tribute to the Confederate Dead".

A son was born to MR. and MRS. JOE GILSTRAP on Sunday night.

Twin sons were born to MR. and MRS. J.W. CANTRELL on the 2 (May).

The Truth, Spartanburg, S.C. says, "MISS LIDIE HAGOOD of Easley, S.C. is the guest of MISS NAN CREIGLER on South Church Street."

An infant child of MR. and MRS. WILL H. ANTHONY of Field, S.C. died Saturday. Burial was at Griffin Church.

The soda water fountain of MESSRS. BOLT and THORNLEY, Druggists, is now in full blast.

A son was born to MR. and MRS. MOSE SIMMONS the 5 (May).

A daughter was born to MR. and MRS. MARION ARNOLD the 5 (May).

A daughter was born to MR. and MRS. DUFF HUDSON the 5 (May).

Notice - Do not hire or shelter my son JOE JEWELL, age 17, who left home without just cause. S. JEWELL.

Notice for bids on the Freeman Bridge, across the Saluda River.

Issue of: Thursday 16 May 1901:

A Memorial Service was held at the Old Stone Church (details).

Article - "Anderson Co., S.C Contracts are Called - Slavery Contracts".

The infant child of JOHN STEVENSON died. Burial was at Griffin Church Burying Ground last Sunday.

Married the 12 May 1901 at the residence of JOHN MURPHREE by J.S. Bowen, N.P., MR. E.T. CASSELL to MISS A.E. MURPHREE all of Pickens County.

Married the 12 May 1901 at the residence of RICK HENDRICKS by M.F. Hester, N.P., MR. VAN GRIFFIN to MISS ANNA EVATT all of Pickens County.

RICHARD SHIRLEY died in Central, S.C. last week.

JERREMIAH LOOPER has secured a nice tomb (stone) for the grave of COL. ANDY GRIFFIN, C.S.A. who was buried at Secona several years ago.

A daughter was born to MR. and MRS. R.H. CRANE on the 12 (May).

JOHN GRIFFIN, colored, was killed on the ELBERTON AIR LINE RAILROAD last Sunday. Burial was at Cold Springs Burying Ground.

Pickens Co., S.C. Tax Sales:
L.M. SMITH - 3 acres in Easley Township to be sold.
W.G. STEPHENS - 2 lots and 2 buildings in the town of Central, S.C. to be sold.
W.A. NEAL - 2 mules to be sold.
NEAL and NEWELL - 1 Nagle engine and 1 Erie City boiler to be sold.

Issue of: Thursday May 23 1901:

Married the 19 (May) Liberty, S.C. at the residence of MR. W.B. McWhorter, N.P., MR. CALTON SUTHERLAND and MISS LULA SUTHERLAND. Miss Sutherland is the daughter of MR. SAMUEL SUTHERLAND of Alabama.

MR. A.N. STONE died at his home near Old Pickens, Oconee Co., S.C. the 14 (May). He leaves a wife and 7 children. Burial was at Six Mile, S.C.

DAVID DORSEY died the 7 (May) at about 25 years of age. He leaves a wife and 3 children.

J. SAM LARK, Confederate Veteran sends a letter from Valley View, Texas.

Issue of: Thursday 30 May 1901:

Article - "Pickens Graded School".

Married the 19 May at the residence of Rev. J.T. Dobson, THOMAS BLACK of Anderson Co., S.C. and MISS LUGENIA SUMMEY of this county.

Married the 19 May, MR. ROWLEY WILLIAMS and MISS DREW GRANT at the bride's residence. Rev. Thomas Looper officiated.

JOHN GLENN, colored, of the Pumpkintown Township has found on his place a mine in which he says there is gold. Various prospectors have examined it and have decided that there is gold in sufficient quantity to be profitably mined.

PROF R.T. HALLUMS of Liberty, S.C. has been teaching in Wannamaker, S.C.

Married the 26 May at the residence of ALFRED SANDERS of Pickens Co., MR. JOHN JOHNSON and MISS MARY COOPER. M.F. Hester, N.P., officiated. This makes 184 couples Mr. Hester has married in the last 14 years.

The "Long Distance" telephone men have reached Easley, S.C. The line will put New York and New Orleans in direct communication with all immediate points.

The Unveiling of a Monument to South Carolinians at Chickamauga, Georgia (details).

Issue of: Thursday 6 June 1901:

TILLMAN and McLAURIN and the Gaffney Episode (details).

The bridge over Wolf Creek near Cross Roads is still not there.

Pickens Co., S.C. Citation Notice - THOMAS DURHAM filed for Letters of Administration for the estate of CARTER DURHAM, deceased.

A twelve pound girl was born to MR. and MRS. CHARLEY T. HUGHES on the 2 (June).

The eleven month old son of EDDIE STEELE died on Monday.

A son was born to MR. and MRS. T.T. HUGHES of Hughes, S.C. the 4 June.

Married the 2 June at the residence of the bride's parents, by Rev. P.S. Little, MISS MARY E. LOWERY to MR. FRANK MOORE all of Central, S.C.

Married the 19 (May), MISS LEVEY JARRET to MR. SNOW MASTERS, at the home of JOHN L. GRAVELEY of Sunny Dale, S.C. John A. Robinson, N.P. officiated.

EARLE FERGUSON of Easley, S.C. died on Wednesday (see issue of the 13 June 1901).

Notice - Do not harbor my son, TOM DAVIS, age 16, who left home without just cause. JESSE DAVIS (colored).

Issue of: Thursday 13 June 1901:

Tribute to WILLIAM T. KING, born near Belton, Anderson Co., S.C. the 15 Jan. 1815, moved to Pickens Co. in 1851. At the organization of George's Creek Baptist Church, he was a charter member. Mr. King died the 8 Feb. 1901 and the funeral service was conducted by Brother D.W. Hiott. Burial was at George's Creek with MASONIC HONORS. He was buried beside his wife who died a few years age. There were 2 sons and 3 daughters in the family.

A son was born to MR. and MRS. ROBERT BAGWELL the 8 (June).

W.A. CHRISTOPHER was re-elected teacher at Lathem for the summer term.

MRS. JAMES RICE about 25 years of age, died at her home near Alexander, S.C. last Sunday.

The two year old son of JOHN HAYNES of near Liberty, S.C. died last Monday. Burial was a Bethlehem.

MRS. LONEY CANNON, colored, relict of the late THOMAS CANNON died the 11 (June) and was buried at Bethlehem. She leaves several children.

Married at the home of Rev. C.T. Miller the 6 (June), JOHN PRATHER to DORA BOWEN both of Toccoa, Georgia. All colored.

GEORGE CURETON, clerk at the drug store of BOLT and THORNLEY, left Friday for Sewanee, Tennessee.

Married the 2 (June) at the home of the bride's father MR. G.W. NABORS by J.D. Simmons, N.P., MR. JAMES HALL of Ambler, S.C. to MISS KATIE NABORS, of Field, S.C.

MRS. LILLIE JOHNSON wife of CALEB JOHNSON died at her home in Pelzer, S.C. the 1 (June) at the age of 28 years. She was buried at Piedmont, S.C. and leaves a husband and 2 children.

WEST HEAD implicated in the murder of JOSEPH KELLEY, two years ago, will serve two years.

Married, MR. ISAAC HENDERSON of North Carolina to MISS TEXAS McCALL of Easley, S.C. the 9 (June). Mr. A.M. Folger, N.P. officiated.

MR. EARLE FERGUSON of Easley, S.C. died the 4 (June). He was found dead in his bed on Wednesday. Mr. Ferguson was a brother of MRS. JOB SMITH. (see issue of the 6 June 1901)

From Fairview, Oconee County, S.C.
We have erected a house of worship in our neighborhood which was given the name of Rock Hill.

Pickens Co., S.C. Final Settlement - Estate of W.B. CHILDRESS, deceased by CHARLES CHILDRESS and J.T. CHILDRESS, Administrators.

Pickens Co., S.C. Guardianship Settlement - ELIZABETH C. JACKSON, Ward and J.D. JACKSON, Guardian.

Widow of WADDIE THOMAS dies in a fire in Jacksonville, Florida (details - date not given).

Issue of: Thursday 20 June 1901:

Article - "The Piedmont Region's Name".

A daughter was born to MR. and MRS. R.E. OLLIVER the 17 (June 1901).

A son was born to MR. and MRS. J. HUBERT NEWTON the 14 (June).

MRS. HENSE VAUGHN and children of Weatherford, Parker Co., Texas are on a visit to relatives in this county.

The grandfather of MRS. T.B. HIGGINS of Seneca, S.C. was JERRE LOOPER.

Married the 16 June 1901 at the residence of HAMPTON BLYTHE, MISS QUEEN BLYTHE to MR. GEORGE TERRELL, A.L. Edens, N.P., officiated.

Married at Easley, S.C. the 16 June 1901 by Magistrate J.M. Jameson, MISS TOONEY HAGOOD to MR. ELIAS ADDISON all of Pickens County.

ANN HAGOOD widow of UNCLE BUCK HAGOOD, colored, died the 13 (June). Burial was at Cold Springs.

The summer term of the Bethlehem School District #20 will be taught by PROF. R.T. HALLUM.

JOHN I. MILLER, (colored), son of CLARK T. MILLER, recently a first honor graduate in the English course at Howard University in Washington, D.C., will teach the Griffin Ebenezer School beginning in July.

C.T. MILLER, colored, preached at the Poor House last Sunday. He has been elected to teach the Colored Wolf Creek Public School.

W. ERVIN ALEXANDER died at his home on Mile Creek near Stewart Post Office, S.C. the 14 June at about 60 years of age. Burial was at Crow Creek Church. Mr. Alexander's wife died about a year ago. He leaves 6 daughters and 2 sons.

A Negro named JOHNSON was shot last Sunday by BAYLIS BLAKE, colored. He died at the home of ABNER LOOPER in the Dacusville Section.

MRS. JULIA L. TOWNES wife of J.T. TOWNES died the 14 (June) at her home near Porter's Chapel. She was 60 years old. The funeral service was conducted by Rev. R.R. Dagnall and

Rev. J.T. Lewis. Burial was at Porter's Chapel.

CAPTAIN WILLIAM HUNTER died at his home on Golden Creek the 15 (June) at the age of 86 years. Burial was at Old Liberty Cemetery. He came from Pennsylvania at the age of 2 years, was a Mason and a Confederate Soldier. Captain Hunter reared a large family.

Issue of: Thursday 27 June 1901:

A daughter was born to MR. and MRS. T.D. HARRIS the 23 (June).

A daughter was born the 18 (June) to MR. and MRS. ROBERT LANDRESS.

N.D. TAYLOR a "crack-a-jack" photographer is now stationed in Easley, S.C.

W.P. or W.B. LOOPER, Confederate Soldier from Pickens Co. was wounded in the battle of Averasborough, North Carolina and died a few days after was buried in a family burying ground near the battlefield. He left a wife and 2 children living in Pickens Co., S.C. For more information write Box 91, Laurens, S.C. (no other details).

A 12 year old son of JIM SIMMONS died the 13 (June).

From Beverley
The funeral of MITCHEL DAVIS was preached at Reunion Church the 16 June.

Events in Easley
Married, MISS ROSSIE HOLCOMBE to MR. WILLIAM McKINNEY of Greenville Co., S.C., at the bride's home 3 miles east of Easley, S.C. the 20 June.

For Rent - 4 room house on Grandy Row on West Johnson Street, by REV. B.E. GRANDY.

Issue of: Thursday 4 July 1901:

Pendleton, S.C. - 24 June 1901
"A Confederate Soldier in the Anderson Poor House" by W.R. ROWLAND (details).

Married at the residence of B.D. Garvin, N.P., the 16 June 1901, DOASIA LITTLE to JOHN BOWEN both colored. All of Pickens County.

JAKE MEDLIN died at his home last Thursday near BOROUGH'S MILL in his 18th year. Burial was at Prater's Creek Church.

Married the 30 June at the residence of SHERIFF McDANIEL.

AMANDA SULLIVAN to JOE SMITH both colored. B.F. Parsons, N.P., officiated. Coroner Parsons looks after the living as well as the dead.

WALTER B. WILLIAMS of Anderson Co., S.C., eldest son of ELIZABETH WILLIAMS of this county, committed suicide at his home near Septus on the 29 (June).

A daughter was born to MR. and MRS. BENJAMIN PACE the 27 (June).

ROBERT CRAIG will be principal of Cateechee School.

J.W.W. DANIEL is principal of the male school at Johnston's Chapel and MISS SALLIE MULLIKIN of the female school.

MISS DORA GRAVELEY, daughter of MR. and MRS. W.I. GRAVELEY of Hale Post Office, S.C., died the 29 June at the age of 18 years. The funeral was at Porter's Chapel with the service being conducted by Rev. I. Stone and Rev. C.L. McCain.

AD - Presbyterian College, Clinton, S.C. The next session will start the 26 September.

Issue of: Thursday 11 July 1901:

Article - "Life and Times of FRANCIS W. DAWSON, Editor, Soldier and Patriot".

MRS. L.W. HARRIS of Fairdeal, Anderson Co., S.C. while traveling from Charlotte, North Carolina to Greenville, South Carolina last Sunday was asked to hold a baby boy about 1 year old. The parents never came back. Mrs. Harris is keeping the child hoping to find the parents.

Ground was broken on Monday for the bank building in Liberty, S.C. Business will commence on the 1 September.

A.B. HUGHES died the 4 July at the home of his brother near Pickens. He was 33 years of age. (ALFRED B. HUGHES, born 21 Oct. 1868, died 4 July 1901, buried Carmel Presbyterian Church - Pickens Co., S.C. Cemetery Survey, Vol. 2, p. 172).

An infant daughter of MR. and MRS. J.M. GILSTRAP died at their home near Crow Creek Post Office, S.C. the 3 (July). Burial was at New Friendship Methodist Episcopal Church.

The residence of W.W. AIKEN is about complete. The workmen were: JAMES SMITH, WHIT PALMER and WILL ROPER. Mr. Aiken is now ready for a few boarders.

MRS. IDA GREGORY a former resident of Easley, S.C. died in Columbia, S.C. on Monday. Burial was at Easley Cemetery.

She was a MISS GREEN before her marriage and was about 35 years of age.

Next Sunday the new St. Paul's Church, 4 1/2 miles south of Easley, S.C. in the Bushy Creek Township will be dedicated.

Pickens Co., S.C. Petit Jury List (summer term).

Issue of: Thursday 18 July 1901:

Article - "Trial and Conviction of WILLIAM L. YANCEY" - Stories about an Old Tragedy.

The infant daughter of MR. and MRS. ROBERT STEWART died on Monday. Burial was at Easley Cemetery.

A daughter was born to MR. and MRS. ARTHUR ROBINSON the 9 (July).

A daughter was born to MR. and MRS. WASH ROBINSON the 15 (July).

CLARENCE RICHEY was accidentally killed near his home in Lexington, Kentucky the 25 (June). He was a distant relative of EX-SHERIFF H.A. RICHEY.

ROBERT A. ALEXANDER residing on the Keowee in this county was married the 23 June to MISS BESSIE GRANT. She is the granddaughter of WILLIAM J. GRANT, ESQ., formerly a prominent lawyer of Old Pickens, Oconee Co., S.C. and a daughter of RICHARD GRANT of Oconee County. Rev. W. Reid officiated at his residence near Old Pickens.

MRS. F. SMITH wife of R.S. SMITH died at her home near Pleasant Hill Church the 3 (July) with burial at the church. She was 88 years old and leaves a husband and 7 children. (FRANCES E. SMITH, born 27 April 1811, died 3 July 1901, buried Pleasant Hill Baptist Church - Pickens Co., S.C. Cemetery Survey, Vol. 2, p. 110).

MRS. J. LEE CARPENTER of Greenville, S.C. is visiting her father MAJOR J.J. LEWIS and family.

A son was born to MR. and MRS. DANIEL McJUNKIN of Mica, S.C. the 10 (July). They have 4 sons and 4 daughters.

Issue of: Thursday 25 July 1901:

Article - "Fragments of Our History - Curious Facts of Confederate Days".

CAPTAIN A.H. JENKINS died Sunday. He was a member of the 4th S.C. Cavalry and was born is Colleton Co., S.C. the 8 June 1845. His father was ADAM HUBLEY JENKINS a native of

Lancaster Co., Pennsylvania, who became a citizen of S.C. in early manhood and married MISS MARGARET GLOVER of Charleston, S.C. *Greenville News* - 23 July 1901

ROBERT KENNEDY of the Camden Graded School has lately found the original tombstone of the Revolutionary Hero, BARON DeKALB in the cellar of the Presbyterian Church.

Pickens Co., S.C Final Settlement - Estate of TIMOTHY O'BRIEN, deceased by J.E. HAYGOOD, Executor.

A son was born to MR. and MRS. BERRY PACE the 27 (June).

A daughter was born to MR. and MRS. MORRIS GILSTRAP the 18 (July).

Married the 21 July 1901 at the residence of J.E. GARVIN, MISS BETTIE McALISTER daughter of JAMES McALISTER to MR. JOHN BLACK. All of Garvin Township, Anderson Co., S.C. B.D. Garvin, N.P. of Pickens Co. officiated.

LEWIS CHILDRESS age 5, son of MR. and MRS. L.E. CHILDRESS, died at the home of his grandfather JOHN L. LEWIS the 22 July 1901. Burial was at Enoree Burying Ground in Greenville Co., S.C.

MARTIN BOGGS, age about 35, died at his home near Flat Rock, S.C. the 14 July. Burial was at Liberty, S.C. He was never married.

GEORGE W. WILLIAMS age 90, died at his home in Pickens on Monday. Burial was at Secona.

MISS SALLIE WHITMIRE daughter of G.S. and VALENIA WHITMIRE and niece of HON. J.M. WHITMIRE of Greenville Co., S.C died the 19 July 1901. She lived 4 weeks after being seriously burned.

The *Journal* has moved into its new quarters in the ANTHONY BUILDING on the street leading to Brevard.

MISS VETA CHILDRESS opened a school in Dayton.

W.A. CHRISTOPHER opened the school in Lathem.

MISS NANNIE ROPER is head of Lenhardt School.

AD - R.E. SMITH, Contractor and Builder, Alexander, S.C.

AD - S.B. MANN, Contractor and Builder, Pickens, S.C.

Pickens Co., S.C. Notice - Contract for Steward of the Poor Farm to be let.

Issue of: Thursday 1 August 1901:

Action of the South Carolina State Executive Committee - SENATOR McLAURIN Invited to Resign (details).

Resolutions of Endorsement for REV. T.C. HOLTZCLAW and Refutation by some Members (details).

A son was born to MR. and MRS. BOWER FREEMEN the 29 July.

A son was born to MR. and MRS. FLETCHER BROCK the 24 July.

B.F. FREEMAN is in charge of the summer term at Hagood School.

S.A.S. PORTER secured a patent on his rotary engine on the 3 July 1900 (sic).

MAJOR E.H. SHANKLIN, a life time resident of Pendleton, S.C., died at Hickory, North Carolina the 28 July 1901 at the age of 75 years. During the War Between the States, he served in the 12th Regt., S.C. Infantry and later transferred to the 7th (Haskell's) Regiment of Cavalry, Gary's Brigade. His remains were brought to Pendleton, Major Shanklin leaves 3 sons and 2 daughters. (EDWARD HENRY SHANKLIN, born 21 July 1831, died 28 March (sic) 1901, husband of VIRGINIA ROBINSON, buried St. Paul's Episcopal Church, Pendleton, S.C. - Smith's Book of the Dead, Anderson Co., S.C., p. 342).

NELLIE CRAIG, the 13 month old daughter of REV. and MRS. C.L. CRAIG, died at their home in Walhalla, S.C. the 23 July. Burial was at Griffin Church. She was the granddaughter of MR. and MRS. SHERIFF H. BROWN of this county.

Stewart
Crow Creek has PROF. EARLE MILLER as a teacher.
The Palestine School has PROF. JASON ENTREKIN in charge.

PROF. J.W. DANIEL is in charge of the school in Norris, S.C.

MISS ALMA MAULDIN is attending Johnsonia Female School.

Hazel Items
Married the 14 July 1901 at the residence of CURRAY CHAPMAN, FIELDS R. CHAPMAN to MISS SALLIE LEWIS.
JOHN GILSTRAP died at the home of his mother the 20 July. Burial was at New Friendship Methodist Episcopal Church. The funeral was conducted by Rev. C.L. McCain. John Gilstrap was 16 years old and leaves a mother and 3 sisters.

Beverly
MISS MAMIE BALLENTINE opened the school at Reunion.

MISS MALINDA RICE, age 71, who lived with her brother RANSOM RICE in Jackson Co., North Carolina, died the 17 June 1901. Another brother is JACOB RICE and a nephew is NATHAN ROGERS. She died and was not found for 2 weeks. Burial was under the tree where her remains were found in Oconee Co., S.C. (details).

Issue of: Thursday 8 August 1901:

Dispute Settled - The Boundary Line Between Greenville County and Spartanburg, County, S.C. (details).

RICHARD HARRISON EARL died on Wednesday. He was 76 years old and one of the oldest citizens of Greenville, S.C. He leaves a wife and 7 children.

G.B. GILLESPIE is circulating a petition for the establishment of a GOVERNMENT DISTILLERY in Liberty Township.

WILLIAM CAMPBELL, age about 72 years, died at his home on MAJOR BOYD'S place north of Pickens, last Monday. Burial was at Secona. His son is SANDFORD CAMPBELL of Greenville, S.C.

An 18 month old infant of MR. and MRS. REUBIN STEWART residing on the JERRE LOOPER plantation, died on Monday. Burial was at Secona.

Married the 31 July 1901 at the residence of MRS. REBECCA MASTERS, MR. HAMPTON RIGDON of Pickens Co. to MISS MARY JONES of Greenville Co., S.C. A.L. Edens, N.P., officiated.

NARCISSA ROSEMOND, colored, wife of WILL ROSEMOND and daughter of WILLIAM SIZEMORE, died on Monday at the age of 34 years. Burial was at Cold Springs.

SAMUEL ARTHUR HUNT, Auditor of Pickens Co., died at his home in Pickens on Monday at the age of 29 years. Burial was at the Pickens Cemetery with Rev. Dagnall conducting the service. In Jan. 1900 he married MISS LILLIAN WERTS of Newberry Co., S.C. who with one child survives him. Mr. Hunt was the second son of ROBERT HUNT a life time resident of this county. Mrs. Hunt's brother is EUGENE S. WERTS, Superintendent of Education, Newberry County, S.C. (S.A. HUNT, born 24 Dec. 1867, died 5 Aug. 1901, buried Pickens Sunrise Cemetery - Pickens Co., S.C. Cemetery Survey, Vol. 2, p. 133).

A handsome monument has been erected over the grave of CAPTAIN JOHN L. THORNLEY at the Presbyterian Church Cemetery. It is a work of finest art. The work was extended from the original stone by WHITE and COMPANY of Anderson, S.C.

EASLEY COTTON MILL is having a commodious school and church building erected in a pleasant grove near the mill.

A little son of MR. STONE of Easley Cotton Mill, S.C. died last Wednesday and was buried at Easley Cotton Mill Cemetery. (ROBERT FOUNTAIN STONE, son of B.E.(?) and M.E. STONE, born 16 Oct. 1892, died 30 July 1901 - Pickens Co., S.C. Cemetery Survey, Vol. 1, p. 123).

Pickens Co., S.C. Court of Common Pleas - WILLIAM J. CREW, N.P. CREW, MOSES WILLIAMS vs CATHERINE CANNON, RUFUS F. CREW, et al. Summons for Relief.

Pickens Co., S.C. Foreclosure Sale - PEOPLE'S BANK of GREENVILLE, S.C. vs B.T. JAHNSON (sic) and J.M. HUTCHINS. 821 acres in Pumpkintown Township to be sold.

Issue of: Thursday 15 August 1901:

JAHUE STEWART residing on the JERRE LOOPER plantation is sick with fever.

HARRISON HOLLAND, youngest son of REV. W.P. HOLLAND, died near Six Mile, S.C. the 25 July 1901.

MRS. ABBIE MORGAN oldest member of Gap Hill Church died at her home near Crow Creek Church the 2 Aug. 1901 at the age of about 90 years. She was one of the first member of Gap Hill Church where she was buried.

MISS MARIE FOLGER was named 2nd assistant and MISS MAMIE SWAN first assistant of Pickens School.

Married at the residence of LAFAYETTE PACE the 11 Aug. 1901, MR. JAMES H. PORTER to MISS HATTIE PACE. M.F. Hester performed the ceremony.

Married the 12 Aug. at the home of her parents HON. and MRS. W.T. BOWEN of Coliatta, two miles east of Pickens, MISS MARY IOLA BOWEN to MR. BENJAMIN F. ROBERTSON of Clemson College, S.C. Dr. A.J.S. Thomas officiated. The groom is the 2nd son of MR. THOMAS L. ROBERTSON (details).

MR. and MRS. WILLIAM STEWART are guest of Mrs. Stewart's mother MRS. L.C. FOLGER.

A family reunion for HENRY WILLIAMS was held the 1 Aug. 1901. He has 110 descendants (details).

Letters remaining in the Pickens Post Office, S.C.:
R.L. ANDERSON   MISS MATTIE GORDON
GEORGE DORSEY   MISS ORA I. SMITH
MISS GRI___ FING   MISS BECKIE TROTTER

CORNELL FINCH   HENRY HUNTER
MISS SARIE FING   JOHN GEORGE

Issue of: Thursday 22 August 1901:

Married the 14 Aug. at the residence of Rev. A.S. Whitmire, MISS ENGENIE CANTREL of Mica, S.C. to MR. JONAH SIMMONS of Ambler, S.C.

JESSE ELLIS died at his home near Cedar Rock, S.C. the 16 August. Burial was at Bethlehem Cemetery with the service conducted by Rev. R.R. Dagnall assisted by Rev. S.M. Jones. Had he lived until the 17 Dec. 1901, Mr. Ellis would have been 84 years old. He leaves a widow and 6 children.

MRS. LUTHER RICHARDSON died at her residence, the NORTON place, Old Pickens, Oconee Co., S.C. the ___day of Aug. (1901). She was buried the 19 Aug. 1901 at Seneca, S.C.

OLGA LaBOON, the 3 year old infant of MR. and MRS. B.B. LaBOON, died at her home one mile north of Pickens on Saturday. Burial was at Pickens Cemetery. Dr. A.J.S. Thomas conducted the funeral service.

VICTOR WILSON of Anderson, S.C. age about 20, died by drowning. He was the son of the Presiding Elder, J.B. WILSON of this district.

Picture of the brick barn at J.C. STRIBLING'S place near Pendleton, S.C.

Pickens Co., S.C. Final Settlement - Estate of J.F. FOLGER, deceased by J.McD. BRUCE and A.W. FOLGER, Administrators.

Pickens Co., S.C. Final Settlement - J.McD. BRUCE, Guardian of LUCIA FOLGER and MARIA FOLGER.

Pickens Co., S.C. Final Settlement - A.W. FOLGER, Guardian of ERNEST FOLGER.

Picken Co., S.C. Court of Common Pleas - ANDY G. WYATT, Merchant vs EARLE HARPER.

Issue of: Thursday 29 August 1901:

The Institution at Clemson (details).

A daughter was born to MR. and MRS. LAWRENCE GILSTRAP the 22 August.

A son was born to MR. and MRS. J.H. SEABORN the 24 August.

GARF FINLEY, the 18 month old son of MR. and MRS. JOHN

FINLEY, died at the home on Mile Creek. Burial was at Crow Creek.

The application of J.P. WATKINS of Central Township to establish a Distillery was approved.

Married in Greenville, S.C. the 15 Aug. 1901, MR. GEORGE MORRIS and MISS BLANCHE McCORD at the home of her sister MRS. T.P. DAWSON. The ceremony was performed by Dr. Gardner, Pastor of the First Baptist Church. Mr. Morris is a native of England.

Issue of: Thursday 5 September 1901:

A son was born to MR. and MRS. MOSE HAYES the 31 August.

JOBERY SIZEMORE, colored, died at his home north of Pickens on Wednesday. Burial was at Cold Springs Colored Baptist Church.

MRS. J.D. CURETON has moved her stock of goods and is now doing business in the MASONIC HALL.

Married the 1 Sept. at the residence of M.F. Hester, N.P., MR. MEDICUS F. DAY to MISS BESSIE ROBINSON all of Pickens County. Mr. Day was in the 2nd S.C.V.I., Co. K that invaded Cuba.

ESSIE HARRIS, the little daughter of MR. and MRS. R.L. HARRIS, died the 23 August.

Married last Tuesday at the Presbyterian Church at this place, MISS AURIE HOLLINGSWORTH of Pickens to MR. JONES FULLER of Ninety-Six, S.C. The ceremony was performed by Rev. Thomas H. Medd, assisted by Dr. W.A. Rogers of Orangeburg, S.C. Her sister is MRS. R. FRANK SMITH. The groom was attended by his brother-in-law, SENATOR J. STEELE BRICE of Yorkville, S.C. MRS. F.M. FULLER is mother of the groom. MR. and MRS. FULLER will move to Conway, Arkansas.

MR. J.P. SMITH is having a dwelling built near the factory in Liberty, S.C.

Issue of: Thursday 12 September 1901:

PRESIDENT McKINLEY Seriously Wounded (details).

Article - "History of Pickens County".

An infant of JOE THOMAS died on Tuesday night.

A daughter was born to MR. and MRS. A. MITCHELL the 31 August.

A son was born to MR. and MRS. P.L. MAULDIN the 30 August.

A daughter was born to MR. and MRS. LAWRENCE GILSTRAP the 22 August.

WILLIAM PARROTT died about 2 weeks ago of typhoid fever. (WILLIAM H. PARROTT, born 2 May 1872, died 16 Aug. 1901, buried Prater's Creek Baptist Cemetery - Pickens Co., S.C. Cemetery Survey, Vol. 2, p. 147).

MRS. JOHN G. WYATT died at her home in Greenville, S.C. on the 3 Sept. She once lived in Pickens Co. and was a sister of MRS. W.W. FORD.

HARRISON DURHAM, brother of L.R. DURHAM, died at Dalton, Georgia.

JOSEPH WATERS, 14 year old son of B.L. WATERS, died near Flat Rock, S.C. in an accident the 3 September.

ABSALOM ROPER died at his home near Field, S.C. on Saturday night at the age of 84 years. Burial was in the family burying ground. He leaves a widow and one son. Mr. Roper was thrice married. (ABSALOM ROPER, died Sept. 1907/08, age 84 years, buried Absalom Roper Cemetery - Pickens Co., S.C. Cemetery Survey, Vol. 2, p. 165).

Recent developments on the disappearance in 1842 of TOM ALEXANDER, son of the late ELISHA ALEXANDER. It appears he was stolen and sold as a slave and so served until the close of the war. He is living in Georgia, where he married and reared a family.

A two year old child of MR. and MRS. SILAS DAVIS died last Tuesday. Burial was at Mt. Carmel.

GARFIELD FINLEY, age about 1 year and 8 months, the only child of MR. and MRS. JOHN FINLEY of Stewart, S.C. died the 27 Aug. Burial was at Keowee Cemetery.

Pickens Co., S.C. Notice to Debtors and Creditors - Estate of J.T. YOUNGBLOOD, deceased by ELIJA J. YOUNGBLOOD and W.W. YOUNGBLOOD, Administrators.

Pickens Co., S.C. Citation Notice - J.A. HINTON applied for Letters of Administration for the estate of R.O. HINTON, deceased.

Issue of: Thursday 19 September 1901:

PRESIDENT McKINLEY is Dead (details).

Article - " History of Pickens County", by WILLIAM T. FIELD (continued - details).

Married the 9 Sept. at Calhoun, S.C., MR. THOMAS BARKER to MISS WILLIE DAVIS of Oconee Co., S.C., by T.L. Grant

A 3 year old infant of MR. and MRS. LEWIS G. GILSTRAP died at his home about 6 miles north of Pickens the 9 Sept. of scarlet fever. Burial was at Mountain Grove, by Rev. John T. Lewis.

MRS. MINA GILSTRAP died at the home of JOHN GILSTRAP near Golden Creek the 12 Sept. Burial was at Ruhamah. She was about 60 years old and was married twice. Mrs. Gilstrap leaves a son THOMAS PELFREY, a child of her first marriage. (MINNIE PELFREY, born 1852, died 1901, buried Ruhamah - Pickens Co., S.C. Cemetery Survey, Vol. 1, p. 177).

MRS. DIANA JAMES relict of the late GEORGE W. JAMES died in Columbia, S.C. last Saturday (14 Sept.). She was about 86 years old and leaves no children. Burial was at Secona.

MISS DESSIE MORRIS daughter of F.M. MORRIS died at the home of her father in this city last Friday. She was about 18 years of age. Burial was at Robert's Presbyterian Church, with the service being conducted by Rev. J.W. Bailey. *Anderson Intelligencer* - 11 Sept. 1901

Married, MR. NEWTON MOODY and MISS JANIE MOODY of near Piedmont, S.C., at the residence of Rev. J.W. Sheriff.

Married last Thursday at the residence of N.J. SHERIFF by Rev. J.W. Sheriff, MR. BEN FARMER and MISS STEGALL. Both of the contracting parties are from Crosswell, S.C.

Pickens Co., S.C. Final Settlement - Guardianship - W.M. HAGOOD, Guardian of WILLIAM ALLEN, Ward.

Issue of: Thursday 26 September 1901:

CATHERINE CANNON, colored, wife of WILL CANNON of Twelve Mile River, died last Sunday. She was buried at Bethlehem Cemetery.

Married the 15 Sept., MR. THOMAS WOODS and MISS MAMIE MULLINAX of the south part of Easley, S.C. by A.M. Folger, N.P.

MR. and MRS. W.W. ROBINSON celebrated their crystal wedding (anniversary) the 17 Sept. at their home.

MISS UNITY RIGDON has closed the school in Ambler, S.C. and is attending summer school.

MISS DAISY BOROUGHS is teaches at Prater, S.C.

MISS MARY MARTIN teaches at a school near Easley, S.C.

MR. TOM CHILDRESS of Thomasville, S.C. died last Friday.

MR. and MRS. B.F. ROBERTSON now occupy a handsome cottage recently constructed on Hotel Ridge (Clemson College).

MRS. M.J. SKELTON of Table Mountain, S.C., mother of S.O. SKELTON of Liberty, S.C., died on Saturday. She was about 60 years old and leaves 4 sons and 4 daughters. Her husband died about 9 years ago. The service was conducted at Oolenoy Cemetery by Rev. J. Tyre Singleton.

AD - Opening - Millinery Shop, Liberty, S.C. the 3rd and 4th of Oct., by Mrs. M.J. CHAPMAN.

Pickens Co., S.C. Notice to Debtors and Creditors - Estate of WILLIAM HUNTER, deceased by D.F. BRADLEY.

Issue of: Thursday 3 October 1901:

Article - "Trial of the Man who Shot PRESIDENT McKINLEY".

List of teachers who attended Summer School (see article).

MR. AARON BOGGS of Calhoun, S.C. and father of Clerk of Court, A.J. BOGGS is getting along very well for his advanced age.

Married the 29 Sept., WILL SANDERS and DORA ARIAL. Rev. C.T. Miller officiated. All colored.

LEO COOPER, the 5 year old son of STEVEN COOPER who lives on the E. SMITH GRIFFIN place, died the 28 September. He was buried at Porter's Chapel.

MRS. _____ SLOAN who lately moved to Oconee Co., S.C. from Nine Times, S.C. died the 30 September.

Married the 30 September in Greenville, S.C. at the Methodist Parsonage by the pastor, MR. HUGH KEENAN to MISS MAMIE PARSONS of Liberty, S.C. She is the daughter of B.F. PARSONS.

MRS. THOMAS STEWART died at her home in the Crow Creek Section the 22 Sept. and was buried at Shady Grove. She leaves a husband and 4 children, one an infant about a week old.

MRS. RUTHA ANN STEPHENS wife of L.D. STEPHENS died at her home at Redmond, S.C., three miles west of Pickens the 26 Sept. at the age of 52 years. Burial was at Secona Cemetery with Rev. B.E. Grandy conducting the service. Mrs. Stephens is survived by a husband and 9 children.

Married the 29 Sept. at the home of the bride, W.M. FOLGER

and MISS MAGGIE HILL of Maynard, S.C. Mr. Folger is the son of MRS. L.C. FOLGER of Easley, S.C.

Spencer Post Office, S.C. was discontinued last Saturday.

KATE HUDGENS died the 26 September.

Married the 2 Oct., CAPTAIN ELIAS DAY of Easley, S.C. and MISS LELA McHUGH. Miss McHugh is the daughter of MARGARET McHUGH. *Greenville News*

Land for Sale - Several tracts near Easley, S.C. are being sold by W.A. HAMILTON.

AD - Jewelry, Easley, S.C., by W.H. PICKENS.

Card of Thanks, to neighbors and friend for kindness during illness and death of wife. L.D. STEPHENS.

Notice - Do not hire or harbor my wife EMMA STEPHENS. JACOB STEPHENS.

Ad - MOUNTAIN VIEW HOTEL, Easley, S.C. - MRS. CORRIE M. BLALOCK - Located directly opposite the depot - $2.00 a day.

Ad - EASLEY HOTEL - S.N. WYATT, Proprietor. Just opposite the depot. Reasonable Rates.

Issue of: Thursday 10 October 1901:

A 5 month old infant of JAMES CANTRELL died at his home about 3 miles below Pickens on Sunday. Burial was at Tabor.

Old Stone Church is raising $1,000 to establish an endowment. The 1200 foot stone wall that was recently build cost $540.00.

Pickens Co., S.C. Jury List.

MRS. T.H. VAUGHN who has been visiting her relatives in North Carolina and South Carolina has returned to her home in Witherford, Texas. This was her first visit in 21 years.

For Sale - HENRY GANTT'S 4 acre lot in the town of Pickens, by JOHN FERGUSON.

Pickens Co., S.C. Sheriff's Sale:
ADDIE R. ANSEL vs WILLIAM F. SMITH et al. 22 1/2 acres near Easley. S.C. to be sold.

Pickens Co., S.C. Clerk's Sale:
R.F. SMITH, Administrator, et al. vs JESSE ARTER - 40 acres known as the THOMAS DILLARD place and 1/2 interest in 205 acres on the west side of Twelve Mile River to be sold.

Ad - ANDERSON BABB - Contractor and Builder, Pickens, S.C.

Issue of: Thursday 17 October 1901:

Article - "A Pickensville Muster".

CAROLINE BURDINE died the 28 September. Her sons are B. and D. BURDINE.

A daughter was born to MR. and MRS. JEFF HOLDER the 11 October.

A son was born to MR. and MRS. E.S. (DOC) PORTER the 11 October.

Married at Camp Creek Baptist Church the 6 Oct., MR. MAJOR MAULDIN of Pickens Co. to MISS ESSIE VAUGHN of Texas. Rev. J.B. Trammel officiated.

Married at the residence of the bride's parents the 6 Oct. 1901, MR. J.P. MOORE to MISS BETTIE EVETT. Rev. J.B. Trammel officiated. All of Pickens County.

Invitations are out for the marriage of PROF. W.J. CREW of Easley, S.C. to MISS LOO CANTRELL daughter of H.H. CANTRELL, D.D. of Adaburg, Georgia the 23 October. All colored. W.J. CREW is the son of the late MOSES W. CREW.

Pickens Co., S.C. Citation Notice - ANDY GRIFFIN applied for Letters of Administration for the estate of JOHN GRIFFIN, deceased.

Honor Roll of the Pickens, S.C. Graded School for September:

First Grade
ESSIE FREEMAN	CLIFFORD MORRIS
INEZ MORRIS	EDNA EARLE
ALBERTA YONGUE	FRED JENKINS
ELLEN LEWIS	

Second Grade
BELLE YONGUE	LUCIA EARLE
MAY LEWIS	GEORGE PRINCE

Third Grade
MARY McFALL	MINNIE WELBORN
IRENE JENKINS	CLARISSE KEITH

Forth Grade
ETHEL JENKINS	HENRY McDANIEL
LOUISE McDANIEL	WYATT JENNINGS
LORENA TAYLOR	CHARLIE ROBINSON
HAGOOD BRUCE	GRACE PRINCE
JULIUS BOGGS	ARTHUR LEWIS

Fifth Grade
JOHNNIE CAREY	FRANK KIRKSEY
EVA EARLE	RICHARD FREEMAN
JESSIE LEWIS	HERBERT NEWTON

Sixth Grade

FLORIDE CAREY	WILLIAM WELBORN
EILENE TAYLOR	MAJOR WELBORN
CLAUDE FREEMAN	

Seventh Grade

VESTA ASHMORE	LIZZETTE (sic)
HELEN BOGGS	BERTHA BRIDGES
GUSSIE CURETON	CHILDS MOORE
JAMES CAREY, JR.	EDGAR MORRIS
NELLIE GRANDY	LOIS NEWTON
LILA WILBORN	HATTIE EARLE
ELBERT WILBORN	EARLE LEWIS
FORREST (sic)	WILLIE MAULDIN

Eighth Grade

MATTIE BOWEN	CARRIE BRUETON
CORINNE NEWTON	JENNIE LEWIS
ELIZA McDANIEL	HOVEY EARLE
MARY McDANIEL	FRANK McFALL
BRUCE BOGGS	ERNEST FREEMAN
ROBBIE BOWEN	

Ninth Grade

HESTER CURETON	BRANDON TAYLOR

Pickens Co., S.C. Probate Court - Summons for Relief - A.W. FOLGER and T.W. HILL, Administrators for the estate of R.K. HILL, deceased vs E. OBEDIENCE THORNLEY, S.E. HESTER and MARGARET NIX.

Issue of: Thursday 24 October 1901:

Sale at the residence of the late ANDREW B. WILLIAMS, deceased, by S.E. WILLIAMS and J.M. STEWART, Administrators.

Pickens Co., S.C. Court Proceedings - Minor criminal cases (details).

MRS. W.W. AIKEN is teaching a small subscription school at the AIKEN HOTEL.

Land for Sale - WILLIAM FERGUSON'S farm of 250 acres, 1 mile from Pickens, by JOHN FERGUSON.

AD - BRIDGES & HAMMOND, J.E. BRIDGES and W.W. HAMMOND, Selling General Merchandise. Pickens, S.C.

The WILLIAM HUNTER MILL property will be sold in Dec. by MAJOR D.F. BRADLEY, Administrator.

Issue of: Thursday 31 October 1901:

An infant of MR. and MRS. THOMAS J. LIGON of near Sunny Dale, S.C., died the 21 October. Burial was at Mountain Grove Church with John J. Lewis conducting the service.

Married the 13 Oct. 1901 at the residence of J.C. LENDERMAN, MR. HENRY LENDERMAN to MISS LAURA EVATT all of Pickens County.

Killed, CALVIN SMITH by A.A. ALEXANDER with a gun. Alexander is in jail (details).

MISS ALICE PORTER died at her home in Piedmont, S.C. the 25 October. Burial was at Piedmont Cemetery. She was the daughter of MR. and MRS. DAVIS PORTER.

ELIZA LATHEM the infant daughter of MR. LAWRENCE LATHEM died in Greenwood, S.C. on Wednesday and was buried in the Lathem Burying Ground near Mt. Carmel.

WILLIAM WALTER BOWEN died the 22 Oct. in his 32nd year.

Pickens Co., S.C. Citation Notice - J.M. STEWART applied for Letters of Administration for the estate of CALVIN M. SMITH, deceased.

Notice of the Sale of Personal Property of RANSOM DUKE by JANE DUKE, Administrator.

Issue of: Thursday 7 November 1901:

Pickens Co., S.C. Executor's Sale - Land of G.W. BANKS, deceased by MARY C. BANKS, Executrix. Tract #1 - 31 acres; tract #2 - 57 acres; tract #3 - 29 acres.

A son was born to MR. and MRS. R.B. LUMPKIN the 29 October.

An infant of ____WHITMIRE died at the home of the grandfather J.W. THOMAS the 28 October. Burial was at New Hope.

Married the 4 Nov., by B.D. Garvin, N.P. at his residence, RUBEN ANDERSON to CASTORIA ANTHONY both colored. All of Pickens County.

Street lights have been put up near places of business in Pickens by the merchants.

CLARA A. BARRON, the 3 month old daughter of MR. and MRS. WILLIAM F. BARRON, died at their home in Talley, S.C. the 29 October. Burial was at Secona with Rev. J.M. Stewart conducting the service.

MR. A.M. FOLGER has finished his new home at the corner of Main Street and Piedmont Avenue.

A son was born to MR. and MRS. LUCIAN HENDRICKS the 21 October.

My son ELIJAH GRIFFIN left my premises. I forbid anyone to hire him as he is under age. BEN P. GRIFFIN.

IDA MAGGIE PRINCE, little daughter of MARCUS and LAURA PRINCE, died at their home near Slabtown, Anderson Co., S.C. the 28 Oct., aged 2 years and 14 days. Burial was at Mountain Grove Cemetery.

Married the 3 Nov. at the residence of Magistrate B.D. Garvin, MISS EVA MASSAGALE (sic) and MR. CHARLIE ROPER all of Pickens County.

Pickens Co., S.C. Executor's Sale:
Estate of WILLIAM HUNTER, deceased by D.F. BRADLEY, Executor. Tract #1 - 42 acres near Twelve Mile River; Tract #2 - 72 acres; Tract #3 - 51 1/4 acres near Golden Creek Church; Tract #4 - 70 acres on Twelve Mile River to be sold.

Pickens Co., S.C. Notice to Debtors and Creditors - Estate of RUTHA HENDRICKS, deceased by HARRISON O. HENDRICKS, et al. vs WILLIAM A. HENDRICKS.

Administrator's Sale of Personal Property - Estate of ANDREW B. WILLIAMS by ESSIE WILLIAMS and J.M. STEWART - Mules, Cattle, Wagon, etc. to be sold.

Pickens Co., S.C. Clerk's Sale - Court of Common Pleas:
JAMES E. HAGOOD vs JAMES A. MOORE. 25 acres on Cedar Creek and 4 acres on Keowee River to be sold.
E.H. ACKER, et al. vs M. NETTIE WYATT. 100 ft. in the town of Easley fronting on Table Rock Street to be sold.
A.M. MORRIS vs G.B. DURHAM, et al. 80 acres and 70 acres on Crow Creek to be sold.
LIDIA REEVES, et al. vs ANGELINE POWELL, et al. 250 acres on Big Crow Creek to be sold.
HARRISON O. HENDRICKS, et al. vs WILLIAM A. HENDRICKS. 156 acres in Hurricane Township to be sold.
L.N. GEER, et al. vs A.T. NEWELL and W.A. NEAL, et al. 111 3/4 acres on the north side of Town Creek and personal property to be sold.
AMERICAN BANK vs E.M. HUNT, et al. Tract #1 - 227 acres on Saluda River; tract #2 - 104 acres on Saluda River; tract #3 - 103 acres; tract #4 - 1/2 interest in 80 acres on Saluda River; tract #5 - 100 acres on Saluda River known as the THOMAS HUNT place to be sold.
CAROLINA NATIONAL BANK of COLUMBIA, S.C. vs W.A. NEAL, et al. - Tract #1 - 40 acres near Easley, S.C.; tract #2 - 3 1/2 acres on the edge of Easley; tract #3 - 1/2 acre near the town of Easley; tract #4 - 1 acre the north side of the SOUTHERN RAILWAY near the depot; tract #5 - 62 5/8 acres near Easley to be sold.

Pickens Co., S.C. Sheriff's Sale - Court of Common Pleas:
MARY V. MAJOR, et al. vs E. MARION HUNT, et al. 102 acres

known as Tract #1 in the division of E.M. HUNT'S home plantation; Tract #2 - 74 3/4 acres adjoining Tract #1; Tract #3 - 71 1/2 acres adjoining Tracts #1 and #2 to be sold.

W.J. CREW, et al. vs CATHERINE CANNON, et al. 24 acres in Hurricane Township to be sold.

Estate of CORNELIUS KEITH 353 acres in Pumpkintown Township to be sold (tax execution).

T.C. MARTIN 71 acres in Hurricane Township to be sold (tax execution).

Anderson Co., S.C. Court of Common Pleas - MAMIE CATHERINE ROBINSON, JAMES ALDA ROBINSON, et al. by R.W. SMITH, Guardian vs JAMES A. ROBINSON and CYNTHIA A. ROBINSON, Administratrix of the estate of JAMES H. ROBINSON, deceased. 90 acres on Todd's Creek to be sold.

Issue of: Thursday 14 November 1901:

MRS. MARY MURPHREE died at the home of her daughter the 6 Nov. at the age of 74 years. Burial was at Pickens Cemetery.

Married at the residence of D.C. TOMPKINS near Hughes Post Office, S.C. the 10 Nov., MR. FRANK TOMPKINS to MISS MARTHA CASTLE. Rev. W.C. Seaborn officiated.

Married last Wednesday at the home of the bride's father CAPTAIN A.W. HUDGENS, MISS BLANCHE HUDGENS to MR. HENRY MEETZE. The service was conducted by Rev. R. Weston Hiott.

AD - Heavy and Fancy Groceries Being Sold by D.T. and W.M. CURETON at Table Rock Street near DR. SMITH'S DRUG STORE, Easley, S.C.

Issue of: Thursday 21 November 1901:

A daughter was born to MR. and MRS. SPARTAN CHILDS the 19 November.

Married at the bride's home in Hazel, S.C. the 17 Nov., MR. HENRY GRANT and MISS LOUISE GILSTRAP.

Married at the residence of Rev. T.F. Nelson the 10 Nov., MR. W.C. FOWLER to MISS J.A. CANTRELL.

Married the 14 Nov. at the residence of AUGUSTUS FERGUSON, MR. WILLIAM P. EDENS of Pickens Co. to MISS CALDONA FERGUSON of Greenville County, S.C. A.L. Edens, N.P. officiated.

Married the 20 Nov. 1901 at Liberty, S.C., MISS MARIE ANTOINETTE RICHARDSON eldest daughter of MR. and MRS. E.B. RICHARDSON to ROBERT BRUCE FICKLING. They will live in Blacksburg, S.C.

A three year old infant of MR. and MRS. WILLIAM THACKER died last Monday. Burial was at Bethlehem Cemetery with Rev. R.R. Dagnall conducting the funeral service.

Married the 14 Nov. at Easley, S.C., MISS LIDIE MILES HAGOOD eldest daughter of MR. and MRS. WILLIAM M. HAGOOD to MR. EDWARD HENRY SHANKLIN at the Presbyterian Church. The ceremony was performed by Rev. Thomas H. Medd. Mr. Shanklin is Superintendent of the EASLEY COTTON MILL.

An infant of MR. and MRS. DAVIS HOLDER who live in the Dacusville Section died the 9 November. Burial was near their home.

Pickens Co., S.C. Court of Common Pleas - Estate of G.W. JAMES. His wife was DIANA (ALEXANDER) JAMES (long list of heirs - see issue of the 19 Sept. 1901).

Issue of: Thursday 28 November 1901:

A new building on the site of the old building at Griffin Ebenezer Church is almost complete.

A son was born to MR. and MRS. R.L. HENDERSON at the residence of E. FRANK LOOPER the 25 November.

Wolf Creek Public School will have B.A. ALLGOOD as the principal in charge.

B.F. PARSONS will soon complete a dwelling on Cedar Rock Street, facing the public square.

Married at the home of MR. and MRS. W.E. NIMMONS near Old Pickens, Oconee Co., S.C. the 20 Nov. 1901, MISS ANNIE NIMMONS and MR. BARNETT A. ALLGOOD of Pickens. The ceremony was performed by Rev. D.W. Hiott of Seneca, S.C. The bride is the sister of W.P. and LAWRENCE NIMMONS. *Seneca News* MR. ALLGOOD is the son of MR. and MRS. W.B. ALLGOOD of Pickens County (2 articles in the same issue).

The widow of the late "STUTTERING" ROBERT STEWART died last Wednesday and was buried at the Stewart Family Burying Ground on CAPT. J.J. HERD'S place. She was living in the Six Mile Section at the time of her death.

Died at the Methodist Parsonage the 22 Nov. 1901 REV. C.E. WIGGINS. He was 73 years of age and was buried in Hampton Co., S.C. Rev. Wiggins was the father of REV. W.E. WIGGINS.

RACHEL THOMAS was killed at her home near Salem Church, Oconee, Co. S.C. by unknown parties, last Sunday night.

MR. M.W. COLEMAN of Seneca, S.C. died in Charleston, S.C. the 24 November.

Information about JAMES KELLY of Co. C, Orr's Rifles. His wife was named SARAH (details).

CLARANCE BRUCE THORNLEY infant son of MR. and MRS. L.C. THORNLEY died last Sunday. The funeral was conducted by Rev. T.H. Medd.

A Negro named LADDISON was lynched in Anderson, S.C. He went to the home of MRS. PERRY CRAFT and asked for food which she gave him. He was not satisfied so he shot her. She is severely wounded and may die. He was tracked down and lynched. Several leading citizens took part.

Issue of: Thursday 5 December 1901:

RUTH FREDONIA HOLLAND MILLER youngest daughter of MR. and MRS. JOEL H. MILLER died at her home near Easley, S.C. the 25 Nov., aged 2 years and 7 months. Rev. B. Holder conducted the funeral at Williams Cemetery.

A daughter was born to MR. and MRS. JUDGE M. WELBORN the 28 November.

A son was born to MR. and MRS. WALKER YOUNGBLOOD the 1 Dec. 1901.

A daughter was born to MR. and MRS. LEONARD STEPHENS the 3 Dec. 1901.

Married the 1 Dec. at the residence of Rev. B. Holder, MR. JAMES EVIT (sic) to HARRIET BYARS all of this county.

Married the 1 Dec. 1901 at the residence of Magistrate J.M. Jamison, MISS ADAR GARDNER to CHARLIE ALLEN, colored. All of Easley, S.C.

Married the 1 Dec. 1901 at the residence of M.F. Hester, N.P., MISS NORA PACE of Pickens Co. to WILLIAM RUTLEDGE of Pelzer, S.C.

Married the 1 Dec. 1901 at the home of the bride's father, E. SMITH GRIFFIN, LAWRENCE LATHEM and MISS EULA GRIFFIN. Rev. H.L. Haddock officiated.

RUFUS GRAVELEY, the 4 year old son of MR. and MRS. WILLIAM GRAVELEY, died at their home near Pindor Post Office, S.C. the 28 Nov. 1901. Burial was at Porter's Chapel.

Married the 21 Nov. 1901 at the residence of MR. M.D. FARMER, MR. WILLIAM M. JENKINS to MISS ANNA BARRET. B.D. Mauldin, N.P. officiated. All of Pickens County.

Married the 1 Dec. 1901 at the residence of the bride's

father, MR. C.L. WILLOMAN (sic) to MISS MARJIE ALEXANDER. B.D. Mauldin, N.P. officiated. All of Pickens County.

MRS. WILLIAM FARMER died at her home near Norris, S.C. the 28 Nov. 1901 and was buried at Flat Rock, S.C. She was about 46 years old and leaves a husband and 7 children.

DR. R. KIRKSEY recently removed a cancer from the breast of THOMAS DURHAM who lives near Twelve Mile Camp Ground. The operation was performed without excessive loss of blood or the use of anesthetics.

ORA OWENS wife of ROBERT OWENS died at her home near Norris, S.C. the 28 Nov. 1901. Burial was at Ruhamah with service being conducted by Rev. H.C. Haddock. She was 21 years old and leaves her husband and a 13 month old infant.

Married, MR. SAMMEL (sic) LOOPER, JR. son of SAMMEL LOOPER, SR. and MISS HATTIE ROBINSON daughter of J.P. ROBINSON at the bride's parents near Looper, S.C. on Sunday. Rev. E.J. Mullinix officiated.

AD - General Store, Central, S.C., operated by L. ROSS EATON.

Land for Sale - A 1 horse farm and a 2 horse farm near the Court House, by IVY M. MAULDIN.

Pickens Co., S.C. - Final Settlement - Estate of J.L. THORNLEY by L.C. THORNLEY, Administrator.

Issue of: Thursday 12 December 1901:

REV. W.R. RICHARDSON is the new Editor of the *Southern Christian Advocate*.

Pickens, S.C. Graded School Honor Roll for November 1901:
First Grade
WALTER DICKENS	ELLEN LEWIS
CLIFFORD LEWIS	

Second Grade
GEORGE PRINCE	PAUL HESTER
THERON HESTER	

Third Grade
MAY McFALL	MINNIE WELBORN
NETTIE PORTER	CLARICE KEITH
BELLE YOUNG	

Forth Grade
JULIUS BOGGS	PICKENS McCULLUM
LORENA TAYLOR	HAGOOD BRUCE
ETHEL JENKINS	GRACE PRINCE
PATTE MAJOR	CHARLIE ROBINSON

Fifth Grade
JESSIE LEWIS	EVA EARLE

JOHNNIE CAREY   RICHARD FREEMAN
<u>Sixth Grade</u>
FLORIDE CAREY   OLA RICHEY
CLAUDE FREEMAN   BILLIE WELBORN
ORA McFALL   KATE HESTER
ELLEN TAYLOR
<u>Seventh Grade</u>
ESSIE JONES   LEE COCHRANE
BERTHA BRIDGES   LILA WELBORN
WILLIE MAULDIN   ELBERT WELBORN
EDGAR MORRIS   VESTA ASHMORE
HELEN BOGGS   NELLIE GRANDY
JAMES CAREY, JR.   GUSSIE CURETON
EARLE LEWIS   WILTON HESTER
<u>Eighth Grade</u>
BRUCE BOGGS   HOVEY EARLE
ROBBIE BOWEN   FRANK McFALL
CECIL HESTER   GREGG MAULDIN
<u>Ninth Grade</u>
HESTER CURETON   ESSIE GILLESPIE
BRANDON TAYLOR

Pickens County, S.C. Sheriff's Sale - Court of Common Pleas: J.W. NORWOOD vs RUTHA ALEXANDER, et al. Tract #1 - 200 acres on Crow Creek; tract #2 - 22 acres of land of the estate of E.B. ALEXANDER, tract #3 - 634 acres of land where Rutha Alexander now lives from the estate of BLEV ALEXANDER.

<u>Issue of: Thursday 19 December 1901:</u>

<u>From Liberty</u>
J. MILTON KING has let the contract for a new residence on East Main Street to JOHN O. SHECK.

The *Journal* office is in the rear of McFALL'S STORE in the brick building formerly occupied by ANTHONY and KEITH.

<u>Issue of: Thursday 26 December 1901:</u>

A girl was born to MR. and MRS. THOMAS PORTER the 22 Dec. 1901.

A girl was born to MR. and MRS. JORDAN BREAZEALE the 16 Dec. 1901.

A daughter was born to MR. and MRS. J.P. CARY the 17 Dec. 1901.

Married at the bride's home the 5 Dec. 1901, MISS ALICE GILLESPIE to MR. JAMES H. PORTER of Piedmont, S.C.

Pickens Co., S.C. Assignee's Sale - Assets of the firm of B.E. GRANDY and COMPANY will be sold at public auction to satisfy creditors.

THE PEOPLE'S JOURNAL 1902

Issue of: Thursday 2 January 1902:

Married the 2 Jan. 1902, MR. GEORGE BATES to MISS CLEVIE DODGENS all of Pickens County.

Married the 21 Dec. 1901 at the residence of the bride's father, MISS DELIA SIMONS to MR. R.F. PORTER by Rev. B.F. Murphree.

Married the 21 Dec. 1901 at the residence of the bride's mother on Crow Creek, MISS CORRIE ELLENBURG to MR. B.S. POWELL by Rev. B.F. Murphree.

Married the 18 Dec. 1901 at the residence of O.W. GARRISON, by W.D. Garrison, N.P., MR. JAMES BISHOP to MISS ESSIE JULIAN. All of Pickens County.

Married the 26 Dec. 1901 at the residence of O.W. GARRISON by W.D. Garrison, N.P., MR. H.L. TRIPP of Anderson Co., S.C. and MISS RINDA FREEMAN of Greenville County, S.C.

RICHARD GRAVELY aged about 80 years died at the home of his daughter MRS. NANCY ROBINSON near Pickens the 30 Dec. 1901. Burial was at Holly Springs Cemetery.

MRS. MAGGIE WELBORN wife of ADAM C. WELBORN died Christmas night at her home in Greenville, S.C. at the age of 34 years.

Married the 14 Dec. 1901 at the residence of the bride's father JOSEPH STANSELL by Rev. B. Holder, BAYLIE C. ROBINSON eldest son of MR. C. ROBINSON, ESQ. and MISS ESSIE STANSELL.

Married the 15 Dec. 1901 by B. D. Garvin, N.P. at his residence, MISS WILLIE GILLESPILE (sic) of Anderson Co., S.C. to MR. LAFAYETTE McALISTER of Pickens County.

A meeting of the Colored Teacher's Association will be held at Pickens Court House the 4 Jan. 1902 - J.B. SIMPSON, Principal of the Association.

Married the 22 Dec. 1901 at the residence of B.D. Garvin, N.P., MISS CORA McDANALD (sic) to MR. SAMUEL HUGHES all of Pickens County.

Married the 22 Dec. 1901 at the residence of B.D. Garvin, N.P., MISS BESSIE WHITE daughter of MR. WHITNER WHITE of Anderson Co., S.C and MR. JAMES HOW of Pickens County.

Married the 18 Dec. 1901 at the residence of the bride's father MR. G.A. GARY, MISS SALLIE GARY to MR. MARSHALL

PARSONS. B.D. Garvin, N.P. officiated. All of Pickens County.

Married the 19th (Dec. 1901) at the residence of the bride's father MR. HARVEY CHAPMAN by Rev. W.C. Seaborn, MR. J. DYCE BOLDING to MISS DELIA CHAPMAN. The groom's father is MR. B.M. BOLDING.

Pickens Co., S.C. Final Settlement - Estate of LUCINDA E. JOHNSON, deceased, 30 Jan. 1902. W.F. JOHNSON and T.G. JOHNSON, Executors.

Shooting at SUTHERLAND'S MARKET in South Easley, S.C. Mentioned in a long article, SAM SUTHERLAND, WALTER ELLIS, HAMPTON LaBOON, JAY McMAHAN, POLICEMAN OATES, WILLIAM SHERIFF, ROBERT LaBOON, CONSTABLES JAMESON and MILLER, HAMPTON WHITE, FURMAN JOHNSON, CHIEF OF POLICE SMITH and E.P. McCRAVEY (details - see issue of the 27 March 1902).

MR. H.E. COUCH of Texas died.

JAMES HOPKINS died the 16 Dec. 1901 at the age of 80 years, 10 months and 16 days and was buried in Liberty, S.C. He was wounded in the War Between the States. (JAMES HOPKINS, born 21 Jan. 1821, died 16 Dec. 1901, buried Liberty Cemetery - Pickens Co., S.C. Cemetery Survey, Vol. 2, p. 206).

Issue of: Thursday 9 January 1902:

Married the 30 Dec. 1901 by B.J. Johnston, MR. ALFRED GREEN to MISS ROSA PRESLEY all of Liberty, S.C.

Married at the Easley Parsonage by Rev. W.E. Wiggins the 25 Dec. 1901, MISS MAXIE SMITH of Easley, S.C. to MR. WALKER ELLISON of Anderson, Co., S.C. The bride's aunt is MRS. L.R. DURHAM.

Married at the home of the bride's mother MRS. MARTHA BOROUGHS widow of JAMES E. BOROUGHS the 26 Dec. 1901, MISS DORSIE BOROUGHS and MR. SAMUEL C. BOGGS of Central, S.C., by Rev. W.C. Seaborn (details).

The family reunion of MR. and MRS. MATTHEW HENDRICKS (details).

Quarto Centennial of Ebenezer Colored Baptist Church (details).

Issue of: Thursday 16 January 1902:

Married the 25 Dec. 1901 at the residence of Rev. W.C. Seaborn, MR. JAMES L. PARSONS and MISS DOVIE CASTLE both of Pickens County.

Married the 12 Jan. 1902 at the residence of the bride's father MR. A.B. RIGGINS of Prater, S.C., MR. W.D. CHRISTOPHER to MISS MAGARET (sic) RIGGINS both of Pickens County. Rev. W.C. Seaborn officiated.

Married on Wednesday of Christmas week, MR. SAM WATSON to MISS LIDA GIBSON, Johnson Sheriff, N.P. officiated.

The heirs of DAVID ORR an aged white man who was killed by a freight train in Spartanburg, S.C. a few months ago have entered suit against SOUTHERN RAILWAY for $15,000 damages.

Issue of: Thursday 23 January 1902:

A daughter was born to MR. and MRS. D.T. HOYES (sic) of Pearl, S.C. the 15 January.

Married at Liberty, S.C. the 16 Jan., MISS ANNIE HODDOCK (sic) to REV. S.G. STONE, Rev. W.J. Spearman officiated.

Married at the residence of MRS. BETTIE SIMMONS, MISS DORA SIMMONS to MR. B.E. RIGDON, A.L. Edens, N.P. officiated. All of Pickens County.

Married the 16 Jan. at the bride's residence, MR. CHARLIE RABINSON (sic) to MISS GROGAN. George A. Ellis, N.P. officiated. All of Pickens County.

HON. D.T. REDFEARN, Trustee of Clemson College died.

A baby of MR. and MRS. HENRY RIGGINS died the 14 Jan. and was buried at Six Mile, S.C.

Pickens County, S.C. Church Directory (details).

Issue of: Thursday 30 January 1902:

A son was born to MR. and MRS. W.W. HAMMOND the 23 January.

CODY BOWEN daughter of WILLIAM BOWEN, colored, died at her home in Pickens the 23 January. She was about 20 years old and was buried at Secona.

Married the 26 Jan., MR. JACOB LEWIS to MISS ELLIE KELLEY, by Rev. J.E. Foster at the bride's residence. All of Pickens County.

A seven year old daughter of MR. W.H. GILSTRAP of Anderson, S.C. died the 19 January. She was buried at Bethlehem Cemetery. In the last 12 months Mr. Gilstrap has lost his wife and two children.

Married the 26 Jan. 1902, by M.F. Hester, N.P. at the residence of the bride's father MR. W.C. PORTER, MR. JEFF PACE to MISS MARY PORTER.

CLAUDE FREEMAN age 14, died on Friday morning leaving a mother, little brothers and sisters. He was buried at Pickens Cemetery.

Old AUNT CYNDA REAVES of Anderson Mills, S.C. is at the point of death. She is said to be 95 years old.

MR. JORDAN RICE died the 16 Jan. 1902 at his home on Crow Creek in his 90th year. MRS. RICE died 6 years ago. His daughter MRS. LYCENA RIGGINS lived with him. Rev. B.F. Murphree preached the funeral service.

Issue of: Thursday 6 February 1902:

A daughter was born to MR. and MRS. MELVILLE HOLDER the 1 February.

ANNIE MAY HOLDER, infant daughter of MR. and MRS. JEFF D. HOLDER, died the 1 Feb. and was buried at Pickens Cemetery. Rev. B. Holder conducted the service.

Married, J.W. GRANT to MISS JANIE PORTER, at the residence of the bride's father MR. SMITH PORTER north of Pickens on Sunday, Dec. 1901 (sic). Rev. Pierce Attaway officiated. The groom's parents are MR. and MRS. J.N. GRANT.

Married the 26 Jan. 1902, PROF. A. WHITE SINGLETON to MISS LILLIAN EMILY MILLER oldest daughter of HON. and MRS. JOEL H. MILLER at the bride's home near Cedar Rock, S.C. Mr. Singleton is a resident of Greenville Co., S.C. but originally came from Oconee County, S.C. Rev. S.H. McDaniel officiated.

THOMAS L. ROBERTSON died at his home near Cateechee, S.C. the 1 Feb. at the age of 62 years. He leaves a widow, one daughter and 3 sons. MR. Robertson was in the Confederate Army and served as a member of Orr's Regiment. Burial was in the family burying ground. (THOMAS L. ROBERTSON, born 16 July 1840, died 2 Feb. 1902, buried Phillip Clayton Cemetery - Pickens Co., S.C. Cemetery Survey, Vol. 3, p. 90).

A little son of MR. and MRS. W.A. OLIVER died near Central, S.C. the 31 Jan. and was buried at Mount Zion Cemetery.

An infant of MR. and MRS. SAM OATES died last week. Two more of their children are very sick.

A daughter was born to MR. and MRS. PERRIN PRINCE the 1 February.

J.E. GILLESPIE and J.H. SEABORN have taken the contract for building the Allgood Bridge across the Twelve Mile River.

MR. WARREN D. HENDRICKS, SR. is having a nice dwelling erected at his farm on Caesar's Head Road. M. HENDRICKS and SON have the contract to build it.

MR. J. MARTIN JONES is a furniture maker.

MR. LAWRENCE PACE and his young bride are at home to friends at Farrs, S.C.

Issue of: Thursday 13 February 1902:

JAMES K. SUTHERLAND was born the 18 Feb. 1811 and died the 17 Jan. 1902 at nearly 91 years of age. He leaves 2 daughters, MRS. LAURA SHIRLEY of Honea Path, S.C. and MRS. DR. JOHN WILSON of Williamson, S.C. His only son died in the Civil War and was buried in Virginia. Mr. Sutherland was burial at Oolenoy.

A daughter was born to MR. and MRS. E.F. KEITH the 10 January.

M. OSCAR ELLISON died the 5 Feb. at the home of his brother, J.W. ELLISON. (M.O. ELLISON, born 17 May 1874, died 5 Feb. 1902, buried Easley City Cemetery - <u>Pickens Co., S.C. Cemetery Survey</u>, Vol. 3, p. 36).

MR. WILL N. GANTT and MRS. LORANES WARE were married Sunday morning by Rev. H.C. Haddock. The groom's father is MR. WILLIAM GANTT.

MRS. MARGARET HIGGINS died the 16 Jan. and was buried at Zion Church. The service was conducted by Rev. W.E. Wiggins. Mrs. Higgins lived with her niece MISS MATTIE LESLEY.

MR. LAWRENCE TUMBLIN died at his home in Greenville, S.C. the 25 January. He was buried at Zion (see issue of the 20 March 1902).

Married the 18 Dec. 1901 at the home of the bride's brother, MR. E. CALHOUN BOWIE to MISS JANIE ROBERTSON of Oconee Co., S.C.

Married the 29 Dec. 1901 at the residence of the bride's father MR. COOT DODSON of Transylvania Co., North Carolina, MR. TALLY BALDWIN of this county and MISS EMMA DODSON. Rev. W.C. Boren officiated.

Married the 5 Jan. 1902 at Bethel Baptist Church, MR. J.B. NIX to MISS DELLA GANTT. Rev. B.P. Moore officiated. All of Pickens County.

MAXWELL "TODY" STEWART is in from Montana visiting relatives and friends. It is rumored that his purpose here is to seek a companion. If a man comes all the way from Montana for a wife - well she ought to be a good one.

The firm of M. HENDRICKS & SON has dissolved its Mercantile Business.

Issue of: Thursday 20 February 1902:

A daughter was born to Mr. and MRS. B. LEWIS the 14 February.

CONTRACTOR WYATT turned over the keys to MR. KENNEMORE last week and he and his family moved into their new home Thursday. Easley, S.C. welcomes Mr. Kennemore and his family as new citizens.

REV. H.C. HADDOCK moved into the new manse last week.

Married the 13 Feb. at the home of the bride's father MR. AUGUSTUS FERGUSON, MR. JOHN MASTERS to MISS ANGIL FERGUSON. Mr. Alonzo Edens, N.P. officiated (see issue of the 27 Feb. 1902).

MRS. WILLIAMS died the 7 Feb. at her home in Anderson, S.C. She was a widow and leaves 5 children.

Issue of: Thursday 27 February 1902:

A daughter was born to MR. and MRS. FLEM KELLY the 23 February.

Married the 17 Feb. at the home of Magistrate J.P. Hyde, MR. JAMES SMITH to MISS NETTIE HUDSON. MR. J.P. SMITH is a brother of the groom.

WYATT AIKEN is running for Congress. He fought in the Spanish American War as a private.

A son of MR. JOHN BURGESS died at MONAGHAN COTTON MILL in Greenville, S.C. and was buried at Oolenoy Church the 21 February.

MR. J.W. SUTHERLAND has recently completed an ell to his house and will add other improvements.

An infant son of MR. and MRS. G.W. SUTHERLAND, age about 5 months, died the 16 Feb. and was buried at Oolenoy Church Cemetery.

Six Mile Schoolhouse was consumed by fire last Tuesday night at 12 o'clock. The furniture was all saved.

O.H.C. SMITH is visiting from Banks Co., Georgia. His wife died last November. Mr. Smith draws a pension of $50.00 a year for wounds he received in Confederate Service.

MRS. NIX died the 16 Feb. near Prater, S.C. Burial was at Bethlehem Church.

Issue of: Thursday 6 March 1902:

Pickens Co., S.C. Commissioner's Report of County Expenses for the year 1901 (details).

A son was born to MR. and MRS. C.N. DURHAM the 2 March.

JOHN E. SMITH late of the U.S. 7th Cavalry came home Tuesday and was met by his brother LUTHER D. SMITH of Dacusville, S.C.

ELIM F. TAYLOR was born the 18 Apr. 1845 and died the 2 Jan. 1902. He married MISS VILANTA L. WHITE the 26 Nov. 1878. Mr. Taylor leaves 2 sons and 2 daughters. (Buried Enon Baptist Church Cemetery - Pickens Co., S.C. Cemetery Survey, Vol. 1, p. 102).

JESSE ELLIS died the 16 Aug. last (1901). He left a wife and children. (JESSE H. ELLIS, born 17 Sept. 1817, died 16 Aug. 1901, buried Bethlehem Methodist Church Cemetery - Pickens Co., S.C. Cemetery Survey, Vol. 1, p. 20).

MRS. SARAH MAULDIN who was born the 9 April 1837, died at the age of 64 years, 10 months and 19 days. She was the wife of WILLIAM A. MAULDIN and was buried at Easley Cemetery by Rev. T.H. Medd. Surviving are her husband, one brother and two sisters, MRS. J.W. QUILLION of Buford, Georgia and MRS. MILLER of Greenville, S.C. (see issue of the 13 March 1902).

A new post office is at the home of PHILLIP CHAPMAN, ESQ. on the lower part of the Big Eastatoe. It will be called Eastatoe, S.C.

MR. ANDY GRAY died the 26 Feb. and was buried at Nimmons Burying Ground. He was a member of Eastatoe Baptist Church.

Little J. WELBORN the infant son of MR. and MRS. JOHN WELBORN died on Tuesday morning.

BUCH LEWIS whose house was burned sometime ago has rebuilt on the same site. Buch lives at the same place on which his great grandfather settled nearly 100 years ago.

Married the 19 Feb., MR. TALLY CLARK to MISS NETTIE ROPER at the residence of the bride's grandfather MR. J.E. ROPER. Rev. Andy Whitmire performed the ceremony.

Married the 23 Feb. at the residence of Rev. H.L. Fortner, MR. JOHN MEDLIN to MISS CORBIN.

An eleven month old baby of JOHN F. BURGESS died the 22 Jan. Mr. Burgess had just lost a 10 year old son. His wife and another child are very sick. They live at Monaghan Mills, S.C.

The Olga Post Office, S.C. that was established at REV. J.E. FOSTER'S 5 years ago with MISS MILLIE FOSTER, Postmaster has moved to R.M. FOSTER'S with MRS. R.M. FOSTER, Postmaster.

Issue of: Thursday 13 March 1902:

A daughter was born to MR. and MRS. THOMAS FREEMAN the 8 March.

JACOB KENNEMORE is sick from the effects of measles he had in the Civil War.

FURMAN ANTHONY the 5 year old son of JAMES R.J. ANTHONY died the 6 March.

MRS. SARAH MARTIN MAULDIN wife of W.A. MAULDIN died Friday 28 (Feb.) (SARAH MARTIN MAULDIN, born 9 April 1837 in Greenville Co., S.C., died 28 Feb. 1902 in Easley, S.C. wife of WILLIAM A. MAULDIN, buried Easley City Cemetery - Pickens Co., S.C. Cemetery Survey, Vol. 3, p. 38).

Married, MR. W.M. STEWART to MISS ELLA PRICE eldest daughter of WILLIAM R. PRICE of Sunny Dale, S.C., on Thursday by Rev. B.F. Murphree. Mr. Stewart lives in the far north west, Red Rock, Montana. The couple left the 6 March accompanied by MESSRS. ARTHUR GRAVELY, LEIGH AIKEN and LAWRENCE and ROBERT STEWART.

A son was born to MR. and MRS. ALONZO WILLIAMS the 28 February.

A divorce was granted GEORGE SIMPSON against CARRIE SIMPSON.

Reunion School is in a prosperous condition under the management of MISS MAMIE BALLENTINE.

A new road has been opened from Easley, S.C. to Liberty, S.C.

A son was born to MR. and MRS. ANDREW ROPER the 1 March.

The LONG DISTANCE TELEPHONE CO. is sending men through to measure the line and number the posts.

An infant, about two months of age, of MR. and MRS. COLE BRISSEY died.

MISS NANNIE ROPER'S school had been suspended because of bad weather but reopened this week.

MISS UNITY RIGDON is in charge of the Ambler Schoolhouse.

Issue of: Thursday 20 March 1902:

A daughter was born to MR. and MRS. THOMAS FREEMAN the 8 March.

A son was born to MR. and MRS. SMITH PORTER the 11 March.

MRS. D.J. GREER died at her home the 10 March. She was 40 years of age and leaves a husband and 4 children. Mrs. Greer was a member of the Presbyterian Church.

LAWRENCE RUFUS TUMBLIN the only son of S.J. and ISABELLA (WOLFF) TUMBLIN died the 25 Jan. 1902. He was born the 29 April 1877 and was buried at Zion Methodist Church (see issue of the 13 Feb. 1902).

MRS. EVELINE WILLIAMS died the 11 March at her home near Mica, S.C. She leaves a husband T. AUGUSTUS WILLIAMS and a son. Burial was at Mt. Tabor Baptist Church.

MISS ZILPHY NABORS died at her home last Friday. Burial was at Peter's Creek.

Pickens Co., S.C. Final Settlement - Estate of RANSON DUKE, deceased by JANE DUKE, Administrator.

H. SNIDER does watch and jewelry repair in Easley. S.C.

Issue of: Thursday 27 March 1902:

JACOB LINCH, colored, died at his home north of Pickens, Saturday and was buried at Cold Springs.

Married the 23 March 1902 at the home of Rev. W.C. Seaborn, MR. JAMES C. STEWART to MISS MATTIE E. ALEXANDER both of Pickens County.

MRS. ELIZABETH BOWEN widow of the late REESE BOWEN, now aged 77, is very sick at her home a few miles east of Pickens.

ETTA MAY BANE, infant daughter of PINK BANE, died at Poe Mills, Greenville, S.C. last Wednesday. Burial was at Peter's Creek. Rev. J.E. Foster conducted the service.

MRS. NINA WOOD of Williamston, S.C. died Tuesday night. She was the daughter of MR. and MRS. JAMES E. EARLE of this place (see issue of the 3 April 1902).

O.F. BOGGS has a dwelling underway on the east side of town.

PROF. O'DELLS' school closed Friday.

MISS ELLA WORKMAN will continue a subscription school.

MR. B.A. GREEN of Maynard, S.C. died (see issue of the 3 April 1902).

MR. KILBURN died the 10 March, leaving a widow and 3 children. Burial was at Mt. Zion near Central, S.C.

MRS. T. HOMER BROCK died the 21 March in her 78th year. Burial was at Mt. Zion. She leaves 3 children.

MR. I.A. WHITMIRE has built a new ell to his house and made several other improvements on his place near Pumpkintown, S.C.

Pickens Co., S.C. Citation Notice - Estate of B.A. GREEN, deceased. IDA C. GREEN applied for Letters of Administration.

Pickens Co., S.C. Citation Notice - Estate of W.W. KILBURN, deceased. B.J. JOHNSTON applied for Letters of Administration.

Issue of: Thursday 3 April 1902:

CAPTAIN JOHN M. PATRICK, commandant and teacher in Patrick Military Institute, which was formerly located in Greenville, S.C. but is now in Anderson, S.C. (see issue of the 24 April 1902).

Married the 26 March at the residence of Magistrate Philip Chapman, MISS ANNA STANSELL to MR. JACK GRAY all of Pickens County.

NINA EARLE WOOD died the 25 March at the age of 22 years, 9 months and 11 days at Williamston, S.C. She was the eldest daughter of J.W. EARLE of Pickens. On the 20 Feb. 1899 she married A.C. WOOD. Mrs. Wood leaves a husband and a 2 year old son. The body was shipped to Pickens for burial in the Earle Family Cemetery (see issue of the 27 March 1902).

Married by Rev. W.E. Wiggins at the Methodist Parsonage last Thursday evening, MISS BESSIE SPENCER to J.B.F. CHILDRESS.

Married at the home of MRS. OWENS in south Easley, S.C. on Sunday, MISS MIAMI BROWN to MR. NEWTON WHITE by Rev. D.W. Hiatt.

MISS ALMA KAY is getting along fine with her school in Six Mile, S.C.

MR. B.A. GREEN died the 15 March. He was 34 years of age

(see issue of the 27 March 1902).

CLARENCE LOOPER died from burns the 19 March. He was the son of MR. and MRS. THOMAS J. LOOPER of near Mica, S.C. Burial was at Cross Roads Cemetery (see issue of the 24 April 1902).

Pickens Co., S.C. Clerk's Sale:
AMANDA E. KENNEMORE vs W.T. McFALL, et al. A lot in the town of Pickens known as #46, containing one acre; lot #44 - 1/2 acre; lot # 80 - 1/2 acre to be sold.
Real estate of GEORGE W. JAMES fronting Garvin and Cedar Rock Streets to be sold.

CLARENCE HOLTZCLAW WILLIAMS under contract to WILLIAM ELLIS has left the premises.

Issue of: Thursday 10 April 1902:

Article - "Pickens County, S.C.". Information on Pickens, Easley, Liberty, Central, Cateechee and Pea Ridge or Paradise (details).

DR. NAT LANCASTER died by drowning in the Mississippi River the 12 March. His brother is DR. R.A. LANCASTER, the wife of Dr. R.A. Lancaster is MRS. OLA HOLLINGSWORTH LANCASTER.

SHERIFF J.H.G. McDANIEL was born the 28 Nov. 1847 in Greenville Co., S.C. and was educated there and in Charleston, S.C. He served ten months in the latter part of the Civil War. Mr. McDaniel has been Sheriff of Pickens County for the past nine years.

A. JOHN BOGGS was born the 7 Dec. 1864 in Pickens District (now Oconee County, S.C.) attended the "Old Field" School until he entered the Piedmont Institute at Pickens Court House in 1882 under PROF. W.M. McCASLAN. He married MISS SALLIE LOOPER. Mr. Boggs was elected Clerk of Court in 1900.

AUDITOR E. FOSTER KEITH was born at Pumpkintown, S.C., 36 years ago. He was a student of Piedmont Institute at Pickens under the direction of W.M. McCASLAN and JOHN R. RILEY. He had one term at the Citadel.

WILLIAM W.F. BRIGHT was born the 19 Dec. 1840 near Louisville, Tennessee and was a Confederate Soldier. In 1898 he was elected Superintendent of Schools. Mr. Bright married the 21 Sept. 1871 MISS MARGARET J. WILLIAMS daughter of B.J. WILLIAMS.

Books of subscription to the capital stock of the EASLEY CREAMERY CO. will be open.

PROBATE JUDGE J.B. NEWBERRY was born in Darlington Co., S.C. the 21 June 1837. He married the 10 Jan. 1860 MISS TRIZAH BURDINE of Anderson County, S.C. During the Civil War he was in Co. K, 6th S.C. Regiment. Judge Newberry has one daughter MISS STELLA NEWBERRY (lengthy article).

MR. R. FRANK SMITH was born in Anderson County, S.C. and is the son of the late J.M. SMITH. He studied under JOHN L. KENNEDY and continued thru Adger College in medicine. Mr. Smith's father-in-law is COL. C.L. HOLLINGSWORTH (long article).

MRS. HOGSED died the 25 (March) at 80 odd years. She was the mother of IRA PERRY and FRANK HOGSED. Burial was at Dacusville Methodist Church. She leaves a number of children and grandchildren. (MARY E. MANLY wife of W.P. HOGSED, born 7 July 1818, died 25 March 1902 - Pickens Co., S.C. Cemetery Survey, Vol. 1, p. 84).

Issue of: Thursday 17 April 1902:

WADE HAMPTON died the 11 April at his home in Columbia, S.C.

MRS. HARRIETT McWHORTER widow of GIDEON McWHORTER died at the home of her son WILLIAM McWHORTER near Sandy Springs, Anderson County, S.C. the 8 April at the age of 72 years. Burial was at Sandy Springs, S.C. Mrs. McWhorter leaves one sister MRS. BARNET SMITH and two brothers J.W. and STEPHEN A. MAJOR.

MRS. CAROLINE FREEMAN widow of JOSEPH FREEMAN died at her home three miles south of Pickens Court House the 10 April. Burial was at Cross Roads Church by Rev. J.E. Foster and Rev. W.C. Seaborn. She was 73 years old and leaves 4 sons and 4 daughters: WILLIAM FREEMAN of Arkadelphia, Alabama, MORTON, THOMAS and PROF. B.F. FREEMAN of Pickens, MRS. C.T. HUTCHINS of Liberty S.C., MRS. A.A. MOON and MISSES EVA and JOSIE FREEMAN of Pickens. Her husband died 28 years ago.

MRS. CAROLINA I. CLYDE wife of J.B. CLYDE died the 6 April. She was born the 18 Feb. 1834 and leaves 3 daughters: MRS. HIGGINS, MRS. BALLARD and MRS. KIRKSEY. The service was conducted by Rev. Hiott and Rev. Wiggins, with burial in Easley Cemetery.

MISS MARGARET JOHNSTON died the 5 April at her home near Norris. S.C. at about 53 years of age. Burial was at the Old Johnston Cemetery near her home. She leaves six brothers and sisters.

MISS IDA HENDRICKS closed her school at Rock, S.C. She has been teaching for five months.

A long tribute to WADE HAMPTON from the 12 April issue of the *Greenville Mountaineer*.

Issue of: Thursday 24 April 1902:

Article - "The Burial of Wade Hampton".

BEN F. PARSONS, Coroner was born in Pickens County the 2 June 1857. He was elected Coroner in 1900.

REPRESENTATIVE CHARLES E. ROBINSON was born the 9 Dec. 1861, in Pickens County at the Parsonage of Carmel Presbyterian Church. He went to school at the Academy in Liberty, S.C. and read law under his uncle R.A. CHILD. In the year 1883 he was admitted to practice.

IVY M. MAULDIN was born the 17 Dec. 1875 near Pickens. He graduated from Clemson College in 1895 (first class to graduate). Mr. Mauldin served in the 2nd Regt. in the Spanish War and was Captain of Co. K. He was elected to the S.C. Legislature in 1900.

SENATOR W.T. BOWEN son of REESE and ELIZABETH BOWEN resides in Callatta, S.C., about three miles south east of Pickens. He is about 60 years of age and is married to the former MISS REBECCA ALLGOOD. They have three sons and two daughters.

SUPERVISOR LEONARD D. STEPHENS was born the 16 Feb. 1846 in Pickens County and is married to the former MISS RUTHA A. STEWART. She died in 1900, leaving nine children.

A. JEFFERSON WELBORN is about 46 years of age and resides near Easley, S.C. He married MISS LIZZIE ARIAIL daughter of the late LUKE ARIAIL by whom he has five children.

COUNTY COMMISSIONER ROBERT STEWART was born the 21 March 1844 in Pickens County and is now living about 3 1/2 miles from the place where he was born. His mother died when he was 11 years old. Mr. Stewart enlisted in the Confederate Army in March 1862 at the age of 18 under CAPT. R.A. THOMPSON in the 2nd Rifle Regt. and COL. JAMES V. MOORE. He received a musket ball in the left arm at the Battle of 2nd Manassas. DR. JAMES SLOAN extracted it 14 year and 5 months later. Mr. Stewart was also postmaster at Alexander, S.C.

MAJOR J.M. STEWART a native of Pickens County is in his 62nd year. He was educated at Old Field School and went into the Civil War as Captain where he was promoted to Major. In 1880 he was ordained as a minister and in 1888 elected Clerk of Court, Pickens County, S.C.

S.D. CHAPMAN was born the 1 Dec. 1861 in Pickens County and educated at Piedmont Institute at Pickens under W.M.

McCASLAN. In 1900 he was elected Treasurer of Pickens County, S.C.

MAJOR JOHN J. LEWIS was born in Pendleton, S.C. in 1837. He served in Trenholm's Squadron, 7th Regt. S.C. Cavalry, during the Civil War. His father JESSE P. LEWIS moved to Pickens from North Carolina and settled where J.C. STRIBLING now lives in Sleepy Hollow, S.C. He was elected Clerk of Court of Pickens County in 1876 and held the office for 12 years (details).

The GILREATH HOUSE, MRS. EMMA A. GILREATH, Proprietress is located on West Main and charges $2.00 a day.

The EASLEY HOTEL, S.N. WYATT, Proprietor charges $2.00 a day.

Article - "Crow Creek Section, Pickens Co., S.C."

Article - "The Oldest Working Society of Farmers in America". *Clemson College Chronicle*

W.T. McFALL went to Atlanta, Georgia on Monday. He carried with him his little daughter IVY and young ERNEST FREEMAN for treatment in the National Surgical Institute at that place.

ROBERT ARIAIL, colored, died at his home on T.D. HARRIS' place the 21 April and was buried at Enon.

MRS. ELIZABETH BOWEN widow of REESE BOWEN died at the home of her daughter MRS. ISAAC NIMMONS 8 miles north west of Pickens the 17 April in her 79th year. She was MISS ELIZABETH BLASSINGAME daughter of JOHN BLASSINGAME. Surviving are 11 children: SENATOR W.T. BOWEN, R.A. BOWEN, G.W. BOWEN, REESE BOWEN, JR., M.H. BOWEN, MRS. N.E. NIMMONS and MRS. ANNIE ALLGOOD of Pickens County and MRS. MARTHA NIMMONS of Oconee County, S.C. JOHN BOWEN, PICKENS BOWEN and LAWRENCE BOWEN of Texas. Mrs. Bowen was buried at Tabor Church with Rev. J.E. Foster conducting the service (see issue of the 1 May 1902).

Article - "Pickens Baptist Church".

Pickens Graded School has PROF. W. ERSKINE DENDY as principal and MISS MARY SWARN (sic) as assistant (details).

Pickens Colored Graded School, with R.K. MOON as principal, has 83 students (details).

Easley Graded School (details).

Article - "Traveling Libraries - Free Traveling Libraries of the SOUTHERN RAILWAY" (details).

Article - "Glassy Mountain Section, Pickens Co., S.C.".

S.P. FREEMAN makes furniture.

L.T. WIMPEY, J.B. FINLEY, GEORGE ADKINS, and B.F. FARMER make "jug ware".

Extract from an act of the Legislature, 27 Feb. 1902: "To further regulate the working and maintaining of highways and bridges of this state, all persons from the age of 18-50 except those exempted, shall be liable to road duty."

Pickens Co., S.C. County Commissioner's Sale:
Land belonging to Pickens County in the town of Pickens - Lot with building on the south side of Main Street adjoining the MASONIC BUILDING, about 1/4 acre; about 2 acres on the lot where the jail now stands (to be sold in 1/2 acre lots).

AD - EASLEY BICYCLE REPAIR SHOP, P. CEMP JOHNSON.

AD - JOHN F. HARRIS, General Merchandise, Pickens, S.C.

AD - MEAT MARKET, F.M. COUCH, Easley, S.C.

AD - MRS. KATE L. CURETON, General Merchandise, Pickens, S.C.

AD - THORNLEY'S PHARMACY, B.K. THORNLEY, Proprietor.

AD - CHARLES T. TOLBERT SHOE SHOP. Over JOHN F. HARRIS' STORE, Pickens, S.C.

AD - JAMES P. CAREY, Lawyer, office at rear of HEATH, BRUCE & MORROW CO.

AD - DRUG STORE, DR. R.F. SMITH, Easley, S.C.

AD - CRAIG BROTHERS, Pickens, S.C., One Price Cash Store.

AD - HAYGOOD & CO., General Merchandise, Easley, S.C.

AD - TAYLOR PHOTOGRAPHY STUDIO, Over ELLISON BROTHERS, Easley, S.C.

AD - EARLE'S DRUG STORE, Pickens, S.C., G.W. EARLE.

AD - JAMESON'S, A.S. JAMESON, Easley, S.C., Selling Goods.

AD - A.M. MORRIS, Pickens, S.C., General Merchandise.

AD - A.G. WYATT & CO., Groceries, Dry Goods and Everything.

AD - C.T. MARTIN, Lumber, Guano, etc., Easley, S.C.

AD - H.A. RICHEY, THE CORNER STORE, on Main and Ann Streets, Pickens, S.C. General Merchandise.

AD - KEEN EDGE BARBER SHOP, JAMES P. WARE, over EASLEY DRUG STORE.

AD - W.T. McFALL, General Merchandise, Pickens, S.C.

AD - ELLISON BROS., General Merchandise, Easley, S.C.

AD - W.A. HAMILTON, Real Estate, Easley, S.C.

AD - J.E. ROBINSON, Main Street, Easley, S.C. General Merchandise.

AD - O'DELL'S STORE, next to the Post Office, Easley, S.C.

AD - FOLGER & THORNLEY, General Merchandise, Buggies and Wagons.

AD - SKELTON & SMITH, S.O. SKELTON and JOE F. SMITH, General Merchandise, Furniture and Coffins, Liberty, S.C.

AD - NORTH SIDE BARBER SHOP - JOHN W. CHAMBERS, Main Street, 2nd door west of MOUNTAIN VIEW HOTEL, Easley, S.C.

AD - DAVIS, High Grade Shoe Man, W.F. DANIEL, Manager, Anderson, S.C.

AD - SULLIVAN HARDWARE CO., Anderson, S.C.

AD - ANDERSON PRINTING and STATIONERY CO., Anderson, S.C.

AD - B.E. GRANDY, Lumber Yard, Plaining Mill and Contractor, Pickens, S.C.

AD - W.H. JOHNSON, Sewing Machines and Bicycle Supplies, Pickens, S.C.

AD - D.T. & W.M. CURETON, Groceries, Vegetables and Fruits, Easley, S.C.

AD - ANDERSON PHOSPHATE & OIL CO., FRED G. BROWN, President and Treasurer; ELLISON A. SMITH, Vice President; CHARLES A. GAMBRILL, Secretary; and FRANK A. BURBAGE, Superintendent of the Chemical Department, Anderson, S.C.

Issue of: Thursday 1 May 1902:

Article - "The Alexander Section, Pickens Co., S.C." .

Article - "Mount Pisgah Baptist Church".

Article - "Old Liberty".

MRS. ELIZABETH BOWEN died at the home of her daughter MRS. N.J. NIMMONS on Thursday the 17 April. She was buried at Tabor Methodist Church (see issue of the 24 April 1902).

B.E. GRANDY a native of Barnwell County, S.C. came to Pickens County in 1898. He is a dealer in lumber supplies and was the first man to receive a car-load of freight over the PICKENS RAILROAD. Mr. Grandy built the bank, the FREEMAN BUILDING, HEATH-BRUCE-MORROW CO. building, known as the "BIG STORE", the residences of JUDGE J.B. NEWBERRY, BEN F. FREEMAN, DR. J.L. BOLT, J.L. THORNLEY, J. McD. BRUCE and others.

There are now 248 pensioners in Pickens County as against 244 last year.

Married, MR. JOSEPH SMITH and MISS LIZZIE GANTT, at the home of the bride's father MR. WILLIAM N. GANTT 4 miles south of Pickens the 27 (April). Rev. H.C. Haddock officiated.

Liberty Local
DR. CLARK RICHARDSON of Texas died the 18 (April). He was a brother of E.B. RICHARDSON and left here 25 years ago.
Married, MR. ED BALLINGER of N.C. to MISS MATTIE ROWE of Liberty S.C. the 23 (April).

Married, MR. J.N. GANTT and MISS DORCAS MOORE the 24 (April).

Article - "Pickens Methodist Church".

Article - "History of Cedar Rock".

JULIUS E. BOGGS was born the 14 Feb. 1854 in Pickens County, married MISS MINNIE LEE BRUCE the 24 Dec. 1882 (details).

AD - BRIDGES & HAMMOND, General Merchandise, Pickens, S.C.

Article - "Fourteenth Annual Reunion of United Confederate Veterans Association in Dallas, Texas".

Issue of: Thursday 8 May 1902:

Trouble at Clemson - The Sophomore Class leaves the College (details).

Married the 30 April 1902 at the residence of the bride's father MR. O.P. WILLIAMS, MR. HAMPTON FIELD and MISS PEARL WILLIAMS. W.C. Seaborn officiated. All of Pickens County.

Married, MISS MELONEE THORNLEY youngest daughter of MRS. N.E. THORNLEY of Pickens and MR. WILL E. WHITE of Anderson, S.C., at the home of the bride's mother the 30 April.

MRS. MALINDA WILLIAMS relict of the late JOSEPH WILLIAMS died at her home in the Dacusville Section the 1 May. She was about 55 years of age. Rev. J.E. Foster conducted the service at Oolenoy. Mrs. Williams leaves several children.

Pickens County, S.C. Convention of the Democratic Party. W.T. O'DELL was elected temporary chairman (details).

Vineland
An infant of MR. and MRS. ROBERT PERRY died last Thursday and was buried at George's Creek Cemetery.

A letter to the Editor from a subscriber in Silverton, Texas gives information on G.R. HENDRICKS (details).

Issue of: Thursday 15 May 1902:

Article - "WADE HAMPTON".

EARLE MILLER late cadet in Clemson College has been engaged to teach school for the summer.

Vineland School has PROF. J.F. FOLK in charge.

DR. WALTER M. SMITH died at his home in Liberty, S.C. on Tuesday morning. He was 35 years old and leaves a widow and one child.

Married, GEORGE D. CURETON to MISS DICIE SMITH of Belmont, North Carolina, the 6 May in Gaffney, S.C.

WILLIAM B. LIGON died at the home of SHERIFF J.H.G. McDANIEL in Pickens the 10 May at the age of 61 years. He leaves a widow and 7 children in Texas. Capt. J.T. Taylor conducted the service with burial at Secona Cemetery. Mr. Ligon was a brother-in-law of Sheriff McDaniel.

MISS ELLA WORKMAN'S school is out in Liberty, S.C. and she has returned to her home in Virginia.

COL. W.E. WELBORN died the 8 May at the home of his daughter MRS. W.W. McWHORTER near Pickens. He was born the 8 July 1817 near Pelzer, S.C. and served in the Confederate Army for 4 years. Mr. Welborn leaves 5 daughters and 5 sons: MRS. STRICKLAND and MRS. ELROD of Pelzer, S.C., MRS. FERGUSON of Texas, MRS. HUGHES, MARTIN J. WELBORN, THOMAS WELBORN, MRS. W.W. McWHORTER and JUDGE M. WELBORN of Pickens, ADAM C. WELBORN of Greenville, S.C. and JOHN WELBORN of Toccoa, Georgia. Burial was at Enon, by Rev. Hiott and Rev. Seaborn. *Greenville News* - 9 May

MR. J.T. CRAIG died the 11 March 1902, he leaves a widow.

(J.T. CRAIG, born 11 June 1862, died 11 March 1902, buried Tabor Methodist Church - <u>Pickens Co., S.C. Cemetery Survey</u>, Vol. 2, p. 162).

MR. FRANK GREEN died of pneumonia the 22 April in Calhoun, S.C.

REV. T.C. LIGON, Methodist Minister in charge of the Gospel Tabernacle, died here today (12?), Columbia, S.C.
Greenville News - 13 April 1902

Issue of: Thursday 22 May 1902:

PICKENS RAILROAD Timetable.

MRS. HARRIETT JONES died at her home near Liberty, S.C. the 14 May. She was a full pensioner, but death came before the pension money was ready for distribution. (HARIT E. JONES, born 26 Jan. 1839, died 14 May 1902, buried George's Creek Baptist Church Cemetery - <u>Pickens Co., S.C. Cemetery Survey</u>, Vol. 2, p. 183).

Married at the residence of Rev. J.E. Foster the 11 May, MR. WASH NIMMONS and MISS UNITY RIGDON all of Pickens County.

Pickens Co., S.C. Citation Notice - J.P. SMITH applied for Letters of Administration for the estate of W.M. SMITH, deceased.

Issue of: Thursday 29 May 1902:

SLOAN HAGOOD, colored, died at his home in Pickens the 27 May at about 35 years of age. He was buried at Cold Springs.

MISS MARY ANN HALLUMS of Liberty, S.C. died the 20 May and was buried in the family burial ground. (MARY ANN HALLUMS, born 7 Nov. 1829, died 20 May 1902, buried Hallum Cemetery - <u>Pickens Co., S.C. Cemetery Survey</u>, Vol. 1, p. 254).

Issue of: Thursday 5 June 1902:

Married the 1 June at the bride's home near Glassy Mountain, S.C., GARFIELD BRECKENRIDGE to ROXIE BLAIR, both colored. G.H. Hendricks, N.P. officiated.

Married the 28 May at the home of the bride's father MR. JOCCA (JACOB) ALEXANDER, MISS ABBE ALEXANDER to MR. J.B. BURGESS. The service was conducted by Rev. B.F. Murphree.

BERRY GARY moved into his new house last week in Liberty, S.C.

Married, MR. EUGENE ZACHARY and MISS LOLA GAINES daughter of MR. JAMES H. GAINES of Central, S.C., on Thursday at the Methodist Parsonage at Pendleton, S.C. The ceremony was performed by Rev. J.E. Beard. Mr. Zachary is a conductor on the SOUTHERN RAILROAD and is a native of North Carolina.

A little child of MR. JAMES HARVEY died in Greenville, S.C. and was brought to Central, S.C. for burial.

An heir was born to MR. and MRS. M.F. DAY the 23 (May).

Issue of: Thursday 12 June 1902:

MISS UNITY NIMMONS will teach the summer term at Ambler School.

JAMES H. HUGHEY died the 2 June. He was a Confederate Soldier for 4 years and the father of six children, five of whom have died leaving only one son, JOHN A. HUGHEY and his wife. He was 72 years of age and was buried at George's Creek Cemetery. Rev. D.W. Hiott conducted the service.

Clemson and its Commencement as seen by an alumnus (details).

Issue of: Thursday 19 June 1902:

Married yesterday at the home of Rev. T.H. Posey, MR. NORMAN Z. ABBOTT of Central S.C. and MISS DAISY M. PARSON of Cateechee, S.C. (twice in same issue).

A son was born to MR. and MRS. HOVEY NEALEY the 11 June.

ENGINEER JEANES will soon have one of the prettiest cottages in Pickens. It is the work of B.E. GRANDY.

MRS. JAMES GRIFFY and her child died last Saturday on DR. HOLLINGSWORTH'S place. They were buried at Slabtown, S.C.

A baby of J.T. WILLIS died last Wednesday and was buried at Liberty Cemetery. The service was conducted by Rev. H.C. Haddock.

Issue of: Thursday 26 June 1902:

EDWARD DePRIEST the 13 month old baby of MR. and MRS. E.F. DePRIEST died the 17 June, burial was at Friendship.

Married the 22 June by B.D. Garvin, N.P., MISS LULA HUDGENS to MR. WALKER JAMES both of Cateechee, S.C.

Married the 18 June at the Methodist Parsonage at west end, MR. C.M. BOWEN and MISS EVA TRAYLOR (sic).

Cedar Rock School will have MISS OLA MAJORS in charge this summer.

Article - "Negro Superstitions".

Issue of: Thursday 3 July 1902:

A son was born to MR. and MRS. CHARLES RAGSDALE the 29 June.

Pickens County is accepting bids for a new jail.

Married the 25 June at the home of the bride's parents MR. and MRS. L. ROSS EATON of Central, S.C., CAPTAIN IVY M. MAULDIN of Pickens and MISS VERA EATON. Rev. O.M. Abney officiated.

Teachers in Pickens Co., S.C. (details).

IVY STANSELL, a nine month old son of MR. and MRS. JAMES STANSELL of Ambler, S.C., died the 14 (June). He was buried at Oolenoy Baptist Church.

Little J. FRANK MITCHELL the son of MR. and MRS. A. MITCHELL died the 17 (June) at the age of 12 years, 8 months and 17 days.

MISS NANNIE ROPER will teach at Lenhardt School this summer.

Issue of: Thursday 10 July 1902:

ISAAC H. McCALLA born near Lowndesville, S.C., son of CAPTAIN GEORGE R. McCALLA will run for Congress (lengthy details).

C.T. MILLER, colored, has been elected to teach Cold Springs Summer School term for the public school.

MISS JENNIE WAKELIN died at the home of her sister in Oklahoma while on a visit. She leaves her parents.

List of Pickens Co., S.C. Voting Boxes (details).

Married at the home of the bride's parents the 6 July, MR. HENRY HENDRICKS and MISS NINA CRENSHAW by Rev. McDaniel.

Married the 6 July, MR. THOMAS SAMMONS to MISS EULA WILLIAMS, daughter of MR. SILAS WILLIAMS by Rev. S.A. Whitmire.

Vineland School formerly taught by PROF. J.F. FOLK will open the 18 July under PROF. BOLLAND of Slighes, S.C.

Issue of: Thursday 17 July 1902:

MRS. K.L. CURETON will teach at Town Creek School.

Married the 13 July 1902 at the home of the bride's father MR. WARREN ABBOTT by Rev. W.C. Seaborn, MR. ARTHUR H. ARNOLD to MISS GERTRUDE E. ABBOTT both of Central, S.C.

The bridge at Burch's Ford will be iron. The contract was let to the Virginia Bridge and Iron Co. of Roanoke, Va.

Married the 10 May 1902, MR. LEIGH HUNT of the Dacusville Section to MISS MELLA HENDRICKS the 3rd daughter of MR. and MRS. D.E. HENDRICKS at the home of Rev. D.W. Hiott.

Pickens Co., S.C. Court Proceedings - Criminal cases (details).

A son of M.H. "DOCK" and LIZZIE LEWIS died the 10 July and was buried at Mountain Grove Church.

AD - CAESAR'S HEAD HOTEL, J.E. GWINN, opened from 1 June to the 1 Oct., Caesar's Head, S.C.

Issue of: Thursday 24 July 1902:

MRS. AMANDA BILLINGSLEY widow of WILLIAM BILLINGSLEY died at her home near Dalton Post Office, the 14 July at the age of about 53 years. She leaves one daughter, MRS. JOSEPH PERRY and 3 sons. Burial was at Keowee Baptist Church.

THOMAS H. BOGGS died at his home in Fernandina, Florida the 15 July at the age of 44 years. He was buried at Old Liberty Cemetery. He is survived by his wife the former KATE ARIAIL and two children. Mr. Boggs was a brother of HON. JULIUS E. BOGGS of this place.

A daughter was born to MR. and MRS. FIELDS R. CHAPMAN the 12 July.

Issue of: Thursday 31 July 1902:

Article - "NANCY HART".

B.E. GRANDY received the contract to build the new jail.

A son was born to MR. and MRS. MACK GRAVELY the 26 July.

A welcome to the *Easley Progress* on its initial issue.

COL. JOHN SLOAN of Columbia, S.C. is a candidate for Lieutenant Governor of South Carolina. He was born in Pendleton, S.C. in 1846 and was educated at the Academy in that place. He left school at the age of 17 to join the

Confederate Army and was a member of Co. A., 7th S.C. Cavalry (lengthy details).

Issue of: Thursday 7 August 1902:

Quarterly Report of Pickens Co., S.C. Disbursements.

Married 3 Aug. 1902 at the home of M.F. Hester, N.P., MR. ELFORD CLARK to MISS LIZZIE SIMMONS daughter of MR. FRANK SIMMONS of Pickens County.

TONY WILLIAMS, colored, of upper Anderson Co., S.C. died in Liberty, S.C., Monday morning last at the home of W.H. CHASTAIN, colored.

MISS MAY ROBINSON is teaching at Bethlehem School and MISS IDA HENDRIX has charge of Oolenoy Academy.

Issue of: Thursday 14 August 1902:

Article - "Confederate Veteran's Reunion, Greenville, S.C."

WILLIAM ARTHUR CHRISTOPHER will teach at the Easley Cotton Mill School.

HON. G.E. PRINCE is running for Congress. He is the son of the late W.L. PRINCE a Confederate Soldier. His mother was a CLINKSCALES and both his grandmothers were surnamed BLACK (details).

Pickens Co., S.C. Sheriff's Sale - Tax Executions:
L.A. SLATENS - 137 acres, Eastatoe Township to be sold.
MITTIE SMITH - 48 acres, Liberty Township to be sold.
FRANK L. ALEXANDER - 130 acres, Hurricane Township.
J.F. ABERCRUMBIE - 65 acres, Hurricane Township to be sold.
DAVID B. MURPHREE - 50 acres, Eastatoe Township to be sold.

Issue of: Thursday 21 August 1902:

Article - "Story of Cultivation of Rice in South Carolina".

Information on these candidates for office:
J.J McMAHAN
WILLIAM N. GRAYDON
M.F. ANSEL
R.F. SMITH
WYATT AIKEN
MAJOR G.M. LYNCH
S.A McALISTER
A.J. WELBORN
J.J. HERD
A.B. TALLEY, JR.
ROBERT STEWART
J.R. ROSS
N.C. "DOC" PARSONS
J.A. HINTON
W.N. BOLDING
MATTHEW HENDRICKS
IVY M. MAULDIN
FRED WILLIAMS
C.E. ROBINSON
C.H. CARPENTER
LABAN MAULDIN
J.T. GANTT
W.G. MAULDIN

Issue of: Thursday 28 August 1902:

Pickens Co., S.C. Election Returns (details).

The little five year old daughter of MR. BEN BANKS who lives about 3 miles south of Pickens died on Sunday. Burial was at Secona.

MRS. AMANDA ALEXANDER widow of JAMES ALEXANDER died last Thursday at her home near Martin School. She was 61 years old and leaves four daughters and two sons, all grown. Burial was at Shady Grove with the service by Rev. B.F. Murphy and Rev. M.C. Winchester.

MISS OLIVIA McHUGH is teaching at the Saluda Hill School.

HON. WILLIAM W.F. BRIGHT died the 25 Aug. 1902. He was born the 19 Dec. 1840 in Blount Co., Tennessee, the son of DAVID and JANE KAY BRIGHT. Mr. Bright was distantly related to F.S. KEY, author of "The Star Spangled Banner". He was a Confederate Soldier in Co. E, 5th Regt., Tenn. Cavalry and served as a private. He was a resident of Pickens County and was 62 years of age. Burial was at Cross Roads Church. Surviving are five daughters: MISSES HANNAH, LIZZIE, JANIE, MAGGIE and EUNICE BRIGHT.

Issue of: Thursday 4 September 1902:

JAY WELBORN, a five year old son of JUDGE M. WELBORN and MRS. WELBORN, died on Sunday. Burial was at Secona.

TOM COHEN, colored, was identified as wrecking the passenger train of the SOUTHERN RAILWAY the 24 August.

Married in Atlanta, Georgia the 1 Sept., MR. CLAUDE H. ALEXANDER of Pickens and MRS. LAURA HAGOOD O'NEAL of Birmingham, Alabama. Rev. Alonzo Monk officiated at his residence.

Public School in Liberty, S.C. - PROF. DuBOSE of Virginia is principal and MISS ANNIE FERGUSON of Pickens is the assistant.

Pickens Co., S.C. Citation Notice - MARGARET J. BRIGHT applies for Letters of Administration for the estate of W.W.F. BRIGHT, deceased.

Issue of: Thursday 11 September 1902:

ABNER O'DELL died at his home in Liberty, S.C. the 8 Sept. at the age of 76 years. He was thrice married and leaves a widow and two sons. Burial was at Kennemore Burying Ground (see issue of the 18 Sept. 1902).

WADDY MAULDIN McFALL infant son of MR. and MRS. W.T. McFALL died last Saturday. Rev. O.M. Abney conducted the service.

Article - "Old Pickens", Pickens District, S.C. (now Oconee County). The following information is given: ROBERT F. MORGAN had the first hotel, was deputy sheriff, constable and a Confederate Soldier. His children are: FRANK MORGAN and JEFF MORGAN of Central, S.C. and J.D. MORGAN of Seneca, S.C.
ROBERT KNOX was the long time jailor of the Old District. He was an old man at the beginning of the war. His children were: JOHN KNOX and JAMES KNOX who were both killed in the Civil War. ARTHUR KNOX and HARRISON KNOX, younger sons, have died since the War. MRS. CATHARINE BOGGS, widow of MONROE BOGGS, of Newry, S.C. and MRS. BOYD wife of JAMES L. BOYD of Oconee Co., S.C. are both daughters. There was also a son BENJAMIN KNOX now deceased.
MATTISON HUNNICUTT was also a former resident of Old Pickens. His children were: WARREN HUNNICUTT, THOMAS HUNNICUTT, JOE BERRY HUNNICUTT and WILLIAM JOHN HUNNICUTT.

AD - Pickens Graded School, Colored Department, R.K. MOON, Principal.

Issue of: Thursday 18 September 1902:

To Cross the Blue Ridge - A Railroad from Anderson to the Tennessee Coal Fields (details). *Anderson Daily Mail*

C.T. HUTCHINS is building a residence on the west side of Liberty, S.C.

A. O'DELL died the 8 Sept. at nearly 80 years of age. Burial was at Kennemore Bury Ground. The service was conducted by H.C. Haddock. Surviving were sons, J.C. O'DELL and J.S. O'DELL of Georgia. (ABNER O'DELL, born 8 June 1825, died 8 Sept. 1902 - Pickens Co., S.C. Cemetery Survey, Vol. 1, p. 197 - see issue of the 11 Sept. 1902).

AD - Central Graded School. L.G. CLAYTON, Chairman of the Board of Trustees.

Issue of: Thursday 25 September 1902:

Twenty-seven converts were baptized at the pool at Griffin Ebenezer Baptist Church, colored. REV. H. WATKINS is the minister.

Married the 21 Sept. 1902 at the residence of the bride's father MR. JAMES DURHAM, MR. EUPHA COCHRAN and MISS LULA

JANE DURHAM all of Pickens County. Rev. W.C. Seaborn officiated.

The EASLEY HARDWARE CO., Easley, S.C. has been established.

The school in Central, S.C. has PROF. DOMINICK as principal.

South Carolina has an exhibition at St. Louis, Missouri (details).

What's going on in the business way in Pickens, S.C. (details).

Death of a stranger from Kokomo, Indiana from an overdose of morphine. He was found in a dying condition near the depot and gave his name as WILLIAM SMITH. Burial was at the Poor Farm in Pickens County.

Issue of: Thursday 2 October 1902:

WILLIAM FIELD BLASSINGAME died the 27 Sept. He was born the 4 Nov. 1868 in Anderson Co., S.C. and graduated from Furman University. On the 25 Oct. 1893 he married MISS EVA GREGORY of Union Co., S.C. who died within a year. Surviving are his father, MR. B.F. BLASSINGAME, one brother, J.T. BLASSINGAME and one sister, MRS. MAMIE CURETON of Greenwood, S.C. Burial was in Greenville, S.C.

MISS EULA BOGGS died last Saturday at the home of her father MR. BENJAMIN BOGGS four miles below Pickens. She was a sister of WALTER J. BOGGS. Rev. Thomas H. Medd conducted the service. Burial was at Ruhamah.

MR. O.H.P. FANT died at his home in Anderson, S.C. the 28 Sept. at the age of 85 years. He is survived by REV. HANDY B. FANT, J. REESE FANT and MRS. CASHIN of Anderson, S.C., WAYNE FANT of Townville, S.C., MRS. CARY of Seneca S.C. and MRS. EVA THORNLEY of Pickens. Burial was at Silver Brook Cemetery in Anderson, S.C.

Married the 25 Sept., MISS MYRA LAY of Westminister, S.C. and W.N. COX in the Presbyterian Church. Rev. W.S. Hamiter of Seneca S.C. officiated. Mr. Cox lives in the historic HORSE SHOE ROBINSON old house at the Horse Shoe Bend on the Chauga River.

Pickens Co., S.C. Final Settlement - Estate of ABSOLEM ROPER, deceased by JOHN ROPER, Administrator.

Pickens Co., S.C. Notice to Debtors and Creditors - Estate of B.A. GREEN, deceased by IDA C. GREEN, Administratrix.

Pickens Co., S.C. Citation Notice - A.J. BOGGS C.C.P. filed for Letters of Administration for the estate of J.T. CRAIG, deceased.

Pickens Co., S.C. Citation Notice - R.A. BOWEN filed for Letters of Administration for the estate of REESE BOWEN, deceased.

Issue of: Thursday 9 October 1902:

Married the 5 Oct. at the home of the bride's father MR. MOORE near Central, S.C., MR. SILAS A. ALEXANDER to MISS ELLA MOORE both of Pickens Co. W.C. Seaborn officiated.

MRS. HESTER ANN SMITH relict of the late J. MONROE SMITH died at the home of her son-in-law DR. L.G. CLAYTON at Central, S.C. the 4 Oct. She was buried at the cemetery in Slabtown, Anderson Co., S.C. Services were conducted by Rev. P.L. Grier of Due West, S.C. Mrs. Smith was 76 years of age and is survived by sons: J.P. SMITH and L.J. SMITH of Liberty, S.C. and DR. R.F. SMITH and W.C. SMITH of Easley, S.C. and daughters: MRS. J.P. GREEN of Slabtown, MRS. J.C. WATKINS of Anderson, S.C. and MRS. L.G. CLAYTON of Central, S.C. She is also survived by three brothers.

Article - "Story of the Sword of DR. J.D. CURETON".

MRS. POLLY STANSELL died at the home of her son H.C. STANSELL of Piedmont Cotton Mills, S.C. the 22 Sept. Her daughter is MRS. JANE WINCHESTER. Burial was at Holly Springs beside her husband.

Honor Roll for Pickens Graded School September 1902:
First Grade
FEDDIE McDANIEL   JANET BOLT
FAY McHUGH   FURMAN PACE
EUGENE YONGUE   RALPH HESTER
Second Grade
INEZ MORRIS   WALTER DICKENS
ELLEN LEWIS   ALBERTA YONGUE
MEDA BOGGS   EDNA EARLE
Third Grade
THERON HESTER   PAUL HESTER
CLIFFORD LEWIS   MARY LEWIS
GEORGE PRINCE
Fourth Grade
KATIE McDANIEL   BELLE YONGUE
MAY McFALL
Fifth Grade
PATTIE MAJOR   HENRY McDANIEL
HAGOOD BRUCE   LOIS HESTER
LOUISE McDANIEL   JULIUS BOGGS
WYATT JENNINGS   GRACE PRINCE
JOHNSON CRENSHAW   OTIS KEITH

LORENA TAYLOR

<u>Sixth Grade</u>

ORA McFALL	JESSE LEWIS
MAKA BOGGS	DICK FREEMAN
GLADYS MAULDIN	FURMAN MORRIS
EVA EARLE	JACK LEWIS

<u>Seventh Grade</u>

FLORA CAREY	OLA RICHEY
EILENE TAYLOR	JAY ROBINSON
KATE HESTER	LIZZETTE WELBORN

<u>Eight Grade</u>

BERTHA BRIDGES	HATTIE EARLE
GUSSIE CURETON	NELLIE GRANDY
VESTA ASHMORE	EDGAR MORRIS
JAMES CAREY, JR.	WILLIAM JONES
ELIZA McDANIEL	LOIS NEWTON
MARY McDANIEL	

<u>Ninth Grade</u>

CORRINNE NEWTON	BRUCE BOGGS
CECIL HESTER	EDWIN EARLE
JENNIE LEWIS	HOVEY EARLE

<u>Issue of: Thursday 16 October 1902:</u>

J.T. WATKINS of Nashville, Tennessee brought one of his daughters to Slabtown, Anderson, Co., last week to be buried.

Pickens Co., S.C. Clerk's Sale - Court of Common Pleas: J.R. KEITH vs WILLIS GLENN, SR. - 14 acres to be sold.

Pickens Co., S.C. Petit Jury List.

<u>Issue of: Thursday 23 October 1902:</u>

Married at the residence of the groom, MR. WILLIAM FARMER to MISS MISSOURI RACKLEY, B.J. Johnson, N.P. officiated. All of Pickens County.

Married at the residence of Rev. J.E. Foster the 12 Oct., W.H. WILLIAMS of this place and MISS CORA ELLIS of Locust, South Carolina.

Article - "JEFFERSON DAVIS' Private Secretary, The Story of a Faithful Slave named BEN MONTGOMERY".

Valuable land for sale - Tract #1 - The home place on Carpenter's Creek - 327 acres; tract #2 - Known as the JONES place - 15 acres, 2 good tenant houses; tract #3 - known as the CART place, 65 6/10 acres with one tenant house. This is the estate of JOSEPH F. WILLIAMS and MATILDA ANN WILLIAMS, both deceased. Sold by T.A., G.A., J.I., L.B., J.F., and H.L. WILLIAMS and J.W. CLEMENTS.

Issue of: Thursday 30 October 1902:

Pickens Co., S.C. Final Presentation of the Grand Jury for the fall term of 1902. Report on road conditions and recommendations. Observations that the railroad is violating the law by operating their freight trains on Sunday. They ask that this section of the report be turned over to the proper authorities.

EVA NEAL is to open the Roanoke Public School, Monday the 10 November.

Issue of: Thursday 6 November 1902:

Married the 2 Nov. at the residence of BOWER MARTIN by Rev. B. Holder, MR. I.B. BANKS to MISS ELLA STATON all of Pickens County.

ROBERT CONNER, colored, drowned near J. SAM WILSON'S place last Saturday night.

MAJOR J.J. LEWIS is ill at the home of his daughter MRS. J. LEE CARPENTER of Greenville, S.C.

Last Saturday night NERO HALLUMS, colored, died of gun shot wounds (details).

J.D. LOOPER, the two year old son of MR. and MRS. M.O. LOOPER, died the 4 Nov. at the home of his grandfather J.L. MOON three miles below Pickens. Burial was at Secona.

Pickens Co., S.C. Notice to Debtor and Creditors - Estate of CATHERINE CANNON, deceased by A.J. BOGGS, C.C.P.

Pickens Co., S.C. Final Settlement - Estate of JULIA BOGGS, deceased by S.C. BOGGS and J.C. BOGGS, Executors.

Executrix Sale - Estate of G.W. BANKS by MARY C. BANKS, Executrix. 31 acres and 57 acres to be sold.

Sale of Personal Property of J.F. and MALINDA ANN WILLIAMS at the home place now the residence of J.I. WILLIAMS - household effects, mule, wagon, corn, etc. to be sold.

Pickens Co., S.C. Notice to Debtors and Creditors - Estate of W.F. BLASSINGAME by W.T. FIELD, Executor.

Issue of: Thursday 13 November 1902:

Pickens Co., S.C. Supplement Statement of Expenditures of the Office of the County Commissioners (details).

Pickens Co., S.C. Citation Notice - ISAAC HALLUM, colored, applied for Letters of Administration for the estate of NERO HALLUM, deceased.

Pickens Co., S.C. Probate Sale:
R.A. BOWEN, Administrator of the estate of REESE BOWEN, SR. vs JOHN Y. BOWEN, et al. 222 acres known as the Reese Bowen homeplace to be sold.

Pickens Co., S.C. Clerk's Sale - Court of Common Pleas:
CHANEY McKINNEY, et al. vs W.M. BROWN, et al. 134 acres on Toxaway River to be sold.

Pickens Co., S.C. Clerk's Sale - Court of Common Pleas:
EMMA WILLIAMS, et al. vs JOHN WILLIAMS, et al. 13 lots, each 1 acre near Norris Station on the SOUTHERN RAILWAY, part of the estate of A.B. WILLIAMS, deceased, to be sold.

Pickens Co., S.C. Clerk's Sale - Court of Common Pleas:
JULIA WATKINS, et al. vs JOHN C. BOGGS et al. 225 acres of land in Central Township to be sold.

Pickens Co., S.C. Sheriff's Sale - Court of Common Pleas:
JAMES K. LATHEM vs JAMES R. LATHEM. 45 acres in Easley Township and 45 acres adjoining the above, deeded to JAMES R. LATHEM by his sister ANN CHILDRESS to be sold.

Issue of: Thursday 20 November 1902:

Married the 9 Nov. at the home of the bride's father MARION STEPHENS by Rev. W.C. Seaborn, MR. WILLIAM ATKINSON to MISS NORA STEPHENS both of Pickens County.

A Mass Meeting at Norris, S.C. - Requesting the Governor to offer a reward for the person or persons who killed NERO HALLUM (details).

Issue of: Thursday 27 November 1902:

Sketch - "Old Pendleton".

MRS. S.E. ERVIN of Richland, S.C. died. She was the sister of PROF. W.E. DENDY. (FLORENCE IRENE ERVIN, daughter of THOMAS and LUCY DENDY, age 35 years, died 20 Nov. 1902, buried Richland Presbyterian Church - Oconee Co., S.C. Cemetery Survey, Vol. 1, p. 255).

Married the 20 Nov., MR. WADE H. BOGGS and MISS ESSIE GANTT, all of this county. Rev. H.C. Haddock officiated (error - see issue of the 4 Dec. 1902).

Pickens Co., S.C. Notice to Debtors and Creditors - Estate of W.E. ALEXANDER, deceased by B.F. ALEXANDER, Administrator.

Issue of: Thursday 4 December 1902:

Pickens Co., S.C. Executor's Sale:
Land of WILLIAM HUNTER, deceased on Twelve Mile River to be sold, by D.F. BRADLEY.

Married at the residence of MR. W.M. HAGOOD the 27 Nov., MR. H.C. HAGOOD and MISS VIOLA RUNION by Rev. J.C. Shive.

Married the 23 Nov. at the home of the bride's grandfather MR. N.M. MADDEN, MR. W. PAUL ARNOLD of Pickens Co. to MISS CORA E. MADDEN of Anderson, S.C., by Rev. W.C. Seaborn.

Married the 30 Nov. at the residence of M.F. Hester, N.P., MR. TYLER BEARDEN to MISS LILLIE CLARK all of Pickens County.

MR. ROBIN S. SMITH age 84 years, died at the home of his son OLIVER S. SMITH the 26 November. He served in the Civil War. Burial was at Pleasant Hill Baptist Church. Mr. Smith leaves seven children (two items in same issue).

MISS ESSIE GANTT married MR. ARTHUR BOGGS not WALTER H. BOGGS. (error in issue of the 27 Nov. 1902).

MISS LILA FOLGER is teaching at Mt. Tabor.

J.H. PAYNE of Calhoun, S.C. died at the State Hospital the 24 Nov. at the age of 47 years. Burial was at Mt. Zion Church. He leaves a wife and two children (see issue of the 11 Dec. 1902).

Pickens Co., S.C. Final Settlement - J.A. HINTON, Administrator for the estate of R.O. HINTON, deceased.

Issue of: Thursday 11 December 1902:

WILLIAM P. FINDLEY age 30 and a son of MR. C.B. FINDLEY died the 23 Nov. He leaves a father, two sisters and five brothers. Service was by B.A. Lewis, his pastor, with burial at Keowee Cemetery.

Hazel News
Married the 12 Nov. at the residence of the bride's mother MRS. HARRIETT BOWIE, MR. WADE LEWIS to MISS MARGIE BOWIE. Rev. J.P. Attaway officiated.

Calhoun Items
JERRY H. PAYNE died. He was born in Cleveland, White Co., Georgia, and came to Central, S.C. with his parents when he was 18 years old. Mr. Payne married MISS MYRA BOGGS of Pickens Co. the 15 Aug. 1883 (see issue of the 4 Dec. 1902).

This Issue in Poor Condition.

Issue of: Thursday 18 December 1902:

Married at the residence of the bride's parents the 10 Dec., MR. MARION EVAN to MISS LOLA KENNEMORE all of Pickens County. Rev. J.M. Stewart officiated.

Married at the residence of W.N. HUGHES the 7 Dec., MR. JOSEPH TROTTER to MISS CORA AIKEN of Table Mountain, S.C. W.N. Hughes performed the ceremony.

Pickens Co., S.C. Clerk's Sale:
WILLIAM M. CANNON, et al. vs LONZO D. CREW. 20 acres in Hurricane Township, part of the old homestead of MOSES W. CREW to be sold.

Pickens Co., S.C. Sheriff's Sale - Court of Common Pleas:
WILLIAM B. LOOPER, SALLIE JULIAN, GEORGE W. F. ROBINSON, et al. vs A. ROBINSON. Real estate of the late SARAH E. ROBINSON - 140 acres on Gregory's Creek to be sold.

Most of this Issue Missing.

NO PAPER FOUND FOR 25 DECEMBER 1902.

THE PEOPLE'S JOURNAL 1903

Issue of: Thursday 1 January 1903:

Article - "The New White House".

Article - "Palmetto Gleanings - Events of the Week in Brief".

Special - Greenville, S.C.
Lynching of a Negro and his wife for the killing of W.K. JAY of the Troy Section (details).

A. BRANDON TAYLOR of Furman University spent the holidays with his parents.

W.F. MAULDIN a Clemson College student spent the holidays at his home in Pickens.

MRS. K.L. CURETON is teaching at Town Creek School.

MISS JOSEPHINE STEPHENSON a student of Williamston Female College spent the holidays with her parents in Pickens.

T. CHRISTIE ROBINSON, head clerk of the BEN-DELLA HOTEL, Laurens, S.C. spent the holidays with his father and family.

Married the 28 (Dec. 1902) at the residence of S.J. MADDEN, MR. J.Z. MADDEN to MISS ANNA ALEXANDER by Rev. B.F. Murphree. All of Pickens.

R.T. HALLUM, School Superintendent, has moved to Pickens and occupies the dwelling formerly occupied by H.W. FARR who has moved into the WILLIAM MARTIN residence.

DRAYTON EARLE a Clemson College student visited his uncles DR. G.W. EARLE and J.W. EARLE of Pickens.

Married the 17 Dec. 1902 at the residence of the bride's father CAPTAIN W.B. ALLGOOD by Rev. J.M. Stewart, MR. BLUFORD ALEXANDER to MISS BETTIE ALLGOOD.

S.G. HIGGINS died the 22 (Dec. 1902) from an accident on the railroad from Asheville, North Carolina to Spartanburg, South Carolina. He was buried at Easley, S.C. (SAMUEL G. HIGGINS, born 30 Jan. 1874, died 22 Dec. 1902, buried Easley City Cemetery - Pickens Co., S.C. Cemetery Survey, Vol. 3, p. 53).

Central
MISS MATTIE MAE MORGAN a student at Columbia Female College was at home for the holidays.

MISS SALLIE BROWN daughter of MRS. BROWN died the 25 Dec. 1902, at her home and was buried at Mt. Zion Cemetery.

MR. A.W. ROCHESTER is at home from Newman, Georgia.

Pickens Co., S.C. Executor's Sale:
Estate of WILLIAM HUNTER, deceased by D.F. BRADLEY, Executor. Tract #2 - 70 acres, corn mill, wheat mill, saw mill, ginnery and machinery connected with these mills (details).

Pickens Co., S.C. Auditor's Notice (details).

Pickens Co., S.C. Treasurer's Report (details).

AD - Pickens Co., S.C., DRUG STORE, J.L. BOLT, M.D. and J.N. HALLUM, Pharmacist.

Issue of: Thursday 8 January 1903:

Article - "Palmetto Gleanings - Events in Brief of the past Week".

Article - "Social Life in Pickens" by JULIUS E. BOGGS. *News and Courier*

MISS MARY E. SWANN is teaching the graded school in Pickens.

J.M. GILLESPIE, Pickens County farmer, is in town entering his daughters MISSES ADA and OLIVE in the graded school.

The PICKENS BRICK YARD is located near town.

Married the 24 Dec. (1902) at the residence of the bride's father MR. SPENCER ROPER by J.E. Foster, MR. ARTHUR RAMPEY to MISS SUE ROPER (details).

Married the 30 Dec. (1902) by G.R. Hendricks, MONROE JAMISON and MISS BYRD.

Married at the residence of M.F. Hester, N.P., MR. FRANK DAY to MISS LEILA CLARK all of Pickens.

Married the 4 Jan. 1903 at the residence of the bride's parent MATTHEW RIGDON by Rev. B. Holder, JOSEPH STANSELL to MISS SARNIE RIGDON all of Pickens County.

A.B. TALLY, JR., County Commissioner-Elect, is moving to Pickens. He will occupy the DR. EARLE house beyond JUDGE NEWTON'S.

The schoolhouse in Garvin District #25 was destroyed by fire Thursday night the 1 (Jan.). ROBERT CRAIG is in charge of the school.

300

New Pension Laws (details).

Card of Thanks, to neighbors and friends at the time of the death of S.C. McWHORTER on the 30 Dec. 1902, from his family.

Issue of: Thursday 15 January 1903:

Article - "Palmetto Gleanings - Events in Brief of the Past Week".

CHIEF JUSTICE HENRY McIVER died Monday at his home in Cheraw, S.C. (details of his life).

GEORGE WILLIAMS died the 6 (Jan.) in Charleston, S.C. at the age of 83 years.

PINK JOHNSON has a livery stable in Easley, S.C.

JESSE JENNINGS is home for a brief visit. He has been with OLIVE & CO. in Birmingham, Alabama. Mr. Jennings will leave in a few days for Columbia, S.C. where he will accept a position with the SOUTHERN RAILROAD.

W.L. LaBOON of Anderson, S.C. will practice law in Pickens. He was admitted to the bar the 10 Dec. 1902.

Married Thursday the 8 Jan. 1903 at the residence of the bride's father MR. JACOB MARTIN by Rev. W.C. Seaborn, MR. GEORGE T. WATSON of Anderson Co., S.C. to MISS CORA J. MARTIN of Pickens County.

Married Sunday the 4 Jan. at the residence of the bride's father, by George A. Ellis, N.P., MR. JACOB BEARDEN to MISS AMANDA TURNER.

Liberty
BEVERLY GRANITE WORKS started up again.
JOKE (sic) ALLGOOD will soon have his residence ready for occupancy on the west end.
School opened Monday with MISS CALHOUN of Clemson, S.C. as principal and MISS REEMS of Tennessee as assistant.
C.T. HUTCHINS now occupies his new residence on the west end. When the house is completed it will be the best residence on that end of town.

J.F. JENNINGS has sold his residence to ABB YOUNG. He has bought HUNTER'S lot where the HUNTER STORE burned a few years ago.

The Governor's Annual Message - Clemson College, New Mansion, Winthrop, Finance, Taxation, etc. (details).

AD - JOHN T. BOGGS, Jeweler and Job Printing, Liberty, S.C.

Issue of: Thursday 22 January 1903:

N.G. GONZALES, Editor of the *Columbia State* died Monday. He was shot the 15 Jan. by JAMES H. TILLMAN (details of his life).

There is a smallpox scare in Pickens County.

B.E. GRANDY is building a "PALACE CAR" for the county chain gang. We have not been informed as to whether the sleeping apartments will be on the "WAGNER" or the "PULLMAN" style but finishing inside and out will be of "native pine".

Reunion Schoolhouse near BEVERLY GRANITE WORKS was destroyed by fire Friday night. MISS MORRISON of Clemson College, S.C. had been in charge (details).

JEFF RICHARDSON was appointed postmaster at Greenville, S.C. (details).

DICK HENDRICKS, colored, died Friday. He was living a few miles north west of Pickens. It is thought he died of smallpox (details).

CAPTAIN L.M. GRIST died at his home in Yorktown (sic), S.C. last Thursday. He was manager of the *York Enquirer*. Captain Grist was in the Confederate Army and was wounded in the Second Battle of Manassas. He was a member of the Associate Reform Presbyterian Church.

DR. GEORGE W. EARLE died Tuesday. He was born the 3 Sept. 1837 in Slabtown, Anderson Co., S.C. Dr. Earle was the son of DR. JAMES W. EARLE and his mother was the former MISS AMANDA BENSON of Pendleton, S.C. She was the daughter of E.B. BENSON. Dr. Earle served in the Confederate Army as a Pvt. Palmetto Riflemen, 4th S.C. Regt. He married in 1874 MISS JEANNETTE BREAZEALE of Belton, Anderson Co., S.C. There are five children: MISSES EVA EARLE and ESSIE EARLE, LOUIS EARLE, EDWIN EARLE and CECIL EARLE all living. His brothers are: JAMES W. EARLE who lives near Pickens and BERRY EARLE, deceased. His three sisters are: MRS. AUSTIN of California, MRS. KING of Charlotte, North Carolina and MRS. O'NEAL of Texas. Dr. Earle was predeceased by three sisters: MRS. BOMAR, MRS. BROWN and MISS ELLA EARLE. He was a member of the Presbyterian Church. (GEORGE W. EARLE, born 3 Sept. 1836, died 20 Jan. 1903, buried Pickens Sunrise Cemetery - Pickens Co., S.C. Cemetery Survey, Vol. 2, p. 133 - two articles in this issue).

Norris
There is a flourishing school here.
Mr. W.R. JOHNSON is in the merchandise business at this place.

CAPTAIN JOHN H. BOWEN of Pickens County died last Thursday, at his home on the Saluda River about 15 miles from Pickens, at the age of 65 years. He died of cancer of the throat. Captain Bowen was Treasurer of Pickens County for several years and had been in the State Legislature from Pickens County. He served in the Confederate Army in COL. HOLLINGSWORTH'S Company and transferred to CAPTAIN R.Y.H. GRIFFIN'S Company. At the death of Captain Griffin, Lt. Bowen became Captain. He was married three times, first to MISS HOLCOMBE, second to MISS BURDINE and third to MRS. HUNT who survives. He is survived by 5 brothers: Col. R.E. BOWEN, WILLIAM BOWEN, THOMAS BOWEN, SAMUEL BOWEN and LaFAYETTE BOWEN, three of whom live in Texas. The funeral was at George's Creek Baptist Church where he was a deacon.

Central
There is concern over the appearance of smallpox among the Negroes near town.

R.L. SMITH has a new market in Pickens.

Issue of: Thursday 29 January 1903:

HOMER ALONZO RICHEY died last Thursday.

MRS. FLORA LATHEM and her two little daughters came from the THORNWELL ORPHANAGE on the sad mission of attending the burial of HOMER A. RICHEY, JR. (see below).

HOMER A. RICHEY of Pickens died Thursday at the age of 28 years. Since March of 1897 he has been connected with his brother-in-law J.L.O. THOMPSON of the *Pickens Sentinel* and with his father in the firm of H.A. RICHEY & SONS. Mr. Richey was a member of the town council. He leaves a father, mother, one brother, JAMES T. RICHEY and 7 sisters, MRS. MARTIN, MRS. FLORA LATHEM, MRS. J.L.O. THOMPSON, MRS. B.B. LaBOON, MISSES OLGA, SADIE and OLA BELLE RICHEY. He was buried with the MASONIC RITUAL of the Keowee Lodge. (HOMER A. RICHEY, born 6 Oct. 1874, died 22 Jan. 1903, MASON, buried Pickens Sunrise Cemetery - Pickens Co., S.C. Cemetery Survey, Vol. 2, p. 132).

A. "ART" R. CRAIG froze to death in December. He served in the Confederate Army and was Deputy Sheriff of Oconee Co., S.C. Mr. Craig moved from Walhalla, S.C. to his large plantation on the Keowee River. He leaves a widow, 1 son and 1 daughter. *Keowee Courier* (ARTHUR R. CRAIG, born 18 May 1846, died 16 Dec. 1902, buried Craig Family Cemetery - Pickens Co., S.C. Cemetery Survey, Vol. 1, p. 230).

Letter to the Editor from THOMAS LYNCH of Menan, Freemont Co., Idaho, dated the 8 Jan. 1903 (details).

MISS SARAH GROGAN of Elberton, Georgia is visiting the family of J. McD. BRUCE.

A new design for the postage stamp will be issued early in February and is much more handsome than the ones now used.

The anniversary of the death of GENERAL WADE HAMPTON was observed Friday last by the S.C. State Legislature.

WILTON HESTER has resigned his position with the PICKENS RAILROAD CO. and is going to try his fortune in the "Gate City". CARLISLE NEWTON has been selected to fill the vacancy.

J.R. ROSS died at his home about 15 miles west of Pickens at the age of 55 years. He leaves a wife and several children. Mr. Ross was a member of the Six Mile Baptist Church. (JESSE RICHARD ROSS, born 2 Feb. 1846, died 23 Jan. 1903, Pvt., 1st Orr's Regt. S.C. Rifles, CSA, buried Old Pickens Presbyterian Church Cemetery, Oconee Co., S.C. - Pickens Co., S.C. Cemetery Survey, Vol. 1, p. 228).

JOHN HARRISON, a Negro, of Pickens Co., S.C. received a pardon (details).

MRS. JULIUS R. NEWTON died at Athens, Georgia last Thursday. Her husband is a brother of our townsmen JOHN H. NEWTON and MARION NEWTON of the Bethlehem Section. She was the daughter of GIDEON ELLIS and was 39 years old. In a family of 5 sisters, MRS. J.M. GILLESPIE is the only one to survive. Mrs. Newton leaves a husband and 6 children.

Finishing touches are being put on the cottage of W.H. JOHNSON, one of the neatest cottages in town.

T.D. HARRIS will build a commodious dwelling on the lot where he now resides.

DR. I. CRIMM, eye specialist of Greenville, S.C. will be at the GILREATH HOUSE in Pickens the 2nd and 3rd of February.

MRS. T.A. WIDEMAN, eldest sister of MR. W.T. McFALL of this place, died the 20 (Jan.) at her home at Orphan's Home, Texas. She was 75 years old. Mrs. Wideman leaves a husband and a large family of children.

Liberty
ABB YOUNG who recently bought the J.F. JENNINGS place has moved to his new dwelling on the west end of town.
F.F. BOGGS of Raleigh, N.C. is visiting at his old home.

Pickens Co., S.C. Citation Notice - L.E. HUNT applied for Letters of Administration for the estate of J.H. BOWEN, deceased.

AD - New Store, Meat Market, R.L. SMITH.

Issue of: Thursday 5 February 1903:

Article - "THOMAS JEFFERSON Honored - A Monument to be Erected".

Information on the Pension Bounty (details).

Pickens Co., S.C. Citation Notice - TEXAS ANDERSON made application for Letters of Administration for the estate of ANDREW ANDERSON, deceased.

BEN A. HAGOOD will soon erect a splendid 10 room residence in Pickens.

SHERIFF J.H.G. McDANIEL will erect a commodious home on his farm near town in the early spring.

SOLICITOR JULIUS E. BOGGS will erect a handsome home on his lot opposite COL. HAGOOD'S. B.E. GRANDY will be the contractor.

AUNT LOU GRIFFIN, colored, wife of JAKE GRIFFIN, died Tuesday at the home of her son JACK ALLGOOD of pneumonia. She was 55 years old. Burial was from Cold Springs.

JULIUS E. PARSONS has purchased a lot from R.E. YONGUE and will erect a handsome cottage. The lot is between Mr. Yongue's and B.B. LaBOON'S lots. The street is noted for pretty cottages.

MRS. N.E. THORNLEY received a telegram Sunday from her son-in-law RALPH OLIVER calling her to Nashville, Tennessee on the account of the death of MRS. W.J. OLIVER whose home is in Illinois. She left Monday and was accompanied as far as Atlanta, Georgia by her son LARRY C. THORNLEY (details).

Teacher's Salaries at Clemson College (details).

W.T. LOOPER of Pickens who has been with H.K. STURDEVANT CO. of Greenville, S.C. is now with MAHON & ARNOLD.

STONEWALL JACKSON'S HOME in Virginia has been purchased from the widow of GENERAL JACKSON by the UNITED DAUGHTERS OF THE CONFEDERACY and will be converted into an old soldier's home.

The 10 month old infant of MR. and MRS. EARLE GILSTRAP died Friday the 30 (Jan.) at their home near McFARMERS' residence a few miles east of Pickens.

FRANK JENNINGS is home on a visit. He was recently in Chicago, Illinois (details).

GEORGE W. SHAW, a colored man, at Clemson College, S.C. won a prize for raising the largest amount of corn from 1 pound of seed (details).

Liberty
R.C. ROBINSON has moved his stock of clothing to the old SMITH stand next door to the bank.

MRS. LOU HAWKINS wife of J. FRANK HAWKINS died the 7 Jan. at her home near Mayfield, S.C. and was buried at Ebenezer Church. She leaves a husband, 1 son and 3 daughters.

MRS. AMELIA COLEMAN wife of T.D. COLEMAN died Sunday the 11 January. She was a member of Peter's Creek Church and was buried from there.

MRS. ENNIE FREEMAN was buried from Peter's Creek Church, of which she was a member, the 14 January. She leaves a husband and 3 children.

P.H. JONES died the 13 (Jan.) at the age of 27 of pneumonia. He was buried at Peter's Creek Church Cemetery. Mr. Jones leaves 1 sister and 5 brothers.

MRS. SUSAN HUNT wife of H. HUNT died at her home near Olga, S.C. the 20 Jan. and was laid to rest at Nine Forks Cemetery. She leaves a husband and 6 children.

Statement to stockholders of the PICKENS BANK.

Issue of: Thursday 12 February 1903:

The Opportunity of Pickens Co., S.C. (details).

WILLIE MAULDIN has gone to Greenville, S.C. where he has accepted work with his brother-in-law LUTHER GRANDY.

JOHN L. THORNLEY has moved his market from the ANTHONY BUILDING, up on Ann Street into the building formerly occupied by J.F. BROCK.

JOHN TILLMAN, a grand uncle of U.S. SENATOR B.R. TILLMAN, died last Monday at the age of 70 years in his one room hut in St. Paul, Minnesota (details).

MRS. AMANDA FREEMAN has moved up on Main Street into the AMBLER HOUSE.

J.F. BROCK has disposed of his stock of fancy groceries but will continue his jewelry business in the DR. G.W. EARLE BUILDING.

MR. JONES FULLER and wife will move to Easley, S.C. where he has purchased a house and lot. He has a position with the EASLEY LOAN and TRUST COMPANY.

DR. WEBB has withdrawn from the PICKENS DRUG COMPANY.

W.H. PICKENS died at Easley, S.C., Friday. He had a china and hardware store (minor details). (W.H. PICKENS, born 19 June 1850, died 30 Jan. 1903, buried Easley City Cemetery - Pickens Co., S.C. Cemetery Survey, Vol. 3, p. 43).

Article - "Views of the Pension Laws", by J. LOOPER.

COL. J.E. HAGOOD resigned his Clerkship in the U.S. Court on Saturday (details).

AD - R.G. GAINES & GASSAWAY BROS., Central, S.C. Selling mules, horses, etc.

Issue of: Thursday 19 February 1903:

Norris
H.B. BOWEN LUMBER CO. is located on the SOUTHERN RAILROAD between Norris, S.C. and Central, S.C. (details).

MISS CORA BOWEN is teaching at the Cedar Rock School.

PROF. A. WHITE SINGLETON is teaching the Mauldin School near Liberty, S.C.

MRS. ELMIRA THOMAS wife of JOE THOMAS died at her home 4 miles south of Pickens on Saturday and was buried at Prater's Church. She leaves a husband and 5 children.

MISS ANNA TURNER is teaching in Greenville, S.C.

MISS MAY ROBINSON is teaching at Holly Springs, S.C.

CLAUDE H. ALEXANDER has accepted a position with the PICKENS BANK.

Garvin District #24 is building a new schoolhouse - the old one burned a short time before Christmas.

Married Saturday the 15 Feb. at the residence of the bride's father MR. M.D. CANTRELL by Rev. A.J. Manly, MR. JOHN PORTER to MISS NETTIE CANTRELL.

MISS JOSEPHINE STEVENSON eldest daughter of MR. and MRS. W.E. STEVENSON returned to Williamston Female College.

Article - "The Death of GEORGE WASHINGTON".

Land for Sale - D.A. COOPER'S home place, 47 acres located 4 miles north of Pickens Court House on Sassafras Road, by T.J. MAULDIN and IVY M. MAULDIN.

Pickens Co., S.C. Court of Common Pleas - Summons for Relief - W.F. DURHAM, Plaintiff vs W.C. SEABORN, THOMAS M. DURHAM, et al., Defendants.

Notice - Resolutions of the Board of Directors of the LIBERTY COTTON MILLS.

Pickens Co., S.C. Citation Notice - F.B. MURPHREE applies for Letters of Administration for the estate of J.N. MURPHREE, deceased.

A terrible storm struck Honea Path, S.C. on Tuesday afternoon. The large two story brick furniture store of W.A. SHIRLEY was a total wreck. The walls fell on EARLE McGEE, BURT AUSTIN, A.C. STONE and EDGAR DONALD. McGee and Austin were killed.

Pickens Co., S.C. Citation Notice - M. ELIZABETH BOLDING and J.M. PERRY apply for Letters of Administration for the estate of J.R. ROSS, deceased.

Pickens Co., S.C. Citation Notice - MRS. M. PRITCHARD applies for Letters of Administration for the estate of W.L. PRITCHARD, deceased.

Issue of: Thursday 26 February 1903:

South Carolina New Acts (details).

Picture of the Monument to NANCY HANKS LINCOLN, Mother of ABRAHAM LINCOLN Lincoln City, Indiana.

Sketch - "Life of CAPTAIN JOHN H. BOWEN". He was born the 20 Oct. 1838 in Pickens Co., S.C. Entered the Confederate Army as Lt. and came out as Captain. Captain Bowen was a member and deacon of George's Creek Church. He was County Treasurer and a member of the Ebenezer Lodge #101 in Marietta, Greenville Co., S.C. (details). (JOHN H. BOWEN, born 8 Oct. 1838, died 15 Jan. 1903, buried George's Creek Baptist Church Cemetery - Pickens Co., S.C. Cemetery Survey, Vol. 2, p. 183).

REV. WADE is the newly called pastor of the Pickens and Easley Presbyterian Churches.

Married Thursday the 19 (Feb.) at the home of MR. W.R. PRICE, MISS ANNA PRICE to MR. WADE H. CHASTAIN. A reception was given the next day by MRS. M. CHASTAIN the mother of the groom (details).

J.D. HOLDER & CO., Real Estate Dealers, located at the depot in Pickens.

Runaway Boy, CAREY LAWRENCE son of JETER LAWRENCE.

REV. R.A. CHILD, Presiding Elder of the Greenville District (details).

Issue of: Thursday 5 March 1903:

T.L. BIVENS has moved into the new DR. EARLE house while J.C. JENNINGS now occupies the house vacated by Mr. Bivens.

RUBEN S. PITTS, Principal of the Inman School, Spartanburg Co., S.C. shot and killed ED FOSTER one of his pupils (details not known).

Married on Sunday the 1 March at the home of MR. P.G. THOMAS of near Golden Creek, by Rev. S. Atkinson, MR. P.O. THOMAS and MISS M.D. MOORE all of Pickens.

Married on Wednesday the 25 (Feb.) 1903 at the residence of the bride's father N.M. MADDEN by Rev. W.C. Seaborn, MR. J. LUTHER KELLEY and MISS ANNA V. MADDEN both of Pickens County.

Pickens Co., S.C. Salesday - No land sold.

DR. G.B. MOORE, Professor of Political Economy at Furman University, has resigned to become Superintendent of the VIRGINIA ANTI-SALOON LEAGUE. He leaves for Richmond, Virginia on the 1 April.

Married Wednesday afternoon at the residence of the bride's uncle J.B. BURGARD on Thurston Street (place not given), by Rev. A.R. Mitchell, Rector of Christ Church, MISS BESSIE B. BRIGHT of this city to ROBERT R. ROARK of Pickens. Miss Bright is employed at the law office of JAMES P. CARY of Pickens. Mr. Roark is a leading merchant of Pickens having recently purchased the stock of goods formerly belonging to A.M. MORRIS.

Married, last Thursday the 19 (Feb.) in South Easley, S.C., by Rev. D.W. Hiott, MR. DUDLEY J. GREER of Liberty, S.C. and MISS SALLIE HOLDER of Easley, S.C.

W. SILAS KIRKSEY died (accident) at his home Thursday night at the age of 66 years. He served in the Confederate Army. Mr. Kirksey leaves a wife and 7 children, 4 sons and 3 daughters. He leaves one brother JAMES KIRKSEY. Burial was at Secona Church Cemetery.

MR. RALPH C. CARTER of Westminster, S.C. opened a line of general merchandise. For the present he will occupy the

SHIRLEY old stand but after the 1 May will be located in the new BROWN BUILDING.

Pickens Co., S.C. Jury List.

A. YOUNG completed his storehouse near the factory and is putting in a stock of goods.

Pickens Co., S.C. Citation Notice - AUGUSTA A. HIGGINS applied for Letters of Administration for the estate of S.G. HIGGINS, deceased.

AD - SOUTHERN RAILWAY - The finest Dining Car Service in the world.

Issue of: Thursday 12 March 1903:

COL. D.K. NORRIS Pioneer in cotton mill building in Pickens Co., S.C. plans to build the NORRIS COTTON MILLS at Cateechee, S.C. (details).

B.E. GRANDY will build a handsome home for BEN A. HAGOOD, ESQ.

W.O. HESTER has moved up into the BYARS house.

Due to smallpox, court has been postponed in Walhalla, S.C. until July.

LEO D. GILLESPIE was admitted to the bar sometime ago. He has located in Pickens and his law office is over BRIDGES & HAMMONDS.

MRS. HAMILTON widow of the late WARREN HAMILTON died last Tuesday the 3 March at her home one mile east of Easley, S.C. She leaves several children (minor details).

MISS NETTIE WALDROP, daughter of W.T. WALDROP who lives near Boggs Mountain, died last Friday night. She was buried from Porter's Chapel.

T.D. HARRIS has a large force of hands working on his new house.

R.C. CARTER has opened a store at Liberty, S.C.

The UNITED DAUGHTERS OF THE CONFEDERACY are organized in Pickens.

Honor Roll of the Pickens, S.C. Graded School February 1903:
First Grade
JANET BOLT   ABSALOM TALLEY
ROBERT BAKER   EARLE HUGHES
EUGENE YONGUE

Second Grade
ELLEN LEWIS ALBERTA YONGUE
INEZ MORRIS EDNA EARLE
MEDA BOGGS ROY NEALY

Third Grade
GEORGE PRINCE THERON HESTER
LUCIA EARLE MARY LEWIS
EVIE SMITH EUGENE TALLEY

Fourth Grade
MAY McFALL BELLE YONGUE
KATE McDANIEL

Fifth Grade
WYATT JENNINGS ARLIE WELBORN
HAGOOD BRUCE FRANK KIRKSEY
PATI MAJOR CHRISTINE SUTHERLAND
HENRY McDANIEL LOUISE McDANIEL
LORENA TAYLOR CHARLIE ROBINSON
GRACE PRINCE

Sixth Grade
ORA McFALL INA BOGGS
EVA EARLE GLADYS MAULDIN
WILLIAM WELBORN JESSE LEWIS
MAKA BOGGS FURMAN MORRIS
JONNIE CAREY MARVEL SIMMONS
DICK FREEMAN

Seventh Grade
FLORIDE CAREY JAY ROBINSON
ADDIE ANTHONY ELBERT WELBORN
NANNIE ROBERTSON KATE HESTER
LELA WELBORN

Eight Grade
VESTA ASHMORE LELA GARRETT
GUSSIE CURETON ELIZA McDANIEL
THOMAS GARRETT NELLIE GRANDY
MARY McDANIEL JAMES CAREY
BERTHA BRIDGES EDGAR MORRIS
HATTIE EARLE

Ninth Grade
CECIL HESTER ADA GILLESPIE

AD - MISS HUGHES, Millinery Goods, HEATH, BRUCE & MORROW CO., Pickens, S.C.

Issue of: Thursday 19 March 1903:

"Palmetto Gleanings - Minor Events of the Week in Brief".

As the Pickens Co., S.C. portable caravansary, made for the county chain-gang, passed through Pickens on Saturday the earth trembled. It might prove a solution of the road problem, if enough mules could be attached to it to draw it over the county. It is a road packer.

Article - "Pickens Co., S.C. Moving for Growth".

C.T. HUNTER of Oconee Co., S.C. opened a barber shop over the PICKENS DRUG COMPANY.

FOLGER & THORNLEY put on the street a very handsome delivery wagon.

MR. H. LANGLEY CLAYTON has issued invitations to the marriage of his sister MISS PRUDENCE CLAYTON to MR. ERNEST WILLIAM STRATMANN of New York. The wedding will occur Thursday the 2 April at Liberty, S.C. (see issue of the 9 April 1903).

The Walker - McElmoyle School has 125 students. This is a county line school. Mrs. WALKER donated 120 acres about 15 years ago for the education of the children of the community.

H.A. McCAIN is superintendent of construction for the new bridge over the Keowee. It is uncertain when it will be completed (details).

Pictures of the tombstones of PRESIDENTS MADISON, GARFIELD and FILLMORE.

Pickens Co., S.C. Court Proceedings - Minor criminal cases (details).

Pickens Co., S.C. New County Treasurer - HENRY W. FARR.

Issue of: Thursday 26 March 1903:

"Palmetto Gleanings - Minor Events of the Week in Brief".

MISS ESSIE HUGHES taught at Hagood School.

Article - "UNITED DAUGHTERS OF THE CONFEDERACY".

W.L. JENKINS, ESQ. has been in Greenville, S.C., for the burial of his mother MRS. MARY LOUISE JENKINS. She died Tuesday night at the home of her daughter MRS. J.W. ROBERTS in Greenville at the age of 82 years. Mrs. Jenkins was the mother of 9 children, 6 sons and 3 daughters. All the children are living and were at her bedside. She was buried at Fork Shoals, Greenville Co., S.C.

THE BIG STORE will open the 3rd and 4th of April with complete stock.

MARY WALKER HAGOOD, the 2 year old daughter of MR. and MRS. A. HAGOOD, died at the home in Charleston, S.C. She was buried in the family burying ground three miles from Pickens.

Pickens Co., S.C. Court Proceedings - Minor criminal cases (details).

Pickens Co., S.C. Report of the Grand Jury. Report on conditions at the poor house, jail, and conditions in general in Pickens County.

Issue of: Thursday 2 April 1903:

"Palmetto Gleanings - Minor Events of the Week in Brief".

J.F. BROCK, Jeweler, has moved his office from EARLE'S DRUG STORE to the "upstairs" over CAREY'S old law office.

Married on Wednesday the 25 March at the residence of the bride's father MR. R.A. BRAZEALE of Broadway Township, Anderson Co., S.C., by Rev. O.L. Martin, MISS NINA BRAZEALE to MR. J.H. RICHARDSON of Liberty, S.C.

The PICKENS BRICK CO., GREER and STEPHENSON, Proprietors, has begun active operation.

BRANDON TAYLOR is working with the PICKENS RAILROAD.

EARLE LEWIS will work at the WEST END DRUG STORE, Greenville, S.C.

ARTHUR LEWIS who is in the railroad service with headquarters at Jacksonville, Florida is visiting his father F.A. LEWIS.

There will be no football between South Carolina College and Clemson College on Thanksgiving.

Married Sunday at the residence of the bride's uncle REV. J.P. ATTOWAY, MR. DRAYTON McCONNELL of Anderson Co., S.C. and MISS JANIE ATTOWAY of this county, daughter of the late REV. McSWAIN ATTOWAY.

Contract to be let for rebuilding a pier under the iron bridge at Old Pickens, Oconee Co., S.C. over the Keowee River.

The partnership of L.N. GREER, L.M. MAHAFFEY and W.E. STEPHENSON is dissolved.

Issue of: Thursday 9 April 1903:

"Palmetto Gleanings - Minor Events of the Week in Brief".

Anderson, S.C. - Special
MR. CHARLEY MILLFORD living on the plantation belonging to MR. BAILEY DRAKE died from a wagon accident on Friday night (details).

The Greenwood, S.C. Graded School Burned (details).

RUFUS DURHAM son of ISAAC DURHAM entered the graded school.

AARON BOGGS of Calhoun, S.C. is now 81 years old.

UNITED DAUGHTERS OF THE CONFEDERACY of Pickens, S.C. received their charter.

JOHN L. THORNLEY has moved his meat market to the HOLLINGSWORTH BUILDING in the rear of BRIDGES and HAMMONDS.

J.D. CAREY has returned from Greenville, S.C. and has opened a business in the CAREY BUILDING.

L.O. MAULDIN graduated from the South Carolina Medical College, Charleston, S.C.

Elections in the Town of Pickens, S.C. (details).

Central, S.C. will have the ISSAQUEENA COTTON MILLS.

MISS S. JANE STANSELL, aunt of W.L. JENKINS, died last Friday the 3 April 1903 in Greenville, S.C. at the home of her sister MRS. J.W. ROBERS (sic) (?Rogers) of pneumonia. Miss Stansell who was about 66 years old was a maiden lady and teacher in Georgia. She had come home to attend the funeral of her sister MRS. MARY JENKINS. MR. and MRS. W.L. JENKINS attended the funeral which took place at the Washington Baptist Church in Greenville Co., near Pelzer, S.C.

Married the 2 April at the home of her brother H.L. CLAYTON of near Central, S.C., by Rev. Dr. Riley of Greenville, S.C. and assisted by Rev. Mr. Porter of Greer, S.C., MR. ERNEST W. STRATMAN of Brooklyn, New York to MISS PRUDENCE "Dence" CLAYTON (see issue of the 19 March 1903).

Pickens Co., S.C. Court of Common Pleas - Non-Resident Summons - M.F. HESTER, Plaintiff vs CLINGMAN POWELL, MARY A. ALEXANDER, MARY AIKEN, etc. (details).

Pickens Co., S.C. Final Settlement - Estate of W.W. KILBURN, deceased by R.J. JOHNSTON, Executor.

Pickens Co., S.C. Final Settlement - Estate of FRITZ DORNBURG, deceased by JOHN A. HAUPFEAR, Administrator.

Issue of: Thursday 16 April 1903 (torn and much missing):

The *Sentinel* office is now in the ANTHONY & KEITH BUILDING in the rear of McFALL'S STORE.

N.D. TAYLOR, photographer of Easley, S.C. will be in Pickens part time. He has rented a building - the upstairs - of the old CARY office.

Article - "Story of CATEECHEE and the Naming of OLD NINETY-SIX".

Land for Sale - 1 nice 3 room house at Six Mile, S.C., will sell 5 - 10 acres of land with house, by C.W. GARRETT, Six Mile.

NO OTHER ISSUES LOCATED FOR 1903.

BIBLIOGRAPHY

Smith, R.M. *Book of the Dead, Anderson County, S.C.*
    Anderson, S.C.: Stenciled by R.M. Smith, 1966.
South Carolina Genealogical Society, Pendleton Chapter.
    Oconee County, S.C. Cemetery Survey, Vol. 1.
    Greenville, S.C.: A Press, Inc., 1983.
South Carolina Genealogical Society, Pendleton Chapter.
    Oconee County, S.C. Cemetery Survey, Vol. 2.
    Greenville, S.C.: A Press, Inc., 1984.
South Carolina Genealogical Society, Pendleton Chapter.
    Pickens County, S.C. Cemetery Survey, Vol. 1.
    Greenville, S.C.: A Press, Inc., n.d.
South Carolina Genealogical Society, Pendleton Chapter.
    Pickens County, S.C. Cemetery Survey, Vol. 2.
    Greenville, S.C.: A Press, Inc., n.d.
Rich, Peggy Burton, Marion Ard Whitehurst and Jerry L.
    Alexander. *Alexander Families of Upper S.C.* Authors,
    P.O. Box 1185, Clemson, S.C., 1988.

INDEX

Name may appear more than one time on a page.

AARIAL, Lou, 47
ABBECRUMBIE, Daniel, 37
ABBEVILLE
  Mail Delivery, 182
ABBOTT
  Gertrude E., 287
  Norman Z., 285
  Warren, 287
ABECROMBIE
  Arwell, 85
  C.R., 40
  J.H., 107, 186
  J.H., Jr., 122
  John, 18, 35
  Mrs., 18
  Orwell, 186
  Susan, 85
  V.G. (Miss), 117
ABERCRUMBIE
  J.F., 288
ABNEY
  O.M. (Rev.), 286, 290
ACKER
  E.H., 260
  Nancy, 234
ADAMS
  Miss, 227
ADCOCK
  J.W., 105
ADCOX
  J.T., 167
  Martha, 45
ADDISON
  Elias, 243
ADGER
  Family, 173
  John B. (Rev.), 173, 174
ADKINS
  George, 280
AGNEW
  James, 199
AIKEN
  A.S., 87
  Albert, 156
  Benjamin, 94
  Cora, 297
  D. Wyatt, 10
  Eliza, 74, 167

  Leigh, 273
  Mary, 313
  Mrs., 161
  Tomps, 156
  W.T., 119
  W.W., 56, 96, 158, 230, 245
  W.W., (Mrs.), 258
  Wyatt, 178, 271, 288
ALABAMA
  Pickens "Colony", 53
ALAMO
  Fall of, 56
ALDRICH
  A.P., 130
  Alford, 130
  Robert, 130
  Rose, 130
ALEXANDER
  A.A., 41, 77, 259
  Abbe, 284
  Adaline, 49
  Alice, 184
  Amanda, 289
  Anna, 298
  B.F., 295
  Blev, 265
  Bluford, 298
  Brothers & Co., 50
  Caroline Elizabeth, 216
  Claude H., 289, 306
  Daniel, 12
  Diana, 262
  Doc, 117
  E.B., 265
  E.M., 49, 168
  Elisha, 33, 253
  Frank L., 288
  G.W., 49
  I.P., 183
  Ida, 72
  Irvin, 72
  Irvin (Mrs.), 216
  J.B. (Mr. & Mrs.), 126
  J.C. "Sweet", 125
  Jacob, 35
  Jake, 145
  James, 289

James (Mrs.), 150
Jim, 33
Jocca (Jacob), 284
John P., 89
Josie, 158
L.A. (Mrs.), 165
Liceney A., 108
Lila, 50
Lizzie, 189
Maria, 204,
Marjie, 264
Mary A., 313
Mary E. "Polly", 145
Mattie E., 274
Mrs., 77
Nora E., 35
Norman, 7
P.E., 76, 173
P. Eugene, 66, 79
Sallie, 73, 76
Robert A., 246
Rutha, 265
Section, 281
Silas A., 292
Thomas, 34
Tom, 253
W.E., 73, 76, 295
W.E. (Mr. & Mrs.), 111
W. Ervin, 243
W.T., 126
William (Mrs.), 123

ALLEN
Arthur, 220
Charlie, 263
H.M. (Rev.), 176
W., 43
William, 254

ALLEY
A.B., Jr., 288

ALLGOOD
Annie, 279
B.A., 27, 43, 57, 83, 199, 262
Barnett A., 262
Bettie, 215
Emma, 142
Forest, 116, 144
Jack, 304
Joke, 300
Mary, 21, 47, 79
Miles (Prof.), 153
Rebecca, 278
T.O., 72
W.B. (Capt.), 49, 298
W.B. (Mr. & Mrs.), 79, 262

ALLISON
E. (Rev.), 84
Sarah, 6

ALTOM
Mattie, 104

AMBLER
House, 147, 152
J.H., 171
Major, 125, 178
R.L., 127
Sis, 3
Willie, 178
Willis, 3, 77

AMERON
Mr., 166

ANDERSON
Andrew, 1, 304
Butler, 166
Florence, 79
H.G., 166
J.F. (Rev.), 41, 66, 88, 108, 110, 116, 119,
J.T., 64, 192
Julius, 222
Lucy, 1
Oil Co., 281
Phosphate Co., 281
Printing Co., 281
R.L., 250
Richard, 186
Ruben, 259
Texas, 304
W.L. (Rev.), 127, 155
Will, 180
William, 138

ANDERSON CO.
Campaign Meeting, 22, 150
Candidates, 22
Court of Common Pleas, 261
Election News, 25
Labor Contracts, 234
Memorial Day, 140
Poor House, 244
Slavery Contracts, 239
Stockades, 233, 235

ANSEL
Addie R., 256
Cothran, 46
M.G., 10
M.F., 288
M.F. (Mrs.), 41
Solicitor, 41, 46

ANTHONY, 190, 247, 265, 305, 313
ANTHONY
  Addie, 310
  Blanche, 90
  Castoria, 259
  E.O., 42
  Furman, 273
  H.G., 46
  H.H., 36
  H.J., 42
  Henry J., 18
  J.F., 117
  J.T., 11, 142, 167, 189, 192
  James R.J., 273
  John T., 18, 36, 42
  Ola, 101
  Richard, 100
  Richmond, 101
  Robert, 182
  W.B. (Mr. & Mrs.), 90
  Will H. (Mr. & Mrs.), 239
  William, 11
ANTIETAM, 168
ARIAIL, 205
ARIAIL (ARIAL)
  A.H. (Mrs.), 107
  Albert, 106
  Dave, 18
  Dora, 255
  Ed, 71
  Grada, 224
  Kate, 287
  Lizzie, 278
  Luke, 278
  Mrs., 106
  Robert, 279
  Will, 125, 188
ARMSTRONG, 69
ARNOLD, 176, 304
ARNOLD
  Andrew, 120, 217
  Arthur H., 287
  Cornelia, 217
  Emma, 120
  Hope, 137
  Jefferson, 186
  John F. (Mrs.), 34
  Marion (Mr. & Mrs.), 239
  Milton, 185
  Reuben, 133
  T.T., 235
  Turner, T., 212
  W.A., 26
  W. Paul, 296
  William, 137
ARTER
  Balus, 82
  Baylus, 116
  Foster, 116
  Jesse, 256
  Nettie, 131
  Ralph C., 308
ARTHUR
  Forest, 1
  Ida, 132
  Jasper, 46
  Sallie, 133
ASHMORE, 98, 197
ASHMORE
  Rufus, 154
  Sam J., 15
  Vesta, 258, 265, 293, 310
  W.H. (Mrs.), 220
  W.W., 100
ASTISON
  Julia, 178
ATES, Mary A., 227
ATKINSON
  S. (Rev), 308
  Seabrook (Rev.), 172
  William, 295
ATTAWAY
  A. McSwain (Rev.), 204
  J.P. (Rev.), 296
  J.P., 204
  John (Rev.), 44
  Pierce (Rev.), 269
  Rev., 210
ATTOWAY
  J.P. (Rev.), 312
  Janie, 312
  McSwain (Rev.), 312
AUSTIN
  Burt, 307
  Charley, 54
  Mrs., 301
  W.F. (Dr.), 11, 31, 42, 78, 172
  William, 54
AVERY
  Albert, 18
  Daniel (Rev.), 210
  Mrs., 18
AYERS
  Lewis M. (Gen.), 49
  Martha, 130

BABB
    A., 144
    Albert, 186
    Anderson, 129, 257
    John, 222
BABB BROS., 21, 23
BACON
    O.F. (Mrs.), 226
BAGWELL
    Adolphus, 163
    Calvin, 114
    Elijah, 195
    F., 186, 225
    Mr., 210
    Robert (Mr. & Mrs.), 242
    William (Mr. & Mrs.), 218
BAILEY
    J.W. (Rev.), 254
    Lily, 11
BAKER
    Amanda E., 26
    B.C., 129, 150
    B.C. (Mr. & Mrs.), 221
    Jas. (Mr. & Mrs.), 156
    John A., 25
    L.M., 129
    Laura, 129, 132
    Lemuel, 129
    Lizzie, 37
    Martha, 67
    Mrs., 236
    Robert, 309
    W.H., 236
    William, 37
    Willie P. 26
BALDWIN
    A.J. (Miss), 208
    Daniel, 8
    Rev., 99
    Tally, 270
BALL
    B.W., 55
    W.W., 130
BALLARD
    Mrs., 277
BALLENGER
    Shady, 221
BALLENTINE
    Mamie, 248, 273
    Mary, 83
    N.E., 164
BALLINGER, 112
BALLINGER
    Ed, 282

BANE
    Etta May, 274
    Pink, 274
BANISTER
    J.F., 129
BANKS
    Abraham, 34
    American, 51, 260
    Anna, 169
    Ben, 289
    Carolina National-
        Columbia, 260
    City National-Greenville,
        118, 120
    Easley, 35, 76, 83, 86
    G.W., 211, 259, 294
    I.B., 294
    Liberty, 236, 245
    Mary C., 259, 294
    People's Bank Greenville,
        233, 250
    Pickens, 282, 305, 306
    Planters, 56, 96
    Seneca, 198
BANNISTER
    J.F., 131
    Jack (Maj.), 121
BAPTIST ASSOCIATION
    Twelve Mile, 70
BARBER SHOPS
    Wood, J.A., 132, 149
BARKER, 148
BARKER
    A.P., 236
    Elizabeth, 73
    Frank H., 224
    Hassie, 222
    J.S., 209
    J.S. (Mrs.), 51
    Sudie, 209
    Thomas, 254
    W.H., 236
BARKLEY
    W., 40
BARNES, 170
BARNES
    Ada, 134
    Mr., 127
    Mr. & Mrs., 134
BARNETT
    C.P. (Mrs.), 61
    D., 195
    J.H. (Mrs.), 233
    Rial, 195

BARNUM & BAILEY CIRCUS, 139
BARR (BARRE)
  J.M., 162
  John M., 64
  M.A., 186
  Samuel, 162
  Samuel A., 124
  W.A., 30
  Will, 165
BARRET
  Anna, 263
  Farm, 210
BARRETT
  Frances, 67
BARRON
  Clara A., 259
  William F. (Mr. & Mrs.), 125, 259
BARTON
  E.H., 199
  Harlston, 43
  Kanie, 161
  M., 104
  Mary E., 44
  Maud, 44
  Melville, 44, 125
  Miss, 43
  W.E., 29
BATES, 197
BATES
  Charles R., 91
  E.H., 68
  E.S., 46
  George, 266
BATSON
  Henry E., 41
  Jerry, 45
BAYNE
  Lum, 93
BEARD
  J.E. (Rev.), 285
BEARDEN (BEARDIN)
  Jacob, 157, 300
  John, 231
  John (Mr. & Mrs.), 206
  Mattie, 229
  Riley, 11
  Susannah, 231
  Tyler, 296
BEASLEY
  D.F., 155
BEATTIE, 30
BEATTIE
  Mr., 27

BEATTY
  W.F., 47
BECK
  J.J. (Rev.), 71
BECKUTE
  A.M. (Mrs.), 147
BEE
  Hampton P. (Gen.), 160
BELL
  Contractor, 148
  G.W., 95
  J.R., 235
  Mr., 128
BENDING FACTORY, 219
BENJAMIN
  J.T., 229
BENNETT
  W.C. (Mrs.), 151
BENSON
  Amanda, 301
  E.B., 301
BENTLY (BENTLEY)
  Isaac, 54, 175
BENTZ
  R.L.R., 159
  R.L.R. (Mrs.), 147
BERKLEY
  John, 89
BERRY
  Jessie, 69
  L.M., 21
  Miss, 21
BEVERLY GRANITE WORKS, 111, 119, 162, 300, 301
BICYCLE SUPPLIES, 281
BILLINGSLEY
  Amanda, 287
  William, 287
  William H., 204
BILTMORE HOUSE, 79
BIRD
  Henry, 57
BISHOP
  Aaron, 66
  James, 266
BIVENS
  T.L., 308
BLACK, 288
BLACK
  H.R. (Miss), 65
  John, 247
  Thomas, 240
BLACKERBY
  Nannie, 176

BLACKSMITH, 127
BLACKSTON
  Andrew (Mr. & Mrs.), 196,
  John (Mr. & Mrs.), 214
BLAIR
  Roxie, 284
  William, 11
BLAKE, 50
BLAKE
  Baylis, 243
  Ed, 97
  George, 133
  Mariah, 97
BLAKELY
  Eliza, 49
BLALOCK
  Corrie M., 256
BLANTON
  Mr., 34
BLASSINGAME
  Ad, 125
  B.F., 291
  D.W., 125
  Elizabeth, 279
  J. Paul, 95
  J.T., 291
  John, 279
  Pink, 4
  Robert, 125
  Samuel, 18, 36, 42
  W.F., 96, 107, 294
  William Field, 291
BLAYLOCK
  Corrie J., 73
  Corrie M., 86
BLYTHE
  A. (Capt.), 179
  Hampton, 243
  Queen, 243
BOARDING HOUSES
  Aiken, W.W., 245
  Brown, J.H., 88
  Calhoun, 9
  Hendricks, 173
  Kirksey, J.K. (Mrs.), 48
  Liberty, 81
  Smith, J.M., 95
BOATWRIGHT (BOATRIGHT)
  46, 104
BOATWRIGHT (BOATRIGHT)
  Annie, 221
  Edith, 117
  J. (Mr. & Mrs.), 72, 117
  Joseph, 35, 42
  Margie, 72
BOEN
  Nettie, 113
BOGGS, 26, 92, 98, 105, 108,
  110, 128, 130
BOGGS
  A.J., 101, 109, 198, 218,
    255, 292, 294
  A. John, 276
  A. Matthew, 234
  Aaron, 177, 184, 255
  Aaron (Mr. & Mrs.), 204
  Alice, 25
  Arthur, 6, 296
  Arthur W., 6
  B.D., 30
  Benjamin, 291
  Bruce, 258, 265, 293
  Catherine, 290
  E. Pauline, 216
  Eliza A., 234
  Ella, 6
  Estelle, 159
  Eula, 291
  F.F., 303
  Flora, 6
  Frank, 6
  G.L., 2
  Georgia, 27
  Hamilton, Jr., 25
  Hattie, 6
  Helen, 258, 265
  Henry, 224
  Ina, 310
  J.A., 4, 9, 43, 216
  J. Addison (Mrs.), 210
  J.E., 35, 38, 39, 47, 69,
    73, 76, 86, 117, 152,
    159, 161, 162, 168
  J.E. (Mrs.), 68
  J.C., 294
  Jay, 9
  Jay L., 168
  John C., 295
  John T., 59, 156, 215, 300
  Julia, 294
  Julia A., 234
  Julius, 257, 264, 292
  Julius E., 282, 287, 299,
    304
  Julius F., 115
  Junius, 14
  Lila, 125
  Lizzie, 30

M.A., 30
M.R., 234
Maka, 293, 310
Martin, 247
Mary, 3
Meda, 292, 310
Minnie, 38
Miss, 114
Monroe, 290
Myra, 296
O.F., 274
Oscar, 6
Pauline, 216
R.E., 22, 83, 58
R.L. (Mr. & Mrs.), 224
Ralph Erwin, 222
Ross, 9
S.C., 294
Samuel C., 267
T. Addison, 4
T.B., 176
T.G., 167
T.H., 115
T.J. (N.P.), 114
Thomas (Mrs.), 97
Thomas H., 287
W.J., 24
W.J. (Mr. & Mrs.), 238
W.J. (Prof.), 147
W.K., 115, 159
W.L. (Mrs.), 4, 8, 14
Wade H., 295
Walter, 43
Walter H., 296
Walter J., 79, 208, 291
Warren, 14
BOHART
  J.C. (Mr. & Mrs.), 237
  Kate, 237
BOLDING
  B.M., 37, 71, 267
  Elfred M., 37
  Emma, 37
  J. Dyce, 267
  M. Elizabeth, 307
  Mattie, 183
  Tom, 71
  W.N., 288
BOLEN
  Norra, 151
BOLLAND
  Prof., 286
BOLT, 239, 242

BOLT
  Dr., 188, 230
  J.L. (Dr.), 173, 216, 282, 299
  Janet, 292, 309
  Mamie, 10, 86, 87
  Sheriff, 178
  Thomas A., 216
  William, 216
  J.L. (Dr.), 187
BOMAR
  Mrs., 301
BOND
  J.A. (Rev.), 190
BONHAM
  Milledge (Mrs.), 130
BONHEUR
  Rosa, 185
BOOK
  T.J. (Rev.), 85
BOREN
  Cling (Rev.), 140
  Connie, 140
  W.C. (Rev.), 270
BORNEST
  Laurie M., 24
BOROUGHS (BOROUGH, BOUROUGHS)
  Daisey, 180, 254
  Dorsie, 267
  Earnest J., 111
  J.E. (N.P.), 45, 99, 142, 157
  James E., 11, 79, 118, 267
  Martha, 267
  Mary Myrtie, 111
  Myrtie, 27, 99
BOSWELL
  Matilda, 233
  Simeon, 233
BOSTICK
  C.W., 85
BOUNDARY LINE
  Greenville & Spartanburg, 249
BOWDEN, 3
BOWEN
  A.G., 28, 217
  B.A., 5
  Barnett, 39
  Bettie, 95, 123, 125
  Butler, 139
  C.M., 285
  Charles, 142

Charles M., 161
Charlie, 114
Cody, 268
Cora, 6, 48, 83, 85, 118, 191, 193, 200, 306
Dora, 242
Elizabeth, 274, 278, 279, 282
Ella, 78
Elowee, 135
Elvira Hunt, 208
Florence, 27, 118, 164, 204
G.W., 59, 92, 279
H.B. Lumber Co., 306
H.O., 3, 11
J.B., 41
J.H., 78, 303
J.S. (N.P.), 239
J.T., 32
Joel (Dr.), 41
John, 208, 244, 279
John H., 86, 302, 307
John Y., 295
Lafayette, 302
Laura, 63
Laurence, 92
Lawrence, 112, 279
Lena, 9, 129
Lena Lucille, 131
Lida, 138
Lidie, 132
M.D., 81
M.H., 279
Mancy E., 41
Martha A., 118, 119
Martin (Mr. & Mrs.), 98
Martin H. (Mr. & Mrs.), 39
Mary, 24, 79, 113, 224
Mary Iola, 250
Mattie, 258
Nancy, 149
Ora Lee, 98
Pickens, 279
R.A., 87, 92, 108, 114, 122, 279, 292, 295
R.A. (Mrs.), 10, 86
R.E., 208, 302
R.E. (Mrs.), 134
R.H., 218
Reese, 155, 214, 274, 278, 279, 292
Reese, Jr., 279
Reese, Sr., 295
Robbie, 258, 265
Robert A., 131
Samuel, 302
Stella, 12
T.W. (Hon.), 92
Texie, 159
Thomas, 302
Thomas H., 41
W.H. (Rev.), 125
W.J. (Mr. & Mrs.), 233, 250
W.R., 113
W.T., 41, 113, 123, 125, 278, 279
W.T. (Hon. & Mrs.), 250
William, 70, 268, 302
William Walter, 259
BOWEN & WYATT, 61
BOWIE
E. Calhoun, 270
Harriett, 41, 80, 117, 296
Lillie, 48
Margie, 296
BOWLIN
Ben, 182
J.M., 186
Noah G., 217
BOYD
Amanda, 33
Belle, 214
Daniel, 49
James L., 290
Major, 249
Mrs., 290
Waren (Maj.), 33
Warren, 45, 114, 186
BOYDE
Benjamin, 34
D.P. (Rev.), 203
BRACHER
Mollie, 178
BRADLEY, 155, 196
BRADLEY
A.J., 186, 220
D.F., 86, 108, 118, 119, 157, 255, 258, 260, 296, 299
E.D., 142
Fitzhugh, 87
J.W., 36, 39
Ray, 220
Thomas, 156
Thomas D., 220

Thomas W., 49
BRAGG
  Jas. O., 111
BRAMBLETT, 120, 139
BRAMBLETT
  Andrew, 29, 68, 106, 146
  Henrietta, 108
  Martin C., 186
  Squire, 117
  W.B., 108, 128
  W.C., 12, 15, 27, 77, 82,
    87, 89, 94, 106
  W.J. (Dr.), 73
BRANCH
  Bun, 70
  Mary, 95
BRANDT
  H., 178
  Julia Anna, 178
  L., 178
BRASS BAND, 22
BRAWNER
  A.E. (Mrs.), 149
BRAZEAL (BRAZEALE)
  John, 17
  Jordan (Mr. & Mrs.), 187
  Nina, 312
  R.A., 312
BREAZEALE (BREAZELE)
  George (Mr. & Mrs.), 170
  Jeannette, 301
  Jordan (Mr. & Mrs.), 128,
    265
  Mr., 37
BRECKENRIDGE
  Doc, 176
  Garfield, 284
BREVARD, N.C., 133
BRICK YARDS
  Bowen & Wyatt, 61
  Neal & Richey, 185
  Pickens, 299, 312
  Stribling, Neil, 62
BRIDGES
  Allgood, 270
  Bertha, 258, 265, 293, 310
  Bids, 59
  Burch's Ford, 287
  Coon Creek, 135
  Dodd's on Keowee, 107
  Easley, 78, 95, 97
  Freeman, 239
  Hagood, 213
  J.E., 258

  Keowee, 97, 311
  Maw, 205
  Old Pickens, 312
  Saluda River, 78
  Twelve Mile Creek, 66, 83
  Wolf Creek, 23, 241
BRIDGES & HAMMOND, 282, 309,
  313,
BRIGGS
  Henry, 163, 183
  Mrs., 124
  Nancy, 107
  W.D., 107
BRIGHT
  Bessie B., 308
  David, 289
  Eunice, 289
  Hannah, 289
  Jane Kay, 289
  Janie, 206, 289
  Lizzie, 289
  Maggie, 289
  Margaret J., 289
  O.P., 167, 169
  W.W.F., 68, 119, 148,
    289
  William W.F. (Hon.), 289
  William W.F., 276
BRINSDON
  John, 145
BRISSEY
  Cole (Mr. & Mrs.), 273
  W.W., 178
BRITISH-AMERICAN MORTGAGE
  CO., 223
BRITTON
  Etta, 215
BROADUS
  John A. (Dr.), 50
BROCK
  Andrew (Capt.), 101
  Caroline, 128
  Ellen, 101
  Fletcher (Mr. & Mrs.), 248
  George, 128
  J.F., 305, 312
  J.O., 143, 152, 195
  John W., 89
  T. Homer (Mrs.), 275
BROOK
  J. Fletcher, 211
BROOKINS
  Richard, 16
BROWN, 309

BROWN
  Bud, 1
  C.C. (Rev.), 39
  Davis, 18
  Frank, 210
  Fred G., 281
  G.A., 59
  Harbin, 124
  Hattie, 236
  J.A., 194
  J. Alonzo, 181, 202, 205
  J.E., 7, 57
  J.H., 28, 44, 51, 88, 92,
    105, 113, 126, 136, 144,
    157, 183
  James A., 78
  Jim, 98
  Joe, 92
  John, 194
  Joseph Emerson, 38
  L.A., 111
  Lida, 160
  Malinda, 210
  Miami, 275
  Mr. & Mrs., 99
  Mrs., 299, 301
  Nancy C., 127
  Parker, 6
  R.B., 194
  R.E., 30
  S.H., 127, 194
  Sallie, 299
  Sam, 99
  Sam (Mrs.), 99
  Samuel, 193, 194, 195
  Sheriff (Mr. & Mrs.), 160
  Sheriff H. (Mr. & Mrs.),
    248
  W.M., 295
  W. Silas, 124
BRUCE, 168, 214, 220, 280,
  282, 310
BRUCE
  A.M. (Mrs.), 192
  Alice, 189
  Corrie, 38, 68, 232
  Emma, 38
  Hagood, 257, 264, 292, 310
  J.F., 192
  J. McD., 38, 45, 53, 68,
    110, 138, 154, 168, 188,
    190, 251, 282, 303
  Julian, 38
  Julian W., 68, 69
  Minnie, 2
  Minnie Lee, 282
  Mr., 139
  S.P. (Esq.), 38
  Sidney, 69
  Winnie, 4
BRUETON
  Carrie, 258
BRUMBY
  Thomas M. (Lt.), 201
BRUNSON, 99
BRYAN, 118
BRYAN
  George D., 68
BRYANT
  Auditor, 22
  Hemp (Mr. & Mrs.), 224
  John P., 40
  Lillie, 75
  Mrs., 191
  Robert L., 183
  Talbert, 191
  W.H., 68
  W.T., 20, 68
BRYCE
  J. Steele (Senator), 252
BRYSON
  Eddie, 90
  John A., 90
BUILDINGS
  Anthony, 190, 247, 305
  Anthony & Keith, 313
  Brown, 309
  Carey, 312, 313, 314
  Doyle, 126, 146
  Earle, G.W., 305
  Freeman, 17, 31, 110, 128,
    132, 137, 184, 282
  Hollingsworth, 57, 94, 96,
    313
  Lewis, 102, 121
  Masonic Hall, 16, 112,
    220, 252
BURBAGE
  Frank A., 281
  S.P., 167
BURCHMEYER
  Mr., 24
BURDETT
  W.A., 171
BURDINE
  B., 257
  Caroline, 257
  D., 257

J.R., 163, 175
　　J.T., 157, 163, 206
　　James M., 7, 46
　　James T. (Rev.), 11, 58,
　　　162
　　Mason, 7
　　Mason B.T., 120
　　Miss, 302
　　Mrs., 162
　　Robert, 162
　　Stephen, 113
　　Trizah, 277
BURGARD
　　J.B., 308
BURGE
　　Mrs., 179
BURGESS
　　Elzarie, 52
　　Gertrude, 24
　　Hampton, 58
　　J.B., 284
　　J.D., 60
　　J.M., 197
　　John, 271
　　John D., 157
　　John F., 273
　　Joshua, 52
　　Louis, 158
　　Rev., 178
　　Sampson, 104
　　Sarah C., 60
　　Sarah Angeline, 97
　　W.A., 197
　　William, 158
BURLEY
　　Noah A. (Mrs.), 226
　　W.W. (Mrs.), 226
BURNS
　　Ben E., 18
　　Luther, 172
　　Sidney, 209
　　Willie, 148
BUROUGHS (BURROUGHS)
　　Daisy, 27
　　James E., 110, 111
BURR
　　Aaron, 60
BURRLES
　　Clint, 116
BURTON
　　W.J.M., 186
BUTLER
　　A.J. (Mrs.), 25
　　Mr., 127

　　P.S. (Rev.), 233
BYARS, 150, 309
BYARS
　　Canna, 164
　　D.D. (Rev.), 179
　　Harriet, 263
　　James, 41
　　Lillie, 110
　　Miss, 41
　　P.H., 179
　　William, 99
BYNAM
　　Turner, 146
BYRD
　　Jack, 136
　　Miss, 299
CAESAR'S HEAD, 63, 103
CAESAR'S HEAD HOTEL, 287
CALHOUN, 232
CALHOUN
　　A.W. (Dr.), 177
　　B.H., 111
　　Ball, 126
　　Christmas Tree, 126
　　Estate, 91
　　John C., 238
　　John Edward, 91
　　Julia, 8
　　Literary Society, 177
　　Miss, 300
CALLAHAM, 92
CALLAHAN (CALAHAN)
　　B.H., 125, 128
　　Julia, 8
CAMEL
　　W. Preston, 137
CAMERON
　　Feaster, 231
CAMPBELL
　　James, 107
　　Naomi, 5
　　Sandford, 249
　　Thomas P., 7
　　W.H., 186
　　William, 186, 249
CAMPS
　　Wolf Creek, 53
CANNON
　　Catherine, 250, 254, 261,
　　　294
　　Jackson, 33, 35
　　Loney (Mrs.), 242
　　Thomas, 11, 86, 135, 213,
　　　242

Will, 254
  William, 213
  William M., 297
CANTREL
  Engenie, 251
CANTRELL
  Ben, 217
  H.H., 257
  Hannah, 119
  J.A. (Miss), 261
  J.T., 186
  J.W. (Mr. & Mrs.), 239
  James, 256
  James (Mr. & Mrs.), 82
  John J., 71
  Laura E., 209
  Leoto, 195
  Lizzie, 229
  Loo, 257
  M.D., 306
  Mack, 229
  Martha, 200
  Mary Ann, 15
  Mrs., 13
  Nettie, 306
  Robert, 96
  William A., 66
CAPEHART
  Elizabeth A., 207
CAPERS
  Bishop, 34
  John G., 34
  Mr., 105
CAPPS
  J.W., 119, 137
  Martha, 30
CAREY, 312, 313
CAREY
  Flora, 293
  Floride, 258, 265, 310
  J.D., 313
  J.P., 35, 73, 76, 158,
    161, 162, 220
  James, 310
  James, Jr., 258, 265, 293
  James, P., 280
  Johnnie, 257, 265
  Jonnie, 310
  Louis W., 158
CARPENTER, 8
CARPENTER
  C.H., 8, 79, 104, 288
  C.H. (Mrs.), 8
  J.B. (Dr.), 39

  J. Lee (Mrs.), 246, 294
CARR
  Effie, 219
CARROLL, 8
CARSON
  A.C. (Mrs.), 205
  S.B., 186
  V.S., 214
CART, 293
CARTER, 126
CARTER
  D.J., 207
  F.H., 146
  Frank, 126
  Lida, 98
  R.C., 309
CARUTH
  Wales, 104
CARY
  Frank M. (Mr. & Mrs.), 195
  J.P., 183
  J.P. (Mr. & Mrs.), 265
  James P., 308
  John C. (Mrs.), 43
  Mrs., 291
CASHIN
  Mrs., 291
CASSELL
  Ben, 166
  Doc, 166
  E.T., 239
  F.M., 186
CASSON
  Betsy, 32
CASTLE
  A.A., 89
  Dovie, 267
  Martha, 261
CATEECHEE, 276, 314
CATO
  Anna E., 228
CAUBLE
  H.A., 134
  J.O., 134
  Jane E., 134
  Mr., 11
CAULEY
  Jamee F., 30
CAUWELL
  Frank, 203
CEDAR ROCK
  History, 282
CELEY
  Hampton, 70

CELY & CO., 154
CENSUS, 180
CENTER
    Benjamin, 141
CENTRAL, S.C., 232
CENTRAL, S.C.
    Article, 276
    Smallpox, 302
CHAMBERLIN, 110
CHAMBERS
    John W., 281
CHANDLER
    Belle, 124
    Elizabeth, 31
    J.J., 31
CHAPMAN, 92
CHAPMAN
    Camie, 183
    Curray, 248
    Delia, 267
    Emma, 31
    Fields R., 248
    Fields R. (Mr. & Mrs.), 287
    Harleston, 31
    Harvey, 267
    Henson, 186, 203
    J. Harvey, 145
    J.R., 8
    James, 104
    Jno., 52
    Joseph, 44
    Josiah, Jr., 102
    M.J. (Mrs.), 221, 255
    Mary, 44
    Mary J., 192
    Mary Jane, 181
    Mr., 24
    Philip, 232, 272, 275
    Rachel, 145
    S.D., 278
    S.H., 223
    Sallie, 194, 237
    Samuel, 21, 84
    Sarah, 9
    Sharp, 11
    Visa A., 11
    W.D., 73
    W.H., 8, 152
CHAPPELL
    Anderson, 186
CHASTAIN
    A.B., 198
    Friendly, 49, 50
    J.J., 175, 206
    Joseph M., 11
    M. (Mrs.), 307
    Malinda, 198
    Nettie, 14
    Rowland, 182
    W.H., 288
    Wade H., 307
CHICAMAUGA
    Story, 44
CHILD
    Elizabeth, 180
    Ida T., 151
    James W., 180
    John (Mr. & Mrs.), 32
    Mamie, 79
    R.A., 180, 278, 308
    R.A. (Mrs.), 151
    R.R., 79, 180
    Thomas, 186
CHILDRESS
    Ann, 295
    Anna, 90
    B.S., 10
    Berry, 149
    Charles, 51, 150, 242
    J.B.F., 275
    J.H., 186
    J.T., 150, 242
    James (Mr. & Mrs.), 208
    L.E., 3, 9, 29
    L.E. (Mr. & Mrs.), 247
    Lewis, 247
    Mr., 150
    Ora L., 186
    Oscar, 104
    Tom, 255
    Veta, 247
    W.B., 150, 242
    W.P. (Mr. & Mrs.), 104
    W.W., 35
    W.W.H., 165
CHILDS
    John (Mr. & Mrs.), 141
    R.A. (Rev.), 3
    Spartan (Mr. & Mrs.), 261
    Thomas J., 73
CHRISTOPHER
    Arthur, 132, 191, 224
    Auditor, 77
    Elbert (Mr. & Mrs.), 159
    N.A., 35, 233
    Thomas, 76
    W.A., 148, 224, 242, 247

W.D., 268
William Arthur, 288
CHURCHES, 256
CHURCHES
   Carmel Baptist, 141
   Clemson Presbyterian, 90
   Corinth #1, 157
   Cross Roads, 20
   Easley, 250
   Easley Presbyterian, 307
   Eastatoe, 235
   Ebenezer Colored Baptist, 267
   Fairview Methodist, 20
   Flat Rock, 110
   Friendship, 193
   Gap Hill, 150
   Gospel Tabernacle, 284
   Griffin Ebenezer, 262
   Griffin Ebenezer Baptist, 100, 290
   Liberty Baptist, 8
   Liberty Methodist, 8
   Methodist (Colored), 59
   Mount Pisgah Baptist, 281
   New Olive Grove Baptist, 224
   Old Stone, 114, 141, 175, 238, 239
   Oolenoy River Colored, 121
   Pendleton Episcopal, 113
   Perritt Chapel, 207
   Pickens Baptist, 279
   Pickens Methodist, 282
   Pickens Presbyterian, 54, 307
   Presbyterian Camden, 247
   Quarto Centennial, 267
   Rock Hill, 242
   Secona, 114
   Six Mile Baptist, 7, 104
   St. Paul's, 246
   St. Phillip's, 153
   Tabor Methodist, 23
   Twelve Mile Baptist, 70
CISSON
   Calvin, 197
   Charles, 197
   Friendly, 49, 50
   J.A., 79
CIVIL WAR, 174, 191
CIVIL WAR
   Antietam, 168
   Battle-Horseshoe, 62
   Battle-Manassas, 64
   Battle-Staunton River Bridge, 58
   Battle-Williamston, 198
   Notable Women, 100
CLAPP
   Milton, 137, 139
   Rev., 139
CLARDY
   Charles, 222
   Ettie, 40
   J.B., 39
   J.L., 46
   James, 192
   John B., 35, 46
   John L., 35
   John L. (Mr. & Mrs.), 222
   John W., 192
   Minnie, 192
CLARK
   Elford, 288
   J.E., 201
   Leila, 299
   Lillie, 296
   M.E., 201
   Manley, 201
   Porter, 208
   Rebecca, 89
   Stella, 54
   Tally, 272
CLAYTON
   A.I., 215
   A.T., 154
   Annie, 136
   Dor, 100
   F.V., 16, 117, 212
   H. Langley, 311
   H.L., 313
   Iola, 37
   J.H., 37
   L.G., 137, 235, 290, 292
   L.G. (Mrs.), 292
   Lang (Prof.), 19
   Lucy, 46
   Martha, 16
   Naomi L., 122
   Naomie L., 120
   Prudence, 311, 313
   S.W. (Dr.), 136
   T.C., 154
   W.S., 27
   W.W., 164

CLEMENTS
  Bettie, 51
  Cordelia, 72
  J.W., 293
  James, 72, 107
  James W., 49
  John S., 31
  Mary Jane, 136
  S., 124
  Salathiel, 126
  V. Greer, 115
CLEMSON FARMS, 100, 102
CLEVELAND
  W.C. (Mrs.), 57
CLIFTON MILLS, 136
CLINKSCALES, 288
CLYDE, 126, 143
CLYDE
  Carolina I., 277
  J.B., 3, 16, 34, 277
  J.T., 116, 163
  Mary W., 108
  Mrs., 129
  Samuel T., 121
  Sarah A., 58
  T.E., 139
  Thomas J. (Rev.), 121
  W.A., 58, 163
  W.L., 32
CLYDE & NALLEY, 126
COAL FIELDS
  Tennessee, 290
COCHRAN
  Eupha, 290
  G.B., 198
  Georgia, 198
  J.W., 198, 218
  John W., 184
  John Wesley, 184
  Leland A., 198
  Mamie, 198
  Mary Alice, 184, 198
  Mattie, 209
  R.A., 229
  R.B., 229
  Rosa, 198
  Sallie Bessie, 198
  T.W., 209
  Thurman, 198
  Walter D., 198
COCHRANE
  Lee, 265
COFFINS, 281

COHEN
  Tom, 289
COLEMAN
  Amelia, 305
  Bud, 156
  I.D., 186
  Jennie, 209
  M.W., 262
  T.D., 305
COLLEGES
  Adger, 277
  Baltimore Medical, 200
  Charleston Medical, 115
  Chicora, 238
  Citadel, 89
  Clemson, 11, 12, 16, 17,
    19, 32, 37, 38, 64, 65,
    89, 90, 94, 100, 102,
    112, 132, 135, 137, 138,
    143, 146, 157, 159, 162,
    182, 197, 251, 255, 268,
    278, 282, 285, 300, 304,
    305, 312
  Clemson New President, 156
  Columbia Female, 298
  Columbia University, 154
  Converse, 103
  Erskine, 193
  Furman, 31, 154
  Greenville & Tusculum, 79
  Howard University, 243
  Presbyterian, 245
  South Carolina, 312
  South Carolina Medical,
    313
  South Carolina State, 75
  Tuskegee Institute, 201
  West Point Military, 144
  Williamston Female, 6
  Winthrop, 16, 61, 64, 300
  Wofford, 103
COLLINS
  Hester, 84
  Sydney, 155
  W.A., 186
COLORED PEOPLE
  Concert, 205
COLORED TEACHERS, 217
COLYER
  Permelia, 43
CONFEDERACY
  Last Cabinet Officer, 98
CONFEDERATE
  Army-Monument, 185

Army-Winchester, Va., 185
Battles-Antietam, 168
Battles-Manassas, 64
Battles-Williamsburg, 198
Chickamauga, Ga., 241
Commissioners, 106
Days, 246
Dead-Tribute, 239
Flag, 17
Generals, 146
Gold, 65
Graves, 238
Monuments, 17, 185
Museums, 77
Pension Laws, 300, 306
Pensioners, 121, 282
Pensions, 94, 96, 164, 179
Pensions-Pickens Co., 186
Picnic, 107, 153
President, 81
Records, 84
Reunion, 63, 103, 153, 212, 282, 288
Rolls, 162
Seal, 185
Soldiers, 53, 196, 244, 263, 276, 277, 278, 279, 288, 289, 290, 296, 301, 302, 303, 307, 308
Soldier's Home, 8
Soldier's Memory, 106
Spy, 214
Story, 156
Times, 137
Tribute, 55
Veterans, 56, 75, 95, 136, 138, 177, 184, 191, 194, 203, 240, 248, 267, 269, 272, 283, 285
Veterans Convention, 145
Wagon Factory, 221

CONLEY
  John, 183
CONNELLY
  John F., 186
CONNER
  Alice, 238
  L.H.T., 224
  Robert, 294
  Texie, 1
  Thomas, 223
  William, 67
CONVICTS, 152

COOK
  Dora, 170
  John T., 174
  Newt, 205
  Ora, 222
  W.W., 217
COOPER, 73
COOPER
  D.A., 39, 307
  E.C., 201
  Elizabeth, 73
  George (Mr. & Mrs.), 202
  George McD., 140
  Hannah, 37
  James, 170
  James (Mr. & Mrs.), 189, 196
  Leo, 255
  Mary, 241
  Mrs., 205
  Nancy, 212
  S.D., 35
  Steven, 255
CORBIN
  Miss, 273
  William, 205
CORN
  E.M., 96
CORN MILLS
  Griffin-Calhoun, 148
COTHRAN
  Ex-Judge, 167
  George, 75
  N.A., 107
  Oscar, 151
  S.O. (Mr. & Mrs.), 197
COTTON
  Damaged, 59
  Died out, 55
  Sorry, 56
COTTON GINS
  Ballinger & Gillerson, 112
  Cely & Co., 154
  Looper's, 119
  Norris, 48, 53, 62, 66, 83, 91, 174
  Pelzer, 5
  Repairs, 188
  Spartan, 7
  Walhalla, 93
  Warehouse, 87
  Weighers, 64

COTTON MILLS
  Easley, 196, 203, 226, 250, 262, 288
  First, 225
  Issaqueena, 313
  Liberty, 235, 307
  Monaghan, 271
  Norris, 309
  Westminster, 195

COTTON PICKERS
  Monkeys, 175

COUCH
  D., 184
  Emma, 237
  F.M., 165, 280
  H.E., 267
  Henry, 173
  Henry S., 179
  Oscar, 237

COURTNAY MANUFACTURING CO., 69

COWARD
  Margaret M., 43

COWPENS
  Battle, 179, 185

COX
  Essie, 91
  F.E., 146, 171
  Frank, 68
  Frank E., 124, 127, 154, 164, 223
  George, 161
  Isaac, 53
  Isaiah, 99
  J.E. (Mr. & Mrs.), 117
  J.L., 72
  Julia, 72
  Lener, 15
  Miss, 165
  S.M., 33, 72
  Samuel, 160
  W.A. (Dr.), 33
  W.H., 182
  W.N., 291
  Walter, 132
  Zade, 10, 117

CRAFT
  Perry (Mrs.), 263

CRAIG, 220

CRAIG
  Art R., 302
  Arthur R., 302
  Bros., 190, 280
  C.L. (Mr. & Mrs.), 190, 248
  C.L. (Rev.), 86, 182
  Charles L. (Rev.), 160
  E.T., 135
  Hamilton, 121
  Hampton, 193
  J.A. (Mr. & Mrs.), 41
  J.E., 41
  J.T., 283, 284, 292
  James, 138
  John, 27, 88, 132
  Josephine, 135, 157
  Laura, 132
  Margaret, 132
  Nellie, 248
  Robert, 245, 299
  Sallie, 191
  Sarah, 41
  T.E., 157

CRAIGHEAD
  E.B., 143

CRANE
  Frank, 113, 150, 230
  Frank (Mr. & Mrs.), 195
  Frank P., 186
  J. Frank, 203
  Jennie, 230
  R.H. (Mr. & Mrs.), 240
  Redden, 129

CRAWFORD
  Ben, 129
  F., 197
  R.C., 186
  Rebecca G., 39

CREIGLER
  Nan, 239

CRENSHAW
  Elizabeth, 229
  Jesse, 36, 39, 52
  Johnson, 292
  Nina, 286
  W.F., 18
  W.J., 35

CRESWELL
  W.E., 195

CREW
  Lonzo D., 297
  Moses, 55, 257
  Moses W., 297
  N.P., 250
  Rufus F., 250
  W.J., 257, 261
  William J., 250

CRIMM
  I. (Dr.), 303
CRISP
  L.P., 109
  L.W., 121, 136
CROW
  Corrie, 228
CROW CREEK SECTION, 279
CROWFORD
  W.R. (Constable), 90
CRUMPTON
  Daisy, 111
  Lidia M., 202
  Nancy, 202
CUBA, 182, 252
CULBERSON
  Annie, 75
CUMMINGS
  C.C. (Mrs.), 135
  C.W., 138
  Casley W., 172
CUNNINGHAM
  Annie, 102
CURETON
  A.H., 6
  Annie, 102
  C.D., 58
  C.L., 215, 221
  Charles L., 134
  D.T., 261, 281
  George, 242
  George D., 283
  Gussie, 258, 265, 293, 310
  Hester, 258, 265
  J.D. (Dr.), 3, 78, 120, 292
  J.D. (Mrs.), 79, 120, 176, 252
  Justice, 73
  K.L. (Mrs.), 287, 298
  Kate L., 280
  Lizzie M., 6
  Magistrate, 86
  Mamie, 291
  T.J., 30
  W.M., 261, 281
CURRY
  Dr., 10
  Miss, 195
CURTIS
  Addie, 188
  Charles H., 212
  Eugenia, 28
  Rebecca, 24

  Silas, 24, 28, 47
DACUS
  Minnie, 202,
DAGNALL
  R.R. (Mrs.), 233
  R.R. (Rev.), 209, 211, 215, 221, 227, 234, 243, 251, 262,
  Rev., 249
DAILY
  Van, 47
DALTON
  Fannie, 29
  Lewis H., 186
  Lila, 182
  Rex, 117
  Tama, 117
DANIEL (DANIELS)
  J.B. (Prof.), 191
  J.W., 248
  J.W.W., 245
  Prof., 192
  W.F., 281
DARAGAN
  J.F. (Mrs.), 26
  Maggie, 26
  Prof., 148
DARBY JOB OFFICE, 11
DARK
  Janie, 78
DARNELL (DARNOLD)
  Laura, 131
  William, 185
DARWIN
  J.T., 88
DAVENPORT
  M.B., 17
DAVIS, 281
DAVIS
  A.E. (Mrs.), 9
  A.T., 90
  Andrew S. (Rev.), 228
  C.B. (Mrs.), 116
  Charles A., 116
  D.H. (Mr. & Mrs.), 214
  D.H. (Mrs.), 177
  Dora, 214
  E.E. (Mrs.), 231
  Ed, 6
  Goodloe, 46
  Henry, 224
  Horace, 177
  J.A. (Mrs.), 99
  J.H., 186

Jefferson, 293
Jesse, 241
John O., 21, 45, 49, 65, 74, 75
Joseph, 164
Lon (Mr. & Mrs.), 4
Mitchel, 244
Mr., 81
Mrs., 14
Polly, 46
Robert, 5, 71
Sidney, 224
Silas (Mr. & Mrs.), 253
Silas M., 107
Tom, 241
W.D., 164
W.R., 231
W.S., 186
Walter, 119
William C. (Mrs.), 147
Willie, 254

DAWKINS
C.M., 222

DAWSON
Amanda, 6
Bettie, 6
Francis W., 245
J.W., 2
May, 6
T.P. (Mrs.), 252

DAY
Anna, 59
Bass, 236
Ben Hill, 230
Elias, 167, 178, 199, 229, 256
Elias (Mrs.), 178
Frank, 299
Fred P., 142
Gussie, 132
Henry, 236
Hester, 229
Jeanette, 112
M.F. (Mr. & Mrs.), 285
M.V., 112
Marion, 148
May, 199
Med F., 182
Medicus F., 252
R. Bolt (Dr.), 167
S.R., 186
S.R. (Mr. & Mrs.), 166
W.T. (Mr. & Mrs.), 192
Zara, 166

DEAN, 171
DEAN
Anna, 59
J.H., 212

DeKALB
Baron, 247

DELIVERY WAGON, 311
DEMOCRATIC CANDIDATE FOR V.P., 218
DEMOCRATIC CONVENTIONS, 22, 26, 102, 106, 283
DEMOCRATS, 54

DENDY
Lucy, 295
Thomas, 295
W.E., 219, 295
W. Erskine (Prof.), 215, 279

DePRIEST
E.F., 96
E.F. (Mr. & Mrs.), 285
Edward, 285

DEWEY
Admiral, 201

DICHERT
W.M., 186

DICKENS
Walter, 264, 292

DICKERSON
James R., 186

DICKSON
E.B., 51, 56
J.M., 56
James M., 51
Mrs., 203
S.C., 118, 120
W.F. (Mrs.), 60

DILLARD
Corrie, 227
Daisy, 179
F.B., 211
John, 217
Kate, 65
Mamie, 199, 224
Thomas, 256

DILWORTH
B.F., 47
Mary, 47

DISPENSARY, 64
DISTILLERIES
Central, 252
Ellison, E.F., 11
Government, 117, 121, 164, 249

Holcombe, 199
Ponder's, 53
DIXIE
Origin, 192
DIXON
William (Mrs.), 97
DOBBINS
Carry, 103, 206
Jesse, 121
Lettie, 121
Mattie, 121
DOBSON
Clayton, 55
J.T. (Rev.), 69, 147, 158, 184, 202, 240
William, 222
DODD
T.M., 113
DODGENS (DODGINS)
Amos, 182, 211
Clevie, 266
Joseph, 53
Joseph C., 159
Riley, 41
DODSON
Coot, 270
Emma, 270
DOGGETT
W.A.C. (Maj.), 8
DOGNALL
W.A. (Prof.), 46
DOLSON
J.T. (Rev.), 225
DOMINICK
Prof., 291
DONAGHEY
John, 174
DONALD
Edgar, 307
DORICH
Ella, 155
DORNBURG
Fritz, 313
DORR
G.W., 61
DORSEY
David, 114, 240
George, 250
Mary, 202
William, 202
DOUGLAS
C.B., Jr., 184
DOWNS
Robert, 133

DOYLE, 126, 146
DOYLE
E.C. (Dr.), 158
O.M. (Dr.), 158
O.R. (Dr.), 158
Ramsey, 130
W.R. (Dr.), 158
DRAKE
Bailey, 312
Eugene Gary, 130
John J. (Mr. & Mrs.), 130
DREIFUS
S., 68
DREIFUS & CO., 68
DRIVER
J.H., 1
DRUCKENMILLER
Family, 148
DRY CLEANERS
Arnold, Milton, 185
DRYMAN
Mary, 237
DRYMOND
Frank, 212
DuBOSE
Prof., 289
DUCKWORTH, 150
DUCKWORTH
J.M., 127
Lemuel, 171
Marcus, 125
Miss, 136, 159, 169
DUCKWORTH & PALMER, 160
DUELS
Bynum, Turner, 146
DUFFIE
R.L. (Rev.), 224
DUKE
Jane, 259, 274
Ransom, 39, 234, 235, 259
Ranson, 274
Russell, 23
Thomas, 55, 166
DULIN
A.H. (Mr. & Mrs.), 102
DUNCAN (DUNCANS)
B.D., 172
David A., 226
E.M., 55
Ellen, 46
Jennie, 75
John, 69
L.A. (Miss), 105
M.B., 221

Pinkney, 52
W.A., 75
W.D., 105
William (Mrs.), 130
DUNWOODY
  Keziah, 164
DuPRIEST
  E.F. (Prof.), 151
DURANT, 60, 125
DURANT
  Henry A., 55
  O.L., 55
  Olin L. (Rev.), 78
DURHAM
  A.C., 107
  Allen, 46, 57, 58, 123
  Bill, 58
  Buck, 101
  C.A., 106
  C.N. (Mr. & Mrs.), 272
  Carter, 63, 150, 241
  Charles, 106
  Charles N., 34, 229
  Daniel C., 213
  Daniel D., 207
  Effie, 145
  Emma, 207
  Essie, 219
  G.B., 260
  Gazelia, 123
  Gus (Mr. & Mrs.), 169
  Harrison, 253
  Isaac, 313
  J.E., 229
  J.L., 80
  James, 290
  L.R., 253, 106, 107
  L.R. (Mr. & Mrs.), 229
  L.R. (Mrs.), 267
  Lula Jane, 291
  Mack (Mr. & Mrs.), 190
  May, 106
  Mrs., 63, 101
  Rebecca, 106
  Rufus, 313
  Thomas, 241, 264
  Thomas M., 307
  W.F., 307
  W.S., 110, 115, 145
DURRANT
  Eddie, 70
EADES (EADS)
  Della, 210
  Eula, 204
  Mindie, 91
EARLE, 312
EARLE (EARL)
  A.B. (Rev.), 117
  Annie W., 182
  Berry, 301
  Cecil, 301
  Clifton, 145
  Dr., 17, 180, 185, 308
  Drayton, 298
  Edna, 257, 292, 310
  Edna, 292, 310
  Edwin, 293, 301
  Ella, 301
  Essie, 28, 57, 75, 103, 301
  Eva, 257, 264, 293, 301, 310
  G.W., 55, 146, 161, 166, 180, 189, 196, 198, 280, 298, 305
  George W. (Dr.), 301
  Hattie, 258, 293, 310
  Hovey, 258, 265, 293
  I.N., 110
  J.N., 186
  J.W., 77, 177, 189, 298
  J.W., Jr., 189
  J.W. (Mr. & Mrs.), 145, 200
  J.W. (Mrs.), 129
  James E. (Mr. & Mrs.), 274
  James W. (Dr.), 301
  Joseph E., 112
  Joesph H. (Sen.), 141
  Lewis, 225
  Louis, 301
  Lucia, 257, 310
  Lucius, 200
  Nina, 177, 275
  Pink, 208,
  Richard Harrison, 249
  Samuel, 1
EASLEY, 232, 238
EASLEY
  Article, 276
  Creamery Co., 276
  Loan & Trust Co., 306
EASLEY-LIBERTY ROAD, 273
EATON
  L. Ross, 7, 264
  L. Ross (Mr. & Mrs.), 286
  Roswell Gaillard, 43
  Vera, 286

EBAUGH, 125
EDENS, 150
EDENS
  A.L., 38, 51, 58, 60, 86,
    133, 200, 204, 205, 230,
    243, 249, 261, 268
  Alonzo, 32, 133, 271
  Bros., 150
  Cato, 194
  E.C., 25
  Elijah, 38
  John D., 30, 200
  Magistrate, 89, 123
  Mary L., 66, 121
  Mathew (Mrs.), 190
  Missouri, 194
  S.M., 121
  S.S., 233
  Samuel, 14, 36, 38, 56, 74
  Samuel M., 66
  Samuel S., 39
  Sidney, 32
  Susan, 74
  Thomas, 204
  Warren, 56, 58
  Warren D., 60
  William P., 261
EDWARDS
  John, 59
EICHELBURGER
  Allie, 231
ELECTORAL VOTE
  By States, 118
ELKINS
  W.J. (Rev.), 78
ELL
  Adolphus (Mr. & Mrs.), 216
ELLENBURG, 117
ELLENBURG
  Bessie, 89
  Corrie, 266
  Francis M., 70
  Joanna, 164
  M.L., 186
  Mahaley, 212
  Pet, 104
ELLERBE
  Governor, 175
  W.H. (Gov.), 185
  William H. (Gov.), 128
  William Haselden, 110
ELLIS
  Cora, 293
  D.H., 81

  E.T. (Miss), 81
  G.A., 172
  G.W. (N.P.), 189
  George A. (N.P.), 268, 300
  Gideon, 117, 303
  J.H., 186
  Jesse, 251
  Jessie H., 272
  John L., 116
  Laura, 12, 116, 117
  Mary, 231
  Walter, 267
  Williams, 276
ELLISON, 34, 42
ELLISON
  A., 155
  Bros., 280, 281
  Claude R., 182
  E.F., 11
  Elias F., 198
  Hugh (Mrs.), 100
  J.W., 270
  Jim, 185
  L.P., 54
  M.O., 54
  M. Oscar, 270
  Marion, 31
  Nettie, 31
  Van B., 198
  Walker, 267
  Wylie, 152
ELROD
  Mrs., 283
  Richard, 220
  T.M., 30
ELWED
  S.P.H. (Rev.), 206
ELWELL
  S.P.H. (Rev.), 206
ENGLISH
  C.N., 111
ENSOR
  Dr., 81
  Joshua F. (Dr.), 144
ENTREKIN
  Henry, 202
  Jason (Prof.), 248
  John, 210
  Mr., 210
  Mrs., 210
EPPS
  A.F., 186
  A.T., 186
  Fannie, 120

Isaac, 120
Lem, 202
ERVIN
    Florence Irene, 295
    J.B., 186
    S.E. (Mrs.), 295
ESKEW
    Kate, 167
EUBANKS
    James, 131
EVAN (EVANS)
    Effie, 114
    Ellenoe, 172
    Ex-Governor, 169
    Governor, 44, 48, 54, 93
    James, 81
    John Gary, 158
    Marion, 297
    Nannie, 86
EVATT (EVETT, EVIT)
    Addie, 70
    Anderson, 99
    Anna, 239
    Bettie, 257
    Effie, 70
    Elvira, 99
    Fannie, 225
    James, 263
    John, 164
    Laura, 259
    Maggie, 77
    W.H., 70
EXPOSITION DOTS
    Atlanta, 70
FACTORIES
    Canning, 52
    Shuttle, 52
    Towns-Incorporation, 69
FANT
    Eva, 232
    Handy B. (Rev.), 291
    J. Reese, 218, 291
    Mildred Ann, 218
    O.H.P., 39, 218, 232, 291
    Wayne, 291
FARMER
    B.F., 280
    Ben, 254
    Cornelia, 221
    M.D., 48, 263
    William, 221, 293
    William (Mrs.), 264
FARMERS OF AMERICA, 279

FARMERS PUBLISHING CO., 119
FARR
    Alice, 45
    Boyce Eugene, 118
    Delilia, 131
    Frances, 131
    Francis (Mrs.), 45
    G.W., 153, 206
    George Washington, 131
    H.W., 298
    H.W. (Mr. & Mrs.), 185
    Henry W., 311
    J.P., 131, 153, 206
    S.E. (Mr. & Mrs.), 118
    Stokely, 78
    W.H., 110
FATE
    W.P., 35
FEATHERSTONE
    Will, 190
    William, 108
FENDLEY
    Annie, 128
    J.P., 128
FENNELL (FENNEL)
    L.G., 186
    N. Elizabeth, 158
    Tillman G., 71
    W.M. (Mrs.), 226
FERGUSON, 104, 205
FERGUSON
    Angil, 271
    Annie, 289
    Augustus, 261, 271
    C.A., 233
    Caldona, 261
    Charles R., 167
    Deannie, 233
    Earle, 241, 242
    Effie, 179
    Frank, 112, 190
    Frank (Mr. & Mrs.), 144
    Hattie, 185
    J.G., 59
    James M. (Maj.), 57, 59
    Janie, 215
    Jefferson, 1
    John, 5, 20, 21, 59, 173,
        185, 190, 200, 256, 258
    Mrs., 283
    Pete, 130
    Thursie, 200
    Toney, 5
    Tucky, 96

V.A., 130
V.A. (Mr. & Mrs.), 96
W.M., 233
William, 4, 77, 258
FEW
  I.C., 227
  Ira, 139
FICKLING
  Robert Bruce, 261
FIELD (FIELDS)
  A.A., 124
  Dr., 75, 109
  Hampton, 282
  Janie, 56, 151
  O.P., 56, 192
  O.P. (Mr. & Mrs.), 151
  W.G., 56
  W.T., 1, 26, 204, 294
  W.W.H., 182
  William T., 253
FILLMORE
  President, 311
FINCH
  Cornell, 251
FINDLEY (FINLEY)
  Ben, 45
  C.B., 296
  Charles B., 33
  Elizabeth, 33
  Garf, 251
  Garfield, 258
  Henry M., 185
  J.B., 48, 280
  Joe, 80
  John (Mr. & Mrs.), 252, 253
  John W., 77
  W.H., 48
  William P., 296
FING
  Gri-- (Miss), 250
  Sarie (Miss), 251
FINNEY
  D.B., 166
  D.B. (Mrs.), 196
FISHER
  Canzada, 166
  Jack, 58
  W.T. (Dr.), 115
  W.W. (Prof.), 111
FLEMING
  C.E. (Dr.), 19
FLOWERS
  Mr., 36

FOLGER, 311
FOLGER
  A.M., 142, 242, 254, 259
  A.N. (Mr. & Mrs.), 102
  A.R. (Mr. & Mrs.), 195
  A.R.N., 30, 51
  A.R.N. (Mr. & Mrs.), 61, 84, 222
  A.W., 87, 95, 216, 251, 258
  Alonzo M. (N.P.), 192, 214
  Dora, 67
  Dora A., 65
  Elmer, 152, 171
  Ernest, 251
  Estelle, 165
  Floy, 238
  Gus, 87
  J.F., 251
  Kate, 222
  L.C. (Mrs.), 250, 256
  Lila, 296
  Lizzie Winona, 76
  Lou, 139
  Lucia, 251
  Lucy, 165
  Mamie, 137, 139
  Maria, 251
  Marie, 250
  Orlando C., 139
  Paul, 84
  Reuben, 21
  T.W., 91
  W.A., 76
  W.W., 255
FOLGER & THORNLEY, 281
FOLK
  J.F. (Prof.), 283, 286
FONTAIN
  Lamar, 94
FORD
  J.T. (Mrs.), 9
  Jesse, 6
  Strother, 184
  Vera, 6
  W.S.B. (Rev.), 222
  W.W. (Mrs.), 253
FOREST
  Luda, 127
FORSYTHE
  J. Adger, 48
  Mr., 48
FORT GEORGE, 105
FORT GEORGE SPRINGS, 99

FORTNER
  Alonzo, 60
  H.L. (Rev.), 273
  H.M. (Rev.), 52
  Henry, 18
  James Henry, 18
  Malissa, 60
  Nancy, 170
FOSTER, 148
FOSTER
  B.A., 161
  Bill, 236
  C.N., 23
  Charles, 227
  Ed, 308
  Elijah, 19
  J.E. (Rev.), 1, 17, 18,
    45, 66, 81, 93, 119,
    120, 125, 126, 141, 150,
    178, 180, 182, 193, 202,
    209, 214, 225, 227, 236,
    268, 273, 274, 277, 279,
    283, 284, 293, 299
  J.R. (Rev.), 60
  Javann, 235
  Millie, 273
  Minnie, 156
  Ola, 210
  R.B.A., 210
  R.M., 273
  R.M. (Mrs.), 273
  Robert, 154
FOWLER
  A.B. (Rev.), 60
  A.R., 140, 141
  W.C., 261
FREEMAN, 17, 31, 92, 110,
  132, 137, 143, 184, 197
FREEMAN
  Amanda, 305
  Amanda E., 229
  B.F., 248, 277
  Ben F., 115, 282
  Ben Frank (Mr. & Mrs.),
    217
  Bentan S., Jr., 28
  Benton, 28
  Bower (Mr. & Mrs.), 248
  Caroline, 81, 277
  Claude, 258, 265, 269
  D.C., 12, 138
  Dick, 293, 310
  Emps, 162
  Ennie (Mrs.), 305
  Ernest, 258, 279
  Essie, 257
  Eva, 277
  J.B.R., 91, 117, 120, 127,
    128, 153, 229
  J.B.R. (Mr. & Mrs.), 70,
    144
  J.B.R. (Mrs.), 207
  J.G., 146, 147, 203
  James B.R., 226
  James F., 162
  James G., 163
  John, 136
  John M., 136, 137
  Joseph, 277
  Josie, 277
  M.E., 118
  Mattie, 81, 118
  Morton, 277
  R.P., 91, 146
  Richard, 257, 265
  Rinda, 266
  Robert P., 100, 140
  S.P., 42, 153, 280
  T.M., 118
  Thomas, 277
  Thomas (Mr. & Mrs.), 210,
    273, 274
  W.B., 146, 162, 163, 203
  W.B. (Mr. & Mrs.), 194
  W.T., 96
  William, 277
  William Benton, 194
FRICKS
  C.C. (Rev.), 176
  David, 4, 119
FRIDDLE
  J.W., 186
  James, Jr., 77
FROST
  White, 54
FULLER
  Corrie, 125,
  Daniel, 125
  E.B. (Capt.), 102
  F.M. (Mrs.), 252
  Jones, 252, 306
FURMAN UNIVERSITY, 23
FURMAN UNIVERSITY
  New President, 154
FURNITURE MAKERS
  Freeman, S.P., 280
  Standard Furniture
    Factory, 153

FURR
  P.F.M., 115
GAFFNEY, 128, 179
GAFFNEY
  Episode, 241
GAILLARD
  A.D., 161
  B.H., 57
  B.H. (Mr. & Mrs.), 206
  David Franklin, 206
  Elizabeth, 57
  Henry, 218
GAINES (GAINS)
  Bettie, 84
  E.P., 124
  Fred, 211
  James H., 285
  Joseph, 40
  Lewis & Co., 156
  Lola, 285
  Lucy, 202
  Mariah, 79
  Mary, 217
  R.E., 157
  R.G., 8, 79, 155, 157, 176
  R.G. & Gassaway Bros, 306
  W.B., 186
  William, 84
  Willie, 11
GALLION
  Parmelia, 123
GALLOWAY
  Adaline, 111
  Cannie, 124
  Jeff, 150
  John, 38
  Kannie, 85
  S.E. (Mrs.), 194
  Stephen (Mr. & Mrs.), 64
  W.E., 84
GAMBRILL
  Charles A., 281
GAMEWELL
  J.A. (Prof.), 65
GANTT (GANT)
  Annie, 6
  Bros., 150
  Clifford, 6
  Della, 270
  Essie, 6, 295, 296
  Henry, 225, 256
  Ida, 6
  J.N., 282
  J.T., 288

  James, 58
  Jonnie, 6
  Lizzie, 282
  Will, 113
  Will N., 270
  William, 270
  William N., 282
GARDNER
  Adar, 263
  C.S. (Dr.), 129
  Dr., 252
GARFIELD
  President, 311
GARLINGTON
  E.A. (Mrs.), 102
  Ernest A. (Maj.), 55
GARRETT
  Aaron, 114
  C.W., 314
  Dora M., 40
  Emma, 114
  Etta, 13
  J.C., 203, 205
  James (Mr. & Mrs.), 14
  Laron, 38
  Lela, 310
  Lula, 203
  M.B., 40
  Nancy Ann, 120
  Nelson, 199
  Rosa, 26
  Thomas, 120, 310
  W.M., 223
  W.R., 40
GARRICK
  Edward, 203
  J.C., 228
  Mary P., 35, 228
  Mellie, 203
GARRISON
  C.W., 42
  Charles W., 41
  D.W. (N.P.), 82
  Henry, 190
  James N., 42
  O.W., 266
  Varina, 42
  W.D. (N.P.), 201, 266
GARVIN
  B.D., 1, 40, 52, 55, 59,
    61, 64, 78, 83, 84, 95,
    96, 114, 121, 177, 197,
    202, 203, 211, 217, 219,
    222, 224, 227, 244, 247,

GARVIN (Cont'd)
  259, 260, 266, 267, 285
  F.L. (Capt.), 36
  Fred (Hon.), 136
  Frederick (Gen.), 137
  Georgia, 136
  J.E., 247
  J.J., 157
  James J., 5
  Magistrate, 155, 216
  Mandanah, 137
  Mrs., 199
GARY
  Berry, 284
  Etta, 49
  G.A., 266
  J. Frank, 190
  J.L., 49
  J.L. (Mr. & Mrs.), 49
  Sallie, 266
  William, 9
GASSAWAY
  Bros., 157, 306
  C.L., 137
  Charlie, 203
  J.T., 59
  Joseph S., 137
  S.J., 186
GASTON
  Daniel, 56
GEDDES
  John, 15
GEER
  B.E. (Prof.), 226
  John M., 226
  L.N., 260
GEIGER Emily, 209, 222
GEORGE
  John, 184, 251
GIBSON
  Lida, 268
  W.C. (Mrs.), 134
GIGNEY
  W.A. (Rev.), 183
GILES
  C.D. (Mr. & Mrs.), 128
  Leila, 128
GILLARD
  John D. (Mrs.), 98
GILLERSON, 112
GILLESPIE
  Ada, 299, 310
  Alice, 265
  Amanda, 94
  Ella, 75
  Essie, 265
  Francis (Mrs.), 225
  G.B., 249
  Ida, 158
  J.E., 270
  J.M., 299
  J.M. (Mrs.), 303
  Janie, 136, 147
  Joseph A., 94
  L.D., 197
  Leo, 147, 172, 226
  Leo D., 309
  Moses, 184, 186
  Mrs., 224
  Olive, 299
  Prudence, 222
  R.L., 161
  Sherman, 196
  Tyler, 224
  W.A., 100
  W.L. (Mr. & Mrs.), 191
GILLESPILE
  Willie (Miss), 266
GILLIARD
  Janie, 181
GILLILAND
  Dr., 200
  J.R. (Dr.), 55
  Minnie, 185
  Nancy, 104
GILREATH
  Emma A., 279
  Mattie, 134
  W.A., 237
  W.W., 96
  William, 178
GILSTRAP
  B.B., 129
  Bright, 44
  David, 186
  Earle (Mr. & Mrs.), 218, 304
  Earle Bryan, 106
  Elisha, 106
  Ephriam, 35, 76, 204
  G.R., 225
  Hardy, 174, 232, 233
  J.A., 186
  J.H., 181
  J.M. (Mr. & Mrs.), 245
  Jay, 61
  Joe (Mr. & Mrs.), 239
  John, 61, 248, 254

Joseph (Mrs.), 98
Josie, 232
Lavina, 232
Lawrence (Mr. & Mrs.),
  251, 253
Lewis G. (Mr. & Mrs.), 254
Louis, 124
Louis (Mrs.), 109
Louise, 261
Mary Ann, 232
Mina, 254
Morris (Mr. & Mrs.), 247
Robert L., 103
W.H., 268
W.R., 186
William, 232
GILSTRAY
  Josey, 224
GIN & MILLING COS.
  Liberty, 108
GIRLS STATE, 61
GIN MILLS
  Chamberlin & Boggs, 110
GLASPIE
  Mansel, 69
GLASSY MOUNTAIN
  Section, 280
GLAZENER
  Ella, 193
  Lula, 22, 78, 109
GLENN, 142
GLENN
  Alice, 64, 115
  Bessie Marie, 234
  Frank, 14
  Frank M., 61
  J.M., 61
  J.M. (Mrs.), 139
  Jerry, 225
  Jessie, 235
  John, 240
  John M., 136, 139
  Robert, 58
  S.D., 55, 57, 97
  W.D., 136
  Willis, 64
  Willis, Sr., 293
GLOVER
  Margaret, 247
  Sanders (Maj.), 25
GOLD, 153
GOLD MINES, 159, 240
GOLD PIECES
  History, 103

GOLDMAN
  Richard A., 45
GOLDSMITH
  May, 129
  William, 129
GONZALES
  N.G., 301
GOOD
  Emma, 224
  I. (Mr. & Mrs.), 224, 235
  Laura, 235
GOODMAN
  W.W., 235
GOODWIN
  Lily, 127
GORDAN
  John B. (Gen.), 188
  Mattie (Miss), 250
GOSLIN
  Lewis, 4
GOSNELL
  S.A., 162, 168
GOSS
  William, 152
GOSSETT
  John, 151
  John R., 207
  Pinckney, 191
  Pink, 41
  Sallie T., 41
  S. Homer, 165
  T.F., 193
  W.P., 191
  W. Pinckney, 193
GOUDELOCK
  Ada, 132
  M.N. (Mr. & Mrs.), 197
  Thurman, 197
GOWENS (GOWEN)
  Baylus, 230
  Hattie, 230
  Lake, 123
  R.P., 123
GRADY
  B.E., 227
  H.C., 143, 166, 196
  Hattie, 196
  Henry W., 13
  John, 13
GRANBY
  J.D., 110
GRANDY
  B.B., 179,
  B.E., 173, 188, 193, 199,

GRANDY (Cont'd)
    202, 212, 215, 217, 229, 244, 255, 281, 282, 285, 287, 301, 304, 309
  B.E. & Co., 265
  Contractor, 203
  J.D., 71
  Luther, 305
  Mr., 197
  Nellie, 258, 265, 293, 310
  P.E. (Rev.), 230
GRANGER
  Lawrence, 141
  M.B., 186
GRANT
  Bessie, 246
  Drew (Miss), 240
  Henry, 261
  J.N. (Mr. & Mrs.), 269
  J.W., 269
  Lincoln, 43
  Lizzie, 44
  M.A. (Mrs.), 225
  Richard, 246
  T.L., 254
  Thomas L. (Mag.), 209, 222, 224
  William J., 246
GRAVELEY
  Axie, 98
  C.M. (Mr. & Mrs.), 211
  Dalla, 170
  Dora, 245
  J. Conney (Mr. & Mrs.), 238
  John L., 241
  John L. (Mr. & Mrs.), 170
  L.B., 90
  Lucy, 208
  M.C., 44
  Nancy, 229
  Niles, 204
  R.A. (N.P.), 237
  Rev., 71
  Rufus, 263
  W.A., 90
  W.I., 223
  W.I. (Mr. & Mrs.), 223, 245
  William (Mr. & Mrs.), 263
GRAVELY
  Arthur, 273
  Connie, 95
  Mack (Mr. & Mrs.), 287
  Mr., 51
  Niles (Mr. & Mrs.), 64
  Richard, 266
  Sarah, 221
GRAY
  Andy, 272
  Frank (Mr. & Mrs.), 233, 234
  J. Walter, 68
  Jack, 275
  Jake, 238
  Samuel, 78
GRAYDON
  William N., 288
GREELEY
  Horace, 57
GREEN
  Alfred, 267
  Aliene, 6
  B.A., 8, 68, 93, 275, 291
  Frank, 284
  Garrien, 181
  Gen., 222
  Ida C., 275, 291
  J.P. (Mrs.), 292
  Jeff, 49
  Lewis, 44
  Miss, 246
  Philip, 49
  William, 175
GREENVILLE
  Campaign Meeting, 109
GREENVILLE COUNTY
  Legends, 64, 65, 67
  Master's Sale, 42
GREER
  D.J. (Mrs.), 274
  Dudley J., 308
  L.N., 312
GREER & STEPHENSON
  Brick Yard, 312
GREGORY
  Eva, 291
  Ida, 245
GRESHAM
  Elizabeth, 38
  Mrs., 46
  W.A., 129
  W.A. (Mr. & Mrs.), 209
  W.A. (Mrs.), 183
  Walter Quentin (Gen.), 55
  William A., 74
GRICE
  Daniel, 114

Lettie, 28
  Miss, 67
GRIER
  Dr., 198
  William Moffett (Dr.), 193
GRIFFIN, 4, 112, 120, 143, 153
GRIFFIN
  A.E., 160
  Alva, 113
  Ambrose E., 130
  Andy, 240, 257
  B.M., 73, 146, 159, 167, 197
  B.P., 4, 9
  Ben B., 113
  Ben M. (Mr. & Mrs.), 213
  Ben P., 260
  Calhoun, 148
  E., 78
  E.S., 16, 135
  E.S. (Mrs.), 84
  E. Smith, 255, 263
  Elijah, 260
  Eliza, 57, 58
  Emma, 78
  Eula, 263
  Florence, 10, 85
  Frank, 103
  George, 166
  George (Mr. & Mrs.), 226
  Henry, 186
  Jake, 304
  James, 50
  James A. (Capt.), 82, 130
  John, 240, 257
  Lake, 135
  Lou "Aunt", 304
  Maria, 76
  Mr., 140
  R.Y.H. (Capt.), 302
  Smith, 110
  Thomas, 114
  Van, 239
  W.A., 81
  W.D., 136
  W.T., 228
  W.T. (Mrs.), 207
  Walter, 110
  William, 30
GRIFFY
  James (Mrs.), 285
GRIST
  L.M. (Capt.), 301
GROGAN
  Dora, 150
  L.B. (Rev.), 237
  Miss, 268
  Polly, 212
  Sarah, 303
  Tilda, 210
GUANO, 280
GUANO BUSINESS
  Carroll & Carpenter, 8
GUNNELS
  J.H., 81
GUNTER
  Nancy, 119
GURLEY
  Lula, 82
GWINN
  J.E., 287
GYPSIES, 138
HADDEN
  Henry, 49
HADDOCK
  H.C., 264, 270, 271, 282, 285, 290, 295
  H.L. (Rev.), 263
HAGOOD, 45, 82, 168, 195, 213
HAGOOD
  A. (Mr. & Mrs.), 311
  Ann, 243
  B.A., 103
  Ben A., 304, 309
  Buck "Uncle", 238, 243
  C.B., 197
  Col., 304
  Gertrude, 11
  H.C., 296
  J.E., 4, 65, 67, 85, 103, 168, 306
  J.E., Jr., 65
  James E., 260
  Lidie, 239
  Lidie Miles, 262
  Loui, 19
  Mary, 25
  Mary Walker, 311
  Place, 123
  Reunion, 184
  Sloan, 284
  Thomas, 46
  Tooney (Miss), 243
  W.M., 43, 82, 86, 254, 296
  W.M. (Mr. & Mrs.), 19
  W.M. & Co., 76

William, 238
William M. (Mr. & Mrs.), 262
HAINES
  Nettie, 118
  Thomas, 118
HALL
  J.M., 135, 139
  James, 242
  M.P., 31
  Marion, 12, 13,
HALLOWAY
  O.W., 186
HALLUM (HALLUMS)
  Baz, 218
  Isaac, 218, 295
  J.M., 151, 175
  J.N., 299
  John W., 197
  Mary, 216
  Mary Ann, 284
  Nero, 100, 294, 295
  Ninevah, 202
  R.F., 32
  R.T., 46, 151, 175, 200, 217, 240, 243, 298
  Richard, 7, 14
  Richard T., 3, 203
  Squire, 85
HAMILTON, 108, 156
HAMILTON
  A.R., 114, 122
  Andrew, 216
  C.E., 30, 105, 127, 168
  Clinellia, 93
  E.L., 32
  Homestead, 114
  James S. (Mrs.), 75
  L.G., 122
  Lemuel, 93
  McDuffie, 137
  Mrs., 309
  W.A., 93, 114, 122, 165, 256, 281
  W.H., 159
  W.R. (Mr. & Mrs.), 230
  Warren, 132, 309
  Willie, 132
  Z.P. (Rev.), 214
HAMITER
  W.S. (Rev.), 291
HAMLEY
  T.H., 186

HAMMETT
  H.P., 85
HAMMOND (HAMMONDS), 282, 309
HAMMOND
  G.E., 91
  James, 186
  W.W., 150, 258
  W.W. (Mr. & Mrs.), 206, 268
HAMPTON
  Wade, 277, 278, 283, 303
HANBY
  Mr., 196
HANCOCK
  Sophia, 230
HANES
  Dora, 172
HANGING
  Laddison, 263
HANGINGS, 68, 77, 174, 229, 298
HANNAH (HANNA)
  Earle, 2
  Oliver, 2
  Oliver (Mr. & Mrs.), 89
  Oliver M., 143
HARD
  Charles F., 152
  Clara T., 152
  Elizabeth W., 152
  Ella S., 152
  Ella W., 152
  Harriet J., 152
  Mary E., 152
HARDIN (HARDEN)
  Joseph, 30
  W.M. (Rev.), 131, 136, 139, 143, 171
HARKNESS
  Nannie, 3
HARPER
  Earle, 251
  John, 114
  Mrs., 94
  W.C., 194
HARRIS, 122
HARRIS
  A.C., 161, 166
  A.R., 27
  Benjamin (Gen.), 235
  Cling, 160
  Clingman, 159
  Essie, 90, 252
  Fannie, 25

Hattie, 170, 207
J.R., 189, 228
J.T., 170
James R., 47, 207
John D. (Mr. & Mrs.), 188
John F., 280
John F. (Mr. & Mrs.), 202
L.W. (Mrs.), 245
Lila, 207
M.J. (Mrs.), 90, 170
Mrs., 177, 221
Pickens, 93, 193
R., 93
R.L. (Mr. & Mrs.), 148, 252
Rachael, 207
Robert L. (Mr. & Mrs.), 25
Sallie, 47
Sunie, 93
T.D., 90, 102, 107, 121, 125, 141, 170, 208, 235, 279, 303, 309
T.D. (Mr. & Mrs.), 244
HARRISON
  Dr., 6
  James (Dr.), 6
  James H., 5
  John, 303
  Lewis, 164
HART
  C.M., 168
  Nancy, 287
HARTZOG
  Henry S., 155
HARVEY James, 285
HAUPFEAR
  John A., 313
HAWKINS
  J. Frank, 305
  John, 186
  Lou, 305
  William, 186
HAWTHORNE
  George, 59
  J. Ludlow, 233
  Jasyer (Jasper) N., 233
HAYES
  D.T. (Rev.), 228, 229, 231, 233, 235
  J.M., 93
  James, 178
  Lila, 178
  Mamie, 219
  Mode, 213

Mose (Mr. & Mrs.), 252
R.B. (Rev.), 210
Richard, 132
T.B., 109
W.F., 93
HAYGOOD
  Atticus G., 85
  J.E., 247
HAYGOOD & CO., 280
HAYNES
  Edward, 217
  Flavor, 81
  James M., 76
  John, 242
  John (Mr. & Mrs.), 195
  W.J.F., 83
HAYWARD
  E.C., 186
HEAD
  West, 201, 242
HEATH, 280, 310
HEATH, BRUCE, MORROW & CO., 214, 220, 282
HEATHERBY
  James, 217
HEATON
  Wade, 26
HEINITSH
  Dr., 81
HELLAM, 89
HELLAMS
  Eliza, 233
  Thomas V., 176
HEMPHILL
  R.R., 182
HENDERSON
  Isaac, 242
  J.G. (Rev.), 207
  L.O., 103
  Mr., 124
  R.L., 183
  R.L. (Mr. & Mrs.), 215, 262
  Redmond, 113
  Ross, 41
HENDRICKS, 143, 150, 173
HENDRICKS
  B.L., 74, 91, 117, 170
  Commissioner, 233
  D.E., 91, 109, 125, 161
  D.E. (Mr. & Mrs.), 151, 287
  D.F., 109

Daniel, 187
Dave, 9, 140
David, 73
David, Jr., 98
Dick, 301
E.E., 180
E.H. (Mrs.), 180
Earl, 167
Ed, 125, 129
Ed (Mr. & Mrs.), 214
Eddie (Mr. & Mrs.), 104
Emma, 174
Essie, 9
Family Reunion, 267
Frank, 190, 198
G.H., 93, 140, 166, 217, 284
G.R., 182, 186, 283, 299
G.T., 100
George, 2, 220
George H., 26, 27, 135, 218
George K., 35, 91
H. (N.P), 185
H.B., 16, 32, 33, 73, 91, 138, 195, 204
Harrison O., 260
Henry, 286
Henry D., 1
Ida, 277
J.F., 102, 204
J.S., 189
J. Mason, 196
J. Salter, 190
James, 1, 34, 47, 174
James (Mrs.), 207
James F. (Mr. & Mrs.), 1, 80
Joe, 93
John, 128
John A., 195
John M. (Mrs.), 4
Larkin, 73
Leona, 233
Lillie, 36
Lou, 161
Lucian, 195
Lucian (Mr. & Mrs.), 259
M. & Son, 270, 271
Matthew, 66, 93, 97, 288
Matthew (Mr. & Mrs.), 267
Mella, 287
Millie, 45
N.A., 223

Noah, 80
Noah R., 1
Nora, 151, 190
Pollie C., 220
R.M., 88
Rachael, 164
Rebecca J., 76
Rick, 239
Rufus N., 120
Rutha, 260
Supervisor, 47
Susan, 74
Susanah, 74
Talitha, 75
W.E., 29, 160, 178
W.F., 25, 87, 115
W.F. (Mr. & Mrs.), 112
W.F. & Bros., 228
Ward, 140
Warren D., Sr., 270
William, 224
William A., 260
William Walker, 196
HENDRIX
Henry, 2
Ida, 288
John (Mrs.), 2
T.R., 89
HENRY
B.A. (Mrs.), 72
D.R., 72
Ella, 113
W.M., 167
HERD
David A., 80
J.J., 97, 121, 262, 288
John, 79
T.J., 79
HESTER
B.M. (Mrs.), 216
Captain, 18
Carr, 86
Cecil, 265, 293, 310
Elizabeth, 86
James W., 182
Jane, 11
Joeberry, 186
Kate, 265, 293, 310
Lois, 292
Louisa, 113
M.F., 1, 16, 23, 32, 34, 42, 79, 80, 82, 86, 91, 124, 135, 166, 170, 181, 206, 211, 213, 219, 221,

HESTER (Cont'd)
  227, 231, 238, 239, 241,
  250, 252, 263, 269, 288,
  296, 299, 313
  M.F. (Mr. & Mrs.), 66, 183
  M.W., 113
  Mary, 18
  Mary T., 80
  Mattie, 183
  Miss, 23
  Paul, 264, 292
  R.A., 73
  R.A. (Mr. & Mrs.), 165
  Ralph, 292
  S.E., 223, 258
  Samuel J. (Dr.), 50
  Theron, 264, 292, 310
  Thomas, 11, 186
  W.H., 2, 114, 151, 155, 157
  W.O., 182, 309
  Walter O., 11, 229
  Wilton, 265, 303
HIATT
  D.W. (Rev.), 275
HICKS
  John O. (Prof.), 234
HIGGINS
  Augusta A., 309
  J.A. (Mr. & Mrs.), 171
  Lena, 171
  Margaret, 270
  Mrs., 277
  S.G., 309
  Samuel G., 298
  T.B., 145
  T.B. (Mrs.), 243
HILL
  A.P. (Gen.), 100
  Alice, 222
  Belle, 222
  Bennett, 151, 187
  Biddie, 172
  Dick, 215
  F.G., 36
  Felix, 222
  Frank, 222
  G.W., 222
  George, 237
  J. Bennett, 56
  J.E., 25
  J. Tyler, 237
  Jennie, 222
  John Elford, 62
  Johnnie, 222
  Lewis, 222
  Louis, 15
  Maggie, 256
  Margaret, 119, 222
  R.K., 216, 223, 258
  R.K. (Mr. & Mrs.), 119
  R.R., 23
  R.S., 114
  Richard (Mr. & Mrs.), 172
  Richard K., 215, 216
  Roswell, 223
  Susa, 15
  Susan, 15
  T.M., 216
  T.W., 258
  Thomas, 172, 216
  Tyler, 20
  Victoria, 199
HIMES
  J.S., 29
HINES
  E.A. (Dr.), 138
  E.A. (Dr. & Mrs.), 130
HINKLE (HINCKLE)
  Leonia, 88
  Silas, 32, 88, 205
  Srlas (Mr. & Mrs.), 71
HINSON
  George E., 69
HINTON
  Ashmore, 153
  F.M., 65
  J.A., 253, 288, 296
  J.T., 158
  J.T. (Mrs.), 158
  Levisa, 193
  Mrs., 35
  R.O., 253, 296
  S.P., 193
  Samuel, 35
  W. Elbert, 45
HIOTT
  D.W., 178, 223, 241, 262, 285, 287, 308
  D. Weston (Rev.), 17
  Deal, 48, 75, 185
  Myrtle, 178
  R. Weston (Rev.), 261
  Rev., 277, 283
HITT
  E.C., 186
HOBART, 119

HODDOCK
  Annie, 268
HODGENS
  A.W. (Capt.), 165
HODGES
  W.H. (Rev.), 222
HOESH
  Marie, 218
HOGSED
  Frank, 277
  Frank W., 148
  Ira Perry, 277
  Mrs., 277
  W.P., 148, 277
HOLCOMBE (HOLCOMB)
  B.F., 88
  Berry, 151
  C.A., 119
  C.T., 164, 186
  Frank, 151
  George, 98
  James B., 232
  Joseph, 15
  Kate, 98
  M.E., 35
  Martha E., 35
  Martha Elvira, 19, 31
  Miss, 302
  R.E., 46, 210
  R.W., 35
  Robert E.T., 19
  Robert H., 213
  Rossie (Miss), 244
  Stella, 210
  Sue Lee, 119
  W.E., 46
HOLDEN
  B.F., 186
  Hattie, 68
  J.D., 68
  Naomi, 192
  William, 223
HOLDER, 220
HOLDER
  Annie May, 269
  B. (Rev.), 1, 13, 39, 41,
    77, 104, 132, 143, 166,
    179, 216, 263, 266, 269,
    294, 299
  B.L., 46
  Davie, 180
  Davis (Mr. & Mrs.), 262
  Elizabeth, 34, 164
  Emma, 89
  I. (Rev.), 12
  J.D. (Mr. & Mrs.), 189
  J.D. (Mrs.), 214
  J.D. & Co., 308
  James, 51
  Jeff (Mr. & Mrs.), 148,
    257
  Jeff D. (Mr. & Mrs.), 269
  John, 51
  Lola, 66, 81, 138, 143
  M.M., 19, 166
  Martin, 186
  Mary E. "Polly", 145
  Mazilda, 174
  Meady, 194
  Melville (Mr. & Mrs.), 269
  Melvin M., 3
  Nora, 193
  Sallie, 308
  Tyler, 194, 204
  Tyler (Mr. & Mrs.), 233
  Tyra, 186
  Vallenie, 34
HOLLAND
  Harrison, 250
  Ruth Fredonia, 263
  W.P. (Rev.), 250
HOLLIDAY
  Eliza, 110
  J.I., 1
  Lillie E., 1
HOLLINGSWORTH, 44, 94, 168,
  313
HOLLINGSWORTH
  Aurie, 252
  C.H., 168, 180
  C.L., 15, 42, 52, 58,
    86, 162, 175, 173, 277
  C.L. (Mr. & Mrs.), 20, 101
  Colonel, 54, 189, 302
  Columbus L., 173
  Dr., 285
  M.A. (Mrs.), 175
  Ola, 10, 101, 276
  W.R., 76, 95, 130
HOLLMAN
  G.C., 47
HOLLOWAY
  Elizabeth, 181
  Elizabeth H., 181
  O.A., 181
HOLSTEIN
  M.A., 196

HOLTZCLAW (HOLSCLAW)
  T.C. (Rev.), 155, 167,
    198, 210, 235, 248
HOMUTH
  Mr., 188
HONEA PATH
  Storm, 307
HONEY
  George, 189
HOOD
  John, 231
HOOK
  Rescie C.M., 218
  Ressie E. Miller, 184
HOPKINS
  D.W., 57, 115, 119
  Des, 170
  Des W., 160
  J.W., 186
  James, 186, 267
  Malinda, 110
  Miss, 210
HORSE SHOE ROBINSON, 291
HOTELS
  Aiken, 258
  Ambler House, 26, 147,
    152, 237, 305
  Armstrong, 69
  Ben-Della, 298
  Brown, J.H., 92, 105, 126
  Caesar's Head, 103, 287
  Central, 175, 199
  Clemson, 2, 30, 114
  De McDaniel, 87
  Easley, 68, 90, 195, 199,
    256, 279
  Gilreath House, 279, 303
  Greenville, 95
  Headrick, 65
  Keowee, 34, 183
  Liberty, 81
  Mountain View, 18, 86,
    256, 281
  Nield, 73
  Pickens, 231
  Railroad, 4
  Table Rock, 188
  Thornley, 219
  Westminster, 114
HOTLSCLAW
  T.C. (Rev.), 233
HOUSES
  Ashmore, 44, 98
  Babb, 32, 33
  Bell Shoal, 33
  Biltmore, 79
  Bradley, 155, 196
  Bramblett, 120
  Brown, 132
  Byars, 309
  Calhoun, John C., 238
  Chapman, 39
  Clyde, 32
  Durant, 32
  Earle (Dr.), 299, 308
  Folger, 32
  Fort Hill, 238
  Hagood, 78
  Hamilton, 114
  Headrick, 65
  Hester, 10
  Jackson, Stonewall, 304
  Jones, 165
  Leslie, 105
  Major, 54
  Newberry, Judge, 197
  Norton, 251
  O'Dell, J.S., 90
  Palmer, 53
  Robinson, Horse Shoe, 291
  Southerland, 188
  Stewart, D.B., 90
  Talley, 165
  Thode, 154
  Thornley, 10
  Trotter, 165
  White House, 298
HOW
  James, 266
  Minnie, 147
HOWARD, 76
HOWARD
  J.C., 210
  J.N., 88
  Mr., 205
  S.W., 186, 204
HOYES
  D.T. (Mr. & Mrs.), 268
HOYT
  James A., 157
HUBBARD
  Miss, 193
HUDGENS (HUDGEN)
  A.W. (Capt.), 63, 139, 261
  A.W. & Son, 149
  Blanche, 148, 204, 261
  Kate, 256
  Lula, 285

T.K., 63, 76, 152
Thomas K., 139
V.E., 73, 85, 170
Vic, 90
HUDSON
   Duff (Mr. & Mrs.), 239
   Hill, 153
   J.H., 97, 196
   Jenkins A., 174
   Milton T., 192
   Nettie, 271
   Ruth, 217
   W.A., 143
   W. Austin, 192
HUFFMAN
   Marie, 195
HUGENS
   T.K., 165
HUGHES
   Alfred B., 245
   C.T. (Mr. & Mrs.), 200
   Charley T. (Mr. & Mrs.), 241
   Charlie, 223
   Constant, 74
   Earle, 309
   Essie, 311
   Hester, 61
   J.G. (Mrs.), 184
   Laura, 71
   Messrs., 28
   Minnie, 51
   Miss, 310
   Mrs., 283
   Robert, 90
   Robert (Mr. & Mrs.), 34
   Samuel, 266
   T.A., 61
   T.T. (Mr. & Mrs.), 241
   Terza, 45
   Tirzah, 99, 111, 156
   W.N., 48, 75, 109, 127, 174, 199, 297
   Walter, 114
HUGHEY
   James A., 186
   James H., 285
   John A., 285
   Ola, 142
HUMBERT
   D.G., 197
   David G., 13
HUNNICUTT
   Joe Berry, 290
   Mattison, 290
   Thomas, 290
   Warren, 290
   William John, 290
HUNT
   A.R., 52, 63, 66, 81
   Amanda, 153, 162, 168, 171
   Arthur, 203
   Arthur (Mr. & Mrs.), 221
   Auditor, 215
   Carrie, 75
   Corrie, 164
   E.M., 108, 206, 260, 261
   Earle, 34
   Elias, 98
   Elvira, 208
   Emeziah, 187
   Emma, 86
   Ethel Amber, 235
   Eva, 132
   Ezekial, 164
   Francis (Mrs.), 129
   Frank, 6
   H., 305
   H.C., 74
   Heyman, 26
   J., 81
   J.H., 186
   James, 82
   Jas. T. (Mr. & Mrs.), 34
   Jay, 152
   Jesse, 153
   John, 199, 209
   John F., 160
   Joseph, 99
   L.E., 303
   Lee, 26
   Leigh, 287
   Luther, 78
   M. (Mr. & Mrs.), 132
   M.H., 6
   M.L. (Mrs.), 8
   M.V., 35
   Marion, 260
   Mark, 164
   Martin, 26
   Maud Lee, 7
   Maude, 164
   Mrs., 302
   Permelia, 82
   Raymond O., 153
   Rebecca, 83, 85
   Robert, 249

Robert G., 35
S.A. (Prof.), 148
S. Arthur, 203
Samuel Arthur, 249
Susan, 305
T.F., 153
T.J., 6, 26
T.J. (Mrs.), 112
Thomas, 260
Virginia, 127
W.E., 75, 193
W.P., 128, 161, 164
William U., 26
HUNTER, 26, 98, 108, 156, 300
HUNTER
  Anderson, 189
  C.T., 311,
  Edward, 12
  Emily, 170
  George J., 178
  H.B., 92
  Harrison, 7, 14
  Henry, 251
  J.W., 186
  John, 14, 30
  Mary, 14, 196
  Mr., 100
  N., 170
  Philip, 76
  T.N., 30, 43, 92, 105, 111, 133, 216
  Thomas, 228
  W.H. (Capt.), 196
  Wash, 92, 105
  William, 30, 92, 244, 255, 258, 260, 296, 299
HUTCHINS, 134
HUTCHINS (HUTCHENS-HITCHINGS)
  C.T., 142, 148, 290, 300
  C.T. (Mrs.), 277
  Charles T., 3
  Charley, 94
  Charlie, 95
  J.M., 233, 250
  John, 162, 170
HYDE
  J.P., 191, 271
  Lizzie, 55, 97, 167
IMMIGRATION 1900, 227
INABINET (INABINETT)
  Anna Marcella, 197
  Caroline, 197
  L.L. (Rev.), 113, 197, 213, 221, 227
  L.L. (Rev. & Mrs.), 160
  Mary Caroline, 197
  Rev., 90
INDIAN
  Empire, 17
INDIANS, 194
INDIANS
  Catawba, 61
  Cherokee, 65
INGERSOLL
  Robert G. (Col.), 189
INTERNAL REVENUE SERVICE, 21
INTREKIN
  J.M., 186
IRVIN
  Stewart T. (Rev.), 209
JACKSON
  Andrew, 60, 87, 91
  Elizabeth C., 242
  Forest Bryan, 107
  J.D., 242
  J.R., 107
  Jack, 205
  Stonewall, 146, 219, 304
JAHNSON
  B.T., 250
JAIL, 129, 286, 287
JAIL
  Hotel De McDaniel, 87
  Palace Car, 301
  Portable, 310
JAMES
  Diana, 254, 262
  Eva, 68
  G.W., 262
  George W., 254, 276
  George W., 276
  J.F., 83
  John, 175
  Julia, 175
  L.P., 203
  Mrs., 125
  T.E., 203
  W.D., 100, 102
  Walker, 285
JAMESON (JAMISON)
  A., 165
  A.S., 280
  Archibald, 222
  Columbus, 202
  Constable, 267
  Ella, 222

Emaline, 130
J.B., 9, 161
J.J., 186
J.M. (Mag.), 243, 263
James, 9
John, 134
John J., 136
Monroe, 299
Mrs., 134
Nora, 120
Samuel, 4
T.O., 120
JARRET (JARRETT)
  Hellen, 203
  Levey (Miss), 241
JAY
  W.K., 298
JEANES
  Engineer, 285
JEFFERIES
  John R. (Hon.), 7
JEFFERSON
  Thomas, 304
JENKINS
  A.H. (Capt.), 246
  Adam Hubley, 246
  Constable, 90
  Daisy, 178
  Ethel, 257, 264
  Fred, 257
  Howard, 5, 84, 193
  Irene, 257
  L.A., 24
  Magistrate, 142, 157
  Mary, 313
  Mary Louise, 311
  T.N., 178
  Thomas, 35, 89
  W.L., 5, 14, 84, 144, 311
  W.L. (Mr. & Mrs.), 313
  William M., 263
JENNINGS
  Frank, 304
  J.C., 146, 155, 182, 308
  J.C. (Mr. & Mrs.), 62
  J.C. (Mrs.), 173, 207
  J.F., 300, 303
  Jesse, 300
  Mrs., 7
  Wyatt, 257, 292, 310
JETT
  Bell, 48
  J.B., 48

JEWELL (JEWEL)
  Joe, 239
  Lewis, 50
  S., 239
  Thomas, 50
JOHNSON, 218, 243
JOHNSON
  B.J., 182, 205, 293
  B.T., 233
  C.L., 187
  Caleb, 242
  Cemp, 165
  David (Judge), 21
  Emily, 152, 165
  Furman, 267
  George, 213
  George T., 164
  Ira, 60
  J.W., 230
  John, 199, 241
  Lillie, 242
  Lucinda E., 267
  Martha, 230
  Mary, 64
  Mattie, 182
  Miss, 202
  P. Cemp, 280
  Pink, 300
  R.J., 313
  T.G., 267
  Thomas (Mrs.), 176
  Thomas (Rev.), 134, 164
  Thomas C., 83
  W.F., 267
  W.H., 281, 303
  W.R., 301
JOHNSTON
  B.J., 211, 221, 267, 275
  Lucinda E., 211
  Margaret, 277
  Thomas G., 197
JONES, 165, 293
JONES
  A.A. (Mag.), 172, 195
  A.J., 8, 94
  A.L. (Rev.), 45
  Bob, 225
  C.C. (Dr. & Mrs.), 158
  Carrie, 91
  D.B., 77
  D.D.B., 86
  Dora, 145
  Elbert, 126
  Ella E., 108

Essie, 265
Grady, 170
Harit E., 284
Harriett, 284
Harrison, 187
Haynes, 199, 214
I.B. (Rev.), 50
J.H., 178
J. Martin, 270
J.P., 39
J.R., 157
James, 104, 150
James B., 163
James, Jr., 150
James P., 36
James T., 172
Jasper, 174
L. (Rev.), 35
M.L., 37, 44, 61, 71, 75, 98, 99, 122, 126, 127, 129, 160, 163, 164, 185, 207, 214
M.L. (Mrs.), 71
Magistrate, 163
Malinda, 174
Manning (Capt.), 139
Manning (Mrs.), 141
Mary, 249
Miss, 126
Mrs., 139
N.H., 14, 28, 85, 137
P.H., 305
S.M. (Rev.), 251
Telitha G., 139
Thomas, 145
W.D., 172
W.D. (Mr. & Mrs.), 108
Warrie Russell, 85
William, 293
JORDAN, 125
JORDAN
M. (Miss), 24
T.R. (Mrs.), 24
Thomas (Gen.), 76
JUDSON
C.H., 35
JULIAN
Essie, 266
Jesse, 54
Matt, 95
Sallie, 297
Washington, 102
KAY
A.W., 122, 187

Albert, 207
Alma, 1, 11, 28, 275
Doran, 131, 132
F.M. (Mrs.), 157
J. Thomas, 116
Katie, 116
Maggie, 170
Margaret, 131, 132
Margaret M., 135
Mattie, 3, 15
Vesta, 122
Wester, 173
KEELER
Annie, 143
KEITH, 150, 265, 313
KEITH
Adeline, 49
Clarice, 264
Clarisse, 257
Cornelius, 144, 261
E.F. (Mr. & Mrs.), 270
E. Foster, 36, 276
E. Foster (Mr. & Mrs.), 237
George W., 116
Harriet, 144
J.D.M., 25
J.M., 226
J.R., 293
James Newberry, 237
Jennie, 156
John J., 226
L.A. (Miss), 157
Marcus, 19
Marcus D., 19
Marquis D., 25
Otis, 292
Roe, 22
W.C. (Mr. & Mrs.), 214
KELLEY (KELLY)
A.E., 44, 113, 119
Anna, 197
Ashbury, 197
Charles, 62
Elisha, 117
Ellie, 268
Emma, 38
Flem (Mr. & Mrs.), 271
G.A., 117
Ida, 221
J. Luther, 308
J.R., 202
James, 263
Joe, 201

Joseph, 242
Julia, 147
L.K., 218
Lizzie, 87
M. Carrie, 113
Maggie, 44
Robert (Mr. & Mrs.), 223
Samuel, 38
Sarah, 263
Thomas, 119
Thomas (Mr. & Mrs.), 147
William, 63
William (Mrs.), 219

KENNAN
Hugh, 255

KENNEDY
D. McD., 35
John D. (Gen.), 97
John L., 277
Robert, 247

KENNEMORE
Amanda E., 276
D.H. (Rev.), 77
E.E., 54
E.M., 21
Earle N., 70
George, 23, 65
J.H., 77
Jacob, 186, 273
Lola, 297
M.S., 68
Michael Smith, 52
Mr., 271
N.R., 200
Olive, 54
Sula, 200
William, 46

KENNEMUR
E.F., 139
W.R., 35

KERSHAW
J.B. (Gen.), 13

KESTER
Walter, 206

KEY
D.W. (Rev.), 222
F.S., 289

KILBURN
Mr., 275
W.W., 275, 313

KILBY
Essa, 18

KILE
J.H. (Mrs.), 226

KINCH
J.E., 28, 44, 236
J.E. (Mr. & Mrs.), 57, 212
Joe E., 22

KING
Elizabeth, 39
Isaac, 215
J.B., 182
J. Milton, 129, 265
J. Monroe, 33, 52, 139
Jacob M., 33, 52
John T., 231
Lillie, 139
M.M. (Dr. & Mrs.), 131
Margaret, 39
Margaret C., 33, 36, 39, 52
Mary J., 164
Mrs., 301
Old Stand, 56, 96
Sarah M., 181
Vesta, 88
Vesta Elizabeth, 36
W.J., 164, 186
Warren, 182
William T., 231, 241

KIRBY
John, 91

KIRKLAND
Ella, 147
George, 147

KIRKSEY (KIRKSAY)
Dr., 127
Frank, 257, 310
J.K., 124
J.K. (Mrs.), 48
James, 308
James K., 127
Kitty, 44
Mary, 23, 94, 96, 215
Minnie, 19, 84, 176
Mrs., 277
Nannie, 9, 29
R. (Dr.), 51, 264
Robert (Dr.), 10, 18, 41, 68
Thomas, 36
W.S., 153, 187
W. Silas, 308

KLUGH
J.C. (Judge), 129
W.W., 197

KNIGHT
Amanda, 172

Jacob, 204
M.M., 210
W.W., 172
KNOX
Arthur, 290
Benjamin, 290
Harrison, 290
James, 290
James E., 33
John, 33, 290
Robert, 290
Robert E., 33, 80
KRUSE
John Gabriel Christopher, 156
KUYKENDALL
Alice, 29
LaBOON
B.A., 144
B.B., 304
B.B. (Mr. & Mrs.), 251
B.B. (Mrs.), 302
Ben (Mr. & Mrs.), 222
Hampton, 267
Olga, 251
Robert, 267
W.L., 300
LADD
Catherine, 81, 176
E. (Mrs.), 176
Millie, 229
Mr., 82
LADDISON, 263
LAFOY
Averilla, 45
J.L., 45
LANCASTER
Dr. & Mrs., 20
Nat (Dr.), 276
Ola Hollingsworth, 276
R.A. (Dr.), 276
R.A. (Mrs.), 101
Robert (Dr.), 10
LANCE
Eula, 65
William, 102
LAND
Calvin, 158
Cordelia Ann, 72
Milton W., 72
LANDERS
George, 1
LANDRESS
Robert (Mr. & Mrs.), 244

LANGFORD
Frank, 60
LANGLEY
N.J. (Miss), 124
LANGSTON
Bailey A., 146
Henry, 153
Henry (Mr. & Mrs.), 164
Isaac, 187
J.T., 72, 84, 146
J.W., 223
John T., 84
P.B., 140
P.B. (Mr. & Mrs.), 195
W.J. (Rev.), 161
LARK
Frank, 131
J. Sam, 240
L.A., 12
Mary, 12
Sam, 228, 229
W.R., 91
LaROCHE
Dora, 147
LAROY
Dave, 229
LASH
Clarinda, 187
LATHEM (LATHAM)
E.B., 31, 36, 82
Eliza, 259
Eliza Ann, 63
Ellen Clements, 36
Ellen S., 31
Enoch, 31
Flora, 144, 196, 199, 302
G.W., 68
J.F., 79, 116, 135,
J.K., 68, 83, 116, 135, 149, 160, 174
J.S., 39, 83, 116, 135
J.T., 143
James F., 83
James K., 148, 295
James R., 295
John, 76
Judge, 129
L.O., 47
Lawrence, 259, 263
Lawrence (Mrs.), 205
Nancy L., 68, 149
Nannie L., 174
R.E., 64
Susan E., 31

Will, 29
LATIMER
  A.C., 215
  George E., 6
LAWMAN
  A.W., 115
LAWRENCE (LAURENCE)
  Carey, 308
  James H. (Rev.), 235
  Jeter, 308
  William (Mr. & Mrs.), 150
  Willie, 42
  Zedar, 144
LAWYERS
  Negro Woman Tenn., 157
LAY
  J.F., 206
  James F., 41, 69, 109, 115
  Mary, 109, 115, 117
  Myra, 114, 291
  Savilla, 109, 115, 117, 206
LEA BROS. & CO., 165
LEACH
  Marion G., 108
LEAVELL
  Robert E., 222
LEE
  R.E. (Gen.), 153
  Robert E., 168, 230
LEMONS
  Bill, 80
LENDERMAN
  Henry, 259
  J.C., 259
LENDHARDT (LENHART)
  B.D., 23
  Richard, 19, 31, 35, 73, 76, 198
LEONARD
  J.A., 117
LESESNE (LESENE)
  Lafayette, 124
  Prof., 57
LESLIE, 105
LESLEY (LESLIE)
  Alice, 76
  Anderson, 211
  Dennis, 76
  G.W., 187
  Hassie, 23
  J.F. (Prof.), 213
  John, 187
  Mattie, 270
  Nora, 213
  Sallie, 169
  Saluda, 77
  W.A. (Mr. & Mrs.), 23
  W. Anderson, 169
LESTER
  Andy, 27
LEWIS, 102, 121, 146, 149, 156
LEWIS
  A.B. (Mr. & Mrs.), 4
  Arthur, 257, 312
  Artie, 112
  B., 94, 207
  B. (Mr. & Mrs.), 271
  B.A., 296
  Bee, 134, 155
  Buch, 272
  Clifford, 264, 292
  Cornelia, 143
  D., 35
  Dock, 287
  E.E., 32
  Earle, 258, 265, 312
  Effie, 233
  Ellen, 257, 264, 292, 310
  F.A., 32, 187, 312
  H.J., 15
  H.J. (Mrs.), 143
  H.L., 59
  Henry J., 209
  Hester, 42
  J.J., 13, 14, 167, 246, 294
  J.J. (Mrs.), 145
  J.P., 70
  J.T. (Rev.), 134, 151, 219, 236, 244
  J.T. & Sons, 94
  Jack, 293
  Jacob, 268
  James D., 61
  Jas. P., 102
  Jennie, 100, 258, 293
  Jesse, 293, 310
  Jessie, 100, 164, 257
  Jesse J. (T.J.), 14
  Jesse P., 279
  John J., 100, 247, 258, 279
  John L., 247
  John T., 46, 52, 94, 174, 204, 209, 228, 254
  John T. & Sons, 17

Kate, 9
L.T. (Rev.), 9
Lasiene, 113
Lizzie, 287
M.A., 37
M.E. (Miss), 15
M.H., 287
Maggie, 79
Mary, 257, 292, 310
Miss, 209
N.J., 143
Omecca, 119
Overton, 72
R.K., 15, 59
R.S. (Capt.), 79
Rev., 69
Robert, 119
Rosa, 10, 17
S.E. (Mrs.), 113
Sallie, 248
Stand, 127
Theodore (Mr. & Mrs.), 99
Thomas L. (Dr.), 72
Thomas Lawton (Dr.), 165
Trial Justice, 41
Wade, 296
Warehouse, 160
LEWIS & SONS, 12
LIBBY
  J.E., 7
LIBERTY, 232
LIBERTY
  Article, 276, 281
  Brass Band, 22
  Business Tour, 92
  Depot, 109, 154
  Depot Agency, 111
  Oil Mill, 144
  Passenger Depot, 105, 107
  Tornado, 61
LIBERTY BELL, 85
LIBRARIES
  Southern Railroad Travel, 279
LIFE INSURANCE BUSINESS, 160
LIGON
  J.T., 74
  James, 198
  Mamie, 14
  T.C. (Rev.), 284
  T.J., 121, 186
  Thomas J. (Mr. & Mrs.), 258
  Virginia, 29

William B., 283
LINCOLN
  Abraham, 64, 101, 307
  Nancy Hanks, 307
LINDSAY
  John James (Dr.), 195
  Peter, 100
LINEBURGER
  Harry, 115
LINK
  Joe, 134
LITTLE
  Doasia, 244
  P.S. (Rev.), 241
LITTLEJOHN
  (Dr.), 188
  William, 182
LIVERY STABLES, 150, 159
LIVERY STABLES
  Bates & Freeman, 197
  Central, 7
  Hagood, 195
  Hagood & Thornley, 4
  Hollingsworth, 44
  Johnson, Pink, 300
  Parsons, W.A., 113
  Pickle, 45
  Thornley Bros., 65
LIVINGSTON
  Mrs., 43
LOCKHART
  George, 225
LOCUST, 15
LOGAN
  John A., 135
  W.M., 89
LOGGINS
  Calvin, 142
  Tabitha, 135
LOLLIS
  Joe, 217
LONE STAR STATE, 225
LONG
  Mrs., 193
LONGSTREET
  James (Gen.), 155
LOOPER
  Abner, 225, 243
  Anderson, 154
  Bros., 119
  Charlie, 145
  Clarence, 276
  Daniel, 106
  E.F., 107

E.F. (Mr. & Mrs.), 29, 183
E.F. (Mrs.), 129
E. Frank, 262
Ellen, 37
Frank, 94
G.B., 49, 83, 220
George B., 80
Ger, 27
H.M., 97
J., 306
J.B. (Mr. & Mrs.), 145
J.D., 294
J.M., 24, 84, 109
J.T. (Rev.), 131
Jerre, 51, 99, 243, 249, 250
Jerrimiah, 154, 240
John, 153, 203
John W. (Mr. & Mrs.), 84
Jos. L., 11
Joseph, 51, 63
Joseph (Mrs.), 13
Joseph, Jr., 13
Lawrence, 154
Lizzie Esther, 29
M.O. (Mr. & Mrs.), 294
Marcus O. (Mr. & Mrs.), 188
Mary, 164
Matilda, 159
Merritt (Mr. & Mrs.), 22
Mrs., 194
Offrey, 6
Sallie, 220, 276
Sammel, 264
Sammel, Jr., 264
Shop, 153
Solomon, 209
Supervisor, 176, 215
T., 128
Thomas, 37, 51, 86, 90, 122, 131, 141, 142, 170, 240
Thomas J. (Mr. & Mrs.), 276
Viola, 29, 183
W.B., 244
W.B. (Mr. & Mrs.), 146
W.P., 244
W.T., 304
Will, 159
William, 194
William B., 297
LOST BOY, 124

LOVETT
　John Thompson, 216
LOWERY
　Etta, 78
　Mary E., 241
LUCKIE
　Dan, 88
LUMBER YARD, 281
LUMPKIN
　R.B. (Mr. & Mrs.), 259
LYNCH, 150
LYNCH (LINCH)
　B.S., 11, 193
　Baker (Mr. & Mrs.), 190
　Bannister, 131, 191
　Bannister S., 62
　Calvin, 191
　Elizabeth, 193
　Emma, 225
　Freeman, 149
　G.M., 48, 288
　Gideon, 178, 191, 229
　Gideon M., 80, 136
　Hester, 117
　Holbert, 32
　Jacob, 274
　Jane, 217
　Lilly L., 11
　Lucas, 219
　Nathaniel, 192
　R. Lucus, 219
　Robert, 79
　Robert (Mr. & Mrs.), 219, 234
　Sarah, 131
　Thomas, 178, 302
　Thomas (Mr. & Mrs.), 205
　Thomas C., 96
　W.R. (Mr. & Mrs.), 190
LYNCHINGS, 149
LYNCHINGS
　Johnson, Ira, 60
MADDEN
　Anna V., 308
　Cora, 296
　J.Z., 298
　N.M., 42, 97, 296, 308
　Ossie, 140
　S.J., 298
　Thomas, 34
MADDOX
　J.I., 177
　J.R., 227

MADISON
　President, 311
MAHAFFEY (MAHAFFY)
　D.T., 187
　L.M., 312
　Rufus, 233
MAHON, 176
MAHON & ARNOLD, 304
MAHONE
　William (Gen.), 70
MAIL ROUTES, 105
MAJOR, 28, 54
MAJOR
　Harriett, 277
　J.W., 277
　Mary V., 260
　Miss, 163
　Ola, 286
　Pati, 310
　Patte, 264
　Pattie, 292
　S.W., 103
　Stephen A., 277
　W.R., 3, 163
MALONE
　Mr., 89
MANASSAS
　Battle, 64
MANLEY (MANLY)
　A.J. (Rev.), 203, 205, 306
　Basil (Rev.), 28
　Charles (Rev.), 28
　H.N., 69
　Mary E., 277
　Sarah M., 28
MANN
　Milstead, 110
　S.B., 109, 247
　W.B., 230
　William, 110
MANSEL (MANSELL)
　Adam, 228
　J.C., 47
　Jane, 47
　Joseph Lawrence, 47
　Samantha, 199
MARBLE BUSINESS, 15
MARCHBANKS
　Georgia, 80
　Peter C., 52
MARSH
　J.B. (Rev.), 210
MARSHALL
　Mr., 105

MARTIN
　B.F., 78
　Benjamin F., 21
　Billy "Uncle", 82
　Bower, 294
　C.B., 78
　C.T., 113, 280
　Carrie, 177
　Clayton, 55, 56
　Clayton (Mr. & Mrs.), 238
　Cora, 119
　Cora J., 300
　Cynthia, 133
　Edmund, 133
　H.H., 108
　H.J., 103, 206
　Hattie, 186
　I.M. (Capt.), 185
　J.H. (Jake), 86, 159
　J.H. (Mr. & Mrs.), 144
　Jacob, 300
　Lizzie, 202
　Mary, 147, 202, 254
　Miss, 113
　Mrs., 179, 302
　N.T., 121
　O.B., 170
　O.L. (Rev.), 198, 312
　P., 12
　S.M., 197
　Sarah, 273
　Sarah E., 112, 156
　T.C., 261
　W.W., 64, 112, 156
　Warren, 117, 203
　Warren C., 177
　William, 298
　William W., 110
MASON, 244
MASON
　Robert (Rev.), 180
MASONIC
　Building, 280
　Hall, 16, 112, 220, 252
　Honors, 101, 149, 168, 241
　Lodge, 190
　Ritual, 181, 302
　Temple, 112
MASSEY
　Miss, 55
MASSINGALE (MASSAGALE)
　Arthur (Mr. & Mrs.), 210
　Dora, 68
　Eva, 260

Jennie, 218
John, 205
Joseph, 179
King, 122
Queen, 132
Tom, 219
MASTERS (MASTER)
  Ben, 145
  Foster, 133
  Henry Grace, 70
  J.C., 70
  John, 271
  Mr., 209
  Rebecca, 249
  Snow, 200, 241
  William, 63
MATTHENEY
  Lesley, 232
MATTHEWS
  Claude (Gov.), 102
MATTISON
  R.J., 196
MATTOX
  Col., 41
  John, 59
MAULDIN
  A.M., 39, 235
  A.M. (Mr. & Mrs.), 166
  Alexander, 187
  Allen, 5
  Alma, 248
  Americus, 24
  B.D., 30, 231, 263, 264
  B. Frank (Mr. & Mrs.), 198
  Belle Z., 213
  Benjamin, 5
  C.W., 197
  Clara, 90
  Cleon, 200
  Damie, 4
  E.J. (Mrs.), 225
  Earle, 176
  Frank, 144
  Frank G., 103
  Gladys, 293, 310
  Gregg, 265
  Guy, 7
  Henry (Mr. & Mrs.), 212
  Hortense, 124
  I.M., 32, 125, 168
  I.R., 179
  Ivy M., 21, 62, 264, 278, 286, 288, 307
  J.A. (Mr. & Mrs.), 103
  J.R., 209
  Joab, 102, 124, 166, 168
  Joab (Mr. & Mrs.), 21
  Joab (Mrs.), 189
  John O., 43
  Joseph, 35, 90
  Julia Vesta, 194
  Kate, 194
  Kirk, 217
  L.O., 177, 197, 313
  Laban, 288
  Leila, 211
  Lidie, 217
  Lizzie, 23, 169, 202, 211
  M. (Capt.), 182
  Major, 257
  Mary, 166
  Mary Elsie, 198
  McDuffie, 183
  Naomi, 5
  Ossie, 106, 181
  P.L. (Mr. & Mrs.), 253
  Perry (Mr. & Mrs.), 211
  Perry J., 194
  Rett, 176
  Rev., 184
  Rhoda, 39
  Riley, 221
  Ruben (Mr. & Mrs.), 207
  Samuel, 173
  Samuel (Mrs.), 6
  Sarah, 272
  Sarah Martin, 273
  T.J., 47, 143, 144, 173, 307
  Tom Joe, 225
  Trainum, 202
  Vinda, 211
  W.F., 298
  W.G. (Rev.), 124, 202, 204, 210, 288
  W.H., 136
  William, 24
  William A., 272, 273
  William A. & Co., 120
  Willie, 258, 265, 305
MAULEY
  Harrison, 187
MAUR
  Mrs., 58
MAW
  Julius, 227
  Mary, 203
  S.P., 187

Willie, 219
MAXEY
    Leo, 54
MAXWELL
    G.K., 73
    P.E., 183
    Priestly, 163
    Priestly E., 163
    Robert (Gen.), 114
    Sue, 73
MAYES
    G.G. (Rev.), 73
MAYFIELD
    G.R., 225
    George R., 179
    Julius, 220
    Kate, 149, 179, 228
    S.G., 179
    W.D., 179
    William, 179
MAYS
    J.A. (Constable), 90
McADAMS
    George, 187
    Place, 116
McALISTER, 30
McALISTER
    Bettie, 247
    Ezekiel, 197
    F.P., 72
    James, 247
    Lafayette, 266
    Miranda, 197
    S.A., 288
McBRIDE
    J.T. (Rev.), 8
McCAIN
    C.L. (Rev.), 245, 248
    H.A., 311
McCALL
    Maggie, 233
    Texas, 242
McCALLA
    George R. (Capt.), 286
    Isaac H., 286
McCANN
    Julia, 155
    Thomas H. (Maj.), 139
McCARLY
    Mr., 151
    W.C., 151
McCASLAN
    Eliza, 46
    W.M., 279

W.M. (Prof.), 276
McCLANAHAN (McCLANAHAM)
    F.R. (Rev.), 194
    Frank R. (Mr. & Mrs.), 87
McCOLLUM (McCOLLUMS)
    Lily, 139
    William, 217
McCOMBS
    John A. (Mr. & Mrs.), 95
    Willie, 95
McCONNELL
    Rev., 127
McCORD
    Blanche, 252
    Henry, 183
McCORKLE
    J.M., 175
    Mrs., 199
    Zeuella, 175
McCOY
    Mr., 165
McCRACKIN
    H.C. (Prof.), 204
    J.L., 221
    R.L., 30
McCRAREY (McCRARY)
    Prof., 43
    Reed, 202
McCRAVEY
    E.P., 267
    O.D. (Mr. & Mrs.), 78
McCULLUM
    Ada Lee, 217
    Daisey B., 227
    Ford, 34
    Pickens, 264
McDADE
    Mr., 10
McDANALD
    Cora, 266
McDANIEL
    B.T., 11, 17, 70, 73, 121
    B.T. (Mr. & Mrs.), 82
    Ben, 95, 98, 121
    Ben M., 53
    Ben M. (Mr. & Mrs.), 64
    Benjamin (Major), 44
    Eliza, 258, 293, 310
    Feddie, 292
    Harry, 87
    Henry, 257, 292, 310
    Isaac, 87
    J.H.G., 11, 276, 283, 304
    J.H.G. (Mr. & Mrs.), 82

James M., 154
Kate, 310
Katie, 292
Louise, 257, 292, 310
Mary, 258, 293, 310
Nora, 82
Permelia, 154
Rev., 286
S.H. (Rev.), 269
Sheriff, 129, 144, 244
W.A., 168, 171
Whit, 179
McDONALD
  D.W., 67
  D.W. (Mrs.), 66
  J.W., 120
  Margaret Unetty, 66
  T. Jeff, 231
McELMOYLE, 148
McELRATH
  J.N. (Mrs.), 175
McELWANE
  Scipio, 147
McFALL (McFALLS), 160, 265, 313
McFALL
  A.C., 177
  Andrew, 214
  Carrie, 214
  Frank, 258, 265
  Ivy, 279
  J.S., 177
  John (Capt.), 177
  Mary, 257
  May, 264, 292, 310
  Miss, 232
  Ora, 265, 293, 310
  Sarah, 59
  W.T., 104, 141, 143, 276, 279, 281, 303
  W.T. (Mr. & Mrs.), 224, 290
  Waddy Mauldin, 290
McFARMERS, 304
McGAHA
  William, 187
McGEE
  Earle, 307
  Mike (Rev.), 167
  Tillman, 218
McGILL
  Ansil, 187
McGOWAN
  Lucia, 151

Samuel (Judge), 151
W.G., 151
McGRAW
  Ella, 147
McGREGOR
  G.T., 184
  Mrs., 97
McGUIRE
  Hunter H. (Dr.), 219
McHUGH
  Fay, 292
  Lela, 256
  Margaret, 256
  Olivia, 289
McIVER
  Henry (Justice), 300
McJAMESON, 2
McJUNKIN
  Daniel (Mr. & Mrs.), 246
  Joe (Rev.), 147
  Lillie, 227
  S.B., 187
  Will, 133
McKEE
  Perry, 54
McKENZIE (McKINZIE)
  B.F., 187, 237
  Emaline, 166
  Frank E., 74
  W.C., 187, 237
McKINLEY, 118, 119
McKINLEY
  Mrs., 169
  President, 133, 169, 252, 253, 255
McKINNEY
  Chaney, 295
  H.E. (Miss), 90
  Mary, 1
  Thomas, 131
  Tom, 132
  William, 244
McKISSICK
  E.M. (Rev.), 1, 11
McLAURIN, 241
McLAURIN
  Senator, 248
McMAHAN
  Cleo, 82
  J.J., 288
  Jay, 267
  Thomas A., 175
McNAMIRE
  E.M. (Mrs.), 80

McNEALEY (McNEELY)
  J.R., 140
  Maud, 219
McPHAIL
  May, 24
McSWEAR'GTON
  John, 187
McSWEENEY
  M.B., 109, 238
McTINDALL
  John, 213
McWHORTER
  B.W., 88, 196
  Eliza, 36
  G.L., 82
  Gideon, 277
  Harriett, 277
  J.A., 22, 55, 75
  Janie, 34
  Mr., 105
  S.C., 234, 300
  S. Cherry, 88
  W.B. (N.P.), 240
  W.W. (Mr. & Mrs.), 229
  W.W. (Mrs.), 283
  William, 277
MEACHAM
  John (Capt. & Mrs.), 99
  Maude, 99
MEARES (MEARS)
  Ella, 30, 55, 64, 206
  John, 4, 182
  W.T., 105, 166, 181
MEDD
  T.H. (Rev.), 263, 272
  Thomas H. (Rev.), 252, 262, 291
MEDLIN
  Berry, 107
  Jake, 244
  James, 170
  John, 187, 273
  Mamie, 69
  Nix, 33
  S., 69
  S.H., 207
  Sarah, 207
  Sloan (Mr. & Mrs.), 221
  V.S., 99, 146
  V.S. (Mr. & Mrs.), 199
  Willie, 79
MEETZE (METTS)
  Henry, 261
  W.K., 191

MEMORIAL DAY, 140
MENDENHALL
  J.K. (Rev.), 108
MERCK, 160
MERCK
  Emma, 208
  Jacob, 114
  Jake (Mr. & Mrs.), 144
  Julia, 63
  Lawrence, 172
  Major, 80
  Trial Justice, 63
  W.K., 1, 63, 80, 81, 114, 140, 157, 191
MERIDITH
  D.C., 187
MERRILL
  J.B., 184
METHODIST CONFERENCE, 170
MICHEL
  Marie H., 24
MILES, 3
MILES
  Frank, 54
  Margaret, 123
  Zim, 230
MILITARY
  Army Regiments, 180
  Negro Regiments, 173
  Orr's Regiment, 263
  Sixth S.C. Regt., 277
  South Carolina, 182
  South Carolina Cavalry, 246
  South Carolina Infantry, 252
  U.S. Army, 272
MILLER
  Anna E., 102
  Boyce, 190
  C.T., 28, 46, 49, 83, 87, 100, 102, 128, 158, 185, 207, 217, 242, 243, 255, 286
  Clark, 83
  Clark T., 243
  Constable, 267
  DeForest, 133
  E.R.B., 1
  Earle, 248, 283
  Ella, 176
  H.C., 218
  Henry, 8, 101
  Henry (Mrs.), 109

Henry C., 184
Irvin, 101, 123, 175
J.N., 24
James, 111
Jesse, 148
Joel H. (Hon. & Mrs.), 263, 269
John I., 243
Lavina, 20
Lillian Emily, 269
Mrs., 272
R.E. (Prof.), 190
R. Earle, 215
Ruth Fredonia Holland, 263
Sarah C., 188
Texie, 138
Thomas A., 8
Tillmon, 188
W.A., 38
Wylie, 182

MILLFORD
Charley, 312

MILLIKIN
Julius, 178

MILLS
Cane, 30, 112,
Clifton, 136
Corn, 231
Daniel, 99, 109, 112
Eugene, 132
Farmer, 48
Flour, 91
Griffin-Smith, 110
Grist, 157
Hagood, 36
Hagood, J.E., 85
Hunter, 258
Liberty, 238
Matilda, 109
Newry, 31, 69
Parson, F.C., 111
Phillips, 48
Pickens Oil, 72
Porter, 85
Rackley, 129
Saw, 218
Shingle, 121
Six Mile Creek, 48

MINER
J.J. (Rev.), 196

MITCHELL
A. (Mr. & Mrs.), 252, 286
A.R. (Rev.), 308
J. Frank, 286

MONK
Alonzo (Rev.), 289

MONROE DOCTRINE, 84

MONTAGUE
Andrew P. (Prof.), 154

MONTGOMERY
Ben, 293

MOODY
F.M., 187
F.N., 75
Janie, 141, 254
Newton, 254
Rachel, 50

MOON
A.A. (Mrs.), 277
Allgood, 81
George E., 73
J.L., 294
Jeff, 150
R.K., 279, 290
Ross (Mr. & Mrs.), 204

MOONEY
B., 77

MOORE, 66

MOORE
B.P. (Rev.), 270
Benjamin P., 67
Bill, 38
Childs, 258
Dorcas, 6, 282
Fannie, 151, 171
Florence, 6, 64
Frank, 241
G.B., 142, 308
George E., 76
J.A., 38
J.D., 142, 157, 217
J.H., 156
J.P. (Rev.), 257
James A., 260
James O., 177
James V., 278
Joicie J., 236
Lettie, 88
Lou, 140, 141
M.D. (Miss), 308
Madalene, 6
Mr., 292
Mrs., 45
Prof., 150
Robert, 44
T.H., 88, 92, 111, 124
T.H. (Mr. & Mrs.), 64
W.B., 1

W.H. (N.P.), 77
MORAN
  Mr., 83
MORGAN
  Abbie, 250
  B.A., 4, 36, 54, 85
  B.F., 36, 85, 118, 119
  B.F. (Mrs.), 10
  Davis, 28
  Frank, 290
  H.N., 91
  Hannah, 182
  J.D., 31, 46, 290
  J.H., 36, 118, 119,
    156, 161
  J.J., 85, 87, 118, 119,
    168
  J.J. (Dr. & Mrs.), 22
  J.N. (Mrs.), 86
  James H., 85
  Jeff, 290
  Jeptha Norton, 36
  John, 100
  M.A., 36, 85
  M.M. (Mrs.), 36, 85, 87
  Martha, 80
  Mattie Mae, 298
  Minnie Eva, 36
  Plantation, 118, 119
  Robert F., 290
  Stallions, 137
MORGAN & BLASSINGAME, 107
MORGAN & ROBINSON, 50
MORHORN
  Effie, 145
  Sam, 145
MOROSO
  Alice, 24
  Bettie, 24
  John A., 71
MORRIS, 134
MORRIS
  A.M., 108, 120, 128,
    143, 161, 260, 280, 308
  Aaron, 110
  Clifford, 257
  Dessie, 254
  Edgar, 258, 265, 293, 310
  F.M., 52, 53, 73, 169,
    170, 254
  F.M. & Co., 42, 52
  Furman, 293, 310
  George, 252
  Inez, 257, 292, 310
  Jesse, 67
  Margaret Unetty, 66
MORRISON
  Miss, 301
MORROW, 214, 220, 280, 310
MORTON
  T. Jackson, 186
MOSELEY (MOSELY)
  Alfred J., 44
  Bailey B., 47
  Hartwell R. (Rev.), 24
  Mattie, 66
  Naomi, 144
  Wiley, 16
MOSER
  E.J., 5
  G.W., 5
MOSS
  Eugenia, 41
  Helen, 234
  James (Prof.), 234
  Miles, 230
  Mrs., 182
MOUNCE
  J.H., 113
MOVING PICTURES, 224
MULL
  Mr., 132
MULLIKIN
  Sallie, 27, 245
MULLINAX (MULLINIX)
  E.J. (Rev.), 264
  J.A., 98, 100
  J.E., 127
  J.L. (Rev.), 68
  Mamie, 254
  Martha, 126
  Ola, 100
  Walter, 127
  William, 179
MUNECH
  F. (Prof.), 64, 65, 67
MURFF
  Charlotte, 30
MURPHREE (MURFREE)
  A.E. (Miss), 239
  B.F. (Rev.), 3, 10, 23,
    55, 56, 88, 190, 217,
    229, 266, 269, 284, 298
  B.T., 15
  David B., 288
  E.B., 307
  Forest, 37
  J.L., 85, 108

J.L. (Mrs.), 107
J.N., 21, 307
John, 239
Joseph H., 174
Joseph T., 195
Mary, 127, 261
Mary M., 223
McD., 121
Myra, 171
Nannie, 172
W.M., 153
W.M. (Mr. & Mrs.), 200
MURPHY
  B.F. (Rev.), 289
  J.N., 61
  Mrs., 125
MURRY
  E.B. (Maj.), 21
MUSTER GROUNDS
  Old Battalion, 52
  Pickensville, 257
NABORS
  G.W., 242
  Katie, 242
  Zilphy, 274
NALLEY, 126, 143
NALLEY
  Bud, 88
  Catherine, 220
  Edward, 165
  Eva E., 231
  George (Rev.), 144
  J.L., 98
  John, 220
  Joseph, 113, 155, 187
  Milton, 98
  Mrs., 53
  W.T., 53
  W.T. (Mr. & Mrs.), 212
  W.W.T., 231
  William (Mr. & Mrs.), 164
NASH
  J.M., 175
  Mr., 160
NATIONAL SURGICAL INSTITUTE, 279
NEAL
  A.M., 31
  Eva, 294
  Florence, 169
  Roy, 310
  Sammit, 186
  Samuel, 71, 169
  W.A., 147, 185, 240, 260

NEAL & NEWELL, 240
NEALEY (NEELY)
  Bart (Mr. & Mrs.), 188
  Hovey (Mr. & Mrs.), 285
NEELSON
  Susie, 118
NEELY
  Octave, 153
NEGROES
  Burning at Stake, 235
  Greenville, 179
  Regiments, 173
  Smallpox, 302
  South Carolina, 60
  Superstitions, 286
  Teacher's Association, 266
NEIGHBORS
  Adeline, 234
  Evsie, 180
  Nancy, 205
NELSON
  Farm, 58
  Sallie, 35
  T.F., 37, 187, 213, 225, 261
  T.F. (Mrs.), 62
NESBITT, 156
NESBITT
  Will, 161
NEUFFER
  Annie Hemphill, 182
NEWBERRY
  J.B., 30, 80, 277, 282
  Judge, 197
  Stella, 45, 188, 277
NEWELL, 240
NEWELL
  A.T., 180, 260
NEWSPAPERS
  Abbeville Medium, 182
  Abbeville Press & Banner, 91
  Anderson Daily Mail, 218, 224, 225
  Anderson Intelligencer, 69, 151, 198, 254
  Anderson Journal, 135
  Anderson People's Advocate, 14, 25, 70, 84, 142, 172, 175, 212
  Atlanta Journal, 72
  Baptist Courier, 22, 135
  Boston Herald, 17
  Brevard Hustler, 106

Brevard News, 85, 103
Carolina Spartan, 64
Carolinian, 105
Central Tyro, 18, 34
Charleston Sun, 130
Clemson College Chronicle, 279
Columbia Register, 30, 44
Columbia State, 159, 301
Cotton Plant, 157
Daily News, 27, 181
Daily Record, 139
Democrat, 210
Easley Democrat, 13, 23
Easley Messenger, 63, 66, 70, 73, 76
Easley News, 236, 237
Easley Progress, 287
Evening Telegraph, 237
Greenville Mountaineer, 24, 67, 141, 161, 222, 278
Greenville News, 6, 22, 30, 36, 44, 46, 50, 60, 61, 62, 65, 71, 72, 74, 75, 78, 125, 128, 129, 130, 131, 134, 158, 161, 164, 177, 179, 201, 214, 225, 226, 235, 247, 256, 283, 284
Hampton Guardian, 158
Journal, 17, 27, 34, 139, 156, 247
Keowee Courier, 4, 20, 73, 86, 93, 159, 223, 224, 226, 232, 235, 302
Kershaw New Era, 99
Marlboro Democrat, 3
News and Courier, 62, 71, 115, 169, 222, 299
News and Observer, 8
Observer, 81, 210
Oconee News, 33, 52, 130, 135, 152, 154, 177, 178, 183, 218, 226
Pelzer Herald, 140
People's Journal, 23, 61, 86, 125, 133, 200, 225, 228, 230, 265
Pickens Sentinel, 22, 66, 116, 134, 141, 229, 232, 302, 313
Piedmont Headlights, 225
Piedmont Sun-Herald, 114, 210
Progress, 207
Rutherford Herald, 15
San Antonio Daily Express, 160
Seneca News, 262
Southern Christian Advocate, 264
Spartanburg Herald, 15, 159
State, 130
Sylvan Valley News, 131
Times, 206
The Truth, 239
Westminster Banner, 3
York Enquirer, 301
NEWTON
C. Earle, 26
Carlisle, 303
Clayton, 158, 176
Corinne, 258, 293
G.H., 38
Herbert, 257
Hubert (Mr. & Mrs.), 243
I.T. (Rev.), 183
J.C.C., 4, 22
J.H., 42, 46, 143
John H., 303
Judge, 299
Julius R. (Mrs.), 303
Lettie, 4
Lois, 258, 293
Marion, 303
Olive, 214
Olivia, 118
S.B., 63
NICE
Juda, 52
NICHOLSON
Allen, 207
NIELD
Charles M., 73
NIMMONS
Annie, 112, 262
Hester, 126
Isaac (Mrs.), 279
Jas., 167
L.A., 41
Lawrence, 262
Martha, 279
N.E. (Mrs.), 279
Unity, 285
W.E., 61, 126
W.E. (Mr. & Mrs.), 262

W.P., 262
Wash, 284
William, 77, 126
NINETY-SIX, 314
NIX
    Amanda, 191
    Harriet, 142
    Henry (Mrs.), 216
    Henry W., 119
    J.B., 270
    Jasper, 78
    John, 172
    Julia, 116
    Margaret, 258
    Miss, 78
    Mrs., 272
    W.D. (Mr. & Mrs.), 191
    William, 187
NORRIS
    D.K., 174, 309
    Factory, 95
    J.A., 118
    James W., 181
    Kate, 225
    Mary, 52, 101, 155
    Thomas, 128
    W.T., 155
    Will, 118
    William, 128
NORTH CAROLINA
    Veterans, 103
NORTHROP
    Lucien B. (Gen.), 8
NORTHWESTERN YEAST CO., 93
NORTON, 251
NORTON
    J.J., 104
    Joseph, 10
    Sally, 10
NORWOOD
    J.W., 188, 265
    W.M. (Dr.), 190
NYE
    Bill, 89
O'BRIEN (O'BRYAN)
    Mrs., 227
    Timothy, 227, 247
O'BRYANT
    J.T., 186
O'DELL, 281
O'DELL
    A., 9, 209
    Abner, 289, 290
    Calvin, 194, 195

F.V., 218
Hendricks, 112
J.C., 8, 290
J.P., 188, 218
J.S., 20, 90, 111, 290
J.S. (Mrs.), 97
John C., 209
L.B., 218
M.A., 218
Mary, 194
Mary Ann, 195
Prof., 275
Ross, 172, 180
S.W., 8, 25, 33, 75
S.W. (Mr. & Mrs.), 189
Senator, 8, 123
W.C., 125
W.T., 154, 215, 283
Wade, 123
Wyatt, 9
O'HANLON
    Prof., 10, 12, 18
O'NEAL
    E.B. (Mrs.), 189
    Laura Hagood, 289
    Mrs., 301
OATES (OATS), 167
OATES (OATS)
    J.E., 167
    Jasper, 167, 168
    Mary, 163
    Mary A., 146
    N., 146
    Newton, 152, 162, 163
    Policeman, 267
    Rufus, 152, 163
    S.G. (Mrs.), 62, 64
    Sallie G., 117
    Sam (Mr. & Mrs.), 269
    W.R., 64, 168
    William R., 62
OCONEE COUNTY
    Dead Town, 148
    Election News, 25
    Officers, 130
ODIORNE
    H.L. (Mrs.), 177
OGLESBY
    Mattie, 225
OIL MILLS
    Liberty, 59, 66, 92,
        110, 144
OLD STONE CHURCH, 114, 141,
    256

OLD STONE CHURCH
   Commission, 175
   Memorial Service, 238, 239
OLIVE & Co., 300
OLIVER (OLLIVER)
   Dr., 134
   Jane E., 134
   Lou, 134
   R.E., 175
   R.E. (Mr. & Mrs.), 200, 243
   Ralph, 304
   W.A. (Mr. & Mrs.), 269
   W.J. (Mrs.), 304
   W.J. & Co., 187
OMBERG
   Ava Stodes, 57
   Sue Gregory, 57
OPTOGRAPH, 224
ORDWAY
   D.P. (Mrs.), 97
ORN
   Jay, 289
ORPHANAGES
   Jennings, 7
   Thornwell, 34, 109, 302
ORR
   David, 268
   L.P. (Mr. & Mrs.), 19
   Lee P., 11, 14, 15, 17, 31, 35
   Leo Hartwell, 19
   S.A.R. (Mrs.), 103, 163
   W.W., 81, 103, 163
ORR'S REGIMENT, 263
OSBORNE
   Lula, 106
   T. (Rev.), 181
   W.K., 106
OSBY
   William, 47
OSWALD
   G.D. (Mrs.), 147
OWENS, 84
OWENS (OWINGS)
   Charles, 200
   Durod, 121
   Emma, 12
   G.W., 187
   J.A., 128
   J.E., 95
   J.L., 66
   John (Rev.), 3
   Leigh, 100
   Lida, 153, 168, 171
   Mamie, 184
   Mrs., 275
   Ora, 264
   Robert, 222, 264
   Sally, 34
   Thomas, 184
   William, 115, 224
PACE
   Alonzo, J.L., 29
   Annie, 12, 13
   Ben, 219
   Benjamin (Mr. & Mrs.), 245
   Berry (Mr. & Mrs.), 247
   Cora, 219
   D.F., 196
   Darcus, 86
   Emma, 163
   Frank, 91
   Furman, 292
   Hattie, 250
   J.W., 152
   Jeff, 269
   Joe (Mr. & Mrs.), 219
   Joseph, 13
   Joseph (Mr. & Mrs.), 170
   Lafayette, 86, 250
   Lawrence, 270
   Myrtie, 211
   Nora, 263
   Sunie, 170
   W.E., 105
PAGET
   James Manchester, 198
PALACE CAR MANUFACTURER, 161
PALMER, 53
PALMER
   Jerome (Mr. & Mrs.), 220
   W.A., 7, 30, 146, 150
   Whit, 245
PALMETTO GLEANINGS, 298, 299, 300, 310, 311, 312
PARADISE
   Article, 276
PARIS MOUNTAIN, 64
PARK
   A.K., 8
PARK & JONES, 8
PARKINS
   C.H., 3, 13, 92
   Thomas (Mrs.), 189
PARROTT (PARRETT)
   David, 38
   J.S., 230

Mamie, 38
Martha, 12
Narnada, 68
William, 37
William H., 253
PARSON (PARSONS), 136
PARSON (PARSONS)
　Andrew (Mrs.), 101
　B.F., 2, 26, 39, 43, 87,
　　245, 255, 262
　Ben F., 278
　Benjamin, 196
　Bros., 133
　Coroner, 245
　Daisy M., 285
　F.C., 21, 30, 111, 112
　Hannah, 196
　J.C.C., 15
　J.E., 99, 143
　J.E. (Mr. & Mrs.), 237
　James L., 267
　Job L., 172
　Julius, 187
　Julius E., 111, 214, 304
　Julius Joel, 214
　Lillie, 214
　Mamie, 255
　Marshall, 267
　N.C. "Doc", 288
　Nettie, 6
　Tunis, 6
　W.A., 113
　W.H., 81
　W.S., 43, 92, 180
　William S., 213
　Willie, 6, 180
PARTRIDGE
　Trope, 213
PATENT
　Rotary Engine, 248
PATRICK
　John M. (Capt.), 275
　Talley, 158
PATRIOTS
　Piedmont Area, 101
PATTERSON
　Elizabeth, 140
　Mrs., 232
　W.E., 103
PAYNE
　J.H., 93, 296
　J.H. (Mr. & Mrs.), 38
　Place, 123
　W.N. (Mrs.), 121

Willie, 38
PEA RIDGE
　Article, 276
PEABODY SCHOLARSHIP, 98
PEARSON
　Mary E., 76
PEEK
　James, 26, 37
PELFREY
　C., 80
　Minnie, 254
　Thomas, 254
PELUM
　B.A. (Mrs.), 233
PELZER COMPANY, 30
PENDLETON
　Memorial Day, 100
　"Old", 295
PENDLETON DISTRICT
　90 Years Ago, 98, 100
PENDLY
　A.J., 212
PENSION BOUNTY, 304
PENSION LAWS, 93, 300, 306
PENSIONERS, 282
PENSIONS
　Ex-Slaves, 179
PEOPLE'S JOURNAL, 61
PEOPLE'S JOURNAL
　Editor, 200
PERKINS, 39
PERKINS
　Corrie, 227
PERRITT (PERRIT), 181
PERRITT (PERRIT)
　Andrew L., 71
　Andrew P., 47
　John, 69
　John P., 71
PERRY
　Bennett, 112
　Capt., 12, 27
　Elbert E., 229
　Fannie, 62
　Ira, 277
　J.M., 307
　John, 172
　Joseph (Mrs.), 287
　Lucia, 229
　Robert (Mr. & Mrs.), 283
　S.J., 112
　S.M., 112, 186
　Samuel A., 202
　W.A., 88

W.H., 62, 187
W.H. (Mr. & Mrs.), 183
William, 37
PETERSON
Tom, 77
PETSCHE
A.H. (Mr. & Mrs.), 24
PETTIGREW
Constable, 60
T.B., 90
PHILLIPS (PHILIPS)
Guy, 82
J.M., 169
Louis (Mrs.), 20
Mattie, 133
R.W., 187
W.P., 82
Wig, 13
William W., 13
PHILPOT
I.H., 4, 176, 186
Lou, 49
Lou M., 25
Minnie Virginia, 176
PHOTOGRAPH
Gallery, 17
PHOTOGRAPHERS, 244
PHOTOGRAPHERS
Henderson, Mr., 124
Kennemur, E.F., 139
Taylor, N.D., 280, 314
PHOTOGRAPHY
Taylor Studio, 280
PICKENS
Andrew (Gen.), 141
J.A. (Mrs.), 233
Maggie, 161
W.C., 20
W.H., 86, 152, 256, 306
PICKENS "COLONY"
Alabama, 53
PICKEN COUNTY
Administrator's Sale, 175
Assignee's Sale, 265
Auditor's Notice, 229
Board of Assessors, 9
Board of Commissioners,
 45, 59, 133
Board of Trustees, 42
Business, 291
Canidates, 24
Chain Gang, 310
Church Directory, 237, 268

Citaion Notices, 16, 31,
 42, 49, 58, 60, 101,
 103, 108, 112, 113, 117,
 118, 126, 132, 135, 137,
 138, 146, 149, 150, 163,
 168, 175, 188, 195, 203,
 204, 211, 216, 220, 235,
 238, 241, 253, 257, 259,
 275, 284, 289, 292, 295,
 303, 304, 307, 309
Clerk of Court, 56
Clerk's Sale, 31, 33, 36,
 42, 52, 73, 80, 96, 115,
 118, 119, 155, 156, 157,
 162, 163, 179, 198, 204,
 209, 222, 256, 260, 276,
 293, 295, 297
Commissioner's
 Expenditures, 294
Commissioner's Meeting,
 61, 69, 81, 83, 99, 130,
 137, 138, 142, 146, 149,
 153, 163
Commissioner's Report, 272
Commissioner's Sale, 280
Commissioner's Township,
 48, 135
Commissioners, 13, 32, 51
Commissioners of
 Elections, 32, 61, 62
Comutation Tax, 80
Convention, 98
Court, 60
Court Actions, 107
Court Cases, 68, 117, 134,
 178
Court House, 59, 61, 163
Court of Common Pleas, 18,
 19, 42, 56, 59, 91, 110,
 136, 152, 153, 176, 212,
 213, 222, 233, 250, 251,
 262, 307, 313
Court of General Session,
 21, 67, 106, 133, 189,
 198, 208, 215, 220, 221
Court Proceedings, 21, 47,
 48, 235, 258, 287, 311,
 312
Court Records, 29, 42, 59,
 90
Court Sessions, 10
Court Sessions Report, 161
Criminal Cases, 117

Democratic Convention, 22, 283
Democratic Exec. Committee, 59
Disbursements, 288
Election, 61
Election Managers, 33, 115, 220
Election Notice, 61
Election Primary, 62
Election Returns, 24, 26, 289
Elections State, 33
Executive Committee, 107, 108, 109, 151
Executor's Sale, 35, 83, 108, 122, 137, 140, 259, 260, 296, 299
Final Setlement, 7, 13, 15, 26, 27, 44, 47, 52, 68, 88, 121, 122, 126, 145, 154, 155, 156, 163, 181, 183, 192, 196, 203, 206, 215, 218, 229, 237, 242, 247, 251, 254, 264, 267, 274, 291, 294, 296, 313
Foreclosure Sales, 250
Government Laws, 179
Grand Jury Report, 29, 48, 294, 312
Growth, 310
Guardianship Settlement, 242
Guardianships, 54, 121
Gypsies, 138
History, 252, 253
Homestead Exemption, 62, 66, 184, 228
Indians, 194
Jail, 144, 163, 286, 287
Jury, 47
Jury List, 9, 20, 25, 27, 49, 59, 66, 88, 105, 115, 131, 146, 159, 160, 234, 256, 293, 309
Land Agency, 152
Land Co., 165
Land Owned, 280
Land Sales, 42
Magistrates - Appointments, 133
Military Co., 63
Militia, 14, 84

Mortagee's Sales, 42, 91, 93, 126
Muster Grounds, 52
Notice, Debtors & Creditors, 25, 26, 33, 109, 137, 153, 157, 162, 165, 172, 173, 179, 184, 187, 193, 195, 228, 229, 253, 255, 260, 291, 294, 295
Old Court House, 15
Opportunities, 305
Pension Rolls, 186
Petit Jury List, 47, 145, 188, 196, 246
Poor Farm, 247, 291
Poor House, 49, 104, 243
Population, 232
Portable Caravansary, 310
Probate Court, 258
Probate Office, 45
Probate Sale, 80, 122, 295
Progress, 73
Public Well, 22
Real Estate Sales, 117
Salesday, 30, 35, 39, 46, 73, 76, 83, 143, 161, 167, 171, 188, 308
Schools, 174
Senate Seat Campaign, 149
Sheriff's Sale, 13, 27, 31, 36, 51, 66, 86, 102, 103, 118, 120, 136, 159, 162, 173, 182, 185, 198, 221, 222, 256, 260, 265, 288, 295, 297
Smallpox, 301
Supervisor's Cabinet, 65
Supervisor's Meeting, 110
Supervisor's Report, 66, 114
Tax Assessment, 2, 43, 121
Tax Assessment Notice, 30, 37, 69, 165, 167
Tax Assessors, 50
Tax Execution Sale, 141, 192
Tax Notice, 113, 119, 126
Tax Sale, 240
Teachers, 286
Town of Pickens, 276
Treasurer, 236, 311
Treasurer's Report, 19, 20, 57, 299

Voter Registration, 54, 97
Voting Boxes, 286
PICKENS, S.C., 232
PICKENS, S.C.
   Bending Factory, 215
   Elections, 313
   Mail Carrier, 22
   Military Co., 15
   "Old", 290
   Post Office, 163
   R.R. Timetable, 284
   Rifles, 47, 53, 54, 55, 65, 135, 144, 154, 163
   Social Life, 299
   Street Lights, 259
   Town Improvements, 13
PICKENSVILLE, 211
PICKENSVILLE
   Muster, 257
PICKLE, 45
PICKLE (PICKEL)
   J.A., 200
   Jacob A., 182
   William, 104
PICKRELL
   Jonathan, 225
   Mary B., 225
PICTURES
   President's Tombstones, 311
PIEDMONT
   Early Days, 114
   Region, 101
   Reigon Name, 243
PILGRIM
   Eliza, 110
   Harlston, 20
   William H., 45
PINKNEY
   Thomas (Gen.), 141
PINSON
   Moses, 201
   W.E., 66
PIONEERS AND HEROES, 175
PITMAN
   Arcis, 141
   Samuel, 141
PITTS
   Ruben S., 308
   Will (Mr. & Mrs.), 117
PLUME
   Emily, 158, 169

PLUMMER
   D.R., 95
PODER
   W.M., 104
PONDER, 53
PONDER
   Honest, 116
   J.M. (Dr.), 228
   Milton, 115
   N.F. (Mrs.), 220
   W.J., 108, 116, 235
   William J., 129
   William J. (Mrs.), 45
POOL
   Sarah, 208
POOR FARM, 212, 291
POOR HOUSE, 49, 213, 243
PORCHER
   Rev., 74
PORTER, 85
PORTER
   Alice, 259
   Anna, 7
   Arthur, 105
   Auther, 39
   B.S., 16, 26, 31, 36, 42
   Barnett (Mr. & Mrs.), 194
   D.F.S., 107
   David, 36, 39, 42
   Davis (Mr. & Mrs.), 259
   David E., 143
   E.R., 7
   E.S. "Doc" (Mr. & Mrs.), 257
   Emma, 140
   F.S. (Dr.), 93, 97
   Fletcher S. (Dr.), 90
   Frank (Mr. & Mrs.), 154
   George B., 226
   J.A., 178
   J.M. (Esq.), 7
   J.S. (Rev.), 176, 177
   James H., 250, 265
   Janie, 269
   John, 306
   John P., 42
   L.D. (Miss), 166
   Lidie, 111
   Lizzie, 7, 35
   Lucinda, 7
   Martha Jane, 91
   Mary, 269
   Mrs., 198
   Nettie, 264

P.A., 36, 39, 42, 45,
R.F., 266
Rev., 313
S.A.S., 52, 248
Sarah Gravely, 221
Smith, 198, 203, 269
Smith (Mr. & Mrs.), 222, 274
Thomas, 228
Thomas (Mr. & Mrs.), 265
W.C., 269

POSEY
  T.H. (Rev.), 285

POSSUM RIDGE, 133

POST OFFICES
  Ambler, 161
  Burdine's, 14
  Clement, 92, 140
  Crow Creek, 245
  Eastatoe, S.C., 272
  Farris, S.C., 43
  Goodwin, S.C., 43
  Hale, 245
  Masonic Hall, 16
  Nine Times, 166
  Olga, 156, 273
  Pearl, 127
  Pickens, 115, 163, 250
  Porter, 141
  Spencer, 256
  Thomas' Store, 17
  White's, 14, 154

POSTMASTERS
  Alexander, S.C., 278
  Brown, Nancy C., 127
  Easley, 142
  Ensor, Joshua F., 144
  Folger, A.M., 142
  Foster, Millie, 273
  Foster, R.M. (Mrs.), 273
  Freeman, Robert P., 140
  Greenville, 301
  Metts, W.F., 15
  Olga, 156
  Smith, J. Theodore, 14
  Spencer, Nena, 43
  Stewart, Robert, 278
  Summey, W.H., 43
  Thompkins, Alice, 15
  White, James W., 14

POTTER
  T.C. (Rev.), 238

POTTERY BUSINESS, 88

POTTERY MAKERS
  Adkins, George, 280
  Farmer, B.F., 280
  Finley, J.B., 280
  Wimpey, L.T., 59, 280

POTTS
  Charles P., 174

POWELL (POWEL)
  Angeline, 260
  B.S., 266
  Clingman, 313
  George W., 11
  Jeremiah, 13
  S.F. (Miss), 18
  Thomas, 237

POWERS, 208,

POWERS (POWER)
  C.A., 161
  William K., 192

PRATHER
  John, 242

PRESIDENT U.S.A.
  Message, 76, 122

PRESSLEY (PRESLEY)
  B.M., 187
  Harry, 6
  J.L., 91
  John G. (Hon.), 62
  Lee, 95
  Mr., 151
  Nancy, 228
  Rosa, 267

PRICE, 60

PRICE
  Anna, 307
  Crayton, 53
  E.A. (Sgt.), 212
  Elizabeth, 121
  Ella, 273
  H.A., 215
  Hardin, 121
  J.C., 51
  J.S.H., 56
  James, 12
  Jane, 185
  Mandy, 12
  Perrin (Mr. & Mrs.), 217, 269
  Snider, 50
  Squire, 46
  T.R. (Mrs.), 53
  Thomas R., 87
  W., 10

W.R., 13, 42, 50, 53, 136, 307
  William R., 273
PRICHARD
  W.L. (Mr. & Mrs.), 206
  Wyatt, 206
PRINCE
  E.J., 5, 110
  G.E. (Hon.), 288
  George, 257, 264, 292, 310
  Grace, 257, 264, 292, 310
  Ida Maggie, 260
  Jere, 40
  Laura, 260
  Lila, 40
  Marcus, 260
  Marcus (Mr. & Mrs.), 192
  Mark, 5
  Mr., 233
  N.J., 236
  Ossie Walton, 236
  R.P. (Mr. & Mrs.), 236
  W.L., 288
  W.M., 161
PRITCHARD
  Gertrude, 18
  M. (Mrs.), 307
  W.L., 307
  W.L. (Mr. & Mrs.), 18
PROHIBITION, 64
PRYOR
  S.T., 5
PUBLISHING CO., 119
PULLMAN, 301
PULLMAN
  George M., 161
QUARLES
  Ira, 27
  John, 27
QUARRY
  Beverly, 111, 119, 162, 300, 301
  Union Rock, 90
QUILLION
  J.W. (Mrs.), 272
RABINSON
  Charlie, 268
RABORN
  J.H., 10
RACKLEY, 129
RACKLEY
  Andrew, 67
  Betsy, 51
  Elizabeth, 51, 81
  Missouri, 293
  Reden, 168, 171
  William, 101
RAGSDALE
  Charles (Mr. & Mrs.), 286
  Mr., 147
RAILROADS, 154
RAILROADS
  Agents, 55, 90, 136
  Air Line, 85
  Atlanta & New York Express, 229
  Columbia & Greenville, 10
  Conductor, 175, 285
  Cross Blue Ridge, 290
  Depot, 105, 107
  Dining Cars, 309
  E.T.V. & G., 49
  Elberton Air Line, 240
  Old South Carolina, 187, 198
  Pickens, 73, 136, 187, 282, 303, 312,
  Pickens Timetable, 284
  Seaboard Air Line, 145
  Service, 312
  Shops-Birmingham, 188
  Southern, 24, 50, 65, 73, 89, 103, 152, 165, 169, 229, 260, 268, 285, 289, 295, 300, 306, 309
  Southern Depot, 85
  Travel Library, 279
RAINES
  Baswell, 93
  Bettie Boyd, 168
  C. Arthur, 24
  Elias (N.P.), 105
  J.H., 187
  James, 23, 24, 32, 33, 34, 156, 168
  James (Mrs.), 20, 156
  Nora, 227
  R.E., 187
  Riley, 192
  Stephen R., 131
  W.A., 227
RAMPEY
  Arthur, 299
  J.M., 17, 87
  J. Matt, 96
  Jannah, 96
  Lillie, 40
  McDuffie (Mrs.), 62

Thomas, 78
W.J., 124
RAMSEY
    Thomas S., 200
RAMSUER
    Nellie, 71
RANDALL
    C. (Mr. & Mrs.), 114
RANKIN
    Thomas, 170
RAY
    Rufus (Prof.), 219, 232
REACH
    R.R., 115
REAL ESTATE
    Hamilton, W.A., 281
REAL ESTATE DEALERS, 308
REAVES
    CYNDA (Aunt), 269
    Josie, 157
    Mary, 63
RECORDS OF THE PAST, 225
REDFEARN
    D.T. (Hon.), 268
REDMOND
    Constable, 90
REED (REID)
    B.P. (Rev.), 175
    Jervey, 212
    Pinkney, 75
    W. (Rev.), 246
REEMS
    Miss, 300
REESE
    D.W., 210
    Marion R., 88
    N.S. (N.P.), 178
    Thomas (Dr.), 175
REEVES
    Allie, 187
    Beckay, 142
    Joseph, 187
    Lee, 232
    Lidia, 260
    Tude, 205
REMBERT
    T.E. (Constable), 90
REPUBLICAN CONVENTION, 103
REVIS
    Hugh (Mr. & Mrs.), 133
REVOLUTIONARY HEROES, 247
REVOLUTIONARY WAR
    Cowpens, 179, 185
    Geiger, Emily, 209

RHODES
    Louisa, 76
    Mamie, 217
RICE
    Jacob, 249
    James (Mrs.), 242
    Jordan, 187, 194, 269
    Malinda, 249
    Mrs., 113, 269
    Ransom, 249
    Rena, 226
RICE CULTIVATION, 288
RICHARDS
    W.L. (Rev.), 170
RICHARDSON
    A.N., 206
    Clark (Dr.), 282
    E.B., 97, 166, 167, 282
    E.B. (Mr. & Mrs.), 261
    Francis, 188
    George, 188
    H. (Mrs.), 55
    Hal (Mrs.), 130
    Hester, 102, 206
    J.H., 312
    James, 23, 29, 130, 168
    Jeff, 301
    John P., 189
    Luther (Mrs.), 251
    Maggie, 185
    Marie, 166
    Marie Antoinette, 261
    Miss, 200
    R.M., 168
    S.L. (Mr. & Mrs.), 223
    W.A., 168
    W.R. (Rev.), 166, 264
    Willie, 223
RICHEY, 160
RICHEY
    Clarence, 246
    Cora, 203
    G.W., 211
    H.A., 23, 62, 143, 144,
        153, 185, 211, 246,
        281
    H.A. (Mr. & Mrs.), 203
    H.A. (Mrs.), 224, 225
    H.A. & Son, 302
    Homer A., 9, 48, 88, 134,
        142
    Homer A., Jr., 302
    Homer Alonzo, 302
    James N., 23

James T., 302
John, 192, 208
John T., 23
Nora, 144
Ola, 265, 293
Ola Belle, 302
Olga, 144, 302
Sadie, 144, 302
W.O., 23
Warren, 23
RIDDLE
George (Mrs.), 193
M.V., 45
Mattie R., 45
Mr., 113
RIGDON
B.E., 268
Hampton, 249
J.B. (Mr. & Mrs.), 219
L.M., 76
Mannie, 219
Matthew, 299
Phillip, 86
Robert, 166
Sarnie, 299
Unity, 125, 254, 274, 284
Vardery, 60
RIGGINS
A.B., 268
A.B. (Mr. & Mrs.), 181
David, 160
Henry, 227
Henry (Mr. & Mrs.), 268
Lycena, 269
Magaret, 268
RIGGS
W.M. (Prof.), 197
RILE
Dr., 10
RILEY
A.B., 60, 136, 190
D.J.R. (Dr.), 139
Dr., 67, 89
Fannie, 60
J.R., 41, 49, 60, 82,
  87, 124, 137, 158,
  159, 165, 171, 172,
  173, 210
John R., 276
Lida, 6
Rev., 175, 313
RIPLEY
Samuel, 99

RIVES
Lily, 23
Mr., 23
ROACH
Bill, 27
ROADS
Road Duty, 280
ROARK, 170
ROARK (ROARKE)
J.L. (Mrs.), 165
Robert R., 308
W.J., 159
ROBERS
J.W. (Mrs.), 313
ROBERTS
J.W. (Mrs.), 311
John T., 208
W.R., 115
ROBERTSON
B.C., 197
B.F., 32, 46, 91, 172
B.F. (Mr. & Mrs.), 255
Benjamin F., 250
Cora, 215
Frankie, 9
Janie, 270
Nannie, 310
S.M., 197
Sam, 172
Thomas J., 159
Thomas L., 250, 269
W.L., 9
Zeila, 169
ROBINS
Alice, 80
Gussie C., 89
J.J. (Mrs.), 80
Mrs., 89
Rosey, 80
ROBINSON, 50
ROBINSON
A., 297
A.P., 95
A.P. (Mr. & Mrs.), 95
Arthur, 97, 205
Arthur (Mr. & Mrs.), 246
Artie, 173
Baylie C., 266
Baylus, 200
Benton, 225
Bessie, 252
Bettie, 71, 189
Bob, 92, 105
Bud, 102

C., Esq., 266
C.E., 1, 24, 27, 35,
   39, 135, 288
C.E. (Mr. & Mrs.), 189
C.T., 113
Charles E., 134, 278
Charles S., 122
Charley, 22
Charlie, 257, 264, 310
Charlie Lang, 229
Corrie, 38
Cynthia A., 261
Darcus P., 198
Dr., 72
E.C. (Mrs.), 159
Ella, 32
Essie, 97
Frankie, 8
G.E. (Dr.), 122
G.W., 53
George, 71, 88
George W.F., 297
H.A. (Mr. & Mrs.), 97
Hattie, 264
Henry, 231
Hettie, 173
Horse Shoe, 291
J.A., 34, 45, 49
J.A. (Mr. & Mrs.), 147
J.B., 35
J.E., 12, 88, 281
J.M., 62
J.P., 264
James A., 261
James Alda, 261
James H., 261
Jay, 293, 310
Joe M., 61
John A. (N.P.), 241
John B., 159
Johnnie, 6
Josie, 5, 25, 51
Lewis F., 79, 148
Louie, 197
Mamie Catherine, 261
May, 113, 227, 231, 288,
   306
Mr. & Mrs., 8
Mrs., 180
Nancy, 266
Nannie, 35
Nettie, 51, 65, 148
Pearcy, 35
Pearl, 6
Percy, 94
R.C., 26, 305
Robert C., 180
Rubie, 95
S.F., 28
Samuel (Mr. & Mrs.), 189
Sarah E., 297
Silas F., 84
T.C., 2, 32, 54, 80,
   117, 164
T. Christie, 298
T.L., 8
Virginia, 248
W.W. (Mr. & Mrs.), 254
Wash (Mr. & Mrs.), 246
ROCHESTER
   A.W., 299
ROE
   Mrs., 69, 170
ROGERS
   Cassandra, 237
   Catherine, 228
   Crecy, 87
   Daniel, 237
   Francis, 87
   Henry, 203, 228
   Ida, 69
   J.D., 203
   Michael, 187
   Michail, 164
   Nathan, 249
   R.J., 203
   R.L. (Rev.), 226
   W.A., 127, 252
   William A., 164
ROOKE
   George, 89
   T.J. (Mrs.), 149
   T.J. (Rev.), 54, 96
ROPER, 88, 167
ROPER
   Absalom, 253
   Absolem, 291
   Addie, 121
   Andrew (Mr. & Mrs.), 273
   Bennie, 147
   Betsy, 66
   Charlie, 260
   Elbert, 188
   Elijah, 150
   Essie, 26
   Field (Mr. & Mrs.), 212
   Frank, 200
   G.W., 187

Hampton, 124
Ira Thomas, 188
J.E., 272
James W., 213
John, 26, 142, 291
Maggie, 3
Marion, 121
Matt, 1
Nannie, 247, 274, 286
Nettie, 272
Rufus, 163
Rufus C., 162
S.C., 152, 163
Sallie, 55
Spencer, 66, 299
Sue, 299
W.O., 81
W.U., 137
Wiley, 202
Will, 245
Wylie, 235
ROSAMOND (ROSEMOND)
  Addie, 45
  Ida, 60
  James, 51
  Jas., 60
  John W., 60
  John W. (Mrs.), 134
  Narcissa, 249
  Rich, 217
  Rich (Mr. & Mrs.), 134
  Richard, 91
  Will, 249
ROSEMAN
  W.R., 76
  Will, 192
ROSS
  J.R., 177, 288, 307
  James, 177
  Jesse, 86
  Jesse Richard, 303
  Maggie, 172
  R.A. (Dr.), 63
ROTARY ENGINE, 248
ROUSE
  Charles B., 77
ROUSHTON
  J.E. (Rev.), 199
ROWE
  Mattie, 282
ROWLAND
  James H., 4, 199
  Jim, 7
  Mrs., 231

Sarah E., 128
W.R., 244
W.T., 18, 128
ROYLSTON
  John, 178
RUNION
  Viola, 296
RUSHTON
  J.E. (Rev.), 178
RUSSELL
  H.E. (Dr.), 51
  H. Earle, 192
RUSSEY
  G.W. (Rev.), 221
RUTLEDGE
  Henry, 61
  William, 263
RYDER
  W.L. (Dr.), 149
SADLER
  Lucy, 225
SALLY
  A.S., Jr., 222
SAMMONS (SAMMON)
  Lee, 64, 105
  Thomas, 286
  W. Lee, 28
SAMS
  Carrie O., 110, 124
SAMSON
  Lee, 30
SANDERS
  Able, 164
  Alfred, 241
  Elisha, 114
  J.E., 53
  J.M. (Rev.), 224
  J.S., 187
  Jack. 171
  Matilda, 10
  Melinda, 53
  Mrs., 171
  Nancy E., 122
  Susan E., 63
  W.H., 53, 116, 118, 122
  Will, 255
SANTA CLAUSE, 122
SARGENT
  J.B. (Mr. & Mrs.), 71
  John (Mr. & Mrs.), 160
  John B., 120
  Lizzie, 71
  Marcus, 71

SATTERFIELD
  Bennett, 172
  Janie, 214
  Lizzie, 172
SCHAID
  J.G. (Rev.), 178
SCHOOLS
  Academy, 154
  Academy Hall, 148
  Aiken Hotel, 258
  Ambler, 7, 29, 125, 254, 274, 285
  Anthony's Fork, 29
  Bethel District, 153
  Bethlehem, 21, 25, 115, 191, 199, 224, 243, 288
  Bethlehem District, 47
  Bishop's Branch, 118, 204
  Bright's Station, 23
  Calhoun, 7, 204
  Camden, 247
  Camp Creek, 181
  Carpenter's Creek, 14, 25
  Carson, 152
  Cateechee, 164, 193, 200, 245
  Cedar Rock, 286, 306
  Centerville, 51
  Central, 291
  Central Graded, 219, 290
  Central High, 136, 150
  Cold Springs, 30
  Cold Springs Summer, 286
  Colored #12, 24
  Columbia, 46
  Commissioners, 85
  Concord, 28, 67
  Crosswell, 190
  Crosswell #1, 6
  Crow Creek, 248
  Dacusville, 48, 83, 224
  Davis Military, 3
  Dayton, 147, 247
  District #32, 29
  Double Springs, 15
  Easley, 46, 250
  Easley Colored, 128
  Easley Cotton Mill, 288
  Easley District, 254
  Easley Graded, 68, 140, 154, 279
  Easley Township, 141
  Eastatoe, 112
  Elgin, Ga., 101
  Factory Hill, 234
  Fairview, 144
  Field, 107
  Gaffney, 124
  Gap Hill, 29, 44
  Garvin, 27, 215
  Garvin District, 190, 299
  Garvin District #24, 306
  Gates, 27
  Gates District, 46
  Glassy Mountain, 12, 180
  Greenville, 78, 306
  Greenville Co., 81
  Greenwood, 313
  Griffin Ebenezer, 158, 243
  Grove, 25, 231
  Hagood, 45, 118, 200, 248, 311
  Hagood District #38, 79, 80, 105
  Hampton, 19, 30, 94, 96
  Hazel, 96
  Hickory Flat, 6
  Holly Bush, 24, 143, 148
  Holly Springs, 44, 306
  Inman, 308
  Johnsonia Female, 248
  Johnston's, 23
  Johnston's Chapel, 78, 118
  Johnston's Chapel Female, 245
  Johnston's Chapel Male, 245
  Keowee, 29, 99, 111, 193, 215
  Keowee Church, 44
  King's, 27, 106
  Lathem, 148, 242, 247
  Lathem Academy, 115
  Lathem District, 85
  Laurens High, 190
  Laws, 101
  Lendhardt, 23, 247, 286
  Liberty, 4, 6, 8, 69, 83, 125, 289, 300
  Liberty Colored, 22
  Liberty High, 132, 138
  Liberty Township, 51
  Liberty White, 22
  Long Branch, 23, 108
  Martin, 29, 193, 215
  Mauldin, 24, 306
  Maynard, 8, 91, 93, 95, 148, 190

Mica, 12, 25, 83, 85, 127
Mile Creek, 28, 215
Mountain Grove, 108
Mt. Tabor, 296
Newton District, 63
Norris, 200, 248, 301
North Greenville Baptist, 48
North Greenville High, 217
Olga, 191, 193, 225
Oolenoy, 25, 136, 147, 190, 227, 233
Oolenoy Academy, 288
Palestine, 206, 226, 248
Parson's Grove, 29
Patrick Military Insitute, 3, 275
Peter's Creek, 200
Pickens, 24, 46, 48, 192, 198, 250, 299
Pickens Colored, 49, 111, 290
Pickens Colored Graded, 279
Pickens Colored High, 207
Pickens County, 174
Pickens Court House, 22
Pickens Graded, 215, 219, 240, 279, 290
Pickens High, 23, 79, 110, 112, 148, 174, 191
Pickens Honor Roll, 257, 264, 292, 309
Pickensville, 22
Piedmont Institute, 278
Pinder, 13
Pleasant Hill, 108
Prater's, 27, 254
Rehoboth, 66
Reunion, 208, 231, 248, 273, 301
Ridge Springs, 78
Roanoke, 12, 25
Roanoke District, 75
Roanoke Public, 294
Roberts, 165
Rock, 149, 277
Rocky Knob, 141
Roseland Academy, 104
Ruhamah, 23, 151
Saluda Hill, 289
Shady Grove, 147
Shoal, 7
Shoal Creek, 27
Shoal Creek Colored, 130
Six Mile, 9, 27, 271, 275
Soapstone, 25, 87
South Carolina, 75
St. Paul, 5
St. Stephens, 24
State Summer, 183
Table Rock, 111
Tabor, 23, 24
Teachers, 255
Three and Twenty, 84
Town Creek, 46, 138, 148, 190, 214, 287, 298
Turner's Hill, 22
Twelve Mile, 29, 51
Twelve Mile Cross Roads, 28
Union, 138
Vineland, 3, 132, 138, 283, 286
Vineland Academy, 133
Walhalla, 234
Walker-McElmoyle, 311
Wannamaker, 240
Westminster High, 108
Winthrop State Normal, 19
Wolf Creek, 27, 63, 147, 199, 215, 223, 262
Wolf Creek Colored, 243
Wolf Creek District, 83, 176
Women's Industrial, 14
Zion, 22, 28, 67, 78, 141
Zion District, 109

SCHULER
F.H. (Rev.), 156
SCOTTY
W.C., 40
SCRUGGS
Butler, 202
SEABOARD AIR LINES, 145
SEABORN
E.M., 75
J.E. (Rev.), 170
J.G., 28, 93
J.H., 270
J.H. (Mr. & Mrs.), 251
James, 147
James G., 67, 99, 111, 149
James G. (Mrs.), 110
James Gaines, 184
Joseph, 149, 158
M.E. (Mrs.), 184
Myrtie, 184

Rev., 283
W.C., 8, 15, 26, 35, 37,
    40, 69, 72, 89, 99,
    119, 120, 127, 137, 147,
    149, 167, 169, 177, 187,
    200, 202, 203, 208, 212,
    213, 227, 236, 261, 267,
    268, 274, 277, 282, 287,
    291, 292, 295, 296, 300,
    307, 308
W.D. (Rev.), 9
SEABROOK
   M.S. (Mrs.), 65
SENECA RIVER
   Flooding, 137
SEWALL
   Arthur, 218
SEWING MACHINES, 281
SEXTON
   John B., 111
SEYMOUR
   R.W. (Rev.), 14
   Robert William, 14
SHACKLEFORD
   G.W. (Rev.), 22
SHAFFER
   G.R., 4, 30, 31, 34, 37,
     38
SHANKLIN
   Edward Henry, 248, 262
   G., 197
SHANNON
   W. M. (Mrs.), 177
SHAW
   George W., 305
SHECK
   Frances A., 152, 168
   John D., 160
   John O., 265
SHELDON
   Dr., 94
   W.A. (Dr.), 74, 76, 130,
     142
   W.H., 37
   Willie, 74
SHELL
   J.W. (Rev.), 170
SHEPPARD, 34, 42
SHEPPARD
   J.A., 152, 155
SHERIFF
   J.W., 173
   J.W. (Mr. & Mrs.), 231
   J.W. (Rev.), 254

Joe, 181
Johnson, 52, 128, 195,
   237, 268
N.J., 254
P.P., 187
W.J., 88, 98, 118, 225
William, 267
SHIELDS
   Lawrence, 50
SHIPMAN
   Emma, 196
   Ida, 183
   M.L., 106
SHIRLEY, 39, 309
SHIRLEY
   H.C., 61, 92, 128
   Laura, 270
   Richard, 239
   W.A., 307
SHIVE
   J.C. (Rev.), 235, 296
SHOEMAKERS, 115
SHOEMAKERS
   Aiken, A.S., 87
   Capps, J.W., 119
   Durham, W.S., 110
   Hopkins, D.W., 57
   Merrill, J.B., 184
   Tolbert, Charles H., 184
SHOE SHOPS
   Capps, J.W., 137
   Hopkins, Des W., 160
   Tolbert, Charles T., 280
SHREWSBURG
   Elizabeth K., 173
SHUEY
   Alexander, 233
   Deannie Ferguson, 233
SILVER MINES, 159
SIMMONS (SIMONS)
   A.M., 179
   Bettie, 268
   Carrie M., 184, 218
   Delila, 266
   Dora, 268
   Elmer, 216
   Frank, 216, 231, 288
   Harlin, 161
   J.D. (N.P.), 242
   J.H., 179
   James, 52, 94, 104
   James (Mr. & Mrs.), 72
   Jesse, 34, 185
   Jim, 244

Jonah, 251
Leiar, 1
Lewis, 187
Lizzie, 288
Marvel, 310
Mary, 45
Matilda, 185
Miss, 179
Mose (Mr. & Mrs.), 239
N.J. (Mrs.), 282
Oscar, 103
Stephen, 65
Texie, 231
W.W., 184, 218
SIMPSON
  Carrie, 273
  Frances, 58
  George, 273
  J.B., 266
  J.W., 22
  R.W., 102
SIMS
  Cater, 236
SINGLETON
  A. White (Prof.), 269, 306
  Dan, 37
  Dan (Mrs.), 37
  Dean, 149
  E.O., 223
  Ella, 108
  Fannie, 105
  George E., 128
  George W., 20, 84
  H.D., 173
  J.T., 154
  J. Tyre (Rev.), 255
  J.T. (Rev.), 219
  John E. (Mr. & Mrs.), 205
  John L., 224
  Leumas, 205
  Lillie, 223
  R.R., 21, 32, 101
  Robert R., 47, 99
  T.P., 108
  W.B., 1, 105, 110, 117,
    120, 128, 129, 167, 173
  W.O., 33
  W.S. (Rev.), 47
  William, 105
SITTON
  J.J., 161, 168
  John D. (N.P.), 189
  William D., 229
SIZEMORE

Jobery, 252
Martha, 127
Norsissie, 192
William, 127, 249
SKELTON, 128, 130
SKELTON
  Elisha, 187
  M.J. (Mrs.), 255
  Mary, 34
  S.O., 109, 126, 197,
    228, 255, 281
SLATENS
  L.A., 288
SLAVES AND SLAVERY, 98
SLOAN
  Ben, 46
  D.B., 7
  Hiram, 208
  James (Dr.), 278
  John, 287
  Mr., 65
  Mrs., 255
  R.E., 46
  S.G. (Rev.), 91
  Sep, 46
  W.P., 113
SMALLEY
  G.B., 182
SMALLPOX, 301, 309
SMILER
  Andy, 192
SMITH, 305
SMITH
  Alexander, 169
  Andrew, 232
  Annie, 6
  Arch, 163, 164
  Barnet (Mrs.), 277
  Bluford, 51, 52
  Calvin, 259
  Calvin M., 259
  Calvin McDuffie, 223
  Chief of Police, 267
  Clarinda, 236
  Clarissa, 93
  Columie, 59
  D.D. (Miss), 81
  Dan, 236, 238
  Dicie, 283
  Dr., 261
  Elijah, 97
  Elizabeth, 126, 238
  Ellison A., 281
  Emma, 126, 205

Evie, 310
Fannie C., 66
Foster, 97
Frances E., 246
Frank, 26
Frank (Mr. & Mrs.), 142
Gaines, 155, 157
H.A., 198
Harve (Mrs.), 162
Hattie, 202
Hester Ann, 292
Hoke, 158
I.L., 164
Irey, 127
J., 28
J.A. (Mrs.), 39, 81
J.D., 26, 33, 35, 80, 92, 133, 179, 228
J.F., 164
J. Foster, 187
J.M., 95, 277
J. Mede, 156
J. Monroe, 161, 292
J.P., 127, 235, 252, 271, 284, 292
J. Theodore, 14
James, 16, 44, 208, 245, 271
Jane, 16
Janie, 68
Jas., 68
Job, 126
Job (Mrs.), 242
Joe, 220, 245
Joe F., 281
John, 23, 204
John E., 272
John N., 187
Joseph, 213, 282
Josiah E., 152
Julius, 173
Julius Eugene, 209
Kate, 6
L.J., 292
L.L., 186
L.M., 240
L.R., 160
L.R. (Mrs.), 157
L. Reid, 28
Luther D., 272
M.L., 186
Mag, 233
Maggie E., 140
Margaret H., 152
Martha, 220
Mary A., 162, 168
Mary Ann, 232
Mary M., 186
Maxie (Miss), 267
Mittie, 288
Moses, 187
Mr., 75, 127, 157
Nannie, 16
O.G. (Mrs.), 140
O.H.C., 272
Oliver S., 296
Ora I. (Miss), 250
R.E., 247
R.F., 199, 235, 256, 280, 288, 292
R. Frank, 277
R. Frank (Mrs.), 252
R.G., 175
R.L., 302, 304
R.S., 246
R.W., 261
Rebecca, 167
Retter, 58
Robin S., 296
Ross, 214
Ruben, 187
Sarah, 96
Sarah J., 221
Stephen, 187
Stovall, 186
T.H., 198
T.M. (Rev.), 97
T.N. (Mr. & Mrs.), 238
Tom "Blue", 228
Thomas, 126
Thomas D., 177
Turner, 238
W.A., 16
W.C., 86, 292
W.G., 186
W.L., 104
W.M., 284
W.N. (Mrs.), 58
W.S., 187
Walter M. (Dr.), 283
Walter Monroe (Dr.), 235
Wiley, 187
William, 54, 97, 190, 291
William F., 256
William L., 210
Z.H. (Rev.), 96
SNELLINGS
  J.W. (Mr. & Mrs.), 185

SNIDER
  H., 274
SNIPES
  Minnie, 111
  W.F., 88
SNODDY
  R.P., 191
SODA FOUNTAIN, 239
SOUTH CAROLINA
  Board of Health, 146, 200
  Chicago Exhibit, 96, 99
  Clemson, 89
  Colored State College, 75
  Constitution, 63, 67, 77
  Constitutional Convention, 62, 67, 68, 69, 70, 71, 72, 73, 75
  Corporate Limits Law, 139
  Democratic Committee Report, 26
  Democratic Convention, 29
  Democratic Primary, 21
  Democrats, 54
  Dispensary Law, 93
  Divorces, 69
  Elections, 110
  Executive Committee, 103, 248
  Exhibition, St. Louis, 291
  General Assembly, 38, 87, 89, 90, 128, 130, 131, 132, 133, 230, 231
  Governor, 110
  Governor's Message, 83, 126, 227, 300
  Governor's Proclamation, 238
  Homestead Exemption, 70
  Inaugural Message, 228
  Legislative Notes, 88
  Legislature Report, 84
  Lt. Governor, 109
  Metropolitan Police, 90
  Milita, 56
  New Acts, 307
  News and Notes, 236
  Palmetto Gleanings, 298, 299, 300, 310, 311, 312
  Penetentiary Board, 180
  Registration Law, 93
  Rice Cultivation, 288
  School Commissioners, 85
  Schools, 75
  State Campaign, 102, 107
  State Convention, 67, 96, 100
  State Fair, 116
  State Museum, 100
  Township Plan, 71
  Volunteer Infantry, 182, 252
  Vote for State Officers, 219
  Voter Laws, 52, 54
  Voter Registration, 53, 54, 56, 57, 63, 70, 72, 105
SOUTHERLAND
  Amos (Mr. & Mrs.), 147
  Mr., 140
  Nettie, 25
SOUTHERLAND & GRIFFIN, 143
SOUTHERN AGRICULTURAL WORKS, 142
SOUTHERN RAILROAD, 152, 165, 169, 279
SPALDING
  E.G., 52
SPAN
  L.D., 182
SPANISH AMERICAN WAR, 271, 278
SPEARMAN
  James, 161
  James M., 227
  Lartie (Lottie), 175
  Levi, 81
  S.J. (Miss), 156
  W.D. (Mr. & Mrs.), 175
  Warren, 49
SPENCER
  Bessie, 275
  Boss, 68
  Charles, 33
  Fannie Z., 201
  Ida, 222
  Maudie, 122
  Nena, 43
  T.C., 94, 222
  T.C. (Mr. & Mrs.), 201
  W.T. (Mr. & Mrs.), 121
SPRINGFIELD
  Robert (Rev.), 6
ST. PHILLIP'S CHURCH, 153
STANCEL
  Mr. & Mrs., 15
STANCELL (STANSELL)
  Anna, 275

Elizabeth, 168
Essie, 266
Ivy, 286
J.E., 105
J.L. (Mr. & Mrs.), 204
James (Mr. & Mrs.), 286
Joseph, 266, 299
Polly, 292
S. Jane, 313
W.M., 187
Willie, 10
STANDARD OIL, 161
STAR SPANGLED BANNER, 104, 289
STARKE
Sallie Lou, 154
STATON
Ella, 294
STEELE (STEEL)
C.C., 157
Eddie, 241
H.W., 12
J.E.M., 158
Jane, 94
John E., 157
Ola, 111
R.E., 105, 157
W.H. (Prof.), 44, 101
STEGALL
John, 52
Miss, 254
Spencer, 237
STEPHENS, 312
STEPHENS
A.C., 187
A.T., 111
Baylus, 89, 93
Berry, 111
Bud, 89
C.S., 7
Catherine, 221
E.B., 186
Earle, 211
Emma, 256
Felix, 144
Frank, 219
Henry, 221
J.D., 187
J.L., 89
Jacob, 256
John, 219
L.D., 93, 255, 256
L.D. (Mr. & Mrs.), 22
Leonard (Mr. & Mrs.), 263
Leonard D., 278
Marcus, 181
Marion, 295
Mary Ann, 114
Nannie, 47
Nora, 295
Rebecca, 128
Rutha Ann, 255
W.G., 240
STEPHENSON (STEVENSON)
John, 239
Josephine, 298, 306
Lila, 228
W.E., 312
W.E. (Mr. & Mrs.), 306
Willis, 228
STEWART
Abraham, 74, 80
Anthony, 20
B.D., 28, 30, 51, 143
Carter, 54
Connie, 6, 125
D.B., 90
D.T. (Mr. & Mrs.), 120
Emma, 80
F.C., 140
J.A., 42
J.B., 158
J.F., 80
J.M., 2, 7, 9, 12, 13, 14, 16, 18, 26, 28, 31, 35, 36, 37, 42, 45, 46, 47, 49, 51, 56, 58, 60, 63, 68, 79, 80, 86, 87, 96, 108, 113, 116, 117, 118, 122, 131, 132, 133, 135, 138, 140, 143, 151, 153, 158, 165, 166, 170, 172, 183, 185, 195, 199, 200, 203, 208, 211, 214, 215, 219, 220, 227, 231, 258, 259, 260, 278, 297, 298
J.M. (Mr. & Mrs.), 176, 230
J.M. (Mrs.), 97
J. Mattie, 141
Jahue, 250
James C., 274
James Ernest, 120
Janie, 166

John, 131, 132, 136, 162
John F., 80, 229
Julia, 62
Lawrence, 54, 273
Lena, 124
Magistrate, 148, 154
Major, 124, 146
Malinda, 96
Mary, 183
Maude, 209
Maxwell, 271
May Alice, 131
O.S., 26, 38, 157
Oscar, 80
Pleasant M., 77
R.A., 31
R.M., 168
Reubin (Mr. & Mrs.), 249
Rev., 220
Robert, 66, 118, 132, 162, 168, 262, 273, 278, 288
Robert (Mr. & Mrs.), 246
Robert W., 78
Rutha A., 278
S.C., 197
S.D., 63, 81, 124
S.S., 42
Sarah, 131
Sarah A., 31, 35
Squire, 50
Susan, 162, 168
T.H., 35
T.W., 62
Tempy C., 73
Thomas, 166, 218
Thomas (Mr. & Mrs.), 183, 209
Thomas (Mrs.), 23, 255
Tody, 271
W.A., 16, 50, 55, 148
W.K., 187
W.M., 273
W.O., 173
W.P. (Mr. & Mrs.), 26
Will, 231
William, 165, 170
William (Mr. & Mrs.), 250
STEWYATT
  Mattie, 81
STOCKADES, 235
STOCKADES
  Allen, 180
  Fowler, 180
  Hammond, 180
  Watson, 180
STOKES
  James E., 227
STONE
  A.C., 307
  A. Calloway, 182
  A.N., 240
  Ardella E., 226
  B.E., 250
  Governor, 60
  I. (Rev.), 245
  I.N. (Rev.), 223, 226, 228
  J.H. (Rev.), 160
  M.E., 250
  Mr., 250
  R.N. (Rev.), 207
  Robert Fountain, 250
  S.G. (Rev.), 268
STORES
  Aiken, W.W., 56, 96
  Alexander Bros., 50
  Alliance, 28
  Ambler & Gilreath, 178
  Anderson, 114
  Anderson Printing Co., 281
  Anthony & Keith, 265
  Ashmore, 197
  Big Store, 220, 282, 311
  Boggs, A.J., 143
  Boggs, John T., 2, 300
  Boggs & Skelton, 109, 128, 130
  Bolt & Thornley, 239, 242
  Bolt, Dr., 188
  Bramblett, W.C., 2, 87
  Bridges & Hammond, 258, 282, 313
  Brock, J.F., 305, 312
  Brock, J.O., 143
  Brown, J.E., 7
  Brown, J.H., 3, 44, 51, 136
  Brown, James E., 2
  Bruce, Mr., 139
  Carter, F.H., 146
  Carter, R.C., 309
  Carter, Ralph C., 308
  Carter Merchandise Co., 126
  Chapman, M.J. (Mrs.), 255
  Chapman & Callaham, 92

Clyde, J.T., 116
Clyde, Mrs., 129
Clyde, T.E., 139
Clyde & Nalley, 143
Corner Store, 281
Columbia, 81
Corporate Co., 48
Couch, F.M., 165, 280
Craig, John, 88
Craig Bros., 190, 220, 280
Cureton, D.T. & W.M., 261, 281
Cureton, J.D. (Mrs.), 252
Cureton, Kate L., 280
Davis Shoe Shop, 281
Dr. Smith's Drug, 261
Drug, 299
Duckworth & Wyatt, 136
Earle, Dr., 180, 185
Earle Drug, 312
Earle, G.W., 146, 180
Earle's, 280
Easley Bicycle Repair, 280
Easley Drug, 281
Easley Hardware Co., 291
Eaton, L. Ross, 264
Ebaugh & Jordan, 125
Edens Bros. & Lynch, 32
Ellison Bros., 152, 155, 280, 281
Finney, D.B. (Mrs.), 196
Folger & Thornley, 281, 311
Freeman & Hendricks, 143
Freeman & Williams, 92
Fricks, D., 4
Glenn, 142
Grady, B.E., 227, 281
Green, B.A., 8
Greenville, 89
Griffin, B.M., 159, 167
Hagood, Bruce & Co., 2, 45, 168
Hagood, J.E. & J.L. Thornley, 4
Hagood, W.M. & Co., 76, 83, 86
Harris, 122
Harris, John F., 280
Harris, T.D., 2, 107, 121, 125, 141, 235
Haygood & Co., 280
Heath, Bruce & Morrow, 214, 220, 280, 310

Hendricks, G.H., 140
Hendricks, G.T., 100
Hendricks, M. and Son, 271
Hollingsworth, W.R., 95
Howard, 76
Hunter, 300,
Hunter, C.T., 311
Hunter & Boggs, 26, 30, 92, 98, 105, 108
Hunter & Hamilton, 105, 108, 156
Hutchins, Charlie, 95
Hutchins & Morris, 134
Lathem, J.T., 143
Lathem, Judge, 129
Looper's Shop, 153
Jameson's, 280
Johnson, B.J., 205
Johnson, W.H., 281
Johnson, W.R., 301
Keen Edge Barber, 281
Lewis, J.T. & Sons, 2, 17, 94
Lewis & Sons, 7, 12
Mahon & Arnold, 176, 304
Martin, C.T., 280
Martin, J.H. "Jake", 86
McAlister & Beattie, 30
McFall, 160, 265, 313
McFall, W.T., 2, 281
Merck & Watson, 160
Moore, J.D., 217
Morgan, F.B., 4
Morgan, J.D., 46
Morgan, J.H. & Bros., 156, 161
Morgan Bros., 4
Morris, A.M., 3, 108, 120, 128, 143, 161, 280
Morris, Aaron, 110
Nesbitt, Trowbridge & Co., 156
New York Racket, 17, 126
North Side Barber, 281
O'Dell's, 281
Orr, Lee P., 15, 17
Orr, Lee P. (Mrs.), 17
Pace, D.F., 196
Parson & Bros., 136
Pickens Drug, 306, 311
Pickens, W.H., 86, 256, 306
Price, W.R., 136

Price & Durant, 60
Quillians, 2
Rampey, J.M., 87
Richey, 160
Robinson, J.E., 12, 281
Sheldon Drug Store, 142
Sheppard, J.A., 155
Sheppard & Ellison, 34,
   42, 152
Shirley & Perkins, 39, 92
Skelton & Smith, 281
Smith, J.D., 92
Smith, R.F., 280
Smith, R.L., 302, 304
Soda Fountain, 146
Stephens, C.S., 7
Stewart, Will, 231
Sturdevant, W.K. Co., 304
Sullivan Hardware Co., 281
Sutherland, D.F. & Bros.,
   19, 32
Sutherland Bros., 54
Sutherland & Griffin, 112,
   120, 140, 143, 153
Sutherland's Market, 267
Thomas, 17
Thomas, John W., 54
Thornley, John L., 305,
   313
Thornley, L.C., 96
Thornley Bros., 65
Thornley's Pharmacy, 280
Walker, T.A. & Bros., 17
Walker & McElmoyle, 148
Walker & Owens, 84
Walker's Cash, 30
West End Drug, 312
Willard & Moore, 124
Williams, W.H. & Co., 131
Williams & Freeman, 140
Williams & Barker, 148
Wyatt, A.G. & Co., 2, 129,
   280
Wyatt, Andy, 86
Wyatt, C.N., 2
Young, A., 309
STRATMAN (STRATMANN)
  Ernest W., 313
  Ernest William, 311
STRATTON
  Catherine, 81
STRIBLING
  Brick Barn, 251
  J.C., 197, 251, 279

  M.F. (Prof.), 108
  M.S., 23, 64, 79, 120
  Marshall, 22
  Mrs., 283
  Neil, 62
  Orah, 160
  Prof., 48
STROUD
  Bettie, 202
  Dora, 45
STURDEVANT
  W.K. Co., 304
STURKEY
  Linda, 213
SUDDETH
  Thomas, 79
SULLIVAN
  Amanda, 245
  Miss, 177
  William, 12
SULLIVAN HARDWARE CO., 281
SUMMER HOMES & RESORTS, 103
SUMMERALL
  J.N.H. (Rev.), 214
SUMMEY (SUMMY)
  Jas., 77
  Lugenia, 240
  Peter, 186
  W.H., 18, 43, 56, 96
SUMTER
  Gen., 222
SURVEYORS
  Parsons, Julius, 187
SUTHERLAND, 112, 153
SUTHERLAND
  A.C., 150
  A.C. (Mr. & Mrs.), 163
  Amos, 14
  Amos C., 106
  Bros., 54
  Calton, 240
  Christine, 310
  D.F., 32, 106, 154
  D.F. & Bros., 19
  D.R., 120
  E., 196
  G.W. (Mr. & Mrs.), 271
  George, 200
  J.D., 208
  J.R. (Capt.), 132
  J.W., 3, 15, 28, 32, 271
  Jack, 208
  James K., 270
  John, 6

Lula, 240
R.D., 209
Riley, 50
Sam, 267
Samuel, 240
SUTHERLAND & GRIFFIN, 120
SWAN (SWANN)
    Mamie, 250
    Mary E., 299
SWANGLING
    Amy, 225
SWANGNAM
    A.A., 187
SWARN
    Mary, 279
SWELLING
    Rebecca, 154
SWORD
    Cureton, J.D. (Dr.), 292
SYMMES
    Whitner, 9, 56, 221
TALLEY, 165
TALLEY (TALLY)
    A.B., Jr., 299
    Absalom, 309
    D. (Rev.), 91
    Eugene, 310
    Zeila Robertson, 169
TATE
    Fannie, 100
    W.P., 31
TAYLOR
    A. Brandon, 298
    Brandon, 258, 265, 312
    E.F. (Mrs.), 210
    Eilene, 258, 293
    Elim F., 272
    Ellen, 265
    G.S.W., 43
    G.W., 42
    J.T. (Capt.), 283
    Lorena, 257, 264, 293, 310
    M.A. (Miss), 23
    N.D., 244, 314
    N. Dana, 122
    Photographer, 280
    William, 111
TEACHERS
    Colored, 217
    List, 255
TEAL
    W.P., 223
TEASLEY
    John, 85

TEAT
    John, 169
TEESE
    John, 97
TEET'S BROS. SHOW, 56
TELEPHONES, 112, 187
TELEPHONES
    Building, 179
    Home Company, 180
    Lines, 224
    Long Distance, 273
    Long Distance-Easley, 241
    Pickens, 227
TEMPLETON
    D.H., 94
    David, 74
    Ida, 74
    Laura, 94
TENNESSEE COAL FIELDS, 290
TERRELL
    George, 243
    John, 178
    Lewis, 76
    M.A., 178
    R.F., 78
TEXAS DUTCHMAN, 188
THACKER
    William (Mr. & Mrs.), 262
THANKSGIVING DAY, 166
THODE, 154
THOMAS
    A.J.S., 135, 212, 250, 251
    C. Eugene, 88
    Col., 212
    E.R. (Miss), 225
    Elmira, 306
    Estelle, 95
    Flora, 183
    G.W., 187
    J.W., 259
    Joe, 252, 306
    John W., 54, 97, 116
    Joseph L., 116
    Lemuel, 116
    P.G., 308
    P.O., 308
    Rachel, 262
    W.H., 34
    Waddie (Mrs.), 243
THOMPKINS
    D.C., 261
    Frank, 261
    S. (Prof. & Mrs.), 99

THOMPSON (THOMSON)
  Herbert, 72
  J.L.O., 3, 13, 134, 190, 302
  J.L.O. (Mr. & Mrs.), 155
  J.L.O. (Mrs.), 302
  James (Mrs.), 20
  James L., 186
  Mr., 196
  R.A. (Capt.), 278
  William, 102, 140, 192
THORNLEY, 219, 239, 242, 281, 311
THORNLEY
  B.K., 280
  Bertran, 142
  Bros., 65
  Clarence Bruce, 263
  E. Obedience, 223, 258
  Eva, 291
  J.L., 4, 264, 282
  J.L. (Capt. & Mrs.), 175
  J.L. (Mrs.), 82, 218
  John L., 232, 249, 305, 313
  John L., Jr., 172
  John L., Jr. (Mrs.), 216
  John Lewis (Capt.), 219
  L.C., 96, 140, 264
  L.C. (Mr. & Mrs.), 263
  Larry C., 94, 232, 304
  Melonee, 282
  N.E. (Mrs.), 282, 304
  Olivia, 175
  Perry F., 109, 159
THORNWELL ORPHANAGE, 109, 302
THREFT (THRIFT)
  Frank, 27
  Robert T., 44
TILDEN
  A.C., 22
TILLMAN, 241
TILLMAN
  B.R., 21, 305
  Benjamin Ryan, 230
  George D. (Hon.), 230
  Governor, 38, 39
  James H., 301
  John, 305
  Sophia Hancock, 230
TODD
  Robert Willis, 135

TOLBERT
  B.R., 184, 217
  Ben R., 205
  Charles H., 184
  Charles T., 280
TOLLISON
  Mrs., 129
  Thomas, 129
TOMBSTONES, 150
TOMBSTONES
  White & Co., 249
TOMPKINS
  Alice, 15, 37
  David C., 37
  John, 117
  Miss, 23
  W.F., 236
TOMPSON
  William, 141
TOWNES
  Collector, 8
  Cornelia J., 209
  J.T., 243
  Julia L., 243
  T.W., 141, 209
  T.W. (Mrs.), 209
  Wade, 142, 143
TOWNSHIP PLAN, 71
TRAINER
  M.C. (Mrs.), 37
TRAINUM
  Jeremiah, 130, 137
  Mr., 28
TRAMMEL
  B.W., 53
  B.W. (Mrs.), 53
  J.B. (Rev.), 257
  Widow, 164
TRAYLOR
  Eva, 285
TRIPP
  H.L., 266
TROTTER, 165
TROTTER
  Alice, 79
  Beckie (Miss), 250
  J.L., 112
  James, 187
  James (Mr. & Mrs.), 202
  John, 77, 142
  Joseph, 297
  Josiah, 153
  Mary Jane, 98
  Mattie, 58

Robert, 168, 179
Suckie, 98
Susan, 131
Thomas, 168
W.O., 75
TROWBRIDGE, 156
TUCKER
    W.H., 93
TUMBLIN
    Isabella Wolff, 274
    Lawrence, 270
    Lawrence Rufus, 274
    S.J., 274
    S.T., 187
TUNNEL HILL, 148
TURNER
    Amanda, 172, 300
    Anderson, 107
    Anna, 306
    Fannie, 37
    John, 145
    John T., 187
    Maggie, 202
    Nancy, 204
    Thomas, 45, 98
    Walter, 227
    Warren, 172, 202
    William, 118
UDC, 304
UDC
    Article, 311
    Charter, 313
    Pickens, 309
UNDERWOOD
    James, 150
    T.G. (Dr.), 181
UNION ARMY
    Christmas Dinner, 80
UNION MEETING, 118
UNION ROCK QUARRY, 90
U.S. MAIL, 135, 167
U.S. MAIL
    Free Delivery, 182
    Postage Stamps, 139, 303
VACCINATION
    Compulsory, 200
VALENTINE
    Harry, 185
VANCE
    Zebulon B. (Sen.), 14
VANDERBILT
    Cornelius, 194
    Family, 79
    George, 94

    Palace, 105, 134
VANDIVER
    Mrs., 49
VAUGHN
    C. (Mrs.), 233
    Dora, 86
    Essie, 257
    Hense (Mrs.), 243
    John (Mr. & Mrs.), 31, 212
    May, 31
    T.H. (Mrs.), 256
VAUGHT
    K.H., 187
VENELL
    W.C. (Rev.), 149
VERMILLION
    Jesse (Rev.), 142
    P.J. (Rev.), 223
VERRELL
    Mrs., 231
VETERINARIANS
    Griffin, B.P., 4, 9
VICKERS
    W.L., 184
VICKERY
    Elizabeth, 67
VIRGINIA ANTI-SALOON LEAGUE, 308
VIRGINIA BRIDGE CO., 287
VORHEES
    Daniel Wolsey, 137
VOTER REGISTRATION, 56, 57, 63, 70, 93, 94, 97, 105
VOTER REGISTRATION
    Negroes, 51
    Qualifications, 72
WADE
    Henry, 174
    Jesse, 127
    Rev., 307
WAGNER, 301
WAGONS & BUGGIES, 160, 281
WAKELIN
    J.J., 168
    Jennie, 286
WALDROP
    E.F., 74
    James, 187
    John (Mr. & Mrs.), 212
    Lula, 167
    Nettie, 309
    Sadie, 206
    Sanford S., 206

W.T., 309
WALHALLA
   Semi-Centennial, 207
   Smallpox, 309
WALKER, 30, 84, 148
WALKER
   Ed, 205
   J.N., 197
   James, 236
   James S., 238
   Jeff, 50
   Mrs., 311
   N.D., 184
   T.A., 125
   T.A. & Bros., 17
WALLACE
   William H. (Judge), 236
WALTHALL
   Lou E., 43
WARD
   Hester, 12
   J.M., 20, 152, 170, 173
   J.M. (Mr. & Mrs.), 213
   Jesse, 104
   Lola, 213
   Mamie, 152
WARE
   James P., 281
   Loranes, 270
WASHINGTON
   B.J., 223
   Ernest, 116
   George, 78, 306
WATERS
   B.L., 253
   Joseph, 253
WATKINS
   H. (Rev.), 290
   Himer, 55
   J.B. (Mrs.), 26
   J.C. (Mrs.), 292
   J.P., 252
   J.T., 293
   James, 45
   John Sims (Rev. & Mrs.), 222
   Julia, 295
   Lavine Frances, 222
   R.J., 26
   Rufus J., 157
   T.L., 4
WATSON, 160
WATSON
   Eva, 235
   G.B. (Mrs.), 214
   George T., 300
   J.T., 187
   John, 117
   L.W., 126
   Maggie, 231
   Nora, 126
   P.B., 42, 43, 204
   P.B. (Mrs.), 214
   Rev., 113
   Sam, 268
   Thomas, 62, 64
WATT (WATTS)
   John G. (Mrs.), 253
   Judge, 44
   R.C. (Mrs.), 44
WEBB
   Dr., 306
WEINBERT
   S. (Mrs.), 60
WELBORN (WELBORNE)
   A.J., 288
   A. Jefferson, 278
   Adam C., 266, 283
   Addie Mae, 234
   Addie May, 231
   Arlie, 310
   Billie, 265
   Elbert, 265, 310
   Florence, 200
   J., 272
   J.M. (Mr. & Mrs.), 234
   Joel, 82
   John, 283
   John (Mr. & Mrs.), 272
   Judge M., 283, 289
   Judge M. (Mr. & Mrs.), 231, 263
   L.T. (Rev.), 119
   Lela, 310
   Lila, 265
   Lizzette, 258, 293
   M. (Judge), 95
   Maggie, 266
   Major, 258
   Margaret, 80, 105, 118, 138
   Martin, 182
   Martin J., 283
   Minnie, 257, 264
   Mrs., 289
   N.H., 187
   Thomas, 283

    Thomas (Mr. & Mrs.), 121,
        200
    W.E., 283
    William, 258, 310
WELCH
    J.F., 104
WELDON
    L.T. (Rev.), 35, 36, 53,
        134, 139, 214
    R.L., 158
    Rev., 78, 89
    W.T. (Rev.), 165
WELLS
    J.F., 24, 33
    J. Frank, 42, 52
WERNER
    Joseph (Mr. & Mrs.), 138
    Robert, 138
    William, 136
WERNICKE
    Louis, 169
WERTS (WERTZ)
    Ada B., 17
    D.B. (Mr. & Mrs.), 203
    Eugene S., 249
    Lillian, 203, 249
    R.M., 105, 116, 144,
        150, 219
    R.M. (Mrs.), 16
    Rufus M., 92
WEST
    Thomas, 126
WEST POINT MILITARY ACADEMY,
    144
WESTFIELD & HELLAM, 89
WHALEY
    J. Swinston (Mrs.), 66
WHAM
    Anna, 213
WHITE
    Bessie, 266
    Bill, 27
    Charles E. (Mr. & Mrs.),
        210
    George, 221
    Hampton, 267
    James W., 14
    John R., 187
    Newton, 275
    Vilanta L., 272
    Walter W., 235
    Whitner, 266
    Will E., 235, 282
    T., 87

WHITE & CO., 235
WHITE & CO.
    Granite Works, 249
WHITE HORSE ROAD, 67
WHITE HOUSE, 298
WHITESIDES, 132
WHITLOCK
    Susie, 6
WHITMIRE, 259
WHITMIRE
    A.S. (Rev.), 98, 131, 208,
        251
    Airy, 53
    Andy, 107, 272
    B.H., 1, 91
    B.M., 91
    Bessie, 177
    Elizabeth, 86
    G.S., 247
    G. Sinclair, 67
    H.M. (Hon.), 247
    I.A., 168, 275
    Lucy, 87
    S.A. (Rev.), 286
    Sallie, 247
    Valenia, 247
    Will, 107
WHITNER
    Barry, 118
    James A., 9
WHITNEY
    A.G., 60
WHITTEN (WHITEN)
    Jas A., 145
    P., 52
WIDEMAN
    J.J. (Mrs.), 6
    T.A. (Mrs.), 303
    W.B. (Hon.), 177
WIGGINGTON
    Lizzie, 196
WIGGINS
    C.E. (Rev.), 262
    Rev., 209, 277
    W.E. (Rev.), 229, 262,
        267, 270, 275
WILBORN
    Elbert, 258
    Lila, 258
WILCOX
    Mrs., 220
WILKES
    James, 120

WILKINS
  William, 77
WILLARD
  Agnes, 6
  Choice, 72
  E.E., 176
  F.E., 72
  Mary F., 176
  T.E., 153
  Thomas E., 167
  W.O., 69, 124, 148,
    167, 176
WILLARD & FREEMAN, 140
WILLIAMS, 92, 148
WILLIAMS (WILLIAM)
  A.B., 234, 236, 295
  A.B. (Mr. & Mrs.), 212
  A.S., 225
  Alonzo (Mr. & Mrs.), 273
  Andrew B., 258, 260
  B.H., 65, 77, 106
  B.H. (Mr. & Mrs.), 20, 113
  B.J., 33, 108, 276
  Benjamin, 137
  Benjamin Josiah, 176
  Dr., 97
  Charles, 88
  Clarence Holtzclaw, 276
  Cordelia, 49
  Darthula, 27, 78
  Dorthula L., 212
  E.L., 2
  Elizabeth, 245
  Elliott (Mrs.), 164
  Emma, 295
  Essie, 260
  Eula, 286
  Eveline, 274
  Fred, 288
  Fred (Mr. & Mrs.), 134
  G.A., 293
  G.W., 187
  George, 300
  George W., 247
  Gus, 174
  H.L., 293
  Henry, 16
  Henry (Reunion), 250
  J.F., 4, 43, 44, 92, 117,
    120, 293, 294
  J.I., 39, 293, 294
  J.M., 164
  J.R., 190
  J.S., 148
  J.W., 23
  James B., 174
  Jeremiah, 225
  Jerry, 224
  John, 295
  John I., 95, 101, 106
  John I. (Mrs.), 167
  John W., 160
  Joseph, 72, 283
  Joseph F., 293
  L.B., 293
  L.S., 31
  Lida, 131
  Lillie, 113
  M.F., 126
  M.F. (Mrs.), 124
  Malinda, 283
  Malinda Ann, 294
  Mandanah, 137
  Margaret J., 276
  Martha, 16
  Matilda Ann, 293
  Mattie, 167
  Minnie, 91
  Miss, 106
  Moses, 250
  Mrs., 159, 271
  N.J., 36
  N.L., 218
  Nathaniel J., 199
  Nellie, 20
  O.P., 282
  Pearl, 282
  R.J., 124, 158
  Rev., 78
  Rowley, 240
  S.E., 258
  Silas, 286
  Susan E., 236
  T.A., 293
  T. Augustus, 274
  T.J., 225
  Thomas, 132
  Thomas H., 14
  Tony, 288
  W.H., 131, 293
  W. Henry, 48
  Walter B., 245
WILLIS, 80
WILLIS
  J.T., 285
  Place, 149
WILLOMAN
  C.L., 264

WILSON
  E., 213
  E. Lydie Ann, 9
  Ed, 193
  J.B., 251
  J.C., 3
  J.C. (Mr. & Mrs.), 28
  J. Sam, 294
  James C., 17
  John (Mrs.), 270
  John D., 211
  John O. (Rev.), 36
  Julia E., 56
  Lucius, 225
  Maggie, 17
  Norma, 28
  P.E. (Miss), 115
  Samuel, 9
  Susan, 211
  Victor, 251
WIMPEY (WIMPY-WIMPHEY)
  John, 45
  L.T., 280
  L.T. & Co., 59
  Mary, 91
WIMPEY & ROPER, 88
WINCHESTER
  A.T., 158
  Abraham T., 183
  Annetta, 190
  Daniel, 52, 110, 167
  David, 157
  Elijah, 3
  Florence, 3
  Ida, 55, 56
  J.M., 10, 56
  J. Mattison, 216
  Jane, 292
  M.C., 58, 289
  Winefred, 10
WITHERSPOON
  I.D. (Judge), 10
WOFFORD
  Dick, 37
WOLFF
  Isabella, 274
WOMAN LAWYER
  Keeler, Annie, 143
WOOD (WOODS)
  Augustus G., 177
  J.A., 132, 149
  Julia, 147
  Mr., 127
  Nina, 274

  Nina Earle, 275
  Thomas, 254
WOOL
  Manufacturer, 174
WOOLEY
  John, 213
WOOTEN
  Nancy, 228
WORD
  Frank H., 10
WORKMAN
  Ella, 275, 283
  J.G., 55
  W.F. (Rev.), 39
  W.H. (Rev.), 43, 72,
    126, 133, 164, 180,
    191, 197
  W.H. (Mrs.), 61
  Willie, 61
WORTS
  R.M. (Mrs.), 16
WREAVES
  Lee W., 232
WRIGHT
  Ada, 217
  Carrie, 77
  Eugene, 12
  Eva, 115
  Henry, 217
  Lula, 236
  Mary, 52
  Mrs., 77
  W.W. (N.P.), 43
WYATT, 61
WYATT (WYAT)
  A.G., 129, 167
  A.G. & Co., 280
  A.T., 76
  Andy, 86
  Andy G., 251
  Carrie, 211
  Contractor, 271
  Dr., 200
  E.F. (Dr. & Mrs.), 165
  Ed (Dr.), 165
  Hattie, 24
  Jane, 18, 125
  John, 95
  John G., 159, 162
  M. Nettie, 260
  Mayor, 165
  Miss, 108, 136, 159,
    169
  R.F., 159, 162

    S.N., 68, 90, 256, 279
    T., 81
    Templeton (Mrs.), 23
    W.C., 180
    Walter, 199
WYER
    Prof., 192
YANCY,
    William L., 246
YATES
    Addie, 79
    Arkeluis, 79
    James, 63
YEAR
    1894 National-State, 41, 42
YONGUE (YONGE)
    Alberta, 257, 292, 310
    Belle, 257, 292, 310
    Eugene, 292, 309
    R.E., 166, 304
YOUNG
    A., 309
    Abb, 300, 303
    Addie, 6
    Belle, 264
    Ela, 144
    J.D., 48
    J.P. (Mrs.), 189
    James, 84
    Lon, 67
    M.A., 217
    R.C., 78
    Rosa Lee, 82
    Will, 36
YOUNGBLOOD
    Eliza, 110
    Eliza J., 238, 253
    H.T., 83
    J.T., 57, 112, 156, 238, 253
    J.T. (Mrs.), 62, 109
    Jennie, 230
    John Tyler, 236, 237
    W.W., 238, 253
    Walker (Mr. & Mrs.), 263
ZACHARY
    Eugene, 285
ZIMMERMAN
    S.H. (Rev.), 71, 120
ZINK
    Eliza, 232

www.ingramcontent.com/pod-product-compliance
Lightning Source LLC
Chambersburg PA
CBHW080533300426
44111CB00017B/2707